London

BARS
PUBS & CLUBS

timeout.com

Contents

Time Out Guides Ltd
Universal House
251 Tottenham Court Road
London W1T 7AB
Tel + 44(0)20 7813 3000
Fax + 44(0)20 7813 6001
guides@timeout.com
www.timeout.com

Editorial

Editor Jan Fuscoe
Deputy Editor Simon Coppock
Copy Editor Anna Norman
Researchers Jill Emeny, Cathy Limb
Proofreader Marion Moisy
Subject Indexer Cathy Heath

Editorial/Managing Director Peter Fiennes
Series Editor Sarah Guy
Deputy Series Editor Cath Phillips
Business Manager Gareth Garner
Guides Co-ordinator Holly Pick
Accountant Kemi Olufuwa

Design

Art Director Scott Moore
Art Editor Pinelope Kourmouzoglou
Senior Designer Josephine Spencer
Graphic Designer Henry Elphick
Digital Imaging Dan Conway
Ad Make-up Jenni Pritchard

Picture Desk

Picture Editor Jael Marschner
Deputy Picture Editor Tracey Kerrigan
Picture Researcher Helen McFarland

Advertising

Sales Director Mark Phillips
Sales Manager Alison Wallen
Advertising Sales Ben Holt, Jason Trotman
Advertising Assistant Kate Staddon
Copy Controller Amy Nelson

Marketing

Marketing Manager Yvonne Poon

Production

Production Director Mark Lamond
Production Manager Brendan McKeown
Production Controller Caroline Bradford

Time Out Group

Chairman Tony Elliott
Managing Director Mike Hardwick
Financial Director Richard Waterlow
TO Magazine Ltd MD David Pepper
Group General Manager/Director Nichola Coulthard
TO Communications Ltd MD David Pepper
Group Marketing Director John Luck
Group Art Director John Oakey
Group Production Director Steve Proctor
Group IT Director Simon Chappell

Contributors

Claire Ainsley, James Aufenast, Simone Baird, Peter Cordwell, Jonathan Cox, Peterjon Cresswell, Simon Cropper, Guy Dimond, Kevin Ebbutt, Will Fulford-Jones, Charlotte Fuller, Kate Fuscoe, Gwynnie, Gilad Halpern, Hallie Hodenfield, Andrew Humphreys, Dean Irvine, David Jenkins, Francisca Kellett, Alexia Loundras, Rhodri Marsden, Jenny McIvor, Norman Miller, Felix Milns, James Mitchell, Rachael Moloney, Anna Norman, Sharon O'Connell, Mark C O'Flaherty, Natasha Polyviou, Sam Pow, Mirelle Saranz, Sco, Adam Scott, James Smart, Andrew Staffell, Sejal Sukhadwala, David Swift, Valentine Taylor, Anne Tillyer, Sandie Tozer, John Watson, Patrick Welsh, Tim Wild. **Features in this guide were written and researched by:** Licensed to spill Rebecca Taylor; **The discreet charm of hotel bars** Sejal Sukhadwala; **Lucky strikes** Tom Lamont; **Wine routes** Alice Lascelles; **Good sports** Peterjon Cresswell; **Chain, chain, chain** Simon Coppock; **Booze talking** Andrew Humphreys.

The Editor would like to thank Nikki Crichton, Guy Dimond, Tris Rees-Boughton.

Maps JS Graphics (john@jsgraphics.co.uk).
Street maps based on material supplied by Alan Collinson and Julie Snook through Copyright Exchange.

Cover and Opener Photography Michael Franke, taken at Kabaret's Prophecy, 16-18 Beak Street, W1F 9RD (7439 2229/www.kabaretsprophecy.com); see page 251.
Photography pages 3, 8, 28, 30, 31, 61, 85, 88, 95, 100, 185, 192, 193, 206, 207, 215, 222, 230, 237, 238, 257 Alys Tomlinson; pages 5, 8, 16, 111, 116, 117, 133, 145, 153, 154, 156, 157, 163, 171, 176, 253 Anthony Webb; pages 7, 10, 14, 15, 16, 21, 54, 55, 64, 65, 67, 70, 73, 106, 107, 141, 150, 199, 229 Ming Tang Evans; pages 16, 128 Britta Jaschinski; pages 16, 48 Michael Franke; page 25 Haris Artemis; page 37 Sam Baily; pages 39, 123, 147 Christian Theisen; pages 79, 101, 181, 211, 235 Viktor Pesenti; page 80 Scott Wishart; pages 243, 244 Ingrid Rasmussen.
The following images were provided by the featured establishments: pages 58, 136, 137, 246, 247.

Repro Wyndeham Icon, 3-4 Maverton Road, E3 2JE.
Printed and bound Cayfosa-Quebecor, Ctra. de Caldes, Km 3, 08130 Sta. Perpètua de Mogoda, Barcelona, Spain.

ISBN
To 31 December 2006: 1-905042-04-3
From 1 January 2007: 978-1-905042-04-3

Distribution by Seymour Ltd (020 7396 8000)

About the guide

This guide is arranged by area, because we reckon that's how most people drink. Area boundaries are often nebulous, so we include brief introductions to each section explaining our take on London geography. If you're after something other than just the closest or most convenient decent pub or ace bar, turn to **Where to go for...** on page 258, a rundown of drinking establishments by theme.

Opening times
We only list the opening times of the bar or pub at the time of going to press. We do not list those of any attached restaurant, brasserie or shop (though these may be the same).

Food served
We list the times when food is served in the bar or pub or, where relevant, in any attached restaurant or brasserie. 'Food served' can mean anything from cheese rolls to a three-course meal. When the opening times and food serving times are run together (Open/food served), it means food is served until shortly before closing time.

Admission
In some cases, particularly in central London, pubs and bars charge admission after a certain hour. Where there is a regular pattern to this, we list the details. Note that more and more venues are becoming members-only after a fixed time (usually when pubs close), although the rules are often blurred. We've chosen not to include in this guide places that are strictly members-only.

Credit cards
The following abbreviations are used: **AmEx** American Express; **DC** Diners Club; **MC** MasterCard; **V** Visa.

Babies and children admitted
Under-14s are only allowed into gardens, separate family rooms and restaurant areas of pubs and wine bars, unless the premises has a special 'children's certificate'. If the establishment has a certificate, children can go in as long as they're with an adult. Those aged 14-17 can go into a bar, but only for soft drinks. It's an offence for a licensee to serve alcohol in a bar to anyone under 18. Unless drinkers can prove they're at least 18, the licensee can refuse to serve them and may ask them to leave the premises.

Disabled: toilet
If a pub claims to have a toilet for the disabled, we have said so; this also implies that it's possible for a disabled person to gain access to the venue. However, we cannot guarantee this, so phone in advance to check.

Function room
Means the pub or bar has a separate room that can be hired for meetings or parties; some charge for this, some do not.

Music
Unless otherwise stated, this means live musicians and no entry fee. For a round-up of the best clubs, *see p245*.

No-smoking room/area
Until such time as smoking is totally banned in pubs (*see p8* **There's no smoke... period**) we are listing those pubs or bars that have a designated no-smoking room or area. Note that these can offer little protection from the usual pub smoke.

TV
We tell you whether or not the pub has a TV, and also whether it's a subscriber to cable or satellite.

During the year-long lifetime of this guide, bars and pubs will inevitably change name, change hands or close. We strongly recommend giving the venue a ring before you set out – especially if your visit involves a long trip.

Reviews featured in this guide are based on the experiences and opinions of *Time Out*'s reviewers. All pubs and bars listed are visited – anonymously – and *Time Out* pays the bill. No payment or incentive of any kind has secured or influenced a review.

ADVERTISERS
We would like to thank the companies that have advertised in this guide. However, we would like to stress that advertisers have no control over editorial content. No bar or pub has been included because its owner has advertised in the guide. An advertiser may receive a bad review or no review at all.

Sarastro Restaurant

"The Show After The Show"

A sumptuous treasure trove hidden within a Grade II listed Victorian townhouse, Sarastro is perfectly located in the heart of London's Theatreland. A wide selection of delicious Mediterranean dishes are served with theatrical flair and passion against the elaborate backdrop of golden drapes and decorative frescoed walls.

Every Sunday matinee and Sunday and Monday evenings there are live performances from up and coming stars of the Royal and National Opera houses and all over the world. Sarastro is ideal for pre- and post-theatre dining and perfect for red carpet parties and celebrations with a menu available at £12.50 for lunch Monday to Saturday. Open for lunch and dinner 7 days a week. A private function room is available for corporate and red carpet occasions (for up to 300 guests).

**126 Drury Lane, London WC2 Tel: 020 7836 0101 Fax: 020 7379 4666, www.sarastro-restaurant.com
E: reservations@sarastro-restaurant.com**

Papageno Restaurant & Bar

"Where the show goes on for the theatre casts and audiences"

Prominently located in the heart of Covent Garden's theatreland, Papageno is ideal for both pre and post theatre dining. Open all day, seven days a week, choose from an extensive European a la carte menu or special set menus from £12.50 available throughout the day and early evening. Papageno is the place to host the party to end all parties! Whether it be an office party, wedding or any other event, Papageno has one of the most stunning and beautiful rooms in London that can cater for up to 700 guests. Open for lunch and dinner 7 days a week.

'Seeing is believing'

**29-31 Wellington S, London WC2 Tel: 020 7836 4444 Fax: 020 7836 0011, www.papagenorestaurant.com
E: reservations@papagenorestaurant.com**

Licensed to spill?

We were promised bladdered yobbos and staggering teenage girls. But – surprise, surprise – the new licensing laws, introduced in November 2005, have so far left the capital's streets relatively unchanged. The new law, introduced to allow bars and pubs to extend the hours they serve alcohol (to up to 24 hours), was supposed to put an end to centuries of archaic practice by which pub closing times remained resolutely at 11pm. Politicians wrung their hands over the changes, fearing they would encourage criminality. In fact, some boroughs – such as Haringey – have actually seen crime rates drop since November, a fact that has been attributed by local police to the changes in the law.

The places that have benefited most from the extension in hours have been petrol stations, off-licences and hotels. Meanwhile, most councils (the bodies that now award licences) have shied away from granting pubs, bars and clubs greatly extended opening times. Here, we take you through the small hours with a potted guide to what is open in London's key drinking areas.

Westminster

Hours have changed very little in London's party centre. In general, pubs are able to serve alcohol till 11.30pm on weekdays and midnight on Fridays and Saturdays. Those that had late licences already, such as the **Spice Lounge** (*see p83*), have simply retained them. Only two Soho clubs have been given 24-hour licences: **Pop** and **Opium** (for both, *see p80*).

Camden

A single venue has been granted a 24-hour licence: the **End** (*see p248*). Most pubs have similar hours to the **Lock Tavern** (*see p162*), which serves alcohol until midnight from Monday to Thursday; 1am on Friday and Saturday; and 11.30pm on Sunday. Those venues that already had late licences, such as **Bartok** (*see p161*), have kept them.

Greenwich

One pub, the **Royal Tavern** (185 Court Road, SE9 4UG, 8857 1716), has a 24-hour licence for Sunday nights only. Most pubs can now serve alcohol till midnight or 1am, with some serving till 2am on weekends. Another ▶

There's no smoke... period

Following a government vote in February 2006, Londoners – along with everyone else in the UK – will be forbidden from smoking in enclosed public spaces from the summer of 2007. That means all pubs, bars and clubs. With their city thriving on its reputation for grimy cool, Londoners might have been expected to have thrust a defiant ciggy between their lips and thrown up their spare hand in horror. But, if a recent MORI poll is anything to go by, nearly three-quarters of the capital's population support such a ban. Indeed, London has been ahead of the game in paving the way for the new legislation. Last year, the Association of London Government (ALG), which represents all the London boroughs, submitted a bill to parliament that would have limited smoking in public, borough by borough.

Although some club- and bar-owners fear that the new legislation will affect business, others are already holding their own smoke-free nights or – following the lead of the Phoenix in Throgmorton Street – have closed their doors entirely to smoking in anticipation of the impending legislation. London's smokers will soon be forced to follow in the footsteps of New York's, who huddle around fire escapes for a quick puff during a night on the town. But, with around 10,500 Londoners dying each year from smoking-related diseases (that's more than one death every hour), it's a small price to pay.

trend is to take into account 'cultural' events – the **Birchwood** (Grovebury Road, SE2 9BB, 0871 984 3732) is now open till 2am on St George's Day, Christmas Eve and for Diwali, and times will be extended by one hour before and after important rugby, cricket and football fixtures.

Hackney

The nearest thing to getting alcohol around the clock in Hackney is the **Ye Olde Axe** (69 Hackney Road, E2 8ET, 7729 5137, www.yeoldeaxe.com), where you can now get served until 6am – but since it's an old-school strip joint you may well think twice. Hackney operates a 'Special Policy Area' around Hoxton and Shoreditch, which means that venues haven't been allowed to greatly extend their hours. **Charlie Wright's International Bar** (see p129) is open until 3am Friday and Saturday, the **Dolphin** (see p151) until 4am at weekends, but most follow the example of Hoxton's **333** (see p257), which serves alcohol only until 1am on a Friday and Saturday, even though it's open until 5am.

Islington

Party on in Islington! **Fabric** (see p248), **Meet** (see p120), **Turnmills** (see p257) and **Aquarium** (see p246) all have 24-hour licences. Elsewhere, you can keep going until 2am (4am on Friday and Saturday) at the **Salmon & Compass** (see p179); at **Medicine** (see p177) you can drink until 2am on Thursday, Friday and Saturday.

Kensington & Chelsea

Most 24-hour licences have gone to hotels (and usually for guests only). The **Notting Hill Arts Club** (see p255) serves alcohol until 2am every night except Sunday.

Southwark

Ministry of Sound (see p255) has a 24-hour licence.

China Tang

The discreet charm of the

hotel bar

Once upon a time the thought of hotel bars conjured up visions of stuffy gentlemen's clubs full of heavy leather armchairs, cigar smoke and newly pressed copies of *The Times* – the sort of place where business clients would rub shoulders (and shoulder pads) with moneyed tourists. Certainly nowhere that the hip, hot and happening would be hanging out.

How things have changed. Like the new craze for burlesque and old-fashioned supper clubs, hotel bars – as the locus for timeless, Hollywood-style glamour – are now in vogue. Recent years have seen an explosion of interest in celebrities and entrenched the passion for cocktails, and the hotel bar is the best place to indulge your taste for chocolate and chilli Martinis or fashionable 'oriental tapas'. These days – with every pub and bar in the city seeming to offer a range of watery, weird or just plain woeful cocktails – the quietly capable hotel bar has come back into its own. For a classic cocktail, reverently mixed, where else is there to go? And, given that the hotels can afford some of the capital's most innovative and best-trained mixologists, the more adventurous drinks may not be cheap, but they're usually exemplary. Add in the sense of instant glamour, drama and exclusivity that you get from drinking in a

fine hotel, not to mention the top people-watching opportunities afforded by a quality hotel, and you have a formula for a fun but civilised night out, for considerably less than the cost of staying in one of their rooms.

For some of the best cocktails in town, we recommend the quiet bar off the lobby at the contemporary Italian-designed **Halkin** (Halkin Street, SW1X 7DJ, 7333 1234) – best known for its acclaimed Thai restaurant Nahm – and the bar at the entrance of the **Zetter** restaurant, inside the hotel of the same name (*see p122*). The Halkin's oriental-themed cocktails, such as a lychee Martini, are superb, while Zetter's cocktails, made with Italian spirits like grappa and limoncello, are unique. Neither are destination bars – the clientele at each is stylishly understated rather than ostentatious – but they're ideal for a pre-dinner snifter before settling down for a meal at their respective restaurants.

If ostentation happens to be what you're after, the blingtastic **Rivoli** (*see p81*) in the famously sumptuous Ritz is the real go. It's a small cocktail bar decorated in art deco-style, with soaring ceilings, gold-lacquered columns and palm trees. The Rivoli seems to be delicately poised at a point in history where a formal jacket-only dress code went without saying – although

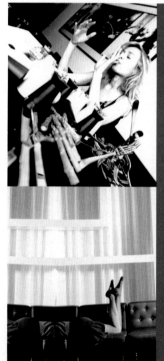

www.zetabar.com

020 7208 4067

35 Hertford Street, W1Y 7TG

www.tradervics.com

020 7208 4113

London Hilton on Park Lane, 22 Park Lane, W1K 4BE

£14 for a cocktail might have caused Bogart to weep bitter tears down his white tuxedo.

Another bar where you'll feel out of place if you're not properly togged is the classic art deco **American Bar** (*see p97*) at the Savoy. Once popular with visiting Hollywood stars, it offers an extensive range of classic and contemporary cocktails, as well as carefully prepared bar snacks. Expect more of the same from the beautiful **Lobby Bar** (*see p98*) at 1 Aldwych, and the glitzy **Homage** at the Waldorf Hilton (22 Aldwych, WC2B 4DD, 7759 4080), but for drinks that are truly exceptional you can't beat the legendary Martinis at the elegant **Duke's Hotel** (*see p80*). Perhaps it has something to do with the fact that they're made from gin or vodka that has been frozen for 24 hours. If all the premium spirits have left you feeling woozy, it may be time to road-test the superb wine list at **Pearl Bar & Restaurant** (*see p49*), within the swish Chancery Court Hotel.

We are able to reveal that there has been a relaunch, after 15 years, of the signature gin-based Cadogan Cooler cocktail at the bar inside the Edwardian-style **Cadogan Hotel** (75 Sloane Street, SW1X 9SG, 7235 7141, www.cadogan.com); we are not, however, at liberty to divulge the recipe. Another hip alternative is the small bar/lounge area inside the trendy **Guesthouse West** (163-165 Westbourne Grove, W11 2RS, 7792 9800, www.guesthousewest.com), a fashionable boutique hotel in the heart of Notting Hill. It has a plain, minimal, fuss-free look, and opens out to a terrace and gardens. The drinks – coffees and wines by the glass join a few classic cocktails – are also rather low on frills.

Following a rather different aesthetic, the **Malmaison Bar & Brasserie** (18-21 Charterhouse Square, EC1M 6AH, 7012 3700, www.malmaison.com), on the lower level of a hotel of contemporary design, is in the style of a traditional French brasserie, with high-backed banquettes and a stone fireplace. There's a short international wine list, and a menu offering French classics such as moules.

Blue Bar

The bar-restaurant at the impeccably British, four-star Pelham Hotel is another venue more suitable for dining than drinking. Located inside this extravagant Georgian townhouse, **Kemps** (15 Cromwell Place, SW7 2LA, 7589 8288, www.firmdale.com) is as popular with passing shoppers as the hotel's guests. Decorated with bright artwork from well-known British designers, it serves breakfast or afternoon tea in the day, but becomes romantically candlelit at night, serving cocktails alongside Mod Euro food.

Rockwell (*see p102*) at the Trafalgar in Trafalgar Square, once a *Time Out* fave, is London's first bourbon bar, specialising in American whiskey and whiskey-based cocktails. Over the last few years, however, it's lost a bit of its lustre – perhaps it's the competition from the newer and shinier **Albannach** (*see p99*), an excellent Scottish whisky bar and restaurant across the Square.

This year, we were also a little disappointed with old favourites, the chic **Claridge's Bar** (*see p66*) and the fashionable **Long Bar** (*see p45*) at the Sanderson Hotel. The right crowd makes all the difference, with the buzz an essential factor in a destination bar's success, and that crowd seems to have moved on, leaving expensive drinks and occasionally surly service. The A-list may also have finally ditched the dimly lit **Met Bar** (*see p69*) at the Metropolitan London – once exclusive but now just difficult to get into. The two most glamorous bar openings this year got them in, though: the luxe **China Tang** bar (*see p66*) at the Dorchester Hotel, remade to look like an old-fashioned cruise liner, and the refurbished and relaunched Brown's Hotel, now boasting the stylish **Donovan Bar** (*see p66*).

The hotel bar doesn't have to be about expense-account Cristal-swigging, gold-leaf sakes and bespoke Martinis, though. Some bars aim squarely at young hipsters who wouldn't be seen within a cigar-stub of a conventional hotel bar. Located near Chelsea's exclusive Brompton Cross, the fashionable myhotel chain has a casual, cosy **mybar** (35 Ixworth Place, SW3 3QX, 7225 7500). It's a feast of purple, furnished with relaxing sofas and designer chairs, decorated with Buddhas

Donovan Bar

and crystals. A new food menu, mybento, has just been launched here, offering oriental-style snacks and light meals during the day. In the evening, the bar serves a good selection of reasonably priced cocktails and wines.

Another hotel that attracts a younger, hipper crowd is the music lovers' haunt K West Hotel & Spa. Next to the lobby of this hip hotel is **K Lounge** (Richmond Way, W14 0AX, 0870 027 4343, www.k-west.co.uk), a favourite bar of music and media folk – perhaps because of the late-night DJs and tail-feather shaking that goes on. Moby and all of Franz Ferdinand have partied here.

On occasion, even the youngbloods pine for a little stiff-spined old-school class. For such moments, we recommend the wonderful **American Bar** (*see p66*). Located to the left of the lobby of the chintzy, Nina Campbell-designed Connaught Hotel (and not to be confused with the hotel's Connaught Bar, which is to the right of the lobby), the American Bar epitomises the clubby feel of the classic hotel bar – hushed, intimate and discreet. It's just right for a business meeting during the day, or a brandy and cigar after dinner. Of course there's no drinks menu – a gentleman knows what he wants, and gets it. The Lanesborough's book-lined **Library** bar (*see p24*) and the handsome **Mandarin Bar** at the Mandarin Oriental Hyde Park (*see p56*) have a similar feel, attracting captains of industry who still have the appetite for a single malt, vintage cognac or cigar after a three-hour, expenses-paid lunch.

So many hotel bars, so little time. Where to start? We've saved the very best until last: our premier recommendation is the Berkeley's gorgeous **Blue Bar** (*see p23*). Strikingly designed by design guru David Collins in periwinkle blue, it is setting the standards for the hotel bar in London. Popular with designers and fashionistas, the Blue Bar has classic contemporary decor, exquisite cocktails and sumptuous snacks. If you only visit one hotel bar this year, make it this one. Just don't bring a hen party.

Hello!

Notable arrivals in the last year.

Annex 3

Princess

Green & Red

Sam's Brasserie & Bar

Central

All Star Lanes
*Victoria House,
Bloomsbury Place,
WC1B 4DA (7025 2676/
www.allstarlanes.co.uk).*
A striking revelation:
bowling has never been
so classy. *See p25.*

Annex 3
*6 Little Portland Street,
W1W 7JE (7631 0700).*
Those *trois* boys have
brought kitschy chic and
an innovative cocktail
list central. *See p42.*

Bloomsbury Bowling
*Basement of Tavistock
Hotel, Bedford Way,
WC1H 9EH (0871
474 5636).*
Upmarket bowling,
without the flash (or
the prices). *See p25.*

China Tang
*Dorchester Hotel, Park
Lane, W1A 2HJ (7629
9988/www.dorchester
hotel.com).*
A sumptuous bar with
A-list guests. *See p66.*

Donovan Bar
*Brown's Hotel,
Albemarle Street, W1S
4BP (7493 6020).*
A £20 million refurb
and Terence Donovan
photographs. *See p66.*

Glass
*9 Glasshouse Street,
W1R 5RL (7439 7770/
www.paperclublondon.
com).*

Glossy black and white
walls, glass chandeliers:
it adds up to one classy
cocktail bar. *See p58.*

**Somerstown
Coffee House**
*60 Chalton Street,
NW1 1HS (7691 9136).*
A superb Grade II-listed
'pub and bistro' in the
hinterland behind the
British Library. *See p53.*

Thomas Cubitt
*44 Elizabeth Street,
SW1W 9PA (7730
6060/www.thethomas
cubitt.co.uk).*
Renovation as it should
be done. Oak panelling,
fireplaces, top drinks
and food. *See p24.*

City

Commercial Tavern
*142 Commercial Street,
E1 6NU (7247 1888).*
Warm, wacky *and*
well stocked – that's
a combination we'd
definitely like to see
more of. *See p135.*

Gramaphone
*60-62 Commercial
Street, E1 6LT (7377
5332/www.the
gramaphone.co.uk).*
Corner bar-restaurant-
club with live comedy,
Mediterranean tapas
and cocktails. *See p135.*

Princess
*76-78 Paul Street, EC2A
4NE (7729 9270).*

Royalty returns to the
East End with this
elegant gastropub.
See p133.

Vinoteca
*7 St John Street, EC1M
4AA (7253 8786/www.
vinoteca.co.uk).*
One of London's best
(and best-priced) wine
lists can be found at this
little gem. *See p121.*

East

Camel
*277 Globe Road,
E2 0JD (8983 9888).*
Find heaven through
the doors of this lovely
old-school boozer.
See p144.

Green & Red
*51 Bethnal Green Road,
E1 6LA (7749 9670/
www.greenred.co.uk).*
Arriba! Arriba! Fine
tequila and Mexican
drinking food. *See p145.*

Pembury
*90 Amhurst Road,
E8 1JH (8986 8597).*
The old Victorian boozer
has returned with 16
handpumps of ever-
changing ales and
ciders. *See p151.*

North

Peachykeen
*112 Kentish Town
Road, NW1 9PX
(7482 2300/www.
peachy-keen.com).*

Get to Camden like
greased lightning for
this special cocktail
bar. *See p165.*

South

Lost Society
*697 Wandsworth Road,
SW8 3JF (7652 6526/
www.lostsociety.co.uk).*
Louche and intimate,
superb drinks list,
impressive food... time
to get Lost. *See p193.*

West

**Sam's Brasserie
& Bar**
*11 Barley Mow
Passage, W4 4PH
(8987 0555/www.
samsbrasserie.co.uk).*
For warehouse-style and
some truly fine wines.
See p232.

Clubs

Kabaret's Prophecy
*6-18 Beak Street, W1F
9RD (7439 2229/www.
kabaretsprophecy.com).*
Another exclusive,
luxurious and swanky
nightclub? Yes, please.
See p251.

Lucky Voice
*52 Poland Street, W1F
7NH (7439 3660/www.
luckyvoice.co.uk).*
This karaoke bar should
endure as long as
Gloria Gaynor survives.
See p253.

Central

Bayswater & Paddington

An area of London that manages to be both great (sizewise it stretches all the way west from Edgware Road to Queensway) yet undistinguished. Praise the Lord, then, for the excellent **Salt Whisky Bar** and regal **Victoria**.

Archery Tavern

4 Bathurst Street, W2 2SD (7402 4916). Lancaster Gate tube. **Open** *11am-11pm Mon-Sat; noon-10.30pm Sun.* **Food served** *noon-3pm, 6-9.30pm Mon-Fri; noon-9.30pm Sat; noon-9pm Sun.* **Credit** MC, V.
This is the kind of pub that features in British movies that want to do well in America, all ornamental china and hanging copper pots. Mercifully, the whole veers away from twee pub tat. Instead, the place has a villagey, local feel, enhanced by the clip-clop of horses' hooves from the adjacent mews. The clientele comprises a mix of readers (there are books on sale for charity in the back room), shooters of the breeze and darts players. Perhaps the darts is a nod to the pub's archery days, when the Royal Toxophilite (from the Greek for 'bow lover') Society filled its coffers regularly. Award-winning ales from the Tanglewood Brewery in Dorset line the bar. The lounge and saloon are no longer doored-off, which gives the pub a quirky, misshapen feel. There's an open fire in the womb-like back room, and a serving hatch that ensures the darts players needn't stray too far from the oche.
Babies and children admitted. Games (board games, darts, fruit machine). Quiz (9pm Sun; £1). Tables outdoors (4, pavement). TV (satellite).

Cherry Jam

58 Porchester Road, W2 6ET (7727 9950/www. cherryjam.net). Royal Oak tube. **Open/food served** *7pm-2am Mon-Sat; 4pm-midnight Sun (times vary, phone to check).* **Admission** *£5 after 8pm Mon-Thur; £6 after 10pm, £7 after 11pm Fri, Sat.* **Credit** MC, V.
The suggestion on Cherry Jam's website to just drop by after work to unwind with a cocktail is a little harder to follow up on these days, with the place only open from 7pm on Friday and Saturday, seemingly to accommodate music – live and DJ – nights. Not the must-go venue it was, the

place still satisfies, its subterranean, alcoved, red-lit seclusion and relaxed staff creating an unselfconsciously decadent ambience. On the cocktail front (from £6.50, which is pretty reasonable), the trads are handled with ease – a Lynchburg Lemonade was tart and boozy – but the house cocktails of Champagne and fruit are what catch the eye. The Cherry Jam – bubbles and cherry liqueur with a sunken maraschino – is great fun. The place may be looking a little ragged these days, even under the subdued lights, with a vibe more Camden Town than Notting Hill, but it's still worth the candle if you can catch it.
Disabled: toilet. Music (DJs 10pm Fri-Sun). Poetry (6pm-12.30am last Thur of mth).

Harlem

78 Westbourne Grove, W2 5RT (7985 0900/www. harlemsoulfood.com). Bayswater or Notting Hill Gate tube. **Open** *11am-2am Mon-Thur; 11am-2.30am Fri; 10am-2.30am Sat; 10am-midnight Sun.* **Food served** *11am-1am Mon-Fri; 10am-1am Sat; 10am-midnight Sun.* **Credit** AmEx, DC, MC, V.
Food and music are the prime reasons for Harlem's existence, with burgers and other hearty fare very much to the fore (we're not sure the soul food tag really applies, though), and a DJ bar downstairs. There's a diner feel upstairs – it can get a little smoky in the small space. A decent spread of reds accompanies the food, there is yellow beer in bottles, and the bar is obedient enough to meet standard cocktail requests. The downstairs bar is really tiny and it will depend on mood as to whether you find it intimate or cramped. It's all relaxed enough – some have said slow when it comes to food service – decked out in dark wood with big windows and a huge newsprint-style sports portrait on the stairs (we assume of one of the Harlem Globetrotters, although no one was able to confirm this). Harlem does a great value lunch deal and offers a takeaway service, this last pointing to a place more concerned with solids than liquids.
Babies and children welcome. Function room (Mon-Thur, Sun). Music (DJs 10pm Mon-Sat; £5 after 11pm Mon-Thur, £5 after 9pm Fri, Sat). Restaurant.

Island Restaurant & Bar

Royal Lancaster Hotel, Lancaster Terrace, W2 2TY (7551 6070/www.islandrestaurant.co.uk). Lancaster Gate tube. **Open** *10am-11pm Mon-Sat; 10am-10.30pm Sun.* **Food served** *6-10.30pm Mon-Sat; 10am-10pm Sun.* **Credit** AmEx, DC, MC, V.
You wouldn't believe this is generally a very dry area on the evidence of the first bar you hit when hanging a right out of Lancaster Gate station. Through an automatic door (very 1960s futuristic) and up a few steps, the Island is a small, bright, simple and stylish bar, with excellent views across to Hyde Park. The atmosphere of exclusivity is enhanced by seating that's raised a few feet above street level for a decadent look-down-on-the-hoi-polloi feel. The nicely balanced cocktail menu (ranging from £6.50 to just under a tenner) doesn't neglect the classics but knows how to have fun, flinging around the framboise, cacao and double cream in a New Forest Gateaux, for example. And only pedants would quibble that the Margarita is served in a Martini glass rather than a coupette, especially given the attentiveness of the staff. A real island paradise, then – you can almost forget it's actually on a traffic island with the Bayswater Road growling nearby.
Babies and children welcome. Disabled toilet. Restaurant (no smoking).

Leinster

*57 Ossington Street, W2 4LY (7243 9541). Bayswater,
Notting Hill Gate or Queensway tube.* **Open** noon-11pm
Mon-Wed; noon-midnight Thur-Sun. **Food served**
noon-6pm Mon-Wed; noon-10pm Thur-Sun. **Credit**
AmEx, MC, V.

Having enjoyed a gay makeover around the beginning of
2004, this secluded little corner pub now treads a careful
line between modern and trad drinking cultures. The traditional pub sign still swings outside, but with cheeky rainbow stripes that make it look like someone's hung a Paul
Smith shirt out to dry. Inside, a three-sided bar gives the
staff little room to operate, but the customers plenty of
space – they are served with alacrity, too. The downstairs
bar, scrubbed and classically plain, with green wood panels and cream walls, is compact, but another bar upstairs
(accessed by a wrought-iron spiral staircase) is both bright
and comfy, with sofas and soft chairs dotted around. Piped
music – Springfield and Streisand for our most recent visit
– is kept to a conversation-friendly level. Difficult to tell,
though, if the horrid upstairs carpet is an ironic wink at
old pub culture or a result of the budget running out.
*Function room. Games (fruit machine). Music (DJs
and cabaret 9pm 1st Wed of mth; free). No-smoking
area. Quiz (7pm 1st Tue of mth; £2). Tables outdoors
(14, patio).* **Map 10 B6.**

Leinster Arms

*17 Leinster Terrace, W2 3EU (7402 4670). Lancaster
Gate or Queensway tube.* **Open** noon-11pm Mon-Sat;
noon-10.30pm Sun. **Food served** noon-9pm daily.
Credit AmEx, MC, V.

At the far end of the bar, two stools with brass plaques that
bear the names of the pub's very own equivalents to *Cheers*
Norm 'n' Cliff (in this case 'Computer Tony' and 'Mind-the-
Gap Graham') sit before a framed collage of regulars getting mad with it at Halloween. Indeed, the pub feels like a
local from the off, even when, after a few visits, one realises
it has just as many transients as any big city boozer. It's
also part of that delicious London phenomenon – the
'secret' watering hole. OK, secret only by virtue of being
some yards off a main drag, but somehow generating their
own pub *Narnia* quality. The contents of the barrels and
spirit selection are rather rudimentary, the decor – standard-
issue Victorian boozer colour scheme and *Punch* prints –
is nothing to write home about. The CD jukebox is a little
predictable, too. But this is one of those pubs that adds
up to far more than the sum of its parts – the whole is
friendly and warm.
*Games (quiz machine, pool). Tables outdoors
(3, pavement). TVs.*

Mad Bishop & Bear

*Upper Concourse, Paddington Station, Praed Street,
W2 1HB (7402 2441/www.fullers.co.uk). Paddington
tube/rail.* **Open** 9am-11pm Mon-Fri; 7.30am-11pm Sat;
8am-10.30pm Sun. **Food served** 9am-9pm Mon-Sat;
8.30am-9pm daily. **No credit cards.**

Compared to the horrors at Charing Cross and London
Bridge, this station pub is almost heaven. It even shows
ambition in the cocktail department, with vermouth bottles stoppered hopefully, pourers at the ready. A roomy
main section encompasses booths, high stools and tables
– the no-smoking area almost achieves cosiness. Best of
all, beer-drinking commuters don't have to wait until they
hit Berkshire for a decent pint: the Mad Bishop wears its
Cask Marque plaque proudly, serving the likes of golden,
organic (and truly honeyish) Honey Dew. Of the solids,
only the own-made soup stands out, and the decor is all
mock-Georgian, but this place should be singled out for
treating even the beer drinker in a hurry as a gourmand.
A touch of real Pullman class.
*Games (4 fruit machines). No-smoking area. Tables
outdoors (8, terrace). TV (big screen).*

Mitre

*24 Craven Terrace, W2 3QH (7262 5240). Lancaster
Gate tube/Paddington tube/rail.* **Open** 11am-11pm Mon-
Thur; 11am-midnight Fri, Sat; noon-10.30pm Sun. **Food
served** noon-3pm, 6-10pm Mon-Fri; noon-4pm, 6-10pm
Sat; noon-4pm, 6-9pm Sun. **Credit** AmEx, MC, V.

Real ale from Adnams, Greene King and Brakspear, with
San Miguel for yellow beer fans, line up in front of a well-
prepared bar that – even though there were few takers –
has its sleeves rolled up ready for moderate cocktail
requests. There's also honest pub grub on offer, with a
cooked-to-requirements burger served on a mini butcher's
block that scored on quality, quantity and imaginative pre-
sentation. With big, plain-glass windows, the place lacks
the clandestine feel of contemporaneous public houses
(such as the Salisbury), but more than makes up for it in
comfort. There are chesterfields in the rear, wing-back
chairs crowd an impossibly cute snug, and there are two
open fires. The off-the-main-drag location gives the Mitre
an additional edge on more famous venues.
*Babies and children admitted (separate room). Function
room. No-smoking area. Music (occasional Wed; phone
for details). Tables outdoors (8, pavement). TV.*

Royal Exchange

*26 Sale Place, W2 1PU (7723 3781). Paddington
tube/rail.* **Open** 11am-11pm Mon-Sat; noon-10.30pm
Sun. **Food served** noon-10pm daily. **Credit** AmEx,
MC, V.

The Royal Exchange is a solid drinking shop, unencum-
bered by the fripperies of design or fashion – no-nonsense
copper-topped tables are the order of the day. Of an afternoon, the place thrums to the rhythm of the horse-racing
on satellite TV, while by night a clientele principally made
up of locals and regulars creates what such a crowd can
often inadvertently negate – a warm, welcoming atmosphere. The pub is Irish-run (in the same hands for 20-odd
years), but mercifully a million miles from the usual high-
street Feck O'Donnell's Green Beer Emporia – we can
easily forgive the odd cartoon of Jack Charlton. There's
Brakspear on tap with, inevitably, both hot and cold running Guinness. The chill cabinet boasts a few bottles of
Champagne – presumably set by for the occasion of a big
win on the horses.
*Babies and children admitted. Tables outdoors (4,
pavement). TV (digital, satellite).*

Salt Whisky Bar

*82 Seymour Street, W2 2JB (7402 1155/www.saltbar.
com). Marble Arch tube.* **Open** noon-1am Mon-Sat;
noon-midnight Sun. **Food served** noon-midnight
daily. **Credit** MC, V.

Whisky, erroneously viewed as the preserve of the roué
and the shadow cabinet grandee, has an image problem.
Thankfully, Salt comes to the rescue, dedicated to the pleasure of whisky in an ultra-modern environment. This sleek,
dark wood bar has ample floor space and perches for a
quick stopover, and comfy sofas upon which to set the
world to rights – for, according to writer William
McIlvanney, if wine is for seduction, then whisky surely is
for philosophy. The classic cocktails are here, impeccably

Central

Blue Bar. *See p23.*

Octave

Live Jazz
Cool Cocktails
Fabulous Food

Octave in Covent Garden is London's hottest new jazz haven with a 2am late license. With live jazz by well known and contemporary artists, Octave has an unmistakable cool vibe and is the perfect place for a night out with friends, a romantic dinner, private parties or a relaxing after-work drink.

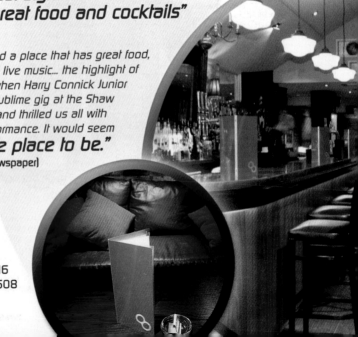

"Octave strikes all the right chords and is set to become one of *London's most significant venues for live music, great food and cocktails"*
(Evening Standard)

"I have finally found a place that has great food, great cocktails and live music... the highlight of the evening was when Harry Connick Junior strolled in after a sublime gig at the Shaw Theatre for dinner and thrilled us all with an impromptu performance. It would seem **Octave is the place to be."**
(The Independent Newspaper)

27-29 Endell St.
Covent Garden,
London,
WC2H 9BA
Tel: 020 7836 4616
Fax: 020 7836 2608
www.octave8.com

mixed (an excellent Rob Roy features an interesting soupçon of dry vermouth) with Glenfiddich as the house standard. Of the fun signature cocktails, go for a Honey Old Fashioned, mixed with ginger and the peaty-fruity delights of the Islay malt Bowmore. Staff are no less expert when juggling the flavoured vodkas, but with more than 200 whiskies on offer – Scotch, American, Irish and Japanese – why diversify?

Function room. Music (DJs 8pm Mon-Sat; free). No-smoking area. Tables outdoors (3, pavement). TV (big screen).

Steam

1 Eastbourne Terrace, W2 1BA (7850 0555). Paddington tube/rail. **Open** noon-1am Mon-Wed; noon-2am Thur-Sat. **Admission** £5 after 11pm Mon-Thur; £7 after 11pm Fri, Sat. **Credit** AmEx, DC, MC, V.
Mind the gap – the gap between style bar and commuter stop-off, that is. Steam's location, attached to both the four-star Hilton hotel and Paddington station, could easily mislead. This isn't somewhere you reel into straight from the office, looking for a quick fix of cooking lager to get you home to Bedfordshire. There's Leffe and Stella on tap, but what the place is really about is the cocktail. The cocktail menu is a helluva read, and errs definitively on the side of the modern (a request for a Rusty Nail on a nippy night was met with a blank look). The decor is heavily 1970s retro in orange and brown, and the odd lava lamp punctuates legions of spirits behind the impressively long, sleek, dark-wood bar. Gin and flavoured vodkas vie for domination, although there is also a surprisingly broad spectrum of American whiskeys.
Disabled: toilet (in hotel). Music (DJs 10pm Fri, Sat). Restaurant. TV (big screen, satellite).

Victoria

10A Strathern Place, W2 2NH (7724 1191). Lancaster Gate tube/Paddington tube/rail. **Open** 11am-11pm Mon-Sat; noon-10.30pm Sun. **Food served** noon-9.30pm Mon-Sat; noon-9pm Sun. **Credit** AmEx, MC, V.
The exterior of this striking corner pub is as distinctive as its interior. Immaculate white frontage conceals a beautiful gin palace, replete with detailed engraved mirrors, brass lamps on the bar and an open fire at either end. Further delights await in the private rooms upstairs – the dainty theatre bar and plush, panelled, gentleman's club-ish library are available for hire, with the Dracula Society among those who meet here regularly. On the taps, Leffe and Hoegaarden rub shoulders with Fuller's Discovery Blonde and the rotating Fuller's Seasonal Ales. The ornate clock above the bar is dated 1864 and the walls are adorned with images of – who else? – our own dear Queen. The menu (hale and hearty fare such as steak and ale pie) suggests that Charlie Chaplin and Winston Churchill were both regulars here, but adds a warning to take tales handed down by pub landlords with a pinch of salt. A nice self-effacing touch, from a pub with a lot to brag about.
Function rooms. Quiz (9pm Tue; £1). Tables outdoors (7, terrace). TV.

Also in the area...

All Bar One 7-9 Paddington Street, W1U 5QE (7487 0071).
Gyngleboy (Davy's) 27 Spring Street, W2 IJA (7723 3351).
Tyburn (JD Wetherspoon) 18-20 Edgware Road, W2 2EN (7723 4731).

Belgravia

The debt of gratitude Belgravia has owed its town planner for giving the place such stately streets back in the 1820s may finally have been repaid: the **Thomas Cubitt** has enjoyed an exemplary renovation. Otherwise, swank with the diplomats at **Blue Bar** or the **Library**.

Blue Bar

The Berkeley, Wilton Place, SW1X 7RL (7235 6000/ www.the-berkeley.co.uk). Hyde Park Corner tube. **Open** 4pm-1am Mon-Fri; 3pm-1am Sat; 4-11pm Sun. **Food served** 4-11pm daily. **Credit** AmEx, DC, MC, V.
One of London's best bars, this deeply stylish venue is located by the lobby of the Berkeley hotel. It's decorated by David Collins in a striking 'Lutyens blue' colour scheme, with a white onyx bar with seats, a black crocodile-print leather floor and a sunken seating area. Juicy olives and caramelised nuts are brought by polite staff as soon as you're seated. The drinks list offers a large selection of high-end Champagnes, classic and contemporary cocktails, wines by the glass, and 50 whiskies. There's also a Grape & Smoke menu that enables the many business clients to match cigars with wines. Bar snacks include upscale 'oriental tapas', such as lime leaf and chicken on coconut crisp with citrus coulis and rice paper (£5.50). Little wonder the bar is enduringly popular with designers and fashionistas.
Disabled: toilet. Function room. Restaurants.

Ebury

11 Pimlico Road, SW1W 8NA (7730 6784/www.the ebury.co.uk). Sloane Square tube/Victoria tube/rail/ 11, 211 bus. **Open** noon-11pm Mon-Sat; noon-10.30pm Sun. **Food served** noon-3.30pm, 6-10.30pm Mon-Fri; noon-4pm, 6-10.30pm Sat; noon-3pm, 6-10pm Sun. **Credit** AmEx, MC, V.
Sunday lunch at this trendy Chelsea gastropub means Bloody Marys, newspapers, meaty roasts and kids running about – the place is packed with young families. There's a bar counter that sells oysters and seafood and, in the ground-floor dining area with its polished wooden floor and funky lampshades, the fine Modern European menu (with game in season) has made the place more dining destination than pub. Nonetheless, drinks are still a reason to drop by: there's a new wine list with a good selection of wines by the glass, conveniently listed under headings like 'juicy and fruity' and 'crisp and dry'. Pre-dinner aperitifs, draught beers, real ales and Champagnes are also available. Cocktails are priced from £6.50 to £9.50, and include classics like Mint Julep and Singapore Sling.
Babies and children admitted. Bar available for hire. Function room. Restaurant (available for hire).

Grenadier

18 Wilton Row, SW1X 7NR (7235 3074). Hyde Park Corner tube. **Open** noon-11pm Mon-Sat; noon-10.30pm Sun. **Food served** noon-2.30pm, 6-9pm daily. **Credit** AmEx, DC, MC, V.
Centuries old, this grand pub plays its military schtick for all it's worth, and then plays it some more. Still, in the grand scheme of schtick, the Grenadier's history lies close to the top. The building was originally the mess for Wellington's men; after one young soldier was (apparently) caught cheating at cards, he was (reputedly) beaten to death by other officers and (allegedly) haunts the place to this day. Military ephemera pokes from every corner of the

minuscule front bar, packed nightly with a mix of toffee-nosed locals and gee-whizz American tourists eyeing up the £19.95 souvenir tankards; further back, tables are set aside for diners chowing down on an array of meaty dishes. The ales are decent (Bombardier, Pride, Adnams Bitter, Greene King IPA) and the Sunday-morning Bloody Marys are legendary, but the rather brusque staff otherwise seem well aware that they don't need to make much effort: on reputation alone, this pub fills itself.
Babies and children welcome (restaurant only). No piped music or jukebox. Restaurant (no smoking).

Horse & Groom

7 Groom Place, SW1X 7BA (7235 6980/www.horse andgroom.net). Hyde Park Corner tube/Victoria tube/rail. **Open** 11am-11pm Mon-Wed; 11am-midnight Thur, Fri. **Food served** noon-8.30pm Mon-Fri. **Credit** AmEx, MC, V.
Tucked away down a tiny private mews in deepest Belgravia, the 19th-century Horse & Groom boasts a rather unexpected location, but the pub itself also surprises. It's far from the posh alehouse you might expect given the neighbourhood: the room is basic and careworn, its banquette seating slightly tatty and its cheap 1970s tables battered almost into submission. The locals appear to be staff from the nearby embassies and hotels, taking the edge off the day with pints of tidily kept ale (it's a Shepherd Neame pub) to a soundtrack of 1980s pop and rock. There's a full menu at lunchtimes; at night, a complimentary tray of sandwiches are dispensed by a wild-eyed barman with a wicked grin.
Bar available for free private hire Sat, Sun. Games (darts). Tables outdoors (10, pavement). TV.

Library

Lanesborough Hotel, Hyde Park Corner, W1J 7JZ (7259 5599/www.lanesborough.com). Hyde Park Corner tube. **Open** 11am-1am Mon-Sat; noon-10.30pm Sun. **Food served** 11am-midnight Mon-Sat; noon-10.30pm Sun. **Credit** AmEx, DC, MC, V.
As its website advertises, the Lanesborough 'captures the gracious style and hospitality of an early 19th-century residence'; guests here are even allocated their own butler. However, the imposing structure on Hyde Park Corner was actually built as a hospital, and only became a hotel while John Major was living at No.10. The whole place is an illusion, then, but it's an undeniably grand illusion, not least in its handsome bar. There are vintage cognacs that date back to 1800. Cognacs with special dates, such as birth dates or significant historical dates are also available. Other drinks include armagnacs, Champagnes by the glass wines and lagers, but if you're spending this kind of money, at least take a look at the cocktail list, a mix of standard classics and more exotic recipes. All are served immaculately by staff whose discreet manners would make them a perfect fit at a library of a rather more traditional stripe. The cigar humidor, which offers rare cigars from Castro's own collection, will have to find a new home in spring 2007; enjoy it while you can. Drinks are served with complimentary canapés.
Disabled: toilet. Function rooms. Music (pianist 6.30pm daily). Restaurant.

Nag's Head

53 Kinnerton Street, SW1X 8ED (7235 1135). Hyde Park Corner or Knightsbridge tube. **Open** 11am-11pm Mon-Sat; noon-10.30pm Sun. **Food served** noon-9pm daily. **No credit cards.**

You're best off arriving at the Nag's Head stone-cold sober; the layout of this poky but undeniably charming little pub, originally stables, is mind-bending enough without alcohol to exaggerate the effect. The floor in the main bar is at least a foot lower behind the bar than it is in front of it, rendering the staff in curious miniature; conversely, from the downstairs room, you can see the bartender's feet as he or she pours immaculate pints of Adnams from the taps upstairs. The pub is cluttered with all sorts of relics, seemingly bought as a job lot from a 19th-century car boot sale: yellowing press cuttings, caricatures of old regulars, horse-grooming gear, farming equipment, a what-the-butler-saw viewing kiosk, even an ancient stove. The best bit? Mobile phones are banned from the place.
Games (antique what-the-butler-saw machine). No mobile phones. Tables outdoors (1, pavement).

Star Tavern

6 Belgrave Mews West, SW1X 8HT (7235 3019/ www.fullers.co.uk). Hyde Park Corner or Knightsbridge tube/Victoria tube/rail. **Open** 11am-11pm Mon-Sat; noon-10.30pm Sun. **Food served** noon-2.30pm, 6-9.30pm Mon-Fri; 6-9pm Sat; 6-8.30pm Sun. **Credit** AmEx, MC, V.
Back in the 1960s, the centuries-old Star Tavern was favoured by some of London's more raffish drinkers: actors, models and even the occasional crim (it's said that the Great Train Robbery was planned in the upstairs room). The drinkers these days may be a little less newsworthy (some local residents, some local workers), but this is still a superior pub. Longstanding landlord TJ Connell left a couple of years ago; happily, though, not much seems to have changed in his absence. The various Fuller's ales remain in excellent nick, the food is still decent English fare from the days before gastropubs and, as ever, there's no piped music. Hidden down a small mews, the Star can be a bugger to find, but once you're in, you won't be in any hurry to leave.
Babies and children welcome. Function room. Games (board games). No piped music or jukebox. TV.

Thomas Cubitt

44 Elizabeth Street, SW1W 9PA (7730 6060/ www.thethomascubitt.co.uk). Hyde Park Corner tube/Victoria tube/rail. **Open** 11am-11pm daily. **Food served** noon-10pm daily. **Credit** AmEx, MC, V.
This is how a pub renovation should be done. Although completely new, the oak panelling, newly laid wooden floors, fireplaces and sturdy bar are perfectly in keeping with the Grade II-listed building. The pub's new name is a homage to the master builder who created much of Belgravia and Pimlico in the second quarter of the 19th century; this pub lies on one of the many streets Cubitt built. The ground floor bustles with people enjoying Old Speckled Hen and Marston's Pedigree, or bar snacks such as oysters or posh sausage and mash. The first floor is occupied by a more ambitious dining room, serving British-accented Modern European food such as scallops pan-fried with pancetta and celeriac purée, or a ballotine of guinea fowl with thyme and veal jus. If every neighbourhood had a pub that was as lovingly cared for as the Thomas Cubitt is, we'd all be happier about going for a pint.
Babies and children welcome. Function room. No-smoking area. Restaurant (available for hire; no smoking). Tables outdoors (8, pavement). TV (big screen).

Central

Lucky strikes

What did bowling in London used to mean? A retail park in the suburbs, usually. Blaring arcade machines. Sticky floors. Fluorescent blue 'raspberry slushes' that came from no earthly fruit. The activity itself took a backseat to birthday parties, chicken nuggets and boy–girl groups of teens, silently testing the waters of mixed-gender fraternity.

Changes are rollin' into town. Perhaps influenced by the stateside success of 'boutique' bowling alleys – darker, less sticky, with bars, dining areas and no kids – Londoners now have two alternatives to the retail parks. **Bloomsbury Bowling Lanes** (in the basement of the Tavistock Hotel, off Russell Square) and **All Star Lanes** (in the basement of an office building on Bloomsbury Square) both opened within the last year, and are doing a roaring trade.

At last! Successful outfits like **Elbow Room** (for pool) and **Bar Kick** (for table football) have shown there's a market for gently accessible sports that anyone can enjoy, regardless of innate athletic talent or blood-to-alcohol ratio. Bowling has been waiting its turn for trendification. It's loud, destructive, but also sociable (providing you're not the one hoofing it towards the foul-line with a 12-pound ball), tapping into the sort of cool that runs through cult films like *The Big Lebowski*, *Kingpin* and a much-loved episode of *The Simpsons*. Before this Bloomsbury twosome, bowlers beyond their wispy 'tache years had to traipse to the rather grim Rowans in Finsbury Park to reel off favourite quotes.

So what's the difference between them? While both are geared towards adults rather than kids – think office parties, suited types letting off steam after work, groups of students from the London universities – All Star Lanes is noticeably aimed at the richer end of the market. Their four bowling lanes (plus two private lanes upstairs) are only part of the set-up: All Star also has a pricey diner-style restaurant (steaks ring in at a whopping £16-£19, while lobster appears at £30) and an even pricier red-leather bar beyond (cocktails climb to £8 and there are no beers on tap). Still, the quality is high and, as long as you can afford it, the bar has buckets more atmosphere than its rival.

Bloomsbury Bowling wins out in other departments, however. With twice as many lanes and hire costs at almost half the price (bowling here costs £5.50 per game at peak time, as opposed to £8.50 at All Star Lanes), this is a less intimidating outfit. The low-key, intentionally grubby decor is less flashy than at All Star Lanes, and the worn booths in the restaurant (burgers £6.75) seem a more authentic representation of Americana than All Star's unspoiled shininess. To top it all, bowling in the daytime (Mon-Wed) only costs £3 per game – surely one of the best prices in London, retail park or not.

All Star Lanes

Their differences mean that All Star and Bloomsbury complement each other well, and they've arrived just at the right time. With capped scorelines, bowling will never be an Olympic discipline (after all, the tally of the sport's best practitioner can be matched by Matey Eightpints on a lucky streak), but as a drink-side pursuit it's exactly what London needs. Fresh and flippant, it makes a worthy alternative to the relentless parade of newborn bars who think beads, bamboo furniture and a new forest fruit in their signature cocktail are a sign of distinction.

All Star Lanes

Victoria House, Bloomsbury Place, WC1B 4DA (7025 2676/www.allstarlanes.co.uk). Holborn tube. **Open** noon-11.30pm Mon-Wed; noon-2am Thur-Sat; noon-11pm Sun. **Bowling** £7.50 (per person per game) before 5pm Mon-Fri; £8.50 after 5pm Mon-Fri; £7.50 all day Sat, Sun. **Map 1 L5**.

Bloomsbury Bowling Lanes

Basement of Tavistock Hotel, Bedford Way, WC1H 9EH (0871 474 5636). Holborn tube. **Open** noon-2am Mon-Wed; noon-3am Thur-Sat; noon-midnight Sun. **Bowling** £3 (per person per game) before 4pm, £5.50 after 4pm Mon-Wed; £4.50 before 4pm, £5.50 after 4pm Thur, Fri; £5.50 Sat, Sun. **Map 1 K4**.

Central

CHARLIE WRIGHT'S INTERNATIONAL BAR

Monday to Wednesday open from 12noon til 1am

Thursday open 12noon til 4am
Live jazz & DJ from 9pm til 4am
Admission free

Friday open from 12noon til 4am
DJ from 10pm til 4am playing soul, R & B funk, classic soul, reggae
Admission free B4 10pm £4 after

Saturday open from 3pm til 4am
DJ from 10pm playing party sound, rock, Northern soul,
country, pop, world
Admission free B4 10pm £4 after

Sunday open from 4pm til late
The Afro Club
Live Africa band plus guest DJ

Admission free B4 9pm £3 after
Sky Sport Live

45 Pitfield St off Old Street. Old St Tube exit 2
020 7490 8345

Bloomsbury & St Giles

Famous for its radical intellectuals, this part of London nowadays combines the contemporary hedonism of terrific club-bar **AKA** with the beauty of pub history at the **Lamb**. You'll also find some mighty fine ale at the **Museum Tavern**, though probably not the next Karl Marx or Viriginia Woolf, and brilliant wines at **Vats Wine Bar**.

AKA

18 West Central Street, WC1A 1JJ (7836 0110/www. akalondon.com). Holborn tube. **Open** 10pm-5am Tue (6pm-5am 1st Tue of mth); Sun; 6pm-3am Wed, Thur; 6pm-4am Fri; 7pm-5am Sat. **Snacks served** 6-11.30pm Tue-Fri; 7-11.30pm Sat. **Admission** £3 after 11pm Tue; £5 after 10pm Thur; £5 after 9pm, £7 after 10pm Fri; £10 after 9pm Sat; varies Sun. **Credit** AmEx, DC, MC, V.

One of London's finest club-bars is tucked away down a dark side street, beside its partner operation, leading nightclub The End. Set in a former Victorian sorting office, this chic two-storey warehouse space has quality stamped all over it. The DJ agenda, the design (one main downstairs bar with a huge drinks counter and a mezzanine for chow and chat), the decor (shiny zinc counter, curved-back seats – comfortable and minimal at the same time), all is done with taste and the customer in mind. And the drinks? A handful of well-crafted cocktails (£7-£9) per spirit, from a Holly Goodhead Martini (Zubrowka Bison, passion fruit, apple and peach) to a Bambi and Thumper (Tanqueray, mango and apple), not to mention the Devaux Champagne varieties of the house – 18 West (with Zubrowka Bison, pear and passion fruit) or Lost In Translation (with sake, passion fruit purée and marmalade) – that are as good as it gets in the capital. Ten well-chosen whites (£12.50-£27), ten well-chosen reds (£12.50-£32), Baltika and Beck's by the bottle, bundles of bourbons, warm chicken salads (£7.95), primavera pizzas with wild rocket and a dozen others (£7.95) – class, class, class.
Bar available for hire. Comedy (7.30pm 2nd Thur of mth; £8). Disabled: toilet. Music (DJs 10pm daily; free). Quiz (8pm 1st Tue of mth; free). Screening facilities (phone for details; prices vary). **Map 1 L6**.

Angel

61 St Giles High Street, WC2H 8LE (7240 2876). Tottenham Court Road tube. **Open** 11.30am-11pm Mon-Fri; noon-11pm Sat; 1-10.30pm Sun. **Food served** noon-9pm Mon-Sat; 1-6pm Sun. **Credit** MC, V.
Tradition itself, the Angel is as popular with the twentysomething post-work crowd as it is with ale-supping darts players fêted with plates of roast potatoes one evening a week. All the elements of the English pub are here: (1) the Victorian decor, tiled indoor courtyard, carved wood and dinky light fittings; (2) the history – in Elizabethan times it was known as the Bowl, as it was where condemned men received their last request; (3) the pints, filled with the standard Young's range of ales and lagers; (4) the nod towards culture, a wall of old theatre posters in the darts room; (5) darts; (6) grub: giant Yorkshire puddings filled with roast beef and veg (£5.75), fish and chips (£5.95), hot baguettes (£3.50) and half-a-dozen vegetarian choices such as spinach and goat's cheese cannelloni with salad and crusty bread (£5.50). Bread with pasta! It couldn't be anywhere else.
Games (chess, darts, cribbage, fruit machine). No piped music or jukebox. Tables outdoors (8, garden). **Map 7 K6**.

Duke

7 Roger Street, WC1N 2PB (7242 7230/www.duke pub.co.uk). Chancery Lane tube. **Open** noon-11pm Mon-Sat; noon-10.30pm Sun. **Food served** noon-10pm Mon-Sat; noon-9.30pm Sun. **Credit** MC, V.
This old corner local – it still has Double Diamond etched on the window – has been converted into a gastrobar of retro character. The gastro element is as superbly executed as the retro, the one best enjoyed at the tables in the back room with a blazing fireplace, the other more visible in a front bar of red Formica tops, a piano similarly painted and pink speakers playing your favourite tunes on the counter. Around each room, pop-art portraits of Audrey Hepburn, Marlene Dietrich, the Rat Pack and other icons. Many come for Bill's kitchen alone. Mains include pea pancakes with roasted balsamic cherry tomatoes and grilled halloumi (£8.95), king prawn and pea risotto (£8.95) and trout stuffed with crab chilli (£9.95), all beautifully conceived. Look out for the fish and game of the week (£12.50), and leave room for £4.25 puddings such as poached pear and ice-cream or vanilla pancakes and cherries. Plenty of wines, eight of each colour by the bottle, four by the glass, plus Adnams and Greene King IPA on tap.
Babies and children welcome. Restaurant (no smoking). Tables outdoors (3, pavement). **Map 3 M4**.

Grape Street Wine Bar

222-224A Shaftesbury Avenue, WC2H 8EB (7240 0686). Holborn tube. **Open** noon-11pm Mon-Fri. **Food served** noon-3.30pm, 5-10pm Mon-Fri. **Credit** AmEx, MC, V.
Run by Clive Allen of Cork & Bottle fame, this well-oiled and well-priced operation attracts the office crowd at the traditional intervals of down time. Wining and dining take place in two rooms, a café-like space at street level, and next door, the more conspiratorial wine-bar basement. Twenty whites and 20 reds are on offer by the bottle, most between £15 and £20, from the humble Chevanceau VdP (£11.50) to a rare Austrian Grüner Veltliner Breiter Rain (£25) and a South Australian Yalumba Shiraz Viognier (£35). Fourteen by the glass allows plenty of room for choice without spending the rest of the afternoon giggling and flirting at your desk. The house Champagne is Pierre Vaudon (£6.25/£31.50), half-bottles and magnums available. No Cristals or Dom Pérignons, just six others in the £40 range – Grape Street is not trying to be something it's not. Chalked up, the specials of the day (£7-£11), imaginative enough to tempt regulars bored with ordering the Grape Street burger (£8.95) again – on this occasion, baked sea bass with cauliflower and potato mash, and baby squid and vegetable risotto. Very tidy indeed.
Babies and children admitted. Function room. Tables outdoors (2, pavement). **Map 1 L6**.

King's Arms

11A Northington Street, WC1N 2JF (7405 9107). Chancery Lane or Russell Square tube. **Open** 11am-11pm Mon-Fri. **Food served** noon-9.45pm Mon-Fri. **Credit** AmEx, DC, MC, V.
Blokes on lunchbreaks fill the regally themed, expansive main bar of this busy corner pub, pleased to be tucking into Thai delights instead of the usual pies and pastas. And very nice it is too, either an £8 platter for two (fish cakes, chicken satay, prawns on toast), a spicy soup (a tom yam hed of lemongrass, mushrooms and fresh chilli, £3.15), a curry or stir-fry. The latter are offered in prawn, beef, pork, chicken or vegetable varieties (£4.90-£6.25), ladled on to jasmine-steamed rice. More blokey blokes can tackle an

Central

King's Arms. *See p27.*

English breakfast or baguette. Adnams, Greene King IPA, Timothy Taylor Landlord or Staropramen are the usual accompaniment, but white-collar workers are able to pick a wine from the half dozen on offer. A rather intricate family tree of English royals down the millennium complements a wall of regal portraits, but most are happier to gawp at groin-strain revelations on Sky Sports than study Stuart history. A large pool room upstairs is unsurprisingly popular – book early or come during the inevitable lull before playtime at five.
Games (darts, pool). Function room. No-smoking area. Tables outdoors (2, pavement). TVs (big screen, satellite). **Map 3 M4.**

King's Bar
Russell Hotel, Russell Square, WC1B 5BE (7837 6470/ www.principal-hotels.com). Russell Square tube. **Open** 7am-midnight Mon-Sat; 8am-11pm Sun. **Food served** 7am-9pm Mon-Sat; 8am-9pm Sun. **Credit** AmEx, MC, V.
'Beyond expectation' runs the blurb for the £20 million refit of the Gothic Victorian Russell Hotel, in whose lobby this still traditional, leather armchair and high tea bar is set. £4.95 is beyond what you would expect to pay for a coffee, £18 beyond the going rate for a steak sandwich. Yet, weirdly enough, said sarnie is twice the price of a very decent Martini indeed, a Long Live The Queen mixed with Grey Goose vodka. In fact, if you choose your drinks judiciously – perhaps a Crocodile Dundee of Stoli, Amaretto and Famous Grouse – and pick a spot by one of the large windows overlooking leafy Russell Square, this isn't a bad place at all for a classy and intimate drink. Beyond expectation though – in fact, beyond belief – are the Did You Knows? on the drinks menu: for example, 'Winemaking

begins in the vineyard and the growing of the grapes. This is crucial to the whole process.' That's priceless.
Babies and children admitted. Disabled: toilet. Dress: no shorts. Function room. No piped music or jukebox. No-smoking area. Restaurant (no smoking). **Map 1 L4.**

Lamb
94 Lamb's Conduit Street, WC1N 3LZ (7405 0713/ www.youngs.co.uk). Holborn or Russell Square tube. **Open** 11am-midnight Mon-Sat; noon-4pm, 7-10.30pm Sun. **Food served** noon-9pm Mon-Thur, Sat; noon-3pm Fri; noon-4pm, 7-10.30pm Sun. **Credit** AmEx, MC, V.
For a taste of old Bloomsbury – and slow-roast lamb shank, pan-seared lamb's liver or prime Scotch beefburgers – the near 300-year-old Lamb is for you. Founded in 1729, a date celebrated with in the naming of its own-made steak and mushroom pie (£8.75), this beautifully restored etched glass and mahogany masterpiece is class itself. Today the snob screens have a decorative role above the horseshoe island bar, but, back in the days when music hall stars were regulars here, they were used to deflect unwanted attention. The stage stars are remembered with two rows of small, gilt-framed portraits running around the walls, and other vintage theatrical touches are provided by a polyphon (the old mechanical musical instrument in the corner), dinky brass balustrades around the bar tables and The Pit, a sunken back area that gives access to a summer patio. The beer is Young's, the wines a well-chosen half-dozen of each colour from Cockburn and Campbell, and the menu seasonal, with most main plates under a tenner.
No-smoking area. Separate room for parties, seats 32. Tables outdoors (3, patio; 3, pavement). No piped music or jukebox. **Map 3 M4.**

Lord John Russell

91 Marchmont Street, WC1N 1AL (7388 0500).
Russell Square tube. **Open** 11.30am-11pm Mon-Sat;
noon-10.30pm Sun. **Food served** noon-3pm Mon-Fri.
Credit MC, V.
A short walk but a world away from the Bloomsbury Set
and the British Museum, Marchmont is a mongrel area
of the low-waged, launderette users and long-time ex-
students. Now and then they pop into this rather splendid
venue, which has all the markings of a gastrobar (bare
boards, sturdy rustic tables, the occasional pew and
plenty of Monet on the walls) but only needs to serve pies
and pasties. The beers – König Pilsener, Budvar, San
Miguel, Director's, Bombardier, John Smith's – cannot be
gainsaid, nor the egalitarian nature of the vibe around the
bar as people sip and sup them. Bottled Belgian brews are
available, too. Some decent music rather than bland radio
would give this place a B+, rather than just a B–, but, as
another ex-student crams his Wranglers into the launderette opposite, it could always do better next term.
*Babies and children welcome (daytime only). Games
(board games, chess, draughts, quiz machine). Tables
outdoors (7, pavement). TV.* **Map 1 L4.**

Museum Tavern

49 Great Russell Street, WC1B 3BA (7242 8987).
Holborn or Tottenham Court Road tube. **Open** 11am-
11.30pm Mon-Thur; 11am-midnight Fri, Sat; noon-
10.30pm Sun. **Food served** 11am-8.30pm Mon-Sat;
noon-8pm Sun. **Credit** AmEx, DC, MC, V.
Although historically linked with the British Museum
opposite, and counting Reading Room veterans Orwell and
Marx among its past regulars, the namesake tavern is of
greater vintage. As the Dog & Duck in the early 1700s, it
was surrounded by marshlands, not the current crocodiles
of cagouled Italians and stench of overpriced hot dogs. A
sumptuous refurb in the mid 1800s resulted in the beautiful pub interior you still see today. Tourists come for tradition; locals for the splendid range of ales. Theakston Old
Peculier, Everards Tiger Best and Original, St Austell
Tribute, Fuller's London Pride and Thwaites Original all
line up on the sturdy dark-wood bar counter, behind which
glint bottles of Budvar and Baltika. Both visitor and regular are pleased with the oven-baked pies and meaty
mains, served from the food counter at the back of the main
bar area. Fine selection of whiskies, too.
*Children admitted (over-14s only before 5pm). Games
(board games). Tables outdoors (5-8, pavement).*
Map 1 L5.

mybar

*11-13 Bayley Street, WC1B 3HD (7667 6000/www.my
hotels.com). Goodge Street tube.* **Open** 11am-12.30am
Mon-Thur, Sun; 11am-1am Fri, Sat. **Food served** 7am-
10.30pm daily. **Credit** AmEx, DC, MC, V.
The bar at this outpost of the myhotel chain is looking
sleeker and has a new cocktail list. On our most recent visit
the barman served us a fruity, brown-sugar-frosted
cachaça confection of his own invention that, as he assured
us it would, tasted of mango though there was no mango
in it. For a classic Martini, we opted for Hendrick's from
half-a-dozen premium gins – classy it was too. Bar snacks
including bowls of 'myfries' (fat chips with ketchup, mayo
and pesto) soak up the damage. The furnishings in the two-
room bar are very glossy, with strangely narrow-backed,
bendy chairs at the tables in the front room, banquettes
and a screen showing random silent films in the smaller
space out back. Globular silver lightshades and light

boxes bearing architectural artwork complete the aesthetic, professionals and the professionally hip make up the
punters. Our grumbles? You wouldn't have to walk far to
get a pair of fine cocktails a lot cheaper than £20. And
something decent on draught wouldn't hurt.
*Babies and children admitted (until 6pm). Bar available
for hire. Disabled: toilet. Function rooms. Tables
outdoors (7, pavement).* **Map 1 K5.**

Oporto

*168 High Holborn, corner of Endell Street, WC1V
7AA (7240 1548/www.baroporto.com). Holborn tube.*
Open/food served noon-midnight Mon-Wed; noon-
1am Thur, Fri; 1pm-1am Sat. **Credit** MC, V.
The once continental Oporto is slowly turning Thai. An
extensive menu from south-east Asia is the latest feature
of this funky little two-floor bar on the corner of High
Holborn and Endell Street. Mixed veg platters (£6.50) of
deep-fried tofu and vegetable tempura, large sharing platters (£12) of chicken satay and prawn-in-a-blanket, thom
kha coconut soups (£4-£4.50), gado gado salads (£6.50),
curries (£5.50-£6), it's all a far cry from the Med-influenced
dishes of yesteryear. As for the drinks, there's now Sabai,
Thai white wine and hibiscus juice – but also, the more traditional of the youngish, reasonably hip regulars will be
pleased to hear, still Boddingtons on tap and eight standard wines of each colour, four by the glass. A Jean Lafite
Chablis and a Conde de Valdemar Rioja Crianza (both £20)
are at the quality end. Lager drinkers can sip San Miguel
while shooting pool downstairs.
*Function room. Games (pool, £1.50 per game). Tables
outdoors (4, pavement). TV.* **Map 1 L6.**

Perseverance

63 Lamb's Conduit Street, WC1N 3NB (7405 8278).
Holborn or Russell Square tube. **Open** 12.30-11pm Mon-
Thur; 12.30pm-midnight Fri, Sat; 12.30-10.30pm Sun.
Food served 12.30-3pm, 6.30-10pm Mon-Fri; 12.30-
3pm Sat, Sun. **Credit** MC, V.
By day a gastropub for diners (apart from a back row of
tables for drinkers), by night the Perseverance is a wine
and beer bar with a quality menu. Sister to Soho's
Endurance, the Perseverance knows where its bread is buttered. The wines chalked up on the blackboard are only a
selection – the full list takes in a Sancerre Domaine de la
Rossignole (£26), a Jean Goulley Chablis (£24.50) and Les
Cailloux Châteauneuf-du-Pape (£30). You can, alternatively, order a Lebeau Chêne vin de pays of either colour
for £3 a glass. The bar menu, served from 6pm to 10pm,
includes a charcuterie platter (£15) – and even the fat chips
(£3) come with Bloody Mary ketchup and harissa mayonnaise. Director's, Deuchars IPA and San Miguel are the
beers on draught. Glugging is hardly encouraged by the
sleek but simple sit-down interior, although the upstairs
dining room is more intimate.
*Babies and children admitted (lunchtime). Tables
outdoors (6, pavement). Restaurant (available for hire;
no smoking).* **Map 3 M4.**

Plough

27 Museum Street, WC1A 1LH (7636 7964).
Tottenham Court Road tube. **Open** 11am-11.30pm
Mon-Thur; 11am-midnight Fri, Sat; noon-10.30pm Sun.
Food served noon-8pm Mon-Fri; noon-5pm Sat, Sun.
Credit MC, V.
'The best fish and chips in London', boasts the blackboard
outside this corner pub in sight of the British Museum, a
short walk explained to tourists in four languages in the

Central

window. Once inside this Taylor Walker pub, though, it's not Queen Mum and corgis, not at all. In fact, thanks to the Young's, Bombardier, Deuchars and Abbot, sport on TV and comprehensive selection of wines in the back bar, locals easily outnumber foreign visitors. Local custom is also generated by, well, fish and chips, but also pies and pastas, and open mic poetry evenings every second Tuesday. These take place in the convivial lounge room upstairs, but most are happy to use the simple front bar, lined with framed old prints. In short, a tourist-friendly pub with character.

Babies and children admitted (upstairs bar). Comedy (occasional Fri; phone for details). Function room. Games (fruit machine). Poetry (7.30pm 2nd Tue of mth; free). Quiz (7.30pm 1st Wed of mth; £2). Tables outdoors (8, pavement). TVs (satellite). **Map 1 L5**.

Point 101

101 New Oxford Street, WC1A 1DB (7379 3112/ www.101bar.com). Tottenham Court Road tube. **Open/ food served** 5pm-3am Mon-Thur; 4pm-4am Fri, Sat; 4pm-2.30am Sun. **Admission** £3 after midnight Fri, Sat. **Credit** AmEx, MC, V.

Once a pre-club bar and lunchtime hangout of some renown, Point 101 is still finding its feet after last year's change of ownership and refit. The change of schedule to evening-only suits it down to the ground, although the purple exterior covering the front windows may not have been wise. There isn't much you can do to embellish Centre Point rising above the place, but the rather minimal, institutional feel of yesteryear somehow fitted. The menu is pretty standard: paninis and dips, regular Daiquiris and Cosmopolitans at £6.50, and ten wines of each colour, three

each by two sizes of glass. The majority of the party-oriented clientele forgoes the £20 Rioja Tempranillo and settles for the simple option of a pint of San Miguel or Kronenbourg. Same sci-fi-esque decor, same stroppy East European staff.

Function room. Music (DJs 10pm daily). Tables outdoors (4, pavement). **Map 7 K6**.

Queen's Larder

1 Queen Square, WC1N 3AR (7837 5627). Holborn or Russell Square tube. **Open** 11am-11pm Mon-Fri; noon-11pm Sat; noon-10.30pm Sun. **Food served** noon-3pm daily. **Credit** MC, V.

Although not exactly sweeping Queen Charlotte from history, the new broom at this landmark pub has cleaned up and modernised the business to such an extent that it's much like any other in the area. The result certainly isn't unpleasant, but the framed posters of mainstream theatrical productions, Sky Sports and the primitive pictorial pub sign grate when compared with the pub's previous incarnation as a historic curiosity dating back 250 years. Going with the unenviable territory of being Mad King George's other half was Charlotte's task of having to hide his medicaments here – hence the Queen's Larder. Until fairly recently, royal portraits adorned the tiny, low-ceilinged cabin of a bar. OK, so now it's not so gloomy, and the pub grub has been upgraded (ribeye steak and chips, £7.95), but something has been lost along the way. Good beers, mind, Greene King IPA and Abbot, pleasantly supped at one of the bench-tables on the cobbled terrace, or in the criminally underused lounge bar upstairs.

Function room. Restaurant. Tables outdoors (7, pavement). TV. **Map 1 L5**.

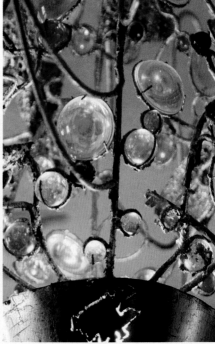

Rugby Tavern

19 Great James Street, WC1N 3ES (7405 1384). Holborn tube. **Open** 11am-11pm Mon-Fri. **Food served** noon-2.30pm, 5.30-9pm Mon-Fri. **Credit** AmEx, MC, V.

Rather upmarket this one, a smart Shepherd Neame pub with modern bar touches. As a pub, it would have been used by the pre-war literary set (Dorothy L Sayers lived next door). As a bar, it's gastronomically inclined, the sporting connection a mere quirk of geographical fate – Rugby Street is nearby. This hasn't stopped the mounting of a wall of contemporary photos of muddy action, incongruously placed around a comfortable alcove of cosy sofas, and a display of Dr Arnold's tie and scorecards. As for the food, there are char-grilled burgers (£5.50), superior sandwiches such as ribeye steak (£4.25) and warm Cumberland sausage (£4), a blackboard of daily specials and fish battered in Shepherd Neame Master Brew and served with hand-cut chips (£6.50). As well as Shepherd Neame beers, there is Dutch Oranjeboom on draught and rare bottles of strong, Swiss Hürlimann lager.

Function room. Games (darts). Tables outdoors (10, pavement). TV. **Map 3 M4.**

Truckles of Pied Bull Yard

Off Bury Place, WC1A 2JR (7404 5338/www.davy.co.uk). Holborn tube. **Open/food served** 11am-10pm Mon-Fri; 11am-3pm Sat. **Credit** AmEx, DC, MC, V.

Nestled in a quiet courtyard otherwise containing camera shops and the excellent London Review Bookshop, Truckles' Bloomsbury branch was once the most traditional of the 16-strong Davy's wine-bar chain. These days the upstairs is modern, dressed in pine and housewives'-television-backdrop yellow, while the basement restaurant maintains its spit 'n' sawdust character. New to the operation are the 30-minute lunch (a plate of ham, hot buttered potatoes, glass of wine and coffee for a tenner), complimentary canapés for pre-booked parties of ten and occasional quiz nights. There has been no dumbing down of the food or wine menus, though: mains of Devonshire dressed crab (£12.95), braised lamb shank with rosemary (£13.95) and wild mushroom risotto (£8.95), starters of Scottish smoked salmon (£5.95) or warm tartlet of spinach, ham and goat's cheese (£5.25), all is as it should be. There are sandwiches, sharing plates and salads, too. A dozen of Davy's own wines – fine French claret (£4.75/£17.75), Australian chardonnnay (£4.85/£18.25), Rioja of Marqués de Vitoria, Alavesa (£4.75/£17.95) – come by the glass or bottle. For special occasions, there is Vieilles Vignes Chablis (£22.95) or a Château Chasse-Spleen '97 (£39.95).

Babies and children admitted (restaurant). Bar available for hire. No-smoking area. Tables outdoors (20, courtyard). **Map 1 L5.**

Vats Wine Bar

51 Lamb's Conduit Street, WC1N 3NB (7242 8963). Holborn or Russell Square tube. **Open** noon-11pm Mon-Fri. **Food served** noon-2.30pm, 6-9.30pm Mon-Fri. **Credit** AmEx, DC, MC, V.

Superb wine bar this – just ask the solicitors and publishers who fill its lived-in two-space interior every lunchtime. The sunken back area is occasionally hired out for private parties, but otherwise the place is tradition itself. Sticking with it, however, is proving frustrating for the more progressive younger element in the management team, who wish to expand a selection dominated by 50 French wines

Cross Keys. *See p35.*

Central

(plus nine Champagnes) and add a few more New World ones to the list. Regulars shouldn't start fiddling nervously with their cravats – the blue-chip food menu of Sussex pheasant-and-venison terrine starters (£5.95) and pheasant, bacon and mushroom casserole mains (£13.95) will not be tampered with. And for uninitiates worried about the bill at the end, 15 carefully chosen wines come by the large glass, all in the £4-£6 range. Outstanding.
Babies and children admitted. Function room. Restaurant. Tables outdoors (4, pavement). **Map 3 M4**.

Also in the area...

All Bar One 108 New Oxford Street, WC1A 1HB (7307 7980).

Chelsea

The golden rule for drinking in Chelsea has long been to get off the King's Road, but there are exceptions: **Apartment 195** and **Nectar** at one end of the scale, **Chelsea Potter** at the other. You'll still need to head into the hinterland for the local boozers and gastros – the justly named **Surprise in Chelsea** and less-attractively monikered (but just as lovely) **Pig's Ear** being good places to start.

Apartment 195

195 King's Road, SW3 5ED (7351 5195/www. apartment195.co.uk). Sloane Square tube/11, 19, 22, 211 bus. **Open** 4-11pm Mon-Sat. **Food served** 4-10.30pm Mon-Sat. **Credit** AmEx, MC, V.
Despite being an upmarket cocktail bar, with buzzed-in access via an ominous black door, this place is open to the public – and surprisingly welcoming. Once you've made your way upstairs, you move into a room that suggests the tasteful mansion of a glam rock star: an enormous fireplace, bordello-like tea lights, aubergine hues and an almost diner-style bar with high stools lined up, waiting. The little flip-book menu of cocktails reveals umpteen Martinis, Latinos, Caipirinhas and classic cocktails, but it's the Mojitos that are renowned here; the Lulo at £8 is particularly wonderful, perfectly balanced with lime and mint. While gentle Latin sounds waft around the room, people lounge on the large sofas or perch coquettishly on settees more suited to a waiting room. Either way, it's the perfect sanctuary.
Function room. Music (DJs 8pm Sat; free).

Beaufort House

354 King's Road, SW3 5UZ (7352 2828/www.chelsea venues.com). Sloane Square tube then 11, 19, 22, 211 bus. **Open** 9.30am-1am Mon-Sat; 9.30am-12.30am Sun. **Food served** 9.30am-3.30pm, 7pm-1am Mon-Wed; 9.30am-3.30pm Thur-Sat; 9.30am-11.30pm Sun. **Snacks served** 7pm-1am Thur-Sat. **Credit** MC, V.
Heaving with gorgeous twentysomethings – and moneyed fortysomethings with gorgeous twentysomethings on their arms – Beaufort House is a civilised affair. A bar counter lit with a beautiful chandelier forms the centrepiece of an otherwise unadorned room. From a reasonably priced, cocktail heavy drinks list, a passion-fruit Martini was too strong; a Blueberry Collins, topped with too much crushed ice, was too watery; but the kiwi fruit Martini was surprisingly non-naff: made with fresh fruit, it was the most successful cocktail we sampled. Bar snacks like croque monsieur and spring rolls were no more than adequate. Our advice is to do what the regulars do: stick to the Champagne.

Babies and children welcome. Function room. Music (singer 10pm Mon-Wed, Sun; free). Tables outdoors (10, heated patio). TV (big screen). Wi-Fi internet connection (free).

Builder's Arms

13 Britten Street, SW3 3TY (7349 9040/www. geronimo-inns.co.uk). Sloane Square or South Kensington tube. **Open** 11am-11pm Mon-Wed; 11am-midnight Thur-Sat; noon-10.30pm Sun. **Food served** noon-2.30pm, 7.15-10.15pm Mon-Fri; noon-3pm, 7.15-11pm Sat; noon-4pm, 7-9pm Sun. **Credit** MC, V.
The Builder's Arms proudly advertises a 'Builder's Bar Snack', although it's anyone's guess when the last actual builder dared set foot across the threshold. This is the good-time pub for posh thirtysomethings of Chelsea. Thankfully it's also a pub for refined palates, with top-notch ingredients fighting for space on the blackboard menu, and an impressive selection of beers, lagers and wines; eight whites and seven reds are chalked up behind the bar, but you're still advised to ask for the full wine list. The place is loud, brash, boisterous and a little tatty around the edges – almost an All Bar One for the jet set. As the evening hots up, a roaring log fire does its best to keep up with the roaring clientele. Hurrah!
Babies and children admitted. Disabled: toilet. Restaurant. Tables outdoors (2, pavement). TV (big screen).

Chelsea Potter

119 King's Road, SW3 4PL (7352 9479). Sloane Square tube. **Open** 11am-11pm Mon-Fri; 11am-midnight Sat; noon-10.30pm Sun. **Food served** 11am-9pm Mon-Sat; noon-9pm Sun. **Credit** AmEx, DC, MC, V.
Unlike the majority of sophisticated watering holes around the King's Road, this is a somewhat dingy establishment, perfect for letting your hair down. A guitar-heavy indie soundtrack and the flickering screens of Sky Sports 2 frame earnest chats at the bar over pints of cheap lager or a couple of the guest ales. In fact, the place feels more like a Camden boozer, almost totally blotting out the chic parade of shops opposite. There are, however, a few gestures towards those who frequent the nearby boutiques: amid the chips and peas on the menu is the odd stem of asparagus and the occasional crushed potato; there's the occasional glimpse of Pimms being sipped while perched on a high stool, and the wines on offer range from Châteauneuf-du-Pape to shiraz, from chardonnay to Sancerre. Oh, and ignore any rumours that Chelsea Potter is Harry's erratic, precocious half-sister.
Babies and children admitted (until 6pm). Games (fruit machines). Tables outdoors (5, pavement). TV (satellite).

Chelsea Ram

32 Burnaby Street, SW10 0PL (7351 4008). Fulham Broadway tube/Sloane Square tube then 11, 19, 22 bus. **Open** 11am-11pm Mon-Sat; noon-10.30pm Sun. **Food served** noon-3pm, 6.30-10pm Mon-Sat; noon-3.30pm, 6.30-10pm Sun. **Credit** MC, V.
They have rocking horses in the windows around here, you know, and this pub absolutely screams 'Berkshire', while the clientele politely murmur 'simply marvellous'. It's a peaceful, elegant Young's pub, with an extensive New World wine selection – nearly 20 by the glass. Smokers are gently ushered away from non-smokers, businessmen either discuss current deals with each other, or recently completed deals with their slightly bored wives, while they all wait for the food to arrive. This is adventurous, seasonal fare, with some reliable pub workhorses such as burgers

Central

Annex 3. *See p42.*

Ruby & Sequoia. *See p76.*

and fish cakes filling in the gaps. There's a slight air of faux sophistication, with the toilet door made up to look like a bookcase and nude sketches on the walls, but the staff are polite, the hubbub relaxing, and the pub quiz predictably difficult.
Babies and children admitted. Function room. Games (backgammon, cards). Restaurant (no smoking). Quiz (7.30pm 1st Mon of mth; free). Tables outdoors (6, pavement). TV (big screen).

Cooper's Arms
87 Flood Street, SW3 5TB (7376 3120). Sloane Square or South Kensington tube. **Open** 11am-11pm Mon-Sat; noon-10.30pm Sun. **Food served** 12.30-2.30pm, 6.30-9.30pm Mon-Fri; 12.30-4pm, 6.30-9.30pm Sat; 12.30-4pm, 5.30-9pm Sun. **Credit** AmEx, MC, V.
The front door advertises the Campaign for Real Food, and it doesn't get much more real than this: tables full of people tucking into hearty portions of own-made shepherd's pie, washed down with pints of Young's Special. But while the regulars sink their ales and Guinness, there are earnest groups of younger customers discussing the merits of the mackerel pâté and the tortellini while sipping on a brace of exotic lagers, and a shiraz so fruity it's like a highly concentrated Christmas cake. Blinds, barometers and bannisters give the place a homely feel, as do the posters advertising great railway days out from 1950s London; the only thing spoiling the overwhelmingly laid-back feeling is sinister stares from the two incongruous animal heads that poke out from a couple of the walls.
Babies and children admitted (until 6pm). Bar available for hire. Function room. TV.

Cross Keys
1 Lawrence Street, SW3 5NB (7349 9111/www.thexkeys. co.uk). Sloane Square tube. **Open** noon-3pm, 7-11pm Mon-Sat; noon-4pm, 7-10.30pm Sun. **Food served** noon-2.30pm, 7-8pm Mon-Fri. **Credit** AmEx, MC, V.
If pubs were judged entirely on decor, this one – on a quiet back street just off Cheyne Walk – would scoop honours galore. It's beautifully lit, with a gorgeous upper gallery, stained-glass windows, comfortable seating and, to top it all, a smoochsome Jeff Buckley track played on the pub stereo; it could be the perfect location for a date. Sadly, the drink selection isn't guaranteed to help you past first base: on our visit, all ales were off, leaving us with an unappetising and unimaginative lager selection. A large chap on a stone mural embedded in the wall appears to be urging you to sample their wine, and some treats can certainly be found if you splash out. If your date seems to be going well, take your beau to the back-room restaurant for some Brit cuisine – and round off the evening feeding each other slabs of aromatic poached pear.
Babies and children admitted. Function rooms. No cigars or pipes (restaurant). Restaurant.

Fox & Hounds
29 Passmore Street, SW1W 8HR (7730 6367). Sloane Square tube. **Open** 11am-11pm Mon-Sat; noon-10.30pm Sun. **Food served** noon-2.30pm, 6.30-9.30pm Mon-Fri. **Credit** AmEx, DC, MC, V.
Sneering openly at the notion that size matters, this minuscule pub makes you forget instantly that you're in London – almost as if a village local has been flown in over Vauxhall Bridge and dumped just around the corner from Sloane Square. It could be someone's living room, with coat hooks, well-used armchairs, bookchairs and paintings adding to the ambience, and only a prominently displayed

Certificate of Employer's Liability Insurance spoiling the informality. The clientele also appear to have come along for the ride from out of town, with guffawing, bearded blokes supping on the full range of Young's ales – and the occasional light 'n' bitter – out of old-style beer mugs. Sustenance comes in the form of soup and doorsteps, bangers and mash, and ploughman's lunches, but that's merely incidental to the main business of steeling oneself for a long evening's drinking.

Lots Road Pub & Dining Room
114 Lots Road, SW10 0RJ (7352 6645/www.thespirit group.com). Sloane Square tube then 11, 19, 22 bus. **Open** 11am-11pm Mon-Thur; 11am-midnight Fri, Sat; noon-10.30pm Sun. **Food served** noon-3pm, 5.30-10pm Mon-Thur; noon-3pm, 5.30-10.30pm Fri, Sat; noon-10pm Sun. **Credit** MC, V.
Curving in a graceful arc around the corner of Lots Road, this much-loved gastrobar is a carefully pitched mix of laid-back and high class. The Team, as the bar staff are known, sweep efficiently between tables wearing smart aprons and scruffy T-shirts, delivering ice-buckets to impeccably coiffed Fulhamistas gorging on riesling and Chablis – which go for a wallet-busting £8.35 and £9 per glass respectively. At one end of the bar they've managed to squeeze in an open kitchen, serving up uncompetitively priced cuisine that is, nevertheless, extremely good. And there's something for all budgets: bar-proppers are perfectly happy with Stella, Carling and Guinness, or a trio of real ales at £2.75 a pint. Away from the bar is a more intimate, gently lit area, perfect for a candlelit dinner if you feel like impressing someone with your choice of food and wine – advised by The Team, of course.
Babies and children admitted. Disabled: toilet. Restaurant (available for hire; no smoking).

Nectar
562 King's Road, SW6 2DZ (7326 7450/www. nectarbar.co.uk). Fulham Broadway tube. **Open** noon-midnight Mon-Thur; noon-2am Fri, Sat. **Food served** noon-9pm Mon-Sat. **Credit** MC, V.
This stylish, open-plan bar, with its retro 1970s wallpaper and pastel-shaded sofas, sits at the western end of King's Road and, to encourage its winsome Chelsea clientele, the fine drinks menu has been enlivened with the inclusion of shots of olde worlde mead alongside the cocktails. Delicious the stuff is too: produced by the West Sussex brewer Largashall, £3 a shot, in honey-sweet, nutmeg-spiced or whisky-tinged varieties. The cocktails (£6-£7, two-for-one Sunday to Thursday) are also decent – like the mead many are honey-infused, though never too sweet: the Honey Orchard, an apple and vodka concoction, was pitched just right. As well as the fine drink selection, there is an Italian snack menu, and an all-you-can-eat brunch on Sunday mornings. Nectar is lively, good-looking and fun.
Babies and children admitted. Bar available for hire. Music (9pm Thur-Sat; £3 after 10pm Fri, Sat). Tables outdoors (6, garden). TV (big screen, satellite).

Orange Brewery
37-39 Pimlico Road, SW1W 8NE (7730 5984). Sloane Square tube. **Open** 11am-11pm Mon-Sat; noon-10.30pm Sun. **Food served** 11am-9pm Mon-Sat; noon-9pm Sun. **Credit** AmEx, DC, MC, V.
Within fruit-lobbing distance of Victoria station and its surrounding offices, the Orange is a perfect place to kick off the evening. The humble, wood-panelled bar is frequented by a mixture of blokes' blokes, local office work-

ers approaching pay day, elderly locals out for some grub, and bohemian dandies in foppish attire – all of them thankful that the prices aren't rounded up to the nearest 5p. The lines of bottles around the ledges tell you that this is a beer lovers' pub, with Pride, Speckled Hen, Greene King IPA and Adnams all on offer, although it's spoilt slightly by the ludicrous aberration that is John Smith's Extra Cold. Care is also taken over the regularly changing 'divine wines' – between £2.80 and £5.80 a glass – and if the wine of the month doesn't tempt you, it's highly likely that the sausage of the week might. Perhaps not a main course pub, but a perfect hors-d'oeuvre.

Babies and children welcome (until 7pm, restaurant only). Function room. Games (fruit machines, quiz machine). Restaurant. Tables outdoors (7, pavement).

Phoenix

23 Smith Street, SW3 4EE (7730 9182/www.geronimo-inns.co.uk). Sloane Square tube. **Open** 11am-11pm Mon-Sat; noon-10.30pm Sun. **Food served** noon-2.45pm, 7-9.45pm Mon-Fri; noon-3.30pm, 7-9.45pm Sat; noon-4pm, 7-9.45pm Sun. **Credit** MC, V.

This is Chelsea, of course, but when the first thing you see in a new bar is a blackboard of specials featuring roasted Toulouse sausage and warm chicory salad, your immediate reaction is that they might be trying a little too hard. Then, when you see that juices come in blackcurrant or apricot varieties, and sample bar snacks are sliced Italian meats or marinated vegetables, your suspicions tend to be confirmed. That said, it's always good to see non-standard lagers in the form of Honey Dew and Warsteiner, there are some gorgeous single malts, and the wines are divided into handy categories such as 'fruity reds'. You'll get a good drink here, but the place is lacking in soul: despite the sofas and table lamps that try to persuade you to the contrary, this is no home from home.

Babies and children admitted. Tables outdoors (7, patio). TV.

Pig's Ear

35 Old Church Street, SW3 5BS (7352 2908/www.the pigsear.co.uk). Sloane Square tube. **Open** noon-11pm Mon-Sat; noon-10.30pm Sun. **Food served** 12.30-3pm Mon-Fri; 12.30-4pm Sat, Sun. **Credit** AmEx, MC, V.

This vaguely continental reworking of the old Front Page pub is a powerful magnet for wealthy locals. On several visits we were barely able get into the place, with routes to and from the bar blocked by South American heiresses supposedly sampling a slice of real British pub life. It may not be particularly authentic – pie and mash displaced by exotic pan-European cuisine that's heavy on the oysters and foie gras – but they could have chosen a lot worse: it boasts a fine real ale from Uley's brewery in Gloucestershire that shares the name of the pub, and the wine list is gigantic in both length and breadth. Upstairs, a peaceful (but fully booked) restaurant is in sharp contrast to the squealing and braying that emanates from downstairs; but whether you decide to go up or down, make sure you arrive early.

Babies and children welcome (restaurant). Function room. Restaurant (available for hire; no smoking).

Sporting Page

6 Camera Place, SW10 0BH (7349 0455/www.front pagepubs.com). Fulham Broadway tube. **Open** 11am-11pm Mon-Sat; noon-10.30pm Sun. **Food served** noon-3pm, 6-10pm Mon-Fri; noon-6pm Sat, Sun. **Credit** AmEx, DC, MC, V.

Don't be put off by the Bollinger signs outside; there's more to this pub than Champagne guzzling. Within, it's surprisingly low-key. An odd array of early 20th-century sporting heroes adorn the walls, and with all the tiled surfaces you'd be forgiven for thinking you'd wandered into the buttery of a redbrick university. An odd array of punters wander in and out, walking an even odder array of dogs – but all are greeted warmly by the Spanish bar staff. Dyed blondes smoking roll-ups get quietly tipsy on a range of Kendall Jackson and Chanson wines, while bar-proppers stick to the reliable pints of London Pride and Bombardier. With a light and airy conservatory feel, it's a perfect lunching pub – with an acceptable spag bol, and cheese fondues or roast skate for the more gastronomically adventurous.

Bar available for hire. No piped music or jukebox. Tables outdoors (12, pavement). TV (big screen, satellite).

Surprise in Chelsea

6 Christchurch Terrace, off Tite Street, SW3 4AJ (7349 1821). Sloane Square tube. **Open** 11am-11pm Mon-Sat; noon-10.30pm Sun. **Food served** noon-3pm, 7-10pm daily. **Credit** MC, V.

'Welcome to the Surprise', it says in large letters on the pub blackboard, so we kicked back with a pint of Adnams and a Virgin Raspini mocktail, and waited. We didn't have to hang around long. While one girl talked about her recent skiing holiday and how she had to courier her passport halfway across the globe, a group of builders loudly extolled the virtues of a local redheaded woman – and, just as you thought the culture clash was complete, a cravatted gent came in and asked for a glass of Champagne and a packet of crisps. A barmy corner of Chelsea, where quaffers of Stella and sippers of champers sit side-by-side – and increasingly comfortably so, after two or three drinks. The bar food is fairly meagre, but the locals are too busy bridging the class divide to care too much.

Babies and children welcome. Games (bar billiards, board games, quiz machine). No-smoking area. TVs (satellite).

World's End Distillery & Restaurant

459 King's Road, SW10 0LR (7351 5834/www.the-worldsend.com). Sloane Square tube then 14, 19, 22 bus. **Open** 11am-midnight daily. **Food served** 11am-10.30pm daily. **Credit** AmEx, MC, V.

This recently reopened pub at the west end of the King's Road would be a prime candidate for a TV series called *When Your Local Goes Gastro*. It's a half-hearted transformation, not wanting to lose the custom of the regular drinkers who gaze over your head at the slightly incongruous screens showing Sky Sports. A slim but appetising menu of four starters and four mains focuses on English fare such as fish pie and lamb shank, with bar snacks and beers to match – jellied eels and platters of ox tongue, washed down with an honest pint of Bombardier. Unusually, there didn't seem to be a wine list on our visit; we were offered just the one, fairly unpalatable, white. With several hundred watts of bright light emanating from the chandelier fittings, the atmosphere doesn't feel particularly homely – but service is fast and friendly.

Babies and children admitted (restaurant). Bar available for hire. Music (indie band 8pm 1st Tue of mth; free). Quiz (8pm Tue; £2). Restaurant (available for hire; no smoking). Tables outdoors (5, pavement). TV (big screen).

Also in the area...

Eclipse Chelsea 111-113 Walton Street, SW3 2HP (7581 0123).

mybar 35 Ixworth Place, SW3 3QX (0871 223 7470).

Pig's Ear

Covent Garden

As a rule of thumb, the further you venture from the Piazza the better the class of pub and bar. In fact, just keep going until you reach Holborn or Soho. However, this is a surprisingly good area for connoisseurs of strange brews, with Cornish ales at the **Cove**, ten rare Irish-brewed beers at the **Porterhouse** and a trio of microbrewed draughts at **Bünker**. Plus there will be at least six different real ales on at the excellent **Lamb & Flag**.

Africa Bar

Africa Centre, 38 King Street, WC2E 8JT (7836 1976). Covent Garden or Leicester Square tube. **Open** 12.30-3pm, 5.30-11pm Mon-Fri; 5.30-11pm Sat. **Food served** 12.30-2.30pm, 6-11pm Mon-Fri; 6-11pm Sat. **Credit** MC, V.
Covent Garden is a Disneyland of naff, internationally themed drinking venues: South African, Aussie, Canadian, Brazilian, American Indian… But this isn't one of them. Within an institutional building not two minutes from the inessential commerce of the Piazza, down a tatty, mural-patterned staircase, a sign points you to the Calabash restaurant, right, and the Africa Bar, left. This claustrophobic red-carpeted corner with matching shabby furniture is what you imagine the Writers' Union bar in downtown Mogadishu might look like, starved of funding but afire with Africans of mixed nationalities in heated debate over tables crowded with beer bottles (the beer is Kenyan Tusker

in this case). On weekend nights the ceiling shudders with the pounding feet of the *jit*-driven dancehall upstairs, while on other nights you might have to push your way through a hallway of assembled black Muslims gathered for an evening lecture. For drinkers with a sense of adventure. *Babies and children admitted (restaurant). Restaurant. TV.* **Map 2 L7.**

Box

32-34 Monmouth Street, Seven Dials, WC2H 9HA (7240 5828/www.boxbar.com). Leicester Square tube. **Open** 11am-11pm Mon-Sat; noon-10.30pm Sun. **Food served** 11am-5pm daily. **Credit** MC, V.
Smart, bright by day and easy-going, Box is a welcoming gay bar-café in which straights can also feel at home. It has an enviable location just south of Seven Dials, displayed to advantage through a fold-back glass frontage or even better, weather permitting, from pavement tables on Upper St Martin's Lane. Table service enhances the West Coast feel and the drinks selection is more sophisticated than most – quality lagers such as Staropramen backed with boutique beers (Hoegaarden, Leffe Blonde), cocktails, a decent wine selection and coffees. There's a decent food menu during the day. Campery is kept to a minimum – a back bar of doll's-house windows filled with bubbling water – although we can't make any guarantees for the clientele's behaviour as the evening wears on. *Babies and children admitted (daytime only). Tables outdoors (3, pavement).* **Map 2 L6.**

Brasserie Max

Covent Garden Hotel, 10 Monmouth Street, WC2H 9LF (7806 1000/www.coventgardenhotel.co.uk). Covent Garden tube. **Open/food served** 7am-11pm Mon-Fri; 8am-11pm Sat; 8am-10.30pm Sun. **Credit** AmEx, MC, V.
Always wanted to go to the Groucho Club but don't know anyone who's a member? Well, you can almost replicate the experience at Brasserie Max. Having to pass through the lobby of the very swellegant Covent Garden Hotel, passing greeters and doorkeepers en route, confers sufficient exclusivity to deter all but the most cocksure. They powwow at polished dark-wood tables over flutes of pink fizz or retire round the corner to banquettes that provide alcove intimacy; all the while a lively buzz centres on the long continental-styled zinc bar counter. For those who care, the celeb count is as high as at most Soho members' clubs (it's a very stylish hotel upstairs, favoured by the likes of Scarlett Johansson and Cate Blanchett). Cocktails are supremely well made, with top-quality brands and fresh fruit, while some 20 wines, categorised into light, medium and full bodied, come by the glass or bottle. Light snacks and bottled beers are also on the menu. Prices are also very exclusive – £10.50 for a Martini. Ouch. *Babies and children admitted. Screening facilities (6pm Sat; dinner plus film £35). Function rooms. Restaurant (no smoking).* **Map 1 L6.**

Bünker

41 Earlham Street, WC2H 9LD (7240 0606/www. bunkerbar.com). Covent Garden tube. **Open** noon-11pm Mon-Wed; noon-11.30pm Thur; noon-midnight Fri, Sat; noon-10.30pm Sun. **Food served** noon-10pm Mon-Sat; noon-4pm Sun. **Credit** MC, V.
One of London's last surviving microbreweries (what went wrong?) and one of only two in the West End (Mash on Great Portland Street being the other), Bünker is to be applauded for its bloody-minded determination to stick to its copper vats. The three house draughts (Red Soho,

Central

Pilsner and Organic) come in pint (£3.10-£3.30) or two-pint forms, with a try-before-you-buy option. They are excellent, particularly the flowery Soho Red. Tragically – and here's the clue to the demise of own-brewing – on the evidence of our recent visits most punters seem to favour the international bottled beers (Budvar, San Miguel, Nastro Azzurro), standard cocktails (£6.50) and shooters (£3.40). This is in keeping with the vibe, which is pumped-up, post-work party, whatever the time, whatever the day. Big communal tables encourage group binging, while the volume on the house sound system is wedged firmly at eleven. (Aren't those umlauts bloody irritating?)

Music (DJs 9pm Fri, Sat; free). TV. **Map 2 L6.**

Café des Amis

11-14 Hanover Place, WC2E 9JP (7379 3444/www. cafedesamis.co.uk). Covent Garden tube. **Open** 11.30am-1am Mon-Sat. **Food served** 11.30am-11.30pm Mon-Sat. **Credit** AmEx, DC, MC, V.

Seeking to be a cut above other local venues serving the nearby Opera House, Café des Amis certainly manages to have higher prices, charging £16 for ribeye steak. The small basement bar has a sleek, dark-wood interior with pictures of ballet dancers covering the walls. The owners are clearly currying favour with pre- and post-theatre visitors, although local office-workers and suits also enjoy the rarefied air here – a world away from central pub chains filled with screaming guys and gals. Here you'll find middle-aged folk squeezing into tight corner seats while juggling a glass of wine chosen from a lengthy, Francophile list on which good wine from the Côtes de Gascogne sits alongside reds such as the lovely Domaine l'Enclos 2002 Côtes du Rhône (£6.50 by the glass). There's a poor choice of rosés and one measly Champagne by the glass, but excellent Martinis make up for that: how about fresh sage mixed with Stoli, lemon and the tropical fruit physallis (£7.50).

Babies and children welcome. Function room. No-smoking area. Tables outdoors (12, terrace). **Map 2 L6.**

Christopher's Martini Bar

18 Wellington Street, WC2E 7DD (7240 4222/www. christophersgrill.com). Covent Garden tube. **Open** 11.30am-11.30pm daily. **Food served** noon-3pm, 5-11pm Mon-Fri; 11.30am-3pm, 5-11pm Sat, Sun. **Credit** AmEx, DC, MC, V.

Christopher's is a classy establishment, with only the legend 'Christopher's Bar & Grill' inscribed on the high frosted-glass windows to mark its presence for the passerby. Consequently, rarely are its half-dozen tables more than half full, meaning that the immaculately attired gents behind the luminous, slatted-wood bar counter can take their time over the preparation of premium-spirit cocktails (£8.50) and Martinis (£8.50), the latter including 'Christopher's Martini' of Grey Goose and vermouth with a twist. The Whiskey Sour (£6.50), made with egg whites to give it a viscous fizz, is one of the best in town, while the house Bloody Mary, made with Absolut Pepper and tomato and lemon juices, also has its fans.

Babies and children welcome. Function room. TV. **Map 2 L7.**

Coach & Horses

42 Wellington Street, WC2E 7BD (7240 0553). Covent Garden tube. **Open** 11am-11pm Mon-Sat; noon-10.30pm Sun. **Food served** noon-2.30pm daily. **Credit** MC, V.

The closest decent boozer to the Piazza, the Coach is a genuine, expat Irish pub – in other words, nothing at all like an O'Neill's. Although it no longer boasts Guinness from Dublin

(it's all from there now), it's a well-pulled pint nonetheless, with a couple of real ale alternatives to the stout. And tiny though the bar area is, it also boasts over 70 malts and whiskies from either side of the Irish Sea. To soak up the booze, hulking great lumps of pork and beef sizzle away on the hot counter, ready for use in sandwiches: hot roast beef, salt beef or Limerick ham at £4.50 a time. Otherwise, sporting talk buzzes around the modestly sized, red-carpeted saloon, regulars putting in their penn'orth before returning their noses to the *Irish Times*. It's the kind of place that could make a fortune from tourism, but doesn't feel it has to. A lovely floral display hangs outside in summer, too.

TV. **Map 2 L6.**

Cove

1 The Piazza, WC2E 8HB (7836 7880). Covent Garden tube. **Open/food served** 11am-11pm Mon-Sat; noon-10.30pm Sun. **Credit** MC, V.

London's only Cornish smugglers' inn is 50 miles from the nearest bit of coastline and several days on horseback from Penzance. In fact, it's above a branch of the West Cornish Pasty Co in Covent Garden. Enter through the back of the shop and up the stairs to three cramped rooms warmed by the smell of baked goods from below and decked out with fake roof beams, assorted maritime and pirate-themed tat and a jukebox of 1980s pop. It would all be a nightmare beyond belief except it has a sizeable terrace overlooking the Piazza and St Paul's church, and also boasts four or five decent real ales on draught by Cornish brewers St Austell (ESB and Tribute) and Skinner's (Betty Stogs and Cornish Knocker) – you won't find them in many other parts of London. Bizarrely, the drinks menu omits any mention of the beers in favour of listing a thousand and one variations on meat and veg wrapped in pastry.

Babies and children welcome. Disabled: toilet. Tables outdoors (3, balcony). **Map 2 L7.**

Cross Keys

31 Endell Street, WC2H 9EB (7836 5185). Covent Garden tube. **Open** 11am-11pm Mon-Sat; noon-10.30pm Sun. **Food served** noon-3pm Mon-Sat; noon-2.30pm Sun. **Credit** AmEx, MC, V.

Possibly the 'most local' of any Covent Garden pub. Its interior is blurry with a Halloween-orange glow that barely illuminates walls and ceiling creaking under the weight of landlord Brian's collection of brasses, portraits, paintings and pop oddities: press cuttings about his successful £500 bid for Elvis Presley's napkin make up the bar counter's centrepiece. The pop pieces are of an age with the clientele, most of whom probably remember the Beatles at the Royal Command Performance in 1963 – the poster is displayed here. The average age drops considerably over summer when the combination of an extravagant floral frontage and benches out on Endell Street attracts drinkers of a fresher bloom. Beers are from Young's and Shepherd Neame.

Function room. Tables outdoors (3, pavement). TV (big screen). **Map 2 L6.**

Detroit

35 Earlham Street, WC2H 9LD (7240 2662/www. detroit-bar.com). Covent Garden or Leicester Square tube. **Open** 5pm-midnight Mon-Sat. **Food served** 5-10pm Mon-Sat. **Credit** AmEx, DC, MC, V.

More than ten years old and in all that time Detroit has hardly changed – but then why should it? It's one of London's most revered style bars, marrying a cool underground interior of a curvacious warren of alcoves with some expert cocktail-making. The three dozen Martinis, flutes

and long drinks (£6.95-£7.95) are created with aplomb and flair; try the house Detroit (Wyborowa vodka, mint and sugar syrup) for a fine example. There's a selection of over-proofs making merry with absinthe (£9.80) and a selection of 'super premium' cocktails involving 'super premium' spirits, such as a Sazerac made with Rémy Martin XO cognac. Beers include Estonian Viru, Japan's Asahi, Italian Peroni and the Belgian Duvel, all by the bottle. The superior snacks, such as Parma ham and honey crostini, are in the £5 range. During Seven-Heaven, from 5pm to 7pm, two cocktails costs £7. Here's to the next ten years.
Function room. Music (DJs 8pm Fri, Sat; free). No-smoking area. Restaurant. **Map 2 L6**.

Freud
198 Shaftesbury Avenue, WC2H 8JL (7240 9933/ www.freudliving.com). Tottenham Court Road tube. **Open** 11am-11pm Mon-Sat; noon-10.30pm Sun. **Food served** noon-4.30pm daily. **Credit** MC, V.
Freud has majored in minimalism since 1986. Accessed by a clanking metal staircase beside the front door of the uten-sils shop of the same name, it's a smallish space leaden in greys of hard slate and wet-look concrete. Changing displays of art liven up the place (sometimes) but otherwise it's down to the cocktails (£5-£6) to add colour and fizz. A huge board up behind the busy, tall bar counter lists myriad options, executed with panache by bar staff who display an accomplished manner with the silver shaker. Beers are all bottled and run to a right mix of nations (Canadian Sleeman, Czech Pilsner Urquell and Staropramen, Italian Peroni, German Warsteiner and Bishops Finger from the UK) – nice, but apart from the last named we challenge anyone to distinguish between them without peeking. Far hipper than anything you'll find in Soho.
Babies and children admitted. Music (jazz 3-5pm occasional Sun; free). No-smoking tables (until 4.30pm). TV. **Map 1 L6**.

Lamb & Flag
33 Rose Street, WC2E 9EB (7497 9504). Covent Garden tube. **Open** 11am-11pm Mon-Sat; noon-10.30pm Sun. **Food served** noon-3pm Mon-Fri, Sun; noon-4.30pm Sat. **Credit** MC, V.
By far the best pub in the Covent Garden area. The problem is that everyone knows it and consequently most evenings, especially in warmer weather, you'll be hard pushed to get anywhere near its 350-year-old (or more) interior. Besides bags of wooden-framed, low-ceiling history, it's got the most picture-perfect location, at the head of a narrow cobbled lane off Garrick Street, with an ancient tun-nelled passageway squeezing down one side. It has a staff that have remained loyal and capable for seemingly decades now, and an excellent line-up of mainly Young's ales supplemented by guests that typically include the likes of Bombardier, Courage Best and Ridley's IPA. There are ploughman's lunches and doorstop sandwiches down-stairs, and full pub grub on red checked tablecloths in the Dryden room upstairs, which is also where a bunch of elderly but lively trad jazzers play every Sunday evening.
Music (jazz 7.30-10.15pm Sun; free). No piped music or jukebox. TV. **Map 2 L7**.

Langley
5 Langley Street, WC2H 9JA (7836 5005/www.the langley.co.uk). Covent Garden tube. **Open/food served** 4.30pm-1am Mon-Sat; 4.30-10.30pm Sun. **Happy hour** 5-7pm daily. **Admission** £3 after 10pm Thur; £5 after 10pm Fri, Sat. **Credit** AmEx, MC, V.

Booze talking
Blue Posts

You are?
Michael Cowell, ex of the King's Head & Dive Bar, Gerrard Street, now the landlord of the Blue Posts, Rupert Street (*see p57*).
What happened to the King's Head & Dive Bar?
The lease ran out and Shaftesbury Estates, which owns most of the area, wanted it back badly. I thought the whole world had finished. It was a very special place. I started in '82 and worked there for 23 years. It's now a Chinese restaurant. And the Blue Posts just happened to come along on the market at exactly the same time. A miracle really.
The Blue Posts was not doing good business – how do you go about turning it around?
I used to come down here on my breaks from the old pub – because I knew it would be quiet. But I used to stand and watch and see little things and realise why it was quiet. They used to blast music out like a discotheque and there was never any consistency – they moved the staff around all the time. We're a bit more hands-on and I think that's the key really. I actually love working behind the bar and I get annoyed when I can't because I've got so many other things to do. There's [also] no lighting outside and you can't see us. We're having lights all the way up the building.
You've got a fair amount of competition.
I'm happy to have the likes of Waxy O'Connor's and O'Neill's around me because a certain type of person goes in those pubs. It filters off what we don't want.
How do you build a crowd of regulars?
I don't quite know how you do it. People just come in, they feel comfortable and they come back. We were also very lucky in that we had quite a lot of regulars in the old pub, the King's Head and Dive Bar, who followed us.

Central

A cut above the other pile 'em in, get 'em pissed venues around Covent Garden, we favour the Langley for its spaciousness and professionalism. Two large underground bar areas, one of bare brick vaulting and thumping music, the other with waitress service and swirly decor, operate the same drinks menu. Cocktails Now (a Yeah Baby of Babycham and crème de cassis, a Cool Melon of Smirnoff and melon schnapps) and Then (Mint Julep with Maker's Mark, Singapore Sling with Gordon's) are each a snippy £5.50, while the standard Champagne cocktails run to £6.95. Bar food is tiered at £3 (fish finger sandwich, hot dog, potato wedges), £4 (tortillas, pitta bread with houmous, veggie spring rolls), £5 (scampi and chips, Thai fishcakes, duck spring rolls) and £6 (gourmet burger, steak baguette, char-grilled chicken and chips). It's simple and it works.
Disabled: toilet. Music (DJs 8pm Wed-Sat). Restaurant. **Map 2 L6.**

Lowlander

36 Drury Lane, WC2B 5RR (7379 7446/www.lowlander. com). Covent Garden or Holborn tube. **Open** noon-11pm Mon-Sat; noon-10.30pm Sun. **Food served** noon-10.30pm Mon-Sat; noon-9.30pm Sun. **Credit** AmEx, MC, V.
The bar counter at 'London's premier Dutch and Belgian beer café' is an absolute vision – no fewer than 15 tall, gleaming chrome beer taps are lined up behind a twinkling array of upturned beer glasses of all shapes and sizes. Draught choices run to pilsners, blondes, wheat beers, red and dark ales, fruit beers and miscellaneous speciality beers. Then there are the more than 40 additional options by the bottle. For the undecided, three third-of-a-pint tasters for £4.80; for the enthusiast, tutored tastings at £19.50 a head. It's a classy establishment through and through, with close rows of light-wood communal tables attended by wait staff in white starched pinnies, overlooked by a mezzanine often hired out for private bashes. Food includes snacks (charcuterie/cheese platters at £4.55/£4.85), mains of the moules frites (£11.95) variety and good value two- and three-course prix fixes.
Babies and children admitted. Function room. No-smoking area. Tables outdoors (4, pavement). TV (big screen). **Map 1 L6.**

Maple Leaf

41 Maiden Lane, WC2E 7LJ (7240 2843). Covent Garden tube. **Open** 11am-11pm Mon-Sat; noon-10.30pm Sun. **Food served** noon-9.30pm daily. **Credit** (over £10) AmEx, MC, V.
The Maple Leaf is apparently London's only Canadian pub. Ah yes, we're excited too. There's a stuffed bear, framed ice hockey paraphernalia and mounted Mounties set within the log-walled bar. The T-shirts worn by the female staff announce that 'Canadian girls kick ass' – which is just as well because the Canadian beers are a lame bunch (Molson and Sleeman Silver Creek on draught, Moosehead by the bottle). It's a sizeable slice of Canada: a large all-in-one bar area and logged lounge, with plenty of snug corners. There are no less than nine TV screens set around the room screening Premiership games, along with American football (NFL) and basketball (NBA) but no NHL owing to logistical problems. Food is the kind of pub grub you'd get anywhere. What really makes the place unmistakably Canadian, though, is the hockey scoreline engraved on the wall: Canada 5, USA 2, Olympics 2002.
Babies and children admitted (before 5pm). Games (fruit machine, quiz machine). No-smoking area. TV (satellite). **Map 2 L7.**

Opera Tavern

23 Catherine Street, WC2B 5JS (7379 9832). Covent Garden tube. **Open** noon-11pm Mon-Sat. **Food served** noon-10pm Mon-Sat. **Credit** AmEx, MC, V.
Two pubs face the Theatre Royal across the road. The Old Nell with its come-hither frontage of a well-dressed bay window attracts free-spending theatre-goers, while two doors down, the less showy Opera is the haunt of bomber-jacketed stagehands. Despite the inevitable games machine and TV, it retains its Victorian good looks (refitted 1879 in dark wood and frosted glass) and has a tiled fireplace down past the end of the bar and a little one-step-up snug at the back, wrapped around with gold and red flock-effect wallpaper. There's a decent and changeable line-up of five real ales, including when we last visited the dubiously named Old Tosser – cue opportunities for much merriment between larky customers and forbearing bar staff. There's also the upstairs Baddeley bar and restaurant where the hungry can revel in the native delights of steak and ale pie or bangers and mash.
Games (fruit machine, quiz machine). Restaurant (available for hire; no smoking). TV. **Map 2 L6.**

Origin

24 Endell Street, WC2H 9HQ (7170 9200). Covent Garden tube. **Open** noon-midnight Mon-Fri; 5pm-midnight Sat. **Food served** noon-3pm Mon-Fri; 5-11pm Sat. **Credit** AmEx, MC, V.
The Hospital is that white elephant of a dining, drinking, studio, gallery and private club complex launched by muso millionaire Dave Stewart and Microsoft billionaire Paul Allen. Origin is the house restaurant and it comes with a bar attached. It's a featureless rectangular space open at both ends with two parades of tables against Coldstream blue leather bench seating. The bar counter is recessed like a cloakroom. On the night we visited (10pm on a Tuesday) the place was completely empty, but we suspect that even the Marx Brothers would struggle to create a party atmosphere here. The drinks are good. A short but well constructed menu accessories the Julep, Bellini and sorbet with the likes of a Fumble of Tanqueray gin, lemon juice and raspberry foam, and a Kentucky Cooler of Buffalo Trace bourbon, vanilla liqueur, apple juice and ginger beer. No good however can ever come of a cocktail called a Tiramisu. Care has also gone into the beer selection with, among others, bottled Bellevue Kriek, St Peter's Organ ic Ale and Melbourn Bros Apricot ale – which is like a fuzzier, sweeter cider. But Sam Smith's lager? Surely not.
Babies and children welcome (until 6pm). Disabled: toilet. Function room. Restaurant. **Map 1 L6.**

Porterhouse

21-22 Maiden Lane, WC2E 7NA (7836 9931/www. porterhousebrewco.com). Covent Garden tube. **Open** 11am-11pm Mon-Wed; 11am-11.30pm Thur-Sat; noon-10.30pm Sun. **Food served** noon-9pm Mon-Sat; noon-7pm Sun. **Credit** AmEx, MC, V.
Vast and multi-levelled, a maze of mezzanines, galleries and walkways, and with glass-fronted cupboards of curious ales, and bannisters and railings fashioned from copper piping, the Porterhouse is one great play pen for would-be inebriates. But the drinks are taken seriously with three each of its own-brewed (that means Dublin-brewed) stouts, bitters and lagers, plus a weissbier, on draught. A glossy 28-page menu lists a gazeteer of alternatives by the bottle which runs from Argentina's Quilmes to Zimbabwe's Zambezi, a fair-minded selection that balances Israel's Macabee with the Palestinian Taybeh. This fine little book-

let also provides instruction on choosing a good beer, and it's worth quoting at length: 'Avoid "lite". Avoid "ice". Avoid "smooth". Avoid beer advertised with words ending in "flow". Avoid beer advertised on TV. Avoid beer with a sports tournament named after it.' We almost forgive them their £10 souvenir baseball caps and £25 rugby shirts. *Disabled: toilet. Function room. Music (bands 8.30pm Wed-Sat; Irish band 4-8pm Sun; free). Tables outdoors (3, pavement). TV (big screen, satellite).* **Map 2 L7**.

Punch & Judy
40 The Market, WC2E 8RF (7379 0923). Covent Garden tube. **Open** 11am-11pm Mon-Sat; 11am-10.30pm Sun. **Food served** noon-7pm Mon-Sat; noon-5pm Sun. **Credit** AmEx, MC, V.
If you've ever puked on a Paris *place*, pissed in the water at Bondi Beach or just been generally boorish in Budapest, this is where the rest of the world gets its own back. In fine weather, in the hallowed neighbourhood of Inigo Jones's St Paul's, one of London's oldest and most perfect little pieces of sacred architecture, a crowd of international youth will fill a balcony opposite the church and get tanked up on lager to bellow, hoot and scream as if they were a bunch of Brits abroad. But then the Punch & Judy is hardly the Reform Club. The vaulted basement recesses of what was once a fruit-market warehouse now house multiple games machines and jukeboxes and are flooded with the aural pap of the hits du jour. The beers are lowest common denominator – the one real ale was off when we last visited – and food is the 'chips-with-everything' variety. *Babies and children admitted. Games (fruit machines, quiz machines). Restaurant. Tables outdoors (6, courtyard). TVs (big screen).* **Map 2 L7**.

Roundhouse
1 Garrick Street, WC2E 9BF (7836 9838). Covent Garden or Leicester Square tube. **Open** 11am-11pm Mon-Thur; 11am-midnight Fri, Sat; noon-10.30pm Sun. **Food served** noon-9pm daily. **Credit** AmEx, MC, V.
Not all chains are anathema to pub lovers. T&J Bernard run some classy houses, including this, the Roundhouse, named for its distinctive hemispherical frontage, which caps a busy, pedestrian-friendly intersection of Theatreland. It started life as the Petters Hotel soon after Garrick Street opened as an access road to Covent Garden market in the 1860s. Now that the market's gone and West End theatre is the preserve of coach parties from Southend, the one-time clientele of luvvies and traders has been replaced by tourists and transients, with a corresponding vacuum where the atmosphere should be. However, the selection of beers is strong – five real ales, including the dangerously mind-befuddling Old Peculier – the pies (beef and Guinness, chicken and stilton) are freshly baked and the wines are well chosen and well priced (from £2.80 a glass and £8 a bottle). *Games (fruit machine). No-smoking area. TVs.* **Map 2 L7**.

Also in the area...
All Bar One 19 Henrietta Street, WC2E 9ET (7557 7941).
Crusting Pipe (Davy's) 27 The Market, WC2E 8RD (7836 1415).
La Perla 28 Maiden Lane, WC2E 7JS (7240 7400).
O'Neill's 14 New Row, WC2N 4LF (7557 9831).
Segar & Snuff Parlour (Davy's) 27A The Market, WC2E 8RD (7836 8345).
Walkabout 11 Henrietta Street & 33 Maiden Lane, WC2E 8PS (7379 5555).

Earl's Court

No Aussie theme pubs, then, though the **King's Head** still has a toehold in the Antipodes. Instead the bohemian **Troubadour** gets our vote – Dylan once played here, you know.

Blackbird
209 Earl's Court Road, SW5 9AN (7835 1855). Earl's Court tube. **Open** 11am-11pm Mon-Sat; noon-10.30pm Sun. **Food served** noon-4pm, 5-8.45pm daily. **Credit** MC, V.
A short hop from the Earl's Court Road exit from the tube station, this pub is a popular and comfortable stop-off for locals. It's a Fuller's pub, so pints of Discovery, ESB, Honey Dew and London Pride are served to customers who sit amid carved mahogany, propping up the octagonal bar counter or in the green studded banquette snugs. There's a dining area at the back, the menu extensive. It's traditional fare, but well executed – own-made fishermen's pies (£8.50), liver and bacon (£7.50), open sandwiches such as mushroom, red pepper and brie (£6.25). A little class is added with the old framed pictures and tagged bottles of vintage ports and wines in a top corner, while decorative pretension is balanced by the honest, working clientele. *Games (fruit machines). TV.*

King's Head
17 Hogarth Place, SW5 0QT (7244 5931). Earl's Court tube. **Open** noon-11pm Mon-Sat; noon-10.30pm Sun. **Food served** noon-9pm daily. **Credit** AmEx, MC, V.
The King's Head may be steeped in Aussie lore (the filming of *Barry McKenzie* here, for instance) but these days it's far more cosmopolitan. It's the kind of well-run, well-priced gastrobar that can be found anywhere in London – this one just happens to be tucked at the end of a narrow alleyway in Earl's Court. Behind a pub façade, the bar furniture is fashionably low and random, the counter at waist level. The main communal area lends itself to chatty drinking (draught Wadworth 6X, Leffe, Adnams Broadside, Sleeman, Leffe, Young's), the intimate one opposite is better suited to your Big Plate of oven-baked butternut squash pie (£6.90) or venison, rosemary and chilli sausages on own-made mash (£8). There are char-grilled burgers too, as well as sharing plates and sarnies. The wine list runs from £11 to £17 a bottle, the dozen varieties by the glass including, among standard French and Italian types, Long Shadow chardonnay (£2.75/£3.90/£10.80) and Deakin Estate merlot (£3.35/£4.70/£12.90) from Oz. *Bar available for hire. Disabled: toilet. Games (retro video games). Quiz (8pm Mon; £2). Music (DJs 7pm Fri; free). TVs (big screen).*

Troubadour
265 Old Brompton Road, SW5 9JA (7370 1434/www. troubadour.co.uk). Earl's Court tube/West Brompton tube/rail. **Open** 9am-midnight daily. **Food served** 9am-11pm daily. **Credit** MC, V.
A great find, this. The Troubadour is a well-run café-bar, part folk club, part tearoom. Its fine (if pricey) menu attracts diners who wouldn't otherwise be seen in public with men in scruffy jumpers and woolly hats smoking roll-ups. While one element tucks into £13.95 steak-frites or a Reviver breakfast (£8.95) in the cosy back alcove, the other is lingering over any one of a dozen teas (ginger oolong, jasmine green, chaya latte with steamed milk) in the bar area by one of two front doors. Coffee is the same Mokital blend used

Central

by the Angelucci family's classic Italian spots in Soho. A bohemian ambience reigns throughout, thanks to the coffeepots and kitchen utensils displayed or dangling everywhere, faux-medieval decorative touches and lived-in feel of the furniture. It's a live venue too, for folk and blues bands mainly, plus poetry. Beers, referred to as 'Talking Water', come by the bottle (Pilsner Urquell, Sheppy's Somerset cider), wines ten of each colour by the bottle, four each by the glass, and there are ten standard cocktails (£5.95).
Club available for hire. Function room. Games (board games). Music (singer-songwriters 8pm Tue, Wed; £2.50-£5; bands 8pm Thur-Sat; £5-£15). Poetry (8-10pm alternate Mon; £4.50-£5.50). Restaurant. Tables outdoors (8, garden; 4, pavement). TV (big screen, satellite).

Warwick Arms

160 Warwick Road, W14 8PS (7603 3560). Earl's Court or High Street Kensington tube. **Open** noon-midnight Mon-Sat; noon-11.30pm Sun. **Food served** noon-3pm, 5.30-11.30pm Mon-Fri; 5.30-11.30pm Sat; noon-3pm, 5.30-10.30pm Sun. **Credit** MC, V.
The quiet pint was invented for the Warwick. Opposite a bloody big Homebase, down the road from an equally huge Tesco, this friendly home-from-home takes customers away from the chores of DIY and shopping. Fuller's beers line the bar counter and a pictorial history of the brewery lines the walls of the bare-brick back room and pristine main one. The wood gleams, the copper sparkles, conversation is low. As well as ESB, Pride and Adnams, there are ten wines, four by two sizes of glass (merlot La Palma £4/£5.10/£15, Rioja Marqués de Griñón £4.30/£5.65/£16.75), with a better choice of red than white. As if to compete with the Thai kitchen of the Young's Britannia Tap down the road, food is provided by RS Executive Indian Cuisine, the tandoori specialities (£4.95-£8.50) and five vegetarian choices (£3.50-£5.50) also available to take away.
Tables outdoors (6, pavement). TV.

Also in the area...
O'Neill's 326 Earl's Court Road, SW5 9BQ (7244 5921).

Fitzrovia

I t's Fitzrovia, OK – not Noho – for under that name the district has been legendary boozing lore from the 1940s. Noho is probably fitting for the properly classy **Hakkasan**, **Long Bar** and **Shochu Lounge**, even the eye-popping **Annex 3**; only Fitzrovia will do for **Bradley's**, the **Newman Arms** or, of course, the **Fitzroy Tavern**; while the jury's out on where such endearing oddities as **Nordic** or the **Roxy** should fall in the classification.

Annex 3

6 Little Portland Street, W1W 7JE (7631 0700). Oxford Circus tube. **Open** noon-midnight Mon-Fri; 6pm-midnight Sat. **Food served** noon-3pm, 6.30-11pm Mon-Fri; 6.30-11pm Sat. **Credit** AmEx, MC, V.
This fantastically decorated bar comes from the three boys who are behind the fabulously camp French restaurant Les Trois Garçons and cocktail bar Loungelover. A similar maximalist, bad-taste chic informs the design, only this time more is less. With its abundance of kitsch art, elaborate furniture, bin-end wallpapers and junk-store muddle of styles, the overall effect is like moving around inside a

pinball machine. The extensive cocktail list is one of the most interesting in the West End, and includes a page of Punches: the Bengal Lancer packs a whopping punch and, the size of a small goldfish bowl, is big enough for two people (£14). A Pisco Sour (£6.50) was less impressive, lacking sufficient egg-white. You can also eat adequate, vaguely Asian dishes. Instead come here to ogle the fittings and furnishings, and maybe the other people if you're lucky. A fun bar, but it's no Loungelover.
Bar available for hire. Restaurant. **Map 1 J5**.

Bradley's Spanish Bar

42-44 Hanway Street, W1T 1UT (7636 0359). Tottenham Court Road tube. **Open** noon-11pm Mon-Sat; noon-10.30pm Sun. **Credit** MC, V.
This scuffed off-Oxford Street landmark is still a Spanish colony, even though many of the tacky decorative trappings went with the old-school barman Luis (framed behind the bar). There's barely a bullfighting poster mounted or gleaming trinket on display. A new generation (dreadlocked and/or pierced) is in charge of this cramped, creaking, two-floor casket of velour, manning the pricey pumps of San Miguel, Cruzcampo, Bitburger and Guinness. They've even learned to show restraint when compiling the old-style jukeboxes in each of the two bars, veering away from The Vines and back towards the Spencer Davis Group. Everyone still loves it, of course, spilling on warm evenings on to narrow Hanway Street in taxi-blocking bonhomie.
Map 7 K6.

Cock Tavern

27 Great Portland Street, W1W 8QE (7631 5002). Oxford Circus tube. **Open** 11.30am-11pm Mon-Sat; noon-10.30pm Sun. **Food served** noon-3pm, 5.30-8.30pm Mon-Thur; noon-3pm Fri; noon-6pm Sat, Sun. **Credit** MC, V.
It may now bear a fashionably sparse, modern, runaround sign brazenly declaring 'The Cock', but this Sam Smith's pub is as traditional as it gets once you set foot on its staid, sturdy floor tiles. A century old or more, the place is a masterpiece of pub interior woodcraft, a grand doorframe topped with a clock dividing the entrance area from the main part of the bar. A fireplace at the back augments the sense of comfort. No surprises on the bar counter, unless you're not yet familiar with the otherwise staunchly traditional Tadcaster brewer's recent decision to call Ayingerbräu lager 'Alpine'. Until the marketing men come up with a snazzier name, ploughman's lunches are served here and in the upstairs lounge bar, open at mealtimes.
Games (fruit machines). No piped music or jukebox. Tables outdoors (3, pavement). **Map 1 J5**.

Crazy Bear

26-28 Whitfield Street, W1T 7DS (7631 0088/www. crazybeargroup.co.uk). Goodge Street tube. **Open/food served** noon-11pm Mon-Fri; 6-11pm Sat. **Credit** MC, V.
Bar of the Year 2005, according to a rival of ours – and they're not far wrong. Über-stylish yet supremely comfortable, the Noho flagship of the namesake Oxfordshire-based hotel-and-pub chain comprises restaurant upstairs and opulent bar below, down an ornate staircase. Choose between a swivel cowhide bar stool, a red padded alcove or low leather armchair and pull up a menu – one for cigars, one for drinks. Actually, one for 'dim sum and drinks', for now the CB has Chaiyong on its books, 'head dim sum chef at the Dusit Thai, Bangkok', and equal emphasis has been placed on all-day £4 offerings such as lou cha har gaij (prawn and green tea) and on the stunningly good cocktails.

wagamama

**fast and fresh noodle and rice dishes
from london's favourite noodle restaurant**

wagamama.com

uk | ireland | holland | australia | dubai | antwerp | auckland | copenhagen

Short and Muddled (£8), Martinis (£8.50) and Champagne varieties (£9.50) are expertly and convivially mixed ('How are you tonight, sir?') with high-end brands, exotic fruits and inventive purées. Time to dish out another award. *Restaurant.* **Map 1 K5**.

Crown & Sceptre
26-27 Foley Street, W1W 6DS (7307 9971). Oxford Circus tube. **Open** noon-11pm Mon-Sat; noon-10.30pm Sun. **Food served** noon-9.30pm daily. **Credit** MC, V.
An excellent place this, creating just the right balance of pub and bar out of what was a standard corner (albeit a large corner) neighbourhood boozer. A sturdy pentagonal bar counter is still the centrepiece of a considerable public space of high ceilings and cosy chatting and dining corners. Upon it, now tagged like Christmas presents with name, provenance, ABV and description, are beer taps including Japanese Kirin, Canadian Sleeman, Amstel, Küppers Kölsch, Deuchars IPA, Spitfire and a few regular others. Wines, eight by the glass and ten by the bottle, are chalked up in each corner, ranging from Silverland chenin chardonnay and Bonarda malbec from Argentina (£2.50/£10) to a New Zealand Spy Valley riesling or brouilly Cave à l'Ancienne (both £15.50) – there's £2 a bottle reduction on the wine of the month. Cocktails (Bees Kiss, Down Hill Racer) are rum-based, using Appleton or Wray & Nephew. And they make equal fuss over the food, whether it's a half-pound Charolais steak burger (£7.50) or snacks ('light') and sandwiches ('between bread'), quesadillas, wedges, fish cakes and the like.
Disabled: toilet. Music (DJ 7.30pm Wed). Tables outdoors (4, pavement). **Map 1 J5**.

Eagle Bar Diner
3-5 Rathbone Place, W1T 1HJ (7637 1418/www.eagle bardiner.com). Tottenham Court Road tube. **Open/food served** noon-11pm Mon-Wed; noon-1am Thur, Fri; 10am-1am Sat; 11am-6pm Sun. **Credit** MC, V.
This New York-style diner-cum-bar, with intimate green booths and Formica tables, is set on split levels. It's a stylish yet unpretentious place that's best used as a diner for breakfast and brunch, and as a cocktail bar in the evening. American-style breakfasts, salads, sandwiches, hot dogs, brownies, cheesecake, shakes and malts are offered on the all-day food menu, while the burgers run to such exotic meats as emu, ostrich, kangaroo and bison. Drinks include bespoke cocktails (including ones laced with tequila and bourbon), American bottled beer (like Dixie, Liberty, Brooklyn and Anchor), bourbons, hot alcoholic drinks, reduced-fat drinks and alcoholic milkshakes with icecream. Cocktails are priced from £6.95 to £8.50, and include a punchy Peanut Butter Martini (£6.95) that would have made Elvis proud.
Babies and children admitted (until 9pm if dining). Music (DJs 7.30pm Wed-Sat; free). **Map 7 K6**.

Fitzroy Tavern
16 Charlotte Street, W1T 2LY (7580 3714). Goodge Street tube. **Open** 11am-11pm Mon-Sat; noon-10.30pm Sun. **Food served** noon-2.30pm, 6.30-9.30pm Mon-Thur, Sat, Sun; noon-2.30pm Fri. **Credit** AmEx, MC, V.
If any place had a pub history it's this one, lending its name via a newspaper gossip column to a then-bohemian area of London. In those days either side of World War II, revered in framed black-and-white glory on the walls of what is now a busy corner establishment, this ornate Victorian pub saw them all: here drank Dylan Thomas, George Orwell and Augustus John, the dissolute shag-

around painter (he would pat any passing children in case they were his) now honoured with his own corner. It closed in 1955. Now it's a Sam Smith's place with the full range of beers from Tadcaster, baguettes and burgers. The outside pub tables and spacious interior, built around a big centrepiece bar counter, fill with nearby employees from the media and building trades. Sneak downstairs to the little function room used for weekly stand-up and you'll still find a picture of Orwell waving goodbye, going off to fight the good fight in the Spanish Civil War.
Comedy (8pm Wed; £7). Function room. Games (fruit machine, quiz machine). No piped music or jukebox. Tables outdoors (9, pavement). **Map 1 K5**.

Hakkasan
8 Hanway Place, W1T 1HD (7907 1888). Tottenham Court Road tube. **Open** noon-12.30am Mon-Wed; noon-1.30am Thur-Sat; noon-midnight Sun. **Food served** noon-3pm, 6pm-12.30am Mon-Wed; noon-3pm, 6pm-1.30am Thur, Fri; noon-4pm, 6pm-1.30am Sat; noon-4pm Sun. **Credit** AmEx, MC, V.
Ensconced in a basement on an unassuming blink-and-you'll-miss-it side-street, Hakkasan is the capital's most glamorous, must-visit Chinese restaurant. Walk past the extravagant floral arrangements by the reception to reach the Ling Ling bar at the far side of the restaurant, where you'll find a moodily brooding space lit with flickering candles. Designed by Christian Liaigre, the stained oak bar is decked out with colourful backlit panels and richly embroidered oriental fabrics. There's a complex cocktail list that was put together by legendary London barman Dick Bradsell. It boasts oriental-themed cocktails (around £8 each) made from sake, oriental spirits and fresh exotic fruit. Try Kumquat Javu (Appleton rum, Mandarine Napoléon, Southern Comfort and kumquats) or Plum Sour (Chinese plum brandy, Chivas Regal and sours). Dim sum is served as bar snacks, and service from elegantly attired staff (uniforms by Hussein Chalayan, no less) is seamlessly efficient.
Babies and children admitted. Disabled: toilet. Function room. Music (DJs 9pm daily; free). **Map 1 K5**.

Hope
15 Tottenham Street, W1T 2AJ (7637 0896). Goodge Street tube. **Open** 11am-11pm Mon-Sat; noon-6pm Sun. **Food served** noon-3pm daily. **Credit** MC, V.
One of several sturdy old boozers north of Noho which rely on the lunchtime and post-work trade, the Hope fills every day of the working week thanks to the quality of its ales (Adnams, Shepherd Neame) and sausages (lamb and rosemary, pork and stilton, venison and wild mushroom, £5.95) – and the two floors of comfort they are enjoyed in. Said sausages are served in threes with a side of chips or mash, peas or beans, either in the quiet of an upstairs dining room decked out in Victorian prints, with a bird's-eye view of street bustle where Whitfield Street meets Tottenham Street, or in a busy downstairs bar otherwise equipped with board games and a television for those lucky enough not to be rushing back to work.
Babies and children admitted (until 7pm). Function room. Games (board games, fruit machine). Tables outdoors (6, pavement). TV (big screen). **Map 1 J5**.

Horse & Groom
128 Great Portland Street, W1W 6PS (7580 4726). Great Portland Street or Oxford Circus tube. **Open** noon-11.30pm Mon-Sat; noon-10.30pm Sun. **Food served** noon-2.30pm, 5.30-8.30pm Mon-Fri; noon-5pm Sat; noon-3pm Sun. **Credit** MC, V.

The back function and fireplace rooms are the attraction here, along with the fact that this is otherwise a standard Sam Smith's local for working types who don't want a wafer in their drink, thank you very much. An obscure sporting heritage is hinted at by the name and mounted pictures of jockeys and sundry team line-ups – once upon a time the Horse & Groom would have been quite grand, given the lovely bay window in what is today the glugging zone of the front bar. A dartboard and glass-topped football table beckon from the back room, while glowing couples and ravenous tradesmen pick at or devour standard pub lunches in relative privacy around the fireplace. A little frosted glass and tidy upholstery out front giftwrap a solidly dependable bar counter equipped with Sam Smith's ale and lager selections.
Function room. Games (darts, fruit machine). Tables outdoors (4, pavement). **Map 1 J5.**

Jerusalem
33-34 Rathbone Place, W1T 1JN (7255 1120/www.the breakfastgroup.co.uk). Tottenham Court Road tube. **Open** noon-11pm Mon; noon-midnight Tue, Wed; noon-1am Thur, Fri; 7pm-1am Sat. **Food served** noon-3pm, 6-10.30pm Mon-Fri; 7-10.30pm Sat. **Credit** AmEx, MC, V.
Once the flagship of the inventive and ambitious bar-owning Breakfast Group, now somewhat overshadowed by their opulent Opium on the other side of Oxford Street in Soho, Jerusalem still fills its spacious basement with punters thanks to its twofer lunchtime deals and £10 early-evening two-course dinners. And the food's not shabby, either. Thai platters for two (£9.80), lamb steak with mash and honey-and-rosemary jus (£10.50) plus the hulking great Ultimate Surf and Turf (£24) of king prawns, chargrilled sirloin and enough meat and seafood to fill an Australian rugby team – it's a pleasure to pig out here. Wines come three of each colour by the glass, eight by the bottle, from the currently ubiquitous Principe de Viana chardonnay or cabernet sauvignon (£3.10/£14.50) to bottles of Australian Gumdale chardonnay or shiraz (£17.50/£16.50). Beer (San Miguel, Grolsch, Kronenbourg) comes by the standard glass size or four-pint jug (£12). The sturdy wooden tables and candlelit decor lend a medieval banqueting ambience.
Music (DJs Thur-Sat; £5 after 10pm Fri, Sat). Restaurant. **Map 1 K5.**

Long Bar
The Sanderson, 50 Berners Street, W1T 3NG (7300 1400). Oxford Circus or Tottenham Court Road tube. **Open** noon-12.30am Mon-Sat; noon-10.30pm Sun. **Food served** noon-11pm Mon-Sat; noon-10pm Sun. **Credit** AmEx, DC, MC, V.
The bright, stylish bar next to the lobby in Philippe Starck's trendy Sanderson Hotel used to attract a hip young crowd, but nowadays the hipsters seem to have moved on – on our visit, the place was packed with tourists, older fellows in suits and gaggles of giggly girls. Service can be snooty, but the long onyx bar remains attractively hip, surrounded by bar stools with Dali-esque eyeball motifs on the back. There are a dozen Martinis, Champagne cocktails and highballs (priced around £10), plus wines by the glass. A seasonally changing food menu includes burgers, charcuterie, meze platters, cheesecake and cookies. Food and drink can be consumed in the bar or in a courtyard that overlooks a Japanese garden.
Babies and children welcome (terrace). Disabled: toilet. Restaurant. Tables outdoors (20, terrace). **Map 1 J5.**

Market Place
11 Market Place, W1W 8AH (7079 2020/www.market place-london.com). Oxford Circus tube. **Open/food served** 11am-midnight Mon-Wed; 11am-1am Thur, Fri; noon-1am Sat; 1-11pm Sun. **Admission** £7 after 11pm Fri; £3 8-11pm, £7 after 11pm Sat. **Credit** AmEx, MC, V.
The West End flagship of the Cantaloupe Group that made its name in Shoreditch. Menus are generic and Latin wherever possible – wines, for example, sold in two sizes of glass and by the bottle, at about £3.50, £4.50 and £14 each, Spanish Viña Rey tempranillo, Chilean Reserva Casanova merlot and Los Prados chenin-semillon from Argentina complement the Latin street-food concept behind offerings from the kitchen. Brazilian seafood casserole moqueca de seruru (£6.50) and gaucho chimichurri rumpsteak sandwich (£6) are interesting finds among the albóndigas and empanaditas – but these are not why this two-floor venue zings nightly: music rules, with a DJ deck manned downstairs, where there is no little flirtatious dancing between the tables. Throw in a couple of quality cocktails (42 Below vodka, Sauza tequila) at £6 and you're in business.
Disabled: toilet. Music (DJs 8pm daily). Tables outdoors (8, terrace). **Map 1 J6.**

Mash
19-21 Great Portland Street, W1W 8QB (7637 5555/ www.mashbarandrestaurant.co.uk). Oxford Circus tube. **Open** 11am-2am Mon-Sat. **Food served** 11am-11pm Mon-Sat. **Admission** £10 after 10pm Fri; £5 after 9pm, £10 after 10pm Sat. **Credit** AmEx, DC, MC, V.
What is going on at Mash? One minute it's breakfast and bento in a box at this style bar, the next the management is renting out prime entrance space to a florist. A florist! The rest of the bar is as was. The copper vats currently contain master brewer Rainer's Belgian wheat, Mash house and Vienna Style Lager beers, plus Great Portland Chocolate Stout. The cocktail menu glitters with 14 Mash originals at £6.50 (Citrus Nail with Chivas Regal and Drambuie, Bazaar with Zubrowka and apple liqueur). Seasonal pitchers (£15.50) and classic cocktails are also made with the likes of Luksusowa vodka and Buffalo Trace bourbon. The food – with a restaurant upstairs – is a cut above (Welsh Black steak sandwich, £6.50; pork terrine with pear chutney and toast, £5.50), as are the fresh blends. Oh yes, and that discombobulating mural of disfigured retro families still dominates the sunken area, overseen by DJs four nights of the week.
Bar available for hire. Dress: smart casual. Music (DJs 10pm Thur-Sat). Restaurant (available for hire). Tables outdoors (4-8, pavement). **Map 1 J6.**

Match Bar
37-38 Margaret Street, W1G 0JF (7499 3443/www. matchbar.com). Oxford Circus tube. **Open/food served** 11am-midnight Mon-Fri; noon-midnight Sat; 3-10.30pm Sun. **Credit** AmEx, DC, MC, V.
Although they are no longer showered with awards, it still takes a lot to match a Match Bar – even this slightly plainer West End branch. The Margaret Street Match makes the most of its narrow space, creating a communal front area with a table spread with newspapers, two levels of corridor tables and a long counter to pose at. No room for murals, but you're here for the painstakingly created cocktails: Classics (£6.50), such as a Rangoon with Plymouth Fruit Cup or Pink Lady with Blackwood's Nordic gin; the Match Originals (£6.50) like Long Mango with Finlandia Mango or Fa'afafene with 42 Below; and the New Season's Creations (£6.25-£9). Old and new show

Central

the hand of cocktail-meister Dale DeGroff, involved with Match since its inception in 1997, and who recently came up with a Bueller of Knob Creek small batch bourbon and Grand Marnier and a Rathbone Gardens featuring Plymouth Navy Strength rum. Sharing bowls (£7, £12 for two, £20 for four) of Burmese chicken curry or giant shepherd's pie temper the urge for sophisticated hedonism. *Disabled: toilet. Music (DJs 7.30pm Thur-Sat; free). Tables outdoors (2, pavement).* **Map 1 J6**.

Newman Arms

23 Rathbone Street, W1T 1NG (7636 1127/www. newmanarms.co.uk). Goodge Street or Tottenham Court Road tube. **Open** noon-midnight Mon-Fri. **Food served** noon-3pm, 6-9pm Mon-Fri. **Credit** MC, V. Despite a modest spruce-up in the poky but historic downstairs bar (a framed picture of former regular George Orwell, some daffy poem by Ken Hilton bemoaning the life of a rep, a smart frontage), the main draw is still the Famous Pie Room upstairs. Duvet-sized puffs of pastry envelop such creative fillings as venison in red wine or pork, apple and cider (to name the specials on the day of review), complementing the seven standards always on offer (beef and Guinness, steak and kidney, and so on). Names of new pies are splashed across the side of the building that forms the narrow alleyway between Rathbone and Newman Streets. What this former brothel and 19th-century tavern doesn't advertise is its role as an alleyway backdrop to Michael Powell's 1960 classic *Peeping Tom* – or as home to a plethora of maverick Fitzrovia characters, bohemian to a fault. Today it's nine-to-fivers chuckling over a pint of Pride or Adnams. *Quiz (6.30pm Mon; free). Restaurant (no smoking).* **Map 1 J5**.

Nordic

25 Newman Street, W1T 1PN (7631 3174/www. nordicbar.com). Tottenham Court Road tube. **Open** noon-11pm Mon-Fri; 6-11pm Sat. **Food served** noon-3pm, 5.30-10pm Mon-Fri; 6-10pm Sat. **Credit** MC, V. A nice little success story, this. A long basement accessed at each end from Newman Street and Passage, this Scandinavian themed bar is kitsch when it needs to be (Ingrid Bergman with reindeer antlers, Max von Sydow triptych), but professional when it comes to cocktails and smörgåsbords. The latter, £9.75 for one, entail Pytt I Panna (sausage and bacon hash), crayfish tails, deep-fried Jarlsberg, the works; the former are works of Arctic art. In the Long and Funky (£6.95) category, the outstanding Northern Light involves Absolut Mandarin muddled fresh mint and purées a gogo; Longberry zings with muddled blueberries, raspberries and strawberries, Finlandia Lime, Lapponia Blueberry liqueur and lingonberry juice. Aquavits feature frozen as an aperitif for lunch, with punch for dessert, or in eight varieties or five tasting bottles if on a bender. Oh yes, plus every Nordic beer, liqueur and vodka you've ever heard of and many that you haven't: Pear Aivy, anyone? *TV (big screen, plasma).* **Map 1 J5**.

Nueva Costa Dorada

47-55 Hanway Street, W1T 1UX (7636 7139/www. costadoradarestaurant.co.uk). Tottenham Court Road tube. **Open/food served** 6pm-3am Mon-Sat. **Credit** AmEx, DC, MC, V. Refitted and renamed, the Nueva Costa Dorada has gone from plain old Costa Dorada, a somewhat tired, tiled (and a tad tacky) Spanish late drinking den and tapas restaurant, to this spanking new lounge bar. The bar area, comprising one-sixth of the cavernous basement space

otherwise given over to lines of wooden dining tables, DJs and occasional flamenco floor shows, is now brown leather seating and dinky little stools. Not a tile in sight. The tapas menu has been downsized but cherry-picked, so that the half-dozen offerings (£6) include chorizo al vino and grated vegetables in stuffed peppers. The Cava is Montesquis (£4.50/glass, £24/bottle) and you can get a decent white Rioja for £4 a glass, £15 a bottle. Hell, there are even bottles of Dom Pérignon (£129). Cocktails, many mixed with Havana Club, are a reasonable £6.50 and similarly priced Martinis now come in Passion Fruit and Espresso flavours. *Music (DJ 8.30pm Tue-Sat; flamenco shows 9.30pm, 11.30pm Thur; 10pm, 12.30am Fri, Sat; free).* **Map 1 K5**.

Oscar

Charlotte Street Hotel, 15 Charlotte Street, W1T 1RJ (7806 2000/www.charlottestreethotel.com). Goodge Street tube. **Open** 11am-11pm Mon-Sat; 5-8pm Sun. **Food served** noon-10.30pm Mon-Sat. **Credit** AmEx, MC, V. Media types scratch each other's backs at this upmarket street-level bar-restaurant of the Charlotte Street Hotel. Watch them in action through the French windows or from a stripy bar-stool vantage point at the chrome bar counter festooned with tall bunches of fresh flowers. Choose from one of half-a-dozen Contemporary Cocktails (£9.50) and enjoy the hit of Absolut Raspberi expertly combined with fresh raspberries and a ginger and mint muddle in an Oriental Passion, or Jack Daniels and Apple Sourz in a Jack and Giles. Observe power powwows go smoothly with Beaumont des Crayères Champagne Bellinis (£10.50) or Martini cocktails (£9.50) such as NZpolitan with 42 Below, lychee liqueur and pomegranate juice. Watch them engage in gentlemanly club chover whose expense account to tab the bar snacks on (Japanese or Moroccan platter, £11.50-£12.50), while picking over the last of the grilled tiger prawns. Done deal – it's a wrap. *Babies and children admitted. Film Club (8pm Sun; £30 incl meal). Function rooms. Restaurant. Tables outdoors (10, pavement).* **Map 1 K5**.

Potion

28 Maple Street, W1T 6HP (7580 6474/www.potion bar.co.uk). Warren Street tube. **Open** 11am-11pm Mon-Wed; 11am-midnight Thur-Sat. **Food served** noon-3pm, 5-9pm Mon-Fri. **Credit** AmEx, MC, V. 'We are one of London's little gems. We are everything you could possibly want in a bar.' (No fresh exotic fruit in the cocktails? No well-chosen background music? No buzz around the bar counter?) These last 'We are…' statements bookending the new menu might grate, but Potion isn't such a bad place. A three-floor bar-diner at Maple and Fitzroy Streets, it offers an alternative to the workaday pubs in the vicinity. Draught beers (such as Kingfisher and John Smith's) are ten in number, bottled types include Asahi and Brahma, wines come three of each colour by the glass, eight by the bottle, from a Emblème d'Argent chardonnay or merlot (£3/£11) to a Pouilly-Fuissé Vieilles Vignes (£21.50) or Rioja Vieja Crianza (£15). Standard cocktails are a standard £5.40, but where Potion wins out is in the food: slow-braised duck in the Sticky Duck pizzas (£7.50), charred Cajun chicken in the Chicken Caesar (£7.50), avocados, bacon and alphabetically ordered all sorts in the ABCCBA burger (£6.45). They push party hire, and you and your colleagues could do far worse. *Babies and children admitted (until 5pm). Function rooms. Tables outdoors (6, pavement). TVs (big screen, satellite).* **Map 1 4J**.

Roxy

*3 Rathbone Place, W1T 1HJ (7255 1098/www.theroxy.
co.uk). Tottenham Court Road tube.* **Open/food served**
5pm-3am Mon-Fri; 9.30pm-3.30am Sat. **Happy hour**
5-7.30pm Mon-Fri; 9.30-10.30pm Sat. **Credit** MC, V.
Embracing tacky, retro, funny and happy-hour cheap, the
Roxy is a sympathetic mix of all. How long it'll be at its
prime off-Oxford Street site is another matter, for there are
always plenty of free tables (a post-work boon towards the
end of the week) around this cavernous basement. For now,
it's fine. Down a staircase muralled with Doherty looka-
likes jumping, through the double doors, a vast bar counter
beckons. On it stand taps of Beck's, Grolsch and
Kronenbourg, the latter pair on twofers till 7.30pm; behind
it, a surprisingly decent selection of wines, a Torres Viña
Esmerelda (£4.75/£16.25) or J Moreau Chablis (£22.50), a
Veramonte cabernet sauvignon (£4.25/£16.50) or Château
Lyonnat St-Émilion (£24.50). House Condessa de Leganza
comes at £3.60/£11.95 in each colour. Pitchers of standard
cocktails (£15.95) are dangerously half-price in happy hour,
making the Costello mural above the DJ decks woozily fuse
with the more-than-welcome indie hits.
*Games (backgammon, chess). Music (DJs 6pm nightly;
admission varies).* **Map 7 K6.**

Ship

*134 New Cavendish Street, W1W 6YB (7636 6301).
Oxford Circus tube.* **Open** 11am-11pm Mon-Fri.
Food served 11.30am-3pm Mon-Fri. **Credit** MC, V.
A recent tidy job on the exterior is the only change in this
gleaming copper cave of a pub interior with a vague nautical theme, festooned with neon signs for little-known
lagers. Bass, Grolsch, Caffrey's and Guinness line the bar
counter – even though a board above it proclaims
'Wenlock's No.1 House' – and punters seem perfectly
happy with their cosy afternoon interlude here. The management even has breakfasts, burgers and jackets brought
round from the Sky 2 caff next door. The somewhat disconcerting 'No Soliciting' sign over the gents' seems somewhat harsh, for although sailors do pass by, they're here
to talk tides and tillers. Outdoor tables in summer.
Function room. Games (fruit machine). TV. **Map 1 J5.**

Shochu Lounge

*Basement, Roka, 37 Charlotte Street, W1T 1RR (7580
9666/www.shochulounge.com). Goodge Street tube.*
Open 5pm-midnight daily. **Food served** 5.30-11.30pm
daily. **Credit** AmEx, DC, MC, V.
The alluring basement bar below award-winning roto-
baki restaurant Roka won *Time Out*'s Best Bar award in
2005, and it's still a hit: the crowd of customers at 7pm on
a midweek evening proved that. It has a lot going for it,
from the louche yet sociable mood conferred by low lighting and a low ceiling to the pioneering focus on Japan's
vodka-like spirit shochu, here tinctured with things like
cinnamon ('for joy of life') or lemon ('for virility') and served
neat or in cocktails by Tony Conigliaro – a Hello Kitty of
shochu, rasperries, rose, lemon and sparkling water, say,
or a Noshino Martini of shochu and sake with cucumber
garnish. The wooden vats and rustic bar counter, low
tables and plush, boxy red seats in enclaves make for a setting that's half 21st-century style bar, half film set for
Zatoichi. It's a shame, then, that the service was by turns
edgy and distracted – an off-note we felt the more keenly
for the near-note-perfect location, food (you can order anything on Roka's menu) and drinks.
*Disabled: toilet. Music (DJs 8pm Thur-Sat). Restaurant
(no smoking).* **Map 1 J5.**

Social

*5 Little Portland Street, W1W 7JD (7636 4992/www.
thesocial.com). Oxford Circus tube.* **Open/food served**
noon-midnight Mon-Wed; noon-1am Thur, Fri; 1pm-
1am Sat; 6pm-midnight Sun. **Credit** AmEx, MC, V.
The same (and as great) as it ever was, these days the
Social is surrounded by flashier venues – note the opulent
Annex 3 bar-restaurant now next door. An unnoticeable,
opaque front still hides this daytime diner and DJ bar of
supreme quality. The diner, its walls dedicated to temporary exhibitions of punky art (previous incumbent:
www.sickhappyidle.com) and its speakers offering aural
gifts from the Heavenly Jukebox, buzzes at lunchtime. Five
rounded booths, tables equipped with Heinz and HP,
accommodate chatty bohos munching into signature
square pies ('Getting Pie on God's Supply', according to the
retro lettering à la caff above the bar). Ruggedly prole
sarnies include fish finger varieties. Both diner and DJ bar
share the same drinks menu: draught San Miguel and
Guinness, bottled A Le Coq and Tsing Tao beer, Breton or
Kopparberg ciders, plus 20 decent cocktails (Pisco Disco,
Perfect Manhattan) at a giveaway £5.40 each. Downstairs,
it's DJs all the way, six nights a week.
*Babies and children admitted (until 5pm). Music (DJs
7pm Mon-Sat; bands 7pm Sun; £3-£5 Sun).* **Map 1 J5.**

Wax

*4 Winsley Street, W1W 8HF (7436 4650/www.wax-
bar.co.uk). Oxford Circus tube.* **Open/food served**
noon-3am Mon-Sat. **Happy hour** 5-7pm Mon-Sat.
Admission £7 after 10pm Fri; £10 after 9pm Sat.
Credit AmEx, MC, V.
Forget whatever happened at work. At Wax you can dis-
count drink like a pig until 7pm every day on £3.10 standard cocktails (categorised 'today' and 'yesterday') and
then get stuck into attracting a potential partner. You even
have one of two bar counters (green- and orange-lit to guide
you), a bar-stool front area and more comfortable lounge
at the back to choose from. Once the Purple Rain (Smirnoff,
Gordon's gin, Bacardi, Archers) wears off (2007?), steady
yourself with a Gourmet Burger or Steak Baguette (£6)
before making back unto the breach with an Asahi or
Michelob and getting serious with a Wax Martini (£5.95)
of Smirnoff and apple schnapps of unknown provenance.
If you're on the pull à deux, share a platter (£13.95) of sticky
barbecue ribs, chicken satay fillets and other comfort sat-
isfiers while lashing into the house red or white (£12.50);
on leaving dos and birthdays, get into the Vallade pinot
grigio (£14.95), Rioja Cosecha (£17.25) or Heidsieck
Champagne (£27.95). You know it makes sense.
*Bar available for hire. Disabled: toilet. Music (DJs 9pm
Thur-Sat).* **Map 1 J6.**

Also in the area...

Jamies 74 Charlotte Street, W1T 4QH (7636 7556).
Lees Bag (Davy's) 4 Great Portland Street, W1N
5AA (7636 5287).

Holborn

Once the preserve of blokish boozers, Holborn's
drinking options are on an upward trajectory.
Roxy Beaujolais's new venture **Bountiful Cow** is
the stand-out, and **Pagliacci** and **Pearl** are plush,
but the blokes can still tut sadly to themselves
in former gin palace the **Princess Louise**.

Mandarin Bar. *See p56.*

Bar Polski

11 Little Turnstile, WC1V 7DX (7831 9679). Holborn tube. **Open** 4-11.30pm Mon; 12.30-11.30pm Tue-Fri; 6-11.30pm Sat. **Food served** 4-10pm Mon; 12.30-10pm Tue-Fri; 6-10pm Sat. **Credit** MC, V.

Other venues may nod towards theme, bung a couple of Cyrillic letters into their name, stick a sticky bowl of tapas into the microwave – but the Bar Polski is the real deal. From the Polish kitchen (bigos, £6.60; barszcz, £5.10; kielbasa, £7.60 – all available until 10pm) to the equally authentic Polish fridge, this sleek and simple, admirable alleyway bar doesn't do dilettante. Speaking of fridge… most at £2.30 a shot, vodkas by the vatload are categorised into 'dry and interesting' or 'nice and sweet' to help the uninitiated. Think of them as meze – try a sweet caraway seed Kwinkowy here, or an Orzechowka infused with unripe walnuts there. Top tapa, at £4.70, is the exclusive N'Luvka, created according to a late 16th-century royal recipe. Bottled beers include Zywiec, Lech and Tyskie. Oh, and little apple-and-cinnamon szarlotka slices just like *matka* used to make.

Tables outdoors (3, pavement). **Map 4 M5.**

Bountiful Cow

51 Eagle Street, WC1R 4AP (7404 0200). Holborn tube. **Open/food served** 11am-11pm Mon-Sat. **Credit** MC, V.

Roxy Beaujolais's new baby is a sassy two-floor diner with a witty and well-sourced bovine theme – retro Vache Qui Rit and Bovril ads, posters for films such as *Cattle Empire*, *Urban Cowboy* and *Cattle Queen*. It's a bar – as opposed to the superb pub, the Seven Stars, she runs by the Royal Courts of Justice – that Roxy herself has described as 'a new public house devoted to beef'. The devotion, though, is sincere. The steaks, both ribeye (£13) and sirloin (£14), are 9oz and succulent to a T, sourced from selected beef hung for two weeks at least. They come grilled as you like or à la Capricorn with melted goat's cheese. Seafood spaghetti (£7.50) was one of four items on the daily specials list on the day of review – it's not all beef, beef, beef. Wines, of course, are well chosen (six of each colour, four by the glass), Adnams should please the ale drinkers, and bottled Budvar and Beck's glint in the fridge. Inconspicuous behind High Holborn – but who outside the legal profession knew about the Seven Stars?

Babies and children welcome. Disabled: toilet. Function room. No-smoking area. **Map 3 M5.**

Old Crown

33 New Oxford Street, WC1A 1BH (7836 9121). Holborn or Tottenham Court Road tube. **Open** 11am-midnight Mon-Wed; 11am-2am Thur, Fri; 6am-2am Sat; 6am-midnight Sun. **Food served** noon-9pm Mon-Fri; 6am-9pm Sat, Sun. **Credit** MC, V.

Once upon a time there was a standard pub on this corner, the Old Crown. A recent quick and clever conversion, using reclaimed materials, has seen fit to turn the place into a funky brown box of a bar. And rather good it is, too. Still finding its feet, it so far boasts a modest cocktail menu of 16 options, divided into 'nuevo' and 'anejo old', all in the £7 range. Interesting new varieties include a Treacle with Appleton Estate 12-year-old rum and cloudy apple juice, an Apple and Vanilla Martini with Zubrowka Bison Grass, and a Cucumber Refresher with Miller's gin, lavender syrup and Devaux Champagne. Open ciabatta sandwiches (£5-£5.50) comprise the bar snacks, Comté cheese a main element, married with marinated chicken, prosciutto or grilled Med veg, while main plates (£7.50-£12.50) feature Prime Argentine ribeye on a bed of rocket and roast shallots (£12.50) and the house signature burger (£8.50) with Aberdeen Angus meat, own-made relish and Isle of Mull cheddar. All in all, this story has legs.

Bar available for hire. Function room. Games (board games, chess). Music (DJs 8pm Thur-Sun; free). Tables outdoors (3, pavement). TV (big screen). **Map 1 L5.**

Pagliacci

77 Kingsway, WC2B 6SR (7405 4433/www.pagliacci london.com). Holborn tube. **Open** 11am-2am Mon-Sat. **Food served** 11am-10pm Mon-Sat. **Credit** MC, V.

A new cocktail bar and restaurant with flair. Bearing as a motif the features of a woman's face, the interior is a large, simple space flooded with natural light and offset by a dark, slate floor and maroon columns. Far more fuss is made over the five dozen cocktails (£6.50-£7), the Strawberry Mules with large, fat fruit muddled with ginger shavings and vodka, the three types of fresh berries mixed with Absolut Kurrant and Chambord in a Kurrant Affair, the Crème de Cassis and Peychaud bitters slammed in with tequila in the Tijuana Sling – all shaken with theatrical glee by reliable bartenders. Fifteen wines, red and white, come by the bottle, five each by the glass, such as a Rioja Tinto Faustino VII (£4.50 or £6.25/£19). Bar snacks cost around £4.

Tables outdoors (5, pavement). **Map 4 M6**.

Pearl Bar & Restaurant

Chancery Court Hotel, 252 High Holborn, WC1V 7EN (7829 7000/www.pearl-restaurant.com). Holborn tube. **Open** 11am-11pm Mon-Fri; 6-11pm Sat. **Food served** noon-2.30pm, 6-10pm Mon-Fri; 6-10pm Sat. **Credit** AmEx, DC, MC, V.

This glamorous bar and restaurant is part of the luxurious Chancery Court Hotel, with a separate courtyard entrance through revolving doors. The bar area has a tiled monochrome floor and stunning lampshades decorated with strings of real pearls. It's furnished with leather chairs and banquettes in a neutral colour scheme, with further – velvet – banquettes inside cosy walnut-wood alcoves and hand-made tables inlaid with mother-of-pearl. The main draw is the wine list, which is one of the best in town. There are 1,400 wines kept fresh by the Cruvinet System nitrogen machine, from which 450 wines by the bottle, over 40 by the glass (priced between £4.50 and £39), and several 'wine flights' are available at any given time. Martinis and other cocktails cost around £9, and Champagne cocktails like the exquisite Pink Pearl (Rémy Martin, elderflower and spiced berry cordials, brown sugar and pink Champagne) will set you back £10.50. Olives and sugared almonds are complimentary with the drinks – which also include blended Scotches, single malts and Canadian whiskies.

Disabled: toilet. Music (pianist 6pm daily). Restaurant (no smoking). **Map 4 M5**.

Princess Louise

208 High Holborn, WC1V 7EP (7405 8816). Holborn tube. **Open** 11am-11pm Mon-Fri; noon-11pm Sat; noon-10.30pm Sun. **Food served** noon-2.30pm, 6-8.30pm Mon-Fri. **Credit** AmEx, MC, V.

One of the better Sam Smith's pubs in central London, the Princess Louise is spacious and ornate, with intricate woodwork, tall, engraved mirrors and a moulded ceiling. Much is made of the food, although it's standard fare – basket meals (£6.25) such as jumbo sausages, scampi and so on, served in the upstairs bar (open only at mealtimes). Sandwiches and baguettes are served in the main bar – avocado and bacon, roast beef and horseradish – as are the ploughman's lunches with a choice of four cheeses and soup of the day. Not sumptuous enough to attract tourists, too staid to bring in young nine-to-fivers, the pub mainly lives from a middle-aged, male clientele who lend the place a somewhat sad air during the day. After work, perhaps *faute de mieux*, it's packed.

No piped music or jukebox. **Map 1 L5**.

Also in the area...

All Bar One 58 Kingsway, WC2B 6DX (7269 5171). **Bierodrome** 67 Kingsway, WC2B 6TD (7242 7469). **Pitcher & Piano** 42 Kingsway, WC2B 6EX (7404 8510). **Shakespeares Head** (JD Wetherspoon) Africa House, 64-68 Kingsway, WC2B 6BG (7404 8846).

Holland Park

There isn't too much to detain drinkers around here, but oenophiles are well served by **Academy** and **Julie's**, and the **Ladbroke Arms** is friendly beyond the call of duty.

Academy

57 Princedale Road, W11 4NP (7221 0248). Holland Park tube. **Open** noon-11pm Mon-Sat; noon-10.30pm Sun. **Food served** noon-3.30pm, 6-10.30pm Mon-Sat; noon-10pm Sun. **Credit** MC, V.

Do you remember wine bars? Academy displays all the classic symptoms: louvre blinds, recessed ceiling lights, tongue and groove walls. Oh, and wine. There's an extensive, well-chosen selection, split 50/50 between the New and Old Worlds, but for a place that majors on the grape, the choice of just five whites and six reds by the glass seems like a missed opportunity. For non-oenophiles, there's Guinness and some lacklustre lagers. The eclectic menu envelops European cuisine in a warm but slightly confused embrace, inexplicably offering 'rustic brie' and 'le brie rustique' within a few lines of each other, but a free view into a kitchen, as there is here, is always an encouraging sign. Academy's biggest asset is that, even on a Friday night, you'll get a seat and prompt service without having to wave a tenner at the bar staff.

Babies and children admitted (until 8pm). Function room. Tables outdoors (8, pavement). **Map 10 Az7**.

Castle

100 Holland Park Avenue, W11 4UA (7313 9301). Holland Park tube. **Open** noon-midnight daily. **Food served** noon-3pm, 5-10pm Mon-Fri; noon-9pm Sat, Sun. **Credit** MC, V.

The Castle's strongest selling point, its proximity to the tube, is also its biggest drawback, as copious passing trade means it fills up very rapidly. Seats are often at a premium, fought over by a mixture of lager-loyal blokes, signet-ringed investment bankers and the odd wildcard, such as El Al air marshals wandering in from nearby hotels. Chandeliers, *Living etc* wallpaper and well-worn banquette seating suggest a half-hearted attempt at boho chic – it's not helped by the playlist, a relentless succession of *Power of Love*-style compilations. The straightforward wine list is predominantly New World and the woeful lager selection is elevated, thankfully, by the presence of Staropramen on tap. Nevertheless, the Castle is a good spot for affordable refuelling – our potato wedges and caesar salad were comfortably above par.

Disabled: toilet. Games (board games). **Map 10 Az7**.

Julie's Wine Bar

135 Portland Road, W11 4LW (7727 7985/www. juliesrestaurant.com). Holland Park tube. **Open** 9am-11.30pm Mon-Sat; 10am-10.30pm Sun. **Food served** 9-11am, noon-3pm, 7-11pm Mon-Sat; 12.30-3pm, 7-10pm Sun. **Credit** AmEx, MC, V.

Central

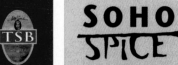

Very little was right about Prince Charles's decision to marry Diana Spencer – except perhaps his choice of engagement party venue, this charming, diminutive hostelry. Inside, its warren of small rooms and alcoves create an environment that's half 1970s Gothic, half imperial Morocco, a look that could see it do effective double duty as the set for *Emmanuelle in Marrakech*. This louche, raffish appeal hasn't been lost on patrons, who have nicknamed one of the downstairs dining spaces the Snog Pit. The food is competently handled modern European, although the pricing's calibrated to match the average income of the moneyed clientele. But they've been cut some slack on the wine list, which is no more expensive than other gastropubs in the postcode (£2.70 to £3.70 for a small glass). The cocktail list is an unadventurous mix of classics; nevertheless, like the place itself, it doesn't have to try too hard to impress. *Babies and children admitted (crèche 1-4pm Sun, free entry for diners). Function rooms. Restaurant. Tables outdoors (10, pavement).* **Map 10 Az7.**

Ladbroke Arms

54 Ladbroke Road, W11 3NW (7727 6648/www.capital pubcompany.com). Holland Park tube. **Open** 11am-11pm Mon-Sat; noon-10.30pm Sun. **Food served** noon-2.30pm, 7-9.45pm Mon-Sat; noon-3pm, 7-9.30pm Sun. **Credit** MC, V.

Most drinking destinations exercise some kind of stealthy, age-related apartheid but at the Ladbroke Arms such segregation laws seem to have been repealed and drinkers of all ages happily cram into the snug, glowingly lit interior. In the bar out front the extremely amiable landlord is kept busy pulling pints of Pride, Flowers, Greene King IPA, Adnams and Abbot, which punters pair with the brief but appealing range of bar snacks. In the dining room at the rear there's a distinct bistro feel, a vibe that owes much to the proximity of the narrow tables; this is the kind of friendly place where you can strike up inter-table chat with the party next to you without someone taking out a restraining order. The French accent extends to the menu, too: simple, unpretentious ingredients are transformed into dishes of Gallic loveliness by deft kitchen staff. *Children admitted (dining only). No piped music or jukebox. Tables outdoors (12, terrace).* **Map 10 Az7.**

Prince of Wales

14 Princedale Road, W11 4NJ (7313 9321). Holland Park tube. **Open** noon-11pm Mon-Sat; noon-10.30pm Sun. **Food served** noon-3pm, 5.30-10pm Mon-Fri; noon-10pm Sat; noon-9pm Sun. **Credit** AmEx, MC, V.

Like the Castle, the Prince of Wales is owned by the Mitchells & Butlers pubco, but this is a more successful deployment of the former's design blueprint – the salvage-yard chic of the handsome interior doesn't feel at all contrived. The pub aims further to distinguish itself by means of 'boutique' touches such as a special gin menu, but instead of adding credibility it seems a bit gimmicky: there's no Pouring Licence, so nothing more interesting can be done with the eight-strong list than serve it in standard gill measures. But, hey, how can you go wrong with a Miller's or Tanqueray Ten G&T. There's a good selection of speciality draught lagers, a well-pitched, broad-spectrum wine list and a menu of simple, Eurocentric dishes, all of which have secured the devotion of a predominantly twentysomething, borderline-cool clientele. Our only reservation is the service, which careers up and down the congeniality scale depending on who takes your order. *Disabled: toilet. Games (board games). Quiz (7.30pm Sun; £1). Tables outdoors (15, garden). TV.* **Map 10 Az7.**

Kensington

If you thought locals with moolah made for ambitious drinking establishments, it's time to visit Kensington. **Tenth Bar** literally, but perhaps not figuratively, reaches the heights; otherwise, the verdicts tend to comfortable but not exceptional.

Abingdon

54 Abingdon Road, W8 6AP (7937 3339). Earl's Court or High Street Kensington tube. **Open** 12.30-11pm Mon-Sat; 12.30-10.30pm Sun. **Food served** 12.30-2.30pm, 6.30-10.30pm Mon; 12.30-2.30pm, 6.30-11pm Tue-Sat; 12.30-3pm, 7-10pm Sun. **Credit** AmEx, MC, V.

Once a rather awkward mix of local pub and gastrobar, the Abingdon has since gone the whole hog and is now a chic spot to sip wine before your meal in the L-shaped diner behind the main bar. Such is its pedigree (opened in 1861) that the trendy, young professional regulars still use it as a destination bar, mixing comfortably with the stylish curves of the interior design. The wine list is nearly 50 strong, with 20 bottles of each colour and a handful of half-bottles, starting with a humble Borgo Selene Bianco or Pic St-Pierre vin de pays (£3/£11.50) and moving up to a £155 Chevalier Montrachet Grand Cru Dom Pillot '99 or Château Haut-Brion Pessac-Leognon (£140). Five reds and whites each come by the glass. The house Champagne is Alain Thienot (£7.50/£29.50), Cristal '99 is £130. The menu changes daily, offering some 15 mains in the £12 bracket. *No-smoking area. Tables outdoors (4, pavement).*

Bar Cuba

11-13 Kensington High Street, W8 5NP (7938 4137/ www.cubalondon.co.uk). High Street Kensington tube. **Open** noon-2.30am Mon-Sat; noon-1am Sun. **Food served** noon-1am daily. **Credit** AmEx, MC, V.

One of London's better Latin bars, the Cuba plays up its ethnicity. There are menus for cigars (from £2.50!) and rums (Bajan aplenty), the bottled beers are Cuban (Palma Crystal), Mexican (Pacifico Clara), Jamaican (Red Stripe) and Brazilian (Bravara), and tequilas (El Conquistador, Olmeca, Herradura) can be picked from a detailed list. Most of all, there are Mojitos (£4.95-£5.95), made with Mount Gay or Santiago de Cuba rums, vanilla- or lychee-infused, traditional or served in a giant goblet (£14.95). Wines too are Latin (Chilean Oveja Negra, Argentine Malbec), best enjoyed in the raised dining area at the back. A dozen house specialities (£7.25-£12.95) include pato Cubana, marinated duck fillet drizzled with Cuban sweet plum sauce or Cajun salmon. DJ decks, a party basement and hundreds of images from Castro's Cuba easily contrive a festive vibe. *Dance classes (7.30-9.30pm Mon-Sat; 6.30-8.30pm Sun). Music (Latin singer 8.30pm Wed; jazz 8.30pm Sun; DJs 9.30pm nightly; occasional bands, phone for details; £3 Wed, Sun, £5 Fri, Sat).*

Churchill Arms

119 Kensington Church Street, W8 7LN (7727 4242). Notting Hill Gate tube. **Open** 11am-11pm Mon-Wed; 11am-midnight Thur-Sat; noon-10.30pm Sun. **Food served** noon-10pm Mon-Sat; noon-8pm Sun. **Credit** AmEx, MC, V.

Halfway between High Street Ken and Notting Hill, the Churchill fills its junkyard interior with many a tourist among old regulars sharing jokes with the cute Polish bar staff. Davy lamps, musical instruments and copper knick-knacks hang from the ceiling in the cramped area around

Central

the bar and over busy tables in the side areas, one of which is warmed by a fireplace. The sense of claustrophobia is relieved by a newly renovated conservatory where the extensive Thai menu (£5-£7), stir-fried curries and the like, is served. Although the tone is unsurprisingly English – pumps of Fuller's ESB, Pride and Discovery on the bar counter, the walls plastered with wartime newspaper cuttings and anything Winnie-related – there's a definite Irish touch, with *Cead Mille Failte* ('A 100,000 Welcomes') signs and team shots of Clare's successful hurling team.
Babies and children admitted. Games (fruit machine). No-smoking area. Restaurant. TV. **Map 10 B7/8.**

Elephant & Castle
40 Holland Street, W8 4LT (7368 0901). High Street Kensington tube. **Open** 11am-11pm Mon-Sat; noon-10.30pm Sun. **Food served** noon-8pm Mon-Thur, Sat; noon-3pm Fri, Sun. **Credit** MC, V.
The quiet crossroads of family homes and little shops festooned with greenery could almost be in a quiet village in Oxfordshire, a comparison you might muse upon as you sip a Wychwood seasonal cask ale, Young's or London Pride on the front terrace. It's a Nicholson's pub, so there's the standard menu of pies and pastas, and no bottle of wine costs more than £12. In this one, a house speciality is the roast beef and horseradish in a long sub roll (£4.95). The interior is lived in, with regulars finding their place on a studded, upholstered banquette, in a wooden booth or in an intimate back room lined with newspaper splashes of seminal 20th-century moments: Laika, Neil Armstrong, the Hindenburg.
Games (fruit machine). No piped music or jukebox. Tables outdoors (4, pavement). TV.

Scarsdale
23A Edwardes Square, W8 6HE (7937 1811). Earl's Court or High Street Kensington tube. **Open** noon-11pm Mon-Sat; noon-10.30pm Sun. **Food served** noon-10pm Mon-Sat; noon-9.30pm Sun. **Credit** AmEx, MC, V.
The tranquil Scarsdale is happy to keep its history to a replica Napoleonic baggage wagon in the back courtyard, a portrait of the Emperor and a modest sign indoors explaining how the pub was built for Bonaparte's officers 200 years ago. Happily they never invaded, and this has been a rather classy pub ever since. Food is crucial to its trade: rugger fans and their girlies tuck into Aberdeenshire Black Gold ribeye steaks (£14.45) or pure-beef beefburgers (£7.75) at one of the dining-area tables at the back, or the wooden tables around the rather cramped bar area of the terrace in the front. There are a dozen wines of each colour, most also by the glass, from a Chenin Blanc Cape Promise from South Africa (£3/£4/£10.90) to a Puligny Montrachet Joseph Drouphin (£28.15) and Rioja Crianza Campo Viejo (£3.80/£4.95/£13.50) to a Gran Riserva (£20.95), but most people are here for ale: Shepherd Neame Spitfire, Young's, Greene King IPA and London Pride are supped patriotically on rugby and cricket afternoons.
Babies and children admitted (restaurant). No-smoking area. Restaurant. Tables outdoors (8, garden). TV.

Tenth Bar
Royal Garden Hotel, 2-24 Kensington High Street, W8 4PT (7361 1910/www.royalgardenhotel.co.uk). High Street Kensington tube. **Open/food served** noon-2.30pm, 5.30-11pm Mon-Fri; 5.30-11pm Sat. **Credit** AmEx, DC, MC, V.
Early evening is the best time to visit the panoramic bar of the Royal Garden Hotel. Not only do you get impeccable sunsets streaked across a wall of window that encompasses London, but also cheap Champagne (weekdays 6-7pm) and bar snacks (oysters, tempura prawns, £7-£8, Mon-Sat 6-8pm). Standard prices (£8.50-£9.25) for the 20 or so cocktails are high – but so is your bar table, alongside a restaurant appealing to moneyed, middle-aged tourists. The drinks menu, changed annually, zings along though, the Martinis (Zubrowka and Cointreau in the apple variety, Stolichnaya and Absolut Citron in the lychee) standing out from the bunch. There are as many Champagnes (£45-£165) as wines, eight by the glass, including a Domaine de l'Eglantière Jean Durup Chablis (£9) and Morgon Domaine de la Chaponne Laurent Guillet (£7.50).
Bar available for hire. Disabled: lift; toilet. Restaurant.

Windsor Castle
114 Campden Hill Road, W8 7AR (7243 9551/ www.windsor-castle-pub.co.uk). Notting Hill Gate tube. **Open** noon-11pm Mon-Sat; noon-10.30pm Sun. **Food served** noon-3pm, 5-10pm Mon-Fri; noon-10pm Sat; noon-9pm Sun. **Credit** AmEx, MC, V.
The beer taps on the bar might just as well say 'Drink Me', because the rooms leading off the main one need you to stoop lower and lower to access them. The layout of the Windsor Castle is as it was when the place was built in 1835, with the Campden, Private and Sherry Rooms filled with wooden pews and booths. The framed pictures have hardly changed either, although Dickens, featured on the a wall, was just starting out when the pub opened. Food is as important as the Adnams, Timothy Taylor Landlord and London Pride on offer, with the slow roast shank of Beltex lamb, chicken breast stuffed with leek and tallegio, sausages such as beef, basil and blackberry all vying for a gastronome's attention. Wines, chalked up on a blackboard, include a Pouilly-Fumé, a Siglo Rioja and a tempranillo, all by the bottle and two sizes of glass. There are seats outside in summer, and a warming fire in winter.
Games (board games). No piped music or jukebox. Tables outdoors (20, garden; 4, pavement). **Map 10 A8.**

King's Cross & Euston
Yes, we've some residual affection for the time when King's Cross was full of scuzz-buckets, but are still glad to say that a couple of years after **06 St Chad's Place** brought the area some much-needed class, the recent arrival of **Somerstown Coffee House** is cheering news.

Harrison
28 Harrison Street, WC1H 8JF (7278 3966). Russell Square tube/King's Cross tube/rail. **Open** 11am-11pm Mon-Fri; 1-10.30pm Sun. **Food served** noon-3pm, 6-9.30pm Mon-Fri; 2-6.30pm Sun. **Credit** AmEx, MC, V.
That a disco ball strikes the sole discord in this otherwise harmoniously conceived pub is one of the best backhanded compliments a pub could get. The Harrison succeeds, in the teeth of the pessimistic adage, by appealing to most of the people most of the time. This is partly due to the pleasing adaptability of the room, with its roomy leather couches, plenty of blond wood and fireplace. It offers 'rapid' and 'gastro' meals and, although of a Monday lunchtime the clientele consisted of one man and his computer, in the evening there's plenty to draw in the crowds and keep them happy: chess on Mondays, DJs on Fridays, and Sundays boast roasts and live music. There is free Wi-Fi access to accompany your Fair Trade coffee and crowd-pleasing wines. There's Young's Bitter and the usual Kronenbourg

and Guinness, with Staropramen a standout. Food is rather more exciting: warm roast vegetable salad with marinated feta and merguez sausage being a tasty example. *Bar available for hire (Sat). Chess club (7pm Mon; free). Games (backgammon, chess). Music (DJs 7.30pm Fri; bands 7pm Sat; musicians 2pm Sun; free-£3). Tables outdoors (7, pavement).*

Head of Steam
1 Eversholt Street, NW1 1DN (7383 3359). Euston tube/rail. **Open** 11am-11pm Mon-Sat; noon-10.30pm Sun. **Food served** noon-2.30pm, 5-8pm Mon-Fri; noon-5pm Sat. **Credit** MC, V.
Trainspotting is a serious business in this drinking den overlooking the bus stops at Euston station. The walls are plastered in train memorabilia, obviously painstakingly arranged by an enthusiast, from ancient timetables and licence plates to cartoons especially commissioned for the pub. Whether it's that or the range of draught lagers and cask ales that attract the older, mostly male clientele is hard to determine, but there weren't many young whippersnappers around on our visit. Holt's and several varieties of Fuller's feature, as well as lesser-known beers such as Phoenix Arizona. Vintage and oak-aged ciders are also available, and the wine list is perfectly adequate. The usual pub dishes (£5.50-£6.25) are on offer, and the TV shows soundless sports. A characterful place, if a little tatty. *No piped music or jukebox. TVs (satellite).*

King Charles I
55-57 Northdown Street, N1 9BL (7837 7758). King's Cross tube/rail. **Open** noon-11pm Mon-Fri; 5-11pm Sat. **Credit** AmEx, MC, V.
There's a laid-back, cosily scruffy feel to this compact pub, created by the open log fire and customers who are clearly loyal regulars. A miniature billiards table in one corner and a stack of games by the bar will help pass the time on quiet evenings – you could go for sedate Scrabble or a compendium of drinking games. The usual beery suspects are available (Foster's, Beck's, Kronenbourg), plus San Miguel and two real ales on rotation. There are no meals on offer, but you can bring your own – or even order at one of the caffs over the road and have them deliver it directly to you. A jukebox covers all corners from Bowie to country (the Stone Roses and AC/DC set the tone when we popped in), while framed comic book art adorns the walls. *Tables outdoors (5, pavement).*

Ruby Lounge
33 Caledonian Road, N1 9BU (7837 9558/www.ruby. uk.com). King's Cross tube/rail. **Open** 4-11pm Mon-Wed, Sun; 4pm-midnight Thur; 4pm-2am Fri, Sat. **Food served** 4-8pm daily. **Credit** MC, V.
Modern-retro is the mood in this cocktail bar, with pop-art likenesses of Elvis hung on the eponymous ruby-red walls. A fabulous shell chandelier is the centrepiece, hanging over a central, circular bar, and the wall-to-wall curved seating means those who are so inclined can engage in the game of seeing and being seen. The token selection of draught beers includes Guinness, Carling and San Miguel, but it's the cocktails that will make you schedule repeat visits. The bartenders are attentive and take pride in the drinks they mix, most of which are priced around the £5 mark. Late opening hours at weekends, when DJs provide the beats with a mix of hip hop and 1980s tunes, plus an anything-goes open decks night, seal Ruby's success: there aren't many places like it, with free entry, in this corner of town. *Music (DJs 9pm Thur-Sat; free).*

06 St Chad's Place
6 St Chad's Place, WC1X 9HH (7278 3355/www.6st chadsplace.com). King's Cross tube/rail. **Open** 8am-11pm Mon-Fri. **Food served** 8-10am, noon-2.30pm, 6-9.30pm Mon-Fri. **Credit** MC, V.
Don't be put off by the approach to this well-hidden bar, down a forbiddingly dark, cobbled alley. This converted Victorian warehouse is a stylish space, with a skylight in the high ceiling setting off exposed brick and polished tiles, and a giant print of a railway platform on the back wall brought to life by the rumble of passing trains. The handful of sofas are outnumbered by rows of wooden tables, indicating that food is the priority; breakfast is served from 8am, there's a Med-leaning gastro lunch menu that changes every week, and each evening sees a new selection of posh finger food. The choice selection of draught beers includes Peroni, Amstel and Brugs Witbier, the wine list ranges from £11 to £45 and the classic cocktails are complemented by innovations like an Espresso Martini (vanilla vodka, a splash of coffee). The atmosphere feels a tad sterile, but service was surprisingly friendly for such a self-consciously design-led place. *Bar available for hire (Sat). Disabled: toilet. Music (DJ 7pm Fri; free). Tables outdoors (3, pavement).*

Smithy's
15-17 Leeke Street, WC1X 9HZ (7278 5949/www. smithyskingscross.com). King's Cross tube/rail. **Open** noon-11pm Mon-Fri. **Food served** noon-2.30pm, 6-10pm Mon-Fri. **Credit** AmEx, MC, V.
This former blacksmith's shop bills itself as 'King's Cross's best-kept secret', and that's not too self-aggrandising a claim. At the end of a dark, narrow street, a small green door opens on to a vista of exposed air ducts, grey iron supports and authentic cobbles. Dimly lit, with matt burgundy walls, chunky candles on every table and dark-wood booths, it's a wine bar that appeals to couples, but not to the exclusion of big groups of both sexes. The clientele is a mixture of trendy designers and grungier twenty- and thirtysomethings. The well-rounded wine list encompasses bottles of either colour from France and the New World, with plenty by the glass and a pleasing three options for rosé drinkers. Beers on tap include London Pride, Greene King IPA, Brakspear Special and Ruddles. A satisfy-all-tastes food menu completes the experience. *Bar available for hire (Sat, Sun).*

Somerstown Coffee House
60 Chalton Street, NW1 1HS (7691 9136). Euston tube/rail. **Open** noon-11pm Mon-Sat; noon-6pm Sun. **Food served** noon-3.30pm, 5.30-10pm Mon-Sat; noon-3.30pm Sun. **Credit** AmEx, MC, V.
In the council estate bounded by the Euston and King's Cross railway tracks, a pub has been reborn. The new French owners have restored this Grade II-listed pub into a handsome, appealing 'pub and bistro'. The pub side is simply but attractively panelled in the original dark wood, and the original fireplace and old windows remain. Real ales include Christmas Cheer, Eagle IPA and Bombardier from Charles Wells, or Courage Directors, plus there's a French-accented bar menu. For more substantial meals, the restaurant serves Gallic dishes such as own-made duck confit or braised lamb. The wine list is limited and and not particularly inspiring, but overall this is a good place to meet, drink and eat. In the summer the front terrace and heated garden should prove an additional draw. *Bar available for hire (Mon-Wed). Restaurant. Tables outdoors (5 tables, terrace; 10 tables, garden).*

Wine routes by Alice Lascelles

London may be the cocktail capital of the world, but when it comes to wine, this city often leaves a lot to be desired. Until recently 'red or white' was about the size of it in your average pub, and many bars didn't do much better. Lack of choice, poor service and storage, and overblown prices meant you were safer sticking to a pint.

Fortunately this is starting to change. The boom in New World wines means there's now far greater variety, and often better value, on offer. Wine menus, with detailed, unpretentious tasting notes are much more common. And anywhere worth its salt now lists at least half a dozen wines by the glass.

A bit of the right food as an accompaniment can really enhance a wine's character and these days a growing number of places also offer good quality bar snacks, canapés or tapas that are specifically tailored to their wine list, so take advantage of it. Or sign up for a tasting – several of the places below organise excellent, reasonably priced events, often including a bespoke menu. If you find what you like, at least two run a wine shop selling the stuff by the case.

Should you feel overwhelmed with choice, never be afraid to ask for guidance – all these places have been recommended as much for their helpful staff as their wine.

Vivat Bacchus

For wine Buffys

Vinoteca is one of the best young, buzzing wine bars around. Take the plunge and try something new from hundreds of well-priced wines from all corners of the world, and a regularly updated list of 20 or so by the glass. While celebrating wine from all over the world, Vinoteca are keen to fly the flag for English wine too: try Chapel Hill 2003 (£7.99 a bottle) from Kent – a lively citrus/pineapple white. Or splash out on a bottle of Château Beaucastel 1989 Châteauneuf-du-Pape (£114). A menu of tapas and more substantial dishes comes with recommended wine pairings, and mixed cases are available to take home.

Overseen by the ebullient South African Gerrie Knoetze, the City restaurant **Vivat Bacchus** was recently expanded to include a more informal wine bar. Naturally enough it has a particularly good selection of South African wines starting at around £15 and including the much sought-after Veenwouden Merlot 1997 from Paarl at £69. Knoetze himself is often on hand for spontaneous tastings or to take you on a cellar tour, while the cheese room, with its own 'sommelier' is a sight to behold. The place hosts a variety of tasting evenings.

An outstanding canteen-style restaurant that sticks firmly to French wine is **St John Bread &** Wine (94-96 Commercial Street, E1 6LZ, 7247 8724, www.stjohnbreadandwine.com). Chop and change among seven wines by the glass at under a fiver, or go for the big time with a bottle of Pomerol's Château Pétrus 1990 at £1,990. Wines are available to buy by the case – but orders must be made in advance.

The jury's largely out on the merits of organic wine – some say it gives less of a hangover – but Islington's eco-friendly **Duke of Cambridge** still has one of the best organic lists in London; and just because it's organic doesn't mean it can't be fun: add some sparkle with the lightly sparkling Prosecco from Bosco del Merlo at £22. English wines are a speciality.

What it lacks in atmosphere, **Wine Wharf** makes up for in education. It's attached to the wine museum Vinopolis and boasts a list of over 300 wines from all over the world, many by the glass. A whopping 150 of the wines on offer are available by the glass. If you are daunted by the task of choosing, try a flight – five 25ml shots (adding up to the equivalent of a glass) of wine around a particular theme (country/grape/style) for between £7.50 and £9.50. Wine Wharf is available for tastings and private events too.

Established in 1890, **Gordon's** is a cramped, candlelit wine bar that has become an institution. The list rarely exceeds £25 a bottle, covering most of the bases, and includes a few surprises. Go off-piste with the Indian wine Grover's 'La Réserve' cabernet shiraz at £16.50 or something more classic such as the Rioja Pierola Crianza at £22.65. The Thames-side terrace is lovely in summer.

Other recommended wine bars include the **Cork & Bottle**, the **Grape Street Wine Bar**, **Cellar Gascon** and the **Bleeding Heart**. Gastropubs with good lists include the **Anchor & Hope** and the ultra-cool **Cow**, while sumptuous **Pearl** offers some 450 by the bottle.

Sherry babies

Forget the annual glass of Bristol Cream at your granny's. Within bright, stylish surroundings **Fino's** (33 Charlotte Street, W1T 1RR, 7813 8010, www.finorestaurant.com) offers a list of around 20 sherries and several dessert wines, by the glass or bottle, as well as a vast array of Spanish wines. Sherry styles cross the spectrum, from the light, tangy Puerto Fino, Solera Reserva, Lustau (£5.50 glass/£16.50 a bottle) through to intense fruity PX sherries such as the 1975 Don Pedro Ximenez, Gran Reserva (£6 glass/£29 bottle). The food is outstanding.

Husband-and-wife team Sam and Sam Clark have done great things for tapas culture in this country at **Moro** (34-36 Exmouth Market, EC1R 4QE, 7833 8336, www.moro.co.uk) and now they're doing it for sherry. Try old favourites such as Tio Pepe Fino (£2.50/£24) as well as very old and aged dated sherries such as Amontillado 1830 El Maestro Sierra (£75 a bottle). Their sherry lunches – every Saturday – include a top-notch four-course meal alongside a range of sherries.

Champagne charlies

The elegant art deco bar **Claridges** boasts a champagne list that's among the best in the world. Prices start at £12.50 for a glass of Laurent-Perrier and run right through into the thousands for rare vintages from the likes of Veuve Clicquot, Krug and Louis Roederer. Staff are extremely knowledgeable, without being snooty, and the detailed, extensive list is updated regularly. Tasting classes are available.

On the right night, the blood-red champagne and oyster bar at **Boisdale of Bishopsgate** (Swedeland Court, 202 Bishopsgate, EC2M 4NR, 7283 1763, www.boisdale.co.uk) is dead sexy. Sit at the marble-topped bar and sip one of 20 champagnes, starting at £6.50 for a glass of house fizz through to £195 for a bottle of Louis Roederer Cristal 1996, alongside a dish of great seafood. The whisky list is also extensive.

Other good places to sip a glass of bubbly are the beautiful **La Grande Marque**, **Vertigo 42** with its panoramic view of London, and the Laurent-Perrier Champagne Bar, which is in the front hall of the **Savoy** (Strand, WC2R 0EU, 7592 1600). This last is the only bar in the UK to stock the entire range of Laurent-Perrier champagnes.

Alice Lascelles writes for *Wine & Spirits International*.

Boisdale

Also in the area...

Davy's of Regent's Place Unit 2, Euston Tower, Regent's Place, NW1 3DP (7387 6622).
O'Neill's 73-77 Euston Road, NW1 2QS (7255 9861).
Positively Fourth Street 119 Hampstead Road, NW1 3EE (7388 5380).

Knightsbridge

The area is a dab hand at sexy and stylish: try the **Mandarin Bar**, **Townhouse**, **V Bar** or **Zuma**. Or, if discreet and hard-to-get are your thing, try the hard-to-find **Swag & Tails**.

Mandarin Bar

Mandarin Oriental Hyde Park, 66 Knightsbridge, SW1X 7LA (7235 2000/www.mandarinoriental.com). Knightsbridge tube. **Open/food served** 10.30am-2am Mon-Sat; 10.30am-10.30pm Sun. **Admission** £5 after 11pm Mon-Sat. **Credit** AmEx, DC, MC, V.

Walk through the glossy marble lobby of the classic but contemporary hotel, past the beautiful fresh flower arrangements, and you'll reach a surprisingly cool bar that's not only ideal for a pre-dinner cocktail or a post-dinner cigar and brandy, but also a destination in its own right. The centrepiece of the bar is a wall of frosted backlit glass panels, behind which you can see shadows of bar staff theatrically shaking fruity cocktails. The bar is furnished with leather armchairs and decorated with mohair, marble, glass, mirrors and wood. Cream silk walls are lined with handcrafted cocktail glasses and ornamental bar paraphernalia. A selection of 45 cigars is offered in an enclosure where international businessmen enjoy single-malt Scotch and complimentary bar snacks.
Music (jazz trio 9pm Mon-Sat; 8pm Sun).

Paxton's Head

153 Knightsbridge, SW1X 7PA (7589 6627). Knightsbridge tube. **Open** noon-11pm Mon-Thur, Sun; noon-midnight Fri, Sat. **Food served** noon-10pm daily. **Credit** MC, V.

The first-floor white masonry windows look like two giant eyebrows over the warmly welcoming chocolate-brown mouth of the front door. Inside is traditional Victorian, with wood and mirrored panels lining the walls. Succumbing to the Thai pub food theme, the Paxton's Head has a pan-Asian restaurant on the first floor and a basic East-meets-West bar menu. Local businessmen share the space with relaxing tradesmen and shop-dropped tourists slurping on pints of Guinness, Amstel, Greene King IPA, Courage, Staropramen, Leffe or Hoegaarden. The wine list has nine of each colour, all available by the glass and surprisingly moderately priced at £12-£16 – the Chilean San Raphael merlot is good value at £13.80, while the joker in the pack is a chenin blanc from Sula, India. Downstairs is a funkier bare-brick space, with leather sofas, a separate cocktail bar and a gas fire.
Games (fruit machines). Music (DJs 9pm Fri, Sat; free). Restaurant (no smoking). TV (big screen).

Swag & Tails

10-11 Fairholt Street, SW7 1EG (7584 6926/www. swagandtails.com). Knightsbridge tube. **Open** 11am-11pm Mon-Fri. **Food served** noon-3pm, 6-10pm Mon-Fri. **Credit** AmEx, MC, V.

A free-spirited pub, hidden a warren of mews cottages, but marked by an abundance of hanging baskets and topiary.

Of course, this is precisely how the locals and regulars like it, generally an affluent bunch who feel at home with all the rustic pine furniture. Old golfing cartoons line the walls and Veuve Clicquot bottles adorn the bar. The beer selection on tap is respectable, with Bitburger, Adnams, Bombardier and John Smith's, plus Guinness and the usual lagers. Sicilian chardonnay is on the expensive side at £14.50 – indeed, most of the wines are around or above the £20 mark and stretch up to £45 – but the good-quality food is surprisingly affordable, with pan-seared foie gras at £10.95.
Bar available for hire (Sat, Sun). Restaurant. Tables outdoors (11, conservatory). TV.

Townhouse

31 Beauchamp Place, SW3 1NU (7589 5080/www. lab-townhouse.com). Knightsbridge tube. **Open** 4pm-midnight Mon-Sat; 4-11.30pm Sun. **Food served** 4-11.30pm Mon-Sat; 5-11pm Sun. **Credit** AmEx, MC, V.

This discreet end-of-terrace bar is exactly what it says on the tin: a thin, converted townhouse – that also happens to be a sexy cocktail bar. The sleek, glowing bar is in the centre, with a couple of chalky brown leather sofas and trendy Perspex tables in the front window and the best seats in the house at the rear. Where the room slightly opens out, good-looking couples sip cocktails like the house special Porn Star Martinis (vanilla vodka, Champagne and passion fruit with a Champagne sidecar, £10) or pear Caipirinhas (muddled with fresh lime and vanilla syrup, £8) in a space that is bordered by a high-backed, dark brown leather banquette. The soundtrack is fittingly electro. There is also an upstairs bar, available for private hire and doused in Burgundy.
Function room. Music (DJs 8.30pm-midnight Tue-Sat; free). Over-21s only. Tables outdoors (2, pavement). TVs (satellite).

V Bar

116 Knightsbridge, SW1X 7JP (7581 6882). Knightsbridge tube. **Open** 6pm-midnight Mon-Sat. **Food served** 6-10.30pm Mon-Sat. **Credit** AmEx, MC, V.

Another in the Knightsbridge tradition of being hard to track down is the downstairs bar of the Viktor restaurant, an alternative sushi joint with secrets in the cellar. The V is quite a find, however. The intimate space, lit by a giant red dome, is ideal for romantic cocktails, particularly for clandestine couples who relax on slinky low-backed red velvet chairs and vibrant Japanese print cushions. The house special is a spiced apple Mojito (£6.50), while Martinis start at £7. But don't miss the Good Girl's Delight, combining vodka, white chocolate liqueur, coffee liqueur, Amaretto and Frangelico (£9). Bottled beers include the obvious Asahi and the unusual Kasteel Cru, a fine Alsace lager brewed from Champagne yeast. Soak up the booze with plates of sushi and sashimi.
Bar available for hire. Restaurant.

Zuma

5 Raphael Street, SW7 1DL (7584 1010/www.zuma restaurant.com). Knightsbridge tube. **Open** noon-11pm Mon-Fri; 12.30-11pm Sat; noon-10pm Sun. **Food served** 12.30-2.15pm, 6-10.45pm Mon-Sat; 12.30-2.45pm, 6-10pm Sun. **Credit** AmEx, DC, MC, V.

Situated at the front of one of the hippest restaurants in London, this contemporary venue attracts a steady stream of A-list celebrities. Zuma offers traditional Japanese izakaya-style informal eating and drinking: izakaya (literally 'sake shops') are like Japanese tapas bars, where

Japanese salarymen take to the low-level seating for swift drinks and snacks after work. The bustling cube-shaped bar here is decked out in green, with a spacious counter surrounded by high seats that are hard to come by in the evenings. The bar area is surrounded by granite-like walls and prettily lit with candles. The drinks list features more than 30 types of sake, shochu and cocktails made from fresh fruit and Japanese spirits. We loved Rubabu (rhubarb-infused ozeki sake, 42 Below vodka, fresh passion fruit). The oriental bar snacks include freshly rolled sushi. A perfect place for people-watching.
Disabled: toilet. Restaurant (no smoking).

Leicester Square & Piccadilly Circus

How things have changed. A few years back we recommended staying away from here altogether. Now we recommend staying away from *most* places in the area. The new cocktail bar **Glass** and revitalised **Astor** suggest an undimmed love for keeping things complicated when it comes to spirits; the **Blue Posts** is a good advert for keeping things simple; and the **Salisbury** makes a case for real-ale drinking as gastronomy.

Absolut IceBar/Below Zero
29-33 Heddon Street, W1B 4BN (7287 9192/www.belowzerolondon.com). Oxford Circus tube. **Open** 12.30-11pm Mon-Wed, Sun; 12.30pm-midnight Thur-Sat. **Food served** 12.30-10pm Mon-Wed, Sun; 12.30-10.30pm Thur-Sat. **Admission** *Icebar* £12-£15. **Credit** MC, V.
The London branch of the Absolut IceBar chain was opened with much flashing of paparazzi cameras in September 2005. A familiar sight in Scandinavia and in glossy fashion mags, an ice venue kept at five below was novelty enough here to entice rave notices from the press corps. So, what's it like? Well, first you must fork out a £10-£15 minimum spend before you don a dinky, silver, fur-trimmed chill-proof cape and enter for your allotted 40 minutes. All that's served, in ice glasses and surrounded by sculptures chipped out of ice shipped in from Jukkasjärvi, Swedish Lapland, is Absolut. Absolut cocktails (£9.50) or flavoured Absolut (£8.50). After another Absolut, you begin to tire of the novelty and wish you were in a bar instead of a fridge. This is the cue to dive into Below Zero next door, the two-floor bar-restaurant serving delicious small plates of fried baby squid with chilli salt (£7) or seabass carpaccio (£8), £10 and fabulous cocktails made with all kinds of high-end spirits.
Bar available for hire. Disabled: toilet. Music (DJs 9pm Fri, Sat; free). No-smoking area. Restaurant. **Map 2 J7**.

Astor Bar & Grill
20 Glasshouse Street, W1B 5DJ (7734 4888/www.astor barandgrill.com). Piccadilly Circus tube. **Open** 5pm-1am Mon-Wed; 5pm-3am Thur-Sat. **Food served** 6-11pm Mon-Sat. **Admission** £10 after 10pm Thur-Sat. **Credit** AmEx, MC, V.
Until very recently, this was the landmark Atlantic, a bar that made its name as a celeb hangout in the mid 1990s, a sought-after venue of VIP ropes and Dick Bradsell cocktails. Now renamed the Astor, it needs to regain its cachet. Decorwise, it has put up a couple of unusual works of art – flattened, crinkly cigarette packets of Gauloises and Belga, a photo of two old drunks snogging over a bottle of

cider. Drinkwise, mixermeister Mario has added zings of ginger, fresh passion fruit and figs to a new selection of contemporary cocktails (£7.50), such as a Headhunter with Havana 3 or Make It Last Forever with Zubrowka vodka. Lychee liqueur features in the signature Lady Astor with Wyborowa Orange. The classics have also been slightly twisted – perhaps an Astor Champagne cocktail with 42 Below and Passion Fruit. Superior bar food comes courtesy of the back restaurants that share the same expansive basement, and exhibitions and DJs are promised at weekends, as well as some unusual shock cabaret on Saturdays.
Function room. Music (musicians 10.30pm Thur; DJs 10.30pm Thur-Sat). Restaurant. **Map 2 J7**.

Blue Posts
28 Rupert Street, W1D 6DJ (7437 1415). Leicester Square or Piccadilly Circus tube. **Open** 11am-11.30pm Mon-Thur; 11am-midnight Fri, Sat; noon-10.30pm Sun. **Food served** noon-9pm daily. **Credit** MC, V.
Not three minutes from London's iconic neon, the Blue Posts is a little hideaway of a pub, frequented by locals. Past landlords are honoured on the walls of the cabin-like wood and bare-brick interior – a framed poem to 'Our Terry', a sterner portrait of early 20th-century incumbent and music hall star Fred D Harris – although the regulars take pride of place at the compact counter. Facing them are pumps of Timothy Taylor Landlord and Fuller's London Pride, and taps of Leffe and Hoegaarden, and a limited choice from the comforting food menu: roast beef, bubble and gravy (£5.25) or individual cottage pie (£3.75) – then again, how individual can one pie be?
Function room. Music (jazz 4-7pm Sun; free). No-smoking area. **Map 7 K7**.

Cocoon
65 Regent Street, W1B 4EA (7494 7609/www.cocoon-restaurants.com). Piccadilly Circus tube. **Open/food served** noon-3pm, 5.30pm-1am Mon-Wed; noon-3pm, 5.30pm-3am Thur, Fri; 5.30pm-3am Sat. **Credit** AmEx, MC, V.
Designed by American designer Stéphane Dupoux, this oriental restaurant has six round dining rooms lined up vertically, decorated in the style of the six-stage life cycle of a butterfly, with subtle cocoon motifs throughout. The circular bar counter, surrounded by bar stools, is located between the third and the fourth dining room. Friendly, flirty mixologists shake oriental-style cocktails with a great theatrical flourish. Watermelon Martini (fresh watermelon, Stolichnaya vodka, shochu, vanilla and honey, £7.50) was fruity and refreshing; many other cocktails are muddled with fresh fruit and come heavily perfumed with rosewater and rose petals. The impressive drinks list also boasts an exquisite selection of saké and shochu, which are used liberally in many of the cocktails (from £5). Champagnes, spirits, a couple of Japanese beers, wines by the glass and interesting alcohol-free cocktails are also available. Bar snacks are oriental. This buzzy, beautiful bar is one of the finest bars in central London for meeting friends, perfect if you want to impress a date.
Disabled: toilet. Function room. Restaurant (no smoking). **Map 2 J7**.

Cork & Bottle
44-46 Cranbourn Street, WC2H 7AN (7734 7807/www.donhewitson.com). Leicester Square tube. **Open** 11am-11.30pm Mon-Sat; noon-11pm Sun. **Food served** 11am-11.30pm Mon-Sat; noon-10pm Sun. **Credit** AmEx, DC, MC, V.

Astor Bar & Grill. *See p57.*

Now in its 35th year, Don Hewitson's homely cellar is a celebration of what good wine is all about – and set the tone for so many others to follow. A window display of magnums of Cordon Rouge Champagne, jammed between a sex shop and a cheap pizza place, beckons you to a discreet glass door, through which a narrow spiral staircase leads to a two-space cellar equally decorated with promotional posters for vintage champers. The 28-page wine list testifies to Don's unpretentious, enthusiastic oenophilia. Average prices are £20 and each specimen, sourced from all over France, Australia, his native New Zealand and elsewhere, is given a personal thumbnail sketch. The bar food is equally exemplary. Timeless.
Babies and children welcome. No smoking. **Map 7 K7**.

De Hems
11 Macclesfield Street, W1D 5BW (7437 2494). Leicester Square tube. **Open/food served** noon-midnight Mon-Sat; noon-10.30pm Sun. **Credit** AmEx, DC, MC, V.
Now part of the Nicholson's family of traditional hostelries, this famous old Dutch pub is set between the gates of Chinatown and the theatrical glitz of Shaftesbury Avenue. Once a refuge for homesick Dutch sailors, the then Macclesfield was taken over by a certain De Hems and became a rallying point for the Dutch Resistance during World War II. Today, this spruced-up dark-wood bar boasts towering beer pumps of Amstel and Oranjeboom, three types of Leffe and the rare draught option of Belle-Vue Kriek. Orval, Rochefort and Vedett are among the multitude of Benelux bottled options. The Dutch range of bar food features pannenkoeken (pancakes either savoury or sweet), bitterballen (meatballs in breadcrumbs, £3-£5) and vitsmitter (poached eggs topped with cheese or ham, £5). Main courses can also be enjoyed in the oyster bar upstairs, the setting for many a musicbiz payola exchange in the 1960s.

Function room. Games (fruit machine). Music (DJ 8pm Fri, Sat; free). TVs (big screen, satellite). **Map 7 K6**.

Glass
9 Glasshouse Street, W1R 5RL (7439 7770/www.paper clublondon.com). Piccadilly Circus tube. **Open/food served** 5-11pm Tue-Thur; 5pm-1am Fri, Sat. **Credit** AmEx, MC, V.
This stunning new cocktail bar is part of Paper, a press-themed restaurant and nightclub venture. Glossy black and white walls and pillars, black glass chandeliers, a heavy wooden floor, padded white alcoves, and a long bar characterise the dimly lit decor. Despite little publicity, it was heaving with young professionals. There's a comprehensive drinks list that includes spirits (including Irish whiskeys and flavoured vodkas), Champagnes, wines and a couple of beers. A sophisticated cocktail list incorporates Martinis, rocks, highballs, Champagne cocktails, shooters and non-alcoholic cocktails. Bramble (Bombay Sapphire gin, fresh lemon juice and blackberry liqueur, £8) was too strong for our taste, but other more contemporary cocktails were a success. The optional service charge is 15%.
Disabled: toilet. **Map 2 J7**.

International
116 St Martin's Lane, WC2N 4BF (7655 9810/www. theinternational.co.uk). Leicester Square tube/Charing Cross tube/rail. **Open/food served** noon-2am Mon-Sat; noon-10.30pm Sun. **Credit** AmEx, MC, V.
This operation is as classy as its prominent St Martin's location suggests. In a stylish interior of cool maroon and brown furnishings, and primitive art in bright colours, a premium selection of drinks and foodstuffs awaits. Cocktails (£6.95-£7.95), categorised by spirit base, feature slight twists of familiar mixes: a Grand Cosmopolitan with Pölstar Sitróna and Grand Marnier or a Raspberry Mojito

with fresh fruit, Bacardi Oro and a Chambord float. The wine list is as comprehensive as the 40-strong cocktail one, with a dozen varieties of each colour, six each by the glass. The bar lunch menu includes Asian, seafood or vegetarian sharing platters (£12.95-£14.95).

Disabled: toilet. Function room. Restaurant. **Map 2 L7.**

Jewel

4-6 Glasshouse Street, W1B 5DQ (7439 4990/www. jewelbarlondon.co.uk). Piccadilly Circus tube. **Open/ food served** 4pm-1am Mon-Sat; 6pm-12.30am Sun. **Credit** AmEx, MC, V.

The rather flashy Jewel now has a sleek, black drinks menu with a pricey selection of cocktails. With its location and starburst chandelier interior, such extravagance is hardly surprising. The prime Top Shelf Diamond cocktail range (such as Jewel Vodka Martini with Grey Goose, Jewel Gin Martini with Tanqueray Ten) is £9.50. The Jewel Bellini, mixed with Devaux Champagne, is £7.90, and the classics (Manhattan, Mai Tai and so on) £7.40-£8.40. A new contemporary range (£7.10-£7.50) features female-friendly creations such as a Debauchery of Courvoisier, Bailey's and Disaronno Amaretto – you're more likely to see garrulous and reasonably glamorous ladies than lads here. Bar snacks (£7) are of the skewered variety.

Disabled: toilet. Music (DJs 8pm Wed-Sat; bands 9pm Mon-Wed; £5 after 9pm Fri, Sat). **Map 2 K7.**

Oxygen

17-18 Irving Street, WC2H 7AZ (7930 0907/www. oxygenbar.co.uk). Leicester Square tube. **Open** 4pm-3am Mon-Sat; 4-10.30pm Sun. **Admission** £5 after 10pm, £7 after 11pm Fri; £7 after 10pm Sat. **Credit** MC, V.

A breath of fresh air is the catch here – as well as a prime location on a corner of Leicester Square. Fresh air comes in little blue canisters, Pure Oxygen, tucked away behind the bar (£10-£14) – you wouldn't notice them as you step across the modest front terrace and through the red interior of the main bar at street level. A basement is used as an end-of-week club or for private hire, while an upstairs room affords more intimacy. The airy gimmick aside, Oxygen is a decent enough late-opening bar, with standard cocktails (£4.75-£4.95/£12.95) by the glass or pitcher, a handful of equally standard wines (£11.95-£15.95), four by the glass, and no surprises among the beers. A number of bars have tried at this same location over the last decade – this one will hope to last after the oxygen joke has run thin.

Bar available for hire. Music (DJs 9pm Thur-Sat). Tables outdoors (4, pavement). TVs (big screen). **Map 7 K7.**

Salisbury

90 St Martin's Lane, WC2N 4AP (7836 5863). Leicester Square tube. **Open** 11am-11pm Mon-Thur; noon-11.30pm Fri, Sat; noon-10.30pm Sun. **Food served** noon-9pm daily. **Credit** AmEx, DC, MC, V.

A Victorian palace of a pub, the corner Salisbury offers fine ales and superior meals, accommodating tourists as well as theatre-goers. The Salisbury was transformed by its namesake leaseholder – the first British prime minister of the 20th century – who had an interior created of beautifully carved mahogany, etched glass and art nouveau lamps. As for the ales, it boasts Everards, Hook Norton Old Hooky, Bombardier, Adnams Explorer, Jennings Golden Host, Marston's Pedigree and St Austell Tribute, as wide a selection as you'll find anywhere in the West End. The kitchen adds lovely touches to standard pub fare.

Function room (no smoking). Games (chess). Tables outdoors (8, pavement). **Map 2 L7.**

Sports Café

80 Haymarket, SW1Y 4TE (7839 8300/www.thesports cafe.com). Piccadilly Circus tube. **Open** noon-4am Mon; noon-3am Tue, Fri, Sat; noon-2am Wed, Thur, Sun. **Food served** noon-midnight daily. **Admission** £5 after 11pm Mon, Tue, Fri, Sat. **Credit** AmEx, MC, V.

First opened in Toronto in 1990, the Sports Café offers beer, bar food and TV sports. One of ten UK venues, the West End branch is large enough to accommodate 125 TV monitors and a scattering of superscreens (including one in the men's toilets), so you can safely surf all the midweek Champions League action by floating around the back bar with your plastic glass of Foster's or Strongbow. A more convivial choice is to book a dining booth with its own mini plasma screen and tuck into one of the shared platters, a 4-4-2 Silver (£13.95) or 4-4-2 Gold (£16.95) of various appetisers. Other dining options involve ribs, steaks and burgers. Memorabilia includes a racing car hanging by the main entrance, a museum's worth of signed football shirts and assorted sports-related Americana. The popular pool room upstairs is available for hire.

Children admitted (until 6pm, dining only). Disabled: toilet. Music (DJs 10pm Mon-Sat). Restaurant (available for hire). TVs (big screen, satellite). **Map 2 K7.**

Waxy O'Connors

14-16 Rupert Street, W1D 6DD (7287 0255/www. waxyoconnors.co.uk). Leicester Square or Piccadilly Circus tube. **Open** noon-11pm Mon-Wed; noon-11.30pm Thur-Sat; noon-10.30pm Sun. **Food served** noon-10pm daily. **Credit** AmEx, DC, MC, V.

'The wonder of Waxy's...', as the board outside says, is why this vast, bland operation is always filled with so many people. And there's so much space to fill – six floors and four bars, all done out with Irish tosh, road signs, plaques, quotations, centrepieced by a bloody big beech tree. The reason would seem to be its prime function as a post-work pick-up joint, liaisons encouraged by Caffrey's, Guinness, Murphy's and Beamish, and sealed over £6.20 plates of Irish stew or crocks of Irish mussels (£6.95). Superior Irish food can be found at the on-site Dargle restaurant: Rossmore oysters, racks of lamb and the like. Aside from the opposite sex, rugby is another attraction, both Six Nations and domestic Irish, with attendant drinks promotions (six bottles of Carlsberg for £12!).

Music (Irish 8.30pm Mon, Tue, Sun; free). TVs (big screen, satellite). **Map 7 K7.**

Also in the area...

All Bar One 48 Leicester Square, WC2H 7LU (7747 9921).

Champagne Charlies (Davy's) 17 The Arches, off Villiers Street, WC2N 4NN (7930 7737).

Hog's Head 5 Lisle Street, WC2H 7BG (7437 3335).

Montagu Pyke (JD Wetherspoon) 105-107 Charing Cross Road & 20 Greek Street, WC2H 0BP (7287 6039).

Moon Under Water 28 Leicester Square, WC2H 7LE (7839 2837).

O'Neill's 166-170 Shaftesbury Avenue, WC2H 8JB (7379 3735).

Pitcher & Piano 40-42 William IV Street, WC2N 4DE (7240 6180).

Tappit Hen (Davy's) 5 William IV Street, Strand, WC2N 4DW (7836 9839).

Walkabout 136 Shaftesbury Avenue, W1D 5EZ (7255 8630).

Central

Marylebone

M arylebone boasts an excellent array of drinking establishments, from the happy restoration of **Inn 1888**, through the traditional charms of **Golden Eagle**, to sheer swank of **deVigne**.

Barley Mow

8 Dorset Street, W1U 6QW (7935 7318). Baker Street tube. **Open** 11am-11pm Mon-Sat. **Food served** noon-3pm Mon-Sat. **Credit** AmEx, DC, MC, V.

Marylebone's self-claimed 'oldest pub' is nothing spectacular, but in some ways its abstention from trying too hard is its principal virtue: you come here for a decent pint and that's what you get: a fact that has earned it a good contingent of loyal locals. The old prints on the walls and shabby wooden furniture lend the Mow a reassuringly traditional character; particularly evocative are the two enclosed booths that flank the bar at the left – if you're lucky enough to get one, it's like having a pub all to yourself. The fruit machine and ample widescreen TV on the wall arguably detract from the vintage character, but they're not serious intrusions. There are few surprises on the drinks front – it's a regular round of ales (Marston's, Adnams, Greene King IPA) and lagers, plus token spirits and wines. Double spirits are a bargainous £3.35.
Babies and children welcome (lunch only). Games (quiz machine). Tables outdoors (4, pavement). TV (big screen).

Beehive

7 Homer Street, W1H 4NU (7262 6581). Edgware Road tube. **Open** noon-11pm Mon-Sat; noon-10.30pm Sun. **Food served** noon-3pm Mon-Fri. **Credit** MC, V.

Bizarrely, two pubs barely a few hundred yards from each other vie over the same name, but this Beehive wins out in the accessibility stakes: it's just off Baker Street, while its namesake is secreted away in a backstreet further west. Inside, the traditional decor – wood panelling, floral carpet, miscellaneous bric-a-brac, faded old prints – is a little marred by the evidence of chain ownership. Still, it's only a small quibble, and the Beehive comes into its own as a place to watch sports: you can see a screen from practically anywhere in the pub (even the solitary leather sofa tucked away at the back), and it doesn't get too rowdy. There are no surprises as far as drinks are concerned, just a regular line-up of draughts, bottles and a few wines.
Tables outdoors (3, pavement). TV (big screen, satellite).

Chapel

48 Chapel Street, NW1 5DP (7402 9220). Edgware Road tube. **Open** noon-11pm Mon-Sat; noon-10.30pm Sun. **Food served** noon-2.30pm, 7-10pm daily. **Credit** AmEx, DC, MC, V.

It's so far west it could almost be Paddington, but the bright, airy, smart Chapel is about Marylebonian civility rather than railway-terminus seediness. The odd shape – a main room adjoined to a narrow bar area – gives it immediate character, which is well supported by the clean, uncluttered modern decor, wood furniture, big skylight, open kitchen and friendly staff. And the fact that it's tucked discreetly into a corner just off the main road adds an extra touch of intimacy. The menu's respectable gastro fare – tapas-like snacks, salads, hunks of meat with veg – is chalked up on a daily changing board. The wine list is good and there's Hoegaarden on tap besides the usual line-up of lagers. It's not always easy to make a big, bright space work as a pub environment, but the Chapel manages admirably.

Babies and children admitted. Function room. Tables outdoors (12, garden; 4, pavement). TV (big screen).

deVigne

Mandeville Hotel, 8-14 Mandeville Place, W1U 2BE (0871 223 2259). Bond Street tube. **Open** 11am-midnight Mon-Sat; 5-10.30pm Sun. **Food served** 11.30am-3pm, 6-8pm Mon-Sat; 6-8pm Sun. **Credit** AmEx, MC, V.

Low lighting, angular Perspex chandeliers, off-the-wall art and splashes of neon define the ultra-modern interior of deVigne, a relatively new opening as part of the refurbished Mandeville Hotel. Such overstated design seems a little out of place in Marylebone, but it matches deVigne's status as the only serious cocktail bar in the area. It's often quiet – perhaps people are put off by the hotel associations – but it's well worth investigating as a more glamorous alternative to the countless pubs hereabouts. An extensive selection of spirits and a carefully chosen cocktail menu are on offer; the whisky selection is notable. There's also Asian-influenced tapas-like bar snacks brought in from the adjacent restaurant deVille.
Disabled: toilet. Restaurant (no smoking).

Dover Castle

43 Weymouth Mews, W1G 7EQ (7580 4412). Oxford Circus or Regent's Park tube. **Open** 11.30am-11pm Mon-Fri; 12.30-11pm Sun. **Food served** noon-3pm, 6-9pm Mon-Fri. **Credit** MC, V.

The Dover Castle benefits from the quaint allure that only a mews location can afford. The interior doesn't disappoint either: the green leather upholstery, the sumptuous carpet and the distressed wood speak of everything that is good about British pub culture. We particularly liked the smaller side room, where the lighting was a little lower, the ambience a little cosier; though we were out of season this time round, the alfresco alcove out back is also delightful. Dover Castle is one of a clutch of pubs in the capital that serve lagers, ales and cider from independent British brewery Samuel Smith – they're produced with natural ingredients, taste great and, what's more, are dirt cheap (a pint is under £2). On closer inspection we found that most of the spirits were esoteric brands too, which further added to the sense that the Dover Castle is the very antithesis of the chain pub. Recommended.
Games (board games, quiz machine). No piped music or jukebox. Tables outdoors (6, pavement).

Duke of Wellington

94A Crawford Street, W1H 2HQ (7224 9435). Baker Street tube/Marylebone tube/rail. **Open** 11am-11pm Mon-Sat; noon-10.30pm Sun. **Food served** noon-3pm, 6-9pm Mon-Fri. **Credit** AmEx, MC, V.

On the sleepier side of Marylebone to the west of Baker Street, the Duke of Wellington is a comfortable and unimposing hangout that is frequented by a cross-section of generally well-heeled locals. It's a thoroughly traditional pub, with all the cosiness that implies – rich carpet, warm lighting, wood panels – but is rescued from ordinariness by the fascinatingly diverse memorabilia arranged in glass cases along the windows and around the walls: mugs, medicine bottles, military paintings, a huge classical bust (of the good Duke, presumably) and more. The list of beers and spirits is decent but unadventurous (ales include Bombardier and Adnams, lagers are Carlsberg and Stella); by the same token, prices are very reasonable: some double spirits are just £2.50.
Tables outdoors (4, pavement). TV.

Absolut IceBar/Below Zero. *See p57*.

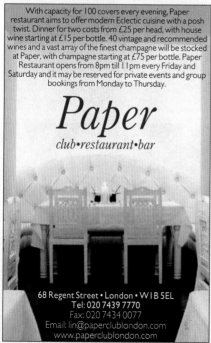

Dusk

*79 Marylebone High Street, W1U 7JZ (7486 5746).
Baker Street tube.* **Open** noon-11pm Mon-Fri; 10am-
11pm Sat; 10am-10.30pm Sun. **Food served** noon-10pm
Mon-Fri; 10am-10pm Sat, Sun. **Credit** (over £10) MC, V.
Formerly the Rising Sun pub, the wryly retitled Dusk has
pretensions of being a bit more like a bar than its traditional predecessor – an ethos evidenced by its neutral, and
in truth rather cold, modern decor. Still, it's a pleasant,
lively place and attracts lots of young professionals,
whether at lunch, after work or off-duty at the weekends.
There's a respectable wine list, with 12 whites and 12 reds,
while on tap is the superb Paulaner wheat beer, plus
Amstel, alongside a good range of bottles. A kitchen turns
out upscale pub grub (eggs Benedict, steak sandwich,
goat's cheese salad). On our last visit we found the smooth
jazz soundtrack a bit wanton, but it didn't stop us staying
for a good few drinks.
Disabled: toilet. Tables outdoors (6, pavement).

Golden Eagle

*59 Marylebone Lane, W1U 2NY (7935 3228). Bond
Street tube.* **Open** 11am-11pm Mon-Sat; noon-7pm Sun.
Snacks served 11.30am-9pm Mon-Sat. **No credit cards.**
Marylebone High Street and its environs have changed radically in the last decade, but just off the main shopping
drag the spirit of Marylebone past remains in the delightful Golden Eagle. That spirit is best observed every
Tuesday, Thursday and Friday night, when the rickety
upright piano in the corner is wheeled out for an old-school
singalong. Younger patrons might not know the words to
the wartime ditties joyously bellowed out by the regulars,
but that doesn't detract from the fun. St Austell bitters are
on rotation, and there's a surprisingly good selection of
spirits, including three gins: Gordon's, Tanqueray and
Bombay Sapphire. The Golden Eagle also proudly touts
its selection of hot 'Proper Cornish' pasties.
*Games (fruit machine). Music (pianist 8.30pm Tue,
Thur, Fri; free). TV.*

Inn 1888

*21A Devonshire Street, W1G 6PG (7486 7420). Baker
Street tube .* **Open** 11am-11.30pm Mon-Wed; 11am-
midnight Thur-Sat; 11am-10.30pm Sun. **Food served**
noon-5pm, 6-9pm Mon-Sat; noon-8pm Sun. **Credit** MC, V.
This pub's illustrious history suddenly vanished when the
venue was converted from a beautifully opulent traditional pub into a totally incongruous, homogenised bar serving
oriental snacks. The resplendent original interior was concealed with false walls, and, like a victim of bad cosmetic
surgery, the venue began its sorry new life. Fortunately the
injustice of the scheme could not be borne for too long, and
Inn 1888 is a pub once more, its native glory exposed for all
to enjoy. The beautiful ceramics, etched mirrors, chandeliers and warm red decor make this one of the most elegant
– and most amenable – pubs in the whole area. Greene King
IPA and Abbot are on tap, there are good wines and an
ample spirit counter, plus bar snacks and coffees. The pub
also takes a selection of newspapers.
Bar available for hire. Tables outdoors (3, pavement).

Low Life

*34A Paddington Street, W1U 4HG (7935 1272/www.
lowlifebar.com). Baker Street tube.* **Open** 5-11pm Mon-
Sat. **Food served** 5-10.30pm Mon-Sat. **Credit** MC, V.
As a basement cocktail bar with decks and DJs, Low Life
is a lone ranger in this rarefied and well-behaved corner of

the capital. That goes some way to explaining why the place
is frequently packed. If there were nearby alternatives for
party-minded young people, we might see them eschewing
this orange sunburst paint-job in favour of something a little classier but, looking on the bright side (and bright's just
the word), there's an extensive drinks list (eight bottled
beers, as many as 23 vodkas, and a catalogue – literally –
of cocktails), cosy little curtained dens to recline in and, in
general, no reason not to come here and just have fun. Staff
are invariably cheery – they'll even let you play your own
music on Monday's open-deck night. Don't bother with the
bar snacks, though, unless you're really hungry.
*Bar available for hire. Games (board games). Music
(open decks 5-11pm Mon; DJs 7.30pm Wed-Sat; free).*

Marylebone Bar & Kitchen

*74-76 York Street, W1H 1QN (7262 1513). Marylebone
tube/rail.* **Open** noon-11pm Mon-Sat; noon-10.30pm
Sun. **Food served** noon-10pm daily. **Credit** MC, V.
Both 'bar' and 'kitchen' give you the wrong impression
about MB&K, for it is not strictly a bar, nor a restaurant,
nor even a gastropub; and its main strength is its general
ambience rather than either the menu or the drinks. Deep
red paint, dark wood furnishings, a subtle oriental touch,
plus comfortable sofas and a pleasantly intimate layout conspire to make this one of Marylebone's cosiest hang-outs.
A respectable wine list is offered alongside a modest selection of draught beers (San Miguel, Red Stripe, Affligem),
and there are often interesting bottles such as the Belgian
9% triple-distilled Delirium Tremens wheat beer (more delicious than it sounds). The food menu (olives, calamares,
gourmet burger) is respectable, but nothing special.
Games (board games). TV (big screen).

Mason's Arms

*51 Upper Berkeley Street, W1H 7QW (7723 2131).
Marble Arch tube.* **Open** noon-11pm Mon-Sat; noon-
10.30pm Sun. **Food served** noon-2.30pm, 6-9pm Mon-
Thur, Sun; noon-3pm, 6-9pm Fri, Sat. **Credit** MC, V.
A plaque outside the Mason's Arms records how the pub
lies on the site of dungeons from which prisoners were
brought, via underground tunnels, to be hanged at the gal-
lows that once stood near the modern site of Marble Arch.
Yet there's no vestige of that inhospitable past in this snug
little drinking parlour. Two open fires and lots of dark
wood set the tone; even more intimate is the little enclosed
cabin behind the bar – though you'll be lucky to find it
unoccupied. Pleasingly, the pub's not afraid to be different
with its beers, and has a good line-up of independents,
including three varieties of Hofbräu (premium, export, regular) and various rotating ales. There's also an excellent
selection of malt whiskies. Average pub grub is served.
*Babies and children admitted (separate area). Games
(fruit machine). Tables outdoors (5, pavement). TV.*

Occo Bar & Kitchen

*58 Crawford Street, W1T 4JW (7724 4991). Edgware
Road tube.* **Open** noon-midnight Mon-Sat; noon-11pm
Sun. **Food served** noon-4pm, 6-11pm daily. **Happy
hour** 5-7pm daily. **Credit** AmEx, MC, V.
A Moroccan-influenced bar may sound like a tenuous prin-
ciple for a new venture amid the upmarket comfort of
Marylebone, but don't be fooled: this is not about sitting
on beanbags, inhaling hookah smoke and shovelling up
mouthfuls of couscous. The North African touch at Occo,
which opened in early 2005, is very subtle, amounting to
nothing more than the odd palm tree here and decorative
flourish there. This is a very good-looking and well-

Central

planned modern bar-restaurant, which impresses on several levels. The wine list is superb, offering 22 white and 22 red bins; there's a cocktail list with some interesting entries such as spiced pear Mojito; and the food, which is based on North African cooking but with modern interpretations, is great (grab the tapas menu for a quick snack). A welcome newcomer.

Babies and children welcome. Disabled: toilet. Function room. Tables outdoors (4, pavement). TVs (big screen).

Prince Regent

71 Marylebone High Street, W1U 5JN (7467 3811). Baker Street tube. **Open** noon-11pm Mon-Sat; noon-10.30pm Sun. **Food served** noon-10pm Mon-Sat; noon-9pm Sun. **Credit** AmEx, MC, V.

Giant pink, fluffy umbrellas here are the only camp, attention-seeking facet of an otherwise well thought-out gastro-style pub. The food is a little too ordinary to earn the place a bona fide gastro stamp, but everything else makes the grade: dark wood, lots of comfortable seating (especially upstairs), warm lighting, extensive wine list hand-chalked on to a big blackboard, and a very impressive selection of wheat beers, such as Leffe, Früli and Franziskaner, alongside more ordinary fare. It's quite rightly been an instant favourite with younger locals and is frequently very busy.

Function room. Music (singer 7.30pm Wed; DJs 7.30pm Sat; free). Tables outdoors (7, pavement).

Queen's Head & Artichoke

30-32 Albany Street, NW1 4EA (7916 6206/www.the artichoke.net). Great Portland Street or Regent's Park tube. **Open** 11am-11pm Mon-Sat; noon-10.30pm Sun. **Food served** 12.30-10pm daily. **Credit** AmEx, MC, V.

Albany Street is a bit of a no-man's-land so it's incredible that such a wonderful pub should be stranded here. However, once you've discovered it, the sense of a well-kept secret only increases its appeal. In terms of decor, the open-plan layout, dark wood and leather sofas are all commendable, but what really brings everything together is the food. Pinchos (little snacks on toast) are available at the bar for just 80p (a formula many gastropubs might copy to their advantage); there's a preposterously long tapas menu, which is serious rather than gimmicky, and a proper gourmet menu too, which changes throughout the week. An extensive wine list accompanies all this, and we're almost more enamoured with the pithy descriptions of the wines ('prosperous chocolate plum', 'brooding cedar cherry', 'glorious apricot brioche') than the wines themselves.

Disabled: toilet. Function room. Restaurant (no smoking). Tables outdoors (4, garden; 8, pavement).

deVigne. *See p60.*

Central

Volunteer
247-249 Baker Street, NW1 6XE (7486 4090). Baker Street tube. **Open** 11am-11pm Mon-Thur, Sun; 11am-midnight Fri, Sat. **Food served** noon-10.30pm daily. **Credit** AmEx, MC, V.

A top-notch modern pub in a rather forgettable location. Perhaps it's the warm, welcoming decor (deep lighting, plenty of wood, a coat of rich brown paint, hints of glitter and opulence) and abundance of comfortable seating that give visitors a good reason to walk the 'wrong' way when emerging from Baker Street station. In terms of drinks, a particular strength is draught beers from the Continent: Paulaner, Erdinger, Früli, Belle-Vue, Staropramen and Amstel are all offered. The team behind Volunteer followed the same formula when they opened the Prince Regent on the High Street, but don't neglect the Volunteer just because the Regent is more accessible – it has a charm all its own.
Babies and children welcome. Games (board games). Tables outdoors (3, benches). TVs (big screen).

Windsor Castle
29 Crawford Place, W1H 4LJ (7723 4371). Edgware Road tube. **Open** 11am-11pm Mon-Sat; noon-10.30pm Sun. **Food served** noon-3pm, 6-10pm Mon-Fri, Sun; 6-10pm Sat. **Credit** MC, V.

A festival of patriotism awaits the visitor to this diminutive pub, with every wall, shelf and corner crammed with relics of the royal family, past and present. There's even a beefeater (just a mannequin, we're sorry to say) presiding over the entrance from within his wooden cabin. However, don't read jingoistic for patriotic – the decor is harmless and welcoming rather than nationalistic and threatening, making for a lively, good old traditional boozer. Everyone seemed right at home on our last visit: the pub clearly has a loyal local following. It's the usual Stella and Carlsberg line-up, plus Adnams and Bombardier; the Thai menu is the only remotely un-British thing about the whole place.
Babies and children welcome. Restaurant (available for hire; no smoking). Tables outdoors (5, pavement).

Also in the area...
All Bar One 5-6 Picton Place, W1U 1BL (7487 0161); 289-293 Regent Street, W1B 2HJ (7467 9901).
Metropolitan Bar 7 Station Approach, Marylebone Road, NW1 5LA (7486 3489).
Ruby Lo 23 Orchard Street, W1H 6HL (7486 3671).
Toucan 94 Wimpole Street, W1G 0EE (7499 2440).

Mayfair

Still the most expensive property on the Monopoly board, Mayfair remains the destination of choice if you want swank bars (often with prices to match). The opening of the fabulous **China Tang** and the **Donovan Bar** at Brown's should guarantee its pre-eminence a while longer.

American Bar
Connaught Hotel, 16 Carlos Place, W1K 2AL (7499 7070/www.savoygroup.com). Bond Street or Green Park tube. **Open** 5-11pm Mon-Sat. **Credit** AmEx, DC, MC, V.
Standing in the lobby of the Connaught Hotel, you wouldn't even know this bar was there. All the action – post-work cocktails, pre-dinner G&Ts – seems to be in the Connaught Bar at the front of the building, where the buzz of conversation battles for supremacy with the ruminative tinklings of a pianist. It's a nice enough place for a drink, but those after a little less company head through the lobby and make a left. There's not much to the American Bar: two small wood-panelled rooms furnished with armchairs, plumped-up sofas and a couple of stuffed and mounted hunting trophies on the wall. But that's precisely the point. There's never anyone here but the attentive bartenders (the silence is truly golden), and the cocktails are made with grace and skill. In a word? Distinguished.
Dress: smart casual.

Audley
41-43 Mount Street, W1K 2RX (7499 1843). Bond Street or Green Park tube. **Open** 11am-11pm Mon-Sat; noon-10.30pm Sun. **Food served** 11am-9pm Mon-Sat; noon-9pm Sun. **Credit** AmEx, DC, MC, V.
This imposing pub is far more welcoming than its exterior might suggest. It's beautifully done out in traditional style, with wood panelling and heavy drapes, and brightly but tastefully lit by ornate chandeliers. It's a perfect post-work boozer, with a broad range of lagers, five tasty real ales – perhaps kept slightly too cold – and a stack of white wines in the cooler, divided up into the ubiquitous sauvs and chards, but with Albariños, Chablis and Sancerres adding depth and variety. Large portions of traditional pub grub – pies, fish, sausages, chips and salads – are served to the predominantly fortysomething clientele up until 9pm, after which the crowd thins out to the hardcore drinkers who begin to sway gently, steadying themselves on the bar while recounting half-remembered office gossip. Nothing flash, but adhering perfectly to tradition.
Babies and children admitted (until 6pm). Function rooms. Games (fruit machines). Tables outdoors (5, pavement). TV.

Cecconi's
5A Burlington Gardens, W1S 3EP (7434 1500/www. cecconis.co.uk). Green Park or Piccadilly Circus tube. **Open** *Bar* 11am-1am Mon-Sat; 11am-11pm Sun. **Food served** 7am-midnight Mon-Sat; 8am-11pm Sun. **Credit** AmEx, DC, MC, V.
This fabulous, chunky marble bar forms the centrepiece of a busy, exclusive restaurant, but bar-proppers are certainly not made to feel like second-class citizens. A warm welcome and a leather-bound menu are quickly proffered, giving you the chance to do a bit of discreet star-spotting in the surrounding dining room. It may be mega-swank, but there's an earthy feel to the place, like a busy working kitchen of a family business, with large joints of ham being

sliced wafer-thin behind the bar. The detailing is exquisite: from art deco lighting to mini-cocktail shakers. And oh the cocktails – the juniper Martini performs tricks with a measure of grappa that we found quite astonishing. There's a large choice of wine at far from extortionate prices, with prosecco on tap at £4.50 a glass. A top notch hangout for any prospective gossip columnist.
Babies and children welcome. Disabled: toilet.
Map 2 J7.

China Tang
Dorchester Hotel, Park Lane, W1A 2HJ (7629 9988/ www.dorchesterhotel.com). Green Park or Hyde Park Corner tube. **Open** 11am-1am Mon-Sat; 11am-midnight Sun. **Food served** 11am-midnight Mon-Sat; 11am-11pm Sun. **Credit** AmEx, DC, MC, V.
Although it had only been open a few months when we visited, the bar adjacent to the sumptuous Cantonese restaurant in the basement of the Dorchester is already heaving with the rich and the famous: the post-scandal Kate Moss, for instance, has been a frequent visitor. As the hotel's main bar is currently closed for refurbishment, China Tang is favoured by the Dorchester's many A-list guests, plus squillionaires and their arm candy. Decked out in chocolate and cream, the smart room looks like an old-fashioned cruise liner, with a few comfy bar stools, and luxurious leather chairs scattered around the thick patterned carpet. There's great range of Champagnes (from £45) and the wines (from £25) include a spice-friendly selection from Alsace and Bordeaux, and aromatic New World varieties.
Babies and children welcome. Disabled: toilet. Function rooms. Music (bands 9pm daily; free). Restaurant.

Claridge's Bar
Claridge's Hotel, 49 Brook Street, W1K 4HR (7629 8860). Bond Street tube. **Open** noon-1am Mon-Sat; 4pm-midnight Sun. **Food served** noon-11pm daily. **Credit** AmEx, DC, MC, V.
Once synonymous with style and elegance, this art deco bar became infamous for Kate Moss's birthday antics a couple of years back and doesn't seem to have recovered. On our visit it was loud and cramped with a *Heat*-reading bridge-and-tunnel crowd, a hen party, and the odd City boy with scantily clad companion. Spread out in two rooms, to which is appended a small function area, the bar has gentlemen's club decor, with comfy leather chairs in browns, creams and British racing green. Despite buying our Bellini at the bar for £13.75, our bill was presented with optional 10% service charge added. When we finally found a seat, service was swift and friendly, and complimentary olives, mixed nuts, grissini, Japanese crackers and parmesan crisps were brought. Drinks include contemporary cocktails, Champagne (including many vintage varieties), spirits (including some single malts) and a few bottled beers. Canapés, caviar, sandwiches, and savoury and sweet finger food make up the rest of the pricey menu.
Disabled: toilet. Restaurant.

Donovan Bar
Brown's Hotel, Albemarle Street, W1S 4BP (7493 6020). Green Park tube. **Open** 11am-1am Mon-Sat; 11am-10.30pm Sun. **Food served** 11am-6pm daily. **Credit** AmEx, MC, V.
After a reported £20 million refurbishment, the legendary Brown's (now owned by Rocco Forte) opened earlier this year to… well, mixed reviews. But that was the restaurant – the bar is much better. Named after the celebrated British photographer Terence Donovan, its design has been

China Tang

inspired by the Helmut Newton Bar in Berlin, and incorporates a Bill Amberg-designed leather bar. Against the backdrop of a stained-glass window, the subtly classy decor boasts black leather chairs and checked fabric banquettes, and the walls are hung with Donovan's iconic photographs. Drop by for a glass from the wide selection of Champagnes available, or settle down with a classic or contemporary cocktail, such as Box Brownie (raspberry purée, raspberry vodka and Champagne).

Disabled: toilet. Function room. Games (board games). Music (musician 7.30pm daily). Restaurant. **Map 2 J7**.

43

43 South Molton Street, W1K 5RS (7647 4343/www. 43southmolton.com). Bond Street tube. **Open** *Club* 10.30pm-3am Thur-Sat. *Members' bar* 5.30pm-3am Mon-Sat. **Food served** *Members' bar* 5.30pm-3am Mon-Sat. *Restaurant* 11.30am-7.30pm daily. **Credit** AmEx, MC, V.

The rope and metal posts outside this bar may give you the impression that you're invading a celebrity première, but you'll need no special pass to access the upstairs bar and spend time alongside glamorous boutique assistants and their self-conscious boyfriends. Arrive early, and you'll be sure of a place around a low, candlelit table, while efficient waiters and waitresses whisk your orders away to the bar around the corner. By all means check the wine list, but the generously proportioned cocktails are king – although descriptions are low on detail: 'A beautiful drink made for a beautiful Mexican lady' doesn't tell you much, and while we suspected that their signature drink, the Cider House Rules, wouldn't contain Strongbow, we had to ask to make absolutely sure. At £8 per cocktail and £4 for bar snacks it's not particularly cheap, but the whiff of exclusivity makes it worth a visit.

Babies and children welcome (restaurant). Music (bands/DJs 10.30pm Fri, Sat; admission varies). Restaurant. Tables outdoors (5, pavement).

Guinea Grill

30 Bruton Place, W1J 6NL (7499 1210/www.the guinea.co.uk). Bond Street or Green Park tube. **Open** 11am-11pm Mon-Fri; 6-11pm Sat. **Food served** 12.30-3pm, 6-11pm Mon-Fri; 6-11pm Sat. **Credit** AmEx, DC, MC, V.

In stark contrast to the English sophistication of the Restaurant & Grill that lurks at the back of this pub, this is a fairly rough and ready boozer, with the slightly unruly customers kept on a short leash by stern, elegant women who operate the bar with speed and efficiency. It's often standing-room only, and large, pot-bellied blokes push past each other unsteadily en route to the gents after sinking their fourth pint of Young's Special in the hour since leaving the office. The wines are fairly undistinguished compared to the more enticing stuff offered to customers of the Grill, but if that was what you were after you probably wouldn't be in the Guinea anyway. It's an unpretentious, no-nonsense drinking den – something all too rare in a West End overpopulated with unappealing chains.

Babies and children welcome (restaurant). Function room. No piped music or jukebox. No-smoking area. Restaurant.

Hush

8 Lancashire Court, Brook Street, W1S 1EY (7659 1500/www.hush.co.uk). Bond Street tube. **Open** 11am-12.30am Mon-Sat. **Food served** noon-11pm Mon-Sat. **Credit** AmEx, DC, MC, V.

If you make the mistake of shinning up the staircase to avoid the fairly pleasant restaurant on the ground floor, you'll be plunged into a hideous maelstrom of deafening music, men wearing dishevelled suits bellowing indiscreetly about Chloë from accounts, while Chloë from accounts stands nearby, sipping her Bellini and clutching a Selfridges carrier bag. It's a vigorous assault on all the senses, with the fluorescent glare of the bar causing retinal discomfort against the extremely dark – and supposedly seductive – seating area. The cocktails are well mixed, and the wines very drinkable, but the place feels like a overpriced provincial nightclub. Hush's wafer-thin veneer of style is perfectly summed up by a drink on the menu, Your Initial, which is described thus: 'Discreetly tell one of our bartenders the initial of the person you intend to receive this truly original Martini, and wait to see the result.' No thanks, I'm off.

Babies and children welcome. Disabled: toilet. Function rooms. Restaurant. Tables outdoors (15, courtyard).

Kilo

3-5 Mill Street, W1S 2AU (7629 8877/www.kilo-mayfair.co.uk). Oxford Circus or Piccadilly Circus tube. **Open** 8pm-3am Fri, Sat. **Food served** noon-11pm Mon-Fri; 6-11pm Sat. **Credit** AmEx, DC, MC, V.

Kilo's main attraction is its restaurant, but they've attempted to turn the reception area for expectant diners into a bar. There are only four tables, draped in black fabric, and enough banquette seating for 20-or-so people – but while businesslike staff whisk people through to their hors-d'oeuvres, there's an amiable barman to tend to the needs of dedicated drinkers. Cocktails are delicate creations served in small measures for a slightly overpriced £8, but they are imaginatively put together, with a Bittersweet Symphony – consisting of gin, Campari and passion fruit – living up perfectly to its name. The strappy-topped, high-heeled brigade stuck to the small wine selection of three reds and three whites by the glass, while their boyfriends toasted their masculinity with bottled beers. You wouldn't want to make a night of it, lest you accidentally get drunk and spend a fortune in the adjoining restaurant, but it's definitely worth a stopover.

Bar available for hire. Music (9pm Fri, Sat; £10). Tables outdoors (7, terrace).

Living Room

3-9 Heddon Street, W1B 4BE (0870 166 2225/www. thelivingroomw1.co.uk). Piccadilly Circus tube. **Open** noon-1am Mon-Sat; noon-11pm Sun. **Food served** noon-11pm Mon-Sat; noon-10.30pm Sun. **Credit** AmEx, MC, V.

This a gorgeous space, large and airy, with open shelving dividing the restaurant area from the bar beyond. Venture past the relatively content diners, however, and you'll find yourself in a frenzy of screaming, shouting and heavy boozing, as the day's office intrigue is disseminated at ear-splitting volume. Remove the human beings and you'd probably have quite a highbrow bar; the menu features a star-studded spirit line-up, dessert wines and even cigars – but any upmarket leanings are blown out of the water by the overwhelming consumption of high-strength lager. The waitresses battle gamely against the odds, while someone is employed solely to go around sweeping up after the rabble – and the later in the week you come here, the more oppressive it gets. The unfortunate glimpse of a Slippery Nipple on the menu indicates the way this place is heading.

Babies and children admitted (restaurant). Bar available for hire. Restaurant (available for hire; no smoking). Music (pianist 8pm Wed-Sat; noon Sun; free). **Map 2 J7**.

Met Bar

Metropolitan Hotel, 18-19 Old Park Lane, W1K 1LB (7447 1000/www.metropolitan.co.uk). Hyde Park Corner tube. **Open/food served** 10am-6pm daily. **Credit** AmEx, DC, MC, V.

We remember the days when this chic bar inside the über-cool Metropolitan London was almost impossible to get into unless you were a celebrity or a hotel guest. Now the A-listers have moved on, but the bar remains a favourite haunt of soap stars and people from the music, media and fashion industries. It's popular for parties and launches, and is open only to members and hotel guests from 6pm. Looking at the interior, you could be forgiven for wondering what the fuss is about: the intimate space has nothing more striking than moody lighting, comfy club chairs, red leather banquettes, burgundy walls with etched glass, and an abstract mural. Drinks include 26 types of Martini (try the excellent Pineapple Martini) and numerous other cocktails that are freshly muddled by friendly, Armani-clad mixologists. Food – salads, sandwiches canapés and bento boxes – is available from the hotel's restaurant Nobu from noon until 10.45pm, but the bar's own upscale snack menu offers the likes of fresh crab and papaya tian with coriander oil. If you are in late at night there's great music mixed by international DJs.

Disabled: toilet (hotel). Music (DJs 10pm Mon-Sat; free). Restaurant.

Mô Tea Room

23 Heddon Street, W1B 4BH (7434 4040). Oxford Circus or Piccadilly Circus tube. **Open/food served** noon-midnight daily. **Credit** AmEx, DC, MC, V.

As with most other establishments on this street, the Moroccan-inspired Mô is generally packed solid with Heddon-ists; the gentle North African fragrances and tranquil lighting do little to calm the excitable throng, and more people can usually be found queuing down the pavement to join them. The interior is decidedly higgledy, and not a little piggledy, with a mass of artefacts the owners have sourced on their travels in the Levant and low-level seating on which the punters perch, contentedly sucking on shisha pipes. To edge towards a vaguely authentic experience you should probably go for their mint tea, but the fruity cocktails are tasty, imaginative and laced with hints of spice. Ideally, you'd kick back with a game of backgammon and murmured conversation would accompany the excellent drinks, but sadly the languid atmosphere you normally associate with a Moroccan tea room is somewhat elusive.

Babies and children admitted. Disabled: toilet. Function room. Music (bands/DJ 9pm Mon, Tue; free). Restaurant. Tables outdoors (10, terrace). **Map 2 J7.**

Polo Bar

Westbury Hotel, New Bond Street, W1S 2YF (7629 7755). Bond Street or Oxford Circus tube. **Open** 11am-1am daily. **Food served** 11am-11pm daily. **Credit** AmEx, DC, MC, V.

It may occupy some dead space at the front of a hotel, but Polo beats many West End bars hands down for a pre-dinner drink. They're catering for the big spenders, with only six wines by the glass but oodles by the bottle – in fact, even spirits are offered by the bottle, with a Wray & Nephew rum for £120 if you feel the need to crash and burn. The classic cocktails include a stunning Martini made with Tanqueray Ten at £11, while the attention to detail even extends to soft drinks, with their apple juice laced with gorgeous hints of cinnamon. The unobtrusive beats provide a gentle, tick-tock backdrop, while the teal velour and art deco motifs of the bar lead you further down the road to relaxation. Don't leave this place to the guests of the Westbury; it makes for a gorgeous mid-week treat.

Babies and children welcome. Disabled: toilet. No-smoking area. Restaurant. TV (big screen, satellite).

Punch Bowl

41 Farm Street, W1J 5RP (7493 6841). Green Park tube. **Open** 11am-11pm Mon-Fri; 11am-6pm Sat. **Food served** noon-4pm, 6-9pm Mon-Fri; noon-5pm Sat. **Credit** MC, V.

There's more variety of pubs within the back streets of Mayfair than in any comparable area of Britain. This one promises much from the street: its cute exterior should conceal a charming, idiosyncratic bar. In fact it's strangely unappealing, with Premiership football games on the TV the main focus of people's attention, and a characterless 1980s soundtrack. The beer-bellied blokes that make up the majority of the drinkers look like they probably work locally rather than live locally, but they're a boisterous, friendly bunch, downing lagers and pints of Bombardier as if their lives depended on it. The wine selection is almost predictably poor, with a pretty undrinkable chardonnay and an unremarkable pinot grigio, but it isn't a bad spot for a pint and a own-made pizza if you're passing at lunch.

Function room. Tables outdoors (3, pavement). TVs (big screen, satellite).

Red Lion

1 Waverton Street, W1J 5QN (7499 1307). Green Park tube. **Open** 11.30am-11pm Mon-Fri; 6-11pm Sat; 6-10.30pm Sun. **Food served** noon-2.30pm, 6-9.30pm Mon-Fri; 6-9.30pm Sat, Sun. **Credit** AmEx, MC, V.

It's got a lot busier in the year since we were last here – a carefully kept Mayfair secret is out, and people from all walks of life are combing the back streets trying to find it. The miniature tables, toby jugs and other knick-knacks give an intimate, front-room feel, although its new-found popularity has slightly lessened its appeal. The landlord is as hospitable as ever, pulling pints of Greene King IPA, Bombardier and Young's ales with a cheeky wink. Honest, unpretentious pub fare doesn't come much better than this, with large plates of steak and ale pie, battered fish and scampi being brought to tables ready-equipped with ketchup and vinegar; if you prefer a quieter meal, you could always scoot through to the more exclusive back room, where they serve up much the same thing for an extra premium – presumably to cover laundry costs for the tablecloths.

Babies and children admitted. Music (pianist 7pm Sat; free). Restaurant (available for hire; no smoking).

Running Horse

50 Davies Street, W1K 5JE (7493 1275). Bond Street tube. **Open** noon-11pm Mon-Sat. **Food served** noon-3pm, 6-9pm Mon-Thur; noon-3pm Fri; noon-4pm Sat. **Credit** AmEx, MC, V.

This extremely handsome room with swanky light fittings, Venetian glass and a glorious roaring fire was made a lot less comfortable on our visit by the presence of grinding, industrial dance music more suited to a Camden nightclub. Far from busy on a Friday evening, it seemed that this one small alteration could completely turn the place around. The wine might be pricey (around £15 a bottle) but it's a varied selection of chenins, picpouls and Riojas; the lagers are plentiful, the ales are well-kept, and the staff set about their few tasks with gusto. A menu of char-grilled steak or grilled chicken sandwiches failed to tempt the few customers in attendance: a mixture of pre-clubbing youths and suited gents trying to look ten years younger. An upstairs

Central

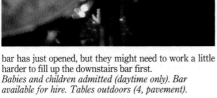

Donovan Bar. *See p66.*

bar has just opened, but they might need to work a little harder to fill up the downstairs bar first.
Babies and children admitted (daytime only). Bar available for hire. Tables outdoors (4, pavement).

Shepherd's Tavern

50 Hertford Street, W1J 7SS (7499 3017). Green Park or Hyde Park Corner tube. **Open** 11am-11pm Mon-Sat; noon-10.30pm Sun. **Food served** 11am-10.30pm Mon-Sat; noon-9.30pm Sun. **Credit** AmEx, MC, V.

A boisterous but inviting place, this. The downstairs room involved heavy drinking and finger-wagging arguments over the choice of sporting entertainment on the pub TV, but there's a quiet smoke-free room upstairs with plenty of seating. This room takes the Victorian theme that dominates the pub and leads it down an almost Tyrolean route, with acres of wood cladding; it's a detail appreciated by a group of Japanese businessmen, happy to work their way through plates of pie and chips in this peculiar but comfortable setting. The other surprise is the wine list: it's big, varied and affordable, with Chablis and Alberiño topping the whites, and a £4.60 glass of Chateauneuf-du-Pape leading the selection of reds. There are also excellent pints of London Pride and Bombardier on tap alongside the usual lagers.
Games (fruit machines). Restaurant (no smoking). TV.

Trader Vic's

The London Hilton, 22 Park Lane, W1K 4BE (7208 4113/www.tradervics.com). Hyde Park Corner tube. **Open/food served** noon-1am Mon-Thur; noon-3am Fri; 5pm-3am Sat; 5-11.30pm Sun. **Admission** £7 after 11pm Mon-Sat. **Credit** AmEx, DC, MC, V.

This chain of bars extends from Atlanta to Taiwan, and makes its London home in the basement of the Hilton. If you haven't been, you should – if only to tick it off your list of preposterous sights in the capital. It's an absurd Polynesian theme bar, framed by bamboo trellis-work from which dangle large glass baubles and, er, a canoe. Rum-drenched cocktails with names like 'Suffering Bastard' come at around £7 each, while bar snacks consist of such unlikely dishes as morel mushrooms en croûte, a snip at £8.50. So, it's something of a financial challenge to get drunk here, but there are lots of laughs: the Hawaiian entertainer and his preposterous banter, the background music playing 1980s classics slightly too fast, and wealthy businessmen attempting to impress pouting girlfriends with a faceful of smoke from a fat cigar. Warning: attempting to access the comedy after 11pm will incur a £7 cover charge.
Babies and children welcome. Disabled: toilet (hotel). Function room. Music (musicians 10.30pm daily). Restaurant (no-smoking area).

Windmill

6-8 Mill Street, W1S 2AZ (7491 8050). Oxford Circus tube. **Open** 11am-midnight Mon-Fri; noon-4pm Sat. **Food served** noon-9.30pm Mon-Fri; noon-3.30pm Sat. **Credit** AmEx, DC, MC, V.

This warm, welcoming pub is in stark contrast to its location – scant metres from the shopping nightmare of Oxford Circus – and its sanctuary status is well valued by the customers who create a busy hubbub at all times of day. The

Windmill comes into its own after work, when office spats are forgotten as lipsmacking Young's ales are slowly knocked back. They love their wine here too: our slightly tongue-in-cheek request for a recommendation was handled without an eyelid being batted, and a truly sumptuous chardonnay it turned out to be. Decor is sub-Victoriana, with portraits of immensely sideburned men, and the food is up to the standard you'd expect from a three-times national steak and kidney pie champion – but it's not just British fare, with grilled halloumi going down particularly well. The atmosphere is so congenial, it's almost enough to make you not resent drinking while standing up.
Function room. No piped music or jukebox. Restaurant (no-smoking area). TV (big screen). **Map 2 J6.**

Windows

28th Floor, London Hilton, Park Lane, W1K 1BE (7208 4021/www.hilton.co.uk/londonparklane). Hyde Park Corner tube. **Open** noon-2.30pm Fri; 5.30pm-2.30am Sat; noon-10.30pm Sun. **Credit** AmEx, DC, MC, V.
It's a room with a view – a spectacular one, from Battersea Power Station right round to the Telecom Tower in the West End – and it would be safe to say that it is the vista that has kept customers whizzing up in the lift to Windows over the years. Sitting on the 28th floor of the Hilton, it has the air of a bar that would rather be members-only, but is wearily forced to accept the hoi polloi wandering up from Hyde Park Corner; so service is efficient, if a little cool, and ten quid cocktails, pricey premium plonk and a post-11pm £7 cover charge are employed to sift the riff from the raff. Summer 2006 sees an attempt to push it further upmarket, as a redesign by the team behind Nobu and the Met Bar are set to transform it into a room which is 'modern, yet luxuriously decadent' – it'll still have the view.
Babies and children welcome (restaurant only). Disabled: toilet. Restaurant (no-smoking area).

Zeta Bar

35 Hertford Street, W1J 7TG (7208 4067/www.zeta-bar.com). Hyde Park Corner tube. **Open** 5pm-1am Mon, Tue; 5pm-3am Wed-Sat. **Food served** 6pm-12.30am Mon-Sat. **Admission** £10 after 10pm Wed-Sat. **Credit** AmEx, MC, V.
This is one of three bars at the Hilton, but the main entrance is via a rather grim windswept sidestreet. Inside, however, it's a glamorous, futuristic bar, lit by what can only be described as golden wicker skittles. On our visit the place was almost empty; strange, because the staff are helpful and welcoming, the music loud but tasteful, and the drink selection unusual but well executed. It's not a place that allows spirits to talk for themselves: each cocktail is combined with spices, herbs and fruit, but to exquisite effect. A £7.50 vanilla Martini came with a whole vanilla pod and tasted like the most sumptuous ice-cream imaginable, while a cucumber version was as refreshing as any gazpacho. Their obsession with flavour extends to soft drinks, with one particular option described as 'a combination of banana, parsley…' – excuse me? – but overall it's an excellent bar in search of a clientele.
Bar available for hire. Dress: smart casual. Music (DJs 9pm Wed-Sat).

Also in the area...

All Bar One 289-293 Regent Street, W1B 2HJ (7467 9901).
Chopper Lump (Davy's) 10C Hanover Square, W1R 9HD (7499 7569).

Hog's Head 11 Dering Street, W1S 1AR (7629 0531).
Mulligan's of Mayfair (Balls Brothers) 14 Cork Street, W1S 3NS (7409 1370).
O'Neill's 7 Shepherd Street, W1J 7HR (7408 9281).
Pitcher & Piano 10 Pollen Street, W1S 1NQ (7629 9581).
Slug & Lettuce 19-20 Hanover Street, W1T 9HG (7499 0077).

Notting Hill, Ladbroke Grove & Westbourne Grove

Whether it's gastropubs or stylish destination bars you're after, the Portobello Road and surrounding streets offer plenty of options. Ladbroke Grove has the lofty **10 West**, while Westbourne Grove has upped its cool quotient with **Metropolitan**, **Crazy Homies** and the fabulous **Ruby & Sequoia**. Even the **Earl of Lonsdale** has had a facelift.

Beach Blanket Babylon

45 Ledbury Road, W11 2AA (7229 2907). Notting Hill Gate tube. **Open** noon-11pm Mon-Sat; noon-10.30pm Sun. **Food served** noon-3.30pm, 7pm-midnight Mon-Sat; noon-4pm, 7-10.30pm Sun. **Credit** MC, V.
Step past the doorman into BBB and you enter one of the most original-looking bars in London. Part Roman villa, part fairy-tale fantasy, this bar boasts curly frescoes, open fires, a cabinet filled with vintage jewellery, and a restaurant at the back reached via a plank-and-chain footbridge and a spiral staircase. The clientele is pretty representative of the area – lots of well-off boys and girls spending a fair whack on pricey bottles of wine (£17 for the house offering) and Champagne. The beer comes in bottles only (Asahi, Budvar, Tiger and Sol). Many areas of this small space get reserved on a Friday and Saturday night, and during the summer tables outside at the front get snapped up in the early evening. There's also a small patio at the back. Given its location on fashionable Ledbury Road, which has filled up with trendy boutiques, this is still a place to see and be seen. BBB will always be the kind of place you either love or hate, but at least it sparks conversation.
Babies and children admitted (daytime). Function rooms. Music (DJ 6pm Sun; free). Restaurant. Tables outdoors (10, garden). **Map 10 A6.**

Cow

89 Westbourne Park Road, W2 5QH (7221 0021). Royal Oak or Westbourne Park tube. **Open** noon-11pm Mon-Thur; noon-midnight Fri, Sat; noon-10.30pm Sun. **Food served** noon-3.30pm, 6-10.30pm Mon-Sat; noon-3.30pm, 6-10pm Sun. **Credit** MC, V.
Owned by Tom Conran, this cosy Irish pub in perennially hip Notting Hill is renowned all over London for its oysters and Guinness. The pub is on the ground floor, with a dining area at the back that serves a simple but well-executed seafood-oriented menu; the more expensive dining room upstairs is especially popular for Sunday roasts. There's an excellent range of wines, spirits and bottled Belgian beers, plus a couple of real ales (Pride and Harveys Bitter). Cow buzzes with local artists, musicians, filmmakers, TV personalities, media folk and young families.
Babies and children admitted (lunch, restaurant). Function room. Tables outdoors (4, pavement). TV. **Map 10 A5.**

Central

Crazy Homies

127 Westbourne Park Road, W2 5QL (7727 6771).
Royal Oak tube. **Open** 6.30pm-midnight Mon-Fri; noon-
midnight Sat, Sun. **Food served** 6.30-11pm Mon-Fri;
noon-11.30pm Sat, Sun. **Credit** MC, V.
Next door to his Lucky Seven diner Tom Conran has
turned a tiny ground-floor space into an attractive bar serving Mexican-style drinks and bar snacks. There are tequila
shots, bottled beers and a short list of Margaritas and
other tequila cocktails that cost £5.50-£6.50. Or there's
Michelada, a mix of beer with citrus juice, salt and sea-
sonings that tastes like a fluid-replacement drink (£4).
Cocktail-making is not a strong point of the smiling staff,
though – one classic Margarita came salt-rimmed, the next
didn't. The bar snacks are well made, but these tiny tacos,
tostados, quesadillas and even the breakfast dish of chur-
ros con chocolate (served here as a dessert) cost around £5-
£7 per nibble. The bar is friendly, but it can feel cramped
when busy: unless you arrive early, you might end up on
one of the child-sized stools, or not get a seat at all.
Bar available for hire. Function room. Jukebox. Table
outdoors (1, pavement). **Map 10 A5.**

Earl of Lonsdale

277-281 Westbourne Grove, W11 2QA (7727 6335).
Ladbroke Grove or Notting Hill Gate tube. **Open** noon-
11pm Mon-Fri; 10am-11pm Sat; noon-10.30pm Sun.
Food served 12.30-3pm, 6-9.15pm Mon-Fri; noon-4pm
Sat, Sun. **Credit** (over £10) MC, V.
This Samuel Smith pub has had a sensitive refurbishment
which retained all that is wonderful about an old boozer
(plenty of etched glass and a host of little dark-wood panelled snugs, all serviced by the island bar and accessed
through little *Alice in Wonderland* doors) while upping its
appeal: the Saloon is a large airy room with not one but
two open fires, plenty of comfy sofas, and tables where you
can be served above-average pub fare such as fillet of cod
in brewery bitter batter or cottage pie. Naturally there's a
reasonable tap range, including Smith's Best, Alpine, Extra
Stout and Wheat Beer, as well as a fine range of spirits and
Fair Trade coffees and chocolate. No wonder it's full of
happy locals most evenings. A gem.
Babies and children welcome (lounge room). Games
(bowling machine). No-smoking area. Tables outdoors
(16, garden). **Map 10 A6.**

Eclipse

186 Kensington Park Road, W11 2ES (7792 2063/
www.eclipse-ventures.com). Ladbroke Grove or Notting
Hill Gate tube. **Open/food served** 4pm-midnight Mon-
Thur; noon-midnight Fri; 9am-midnight Sat; 10am-
10.30pm Sun. **Credit** AmEx, MC, V.
A little corridor of a bar, with leather banquette seating
under Tom Dixon lights on one side, and a cosy open fire
set in a bare brick wall on the other. Part of an expanding
mini chain, Eclipse focuses on classy cocktails, such as a
Blue Velvet of Stolichnaya Vanil, fresh lime, blueberries,
cranberries and elderflower, and a Koshiku of lime-leaf-
infused shochu with sour passion fruit and ginger (both
£6.75); and decent food that ranges from eggs benedict
(£5.50), burgers (served until midnight; the Classic costs
£6.75), Asian snacks (£4) and Moroccan platters (£8.50).
On a wet Tuesday the place was pretty quiet, which suited the slightly more mature folk within, but on the build-
up to the weekend expect DJs playing funky house to heat
the place up in all senses.
Babies and children welcome. Music (DJs 8.30pm Thur-
Sat; free). Tables outdoors (2, pavement). **Map 10 Az6.**

Elbow Room

103 Westbourne Grove, W2 4UW (7221 5211/www.the
elbowroom.co.uk). Bayswater or Notting Hill Gate tube.
Open/food served noon-11pm Mon-Sat; noon-10.30pm
Sun. **Credit** MC, V.
This American-style pool lounge, part of a chain that has
other branches in Islington and Shoreditch (as well as
Bristol and Leeds), is still going strong after ten years. The
original venue on Westbourne Grove remains a laid-back
affair, with lots to offer its punters. There's a long list of
spirits, including the fine Hendrick's gin, and a decent
range of cocktails and shooters on offer. If you work up an
appetite perfecting your bank shots and swerves, there's
a hearty menu on offer, including signature char-grilled
burgers, sandwiches and fajitas. Carling, Coors Fine
Light and Grolsch are on tap, and you can sup the more
unusual Dutch beer Korenwolf. Booths at the front of the
bar give way to a pool hall that contains seven tables. Staff
are reasonably friendly and the crowd is a nice mix of boys
and girls, locals and visitors. The place fills up quickly,
especially on a Friday night, so head here early if you want
to get your name in the booking system for a game.
Bar available for hire. Games (7 pool tables; phone for
details of competitions). Music (DJs 8pm Fri, Sat; free).
TV (big screen). **Map 10 B6.**

Electric Brasserie

191 Portobello Road, W11 2ED (7908 9696/www.
the-electric.co.uk). Ladbroke Grove tube. **Open** 8am-
12.30am Mon-Fri; 8am-1am Sat, Sun. **Food served**
8am-5pm, 6-11pm Mon-Sat; 8am-5pm, 6-10pm Sun.
Credit AmEx, DC, MC, V.
Next to the Electric Cinema, this hip brasserie is a cool
place to hang out with friends, and has proved a major hit
with local celebrities. There's a noisy, bustling bar at the
front with communal tables and benches, and a quieter,
more formal dining area at the back. The all-day menu is
not a world apart from the one at the Wolseley, with its
classic breakfasts, brunches, afternoon tea and contemporary continental fare. The bar sells spirits, beers like Stella
(£1.90 by the half pint, £3 by the bottle), fresh fruit pressés
and wines by the glass, bottle or carafe, organised under
headings like 'fresh and aromatic' and 'rich and robust'.
Cocktails include Martinis (£6.50), Champagne cocktails
(£7.50), long drinks (£6) and short drinks (£6.50). Rose Gin
Fizz (Hendrick's gin, rosewater syrup, fresh mint, lemon
juice and soda water, £6) is perfect for hot weather.
Babies and children welcome. Disabled: toilet. Function
room. No-smoking area. Tables outdoors (8, pavement).
Map 10 Az5.

Elgin

96 Ladbroke Grove, W11 1PY (7229 5663).
Ladbroke Grove tube. **Open** noon-11pm Mon-Thur;
noon-11.30pm Fri; 11am-11.30pm Sat; noon-10.30pm
Sun. **Food served** noon-9pm daily. **Credit** AmEx,
MC, V.
This is a mother of a pub. Everything is enormous, from
the height of the ceilings and size of the rooms – three of
them – to the huge bar that serves them all. It was built
back in 1853 by Dr Samuel Walker, a property-speculating
clergyman. The original Victorian bevelled glass screen
set with chunks of coloured glass, and the wall tiles and
carved mahogany are, however, thanks to William
Dickinson, who acquired the pub in 1892. On our visit no
one was here for the beer (of three rotating real ales, one
was off). There's a small range of spirits, wine by the glass
(from £2.80), bottles of alcopops, and a range of 'Best of

British' pub grub that ranges from pie of the day (£6.95) to egg and chips (£5.45). What we all wanted, and got, was sport (Chelsea v Barça) and plenty of it. There is a fittingly huge screen in each of the rooms, where sofas, tables and chairs variously accommodate. The only bad thing was the 1-2 result.

Function room. Games (fruit machine, pool table, quiz machine). Music (DJs 9pm alternate Fri; karaoke 9pm alternate Sat; both free). No-smoking area. Quiz (6pm Sun; £1). Tables outdoors (12, pavement). TVs (big screen, satellite). **Map 10 Az5.**

Grand Union

45 Woodfield Road, W9 2BA (7286 1886). Westbourne Park tube. **Open** noon-11pm Mon-Sat; noon-10.30pm Sun. **Food served** noon-10pm Mon-Sat; noon-9pm Sun. **Credit** AmEx, MC, V.

Having changed owner and had a brush-up last year, the Grand Union is now pretty similar in feel to other venues in the vicinity that offer a gastropub-style package. Still, thanks to its location perched above the Grand Union canal and the lingering sense of its past (it used to be a characterful boozer for bus workers stationed at the depot nearby), it retains much of its charm. Lots of locals, including families at weekends, come here to cosy up in winter, eat and sink a bottle of wine (from £11.50 for a South African pinotage), or spill out on to the terrace for a barbecue in summer. The beers on draught include Grolsch, Hoegaarden, Staropramen, ESP and London Pride. Under a new chef, the menu is now quite eclectic, with pies sold as a speciality (if you're feeling adventurous, try the camel pie – we were told it tastes like mutton), duck confit, burgers and a few good vegetarian options. The Grand Union's quiz nights are popular, as is the CD jukebox and big-screen TV.

Mô Tea Room. *See p69.*

Central

"*Soul receives from soul that knowledge,
therefore not by book nor from tongue,
If knowledge of mysteries come
after emptiness of mind,
that is illumination of heart*"

- *Rumi 1207-1273*

CORPORATE EVENTS • LAUNCH PARTIES
LEAVING PARTIES • BIRTHDAYS • REUNIONS
ANNIVERSARIES • CHRISTMAS PARTIES

RUMI

531 Kings Road, London SW10 0TZ
Tel: 020 7823 3362
E-mail: info@rumibar.com

www.rumibar.com

Babies and children admitted (until 6pm). Function room. No-smoking area. Tables outdoors (20, canalside). **Map 10 A4.**

Lonsdale

44-48 Lonsdale Road, W11 2DE (7727 4080/www.the lonsdale.co.uk). Ladbroke Grove or Notting Hill Gate tube. **Open** 6pm-midnight Mon-Thur, Sun; 6pm-1am Fri, Sat. **Food served** 6-11pm daily. **Credit** AmEx, MC, V.
Adventurous decor, especially in the upstairs bar, is one of the most enticing features of this former *Time Out* Bar of the Year (2003). Sadly, this space-age pastiche now looks and feels a little lacklustre. On the Saturday night we visited, the service was slow and patchy, despite the presence of an efficient and pleasant manager running up and down stairs (does anyone train their waiting staff these days?). The Lonsdale's clientele is fairly mixed, and no longer made up solely of Notting Hill's beautiful people. In fact, there seemed to be more non-locals present looking to be seen somewhere they deemed hyper-trendy. The cocktail list is long and imaginative (it was originally conceived by London cocktail maestro Dick Bradsell), but the rose petal violet Martini served to us, at a pricey £8, was mixed with a heavy hand. There's a restaurant at the back of the downstairs bar, and the private bar upstairs, Genevieve, is a popular venue for parties.
Disabled: toilet. Function room. Music (DJs 9pm Fri, Sat; free). **Map 10 A6.**

Mall Tavern

71-73 Palace Gardens Terrace, W8 4RU (7727 3805). Notting Hill Gate tube. **Open** noon-11pm Mon-Sat; noon-10.30pm Sun. **Food served** noon-3pm, 6-10.30pm Mon-Thur; noon-3pm, 6-11pm Fri; noon-5pm, 7-11pm Sat; noon-5pm, 7-10pm Sun. **Credit** AmEx, MC, V.
A recent late Wednesday afternoon down the Mall we were eavesdropping on a table, which was occupied by a gent in a cherry-red corduroy jacket and a chain-smoking lady in a slinky golden dress of a type last seen in 1930s Shanghai. He and she – in a voice so cut-crystal she'd have put Her Majesty to shame – were discussing a guest list for their function. Sandy Gall? she suggested. Freddy Forsyth? he returned. And so it went. Harry Pinter. Davey Frost. Stevey Berkoff. Lady Something-or-Otheringtony. Could this be London's poshest pub? It is sufficiently haughty that the three gleaming, surgical-looking beer pumps don't sport any branding and you have to ask what beers they might have (Stella, Hoegaarden and Leffe, is the sniffy response). And your change comes back on a silver plate – although there won't be much of it. Menus on the tables offer Champagne and classic cocktails, but it's really a wine sort of place; we didn't see the list but we don't doubt that it's top-notch. A chalkboard on the wall runs through the cuisine options, which come snacky or haute, to be eaten in the dining room next door. Bright and smart, broadsheets on the counter, fashion mags in a rack, it's a seriously impressive place – we're going to start drinking here when we grow up.
Babies and children admitted (lunch only). Function room. Restaurant. Tables outdoors (5, patio). TV. **Map 10 B7.**

Metropolitan

60 Great Western Road, W11 1AB (7229 9254/ www.realpubs.co.uk). Westbourne Park tube. **Open** noon-11.30pm Mon-Thur; noon-midnight Fri, Sat; noon-10.30pm Sun. **Food served** noon-3.30pm, 6.30-10.30pm Mon-Sat; 1-7pm Sun. **Credit** AmEx, MC, V.

The original pub that stood on the site of the Metropolitan was modernised in 2004 and transformed into what is now one of the most popular drinking establishments in the area. The gastro-centric formula may have been done to death, but the Metropolitan somehow pulls in a bigger crowd than other similarly styled pubs nearby (it has certainly stolen some of the thunder of the Grand Union, located a stone's throw away). There's a reasonable range on tap (from Kronenbourg and Leffe to Red Stripe and Strongbow), as well as Tiger, Corona and Pilsner in bottles. The wine list is decent and starts at £12 for the French house offering. Sunday-night DJ sessions pack out the pub and the patio area at the side gets pretty crowded in summer. The vibe is fairly unpretentious for Notting Hill, and the modern British dishes chalked up on the blackboard menu are above average.
Babies and children welcome (until 7pm). Function rooms. Games (backgammon, chess). Music (DJs 5.30pm Sun; free). Restaurant (no smoking). Tables outdoors (8, heated garden). TV (big screen). **Map 10 A5.**

Number Ten

10 Golborne Road, W10 5PE (8969 8922). Westbourne Park tube. **Open/food served** 5pm-1am Mon-Fri; 11am-1am Sat; 11am-10.30pm Sun. **Credit** AmEx, DC, MC, V.
In what used to be a seedy old bit of Notting Hill, bar/restaurant/private club Number Ten stands three floors tall in the shadow of the iconic Trellick Tower. The ground floor is a small but well laid-out space with a bar and stage, muted lighting, glitterballs and mini chandeliers, red walls and black venetian blinds, 1970s retro furniture, and leather sofas; the upstairs bar is members-only. There is a restaurant on the second floor that serves modern Japanese cuisine, while tapas-style nosh (gyoza, edamame, tempura) is available on the ground floor. For drinkers there are uninteresting draught options including Red Stripe, Stella and Guinness, bottles (Sapporo, Breton cider, Corona), decent spirits (Zubrowka, Hendrick's, Maker's Mark, 18-year-old Glenfiddich) and Japanese-oriented cocktails (£6), as well as a few reds and whites by the glass. On a quietish Tuesday night (not half-bad) new bands were playing and the place had a warm and friendly vibe. It is obviously a well-used and well-loved local.
Babies and children welcome. Function room. Games (arcade games, pool table, table football). Music (bands 7pm Wed, Thur; free-£5). Tables outdoors (5, pavement).

Portobello Gold

95-97 Portobello Road, W11 2QB (7460 4900/ www.portobellogold.com). Notting Hill Gate tube. **Open** 10am-midnight Mon-Thur; 10am-12.30am Fri; 9am-12.30am Sat; 10am-11.30pm Sun. **Food served** 11am-11pm Mon-Sat; 1-9pm Sun. **Happy hour** 5.30-7pm daily. **Credit** AmEx, DC, MC, V.
Situated at the hilly end of Portobello Road, the Gold is a local treasure. Open for business for the past 21 years under the management of the same owner, it has been unaffected by the passing whims of West London. After closing briefly due to a fire in 2004 it reopened the following year, following a low-key renovation. The small bar is properly stocked with around 18 beers, including Spitfire, Brakspear Bitter, Guinness and Leffe on tap and Chimay, Duvel and Thatchers cider in bottles. The wine selection is well considered, with bottles mostly sold by the glass. In addition, there's an impressive selection of Champagne, rum and tequila. Special deals on beer are often available. A renowned restaurant at the back, which once served

Central

Caribbean cuisine, now serves seafood, including oysters. A TV has been installed in the bar area and the live music sessions that the Gold once hosted have recently returned. The pub also hires itself out as a gallery for local artists and photographers, and there's a cybercafé upstairs, as well as a small hotel. If you're in the area, this is one of the best pubs you'll find.

Babies and children admitted (restaurant). Bar available for hire. Internet access. Music (bands/DJ 7pm Wed; free). Restaurant (no-smoking area). Tables outdoors (3, pavement). TV (big screen, satellite). **Map 10 A6**.

Prince Albert

11 Pembridge Road, W11 3HQ (7727 7362). Notting Hill Gate tube. **Open** noon-midnight daily. **Food served** noon-10pm Mon-Sat; noon-9.30pm Sun. **Credit** AmEx, MC, V.

Located a few steps away from Notting Hill Gate tube, beneath the Gate theatre, the Prince Albert revamped itself a few years ago, with new signage, maroon walls, wooden tables and comfy chairs. Once a traditional pub, it's now a more modern affair, which, mostly due to its location, attracts a huge number of shoppers and tourists on their way to Portobello Market. If you don't mind queuing for your drinks, the Prince Albert offers a fair range of ales on tap, including London Pride (though there have been complaints the beer is served too warm). Wines tend to be on the pricey side. The quality of the British and modern European dishes served from the open kitchen can be variable, so it may be best not to order anything too ambitious. One side of the bar has been designated a no-smoking area and there's a small garden at the back. Weekdays and weeknights may be a better bet than weekends if you're in the area and just want to watch the world go by through the large front windows.

Disabled: toilet. Music (DJs 7pm Sun; free). Tables outdoors (8, heated garden). TV. **Map 10 A7**.

Prince Bonaparte

80 Chepstow Road, W2 5BE (7313 9491). Notting Hill Gate or Royal Oak tube. **Open** noon-11pm Mon-Sat; noon-10.30pm Sun. **Food served** noon-10pm Mon-Thur; noon-9pm Fri-Sun. **Credit** AmEx, MC, V.

A busy pub with a good reputation for its food, the Prince Bonaparte is always full. Come on a Friday or a Saturday night and you probably won't get a seat. Call in during the day in winter and you'll have a better chance of grabbing one of the tables near the open fire. The draught beers here are fairly predictable (Carling, Grolsch, Stella, Staropramen), but the wine list is a little more promising, with a good mix of Old World and New World on offer. The Bonaparte's open kitchen serves up well-prepared dishes, such as steaks, seared fish and risotto. Just beware of visiting in the evening if you want a proper conversation – on the Friday night we visited, the DJ was blasting out the music so loud that even the barman said his nerves and eardrums were wearing thin. Still most of the largely local punters seem happy to shout or just nod. The walls at the back are used as a mini-gallery, so you can view what local artists and photographers are up to.

Disabled: toilet. Music (DJs 7pm Sun; free). No-smoking area. TV. **Map 10 A5**.

Ruby & Sequoia

6-8 All Saints Road, W11 1HH (7243 6363/www.ruby. uk.com). Westbourne Park tube/7 bus. **Open/food served** 6pm-12.30am Mon-Thur; 6pm-2am Fri; 11am-2am Sat; 11am-12.30am Sun. **Credit** AmEx, MC, V.

This latest bar and restaurant from the Ruby Lounge folks is ace. The ground floor is impressive enough, with friendly bar staff, modish cocktails and a fun interior that mixes diner-style booth seating with silver and white flock wallpaper in a retro-funky way. The dining area has an ambitious menu, ranging from escabeche of prawns to braised rabbit with mustard, tarragon and bacon, at proper restaurant prices. But it's as a bar that Ruby & Sequoia is best: after 9pm, DJs work the decks in the bigger and more elegant Sequoia basement, which gets busy on Friday and Saturday nights (a doorman, and door policy of sorts, appears on those nights). Sequoia's a great place to spread out on the leather banquettes, admire the studied cool of the Perspex lights, and wonder what the beautiful young people of Notting Hill actually do for a living.

Babies and children welcome (until 6pm). Disabled: toilet. Music (DJs 8.30pm Thur-Sun; free). Restaurant. Tables outdoors (3, pavement). **Map 10 Az5**.

Sun in Splendour

7 Portobello Road, W11 3DA (7313 9331). Notting Hill Gate tube. **Open** noon-11pm Mon-Thur; noon-midnight Fri; 11am-midnight Sat; noon-10.30pm Sun. **Food served** noon-4pm, 6-10pm Mon-Fri; noon-8pm Sat, Sun. **Credit** MC, V.

Perfectly suited to its posh-end-of-Portobello location, the Sun exudes a studiedly boho charm that has obviously taken a lot of effort to get right. Kudos then for the artfully mismatched furniture, the stripped-down flooring and bruised purple paintwork, the Heinz ketchup and HP sauce on the tables, and the line-up of premium beers at the bar (Amstel, Kirin, Sleeman, Hoegaarden and Leffe, not to mention strawberry-flavoured Früli). Fashion portraits up the style quotient – there's even a bit of frisson that comes with the knowledge that the occasionally provocatively posed girls are all locals and some are even regulars. The food menu is a cut above the norm (think mushroom and tarragon sausages, Moroccan spiced chicken on ciabatta, or Italian breads with olive oil, houmous and feta) and, as the menu notes, 'This is a non-smoking pub throughout. We are not sorry.' Except that's not strictly true, as there is a small, partially enclosed garden out back where smoking is allowed.

Games (quiz machine). Music (DJ 8pm Sat; free). No-smoking. Tables outdoors (8, garden). TV. **Map 10 A7**.

10 West

161-165 Ladbroke Grove, W10 6HJ (8960 1702/ www.vpmg.net). Ladbroke Grove tube. **Open** 5pm-midnight Mon-Fri, Sun; noon-midnight Sat. **Food served** 5-11.30pm Mon-Fri, Sun; noon-11.30pm Sat. **Credit** AmEx, MC, V.

Some would call naming a venture after its postcode lazy but this operation, owned by music venue magnate Vince Power and designed by Shaun Clarkson, is no slouch. The easily missed entrance leads into a canvas-covered antechamber, a marquee ready to be opened up in warmer weather. The enormous interior, with lofty ceiling, a mezzanine floor for sit-down eating, and a sweeping, capacious bar with sparsely spread easy chairs that are dwarfed by the palatial walls, bring to mind a movie set – or the Batcave. The no-smoking policy gives the room an extra clarity (puffers must climb to the tented terrace). Cocktails hit both the mark and the wallet. A Champagne and raspberry Gold Digger is a treat (£10), as is the classic Caipirinha and whisky-based Frisco Sour (both £6.50). Things seemed relaxed midweek, with the raised DJ podium unmanned, but get livelier at weekends when the ample space is put to good use.

Babies and children admitted (until 6pm Sat). Music (DJs 8.30pm Mon, Tue, Fri-Sun). Restaurant (available for hire). No smoking. Tables outdoors (12, heated patio). **Map 10 Az5.**

Tiroler Hut

27 Westbourne Grove, W2 4UA (7727 3981/www. tirolerhut.co.uk). Bayswater or Queensway tube. **Open** 6.30pm-1am Tue-Sat; 6.30pm-midnight Sun. **Food served** 6.30pm-midnight Tue-Sat; 6.30-11.30pm Sun. **Credit** AmEx, DC, MC, V.

Given the fact that the rest of Westbourne Grove is giving itself over to multimillion-pound residential conversions and lots of minimalist spas and hair salons, the Tiroler Hut provides some much-needed kitsch. Situated below street level, this family-run bar-restaurant has been trading since 1967 under the same management – the accordion-playing Joseph and his wife Christine. On any given night you might find Joseph, dressed in traditional Alpine garb, yodelling, playing the accordion or tinkling with his Tyrolean cowbells, while boisterous diners in the restaurant tuck into cheese fondue or a plate of bratwurst. The Germanic beers on offer at the tiny bar, where many regulars come just to drink up the atmosphere, include Dortmunder Union on draught (if you are man or woman enough, order a stein, around a litre in size, for £6.50) and Erdinger and Gösser in bottles. There's also a good range of schnapps, and wines such as the Austrian white Zierfandler and red Blauer Zweigelt. Supersnapper Juergen Teller and friends (Kate Moss) have been known to hold a party or two here, and the loyal clientele is a varied crowd of different generations, nationalities and professions. *Babies and children admitted. Music (cowbell show 9pm Wed-Sun; free).*

Tom & Dick's

30 Alexander Street, W2 5NU (7229 7711/www. tomanddicks.com). Royal Oak tube. **Open/food served** 6-11pm Mon-Sat. **Credit** AmEx, MC, V.

Located between Bayswater and Royal Oak, Tom & Dick's just manages to slip into the cool side of camp. Part French boudoir (hand-painted silk wallpaper), part multimedia venue (the sound system is state of the art and art-house film screenings are held regularly), this quirky place hovers somewhere between art deco and the 21st century, and can't help but impress. The service is slick but friendly and the cocktail-led drinks list strikes a good balance between classics (a Bellini was nicely mixed) and innovations (try one of the fruity Martinis). There's a pizza restaurant upstairs, but modern European food is also offered in the bar. This is a fun place to swing by or spend an evening people-watching, but a word of warning – call ahead if you plan to visit on a Friday or a Saturday night, as the entire space is hired out for private parties on a regular basis. *Function room. Restaurant. Tables outdoors (8, pavement).* **Map 10 B5.**

Trailer Happiness

177 Portobello Road, W11 2DY (7727 2700/www. trailerhappiness.com). Ladbroke Grove or Notting Hill Gate tube. **Open** 5-10pm 1st Mon of mth; 5-11pm Tue-Fri; 6-11pm Sat; 6-10.30pm Sun. **Food served** 6-10.30pm Tue-Sat. **Credit** AmEx, MC, V.

This little basement bar resembles an Austin Powers shag pad (plenty of smoked glass, shagpile carpet, retro paintings of Tahitian dusky maidens gazing down from the wall) but is looking more dated than tongue-in-cheek these days. Happily, the clientele are more likely to be here for a good range of cocktails (£6.50) that can be sipped in a cosy atmosphere. House favourites (£7-£15) include a Mitch Martini (Zubrowka with passion fruit, peach, apple and Champagne) and a Mojito Especial (with Havana Club Añejo Especial), while authentically 1950s-style Tikis include a Zombie (five rums, juices, absinthe, syrups, bitters) that is limited to two per person, for obvious reasons. Food – or rather 'TV Dinners' – covers anything from finger food such as a handful of chips to something more substantial along the lines of lamb and lemon racks. *Music (DJs 8pm Wed-Sat; free). Tables outdoors (5, pavement).* **Map 10 Az6.**

Visible

299 Portobello Road, W10 5TD (8969 0333). Ladbroke Grove or Notting Hill Gate tube. **Open** 4-11pm Mon, Tue, Thur; 10am-1am Fri, Sat; 10am-10.30pm Sun. **Credit** AmEx, MC, V.

Towards the end of Portobello Road sits this twinkly little candlelit bar, filled with big leather sofas, a bare brick wall on one side and a brightly painted wall hung with snowscape photos the other. At the end of the corridor-like space is a backlit bar that features an enormous range of spirits – there are at least ten glass flagons of flavoured vodkas, including mango and passion fruit, as well as vanilla-infused gin. So cocktails (£5-£7) are the thing here. How about an Elephant Mud Bath (Stoli, Crème de Cacao and Amarula) or a Cerveza (tequila and San Miguel)? Strange, then, that we were only offered the food menu and a drinks list covering a few draught beers (Stella, Guinness), six red and white wines, and six bottled beers, including Desperados (tequila-flavoured beer, £3.50) – most of the mixed-age crowd were clearly drinking from this one too. All-day food goes from morning breakfasts (tortilla wrap with eggs, bacon and melted cheese, £6.50) to evening burgers (£7.50). Another odd thing: it's so dark in Visible that the menus are anything but. *Babies and children welcome (until 7pm). Music (DJ 9pm Fri; musicians 7pm Sun; free). Tables outdoors (4, pavement). TV (big screen, satellite).* **Map 10 Az5.**

Westbourne

101 Westbourne Park Villas, W2 5ED (7221 1332). Royal Oak or Westbourne Park tube. **Open** 5-11pm Mon; noon-11pm Tue-Sat; noon-10.30pm Sun. **Food served** 7-10pm Mon; 12.30-3pm, 7-10pm Tue-Thur; 7-9.30pm Fri; 12.30-3.30pm, 7-9.30pm Sat, Sun. **Credit** MC, V.

It's still trendy and still full of well-heeled Notting Hillbillies, who are now joined by City boys complete with flash cars parked out front. If this is the kind of clientele you want to rub shoulders with, you won't be disappointed; Friday and Saturday nights are the most popular times to see and be seen. The Westbourne's drinks list helps it retain credibility as a quality pub (Dortmunder Union, Leffe and Old Speckled Hen are on draught, there are good bottled Belgian beers, and the wine list is above average). Located within spitting distance of its well-respected neighbour the Cow, the Westbourne still offers fair modern European-style food and a true-to-form West London experience, which unfortunately can often include rude bar staff (the Westbourne's hired hands generally serve you with plenty of attitude but little charm). Forewarned is forearmed, though: the pub is worth visiting at least once, preferably on a quiet weekday when you can enjoy the best of what is has to offer. *Babies and children admitted. Games (board games). Tables outdoors (14, terrace).* **Map 10 B5.**

Central

Also in the area...

All Bar One 126-128 Notting Hill, W11 3QG (7313 9362).
Corney & Barrow 194 Kensington Park Road, W11 2ES (7221 5122).

Pimlico

Despite having one of this city's poshest postcodes, Pimlico isn't renowned for cutting-edge drinking dens. But you won't need a passport to gain access to some of the best cider (**Chimes**) or whisky (**Millbank Lounge**) in London.

Chimes

26 Churton Street, SW1V 2LP (7821 7456). Pimlico tube/Victoria tube/rail. **Open/food served** noon-2.30pm, 5.30-10.15pm Mon-Sat; noon-3pm, 5.30-10pm Sun. **Credit** AmEx, DC, MC, V.

Chimes sells its apple-based wares in half-pint cups or two-pint jugs, offering one of the better cider selections in London. Its friendly staff and brightly lit space provide an ideal backdrop for exploring the cider menu from draught and keg, while the traditional English restaurant menu offers good pâtés and pies to counteract the high alcohol content. Tour the counties with Worcestershire's Westons Old Rosie (a dry and cloudy scrumpy), then up the ante with an 8% extra dry Biddenden from Kent. Fruit wines also feature on the menu: try the medium-sweet Silver Birch alongside an apple crumble with lashings of cream. Bottled beers in the form of Beck's and Kronenbourg are also available.
Function room. No-smoking area. Restaurant. Tables outdoors (3, pavement).

Gallery

1 Lupus Street, SW1V 3AS (7821 7573). Pimlico tube. **Open** 9.45am-11pm Mon-Sat; 9.45am-10.30pm Sun. **Food served** 9.45am-2.30pm, 5.30-9.30pm Mon-Sat; 9.45am-2.30pm, 5.30-9pm Sun. **Credit** AmEx, DC, MC, V.

Close to both the underground and the Tate is (an original name, this) the Gallery. What may sound like a posh cocktail bar is in fact a neighbourhood pub with fabric upholstery, old carpets and an upstairs mezzanine containing a few prints and IKEA furniture – and euphemistically called the Gallery. The best advice would be to leave the art to the Tate and concentrate on the London Pride, Greene King IPA and Adnams, Hoegaarden or the Kronenbourg Blanc, all available on tap along with standard lagers. The El Coto Rioja looks a good buy at £14.95; there are four wines of each colour in the £12-£18 range. Music is turned down in favour of conversation and the Hoegaarden-battered cod and own-made pies stand out from the basic food menu.
Disabled: toilet. Function room. Games (fruit machine). No-smoking area. Tables outdoors (4, pavement). TV.

Jugged Hare

172 Vauxhall Bridge Road, SW1V 1DX (7828 1543). Victoria tube/rail. **Open** noon-11.30pm Mon-Sat; noon-11pm Sun. **Food served** noon-9.30pm daily. **Credit** AmEx, DC, MC, V.

In the grand old building of a four-columned ex-bank is this Fuller's Ale and Pie house, well stocked with the brewer's finest: London Pride, Jack Frost, Honey Dew and ESP fill the pumps, with specialities like 1845 available in bottles. Scrumpy Jack, Hoegaarden, Leffe and Grolsch are also available. You can also buy Fuller's fruit chutney behind the bar, 'refreshingly good with bangers and mash'. The colour scheme is traditional green and the cathedral-like ceilings are broken up by mezzanine-level seating. On the ground floor, old timers sup glasses of bitter underneath a huge painting of a street scene that depicts fabric-hatted old-timers pulling on flagons of ale and merchants plying their wares... outside the Jugged Hare. *Plus ça change.*
Games (fruit machine). No-smoking area. TV.

Millbank Lounge

City Inn Hotel, 30 John Islip Street, SW1P 4DD (7932 4700). Pimlico or Westminster tube. **Open** 11am-11pm Mon-Sat; noon-10.30pm Sun. **Food served** 11am-10pm Mon-Sat; noon-9.30pm Sun. **Credit** AmEx, DC, MC, V.

Jaded politicians feel particularly at home in this curious mix of travel lodge architecture and speciality whisky bar – jaded politicians being particularly experienced in both fields. The lounge in question is the first floor of the gloomily uninspiring City Inn Hotel; though efforts have been made to liven up the lounge with a shiny, bright-red bar and central thrust of red carpet and furniture, it is impossible to escape from the airport terminal style of the building. That said, people don't come for the architecture but for one of the best collections of whisky in London and an impressive cocktail list (£7.50-£8.50). The 'Whisky Library' was created from the top five choices of eight speciality *Whisky Magazine* journalists, and a 50ml glass will set you back anything from £6.50 for a Bowmore Dusk 50% to £120 for a Glenury Royal 1953 40%. The detailed menu gives a history of Scotch and a 'flights' option by which you can taste five different whiskies for either £15, £30 or £45, or three deluxe whiskies for £100.
Babies and children admitted (until 6pm). Disabled: toilet (hotel). Function room (hotel). Restaurant.

Morpeth Arms

58 Millbank, SW1P 4RW (7834 6442). Pimlico tube. **Open** 11am-11pm Mon-Sat; noon-10.30pm Sun. **Food served** noon-3pm Mon-Fri; noon-4pm Sat, Sun. **Credit** AmEx, DC, MC, V.

This traditional Young's outpost overlooks the river and is allegedly one of the most haunted pubs in London. It is also the place where real-life spooks and Bonds go for a winding-down Martini or pint after a hard day's spying at MI6 across the Thames. The pub is on the site of the former Millbank penitentiary, and there is said to be a vast network of tunnels frequented by the spectre of an escaped prisoner who never found his way out. There is plenty of history on the walls and good Young's ales in bottles and on tap. Wines range from £12 to £16, with an acceptable six of each colour. The first-floor lounge is no-smoking and has good views over the river.
Games (fruit machine, quiz machine). No piped music or jukebox. No-smoking area. Quiz (8.30pm Mon, fortnightly; £1). Tables outdoors (14, riverside terrace). TV.

Page

11 Warwick Way, SW1V 1QT (7834 3313/www.frontpagepubs.com). Pimlico tube/Victoria tube/rail. **Open** noon-11pm Mon-Sat; noon-10.30pm Sun. **Food served** noon-3pm, 6-10pm Mon-Fri; noon-4pm, 6-10pm Sat; noon-4pm, 6-9.30pm Sun. **Credit** AmEx, MC, V.

The pale-wood-lined walls of the Page are decorated with slightly shabby Rothko prints and curtains of a clashing blue that jars the senses. A high shelf of empty bottles of Bollinger tries to add glamour to the jaded surroundings, further cheapened by nylon Bombardier-sponsored

Central

England flags hanging from the ceiling. Though brightly lit and somewhat tired, there are good beers in typical Pimlico style: Hogs Back Brewery Traditional English Ale, Bombardier and London Pride mix with San Miguel, Guinness and Kronenbourg. Funnily enough, Bollinger is the house Champagne, £8.50 by the glass and £40 a reasonable price for a bottle. The Thai menu has been popular in recent years; the main curries are still good but the salads and deep-fried starters have lost their lustre – a bad omen for the upstairs restaurant. Thankfully, the staff are extremely friendly and helpful.
Restaurant (no smoking). Tables outdoors (4, pavement). TV (big screen, satellite).

White Swan
14 Vauxhall Bridge Road, SW1V 2SA (7821 8568). Pimlico tube. **Open** 11am-11pm Mon-Thur, Sat; 11am-midnight Fri; noon-10.30pm Sun. **Food served** noon-9pm daily. **Credit** AmEx, DC, MC, V.
Close to the river on the Vauxhall Bridge Road is this tourist-friendly speciality alehouse, something of a theme in Pimlico. The wood-ceilinged, low-beamed and elongated space is decorated with old pantry stoves, copper pots and brass tankards, and has the faint familiar smell of frying chips and an impressive row of draught ales. Young's Bitter, London Pride, Old Speckled Hen, Bombardier, Greene King IPA and Theakston XB sit comfortably in the pumps, with speciality bottles of Baltika, Brugs Beertje and Grimbergen also available. Seasonal drinks are a nice touch: in winter expect mulled wine and sloe gin. The food is unashamedly English, with several daily varieties of sausage and mash and home-baked pies.
Babies and children welcome (dining only). Games (fruit machine, quiz machine). No-smoking area. Tables outdoors (2, pavement). TV (big screen).

St James's

Historic overtones and classy bars can be found in St James's, where polished traditional pubs rub shoulders with swish hotel bars – **Duke's Hotel** reputedly serves the best Martini in London. Sadly, we were unable to visit upmarket lounge bar **Calma** (23 St James's Street, 7747 9380), as it was closed for refurbishment.

Aura
48-49 St James's Street, SW1A 1JT (7499 6655/ www.the-aura.com). Green Park tube. **Open** 11.30am-3am Tue-Sat (members only Fri); 9.30pm-1.30am Sun. **Food served** 7-9.30pm Tue-Sat. **Credit** AmEx, MC, V.
This upmarket bar-restaurant, in a basement round the corner from the Ritz, puts the fun back into drinking cocktails. The pseudo-erotic fanzine-style drinks menu, a creation in itself, points to someone making gentle mockery of the mixing craze while being handy behind the bar at the same time. At £9 a time, Footlongs feature a Pink Panties of Tanqueray Ten and pink grapefruit, strained through (you guessed it) pink panties. Yoghurt is used in the Berry Yoghurty of Stoli Red and Chambord, the Wiener mix of Bacardi 8, raspberries and lime sugar has been named I Ain't Gettin'On No Plane, Sucka, and Stoli Razberi mingled with various fruits is a Tuppence Licker. It may seem a little juvenile, but better by far than another bland, standard bar offering the same old Sex on the Beach. Pre-Castro Cuban rums sit behind the bar and Fidel's favourite Carlos Salmones cigars are available at £100 each – pricey,

Booze talking
Sun in Splendour

You are?
Simon Pac-Pomarnacki, bar manager of the Sun in Splendour, Notting Hill (*see p76*).
Your pub went no smoking last year. How's that going for you?
Really well. We haven't seen any downturn in trade. In fact early indications are a slight increase in trade on the same time last year. Portobello's a tourist area; a lot of our clientele expect not to be able to smoke.
Has it changed business in any way?
We are selling more food now. People can eat without having a person smoking next to them.
Have you had any problems with people insisting on being allowed to smoke?
No, anybody who's lit up by mistake has been really apologetic and put it out. Or they can go out in the beer garden at the back.
Do you smoke yourself?
No.
And your staff?
Half of them. Not being smokers isn't the reason why we went non-smoking. It doesn't bother me. When I go to pubs I expect smoking. It's the way I was brought up. But the ban is going to happen next year whether we like it or not and it's good to be ahead of the game.
You're owned by the pub company Mitchells & Butlers. Did they back you on the no-smoking policy?
One hundred per cent. The pub is owned by a large company but we are not a brand. It's not like O'Neill's [also owned by Mitchells & Butlers] or anything like that. As manager I get to decide the menus and the drinks. We get given a range and we can choose what we want. Look at the Prince Albert (*see p76*). It's completely different – you wouldn't know that we are the same company.

Central

but these boys know their sources. Twenty wines of each colour by the bottle from £19, three by the glass from £6 and bar food including tempura oysters (£9.50) and foie gras and duck terrine (£9).

Function room. Music (band/DJ 10.30pm Tue; DJs midnight Wed-Sun; both £20). TV. **Map 2 J7**.

Duke's Hotel

35 St James's Place, SW1A 1NY (7491 4840/www. dukeshotel.co.uk). Green Park tube. **Open** noon-11pm Mon-Sat; noon-10.30pm Sun. **Credit** AmEx, DC, MC, V.

What's the secret of a good Martini? The bar of the Duke's Hotel is internationally renowned for doing the best Martinis in London, and the secret seems to be this: use only Tanqueray or Bombay Sapphire gin and Cristal or Smirnoff Black vodka, freeze them for 24 hours, and serve in a cocktail glass that's been frozen before use. Little wonder the relaxing, comfy bar of this elegant, privately owned hotel is popular with American visitors. Other than Martinis, the drinks list offers Champagne and classic cocktails like Pimm's and Bloody Mary. The extraordinary cognac selection includes vintages dating back to the 19th century; some dated to mark particular birthdays or anniversaries are available for the aficionado.

Function room. No-smoking area. Restaurant. Tables outdoors (1, garden).

5th View

5th floor, Waterstone's, 203-206 Piccadilly, W1J 9HA (7851 2468). Piccadilly Circus tube. **Open** 10am-10pm Mon-Sat; noon-5pm Sun. **Credit** AmEx, MC, V.

The makeover of the Studio Lounge, the panoramic café of Waterstone's flagship bookshop on Piccadilly, does justice to its setting on the top floor of this once grand Simpson's

department store. Cocktails (£7.50) are carefully concocted – the own-made demerara syrup in the Mojito, the own-made vanilla sugar in the vanilla Daiquiri – and fired with high-grade spirits, Grey Goose Citron, Havana 3 and the like. Ten wines, all available by the glass and bottle, begin at £3.75/£14 for the house Italian Statua – a decent Chilean Palena merlot or South African Bolland chenin blanc are slightly pricier. Beers (Tiger, Asahi, Pilsner Urquell and Timothy Taylor Landlord, £3-£4) come by the bottle and snacks comprise superior salads and sandwiches (£8.50): smoked chicken, fennel and toasted pine-nut salad or Somerset brie, watercress and tomato chutney baguette. Grab a book and enjoy the view.

Babies and children admitted (until 5pm). Disabled: toilet. Function rooms. **Map 2 J7**.

Golden Lion

25 King Street, SW1Y 6QY (7925 0007). Green Park or Piccadilly Circus tube. **Open** 11am-11pm Mon-Fri; noon-6pm Sat. **Food served** noon-9pm Mon-Fri; noon-5pm Sat. **Credit** AmEx, MC, V.

'Famous for Nell Gwynne and the murder within' runs the snappy blurb of this Nicholson's establishment, referring to the ghost that stalks the 98 steps of the compact pub. In 1823 the tenant's wife Mary Burns kicked a servant to death, although she wouldn't have tried it on today's rather stern Slavic staff. A more pertinent historic detail might be the pub's position opposite the St James's Theatre – for nearly two centuries until its closure in 1957, the upstairs lounge was its bar, serving drinks to Oscar Wilde and Lillie Langtry. Even before that, this was a tavern (where didn't Nell Gwynne drink?), hinted at by the heraldic crests on the glazed windows. Today, somewhat disappointingly, it's a blokes' lunchtime and post-work retreat, serving

Ruby & Sequoia. *See p76.*

Adnams, Pride, Timothy Taylor Landlord and Young's, as well as standard pub meals. Worth popping in for a glimpse at history.
Function room. Games (quiz machine). Restaurant. Tables outdoors (3, pavement). TV. **Map 2 J8**.

Red Lion

23 Crown Passage, off Pall Mall, SW1Y 6PP (7930 4141). Green Park tube. **Open/food served** 11am-11pm Mon-Fri; 11.30am-11pm Sat. **Credit** MC, V.
A real regulars' haunt this, where middle-aged white-collar staff make little marks on their own wine bottle kept behind the bar, perhaps choosing one of the rare malts on a colleague's birthday. Announcing itself as 'London's Oldest Village Inn', the Red Lion is precisely that, with its low-ceilinged, wooden interior and pleasingly lived-in feel. Ornate plates and line drawings comprise the decor, along with a shelf lined with Glenfiddichs from the year dot. It's down a narrow passageway – inevitably, Nell Gwynne was another regular. Ales are still the main tipple here, Adnams the best of them, complemented by the kind of sandwiches (£3) you find at provincial functions – pork and stuffing, pâté and cucumber. Few use the upstairs lounge bar, preferring the conspiratorial banter of the bar ladies, straight out of central casting and on first-name terms with all.
Babies and children admitted (daytime). Function room. No piped music or jukebox. TV. **Map 2 J8**.

Red Lion

2 Duke of York Street, SW1Y 6JP (7321 0782). Piccadilly Circus tube. **Open** noon-11pm Mon-Sat. **Food served** noon-4pm Mon-Sat. **Credit** MC, V.
Just behind Piccadilly stands yet another of London's Red Lions, so renamed, like hundreds of others, in the early 1600s in honour of King James I. Many, such as this one, were later given an ornate Victorian makeover, hence the delicately carved woodwork and etched glass in this compact bar. Two tiny spaces, the front one just big enough to accommodate a couple of tables, are centrepieced by an island bar dispensing Old Speckled Hen, Timothy Taylor Landlord and Fuller's London Pride. Five wines of each colour come by the bottle, including the selection of the month, and the food is generic to the Red Lion's status as a Nicholson's pub – hot steak, sausage or ham and cheese sandwiches (£4.50-£5.50), jacket potatoes (£4.50) and traditional mains, ham and leek or steak and ale pies (£6.95).
Map 2 J7.

Rivoli at the Ritz

Ritz Hotel, 150 Piccadilly, W1J 9BR (7493 8181). Green Park tube. **Open** 11.30am-11pm Mon-Sat; noon-10.30pm Sun. **Food served** 11.30am-10.30pm daily. **Credit** AmEx, DC, MC, V.
You think the lobby is opulent? Wait until you turn it off. Little expense was spared by the Barclay Brothers over the course of an eight-year renovation programme at the Ritz; nowhere is their financial outlay more ostentatiously displayed than the art deco Rivoli Bar, which reopened in 2001 after a spell in the doldrums. Five years later, its gold and glass fittings still dazzle, but the leopard-print armchairs and the presence of a soundtrack better suited to a provincial hair salon cheapen the atmosphere. The cocktails needed to be perfect to justify their price tags, and they weren't: a Red Hot Mexican (£13) was interesting at best, while the Perfect Manhattan (£15) was curiously flat. You, and they, could do better.
Babies and children admitted (lounge area). Disabled: toilet. Dress: jacket, no jeans or trainers. **Map 2 J8**.

Also in the area...

Balls Brothers 20 St James's Street, SW1A 1ES (7321 0882).
Davy's at St James Crown Passage, Pall Mall, SW1Y 6QY (7839 8831).
Tapster (Davy's) 3 Brewers Green, Buckingham Gate, SW1H 0RH (7222 0561).

Soho

This is bar central for London. As well as a host of gay haunts around the Old Compton Street–Wardour Street junction, you'll find classic old-stagers **Coach & Horses** and **French House**, sleek new **Polka** and lovely bar-diner **Boulevard**. Now that karaoke is fashionable again – apparently – embrace **Lucky Voice** (*see Clubs*), or head to all-new **Kabaret Prophecy** (*see Clubs*) for impossible levels of swank.

Admiral Duncan

54 Old Compton Street, W1V 5PA (7437 5300). Leicester Square or Piccadilly Circus tube. **Open** noon-11pm Mon-Thur; noon-midnight Fri, Sat; noon-10.30pm Sun. **Credit** MC, V.
It may be bright pink and slap in the middle of Old Compton Street, but the Admiral Duncan has a more mature, mixed attitude than the get-off-our-faces-and-fuck attitude of other gay venues in the immediate vicinity. It always has had – and not only because of the wreath wrapped over the eternal Christmas light in the entrance with the words: 'The Admiral Duncan will always remember our friends…'. The pub, savagely bombed by a homophobic maniac in April 1999, came out of the atrocity with dignity and its head held high. The AD always brought an older, more mixed crowd together, then and now. And drinking is just as sacrosanct as anywhere else. A score of cocktails are £4 a throw, £5.50 for two and, some of them at least, £8.50 by the pitcher. Pints of Foster's, John Smith's and Stella are quietly supped during the quieter daytimes.
Games (fruit machines, quiz machine). **Map 7 K6**.

Ain't Nothin' But? The Blues Bar

20 Kingly Street, W1B 5PZ (7287 0514/www.aint nothinbut.co.uk). Oxford Circus or Piccadilly Circus tube. **Open** 6pm-1am Mon-Wed; 6pm-2am Thur; noon-3am Fri, Sat; 7.30pm-midnight Sun. **Credit** MC, V.
Suitably scuffed and sombre, Soho's (London's? England's?) only dedicated blues bar is more than just an enthusiasts' rendezvous. Sure, there's music every night from combos such as the Incredible Blues Puppies, Dr Blues & the Prescriptions and Rollo Markee & the Tailshakers, but this is also a characterful space for an early evening Adnams, Red Stripe or Murphy's, hidden from the crowds of Regent Street and the clamour of Soho. A narrow bar is plastered in memorabilia of great bluesmen – bill posters, sheet music and the original Decca 78 by Georgia White of the bar name in question – while a saloon-style back area accommodates a few benches and a Ludwig drum kit. The painted wall of fame around the tiny basement is a nice touch – as are the daily themed food offerings such as Louisiana beef chilli (£6.95).
Music (live blues/jazz nightly; open mic 2pm Sat). **Map 2 J6**.

Central

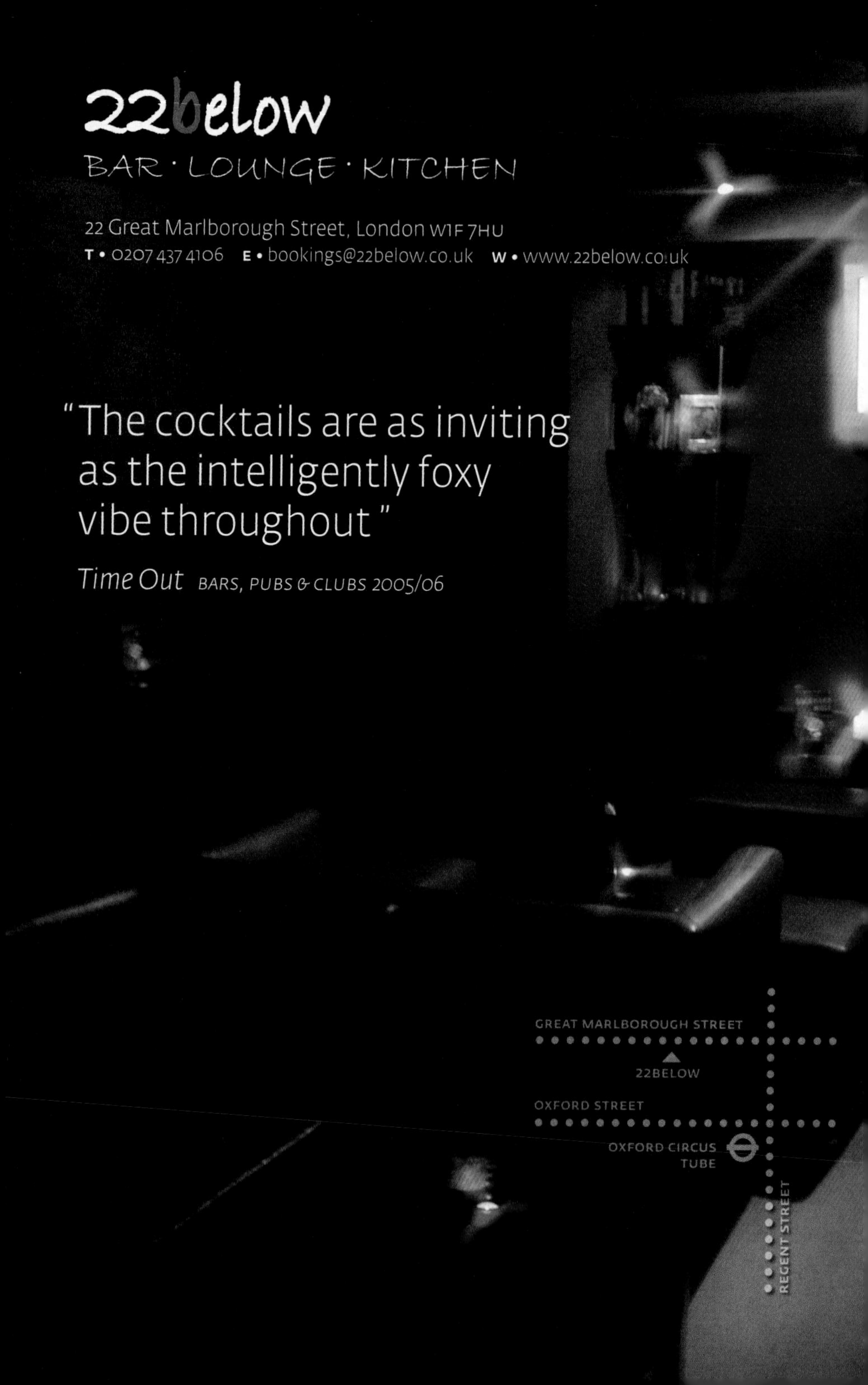

22below

BAR · LOUNGE · KITCHEN

22 Great Marlborough Street, London W1F 7HU
T • 0207 437 4106   E • bookings@22below.co.uk   W • www.22below.co.uk

" The cocktails are as inviting
as the intelligently foxy
vibe throughout "

Time Out   BARS, *PUBS & CLUBS* 2005/06

GREAT MARLBOROUGH STREET

22BELOW

OXFORD STREET

OXFORD CIRCUS
TUBE

REGENT STREET

Akbar

*77 Dean Street, W1D 3SH (7437 2525/www.redfort.
co.uk/akbar). Leicester Square, Piccadilly Circus or
Tottenham Court Road tube.* **Open** 5pm-1am Mon-Sat.
Food served 5-11pm Mon-Thur; 5-11.30pm Fri, Sat.
Happy hour 5-6pm Mon-Sat. **Credit** AmEx, MC, V.
It is no coincidence that this understated but stylish basement cocktail bar should be under one of London's leading
Indian restaurants, the Red Fort – for spices, herbs and fragrances inform the inventive drinks and snacks here. There
are DJs too, and an exotic ambience amid the low-lit alcoves
of Rajasthani sandstone, but most come here for the lemongrass-infused Stoli in the Zafroon Martinis (£7.50) or basil-
infused Bombay Sapphire gin (and date-macerated Havana
3) in the Jahangir long drink (£7). Suitably exquisite bar
snacks – goolar kebabs (£5) of minced lamb with fresh
orange rind, pocha hera jhinga (£7), thinly crisp marinated prawns – can be sampled communally with an Akbar
platter (£15) of assorted spicy bites. Fresh fruit lassis
(mango and ginger, mango and orange, £4.95) and
Kingfisher beer (£3.95) add a final, authentic touch.
*Bar available for hire. Disabled: toilet. Music (DJs 8pm
Thur-Sat; free). Restaurant. TV (big screen).* **Map 7 K6**.

Alphabet

*61-63 Beak Street, W1F 9SS (7439 2190/www.
alphabetbar.com). Oxford Circus tube.* **Open** noon-
11pm Mon-Fri; 5-11pm Sat. **Food served** noon-4pm,
5-9pm Mon-Fri; 5-9pm Sat. **Credit** AmEx, MC, V.
A mainstay on the Soho boho bar circuit, Alphabet suffers
from lack of competition these days. It doesn't do much
wrong, we just know its two floors too well. A wide street-
level dining area is bookended by a bar counter and skylight at one end and a comfy sofa and picture window at
the other; the walls feature regularly changing art for sale.
Downstairs is characterised by fire-sale furniture, a graf-
fitied wall in front of the toilets and the A-Z street pattern
of Soho on the floor. Prime cocktails are the Sparklers
(£7.50), a Paramour of Chambord and Champagne made
with fresh raspberries and blackberries, and the pear
Bellini with pear purée and Eau de Vie de Poire William;
Daiquiris feature spiced pear, pineapple and 'whatever we
have from today's market'. Wines are well chosen, eight of
each colour by the bottle (Argentine Catena Agrelo
chardonnay, Australian Glenguin Stonybroke shiraz, both
£25.50), three by the glass (Minini pinot grigio, £6.10;
South African Graham Beck merlot, £5.90). Beers are bottled and global – Negra Modelo, Cruzcampo – while food
(char-grilled sirloin, £7.70; papaya and duck salad, £7.70)
attracts a ravenous lunchtime and post-work crowd.
*Babies and children admitted (until 5pm). Music (DJs
7.30pm Thur-Sat; free).* **Map 2 J6**.

Amber

*6 Poland Street, W1F 8PS (7734 3094/www.amber
bar.com). Oxford Circus or Piccadilly Circus tube.*
Open noon-1am Mon-Sat. **Food served** noon-
midnight Mon-Sat. **Credit** AmEx, MC, V.
Despite touches of the titular bright resin, colour schem-
ing the decor and embedded in the bar stools, Amber is a
bar of Latin character. In the same family as Alphabet, it
attracts a younger party crowd, accommodated over two
floors. Squeezed in would be more apt for the upper level,
composed of small booths leading to a narrow bar counter.
The choice it offers, though, is extensive. Four dozen cocktails (£6-£7.50) are concocted with quality ingredients such
as Ketel One Citron in the Cosmopolitan and Chivas Regal
in an Old Fashioned. Agavero tequila informs an Agave

Julep muddled with mint and ginger, and a Dirty Sanchez
with Chambord and lime. Wines are similarly South
American or Spanish, ranging from a Casa de Piedra
(£4.50/£13.50) to a Colina Negra cabernet sauvignon
(£23.10), both from Chile. Tapas (boquerones, calamares a
la plancha), mains (costillas de cerdo, brochetas) and beers
(Negra Modelo, Pacifico) have equal Latin allure.
*Function room. Music (DJs 8pm Thur-Sat; free).
Restaurant. Tables outdoors (2, pavement).* **Map 2 J6**.

Argyll Arms

*18 Argyll Street, W1F 7TP (7734 6117). Oxford Circus
tube.* **Open** 11am-11pm Mon-Sat; noon-10.30pm Sun.
Food served 11am-10pm Mon-Sat; noon-9pm Sun.
Credit AmEx, MC, V.
Snug and Oxford Circus may seem incongruous bed-
fellows, but this Grade II listed building slap by one of the
world's busiest pedestrian intersections is the epitome of
Victorian snug pub design. A remodel in mahogany and
etched glass by Robert Sawyer from a pub of the same
name built in the mid 18th century, the Argyll Arms comprises a maze of beautifully carved snugs, designed to separate the unsavoury from the upstanding of fin-de-siècle
society. It's a Nicholson's pub, so the range of beers
(Fuller's London Pride, Adnams) and dinners (toad-in-the-
hole, steak and ale pies) is traditional, keeping the frantic
turnover of locals and tourists happy. Table service at the
equally elegant Palladium Bar upstairs.
*Babies and children admitted (restaurant). Games (fruit
machines). No-smoking area (upstairs bar). Restaurant
(available for hire). Tables outdoors (5, pavement).*
Map 1 J6.

Bar Chocolate

*27 D'Arblay Street, W1F 8EN (7287 2823/www.bar
choc.co.uk). Oxford Circus or Tottenham Court Road
tube.* **Open/food served** 10am-11pm Mon-Sat; noon-
10.30pm Sun. **Credit** MC, V.
Food is now the main ingredient of this former bohemian
hangout. Large placemat menus cover each of the neat
three-legged tables set on an equally pristine tiled floor.
They propose continental delights like a Meze Board
(£9.60), goat's cheese and honey salad (£9) and Tuscan bean
hotpot (£9), and breakfasts all-day (£6), vegetarian (£6) or
served in a focaccia (£5.80). Sohoites still come in to read
battered paperbacks, but their choice of cocktails is limited to a handful of Martinis (£7), long (£7) and short drinks
(£6.50), among which are the signature Bar Chocolate Iced
Tea (Stoli Vanilla, Kahlua and silver tequila) and Bar
Chocolate Martini (Stoli Vanilla with crème de cacao). Wines
come five of each colour by the bottle and glass, from a standard pinot grigio (£3.20/£12) to a Chilean Santa Puerta
sauvignon blanc (£4.40/£17.50), and beer comes out of a silver tap, nothing with labels. Chocolate is still a handy bar
for a rendezvous, but in need of a stiff drink.
*Babies and children admitted (until 6pm). Tables
outdoors (3, pavement).* **Map 1 J6**.

Barcode

*3-4 Archer Street, W1D 7AP (7734 3342/www.bar-
code.co.uk). Leicester Square or Piccadilly Circus tube.*
Open 4pm-1am Mon-Sat; 4-10.30pm Sun. **Happy hour**
4-7pm daily. **Admission** £4 after 11pm Fri, Sat.
Credit MC, V.
Down a dark Soho side street, this two-floor party bar
bristles with action. Muscle boys, steamers, cruisers and
boozers are accommodated with a full programme of entertainment every night of the week, much of it dangerously

Central

discounted drinkwise. Highlights include Thursday night's Homosocial, aka 'Tonker Lite's Thursday Meat Packers' Beer Bust' – we're sure you get the picture – and the downstairs space also hosts some seriously pumping DJ nights at weekends. Upstairs, at street level, two walls are lined with flat-screen computers for internet chat, the other fitted with a bar counter dispensing pints of Kronenbourg, Strongbow, John Smith's and Foster's, bottles of Budvar, Beck's and Corona, and that usual colourful range of alcopops. Wine is either red or white, but an encyclopaedic list of shooters leaves no doubt as to what's on offer here. *Comedy (8pm Tue; £5-£7). Music (DJs 9pm-1am Mon, Wed-Sat).* **Map 7 K6.**

Bar Soho

23-25 Old Compton Street, W1D 5JQ (7439 0439/ www.sohoclubsandbars.com). Leicester Square tube. **Open/food served** noon-1am Mon-Thur; noon-3am Fri, Sat; noon-12.30am Sun. **Admission** £3 after 11pm Mon-Thur; £5 after 9.30pm (£8 for men after 11pm) Fri, Sat. **Credit** AmEx, DC, MC, V.
Not exactly classy, but working at it. Despite a new food and drink menu, starched white tablecloths in one corner and BBC News 24 on the huge TV screen, the Bar Soho is still essentially a party bar and pick-up joint. How could it not be, slap in the middle of Old Compton Street? What the hell does it need newscasters for? The dinky drinks menu is divided into cocktails Classic and New (£7-£7.50), 20 of each. News include a Midori-laced Envy, a Jägermeister-strengthened Jaegerrinha and one described as 'Soho in a cocktail', a Charlie Chaplin. (Wasn't he from Lambeth? In any case, it involves sloe gin.) Wines now extend to an Australian Fifth Leg semillon-sauvignon-chardonnay (£19.50), standard beers come in half-measures (£2.10) or two-pint pitchers (£6.50) and there are late-night eats (pizzas, platters) to dine on à deux in those dark, candlelit recesses.
Babies and children welcome. Function room. Music (DJs 9.30pm nightly). Tables outdoors (4, pavement). TV (big screen, satellite). **Map 7 K6.**

Boulevard Bar & Dining Room

57-59 Old Compton Street, W1D 5HP (7287 0770/ www.boulevardsoho.com). Leicester Square tube. **Open** 11am-1am Mon-Sat; noon-midnight Sun. **Food served** 11am-11pm Mon-Tue, Sun; 11am-midnight Wed-Sat. **Credit** AmEx, MC, V.
Old Compton Street's first real contemporary bar-diner, this one a sister to twins located in Covent Garden. The Boulevard Brasserie and the Boulevard Deli concentrate on alfresco *déjeuners* and artisan loaves – the Bb&dr is cocktail-based. In a street awash with alcopops and overpriced cappuccino, this is no bad thing. At prices reasonably set between £6 and £7, they come in Martini, Chimney, Hi Ball, Flute and Rock varieties, with inventive inclusions such as the Honey and Ginger Martini with Ketel One Citron and Krupnik vodkas; a French Alps with Stoli Razberi, Chambord and double cream; and a Lemon Grass and Ginger Mojito with freshly muddled lemongrass, root ginger and Havana Club 3. From a veritable atlas of wines calibrated for the fine UK-French dining in the quiet back room, five of each colour are available by the glass, from a standard Bergerie de la Bastide VdP (£4.25) to a decent £9 Bordeaux or Henri Bourgeois Sancerre. All takes place in a neat, contemporary space, parcelled off into intimate spaces.
Babies and children admitted (if dining). Music (DJs 8pm Fri, Sat; free). Restaurant. Tables outdoors (3, pavement). **Map 7 K6.**

Café Bohème

13 Old Compton Street, W1D 5JQ (7734 0623/www. cafeboheme.co.uk). Tottenham Court Road tube. **Open** 8am-3am Mon-Sat; 8am-10.30pm Sun. **Food served** 8am-2.30am Mon-Sat; 8am-10pm Sun. **Credit** AmEx, DC, MC, V.
French down to its starched white shirt and black waistcoat, the Bohème is both a *café du coin* and *resto de choix*. The café boasts a whole mess of marvellous Martinis (the French version uses Grey Goose vodka) and Mules (the French one with Martell, the Bohemian one with La Fée absinthe) in the £7 range, as well as wine, wine and more wine. Twenty French varieties of each colour start from a humble £12.95 VdP and run to a Domaine Reverdy Sancerre at £32.50 and a Gigondas Château de Trignon at £36.70; five types come by the glass, two by the half-bottle. There are also varieties from Spain, Italy and the New World. Food, though, is left entirely to the French: Basque fish soup (£5) and foie gras, glazed apple and Rossini sauce (£7.50) among the starters, mains of confit duck, choucroûte and bacon lardons (£12) or boeuf bourguignon (£9.75).
Babies and children admitted (before 7pm). Function room. Music (jazz 4-6pm Thur, Sun; free). Restaurant. Tables outdoors (9, pavement). **Map 7 K6.**

Candy Bar

4 Carlisle Street, W1D 3BJ (7494 4041/www.thecandy bar.co.uk). Tottenham Court Road tube. **Open** 5-11.30pm Mon-Thur; 5pm-2am Fri, Sat; 5-11pm Sun. **Happy hour** 5-7pm daily. **Credit** AmEx, DC, MC, V.
London's long-established lesbian bar is still going strong after a decade. Now with a licence to strip – pole-dancing and striptease shows three nights of the week, girls! – the Candy Bar is sweeter than ever. Its pink façade tucked away in a side street off the Charing Cross Road, the Candy Bar is surprisingly accommodating within. Three storeys comprise an upstairs lounge bar, a long main bar at street level and a sweaty basement dance space. Entry policy is regulated, however – lesbian or bisexual women, and men only if gay and accompanied. Drinks involve strong shots and cocktails, halves of Red Stripe, accompanied by snacks of ciabatta toasties, fuel before the furious interaction downstairs.
Entertainment (strip night 8.30-11.30pm Tue, Thur; 8.30pm-2am Sat; £3-£6; karaoke 9pm Wed; free). Music (DJs 9pm nightly; £5 Fri; £6 Sat). **Map 7 K6.**

Clachan

34 Kingly Street, W1B 5QH (7494 0834). Oxford Circus tube. **Open** 11am-11pm Mon-Sat; noon-10.30pm Sun. **Food served** noon-10pm daily. **Credit** (over £10) AmEx, MC, V.
By the goods entrance for Liberty's, a store it was once part of, the Clachan is one of the classier links in the Nicholson chain of trad pubs. Ale-conscious to a tee – on this visit the Hop Backs were unavailable as the pipes were being cleaned – the Clachan accommodates guest ales (Odyssey, for example) to complement Timothy Taylor Landlord, Shepherd Neame Spitfire and Fuller's London Pride. Sausages (Oxford, Lincolnshire, Pork & Guinness) make appearances on a weekly basis. Chaps and their female colleagues comprise the clientele, interspersed with occasional tourists delighted to find a traditional wooden pub interior. It's divided into two seating areas either side of the bar, with a raised back alcove and upstairs lounge with open fire providing more comfort and privacy.
Function room. Games (fruit machine). Restaurant (no smoking). **Map 2 J6.**

10 West. *See p76.*

Coach & Horses

29 Greek Street, W1D 5DH (7437 5920). Leicester Square or Piccadilly Circus tube. **Open** 11am-11pm Mon-Sat; noon-10.30pm Sun. **Happy hour** 11am-4pm Mon-Fri, Sun. **Credit** AmEx, MC, V.

Panic on the streets of Soho. In 2005 landlord Norman Balon, self-proclaimed rudest landlord in the West End (as if that were something to boast about), announced he was selling up. It made *The Times* and Channel 4 news, and gave half the old soaks at the bar a near heart attack (when they were all hoping to go from cirrhosis of the liver). Not to worry, the pub is back off the market and punters can contentedly continue to fork out £3.20 for a pint of London Pride that can be had over the road for £2.40. The sandwiches remain £1 all day and several of the bar staff continue to fail to understand requests made in English, but that's all part of the charm. Despite being seemingly time-locked in late 1950s London, when bon mots were exchanged for doubles, the Coach has always been the most cosmopolitan of places. It was a refuge for outcasts, misfits and strays long before neighbouring Old Compton Street flew its first rainbow flag. And although he won't thank us for telling you this, Norman's not half as bad as he seems. God bless him and all who sail in him.

No piped music or jukebox. TV. **Map 7 K6**.

Comptons of Soho

51-53 Old Compton Street, W1D 6HJ (7479 7961/ www.comptons-of-soho.co.uk). Leicester Square or Piccadilly Circus tube. **Open** noon-11pm Mon-Sat; noon-10.30pm Sun. **Happy hour** 7-11pm Mon. **Credit** AmEx, MC, V.

The historic, traditional pub frontage on occasionally gaudy Old Compton Street is no mere façade. Comptons, soon to celebrate 20 years since coming out as a gay bar, has history in spades. For 200 years, first as the Swiss Hotel then the Swiss Tavern, it accommodated any number of famous guests – perhaps Wagner, certainly Dylan Thomas – before housing a fringe theatre. Today it's one of Soho's most prominent gay pubs, recently opening the more comfortable and slightly less cruisy Soho Club Lounge upstairs. Without the thudding music or fug of cigarette smoke (nuts and olives, boys!) it doesn't give in to hedonism so earnestly as the spacious downstairs interzone. You can, all the same, gaze at the guys from its picture windows. The saloon at street level is still an amusement arcade of eye-contact games and warm social interaction fuelled by Beck's, Breezers and cheap drinks promotions.

Games (fruit machines, pool table). Music (DJs 8-11pm Mon, Fri, Sat; free). No-smoking area. TV (big screen, satellite). **Map 7 K6**.

Couch

97-99 Dean Street, W1D 3TE (7287 0150/www. massivepub.com). Tottenham Court Road tube. **Open** 11am-11pm Mon-Fri; noon-10.30pm Sun. **Food served** 11am-9pm Mon-Fri; noon-9pm Sat, Sun. **Credit** AmEx, MC, V.

Almost comically unhip – it's the kind of bar that writes crap messages outside ('Always distrust camels – they can go for seven days without a drink'), the Couch is nonetheless immensely popular: just try to find one of its dozen or so tables without a reserved sign on a Thursday or Friday evening. Couples, foursomes and solitary *Standard* readers come for the quality of food and drink, and a waited table in a gastrobar, as opposed to a post-work pub crush. Here you find your table or couch (one of three) and peruse a wine list of ten reds, ten whites, six each by the glass.

Having selected Chilean Tierra Antica cabernet sauvignon (£4/£5.30/£15) or Echeverria chardonnay (£4.60/£6.20/ £17.20), you choose between a vegetarian (£13) or meat (£13.50) platter, or a special of pan-fried cod fillet with crispy bacon on brown rice and lime (£9.50). The ten cocktails (£7) – Rude Cosmopolitan, Espressitini and Orange Mojito – are of equal quality.

Music (DJs 8-11pm Sat; free). **Map 7 K6**.

Courthouse Hotel

19-21 Great Marlborough Street, W1F 7HL (7297 5555). Oxford Circus tube. **Open/food served** 11am-12.30am Mon-Sat; 11am-11pm Sun. **Credit** AmEx, DC, MC, V.

At first glance, this upmarket off-Regent Street Kempinski Hotel wouldn't seem in the least notorious, but the name gives it away. This was the magistrates' court that tried Oscar Wilde, Christine Keeler and Mick Jagger – you can even hire one of three now superbly decorated cells, icebucket urinal and all. The rest of the spacious bar area behind the lobby is equally immaculately furnished with stone, black slate and classy lighting. A long bar counter at the back dispenses superior £8.50 cocktails, a 12.5% charge levied for suitably polite service. Martinis come in blueberry, blackberry, raspberry or strawberry flavours, or a mix of all four – a freedom of choice extended to the Classic Martini (your brand of gin or vodka) and Old Fashioned (any whisky you fancy). Of the Specials, Behind Bars boasts Xanté pear cognac, cream and garnish, while a Parisienne contains fresh grapes, honey, Drambuie and fresh lime. It all makes slopping out seem worthwhile.

Babies and children welcome. Disabled: toilet. Function rooms. Restaurants. TV (satellite). **Map 1 J6**.

Crobar

17 Manette Street, W1D 4AS (7439 0831/www. crobar.co.uk). Tottenham Court Road tube. **Open** 1pm-3am Mon-Sat. **Happy hour** 1-9pm Mon-Sat. **Credit** MC, V.

In a low-ceilinged cabin-like setting not unlike Beavis and Butthead's bedroom, this unreconstructed rock bar round the corner from the Borderline and the Astoria provides a suitable pre-gig fuel stop. Bourbons are a speciality, breeds of Wild Turkey (1855 Reserve, Russell's Reserve, Kentucky Spirit) and JD (Single Barrel, Green Label) complementing labels you couldn't make up: Elmer T Lee, Bulleit Frontier Whiskey and the like. Beers are standard and by the bottle, shooters and cocktails (Lost Bikini, Demon Cleaner) come by the bucket or glass. Thereafter friendly banter turns into bizarre and long-winded anecdotes, such as the one on this particular night about a guy setting his hair on fire in Finland. Sample toilet graffiti: 'Your mother is my dad'. All good, clean fun.

Jukebox. **Map 7 K6**.

Crown & Two Chairmen

31 Dean Street, W1D 3SB (7437 8192). Tottenham Court Road tube. **Open** noon-11pm Mon-Sat. **Food served** noon-7pm Mon-Fri. **Credit** AmEx, MC, V.

'How Low Can We Go?' is the question this traditional corner pub asks as it attempts to attract passing punters by undercutting the wealth of competition deep in Soho. Pints of Carlsberg just shy of the two-pound barrier, Foster's, Carling and Amstel at just over £2, cheap wines, standard, large and king-size lunches at knockdown prices – value is king and royal history is out the window. The name, legend has it, comes from Queen Anne's chairmen, who would deposit her across the road to have her portrait painted

then nip in for a crafty pint. Today's entertainment is provided by all-day Sky Sports, games machines and gawping at the constant pedestrian traffic passing this busy intersection of Bateman and Dean streets.
Comedy (8pm Fri; £10). Function room. Games (fruit machine, golf machine, quiz machine). TV (satellite). **Map 7 K6.**

Dog & Duck
18 Bateman Street, W1D 3AJ (7494 0697). Tottenham Court Road tube. **Open** noon-11pm Mon-Sat; noon-10.30pm Sun. **Food served** noon-9pm daily. **Credit** AmEx, MC, V.
Soho has always been a hunting ground, but back in the day it was actual hounds and hares – hence this pub, originally built in 1734. Still as traditional as it comes, the current carved-wood and glazed-tile appearance dates from its fin-de-siècle makeover. Illustrious past guests include Orwell, who gives his name to the wine bar upstairs. Downstairs, in the tiny bar area and cosy back room, ale rules. Taps of beer from Adnams, Timothy Taylor and Cornish brewer Skinner's line the compact bar counter, where you can also order main dishes such as a half-pound Aberdeen Angus burger or steak and ale pie. It's in the Nicholson stable, so puddings are equally time-honoured, such as chocolate fudge cake and fruit crumbles.
Function room. No-smoking area. Restaurant. **Map 7 K6.**

Edge
11 Soho Square, W1D 3QE (7439 1313/www.edge soho.co.uk). Tottenham Court Road tube. **Open/food served** noon-1am Mon-Sat; noon-11.30pm Sun. **Credit** AmEx, MC, V.
Occupying a strategic corner of Soho Square, the Edge is a continental lunch venue by day and a party (mainly gay) hangout by night. Lunch, taken outside or in the smallish street-level space, comprises tapas (tempura prawns, onion bhajis, any four for £12), daily specials (chicken tikka, pastas, £5), jackets (£3.50) and standard mains (£5.50-£6) such as cod and chips and Edge chicken fillets. Draught Carlsberg, Cobra, standard wines, smoothies and Red Bull-dominated cocktails provide liquid accompaniment. The after-dark afterlife upstairs is hinted at with tacky pop videos on a large screen in the lounge area and flyers in gaudy colours showing phallic bananas. Once the sun sets and punters leave the slops of their convivial pavement pints, the piano bar and dance club kicks off upstairs.
Disabled: toilet. Function rooms. Music (pianist 9pm-midnight Tue-Thur; DJs 9pm Thur-Sun; free). Tables outdoors (6, pavement). TV (big screen, satellite). **Map 7 K6.**

Endurance
90 Berwick Street, W1F 0QB (7437 2944). Leicester Square, Oxford Circus or Tottenham Court Road tube. **Open** noon-11pm Mon-Thur; noon-midnight Fri, Sat; noon-10.30pm Sun. **Food served** 12.30-4pm Mon-Sat; 12.30-4.30pm Sun. **Credit** AmEx, MC, V.
Musos and Sohoites of all stripes gather around the 100-tune jukebox of this Berwick Street market landmark. Bar-like in appearance, bear-like in design with its ursine sign and mounted taxidermy, the Endurance acts as the local pub, the central, octagonal bar counter awash with gossip and chat-up lines. It's gastro too, with superior sea bass and game dishes in the £8-£10 range, best enjoyed at the handful of outside tables. After lunch, though, it's drink only, pints of Pride, Guinness or Deuchars IPA or half a dozen wines of each colour, including an Australian shiraz

(£16.95) and New Zealand sauvignon (£17.50). The black banquettes surrounding the simple interior fill with punters comparing vinyl bargains from the many nearby record stores, chucking the occasional pound coin into the machine for five classic songs. Timeless, really.
Babies and children admitted (before 5pm). Games (darts). Jukebox. Tables outdoors (8, garden). **Map 2 J6.**

Floridita
100 Wardour Street, W1F 0TN (7314 4000/www. floridalondon.com). Tottenham Court Road tube. **Open/food served** 5.30pm-2am Mon-Wed; 5.30pm-3am Thur-Sat. **Admission** £10 after 10pm Thur-Sat. **Credit** AmEx, DC, MC, V.
Constante was the bartender who ran Havana's El Floridita of Hemingway lore. London's Floridita is an equally upscale operation – contemporary restaurant upstairs, fashionable nightspot Bar Constante below – that recreates the glitz and high-level gluttony of those pre-Castro days. Bar Constante concocts faithful renditions of Daiquiris (£6.50-£7.50) with Havana Club Añejo Blanco, limes and sodas, some Maraschino here, some orange Curaçao there, the New Cuban counterparts involving pomegranate, passion fruit and fig purée. Martinis (£13-£25) are made with large measures of Grey Goose, Tanqueray Ten and, fashionably, Kauffman vodka. All are impeccably mixed at an extensive bar counter that runs the length of an expansive basement space sparkling with decorative bling. The food is fabulous – tiny bar snacks (£1.50-£3) of octopus and ceviche, red snapper or warm Brazilian cheesebreads, serious and authentic mains of charcoal-grilled lobsters (half £19, whole £35). Cuban musicians and professional dancers create post-midnight entertainment, and there's an extensive cigar menu.
Cocktail-tasting (monthly, check website for details). Disabled: toilet. Function room. Music (DJ/band 8pm nightly). Restaurant. **Map 7 K6.**

Freedom
66 Wardour Street, W1F 0TA (7734 0071). Leicester Square or Piccadilly Circus tube. **Open** 5pm-3am Mon-Sat; 5-11.30pm Sun. **Food served** 5pm-2am Mon-Sat; 5-9.30pm Sun. **Admission** £5 after 10pm Fri, Sat. **Credit** MC, V.
A gaudy green neon sign shows the way to all kinds of drunken naughtiness at this two-level gay-straight party joint where Wardour, Brewer and Old Compton streets meet. Once exclusive and considerably louche, Freedom can still shake a tailfeather, mainly in a basement DJ bar that's only open half the week. At street level, zebra-striped decor, frilly covers on bar stools and peardrop chandeliers hint at a colourful past. You can get silly during the three happy hours: all cocktails are £5, Bombay Sapphire gin, Ketel One and Zubrowka vodkas giving va-va-voom to the Martinis, Classic and Champagne Cocktails, and Freedom Specialities (otherwise £7-£8). The wines aren't shabby either (Vaucher Père Chablis, £23.90; Bodegas Breton Rioja Crianza, £17.90). Class be damned though, it still gets cruisy – just check one of the many mirrors next time.
Disabled: toilet. Function room. Music (DJs 10.30pm Wed-Sat). **Map 7 K6.**

French House
49 Dean Street, W1D 5BG (7437 2799). Leicester Square or Piccadilly Circus tube. **Open** noon-11pm Mon-Sat; noon-10.30pm Sun. **Food served** *Bar* noon-3pm Mon-Sat. *Restaurant* noon-3pm, 5.30-11pm Mon-Sat. **Credit** AmEx, DC, MC, V.

Central

Freedom. *See p87.*

A little forced these days, the French House. John Claridge's mounted black-and-white photographs of famous guests 'provide a living link with Soho's bohemian past'; Charles de Gaulle's framed declaration, defiantly declaring 'Vive La France', has its English rendition signed off with 'Vive Le French'; and the wine of the week was South African. The French House began between the wars; owner Victor Berlemont invited cabaret stars such as Maurice Chevalier here, creating a French connection strengthened when De Gaulle and his Free French had their office upstairs – a photo from that time still stands behind the bar. Under Victor's son Gaston, a wild post-war era saw Brendan Behan, Dylan Thomas, Francis Bacon and other Olympian drinkers enjoy and endure legendary sessions within its four small walls. Today, with a restaurant upstairs and French House lager on tap, the nearest you'll get is to order up a bottle of Breton cider and set yourself up at the bare table of the back alcove.
Restaurant. **Map 7 K6**.

Intrepid Fox

99 Wardour Street, W1F 0UF (7494 0827). Leicester Square tube. **Open** noon-11pm Mon-Thur; noon-11.30pm Fri, Sat; 3-10.30pm Sun. **No credit cards.**
Why are Goths so ludicrous? Is it the fact that they waste the picture window of a perfectly good and traditional (1784, according to the stone carving outside) public house by covering it with a bloody big parachute? Is it because they wear their own uniform but insist 'no ties, no football shirts' at the door? Is it the skulls, the witches, the Gothic typography of the band names on the gig posters? The Intrepid Fox is how uninitiated foreigners imagine London punk pubs to be, which is why it is full of Spaniards and Swedes and Danes too clueless to find anywhere else. They seem to enjoy it, though, which is more than you can say for the sullen, pierced bar staff.
Comedy (7.30pm Wed; £3). Function room. Games (pool table). Music (DJs 7-11pm Fri, Sat; free). **Map 7 K6**.

Kettners

29 Romilly Street, W1D 5HP (7734 6112/www. kettners.com). Leicester Square or Piccadilly Circus tube. **Open** *Bar* 11am-midnight Mon-Wed; 11am-1am Thur-Sat; 11am-10.30pm Sun. **Credit** AmEx, DC, MC, V.
Pedigree to a tee, Kettners comprises five banqueting suites, a restaurant and a Champagne bar. Founded by Auguste Kettner, former chef to Emperor Napoleon III, it boasts a century-and-a-half of celebrity custom, although these days it's more likely to host a product launch. The Champagne bar (or, rather, rooms – they comprise three different areas) is suitably discreet and tastefully furnished. Of the boasted 26 marques, a dozen come by the half-bottle and two (Brice and Jacquart, £7.75) can be ordered by the glass. Half-bottles (Lanson, Moët, Mumm) are around £25, while bottles run from a £36.50 Lallier Brut to a £480 Cristal '97 magnum. There are cocktails (£7.75-£8.25) too: Kirs, Bellinis and a Kettner Breeze of Champagne and cranberry juice. Ciabatta sandwiches (£6.95) include sirloin steak, parma ham and rocket, and grilled tuna varieties.
Babies and children welcome (restaurant). Function rooms. Music (jazz daily; free). No-smoking area. Restaurant. **Map 7 K6**.

LAB

12 Old Compton Street, W1D 4TQ (7437 7820/ www.lab-townhouse.com). Leicester Square or Tottenham Court Road tube. **Open** 4pm-midnight

Mon-Sat; 4-10.30pm Sun. **Food served** 6-11pm Mon-Sat; 6-10.30pm Sun. **Credit** AmEx, MC, V.
Founded by Douglas Ankrah, the London Academy of Bartending has always been at the forefront of the capital's cocktail scene. Set over two compact floors decorated with a tinge of retro, Lab operates on a huge range of original cocktails, its list recently reinvented. All are £7 or as near as dammit. Its Streets Ahead range now features twisted concoctions such as a KFC Sazerac, using Buffalo Trace with fig jam and caramel liqueur in an absinthe-washed glass; a Plata Passion with Gran Centenario Plata tequila, own-made honey water and passion fruit, served frappé; and a Saga Branca, Sagatiba Velha cachaça, Fernet-Branca and egg white. The Hall of Fame offers further apothecary (Absolut Citron muddled with fresh kumquats in an Absolutely Crushed; 42 Below Manuka Honey and honey liqueur in a Sweet Honey Suckle) – and these are only the tip of a very tasty iceberg. Bar snacks are Thai, a platter for two (£13.95) including prawn sarong, salt and pepper squid, dim sum and dips. Outstanding.
Bar available for hire. Music (DJs 9pm Mon-Sat; free). **Map 7 K6**.

Milk & Honey

61 Poland Street, W1F 7NU (7292 9949/0700 655 469/www.mlkhny.com). Oxford Circus tube. **Open** *Non-members* 6-11pm Mon-Fri; 7-11pm Sat. *Members* 6pm-3am Mon-Fri; 7pm-3am Sat. **Food served** 6pm-2am Mon-Sat. **Credit** AmEx, DC, MC, V.
With the cachet of a members' bar, but without pretension of complete exclusivity, the London incarnation of Manhattan's legendary referral-only destination is of award-winning quality. It isn't just the 40-odd cocktails (although they are exquisitely concocted with just the right touch of Maraschino or egg white, chilled with hand-cut jagged chunks of ice, and surprisingly reasonably priced at £7-£8.50), it's the service that ushers them to your own snug booth, one of six in the main Red Room. Numbers are kept comfortable by the house policy of booking in a limited number of non-members, generally at the start of the week and always before 11pm, according to custom on any given evening – always phone ahead. Monthly changing amuse-bouches (£2-£6) include luxuries such as griddled pheasant skewers and wild mushroom and walnut strudel, some turning up on the two- and four-person platters (£16-£30). Fittingly for the Prohibition-era inconspicuous door entry, jazz plays equally subtly in the background. Members (£300/year) have access to the private bar and games room upstairs.
Function room. **Map 2 J6**.

Old Coffee House

49 Beak Street, W1F 9SF (7437 2197). Oxford Circus tube. **Open** 11am-11pm Mon-Sat; noon-10.30pm Sun. **Food served** noon-3pm Mon-Sat. **Credit** MC, V.
Surrounded by Soho style-bars, the Old Coffee House is old-school hostelry at its most low-key. The finely upholstered front seating, the dark interior decorated with copper knick-knacks, the beady stare of stuffed animals, the long bar counter lined with quiet men supping a slow Marston's Pedigree, Young's Special or Courage Directors – it could pass for a village pub in the Peak District. The Old Coffee House happens to be in one of the world's most fashionable square miles, but that can be explained away by its name and origins. As an establishment, its roots lie deep in the 18th century, when coffeehouses were staid debating chambers for rational political discussion – as opposed to rowdier pubs and taverns. OK, so today regu-

lars no longer muse on the rights and wrongs of slavery or universal suffrage, but a library hush has been carried down the generations. Even though the coffee is instant. *Restaurant. TV (big screen, satellite).***Map 2 J6**.

Opium

1A Dean Street, W1D 3RB (7287 9608/www.opium-bar-restaurant.com). Tottenham Court Road tube. **Open** 5pm-3am Mon-Fri; 7.30pm-3am Sat. **Food served** 6-9.30pm Mon-Fri; 7.30-9.30pm Sat. **Admission** £10 after 9.30pm, £15 after 11pm Thur-Sat. **Credit** AmEx, MC, V.
The indubitably classy Opium is adapting its pricing policy to cope with competition from the new arrivals along Dean and Wardour streets. This is good news for diners, with top-notch Asian cuisine at happy-hour half-price in opulent French-Vietnamese surroundings – and as good news for drinkers, able to sip superbly concocted cocktails from the classic range (Old Fashioneds with Woodford Reserve, Sazeracs with Courvoisier Exclusif and Buffalo Trace) at the same time for under a fiver. The annual fee has dropped to £59, allowing members and two guests to breeze in at otherwise busy weekends. All other times, the Asian-influenced drinks and bar snacks are reliably expensive – but that's star-aniseed-infused Johnnie Walker Black stirred in your Anise Star Manhattan (£11.50) and Cîroc Snap Frost vodka mixed with lychee purée and rose petal syrup in your Kim Cham Frost (£9.50). Bar snacks of marinated tiger prawns (tom nuong xa, £6.50) and barbecued duck pastry parcels (vit banh nuong, £5.50) wipe the floor with the local competition. A treat at twice the price. *Music (DJs 10.30pm Fri, Sat). Restaurant.* **Map 7 K6**.

Phoenix Artist Club

1 Phoenix Street, WC2H 0DT (7836 1077). Leicester Square or Tottenham Court Road tube. **Open** 1-8pm Mon-Fri; 5-8pm Sat. *Members* 1pm-3am Mon-Fri; 5pm-3am Sat. **Food served** 1-9.30pm Mon-Fri; 5-9.30pm Sat. **Membership** £50-£120/yr. **Credit** AmEx, MC, V.
This self-styled 'jewel in the ground' is a classic late-night West End haunt. The trick to enjoying its way-past-midnight hospitality is to arrive before 8pm and stay – slowly sinking pints of Baltika, Red Stripe, Budvar or Bombardier, or sipping a decent Sancerre (£19.95) or Rioja (£15.95) – or cough up an annual membership fee. Early evening, the hand-painted glass panels, theatrical memorabilia and odd rude illustration, dinky dark alcoves and spacious back dining room (platters, sharing plates, steaks and salads) provide more atmosphere than any recently opened Soho bar you care to name. It's at its boho beer-hall best, though, in the wee wee hours, when you can chat, flirt and philander to your heart's content. Priceless. **Map 7 K6**.

Pillars of Hercules

7 Greek Street, W1D 4DF (7437 1179). Tottenham Court Road tube. **Open** 11am-11pm Mon-Sat; noon-10.30pm Sun. **Food served** noon-8pm daily. **Credit** AmEx, DC, MC, V.
As traditional as it comes – but perhaps not as traditional as its mock Tudor façade would have you believe – the cosy Hercules is a manly tavern of fine ales and sturdy lunches. Pumps of Timothy Taylor Landlord, Courage Directors and Fuller's London Pride accompany the regularly changing guest ales (on this occasion Holt's) along the bar counter, the main feature of the narrow corridor linking the back and front areas for drinkers and diners. Although the menu is displayed in four languages on the

front window, don't give up before at least trying the peppered steak and caramelised onion sandwich (£3.95) or veggie burger (£4.35) of goat's cheese, pesto and mushroom. The Big Ben (£5.95) of a 6oz burger, juicy sausage, crispy bacon, fried egg, grilled flat mushrooms and sticky relish can be augmented (£1 supplement) with another burger. Try to waddle through the narrow corridor then. *Games (fruit machine). Music (DJs 6.30pm Wed; free). TV.* **Map 7 K6**.

Player

8 Broadwick Street, W1F 8HN (7292 9945/www.thplyr.com). Oxford Circus tube. **Open** 5.30pm-midnight Mon-Wed; 5.30pm-1am Thur, Fri; 7pm-1am Sat. **Food served** 6-11pm Mon-Fri; 7-11pm Sat. **Credit** AmEx, MC, V.
Bartenders come and go but this classy cocktail den is still one of the great pleasures of London life. Why? Its pedigree and legacy, mainly – founded by Dick Bradsell and recreated by Dale DeGroff. Intelligently crafted drinks are a given. Each basic cocktail (perhaps a Margarita with Sauza Conmemorativo) can be developed two stages, into a Bermejo with Gran Centenario Reposado and then a Joe Crow with Jose Cuervo Tradicional. Upgrades involve drinking economy (a Vodka Martini with Wyborowa, £6.50), business (with Grey Goose, £8) and first-class (with Wyborowa Single Estate, £11). Snacks (£4-£7.50) are created with equal delicacy – for example, the pork fillets marinated in saffron and smoked paprika before being char-grilled and served with a fennel and sage salad. The ambience helps too, as conspiratorial as when Bradsell flew a lone flag here for quality mixing in good company at an hour that suited us. Eight years on, long may it play. *Bar available for hire. Disabled: toilet. Music (DJs 8pm Thur-Sat; £5 after 9pm).* **Map 7 K6**.

Polka

58-59 Poland Street, W1F 7NB (7287 7500/www.polka soho.co.uk). Oxford Circus tube. **Open** noon-11.30pm Mon-Thur; noon-midnight Fri, Sat. **Food served** noon-10pm Mon-Sat. **Credit** AmEx, MC, V.
The Mayfair end of Soho is where to place a new bar, it seems. Responsible for Apartment 195 (*see p31*), the Hartford Group should know. Their venture has its red-fronted façade on the same stretch as Milk & Honey (*see p89*) and opposite Amber (*see p83*). The Polka is sleek, with a simple but attractive interior of fawn-coloured half-booths dotting the main bar. An upstairs lounge operates in the evenings. The cocktails (£6-£7.50), concocted at the counter at the back, involve superior spirits: Grey Goose in the signature Polka Raspberry Cosmopolitan, Cuervo Tradicional in the Blueberry Margarita, Tanqueray and sloe gin in the Polka Collins. The dozen wines of each colour are well chosen; unusually, it's two high-end ones that come by the glass (Californian Rex Goliath merlot, £5.50; Lucien Crochet Sancerre £8). The lunchtime sandwiches (£6.50-£8.50) such as smoked trout and spring onion, mains (£9-£13) of confit duck leg in a red-wine reduction, and evening bites (£6-£8) and plates (£7-£16.50) are certainly ambitious. Will it attract a crowd? Maybe. But not one lively enough to take custom away from Amber, Chocolate or Endurance – it's aiming too high for that. *Bar available for hire. Music (DJs 8pm Fri, Sat; free).* **Map 1 J6**

Pop

14 Soho Street, W1D 3DN (7734 4004/www.the breakfastgroup.co.uk). Tottenham Court Road tube. **Open** 5pm-3am Mon-Thur; 5pm-4am Fri; 8pm-5am Sat;

7pm-midnight Sun. **Food served** 5-11pm Mon-Fri; 8-11pm Sat. **Happy hour** 5-8pm Mon-Fri. **Admission** £3-£9 after 9pm Mon-Thur; £8-£15 after 9pm Fri; £10-£15 guest list only Sat. **Credit** AmEx, MC, V.

The most streetwise of the Breakfast Group group, Pop benefits from an off-Soho Square location – but still struggles to pull a crowd. It's a big space to fill, to be fair, an expansive basement done out in Fanta orange and leading down from a grand staircase. Many descend it for the twice-weekly live music; happy-hour grazers raid the £3 snacks (calamares rings, potato wedges) and £2 bottles of Red Stripe and Tiger. Prices are otherwise West End standard, cocktails at £6.50-£7 (Ketel One in the Cosmopolitan, Plymouth in the gin varieties), wines from £3.50 a glass and £14 a bottle. Pints of San Miguel or 1664 are pretty steep at £3.80, it must be said, but it's a funky little place.

Function room. Music (bands 9pm Mon, Thur; DJs 9pm nightly; phone to confirm). **Map 7 K6.**

Revolution

2 St Anne's Court, W1F 0AZ (7434 0330/www. revolution-bars.co.uk). Oxford Circus or Tottenham Court Road tube. **Open** 11.30am-11pm Mon-Sat; 1-10.30pm Sun. **Food served** 11.30am-10pm Mon-Sat; 1-9pm Sun. **Credit** AmEx, MC, V.

This Russian-themed bar is popularity itself – reserved signs decorate almost every table, even at the start of the week. The place's latest coup is to buy Flagship vodka, triple-distilled and served at the Kremlin, which it manages to sell at post-work glugging prices. Thus the new menu, done up like a James Bond film poster, contains eight £14 pitchers brimming with quality ingredients, while competitors feed the happy-hour masses alcopop slops in a bucket. Cocktails barely break £6, the price tag on a Revolution Martini of Ketel One vodka and a whisper of vermouth. Gimmicks include vodka lolly sticks in sickly flavours (Bubblegum, Bakewell Tart) and instructions as to how to sniff and munch gherkin zakuski to accompany one of 80 vodka brands. The food can be sharing plates (£19.50 for five) or Slavic house specialities like beef goulash with Hungarian spices (£8.25) and salmon and bell pepper skewers (£8.25).

Disabled: toilet. Music (DJs 7pm Mon-Sat; free). **Map 7 K6.**

Romilly Room

Teatro Club, 93-107 Shaftesbury Avenue, W1D 5DY (7494 3040/www.teatrosoho.co.uk). Leicester Square or Piccadilly Circus tube. **Open** noon-3pm, 5.30pm-3am Mon-Sat. **Food served** noon-3pm, 5.30-10.30pm Mon-Sat. **Admission** £10 after 9pm, £15 after 11pm Tue-Sat. **Credit** AmEx, DC, MC, V.

This sought-after, formerly members-only, luvvies' haven one floor up in the heart of Soho has opened its doors to the hoi polloi. Not the Teatro Members' Bar, still off-limits, but the adjoining Romilly Room and Cobra Bar (although on a slow Monday they may close the latter). Each share the same menu and overlook a busy corner of Greek Street and Shaftesbury Avenue; both are spacious and stylish, and, as far as the menus go, exclusivity remains – you won't find better in all Soho. The Boru vodka in a Brewer Street Rascal (£7.50), the Gosling's Family Reserve Old Rum in the house Vintage Vanilla Daiquiri (£7.50), the 42 Below Passionfruit and Stoli Strasberi in a Goodnight Sienna (£7.50)… all are mixed and muddled with fresh fruits and herbs to create 50 classic and contemporary cocktails of supreme quality. Sandwiches

(Teatro classic steak, £7.50) and tapas (Moroccan lamb and prune tagine, £5.50) provide suitable sustenance.

Disabled: toilet. Music (DJs 10.30pm Tue-Sat). Restaurant. TV (big screen, satellite). **Map 7 K6.**

Rupert Street

50 Rupert Street, W1D 6DR (7292 7141). Leicester Square or Piccadilly Circus tube. **Open** noon-11pm Mon-Sat; noon-10.30pm Sun. **Food served** noon-5pm Mon-Thur; noon-6pm Fri-Sun. **Credit** AmEx, MC, V.

Occupying a busy corner of Rupert and Winnett streets, overlooking the sex and theatre trades, Rupert Street attracts relaxed diners and drinkers by day and party animals by night. Light and expansive, it has plenty of scope to offer sit-down meals, as opposed to the scoff-it pre-party stomach lining of other venues nearby. Many spend entire hungover Sundays toying with a Rupert Street full English breakfast (£5.50) of pork sausages, hash browns, the works. Smoked haddock fishcakes (£6.75) come with a sweet chilli dip; cod (£6.75) is battered with Caffrey's and accompanied with proper chips instead of those floppy white things of service-station standard. A grill menu of 8oz Angus beefburgers (£6.50) and rump steak (£6.95), salads such as Caesar with crayfish (£6.50) or chicken and bacon with honey and mustard dressing (£6.50) – it's a serious menu, all right. Even fishfinger baps (£2.95) come with lime and herb mayonnaise. By dusk, professionals mingle over post-work Caffrey's, Guinness or Staropramen, and thereafter, alcopops are popped and shooters shot over pumping music. Tables outside in nice weather.

Disabled: toilet. Tables outdoors (5, pavement). TV (big screen, satellite). **Map 7 K6.**

Shampers

4 Kingly Street, W1B 5PE (7437 1692/www.shampers. net). Oxford Circus or Piccadilly Circus tube. **Open** 11am-11pm Mon-Sat. **Food served** noon-11pm Mon-Sat. **Credit** AmEx, DC, MC, V.

Unashamedly old school (the sign to the toilets says 'Loos'), Shampers is a snug little wine bar and restaurant tucked away just off Regent Street. Of the 166 varieties on the seasonally changing drinks menu, 28 appear (at reasonable prices between £3.25 and £5.50) by the large glass. You can accompany one of five daily special dishes (grilled sea bass, lemon sole or red mullet, £12.75-£13.95) with a Daniel Damet 1999 Chablis for under £20. For lunch, one of eight imaginative starters (£4.75-£6) would suffice – half-a-dozen Rossmore oysters, perhaps, or pan-fried fresh squid in garlic-and-ginger sauce. Bottles start with a standard Penedès or house red Ochoa Tempranillo Garnacha at £11.75 and represent most of the Loire, Rhône and Bordeaux regions, Spain and, interestingly, the Lebanon. Most are in the £20 range. On busy nights, non-diners can be squeezed in at the back – but service remains friendly, at best charmingly eccentric.

Babies and children admitted. Bar available for hire. Function room. Restaurant (available for hire). Tables outdoors (3, courtyard). TV. **Map 2 J6.**

Ship

116 Wardour Street, W1F 0TT (7437 8446). Tottenham Court Road or Leicester Square tube. **Open** noon-11pm Mon-Sat. **Food served** noon-3pm Mon-Sat. **Credit** MC, V.

Even though it is nearly 20 years since the Marquee moved from its location a few doors along in Wardour Street, its classic pre-gig haunt remains in place and in character. Pot-bellied ex-longhairs, balding old punks, pointy-toed

Cantaloupe
Restaurant & Bar

35-42 Charlotte Road Shoreditch London EC2A 3PD
Reservations 020 7613 4411
General enquiries 020 7729 5566
www.cantaloupe.co.uk

market place

11-13 Market Place London W1 8AH
General enquiries 020 7079 2020
www.marketplace-london.com

cargo

Kingsland Viaduct 83 Rivington St London EC2A 3AY
Street Food Cafe 020 7749 7844
General enquiries 020 7739 3440
www.cargo-london.com

dog-eared dolls and obscure bass players still gather within its homely walls, decorated with framed prints of old London. Someone decided it was a good idea to put pirate-related knick-knacks around the bar – it wasn't – but the retro No Dancing sign of a figurine in bellbottoms was a stroke of genius. Beers are decent: Fuller's ESB, London Pride, Green's Discovery and Caffrey's, plus Grolsch for lager drinkers. Bar counter banter tends to be of the 'reissued in '69 under a different label' variety, so for romantic intimacy, grab the table under the stairs.
Games (fruit machine). **Map 7 K6.**

Spice Lounge

124-126 Wardour Street, W1F 0TY (7434 0808/ www.sohospice.co.uk). Leicester Square tube. **Open/ food served** 5pm-3am Mon-Sat. **Admission** £7 after 9pm Fri; £10 after 9pm Sat. **Credit** AmEx, MC, V.
For a new bar to succeed in the cut-throat world of Soho, it has to offer something special – and the late-night dance-and-cocktail basement of this Asian restaurant is struggling to do that. It does little wrong, mind, providing standard cocktails and ones with an Indian twist at under £6 in reasonably cool surroundings (red and slightly retro) – but it has so far failed to get the multitude's mojo in motion. Internet flyers now beckon with £2.50 offers on standard drinks and £3.50 cocktails, Bollywood theme nights and the like, but the drinks are cheap enough anyway – what's lacking is atmosphere. It's all a bit too modest – affordable but unadventurous wines, Cobra or Stella the beer choice. Bar snacks, though, are exemplary, with the restaurant kitchen turning out spiced meats and fish kebabs until 3am.
Disabled: toilet. Music (DJs 9pm Fri, Sat). Restaurant (no smoking). **Map 1 J6.**

Spice of Life

37-39 Romilly Street, W1D 5AN (7437 7013/www.spice oflifesoho.com). Leicester Square or Tottenham Court Road tube. **Open** 11am-11pm Mon-Sat; noon-10.30pm Sun. **Food served** noon-9pm daily. **Credit** AmEx, DC, MC, V.
Standing guard over the entrance to Soho at Cambridge Circus, the Spice is enjoying a revival thanks to an egalitarian policy of daily live entertainment and to upping the ante on food and drink offerings. In its crossroads location, the Spice was always a place for a passing pint – but the decision to throw open its basement Backstage Bar to jazz musicians twice a week, indie bands thrice, bluesers on Tuesdays and open-mic try-outs on Mondays has generated a new community of regulars spanning the generations. On Friday lunchtimes you'll see over-50s queuing for trad jazz; by the evening, it's earnest young indie types. The spacious upstairs bar is a hive of activity, with its all-day kitchen (Big Plates of chicken-and-seafood paella £8.95, sirloin steak £11.95) and fine ales (McMullen AK and Country Best, Deuchars IPA). Six wines of each colour and cheap cocktails too.
Bar available for hire. Disabled: toilet. Music (open mic 6.30pm Mon; blues 8pm Tue; both free; jazz 8pm Wed and Thur, lunch Fri and Sun; £5-£10; acoustic guitar and bands 7.30pm Fri-Sun; £6). Tables outdoors (5, pavement). **Map 7 K6.**

Sun & Thirteen Cantons

21 Great Pulteney Street, W1F 9NG (7734 0934). Oxford Circus or Piccadilly Circus tube. **Open** noon-11pm Mon-Fri; 6-11pm Sat. **Food served** noon-3pm Mon-Fri. **Credit** AmEx, DC, MC, V.

A pleasant mix of corner pub and clubby bar, this once traditional (17th-century) tavern is a smart alternative to either. This being Soho, the clientele is a social jumble – on the afternoon of review, a table of road sweepers, pints of Pride in hand, were debating the rights and wrongs of 24-hour drinking ('All that bloody mess!') with media types mulling over a bottle of South African chenin blanc. Etched glass and dark wood provide a pleasing backdrop to the main bar, adjoined by an understatedly stylish dining area (Thai curries and noodles, £6 range). Should Pride not be your tipple, neat rows of Tiger, Beck's, Hoegaarden and Budvar line the huge fridge backing the bar counter, upon which rest taps of Kirin, Grolsch and Staropramen.
Function room. Music (DJs 7pm occasional Thur, Fri; free). **Map 2 J6.**

Thirst

53 Greek Street, W1D 3DR (7437 1977/www.thirst bar.com). Tottenham Court Road tube. **Open/food served** 5pm-3am Mon-Sat. **Happy hour** 5-9pm Thur; 5-7pm Fri, Sat. **Admission** £3 after 10pm Mon-Thur; £5 after 10pm Fri, Sat. **Credit** AmEx, MC, V.
Thirst is one of Soho's superior music bars. Two floors of post-work, pre-club buzz is generated by quality drinking at fair prices, reasonable even after happy hour. Six cocktail classics (Mojitos with Bacardi Oro), six house specials (Bombay Sapphire in the Thirstinis) and six long drinks (Jose Cuervo Gold in the El Diablos) all feature spirits of distinction, as do the deluxe/super-strength range (£6-£8): Woodford Reserve in the Sazerac and Finlandia Mango in the Urban. The Champagne cocktails (£5.50-£7.50) are topped with Devaux Grand Reserve. Downstairs is always hopping, either round the little bar or in the back room, separated by a doorway and DJ decks; upstairs features a food counter for bar snacks and little booths for pre- and post-dance chat. Wines (from £3.40 a glass) and bottled beers (Pilsner Urquell, San Miguel, £3.10) too.
Function room. Music (DJs 9pm Mon-Sat). **Map 7 K6.**

Toucan

19 Carlisle Street, W1D 3BY (7437 4123/www.the toucan.co.uk). Tottenham Court Road tube. **Open** 11am-11pm Mon-Fri; noon-11pm Sat. **Food served** 11am-3.30pm Mon-Fri; noon-3.30pm Sat. **Credit** MC, V.
It looks like it's been here for centuries, but this Guinness-themed bar just off Soho Square was a sandwich shop until the mid-1990s. The cramped basement was a long-forgotten after-hours disco. All it took was a few toucans and seals from John Gilroy's iconic pre-war advertising campaign for Guinness – plus the black stuff, of course – and this two-floor venue has been a palatable Irish destination bar ever since. Dublin's finest also fills the house cocktails of Black Velvet (with Champagne), Poor Man's Black Velvet (with Magners cider), Black Maria (with Tia Maria) and so on. There is a multitude of Irish whiskies (Clontarf, Erin's Isle, Red Breast) and a museum of vintage brands (26-year-old Midleton, 36-year-old Knappogue Castle). Lunchtime pub grub helps the medicine go down.
TV (satellite). **Map 7 K6.**

22 Below

22 Great Marlborough Street, W1F 7HU (7437 4106/ www.22below.co.uk). Oxford Circus tube. **Open** 5pm-midnight Mon-Fri; 7.30pm-midnight Sat. **Food served** 5-9pm Mon-Wed; 5-10pm Thur-Sat. **Credit** AmEx, DC, MC, V.
Opened in 2004 by bartender to the stars Tim Schofield, this snug basement below the Café Libre at No.22 now has

Central

a regular crowd from CNN and other nearby media offices. Still hard to pick out, even though it's directly opposite the busy estuary into Carnaby Street, 22 Below offers very classy cocktails at reasonable prices (£6-£7), divided according to spirit. Schofield devised the exotic menu – witness the Pisang Ambon liqueur being mixed up with the 42 Below vodka in a Green Hornet, the Agavero liqueur in the Dirty Sanchez – and sourced the Kauffman and Cîroc vodkas, the South gin and the Blanton's Gold bourbon. The result is a crazy scrapbook of bartending lore and imaginative recipes, the like of which you'll find at no other lounge bar within the W1 postcode – make that London, in fact. Asian-influenced bar snacks (dim sum, chicken teriyaki) are on offer and artful photography on display. *Bar available for hire. Music (DJ 8pm Thur, Fri; free). TV.* **Map 2 J6**.

Two Floors

3 Kingly Street, W1B 5PD (7439 1007/www.bar works.co.uk). Oxford Circus tube. **Open** noon-11.30pm Mon-Thur; noon-midnight Fri, Sat. **Food served** noon-4pm Mon-Sat. **Credit** AmEx, DC, MC, V.

Modest though this place is, whatever it does it does rather well. Each of the titular two floors (unpretentious Hoxtonesque bar bohemia at street level, slouch pit in the basement) is kind on the eye and fair on the pocket. There's been no skimping on supplies, either. Kirin, Klug, Brooklyn, Modelo Especial and St Peter's Golden are the ales and beers by the bottle; wines come four of each colour, £3-£4 per glass, £15-£16 per bottle. A comprehensive choice of shots (£4.50) and cocktails (£6) include several variations of the B52 and Caipirinha. Ciabattas (£4), served daytime, involve artichoke, chèvre, Parma ham and olive pâté. A little art, a few candles, some well-chosen tunes spanning all eras and Bob's your uncle.
Bar available for hire. Tables outdoors (2, courtyard). **Map 2 J6**.

Village Soho

81 Wardour Street, W1D 6QD (7434 2124). Leicester Square or Piccadilly Circus tube. **Open/food served** 3pm-1am Mon-Sat; 3-11.30pm Sun. **Happy hour** 3-8pm daily. **Admission** £3 after 10pm Fri, Sat. **Credit** AmEx, MC, V.

A gay landmark since opening in 1991, the thumping Village Soho was the model for so many of its ilk to follow. A byword for go-go glam and good times, VS has two poles, each with its own entrance. Hang out at the chaotic, crowded Brewer Street side, a shambolically camp ambience, all shiny and metallic, and you'll find a crush of non-threatening homosexuality around the bar counter. Blend with the more mixed gang at the top end of the L-shape on Wardour Street, and you can expect an unpretentious time of poppy tack and alcopop heaven. Some 50 cocktails come by the glass (£6) or the jug (£12.50), half-price for five hours every afternoon, and there's hot food too. Pole dancing, DJing and other entertainment occur in the basement. *Entertainment (go-go dancers/pole dancers 11.15pm-1am Thur-Sat). Function rooms. Music (DJs 8pm Thur-Sat). Tables outdoors (4, patio).* **Map 7 K6**.

Yard

57 Rupert Street, W1D 7PL (7437 2652/www.yardbar. co.uk). Piccadilly Circus tube. **Open** 4-11pm Mon-Sat; 4-10.30pm Sun. **Credit** AmEx, MC, V.

Established long before most of the other tackier gay bars in the vicinity, the two-storey Yard bar has a loyal throng of followers. It also has space, the titular five square metres of courtyard a boon in London's most cramped and camp square mile. Sought-after shaded bar tables offer respite from the frazzle of the late-afternoon sun and add a continental touch. Inside, it's a scout hut of simple decor and composition: bar counter, fruit machine, pumping music, take it or leave it. In the smoky loft, accessed through the courtyard, there's a more subdued second bar space with chesterfield seating and colonial-style ceiling fans twirling indolently from a beamed bar roof. Pre-clubbing is key to the weekend trade here, punters warming up with some serious DJing and handed advance tickets for clubs nearby. The Yard is at once respectable and ruthless in its quest for hedonism – just smile at the Russian bouncer whatever your mission.
Function room. Music (DJs 8pm Fri, Sat; free). Tables outdoors (4, covered/heated and open courtyard). TV (big screen, satellite). **Map 7 K6**.

Zebrano

14-16 Ganton Street, W1F 7DT (7287 5267/www. zebrano-bar.com). Oxford Circus tube. **Open** Bar 5pm-midnight Mon-Wed; 5pm-1am Thur, Fri, Sun; 7pm-1am Sat. **Food served** 5-10.30pm Mon-Wed; 5-11pm Thur, Fri; 7-11pm Thur-Sat. **Credit** AmEx, MC, V.

The management describe it as upscale hedonism – and that's not wide of the mark. Zebrano, now boasting a busy street-level bar of the same name, is a foxy hangout for party-goers, either pre-club or instead of. DJs man the decks from Thursday through Saturday, and the sassy red interior zings with social interaction. Prime space for this primeval, if polite, ritual is an intimate alcove at the opposite end from the bar counter where cocktails (£7-£8) short, standard and long are shaken. Grey Goose goes into the French Martini, Stoli Vanil into the Lychee version and Maker's Mark into the Old Fashioned. Wines run from a Zebrano house Lerane in each colour (£3.25/£12) to a Domaine de Vauroux Chablis (£20) and Châteauneuf-du-Pape Chante Cigale (£35). A couple of decent bottled beers (Beck's, Baltika), platters (£12.50) grilled, mixed or Asian, and you have all the ingredients for the perfect party.
Bar available for hire. Music (DJs 7pm Thur-Sat; £5 after 11pm). Tables outdoors (6, pavement). **Map 2 J6**.

Also in the area...

All Bar One 36-38 Dean Street, W1D 4PS (7479 7921).
O'Neill's 38 Great Marlborough Street, W1F 7JF (7437 0039); 33-37 Wardour Street, W1D 6PU (7437 7941).
Slug & Lettuce 80-82 Wardour Street, W1F 0TF (7437 1400).

South Kensington

As well as an exceptionally high quotient of braying Sloanes, South Ken is home to some rather fine pubs, not least the **Anglesea Arms**. Good gastro dining can be had at the **Enterprise** and a spectacular cocktail list at **190 Queensgate**.

Admiral Codrington

17 Mossop Street, SW3 2LY (7581 0005). South Kensington tube. **Open** 11.30am-midnight Mon-Sat; noon-10.30pm Sun. **Food served** noon-2.30pm, 7-11pm Mon-Fri; noon-3.30pm, 7-11pm Sat; noon-4pm, 7-10.30pm Sun. **Credit** AmEx, MC, V.

Strangers to the good ship Codrington will have to navigate the back streets, past austere 1960s factories, to find this linchpin of debonair South Ken society. Its stylish, black-framed windows and unassuming double-breasted front need no hanging baskets or coach lanterns as heralds, but the Admiral would surely approve of the heated outdoor deck to the side. Smart-casual is today's dress code and the preppy jumpers jostle for space around the square central bar whose taps pour several lagers, Guinness, Bombardier and Greene King IPA. The music blandly states middle-of-the-road, but thankfully it is difficult to make out over the Hooray chorus. To the rear is a well-regarded pub-restaurant, entered under a portrait of the Admiral's ship in battle and majoring on meat.
Babies and children admitted. Function room. Games (backgammon, bridge, perudo). Restaurant (available for hire). Tables outdoors (3, garden).

Anglesea Arms

15 Selwood Terrace, SW7 3QG (7373 7960). South Kensington tube. **Open** 11am-11pm Mon-Sat; noon-10.30pm Sun. **Food served** noon-3pm, 6.30-10pm Mon-Fri; noon-5pm, 6-10pm Sat; noon-5pm, 6-9.30pm Sun. **Credit** AmEx, MC, V.

This cosy neighbourhood pub, set back from the main drag, has good courtyard seating in front and the reassuring look of an old-style pub, with 'wines by the glass' emblazoned in gold lettering on the windows. Inside, the cracked green leather benches, framed prints of old London scenes and paintings of dogs and dapper gents all add to its charm. A young media crowd mixes with the locals and the soundtrack is provided by the buzz of busy voices rather than music. There is some seating tucked away to the sides behind wooden divides, but the heart of the pub is open. The ale quota at the Anglesea Arms is admirably filled by pints from Adnams, Young's, Brakspear and Fuller's, and San Miguel is a decent addition to the usual draft lagers. Wines run from £12.50 to £28 and include a good Australian Belltower semillon chardonnay at £14.90. The separate dining room to the rear has an open fire.
No piped music or jukebox. Restaurant (available for hire; no-smoking area). Tables outdoors (12, terrace). TVs (satellite).

Seven Stars. *See p98.*

Central

Cactus Blue

*86 Fulham Road, SW3 6HR (7823 7858). South
Kensington tube.* **Open/food served** 4.45pm-midnight
Mon-Sat; 4.45-11pm Sun. **Happy hour** 5.30-7.30pm
daily. **Credit** AmEx, DC, MC, V.

You enter through a glass-and-steel stairwell that reaches
up the front of the building into a 1980s-era futuristic blue-
lit space, decorated with Navajo fabrics and paintings of
Indians fleeing from Yankees across the American flag.
Above the open fire sits an old Winchester rifle and yellow
blowpipe dating from 1856; a giant wrought-iron candelabra hangs over the bar, which is overlooked by mezzanine seating. The American theme continues with the
drinks: beers come bottled, think Michelob and San Miguel,
with the Indian element being represented by, er, Tiger.
Most people, however, come for the plethora of cocktails.
The house Margarita (£6.50) is sure to make your head
spin, particularly when you look up to see yellow and black
warning tiles on the ceiling; alternatively, try the Yellow
Boy Winchester or Strawberry Ass (£7). The cocktail motif
is 'we shake, we strain, we shoot' and the surprisingly international wine list is divided into diamonds and rubies. Mini
cheeseburgers and firecracker chicken wings (£5) can be
found on the food menu.
*Babies and children admitted (daytime, restaurant
only). Function room. Music (DJs 7pm Thur-Sat; free).
Restaurant. Tables outdoors (4, pavement).*

Collection

*264 Brompton Road, SW3 2AS (7225 1212/www.the-
collection.co.uk). South Kensington tube.* **Open** 5pm-
12.30am Mon-Sat; 5-11pm Sun. **Food served**
6-11.30pm Mon-Sat. **Credit** AmEx, MC, V.

Set back from the road down a small passageway sits this
large African-themed industrial space. You can't miss it:
flaming torches, red ropes and surly door staff wait below
the Veuve Clicquot-sponsored sign. Inside, Fashion TV
plays on high linen drapes above the long brick-backed
copper-topped bar, as an international crowd and skinny
models sip cocktails in the private seating booths underneath the mezzanine restaurant. Carved elephants and
chocolate-colour beaded curtains screen this table-service
area; there are attractively simple low-level wooden stools
and tables, emphasising the tall ceilings of the mezzanine-
free bar area. Don't come for beer unless you like bottled
Peroni: this is a place for cocktails. Glass, uplit shelves
groan under the weight of myriad spirits, one shelf alone
contained 16 varieties of vodka. Cocktails start at £8.
*Babies and children welcome (restaurant). Disabled:
toilet. Function room. Music (DJ 8pm daily; free).
Restaurant. TVs (big screen, satellite).*

Drayton Arms

*153 Old Brompton Road, SW5 0LJ (7835 2301). Earl's
Court or Gloucester Road tube.* **Open** noon-midnight
daily. **Food served** noon-4pm, 6-10pm Mon-Fri; noon-
10pm Sat; noon-9pm Sun. **Credit** AmEx, MC, V.

The magnificent tiled exterior pegs the Drayton as a
period looker, but a glimpse through the flauntingly large
windows reveals a black-box bar, ramshackle furniture,
1960s wallpaper and mismatched lighting. Bizarrely, it
works, drawing a trendy crowd who mix seamlessly with
beer aficionados to sample the draught Spitfire, Adnams,
Hoegaarden, Belgian strawberry Früli, Küppers Kölsch,
Staropramen and Canadian Sleeman Honey Brown lager
which are among the collection. The wine list is comprehensive and well priced (£12-£18). The Brouilly is an interesting choice at £15.50 and eight wines of each colour are

available by the glass. Food is also worthy of mention, particularly roast red pepper and cheese quesadilla (£4.75) and
fish fingers with lime mayo sandwiches (£4.60).
*Music (DJs 8pm Thur-Sun; musicians 3-6pm Sun).
Tables outdoors (6, pavement). TVs (big screen).*

Duke of Clarence

*148 Old Brompton Road, SW5 0BE (7373 1285/
www.geronimo-inns.co.uk). South Kensington tube.*
Open 11am-11pm Mon-Wed; 11am-midnight Thur-Sat;
noon-10.30pm Sun. **Food served** noon-3pm, 7-10pm
Mon-Fri; noon-4pm Sat, Sun. **Credit** MC, V.

This tall, triangular corner house, with its hanging coach
lanterns, resembles a ship – but inside the white wood-panelled walls, decorated with gold-leaf bushels, are more All
Bar One than *Queen Mary II*. The international crowd comprises more than a few suits, but the Duke retains its own
distinct character. It offers an international selection of
beers: Budvar, Warsteiner and Hoegaarden sit next to
Aspall Suffolk cider, Adnams and Sharp's Doom Bar from
Cornwall. White wines are divided by taste, with 'crisp'
and 'creamy' categories, while New World champions like
the Australian merlot Yalumba (£15.20) slug it out with
'fruit-driven' or 'smooth' classic reds. There are 14 of each,
with six of both available by the glass. Plates of spicy
chicken drumsticks (£1.50 for three) and own-made Scotch
eggs (£1.50) are a refreshing take on bar food.
*Babies and children welcome. Quiz (8pm Mon; £1).
Tables outdoors (3, pavement). TVs (big screen).*

Enterprise

*35 Walton Street, SW3 2HU (0871 332 4601). South
Kensington tube.* **Open** noon-11pm Mon-Sat; noon-
10.30pm Sun. **Food served** noon-3pm, 6-10.30pm
Mon-Sat; noon-3pm, 6-10pm Sun. **Credit** MC, V.

Looking like a traditional front-room corner pub on the end
of a Georgian terrace, this pub in residential South
Kensington is initially misleading, but ultimately reward-
ing. The etched windows read 'spirits and fine wines', yet
the interior is largely given over to a thriving restaurant.
The drinking area is confined to a narrow space in front of
the bar, which quickly fills out with a jovial and well-to-do
crowd. One suspects they are locals closely guarding their
territory. The wine list is worth a regular check-out: they
offer three or four bottles of red and white as monthly specials rather than a resident house wine. The main list
strongly favours chardonnay over sauvignon and
Bordeaux over merlot. Bottles start at a pricey £18, with
a Domaine de l'Eglise Pomerol at £45. The hearty menu is
characterised by a ham hock and foie gras terrine at £7.
*Babies and children admitted. Restaurant (no smoking).
TV (big screen, satellite).*

Iniga

*2A Pond Place, SW3 6QJ (7589 6589/www.iniga.com).
South Kensington tube.* **Open** 6pm-midnight Mon-Wed;
6pm-12.30am Thur-Sat. **Food served** 6.30-11.30pm
Mon-Sat. **Credit** AmEx, MC, V.

Italian-run, this cellar bar-restaurant does its best to make
an entrance with a faux garden and lots of potted plants
above its doors, but it still suffers from being off the radar.
Once inside, however, the pulsing red bar, brushed-gold
broken-glass ceiling, purple leopardskin print sofas and
Sinatra soundtrack put you in the mood for pre-dinner
cocktails. Hop on a burgundy bar stool and drain an
Amaretto Sour (£6.50) or a Squeeze Me of Matusalem rum,
fresh mandarin and apricot liqueur (£9). The menu is
divided between tall and short drinks, and themed by base

spirit. The place being Italian, the only available beer is bottled Peroni, but there is an excellent Italian wine list, divided by region and offering tastes from Chianti to Montepulciano. Many of the 40 featured wines are available by the glass. Bottles are priced from £14 to £41, with the reds increasing to £100.
Bar available for hire. No-smoking area. Restaurant (available for hire).

190 Queensgate

The Gore Hotel, 190 Queensgate, SW7 5EX (7584 6601/ www.gorehotel.co.uk). Gloucester Road tube. **Open** *Bar* 5pm-2am Mon-Thur; 5pm-4am Fri, Sat; 5pm-1am Sun. **Food served** *Bar* 5-11pm daily. **Credit** AmEx, MC, V.
Far from the South Ken hub and ideal for combining with a visit to the Royal Albert Hall is this cool and quirky bar. Quite what it is doing out here is a mystery, but one definitely worth a visit to puzzle over. Old paintings, blue, brown and maroon leather sofas and a wood-panelled ceiling suggest an old-style members' club, but the blue-lit spirit bar running the length of the room introduces a sense of cutting-edge sophistication mirrored in the cocktail list. Try the Geisha Girl (rum, fraise des bois, vanilla sugar, strawberries, guava juice and passion fruit, £8.50) or Gingingermon (infused gin and ginger lemongrass cordial, Champagne and a sloe gin float, £10.50). The spirit list is spectacularly extensive, with 24 rums and 12 varieties of tequila. The crowd comprises dazzled hotel guests and the beautiful set, complementing the idiosyncratic old and new setting.
Function rooms. Restaurant (no-smoking area).

Oratory

234 Brompton Road, SW3 2BB (7584 3493/www. brinkleys.com). South Kensington tube. **Open** noon-11pm daily. **Food served** noon-11pm Mon-Sat; noon-10.30pm Sun. **Credit** AmEx, MC, V.
A stone's throw from the Brompton Oratory, this Brinkley's outpost is firmly in the wine bar tradition, with an excellent list. The house wine is £7.50 per bottle and there's a good selection of half-bottles, ranging from a Pouilly-Fumé sauvignon blanc at £7 to a Puligny-Montrachet 1er Cru at £17.50 in the whites. About 30 of each colour are available by the bottle, containing such treats as the Chilean Agustinos pinot noir 2003 at £11.50 and the Château Batailley 1999 Pauillac Grand Cru at £32.50. No wine is more expensive than £45. The intimate and slightly cramped space at the foot of an elaborate mansion block is decorated with gold frames, duck-egg blue walls, multicoloured chandeliers, a shell-studded bar and a faded mirrored mantelpiece; very suitable surroundings for supping wine.
No smoking. Tables outdoors (6, pavement).

Also in the area...

Abbaye 102 Old Brompton Road, SW7 3RD (7373 2403).
Eclipse South Kensington 158 Old Brompton Road, SW5 0BA (7259 2577).

Strand & Aldwych

The Strand itself has little to recommend it except the high-end hotel bars (**Lobby Bar**, **American Bar**), but venture further afield and you'll find superb establishments like the wonderful **Seven Stars**. The **Edgar Wallace**, **Nell Gwynne** and **George IV** are also worth seeking out.

American Bar

The Savoy, Strand, WC2R 0EU (7836 4343/www. fairmont.com/savoy). Covent Garden or Embankment tube/Charing Cross tube/rail. **Open** noon-1am Mon-Sat; noon-10.30pm Sun. **Food served** noon-10.30pm daily. **Credit** AmEx, DC, MC, V.
Tucked inside an elegant five-star hotel, the American Bar is done up in art-deco style. Steeped in history (Harry Craddock of the legendary Savoy Cocktail Book introduced cocktails to the UK from Prohibition-era America), this once talked-about and much-imitated bar is lined with monochrome pictures of Hollywood stars – although on our visit, we had to make do with Martin Clunes. Smartly attired drinkers like to congregate here for well-regarded Martinis (made from Ketel One, Grey Goose or Plymouth, £11.50) and other classic cocktails, wines and Champagnes. Service is unfailingly polite, and olives and nuts are brought to the table as soon as you take your seat. The tinkling piano music in the evenings gives the place a sense of Old Hollywood timelessness.
Disabled: toilet. Music (pianist/singer 7pm-midnight Mon-Thur; 7pm-1am Fri, Sat; £5 cover charge after 8pm). No-smoking area. **Map 2 L7.**

Bank Aldwych

1 Kingsway, WC2B 6XF (7379 9797/www.bank restaurants.com). Holborn or Temple tube. **Open** 11.30am-11pm Mon-Sat; 11.30am-4.30pm Sun. **Food served** noon-2.45pm, 5.30-11pm Mon-Sat; 11.30am-4.30pm Sun. **Credit** AmEx, DC, MC, V.
Located in a converted bank near theatreland and Covent Garden, this spacious, stylish brasserie is open from breakfast, and is hugely popular with an after-work crowd of City slickers. Despite its corporate feel, the bar at the front looks cheerful, with bright red bar stools punctuating a centrepiece curved bar, a large mural of a beach and an attractive glass chandelier. The drinks are fairly safe and populist, with several wines and Champagnes (a few available by the glass), spirits and around 100 classic and contemporary cocktails. The latter are reasonably priced from £6.50. The best-selling Decongestion Charge (Bacardi, Chambord, fresh melon, raspberry purée, passion fruit, lime juice, £7) is as fruity as its name suggests, and fresh fruit Bellinis are priced at £8.65 and are made from a choice of fruits such as watermelon, blueberry and mango. There's a tapas menu offering meat, fish and vegetarian tapas for £12 (for a selection of three), and a full menu of Mediterranean dishes is served from the restaurant located at the back.
Babies and children welcome (restaurant). Disabled: toilet. Music (jazz 11.30am-3pm Sun; free). Restaurant. **Map 4 M6.**

Coal Hole

91 Strand, WC2R 0DW (7379 9883). Embankment tube/Charing Cross tube/rail. **Open** 11am-11pm Mon-Sat; noon-10.30pm Sun. **Food served** noon-10pm daily. **Credit** MC, V.
In its own way almost as exquisite as the Savoy Hotel it used to belong to, this historic hostelry was first frequented by local coal-heavers and later patronised by bacchanalian actor Edmund Kean and his louche Wolf Club fraternity. After Kean died on stage and the coal-heavers left for the Ship & Shovell (*see p103*), the bar was demolished and rebuilt as part of the grand Savoy Hotel complex. It's still grand today, with baronial style wood beams, fancy stained glasswork and Greco-Roman nymph friezes. A stunning art nouveau fireplace sits below a gallery area,

Central

named the Wolf Club. It's a Nicholson's pub, and does the usual tidy range of ales (Shepherd Neame Spitfire, Timothy Taylor Landlord, Adnams, London Pride) as well as Artois Bock, Lanson Champagne by the glass (£5) or bottle (£20), and mulled wine (£2.50) in winter. Hearty all-day meals include a vast Yorkshire pudding stuffed with half a pound of Cumberland sausage (£8.95) and platters (£9.95).
Games (fruit machines). Tables outdoors (2, pavement). TV. **Map 2 L7**.

Edgar Wallace
40 Essex Street, WC2R 3JE (7353 3120). Holborn or Temple tube. **Open** 11am-11pm Mon-Fri. **Food served** noon-8pm Mon-Fri. **Tapas** 4-9pm Mon-Fri. **Credit** AmEx, MC, V.
Renamed after the famous regular and crime writer on the centenary of his birth, the Edgar Wallace has coped reasonably well with the demise of nearby Fleet Street. Much of its daytime trade comes from the Royal Courts of Justice, just as close at hand, so the standard and choice of fare are of superior quality. Draught ales include Shepherd Neame Master Brew, Greene King IPA, Battersea and Sussex, and the wines are well priced, beginning with a £3/£10.50 pinot grigio or merlot – you can order a decent Campo Viejo Rioja for £4/£16.50. New menus (with the iconic profile of the author smoking) offer hearty fare such as rump steak (£6.75) or Dublin coddle (£5.25), finished off with traditional puddings (£2.50) of the sticky toffee or treacle variety. There are framed mementos upstairs of the time when Wallace ran a writers' club there; the adjacent bar opens at lunchtimes.
Function room. Games (golf machine, quiz machine). Restaurant. TVs. **Map 4 M6**.

George IV
28 Portugal Street, WC2A 2HE (7955 7743). Holborn tube. **Open** noon-11pm Mon-Fri. **Food served** noon-10pm Mon-Fri. **Credit** MC, V.
A splendid pub this, with a young, international clientele from the nearby London School of Economics. No promotional lager in plastic glasses here – customers are treated to a decent selection of ales on draught, Shepherd Neame Spitfire and Fuller's London Pride, plus the rarer Timothy Taylor Golden and Young's Waggledance. Food prices are kept reasonable – £2.90 for soup of the day, £3.60 for noodle salads, £3.85 for large poppyseed bloomer sandwiches – and the standard wines start at £3 a glass. It's a traditional pub refit job, so the wood is as shiny as can be around the spacious bar on the ground floor, and thought has gone into creating a relaxing games room upstairs. Nicely located on a traffic-free junction of three streets.
Function room. Games (darts, pool table). No smoking. Quiz (7pm Tue; free). TVs. **Map 4 M6**.

Lobby Bar
One Aldwych, 1 Aldwych, WC2B 4RH (7300 1070/ www.onealdwych.com). Covent Garden or Embankment tube/Charing Cross tube/rail. **Open** 8am-midnight Mon-Sat; 8am-10.30pm Sun. **Food served** 5.30pm-midnight daily. **Credit** AmEx, DC, MC, V.
This large, buzzy bar is one of the most stylish hotel bars in London. It has huge picture windows, contemporary sculptures (including a strange rowing scene) and high-backed chairs. Fashionable and smartly attired young professionals come here to sip top-notch cocktails (including 22 imaginative varieties of Martini), gins and vodkas. Drinks are served with spicy warm nuts, and bar snacks range from sushi to Oscietra caviar. Food is served in the

bar throughout the day, comprising the likes of a continental breakfast (£11.50), organic cakes (£3.90) and sandwiches (£7.75-£8.75 for six pieces). Cold food only (antipasti) is available on Sunday.
Babies and children welcome. Disabled: toilet. Function room. Restaurant. **Map 4 M6**.

Nell Gwynne
1-2 Bull Inn Court, WC2R 0NP (7240 5579). Covent Garden tube/Charing Cross tube/rail. **Open** 11am-11pm Mon-Sat. **Food served** noon-3pm Mon-Fri. **No credit cards.**
'Jerry and Trish welcome you to the friendliest freehouse in the West End', says the sign – the friendliest and surely the smallest. Another sign leads you off the Strand and down a short, tiled passageway to this cubbyhole, just large enough to accommodate a few tables and a prominent counter. On it stand pumps of Old Speckled Hen, Bombardier, Courage Directors and Courage Best, along with taps of San Miguel and Foster's, although most of the customers simply have to nod hello and find their usual spot. Some bother with a lunchtime sandwich, most are happy with just a pint. The historic connection dates from when King Charles II's mistress trod the boards of the theatres nearby, and the cosy interior is dark enough to imagine all kinds of liaisons taking place in a hidden corner.
Babies and children admitted. Games (darts, fruit machines). Tables outdoors (12 chairs, pavement). TVs (satellite). **Map 2 L7**.

Ye Old White Horse
2 St Clement's Lane, WC2A 2HA (7242 5518). Holborn or Temple tube. **Open** 11am-11pm Mon-Fri. **Food served** noon-2pm Mon-Fri. **Credit** MC, V.
A weird place this, abruptly opposed to taking any trade from the nearby London School of Economics – 'No Students' is posted on the front door – but somehow making enough turnover to make ends meet. Although the walls are covered in cartoons with legal themes, there seems to be little trade from the Royal Courts of Justice either – the one main bar is too shabby for that. Still, you couldn't find a better venue for a really quiet pint, Brakspear, Timothy Taylor Landlord or Deuchars, and there's usually a lunchtime spread of pub standards. Voices whisper around the dim, maroon stucco interior, glances get noticed in the mirrors and an occasional cigarette lighter flickers in the frosted glass. It would be the ideal setting for the post-heist scene of a cheap Brit gangster movie – come to think of it, it might make it more lively.
Map 4 M6.

Seven Stars
53 Carey Street, WC2A 2JB (7242 8521). Chancery Lane, Holborn or Temple tube. **Open** 11am-11pm Mon-Fri; noon-11pm Sat, Sun. **Food served** noon-3pm, 5-10pm Mon-Fri; 1-4pm, 6-9pm Sat, Sun. **Credit** AmEx, MC, V.
Roxy Beaujolais' fabulous little pub manages to squeeze the best ales, wines and food into an interior whose compactness is dictated by the constraints of its 1602 construction. It's low-ceilinged and cramped around the main bar counter, but nobody seems to mind, certainly not the jolly clientele from the Royal Courts of Justice across the road. Decent Australian chardonnay and shiraz (£3.65/£15.25), house Duluc (£2.95/£10.50) and draught Dark Star Hophead, Adnams Bitter and Broadside, and Bitburger lager, are consumed with gusto through the afternoon. The blackboard of gastronomic fare (featuring mixed game

stew, £9, and char-grilled ribeye steak, £13.50, on the day of review) and checked tablecloths in the dining areas at either end lend a rustic, French touch. There is just enough room for a decor theme to emerge, as all the film stills and posters on display are of Hovis-era British courtroom dramas. The new knocked-through alcove has a framed collection of cigarette cards, portraits of the Seven Stars pre-war actresses who lent this fine venue its name. *No piped music or jukebox.* **Map 4 M6**.

Also in the area...

Hodgsons 115 Chancery Lane, WC2A 1PP (7242 2836).
Savoy Tup 2 Savoy Street, off Strand, WC2R 0BA (7836 9738).
Walkabout Temple Station, Temple Place, WC2R 2PH (7395 3690).

Trafalgar Square & Charing Cross

Some much-needed glamour was brought to tourist-infested Trafalgar Square when **Albannach** opened its doors at the end of 2004. Now it has upped the ante by opening downstairs cocktail bar **Doon**. Less glamour can be found at **Gordon's**, but there's a great atmosphere and plenty of fine wine, or enjoy the late-night bar privileges of being a member (for a day) of the **ICA**.

Albannach

66 Trafalgar Square, WC2N 5DS (7930 0066/ www.albannach.co.uk). Charing Cross tube/rail. **Open** noon-1am Mon-Wed; noon-3am Thur-Sat. **Food served** noon-3pm, 5-10.30pm Mon-Fri; 5-10.30pm Sat. **Credit** AmEx, DC, MC, V.
This upscale Scottish bar and restaurant opened in the heart of Trafalgar Square to mixed reviews, but we certainly rate the main bar on the ground floor and the newly opened cocktail bar Doon in the basement ('that's the Scottish way of saying "down"', pointed out our Scottish guest). This is no theme bar: Scottish knick-knackery is kept to a minimum, with the venue instead stylishly decked out in dark oak and slate, with thistle-patterned fabrics, stripy banquettes, tartan flourishes, highland heather colours, chandeliers made from antlers, and an illuminated stag. The main bar has one of the capital's best selections of Scottish whisky, including Islay, Lowlands, Highlands and Campbeltown malts and blends. There's also a good range of whisky-based cocktails, Champagne cocktails, Martinis, long and short drinks, and hot alcoholic drinks like Smoked Heather Dram. The first-floor dining room hosts chocolate and whisky pairing evenings, while Doon holds Glamouroke (sparkly karaoke) on Thursday evenings, complete with diamante-encrusted mics and wannabe pop idols in spangly tops.
Babies and children welcome (restaurant). Disabled: toilet. Function room. Restaurant (no smoking). Tables outdoors (3, pavement). TV (big screen, satellite). **Map 2 K7**.

Clarence

53 Whitehall, SW1A 2HP (7930 4808). Embankment tube/Charing Cross tube/rail. **Open** 9am-11pm Mon, Tue; 10am-midnight Wed-Sat; 10am-11pm Sun. **Food served** 10am-9pm daily. **Credit** AmEx, MC, V.

In a line of lucrative faux-historic hostelries reliant on the tourist trade, this at least has a little character. Maybe it's only in the little touches, such as the question of the day or ale of the week chalked up behind the bar – anything that's not trotting out the same old formula. It's got decent ales too – Greene King IPA, Adnams Broadside, Wells Bombardier – and goes to town over its sausages, with combinations such as stilton and mustard. Oven-baked pies (£6.75) are another speciality (lamb and apricot, chicken and stuffing). Few surprises otherwise, certainly not in the decor, the same mock Tudor beams and low ceilings as might depressingly remind you of a school trip to a poorly themed museum.
Babies and children admitted (before 8pm). Function room. Games (fruit machine). Tables outdoors (3, pavement). TV. **Map 2 L8**.

Gordon's

47 Villiers Street, WC2N 6NE (7930 1408/www. gordonswinebar.com). Embankment tube/Charing Cross tube/rail. **Open** 11am-11pm Mon-Sat; noon-10pm Sun. **Food served** noon-10pm Mon-Sat; noon-9pm Sun. **Credit** AmEx, MC, V.
The history of this candelit warren of a wine bar – the oldest in London, established in 1890 – isn't confined to the Coronation-era newspaper clippings or schooners of sherry dispensed from the ageing barrels behind the bar. There's the name itself. When vintner Arthur Gordon founded the place, it already had a history – Samuel Pepys lived here in the 1600s. Rudyard Kipling had a room upstairs. Having established the kind of hideaway where Laurence Olivier would woo Vivien Leigh – it still feels like a cellar of naughty Londoners getting intimately frisky away from the stern torch of the ARP warden – Arthur was then followed by Luis Gordon, no relation. The family of bon vivant, newly departed Luis are still the owners, but little else has changed: fine wines from £3.30 a glass, £11.70 a bottle, detailed in a huge menu, barrels of fino, amontillado and oloroso, port and Madeira, ploughman's lunches and Sunday roasts.
Babies and children admitted. No piped music or jukebox. Tables outdoors (10, terrace). **Map 2 L7**.

Harp

47 Chandos Place, WC2N 4HS (7836 0291). Charing Cross tube/rail. **Open** 11am-11pm Mon-Sat; noon-10.30pm Sun. **Food served** noon-10pm daily. **Credit** MC, V.
Lovely little Irish bar this, with no need to display shillelaghs or signposts to Kilkenny, just titular harps in the glazed front windows, decent ales, a pot of sausages sizzling on the hob and gentle conversation around the bar. Not just any sausages, mind: O'Hagan's award-winning sausages, proudly detailed on the board outside – beef and Guinness, Welsh pork and fresh leek. As for the beers, there's Timothy Taylor Landlord, Harveys and Black Sheep, with a couple of guests, on this occasion Deuchars and Bishops Finger. Decor is provided by portraits of long-forgotten personalities lining the narrow walls of the one main bar, entertainment by the low-volume background of afternoon horse-racing, anticipated from early doors by lazy annotations of the *Sporting Life*.
Function room. No-smoking area. TV. **Map 2 L7**.

ICA Bar

The Mall, SW1Y 5AH (7930 3647/www.ica.org.uk). Charing Cross tube/rail. **Open** noon-11pm Mon; noon-1am Tue-Sat; noon-11.30pm Sun. **Food served** noon-

Central

Good sports

London's celebrated international status is never more clearly illustrated than during a World Cup summer, for better or worse. While pockets of the capital are livened up by their little communities – Portuguese in South Lambeth, Italians in Soho, Poles in Earl's Court and hey, Australia have qualified this year – the Little England nature of the indigenous population in mainly outlying districts comes to the fore. Ructions by suburbanites in Trafalgar Square, riots in Croydon, and all that.

As the 2006 tournament takes place in Germany (and the next European one is a long 12 years thereafter – Wayne Rooney will be 32),

it is estimated by most informed sources that 100,000 England fans will be going over. That's 100,000 England fans who won't be here. London publicans may be able to relax. Maybe.

Between the madness every fourth summer, other sports create reasonably good-natured, boozy bonhomie around the bar counter. This is partly because the main two, cricket and rugby, have a different tempo, temperament and geopolitical logistics to football. A dubious lbw decision isn't going to bring them out on the streets of West Croydon, and the many hostelries that cater for Test matches or the Six Nations – the **Rugby Tavern**, the 14 rugby-

Bar Kick

6071), **Café Kick** and **Bar Kick** all have a football leaning, but without the bias of other boozers. The Sports Café is especially even-handed for quarter-final nights, as you can watch all eight matches, in theory, simultaneously.

Nor is this a city that's shy about personifying its sporting heritage in pub form – witness the **Ring** in Waterloo. Who knows, some entrepreneur might be planning a pan-sports pub at the 2012 site in the Lower Lea Valley.

Sod the Olympics though. The World Cup is the one event that brings everyone on the planet around a TV screen. Whatever the figures are, they're wrong. It's the World Cup. And London is a microcosm – a bloody big microcosm – of all that. Czechs at the bar of the **Czech & Slovak Club** in West Hampstead, Portuguese at the **Bar Estrela** in Stockwell, Dutch at **De Hems** off Leicester Square, Italians at the now licensed **Bar Italia** (22 Frith Street, W1D 4RT, 7437 4520) in Soho, French at **Le Bouchon Bordelais** in Battersea, Poles at the wonderfully obscure **Polish White Eagles Club** (211 Balham High Road, SW17 7BQ, 8672 1723), Swedes at the new **Absolut IceBar/Below Zero** near Piccadilly, expats of many stripes can find their niche here. (Although Swedes are surely the only ones to watch in sub-zero temperatures.) If the Trinidad & Tobago High Commission in Belgrave Square has a bar, that'll be some place to be on match day.

oriented venues of the Tups chain (www.massive pub.com), **Waxy O'Connors**, the **Australian**, the **Barracuda Bar** (133 Houndsditch, EC3A 7BX, 0871 223 5598) – are raucous but rarely troublesome.

There are international sports bars too. The **Sports Café**, the refurbed **Baring**, the **Famous 3 Kings** (171 North End Road, W14 9NL, 7603

Central

Café Kick

2.30pm, 5-10.30pm Mon; noon-2.30pm, 5-11pm Tue-Fri; noon-4pm, 5-11pm Sat; noon-4pm, 5-10pm Sun. **Admission** (non-members) £1.50 Mon-Fri; £2.50 Sat, Sun. **Credit** AmEx, MC, V.

It may cost you half a drink in temporary membership fees but the ICA is worth the outlay. On offer is the best choice of drinks and snacks within a 15-minute radius – bear in mind its proximity to Buckingham Palace, around which no pub or bar may operate without said membership-entry loophole. The bar is a cool, elevated space, slightly institutional, with an international clientele. Cocktails (£5.25-£6.50) are limited but well chosen: three types of Martini (classic, melon, espresso), five long drinks including a Ljub of Southern Comfort, Blue Curaçao, peach schnapps and orange juice, two Champagne varieties. Seven types of red and white wines, most by the glass, pichet or bottle, start with a basic vin de pays (£3.50/£8/£13) and run to a £19 South African Groot Constantia semillon sauvignon and Salice Salentino Taurino. Budvar, Affligem and Paulaner Weiss are the excellent beers on tap, while nibbles and bigger bites include pork and thyme meatballs with field mushroom sauce (£7.95) and an Aberdeen Angus ICA burger (£6.50).

Babies and children admitted. Disabled: toilet. Function rooms. Internet access (free). Music (bands/DJs weekly; check website for details). No-smoking area. **Map 2 K8**.

Lord Moon of the Mall

16-18 Whitehall, SW1A 2DY (7839 7701/www.jd wetherspoon.co.uk). Charing Cross tube/rail. **Open** 9am-11pm Mon-Sat; 9am-10.30pm Sun. **Food served** 9am-10.30pm Mon-Sat; 9am-10pm Sun. **Credit** AmEx, MC, V.

Trouncing all tourist trade in the immediate vicinity – as you walk in there's a price comparison board with the three pubs opposite – this superior Wetherspoon's also benefits from its location in the grand former banking hall of Cocks, Biddulph & Co. Huge high ceilings, reading corners and a beautiful wood-panelled interior lend gravitas; the silly prices generic to this discount-drink chain do the rest. There are unusual beers too: Beartown Brewery Bearly Literate and RCH Old Slug Dark Ale Porter, for instance, not to mention Marston's Pedigree, Frog Island Natterjack or Goff's Jouster, the guests on this occasion. Lavazza coffee, served with a dinky orange biscuit, is a bargain 99p, handy to know if you've had a morning taking the kids to see Big Ben and Westminster Abbey. Food comes in the usual odd prices: £6.09 for a chilli, £6.29 for a chicken jalfrezi, plus the familiar twofer deals.

Babies and children welcome. Disabled: toilet. Games (fruit machine, quiz machine). No piped music or jukebox. No-smoking area. **Map 2 K8**.

Old Shades

37 Whitehall, SW1A 2BX (7321 2801). Embankment tube/Charing Cross tube/rail. **Open** 11am-11pm Mon-Sat; noon-10.30pm Sun. **Food served** noon-10pm daily. **Credit** AmEx, MC, V.

This most modest of tourist-friendly taverns at the Trafalgar Square end of Whitehall hides its history under a bushel. A small plaque hidden as the main door swings back reads 'a pub since 1680', although standard Nicholson's blurb on the menu barely alludes to any history in the pub at all – and, apart from naming its restaurant King Charles I, nor does the pub itself. Its name comes from the days when this was a wine vault, one allowed to dispense drinks under a terrace shade. Today you can sip your pint of Pride, Young's or Timothy Taylor Landlord in a pleasant and surprisingly extensive wood-panelled

interior, on neatly upholstered furniture. Wines come five of each colour by the bottle, two by the glass, with standard Nicholson's pies, toads and tatties to fill a gap.

Babies and children welcome (restaurant). Disabled: toilet. Games (fruit machine). Restaurant (available for hire; no-smoking area). TV. **Map 2 L8**.

Queen Mary

Waterloo Pier, Victoria Embankment, WC2R 2PP (7240 9404/www.queenmary.co.uk). Embankment or Temple tube. **Open** *Summer* noon-11pm Mon-Thur; noon-2am Fri, Sat; noon-10.30pm Sun. *Winter* noon-11pm Mon-Thur; noon-2am Fri, Sat; noon-6pm Sun. **Food served** *Summer* noon-8pm daily. *Winter* noon-8pm Mon-Sat; noon-6pm Sun. **Admission** *Club only* £5 after 8pm Fri, Sat. **Credit** AmEx, MC, V.

Cobalt blue in hue and stern in appearance, the good ship *Queen Mary* is a completely average bar in a way above average setting. At anchor on the Temple tube side of Waterloo Bridge, this sturdy vessel rocks gently with the Thames tide, offering a rare bar-table view of the South Bank. The Wardroom bar in question provides standard drinks – Staropramen, Amstel, Guinness and John Smith's on draught, plonk from £2.35 a glass and £12.99 a bottle – in a prosaic setting that reminds us of school-trip ferries in the days before budget flights and Eurostar. The management has changed the accent from cheap early-week alcopops to a decent selection of food: lamb shank (£6.45) and 8oz Aberdeen Angus burgers (£5.95) being two prime examples. The Hornblower nightclub opposite the Wardroom opens for weekend entertainment.

Babies and children welcome (before 5pm). Function rooms. Games (quiz machine). Music (DJs 9pm Fri, Sat). Tables outdoors (15, deck). TV (big screen, satellite). **Map 4 N7**.

Rockwell

Trafalgar Hilton Hotel, 2 Spring Gardens, SW1A 2TS (7870 2959/www.thetrafalgar.hilton.com). Embankment tube/Charing Cross tube/rail. **Open** 8am-1am Mon-Sat; 8am-10.30pm Sun. **Food served** noon-11pm Mon-Sat. **Credit** AmEx, MC, V.

Named after a fashionable drinking club in West Hollywood that was once popular with film and media stars, Rockwell doesn't look as glamorous as it used to, despite the black leather seats, flickering candles and electric blue lighting. It's London's first bourbon bar, with over 100 varieties of the American whisky on offer. But while it once specialised in whiskies and whisky-based cocktails, now it offers a menu of mainly modish cocktails, good wines and tasty tapas to a smartly attired clientele. Rockwell is also open for brunch, but overall has lost some of its glory since the opening of the much more happening Albannach bar and restaurant (*see p99*) across the other side of Trafalgar Square.

Babies and children admitted (until 5pm). Disabled: toilet. Function rooms. Music (DJs 9pm Tue-Sat; £5 after 11pm Fri, Sat). Restaurant. Tables outdoors (5, roof garden). **Map 2 K7**.

Sherlock Holmes

10 Northumberland Street, WC2N 5DB (7930 2644). Embankment tube/Charing Cross tube/rail. **Open** 11am-11pm Mon-Thur; 11am-midnight Fri, Sat; noon-10.30pm Sun. **Food served** noon-10pm daily. **Credit** AmEx, MC, V.

The mystery of the Northumberland Hotel is an easy case to solve. Why is this former lodgings now a Sherlock

Central

Holmes theme pub? Elementary. It was here that Sir Henry Baskerville stayed when he came to London to meet with Holmes and Watson in the novel named after his hounds. They put together theme pubs with taste in those days (1957, since you ask): displays from various Conan Doyle novels and some of his own family artefacts are still carefully mounted in glass cases or on the walls of this cosy, two-space pub. The themed food – Dr Watson's Favourite of traditional Cumberland sausages (£8.55) or a Sherlock's of 8oz Scottish sirloin beef (£12.95) – is a lamentably modern take. The ale is decent, though (Abbot and Greene King IPA), and outdoor seating in summer provides respite from the tourist rigmarole within – although you'll be missing out on the Basil Rathbone re-runs.
Babies and children admitted (until 6pm). Games (fruit machine). Restaurant (available for hire; no smoking). Tables outdoors (3, pavement). TVs. **Map 2 L7.**

Ship & Shovell
1-3 Craven Passage, WC2N 5PH (7839 1311). Charing Cross tube/rail. **Open** 11am-11.30pm Mon-Fri; noon-11.30pm Sat. **Food served** noon-3pm Mon-Fri; noon-4pm Sat. **Credit** AmEx, MC, V.
At facing sides of the southern end of the Arches, these two nautical themed pubs sharing the same name have historians tied up in knots. Are they named after the coal-heavers who once also frequented the nearby Coal Hole (*see p97*), or after the unfortunate Sir Clowdisley (perhaps Cloudisley) Shovell who received a knighthood despite losing his fleet off the Isles of Scilly in 1707? In any case, both have a maritime theme and, as befits a brewery (Hall & Woodhouse) also founded in the 18th century, both offer decent ales and pub grub in a traditional setting. Ales include Tanglefoot, Dorset Badger and Sussex, while authentic Munich HB is a handy find as far as tap lager is concerned. Superior bloomers or baguettes (£4-£5), baby prawn with sweet red peppers or chicken breast with lime and coriander, are consumed with gusto by white-collar workers on their lunch break. Mains, lamb shank (£7.25) and Florentine gnocchi (£5.95), are also available.
Babies and children admitted (Sat only). Function room. Games (fruit machine). TV (satellite). **Map 2 L7.**

Victoria

Traditionalists will be happy to settle in the fabulous-looking **Albert** or make a selection from the superb range of whiskies at **Boisdale**; those looking for something more contemporary will doubtless find their way to **Bbar** or **Zander**.

Albert
52 Victoria Street, SW1H 0NP (7222 5577). St James's Park tube/Victoria tube/rail. **Open** 11am-11pm Mon-Sat; noon-10.30pm Sun. **Food served** *Bar* 11am-10pm Mon-Sat; noon-9.30pm Sun. *Restaurant* noon-2.30pm, 5.30-10pm Mon-Sat; noon-10pm Sun. **Credit** AmEx, DC, MC, V.
Foreign tourists drifting in from their tours of Parliament and Westminster Abbey may be confused by ale names such as St Austell Tribute and Bombardier, but will be delighted to be able to pay in dollars or euros. Americans among them can order a glass of blush (rosé wine) or cookie dough and cheesecake dessert. Yet such is the ornate nature of this fabulous Victorian creation that we shouldn't be churlish. Steeped in parliamentary tradition, its upstairs carvery contains a division bell and is accessed by a grand, wooden staircase lined with Prime Ministers' portraits. It's a classic 19th-century makeover in carved wood and etched glass. The titular Teuton is honoured with a wedding painting over the fireplace. Traditional food of the steak-and-ale pie variety is executed well enough for the taste of tourist and local, and children will be pleased with the apple and blackberry pie – and a room to get messy in.
Babies and children admitted (children's room). Games (fruit machines). No-smoking area. Restaurant.

Bbar
43 Buckingham Palace Road, SW1W 0PP (7958 7000/www.bbarlondon.com). Victoria tube/rail. **Open** 11.30am-11pm Mon-Fri. **Food served** noon-10.30pm Mon-Fri. **Credit** AmEx, DC, MC, V.
The best choice for a classy drink and dine around Victoria station. Below but not attached to the Rubens Hotel, the Bbar is still tinged with Africana from its original incarnation: framed photographs of zebras and elephants, leopard-spotted lampshades, and a number of southern African wines from the hundred or so on offer. Categorised by taste – 15 crisp and fresh white wines, half-a-dozen aromatic ones, and so on – many are available by two sizes of glass, including a South African Van Zylshof Estate chenin blanc (£4.40/£5.70/£16) and an Australian Miranda merlot (£4.90/£6.50/£18). Other reds come by the magnum (£75-£149) with a complimentary cheese platter. The 60 cocktails in the £7 range are fuelled on quality spirits: Hendrick's gin is used with rosewater and fresh lychees in the Rose Petal Martini and Finlandia vodka muddled with black grapes in the Grape Martini. Although the bottled beers (Budvar on draught) also bear labels from southern African – Castle, Savanna and Namibian Windhoek – the superior food is distinctly Asian, with the Indonesian chicken satay, tiger prawns and oriental duck used in snacks and platters.
Babies and children admitted. Bar available for hire (weekends). Disabled: toilet. Function room. No-smoking area (lunch). Restaurant. Tables outdoors (8, pavement).

Boisdale
13 Eccleston Street, SW1W 9LX (7730 6922/www.boisdale.co.uk). Victoria tube/rail. **Open/food served** noon-1am Mon-Fri; 7pm-1am Sat. **Snacks** £6-£14. **Admission** £10 (£3.95 if already on premises) after 10pm Mon-Sat. **Credit** AmEx, DC, MC, V.
Now with two branches, Boisdale of Belgravia – it's actually round the corner from Victoria coach station – is expanding its empire of quality Scottish bar-restaurants with an impeccable selection of malts and high-end gastronomy mainly sourced from over the border. Here Highland and Island whiskies (18 pages of menu's worth!) are sold by the 50ml glass, most in the £6-£8 range but with historic exceptions. A snifter of Bowmore 1957 will cost you £255.90 (90p is 90p, after all), a Macallan 25 is £59, while an 1841 replica is £33.50. Malt whisky cocktails (£8.50), Flora Macdonald, Highland Sling and so on, are mixed with Laphroaig, Ardbeg and Talisker. Of the few Irish varieties, Jameson is given the honour of being 10p cheaper than the others. Two-course lunches (£14) and the 1780 two-course menu (£17.80) feature Dunkeld wild Scottish salmon, wild Highland game, Inverloch goat's cheese and Loch Ryan oysters among the French and Italian delights. Live jazz and Cuban cigars are additional specialities of the house.
Babies and children admitted (restaurant). Function room. Music (jazz 10pm-midnight Mon-Sat). Restaurant.

Central

Cardinal

23 Francis Street, SW1P 1DN (7834 7260). Victoria tube/rail. **Open** *11.30am-11pm Mon-Sat; noon-10.30pm Sun.* **Food served** *noon-3pm, 5.30-9pm Mon-Fri; noon-3pm Sat.* **Credit** *AmEx, MC, V.*

An obscure Sam Smith's pub this, tucked away behind Westminster Cathedral, its gloomy interior lined with portraits of old cardinals. A roaring fire provides an otherwise-lacking homely touch. The management has seen fit to up the ante on food, taken either in the expansive front bar or in the more accommodating back dining room, separated by a wooden divider. Specials (£7.95) are chalked up on a board by the island bar: lamb shank, traditional fish and chips, plaice goujons. Beers are the usual brewery range, including the renamed Alpine lager, presumably helping the generally blokey clientele here overcome the difficulty of pronouncing what was once Ayingerbräu. Bottles of Young's Waggledance and SS standards such as Old Brewery Bitter are stacked on the back bar.
Babies and children welcome. Function room. Games (darts, fruit machine). No piped music or jukebox. No-smoking area (lunchtime).

Cask & Glass

39-41 Palace Street, SW1E 5HN (7834 7630). Victoria tube/rail. **Open** *11am-11pm Mon-Fri; noon-8pm Sat.* **Food served** *noon-2.30pm Mon-Sat.* **Credit** *AmEx, DC, MC, V.*

Almost village-like in its inner and outer appearance, Shepherd Neame's quaint Cask & Glass sits incongruously behind the brand spanking new office development now dominating Victoria Street. Outside, overflowing hanging baskets of greenery and a cottage-like exterior are embellished with any number of best-bar award plaques. Inside, there's just enough room for a bar counter, half-a-dozen tables, a skirting rail of model aircraft, a wall of framed caricatures and loyal, chatty regulars who make the choice of coming here even though they know they'll be standing up beside the bar counter. The reason? Not just pumps of Shepherd Neame Spitfire, Best and Master Brew, nor wines (from £2.75/£10.50 a glass/bottle) from Todd Vintners, nor snacks and sandwiches served at lunchtimes. It's the warm feel of a no-faff, no-fruit-machine traditional pub, a spot for a pint and a natter, where all outside is gleaming commerce and the desperate rush to and through Victoria station.
No piped music or jukebox. Tables outdoors (4, pavement). TV.

Plumbers Arms

14 Lower Belgrave Street, SW1W 0LN (7730 4067). Victoria tube/rail. **Open** *11am-11pm Mon-Fri.* **Food served** *11am-9.30pm Mon-Thur; 11am-2.30pm Fri.* **Credit** *AmEx, DC, MC, V.*

Unassuming and well run, this corner boozer prefers to offer choice ales, well-priced wines and decent grub than live off its place in the footnotes of history. You can check for upcoming guest ales on the blackboard – currently Ward's Best, Kent's Best and Explorer – as you choose from Bombardier, Young's or Fuller's London Pride. Of the 16 wines, a Ropiteau Chablis comes by two sizes of glass (£4.05/£5.35/£14.65), as does a Rioja Crianza Campo Viejo (£3.55/£4.65/£12.65). Oven-baked pies are the mainstay of a solid menu of all-day meals, served lunchtimes only on busy Fridays. Tradesmen still drink here, as they did when master builder Thomas Cubitt's employees – servants and footmen too – frequented the pub, entered in his honour. The boxy interior relates to their social status and assigned tables. As well as anthropology, the Plumbers Arms does

notoriety, for it was here that Lady Lucan burst in to report the family nanny's murder in 1974.
Function room. Games (board games, darts, quiz machine). Tables outdoors (3, pavement). TV.

Tiles

36 Buckingham Palace Road, SW1W 0RE (7834 7761/ www.tilesrestaurant.co.uk). Victoria tube/rail. **Open** *noon-11pm Mon-Fri.* **Food served** *noon-2.30pm, 5.30-10pm Mon-Fri.* **Credit** *AmEx, MC, V.*

Behind an awning, inconspicuous amid the constant rush of buses and pedestrians, two blue-and-white tiled floors (hence the name) of relaxed imbibing and dining await. The only problem with imbibing is the choice: 20 bottles each of reds and whites, eight each by two sizes of glass, from the humble entry-level Chilean chardonnay and cabernet sauvignon (£3.75/£4.76/£13.50) to a fruity Spanish Alvear Pardina and Argentine Trapiche merlot (both £4.25/£5.50/£15.50) and on to a £27.95 bottle of Domaine Daniel Dampt Chablis and similarly priced Cru Bourgeois Château La Tour de Médoc. Nothing comes over £30 a bottle, unless you start laying into the Tiles Cellar Collection of half-a-dozen French varieties for special occasions, a Vosne Romance 1er Cru Domaine Michel Gros '02 the priciest at £65. Two well-sourced courses are served each day, starters (about £5) including viande des grisons rolled with herbed goat's cheese on rocket, mains (about £10) corn-fed chicken Dijonnaise with smoked bacon, mushrooms, pearl onions and mash.
Babies and children admitted. Function room. Restaurant (available for hire). Tables outdoors (6, pavement).

Zander Bar

45 Buckingham Gate, SW1E 6BS (7379 9797/www. bankrestaurants.com). St James's Park or Victoria tube/rail. **Open** *11am-11pm Mon, Tue; 11am-1am Wed-Fri; 5pm-1am Sat.* **Food served** *noon-2.45pm, 5.30-11pm Mon-Fri; 5.30-11pm Sat.* **Credit** *AmEx, DC, MC, V.*

The sister establishment to Bank (*see p97*) still creates a nice buzz despite a rather hidden location halfway between Victoria and St James's. The 20-odd Zander drinks show zest and imagination. Fashionable prime U'Luvka vodka is stirred with Noilly Prat in the U'Luvka Tini, rare Zacapa 23-year-old rum is slowly flowed with berries in the Guatemalan Blazer, and fresh pomegranate is shaken with Grand Marnier and Absolut Kurant in the Zander Cosmo. Sorbet cocktails are another speciality, perhaps the Frozen one of Mount Gay rum, citrus peel, cinnamon topped with Champagne and Cointreau. Prices are set at £7-£10, but check whether the offer of eight classics at £5 each is still going. Bar food is suitably upmarket: swordfish fishcakes, warm pak choi salad, baby chorizo sausages glazed in honey, plus Greek, Spanish, fish and vegetarian plates (£5.95-£9.50).
Babies and children admitted (restaurant only). Disabled: toilet. Function rooms. Music (DJs 8.30pm Fri, Sat; free). Restaurant. Tables outdoors (60, terrace).

Also in the area...

Balls Brothers 50 Buckingham Palace Road, SW1W 0RN (7828 4111).
Wetherspoons Unit 5, Victoria Island, Victoria Station, SW1V 1JT (7931 0445).
Willow Walk (JD Wetherspoon) 25 Wilton Road, SW1V 1LW (7828 2953).

Waterloo

Despite its proximity to a huge railway terminus, the pubs and bars around Waterloo are surprisingly good. Cocktail paradise awaits at **Baltic**, great food at the **Anchor & Hope** and, at **King's Arms**, all the charm of a great boozer.

Anchor & Hope
36 The Cut, SE1 8LP (7928 9898). Southwark or Waterloo tube/rail. **Open** 5-11pm Mon; 11am-11pm Tue-Sat. **Food served** 6-10.30pm Mon; noon-2.30pm, 6-10.30pm Tue-Sat. **Credit** MC, V.
This bustling gastropub is more of an eating than a drinking destination, even though the venue looks more pub than gastro with its deep red walls and scuffed green velvet furniture. The dining area has a small open kitchen, while the drinking area boasts a solid wooden bar. There's a comprehensive wine list, as well as cocktails, Champagnes and a few decent real ales (Bombardier, Eagle IPA and a guest beer). A no-booking policy has resulted in over-crowding and long waits for tables, but diners have proved themselves perfectly willing to queue up for top-quality, offal-heavy, retro English food (potted shrimps with toast, say, or tripe and chips). Luvvies from the nearby Young and Old Vics love this place.
Babies and children welcome. Restaurant (no-smoking). Tables outdoors (4, pavement).

Archduke
Concert Hall Approach, SE1 8XU (7928 9370). Waterloo tube/rail. **Open** 8.30am-11pm Mon-Fri; 11am-11pm Sat. **Food served** 11am-11pm Mon-Sat. **Credit** AmEx, DC, MC, V.
On the direct route from Waterloo station to the theatres on the South Bank, the Archduke makes a handy stop for theatre-goers and wine lovers alike. Sitting underneath the Victorian railway arches, this split-level bar has a relaxed ambience, with jazz in the evenings and amiable chatter at any time of day. Large, fake plastic plants hang down from baskets and trains rumble overhead. The mix of clientele means it never gets too stuffy. There's an upstairs restaurant, targeted at the pre- and post-Royal Festival Hall crowd, which has jazz-themed sketches hanging from the arch, and there's also an outside conservatory. An impressive array of wines should please most visitors, including those looking for reasonable value.
Babies and children admitted. Function room. Music (jazz 8.30pm Tue-Sat). No-smoking area. Restaurant. Tables outdoors (12, pavement).

L'Auberge
1 Sandell Street, SE1 8UH (7633 0610). Waterloo tube/rail. **Open/food served** noon-midnight Mon-Fri; noon-11pm Sat. **Credit** AmEx, MC, V.
Just next to the exit from Waterloo East, the Waterloo branch of this Belgian chain provides a relaxed setting in which to escape the commuter bustle just a stone's throw away. The wooden bar room, with its scuffed floor, candlelight and low buzz of conversation, is welcoming and feels well used. Continental beer fanciers have a gratifying menu to work from: Chimay Red, Duvel, potent Rochefort, strawberry and cherry varieties (£3.45-£3.95). Kwak (£3.95) is served, according to tradition, in a wooden holder and test tube. Stella, Hoegaarden and Leffe on tap are also available in the two-pint glasses (£5.75-£9.75) known, aptly, in French as *serieux*. Eight wines of each colour are available by the glass. The mainly Gallic menu is experimental and innovative, with a choice of snacks including varieties of mussels, express food, and meat and fish mains.
Babies and children admitted. Restaurant (available for hire; no-smoking area). Tables outdoors (15, roof terrace).

Baltic
74 Blackfriars Road, SE1 8HA (7928 1111/www.balticrestaurant.co.uk). Southwark tube/rail. **Open/food served** noon-11pm Mon-Sat; noon-10.30pm Sun. **Credit** AmEx, DC, MC, V.
Located on the ground floor of a townhouse, this informal, stylish east European bar and restaurant specialises in Russian and Polish food and drink. The decor is cool, with wooden trussed ceilings, exposed beams, a high vaulted glass roof, and a beautiful amber wall. The modish bar, located at the front of the restaurant, buzzes in the early evening with theatre-goers. It offers a regularly changing menu of cocktails based on Russian and Polish spirits, wines by the bottle and glass, east European beers (such as Estonian blond beer Le Coq, £3), premium vodkas (£2.75 per shot) and own-infused vodkas in flavours like caramel, dill and cherry. Bar food includes the excellent khachapuri (Georgian cheese bread with pickled salad, £5.50), as well as blinis, caviar, salads and desserts. The Sunday jazz nights have a popular following.
Babies and children welcome. Disabled: toilet. Function room. Music (jazz 7pm Sun; free). No-smoking area. Restaurant. Tables outdoors (6, terrace).

Cubana
48 Lower Marsh, SE1 7RG (7928 8778/www.cubana.co.uk). Waterloo tube/rail. **Open** noon-midnight Mon, Tue; noon-1am Wed, Thur; noon-3am Fri, Sat. **Food served** noon-3pm, 5-11pm Mon-Fri; 5-11pm Sat. **Credit** MC, V.
Step in from the cold of Lower Marsh into Cubana and – with a bit of imagination – you get a sense of the country that inspired the creation of this lively bar (a few of their well-made Mojitos will assist this process). The Cuban flag is proudly displayed alongside revolutionary slogans, and the decor is fun and colourful (we love the chilli-shaped fairy lights). One bar area is sunk below a huge street-level window and has just enough room to dance. The mound of mint at the bar is regularly plundered for those Mojitos, and there is a comprehensive list of Latin American-influenced cocktails, many of them available by the jug. There's also Sol, San Miguel and Budvar for beer drinkers. Cubana is usually packed in the evening, particularly on nights when there is salsa music, but the bustling crowd only adds to the whole experience.
Disabled: toilet. Music (band 11pm Wed-Sat; £5 after 11pm). Tables outdoors (4, pavement).

Film Café
National Film Theatre, South Bank, SE1 8XT (7928 3535/www.bfi.org.uk). Waterloo tube/rail. **Open** *Bar* 11am-11pm Mon-Sat; noon-10.30pm Sun. **Food served** *Café* 9am-9pm Mon-Sat; 10am-9pm Sun. **Credit** MC, V.
Located right underneath Waterloo Bridge on the increasingly vibrant South Bank, the NFT's glass-fronted bar-café offers a convenient spot overlooking the Thames for pre-film snacks and drinks. Skaters and second-hand book browsers mingle contentedly with theatre-goers and tourists, and there are stools by the window and outside seating from which you can watch the world go by. Inside

the seating stretches across the deli-café, serving hot food and snacks, to the blue-lit bar and coffee shop. It's busy, particularly ahead of film performances. The decor is functional, if somewhat unimaginative, although the NFT promises a new bar-café for autumn 2006 as part of new facilities on-site. At the bar, four wines are available by the glass and Stella, Hoegaarden and Staropramen are available on tap. The choice of eating and drinking options, and the cleanliness and good location, ensure that both older and younger family members are kept happy.

Babies and children welcome. Disabled: toilet. No-smoking area. Tables outdoors.

Fire Station

150 Waterloo Road, SE1 8SB (7620 2226). Waterloo tube/rail. **Open** 11am-11pm Mon-Sat; noon-10.30pm Sun. **Food served** *Bar* 11am-10.30pm Mon-Sat; noon-9.30pm Sun. *Restaurant* noon-3pm, 5.30-11pm Mon-Fri; noon-11pm Sat; noon-9.30pm Sun. **Credit** AmEx, MC, V.

The name pretty much sums it up: the shell of a fire station, built in 1910, has been retained to house a popular bar just metres from Waterloo station. The bar's heritage is lovingly entwined with its present-day function, from the red signage to the fire buckets on display. The long wooden tables inside and benches outside are usually packed, and the bar is never less than busy, filled with the loud chatterings of thirtysomething boozers and a slightly clubby soundtrack (although the crowd at the bar often eases after the post-work rush on a weeknight). The restaurant at the back does steady business, and there's also a reasonable bar menu. The long wine list is chalked up above the bar, and includes a generous six Champagnes. The beers include London Pride, Shepherd Neame Spitfire, Marston's Pedigree and Young's Bitter.

Babies and children welcome. Disabled: toilet. Function room. Games (fruit machine). Restaurant. Tables outdoors (4, pavement). TV (big screen, satellite).

Hole in the Wall

3-5 Mepham Street, SE1 8SQ (7928 6196). Waterloo tube/rail. **Open** 11am-11pm Mon-Wed; 11am-midnight Thur-Sat; noon-10.30pm Sun. **Food served** noon-8pm Mon-Sat; noon-4pm Sun. **Credit** MC, V.

This fairly large, traditional pub could go unnoticed – it's literally a hole in the wall, situated underneath the arches between the bus stops at the rail station. It's not the most glamorous place in the world (in a former life it was a cider house) and is certainly a contrast to the commercial eateries in the station, but it does cultivate a certain scuffed charm, along with plenty of post-work/pre-commute drinkers. The bar in the large, arched, wood-floored main room has a full hand of Adnams bitters, the usual lagers plus Spitfire and Hoegaarden. Pub grub and snacks are basic but priced accordingly (sandwiches £3.95, mains £4.95-£6.95).

Babies and children admitted (until 6pm). Games (fruit machines, quiz machine, pinball). TV (big screen, satellite).

King's Arms

25 Roupell Street, SE1 8TB (7207 0784). Waterloo tube/rail. **Open** 11am-11pm Mon-Wed, Sat; 11am-midnight Thur, Fri; noon-10.30pm Sun. **Food served** 11am-3pm, 6-10.30pm Mon-Fri; 6-10.30pm Sat; noon-4pm Sun. **Credit** AmEx, DC, MC, V.

In Roupell Street, a wonderful Victorian terraced street a short walk from the station, what looks like a friendly but unremarkable boozer from the front hides a treasure. The two-bar interior is tiny and traditional, with stained glass and card-playing locals; the treasure is the discovery of a lovely conservatory at the back, with an open fireplace that roars away, and a long wooden table stretching the length of the room. The walls house a hotchpotch of local memorabilia, a plate collection and random objects such as suit-

Gordon's. *See p99.*

cases hanging from the rafters. Draught Adnams bitters, London Pride and Young's Special are complemented by a fine selection of single malts, and there is a mainly Thai menu (roasts are offered on a Sunday).
Function room (available weekends only). TV.

Laughing Gravy

154 Blackfriars Road, SE1 8EN (7721 7055/www. thelaughinggravy.com). Southwark or Waterloo tube/ rail. **Open** *Bar* noon-11pm Mon-Fri; 7-11pm Sat. **Food served** noon-10pm Mon-Fri; 7-10pm Sat. **Credit** MC, V.
On an isolated stretch of Blackfriars Road, Laughing Gravy houses a restaurant in its roomy glass-roofed back and a small, welcoming bar at the front. Laughing Gravy, the name of Laurel and Hardy's dog, was also a hush-hush synonym for alcohol during the US Prohibition. This bar is a far cry from illicit boozing, though: wooden tables and bohemian curios furnish what is a refined yet laid-back establishment. The cherry-picked beer menu boasts everything from Barbãr Honey Ale from Belgium to Brazilian Bravara (all around £3). Four wines of each colour are available by the glass, and the list also includes oddities like Gumpers' Block shiraz from Australia. Bar snacks and the restaurant are inviting, as is the relaxed atmosphere. A bit of a trek from Waterloo station just for the bar, but a quiet and pleasant place nonetheless.
Babies and children welcome. Disabled: toilet. Games (board games). Restaurant (available for hire). Tables outdoors (2, pavement).

Ring

72 Blackfriars Road, SE1 8HA (7620 0811). Southwark tube/rail. **Open** 11am-11pm Mon-Wed; 11am-midnight Thur-Sat; noon-10.30pm Sun. **Food served** noon-3pm, 6-10.30pm Mon-Sat; noon-5pm Sun. **Credit** AmEx, MC, V.

A surprisingly smart boxing-themed pub, with rows and rows of framed photos of boxers lightening the dark walls, but you're more likely to meet office workers than bruisers here. Far from gloomy or menacing, the theme adds a touch of originality, as well as being a faithful nod to the place's heritage (it used to have a training gym upstairs and has Blackfriars Ring, founded 1910, opposite). It's all hugely entertaining: from curling, sepia photos of moustachioed featherweights to a poster heralding a match with Ted Broadribb, 'Great Britain's outstanding boxing mogul'. The bar, which is a bit of a squeeze, offers a reasonable cocktail menu and Hoegaarden, Staropramen and Leffe on tap, and Thai and non-Thai food.
Babies and children admitted (lunch only). Tables outdoors (8, pavement). TV.

Wellington

81-83 Waterloo Road, SE1 8UD (7928 6083). Waterloo tube/rail. **Open** 11am-11pm Mon-Wed, Sat; 11am-midnight Thur, Fri; noon-10.30pm Sun. **Food served** noon-9pm daily. **Credit** (over £5) MC, V.
What appears from the outside to be a fairly nondescript station pub is in fact a large, warm and comfortable pub – though it certainly couldn't be any closer to the station. A homage to Wellington, complete with an astonishing fresco stretching across its central arch, the place tastefully blends Wellington artefacts with a modern and bright feel. Panelled walls are lit up with lanterns, and wooden floors set off by a good selection of live plants. A reassuring supply of spirits lines the long bar, with the usual draught beers and a small wine selection. Snacks (such as wraps and baguettes, £4.50-£5.25) and regular mains (£6.95) are served until 9pm on weekdays. The varied seating options (comfortable sofas, big and small tables) mean the Wellington's suitable for groups of any size.
Babies and children admitted (until 5pm). Bar available for hire. Games (fruit machine, quiz machine). No-smoking area. TVs (big screen).

Central

White Hart

29 Cornwall Road, SE1 8TJ (7401 7151). Waterloo tube/rail. **Open** noon-midnight Mon-Sat; noon-10.30pm Sun. **Food served** noon-10pm Mon-Sat; noon-9.30pm Sun. **Credit** AmEx, MC, V.

Tucked away on quiet Cornwall Road, this is a terrific pub. A square wooden bar and dark walls are lit up by soft candlelight and bold lampshades, with an eclectic mix of funky yet comfortable furniture (including a retro table computer game). The pub has greatly benefited from an overhaul and a lot of thought has gone into the decor, ambience and menus. The whole feel is intimate and cosy, almost like a lounge bar, and there is plenty to choose from on the menu for both food and drinks. Draught options include ales (Spitfire, London Pride) and boutique beers (Hoegaarden, Leffe, Früli and Küppers Kölsch). The food menu offers light bites, standard sandwiches, salads and mains at around £6-£8. A great place for a date and, if the company's not as enticing as this lovely pub, Waterloo station is just a few minutes' dash away.
Disabled: toilet. Games (arcade machine). Tables outdoors (4, pavement). TV.

Also in the area...

All Bar One 1 Chicheley Street, SE1 7PY (7921 9471).
Hog's Head 52-54 Stamford Street, SE1 9LX (7928 1154).
Slug & Lettuce North Block (1-63), 5 Chicheley Street, SE1 7PJ (7803 4790).

Westminster

Blokey, traditional – and that's just the Houses of Parliament. The drinking establishments round here are much the same, but happily the **Cinnamon Club** restaurant and bar adds a bit of class to proceedings.

Cinnamon Club

The Old Westminster Library, 30-32 Great Smith Street, SW1P 3BU (7222 2555/www.cinnamon club.com). St James's Park or Westminster tube. **Open** *Upstairs bar* 6pm-midnight Mon-Sat. *Downstairs bar* 11am-midnight Mon-Fri; 6pm-midnight Sat. **Food served** noon-2.30pm, 6-10.45pm Mon-Fri; 6-10.45pm Sat. **Credit** AmEx, DC, MC, V.

Tucked into the basement of a Grade II-listed building that was once the Old Westminster library, the bar of this smart Indian restaurant plays quirky scenes from Bollywood films on a back projector. The floor is made of rubber, the walls are leather, and furniture includes hand-crafted Rajasthani sheesham wood tables. Indian snack platters (such as poshed-up kebabs) are offered as bar snacks, and there's a comprehensive selection of wines that are carefully chosen to match Indian food. A great cocktail list includes Indian-themed varieties such as Mango Martini and Lychee Bellini. There's a pool with floating flowers and candles by the entrance, next to a large phallus that's symbolic of the Hindu deity Shiva. A separate lounge bar is located on the ground floor, but as a prelude to dinner in the excellent restaurant upstairs we prefer this one – it's simply more atmospheric.
Babies and children welcome. Bar available for hire. Disabled: toilet. Function rooms. Restaurant (available for hire).

Red Lion

48 Parliament Street, SW1A 2NH (7930 5826). Westminster tube. **Open** 11am-11pm Mon-Fri; 11am-9.30pm Sat; noon-7pm Sun. **Food served** noon-8pm Mon-Sat; noon-6pm Sun. **Credit** MC, V.

As one-time Parliamentary stalwarts such as the Albert (*see p103*) go the whole enchilada for the tourist trade, the Red Lion merely sticks its bar staff in logoed T-shirts. There wouldn't be room for any more people anyway. The smoky main bar (how are the regulars going to cope with the forthcoming ban?) has wooden alcoves full of chatter, haughtily overseen by sideburned ministers framed in Empire-era portraits. Adnams, Young's and Greene King IPA are dispensed from an overworked, stunted bar counter between the front and back areas. The upstairs dining room, with its own entrance on the street, serves sturdy favourites (£8-£9) such as salmon, rump steak and barbecued chicken. A cellar bar is sometimes also opened and in summer a handful of tables appear outside.
Babies and children welcome (dining only). Bar available for hire. No-smoking area. Tables outdoors (5, pavement). TV.

St Stephen's Tavern

10 Bridge Street, SW1A 2JR (7925 2286). Westminster tube. **Open** 10am-11.30pm Mon-Thur; 10am-midnight Fri, Sat; 11am-10.30pm Sun. **Food served** noon-9pm daily. **Credit** MC, V.

Centuries-old brewery Hall & Woodhouse renovated this fading landmark, fittingly traditional all round. Diagonally opposite Big Ben, its carved wood, etched glass, original fixtures and fittings, and high, high ceilings are a pleasure to behold – particularly when viewed from the beautifully upholstered mezzanine with a bird's-eye view of the tourist bustle at ground level. Parliamentarians and lobbyists use it too, but most still prefer the more lived-in atmosphere of the Red Lion (*see above*) round the corner. Here tea and muffins (£4.25) are best taken in the genteel back room, festooned with flowers, where you can also lay in to a full English breakfast (£6.25). This being an H&W pub, the pump ale choice is Tanglefoot, Sussex and Badger; the draught lager authentic Bavarian HB.
Disabled: toilet. Function room. No piped music or jukebox. No-smoking area.

Westminster Arms

9 Storey's Gate, SW1P 3AT (7222 8520). St James's Park or Westminster tube. **Open** 11am-11pm Mon-Fri; 11am-8pm Sat; noon-6pm Sun. **Food served** 11am-8pm Mon-Fri; noon-4pm Sat, Sun. **Credit** AmEx, MC, V.

In combination with the attached Storey's Wine Bar downstairs, this traditional boozer does a steady parliamentary trade, much of it blokey. The beers are similarly masculine – Thwaites Lancaster Bomber, Abbot, Adnams Bitter and Broadside – but there are wines too, starting with a standard Côte de Gascogne in two colours at £3.10/£11.20 and running up to a Californian Rex Goliath chardonnay at £4.50/£17 or Prodigio cabernet sauvignon at £4.10/£15.50. Belly-filling dinners include spicy chilli con carne, beef lasagne and deep-fried scampi (£7.95-£8.95), somehow followed by chocolate fudge cake and cream or treacle sponge with custard (£3.95). Amid all this comfort food for underachieving middle-aged men, a rather dashing display of violins and sheet music of Viennese waltzes seems somewhat incongruous – maybe it has something to do with the rather puzzling Frenchman behind the bar.
Babies and children admitted. No-smoking area. Tables outdoors (4, pavement).

City

Chancery Lane

The prevailing sight around this neck of the woods is that of a drunken lawyer. Happily there's some wonderful architecture to take your mind off all those boring overheard conversations about courts and torts. The **Cittie of Yorke** and **Ye Old Mitre** are particularly lovely.

Cittie of Yorke

22 High Holborn, WC1V 6BN (7242 7670). Chancery Lane or Holborn tube. **Open** 11.30am-11pm Mon-Sat. **Food served** noon-3pm, 5-9pm Mon-Sat. **Credit** (over £10) AmEx, MC, V.
The brassy sign looks a bit tourist-medieval, but the grand old Cittie of Yorke is a fabulously restored historic boozehall. People have been drinking here since 1430, although the current incarnation dates from the 1920s. The first bar on the left is undistinguished and the whitewashed Cellar Bar too like a canteen for cosiness, but the high-ceilinged main bar at the back is gorgeous, with fabulous dark-wood booths opposite a long bar, and an almost theatrical canopy at the top end. Run by Samuel Smith, the pub has a full run of its draught beers: decently priced but hardly exciting. The sheer scale can make it a bit impersonal, but the pub was busy with post-work boisterousness in all three bars on a Wednesday and the staff were very jocular. Industrial food (gammon and egg, £6.95) throughout.
Babies and children admitted (downstairs, until 5pm). Function rooms. Games (darts, fruit machine). **Map 3 M5**.

Ye Old Mitre

1 Ely Court, Ely Place, at the side of 8 Hatton Gardens, EC1N 6SJ (7405 4751). Chancery Lane tube/ Farringdon tube/rail. **Open** 11am-11pm Mon-Fri. **Food served** 11am-9.30pm Mon-Fri. **Credit** AmEx, MC, V.
Deliciously hidden (the tiny alley is marked by a little pub sign between jewellers' shops), this charming pub dates back to 1546. A gruffly cheerful and efficient Scottish barman with a fierce military haircut now runs it on properly old-fashioned lines. The draught line-up is quality (Brains Bread of Heaven improving the more familiar Deuchars IPA, Adnams Bitter and Broadside, plus Carling, Carlsberg

and Guinness if you must) and wood panels, exposed beams and gas-powered hearth fire make for a toasty little lounge bar. Off to one side there's a snug ('Ye closet') sized for half a dozen close friends without fears for their knees, and you can nip outside to a second small bar. Up a tricky staircase past the ladies', the Bishop's Room has the least character and the most room. Gents have an outside facility, off a concrete courtyard with big barrels, to stand at in summer. The bar menu runs to toasties, pork pies and even 60p Scotch eggs. Comfortable as a steamed pudding.
Function room. No piped music or jukebox. Tables outdoors (10 barrels, pavement). **Map 3 N5**.

White Swan Pub & Dining Room

108 Fetter Lane, EC4A 1ES (7242 9696/www.thewhite swanlondon.com). Chancery Lane or Holborn tube. **Open** 11am-midnight Mon-Thur; 11am-1am Fri. **Food served** *Bar* noon-3pm Mon; noon-3pm, 6-10pm Tue-Fri. **Credit** AmEx, MC, V.
The people behind the Well in Clerkenwell and the Gun in Docklands have done a bang-up job here: wood sides and bottom, intricately carved settle, a mirror so vast half of it reaches into the mezzanine above, doubtless thence to the first-floor dining room and beyond. The details (stuffed swan, antlers, ship's bell) bring old-world solidity, while an eight-piece cocktail list (a £6 Polish Martini of vodka, Krupnik liqueur and apple juice) shows an eye for the modern. On draught we found Young's Bitter, Fuller's Pride, Adnams Broadside and Hoegaarden alongside the Guinness 'n' fizz; there were a dozen of each colour of wine, by glass and bottle; and liquor included Tanqueray on optic, G&T fans. Cheerfully intense chatter and diligent *Guardian* reading occupied just three tables on a Monday evening, but doubtless things are busier for the noon-sharp Express Lunch (£15, two courses, one hour); expect the likes of braised pig's cheeks with horseradish mash.
Babies and children welcome (restaurant). Restaurant (available for hire). TV (big screen). **Map 4 N6**.

Also in the area...

Bottlescrue (Davy's) Bath House, 53-60 Holborn Viaduct, EC1A 2FD (7248 2157).
Bung Hole Cellars (Davy's) Hand Court, 57 High Holborn, WC1V 6DX (7831 8365).
Hog's Head 5-11 Fetter Lane, EC4A 1BR (7353 1387).
Penderel's Oak (JD Wetherspoon) 283-288 High Holborn, WC1V 7HP (7242 5669).

Clerkenwell & Farringdon

Just where the City meets the West End, this office-dreary, traffic-clogged area has become a thriving haven for discerning drinkers. You'll find early morning-opening pubs, excellent gastros, pre-club venues and fine wine bars.

Abbaye

55 Charterhouse Street, EC1M 6HA (7253 1612). Chancery Lane tube/Farringdon tube/rail. **Open** 11am-11pm daily. **Food served** noon-11pm. **Credit** AmEx, MC, V.
This Belgian bar-brasserie zeroes in on beer in seemingly infinite varieties, and offers tempting food in the mussels, steak and mash field. Beer fans will find Belle-Vue, Hoegaarden and Leffe on tap, while bottled brews include

dreambagsjaguarshoes. *See p130.*

City

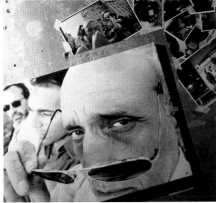

• cocktails • beers • wine • shooters • jugs • bar food •
• spirits • champagne • spirits by the bottle •

40 Hoxton Square, Shoreditch London N1 6PB

alternative entrance at 331 Old Street EC1V 9LE

• Open daily to 2am (midnight sunday) •
• Basement bar available for private hire • No hire fee •
• Deposit and minimum spend required • Table reservation available •
• Runner up best late night bar in Shoreditch - *myshoreditch.com* •
• Pole dancing lessons hosted by www.polestars.net (women only) •

• pr@trafikinfo.co.uk • 020 7613 0234 • www.trafikinfo.co.uk •

flavoured Floris beers: try a passion-fruit or even choco-
late-flavoured concoction, or a more conventional Chimay,
Duvel or de Koninck. Non-beer drinkers won't have a bad
time of it, though, as the spirits list includes such interesting tipples as Genevres gin flavoured with apple or lemon.
The bare-brick walls match the gloomy, religiously themed
imagery on the walls, stark candelabra and studded leather
stools, which all made for a pleasantly darkened drinking
experience, despite the slightly incongruous Indian music
playing on our visit. Abbaye is a mini chain, with outposts
on the Brompton Road and in Bromley.
Babies and children admitted. Function room.
No-smoking area. Tables outdoors (4, pavement).
Map 3 O5.

Al's Café Bar

11-13 Exmouth Market, EC1R 4QD (7837 4821).
Angel tube/Farringdon tube/rail/19, 38 bus. **Open**
8am-10pm Mon, Tue; 8am-2am Wed-Fri; 10am-2am Sat;
10am-11pm Sun. **Food served** 8am-10pm Mon-Fri;
10am-10pm Sat; 10am-9pm Sun. **Credit** AmEx, MC, V.
Primary colours set the tone in Al's: a bar backlit in blue
is framed by yellow columns and set off by red walls,
exposed pipes and fairy lights flashing in time to macho
mid-1990s pop. Subtle it ain't, but that doesn't seem to concern punters in for hearty food like an all-day breakfast at
weekends (halloumi cheese and plantain for £6.75, for
instance). There's a pretty respectable selection of beers on
tap, including Pilsner Urquell, Budvar and Paulaner Weiss
Bier, or you could neck a bottle of Nastro Azzurro, Tiger
or Moretti. Try to nab one of the outdoor tables on
Exmouth Market in summer – they provide a nice spot to
sip Lavazza coffee and crunch some mini amaretti.
Babies and children welcome. Function room. Music (DJ
10pm Thur-Sat; free). No smoking (downstairs, lunch
only). Tables outdoors (12, pavement). **Map 3 N4**.

Apple Tree

45 Mount Pleasant, WC1X 0AE (0871 984 3540).
Chancery Lane tube/Farringdon tube/rail. **Open** noon-
11.30pm Mon-Fri; noon-1am Sat; 6-11pm Sun. **Food**
served noon-3pm, 6-9.30pm Mon-Fri. **Credit** MC, V.
Once the regular haunt of postpeople from Mount Pleasant
sorting office, the Apple Tree has had a sympathetic refurb
with banquette seating, dark-wood flooring and pale green
retro wallpaper. Chandeliers and old-style glass pendant
lamps hang over an attractive back-mirrored bar where a
couple of real ales (Ridley's Prospect, Greene King IPA) are
served, as well as Hoegaarden and Leffe, Strongbow and
Guinness, seven or eight decent red and white wines
(chardonnays, pinot grigios, Riojas) by the glass from
£2.90, and a good range of spirits. There are newspapers,
fresh flowers and a coffee machine. all drawing new
punters: on our visit businessmen were enjoying a better-
than-average lunch (honey-roasted ham and eggs with
own-made wedges, pies from Borough Market) alongside
craftspeople from nearby Cockpit Arts. Perhaps they'd
heard about the original swirly carpet in the loo.
Function room. Music (Americana/bluegrass 7pm-1am
1st, 2nd, 3rd Sat of mth; 6-11pm last Sun of mth; £3).
Tables outdoors (3, pavement). **Map 3 N4**.

Beduin

57-59 Charterhouse Street, EC1M 6HA (7336 6484/
www.beduin-london.co.uk). Farringdon tube/rail.
Open noon-3am Mon-Wed; noon-4am Thur, Fri; 7pm-
4am Sat; 7pm-3am Sun. **Food served** noon-3pm,
6-10pm Mon-Fri; 7-11pm Sat. **Credit** AmEx, MC, V.

Distinguished by its decor, Beduin is a Moroccan-themed
bar that tends to attract moneyed sorts who wouldn't
dream of drinking anything other than Champagne. The
ground-floor bar area is overlooked by a booth-filled
mezzanine, reached by a candle-lined spiral staircase,
and the walls support cracked-glass mirrors. This and the
darker basement room have low tables set with large, oxi-
dised silver trays, and you could go all out with a shisha
pipe and fruit-flavoured tobacco for £11.25. The care
expended on the rest of the decor hasn't, strangely, been
accorded to the seat cushions, which are made of a scratchy
beige sackcloth-type material. Lager drinkers have just bottles of Stella and Corona to choose from, but there's a good
selection of rums and vodkas, including Wray & Nephew,
42 Below and Skyy. Food is a mix of Middle Eastern and
Spanish, comprising tagines and paellas.
Disabled: toilet. Function room. Music (DJs 8pm
Wed-Sat; £5 Fri, Sat). Tables outdoors (4, pavement).
Map 3 O5.

Bishops Finger

9-10 West Smithfield, EC1A 9JR (7248 2341).
Farringdon tube/rail. **Open** 11am-11pm Mon-Fri.
Food served noon-3pm, 6-9pm Mon-Thur; noon-3pm
Fri. **Credit** AmEx, MC, V.
This is a sleek and smart boozer beside Smithfield Market,
peopled by equally well-turned-out office workers. As it's
a Shepherd Neame pub, that brewery's ales dominate the
drinks on offer: Spitfire, Master Brew and, of course,
Bishops Finger are on tap, while bottles of Whitstable Bay
and 1698 are available from the chiller cabinet. Other companies' beers on offer include Oranjeboom and Asahi
draughts, plus Samuel Adams and Hürlimann in the fridge.
The muted decor is solid dark-wood tables and mirrors
framed with chestnut-coloured leather, while the walls support an assortment of pub-of-the-year awards and street
etchings from another era, while vaguely ecclesiastical-
looking candles line the windowsill. A menu dominated by
twelve varieties of sausages (pheasant with tarragon, lamb
with mint and a spicy Tunisian veggie version, all £7.25)
attracts many customers.
Babies and children admitted. Disabled: toilet. Function
room. Tables outdoors (3, pavement). TV. **Map 3 O5**.

Bleeding Heart Tavern

Bleeding Heart Yard, 19 Greville Street, EC1N 8SQ
(7404 0333/www.bleedingheart.co.uk). Farringdon
tube/rail. **Open** 11am-11pm Mon-Fri. **Food served**
Bar 11am-10.30pm Mon-Fri. *Bistro/tavern* noon-3pm,
6-10.30pm Mon-Fri. **Credit** AmEx, DC, MC, V.
A maroon exterior – with the name in golden cursive script
repeated over the big windows – conceals a cosy, dark-
wood bar. Our visits have always uncovered something
exciting from Adnams on draught (this time the terrific
Fisherman joined the usual Bitter and Broadside), but wine
is the place's lifeblood. You're invited to request a full list
of 450 options; the filleted list offers such as Le Marquis
grenache-syrah 2003 (£3.75/£12.75), a Le Clos de Paulilles
Banyuls Red 2003 (50ml, £8.95) and a 2004 sauvignon
blanc from the Bleeding Heart Vineyard in Hawkes Bay
(£4.50/£16.95). Perhaps a bit too mannered (the French-
speaking staff bustle about like waiters in trim black waist-
coats), but the place had a good bustle of post-workers that
died to a knot of die-hards by about 10pm. There's a restaurant downstairs (and another across the courtyard), but
food (of the suckling pig variety) is also served in the bar.
Function room. No piped music or jukebox. Restaurant.
Tables outdoors (10, terrace). **Map 3 N5**.

City

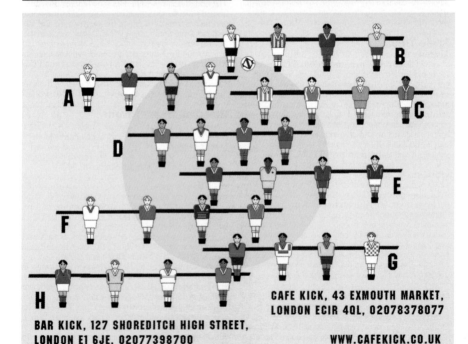

BAR KICK, 127 SHOREDITCH HIGH STREET,
LONDON E1 6JE, 02077398700

CAFE KICK, 43 EXMOUTH MARKET,
LONDON EC1R 4QL, 02078378077

WWW.CAFEKICK.CO.UK

Café Kick

43 Exmouth Market, EC1R 4QL (7837 8077/
www.cafekick.co.uk). Angel tube/Farringdon
tube/rail/19, 38 bus. **Open** noon-11pm Mon-Thur;
noon-midnight Fri, Sat; 5-10.30pm Sun (spring/summer
only). **Food served** noon-3pm, 6-10pm Mon-Fri; noon-
10pm Sat. **Happy hour** 4-7pm Mon-Sat. **Credit** MC, V.
There's always an enjoyably boisterous atmosphere at this
original branch of Café Kick. With fewer groups of lads
hogging the tables than at the Old Street one, it's often
easier to get your kicks on the three Bonzini babyfoot
tables at the front of the narrow bar. If things get too heated
round the tables, head to the bar at the back for decent cool-
ing cocktails and an excellent range of bottled beer from
around the world – Portuguese Sagres and Brazilian
Bravara made our line-up for the evening. Forget the half-
time oranges and go for platters of meat and cheese to
share round one of the titchy tables. A great destination at
any time of the year, this is bound to be one of the best
places to watch the World Cup this summer when the bay
doors will be opened on to the street.
Babies and children welcome (until 5pm). Games
(table football). Tables outdoors (2, pavement). TVs.
Map 3 N4.

Calthorpe Arms

252 Gray's Inn Road, WC1X 8JR (7278 4732).
Chancery Lane tube. **Open** 11am-11pm Mon-Thur;
11am-midnight Fri, Sat; noon-10.30pm Sun. **Food**
served noon-2.30pm, 6-9.30pm Mon, Tue, Thur, Fri;
noon-2.30pm, 7-9.30pm Wed; noon-2.30pm Sat, Sun.
Credit MC, V.
Modestly itself, this quiet Young's pub is on a corner in the
shabbier end of Holborn, behind Mount Pleasant sorting
office. Its pavement tables mark the boundary of the old
Calthorpe estate, whose crest over the door bears the motto
Gradu diverso una via – one way with different steps. Thus
ale lovers, sports fans and unfussy locals can convene over
a bottle of Young's Special Premium Ale, under the low
volume of all-day team news on satellite TV and over £4
lunches with chips (they have to compete with a caff next
door). Specials such as Moroccan chicken or lentil curry
are under a fiver. It's not all just for the price-conscious
punter – although the full Young's range of wines are well
priced. Plenty of room, too, between the brown banquettes
or at a table facing the leafy square opposite.
Babies and children welcome. Function room. Games
(fruit machine). No piped music or jukebox. Tables
outdoors (6, pavement). TV (satellite). **Map 3 M4**.

Castle

34-35 Cowcross Street, EC1M 6DB (7553 7621).
Farringdon tube/rail. **Open** noon-11pm Mon;
noon-midnight Tue-Thur; noon-1am Fri, Sat; noon-
10.30pm Sun. **Food served** noon-10pm daily.
Credit AmEx, MC, V.
The Castle has perfected a mishmash decor that creates an
atmosphere welcoming to everyone. The walls display
sombre, classically painted portraits alongside contemporary photographs of feet, an assortment of pot plants jaun-
tily decorate the window sills, and red toy reindeer are
posed indecently behind the bar. The bar itself is very well
stocked, with two white beers including Erdinger on tap,
plus Young's, Staropramen, Addlestones, Hoegaarden and
Grolsch. Grub is burgers and sandwiches, but the expected
mixed crowd seem more concerned with sampling the good
selection of booze. There's a tabletop Galaxians arcade
game to play when you're bored of staring at the flock

wallpaper, or you can enjoy the piped music if rock classics
and chilled beats make your kind of soundtrack.
Disabled: toilet. Function room. Games (arcade machine,
fruit machine). Music (DJs 7.30pm Fri, Sat; free).
No-smoking area. **Map 3 O5**.

Cellar Gascon

59 West Smithfield, EC1A 9DS (7796 0600). Barbican
tube/Farringdon tube/rail. **Open** noon-midnight
Mon-Fri. **Food served** noon-11pm Mon-Fri. **Credit**
AmEx, MC, V.
Sister establishment of the restaurant on the other side of
Smithfield's market, Cellar Gascon brings the vinous
delights of Gascony to an area more famed for its chops.
A sophisticated Gallic air pervades the stylish interior –
it's not just the Gauloise smoked by the fair share of French
patrons ashing into the large earthenware flowerpot ashtrays, but also the knowledgeable French bar staff who are
happy to advise on the extensive wine list. Divided by
region, there is plenty here to educate the palate. Most are
only available by the bottle, although the dozen or so
whites and seven reds by the glass are well chosen for variety. Superior snacks come in the form of olives and cornets
of chips, although it's worth investigating the seasonally
changing *dégustation* menu – the winter incarnation
included Gascony black ham and some interesting seafood.
Bar available for hire. Tables outdoors (3, pavement).
Map 3 O5.

Charterhouse

38 Charterhouse Street, EC1M 6JH (7608 0858/
www.charterhousebar.co.uk). Farringdon tube/rail.
Open noon-11pm Mon, Tue; noon-midnight Wed, Sun;
noon-1am Thur; noon-4am Fri; 5pm-4am Sat. **Food**
served noon-9.30pm Mon-Fri; 5-9.30pm Sat; noon-5pm
Sun. **Happy hour** 5-7pm daily. **Credit** AmEx, MC, V.
A perennially popular wedge of a bar that has late opening hours and regular DJ nights, making it a good bet either
for those heading to nearby Turnmills or Fabric, or as a
destination in its own right. Post-work drinks on a Friday
evening quickly turn into pre-club sharpeners with the
main ground-floor bar often heaving by 10pm. The bubbly
atmosphere extends into the large upstairs area where DJs
hold court. Midweek and on Sundays the atmosphere is a
bit more chilled and it's possible to enjoy a quietish drink
(San Miguel and Kronenbourg on tap) and some good food
at one of the small tables along the large window.
Function room. Music (DJs 8pm Thur-Sun; free).
Tables outdoors (3, pavement). TV (big screen).
Map 3 O5.

Cicada

132-136 St John Street, EC1V 4JT (7608 1550/
www.cicada.nu). Farringdon tube/rail. **Open** noon-
11pm Mon-Sat. **Food served** noon-3pm, 6-10pm
Mon-Sat. **Credit** AmEx, DC, MC, V.
The heavy glass doors leading into this classy bar may be
there to deter any less-than-stylish visitors entering the
calm, cool interior (stone floors, shiny wood furniture). The
food is Chinese, Japanese and Thai-influenced: bar dim sum
costing £3-£7 or a full menu in the posh diner-like restaurant that occupies one side of the central bar. Asian beers
– Tiger, Asahi and Tsing Tao – fill the fridges, while
Castlemaine XXXX is on tap, no doubt due to the
Australian owner. The cocktail list features imaginative
takes on the East–West fusion theme. A Saketini substi-
tutes saké for vermouth, while the Mekong Mule adds fresh
ginger and coriander to the traditional mix. A minimalist

City

open fireplace provides a focal point on the far wall, while in the basement there's an area available for private hire should you want to impress as many as 75 friends. *Babies and children admitted. Function room. Restaurant (no smoking). Tables outdoors (6, pavement). Map 3 O4.*

Clerkenwell House
23-27 Hatton Wall, EC1N 8JJ (7404 1113/ www.clerkenwellhouse.com). Chancery Lane tube/ Farringdon tube/rail. **Open** noon-11pm Mon-Wed; noon-midnight Thur-Sat; noon-10.30pm Sun. **Food served** noon-10pm Mon-Fri; 6-10pm Sat; noon-7pm Sun. **Happy hour** 6-9pm Mon-Wed; 8-9pm Thur-Sat; noon-10.30pm Sun. **Credit** AmEx, MC, V.
A serious contender for Match's crown as Clerkenwell's king cocktail provider. Just reading the menu induces lusty salivating, and ambrosial recipes such as Blueberry Amaretto Sour don't disappoint. There's a happy hour Monday to Saturday and all-day Sunday, when a selection of these creations go for £3.95 instead of an average of £5.50. In fact, Sunday is full of treats, with a full roast on offer as well as the Cinema Cocktail Club; when we asked what movies were showing, we were offered a selection to choose from. Top marks to the amiable, accommodating staff. Design-wise, monochrome moulded plastic chairs meld surprisingly well with battered wooden floorboards, squishy sofas, psychedelic prints and fittingly funky customers. The open kitchen prepares enticing bites such as a Lebanese meze platter (£12.50 for two to share), which you can work off around the pool tables in the basement. *Bar available for hire (weekends). Games (pool). Music (DJs 7pm Thur, Fri; free). TVs (big screen). Map 3 N5.*

Coach & Horses
26-28 Ray Street, EC1R 3DJ (7278 8990/www.the coachandhorses.com). Farringdon tube/rail. **Open** 11am-11pm Mon-Fri; 6-11pm Sat; noon-3pm Sun. **Food served** noon-3pm, 6-10pm Mon-Fri; 6-10pm Sat; noon-3pm Sun. **Credit** AmEx, MC, V.
Tucked behind the monstrous *Guardian* building, the Coach & Horses has lots of glass to let in daylight, but wood panels and tea-lights lend cosiness of an evening. On a Monday night the place was comfortably full (two tables reserved in the dining half) with a chatty crowd – *Guardian* readers rather than hacks – and the barmen proved sweet and helpful. The draught beers were good if unexceptional (Adnams Bitter, Landlord and Pride the bitters; Leffe, Hoegaarden and Staropramen the best lagers), but a good array of spirits ran to four Irish whiskies and a couple of dozen Scotches. Nibbles range from toasted pumpkin seeds (£1.50) to sprats with horseradish (£5) and Terroni & Sons cured meats (£6), while mains included Bleasedale lamb heart with carrots, watercress and bacon (£13.60). With ur-gastropub the Eagle (*see p118*) up the road, the Coach & Horses needs to be good to survive. It is. *Babies and children welcome. Garden available for hire (covered & heated). Tables outdoors (16, garden). Map 3 N4.*

Cock Tavern
East Poultry Avenue, Central Markets, EC1A 9LH (7248 2918). Farringdon tube/rail. **Open** 6am-11pm Mon-Thur; 6am-2am Fri; 10am-2am Sat. **Food served** 6am-4pm Mon-Fri. **Credit** AmEx, MC, V.
Thanks to special licensing hours, the Cock Tavern has long been a bastion of beer for breakfast for the traders

George & Dragon. *See p130.*

City

and butchers of Smithfield's. It's a subterranean dive, by which we mean an unreconstructed gem. A cross between a pub and a greasy spoon, the place is decorated with pictures of the market through the ages and old butchers' signs. A well-used pool table is tucked in a corner, with the main area of the bar split between a dining space furnished with long wooden tables and a nearly identical area with set tables for morning drinkers. The range of fry-ups on offer is a meat-lover's dream, with Courage Best the pick of the ales to wash it down with.
Babies and children admitted. Bar available for hire. Games (darts, fruit machine, pool table, quiz machine). TV (big screen, satellite). **Map 3 O5**.

Crown Tavern
43 Clerkenwell Green, EC1R 0EG (7253 4973). Farringdon tube/rail. **Open** noon-11.30pm Mon-Wed, Sun; noon-12.30am Thur-Sat. **Food served** noon-5pm, 6-9.30pm Mon-Thur; noon-5pm Fri-Sun. **Credit** AmEx, MC, V.
The pubs of Clerkenwell Green were meeting spots for radical groups in the 19th century, but there's a more conformist feel to the Crown these days. A refurb a couple of years ago retained the Victorian etched glass and dark wooden floor, but implanted a smattering of modern styling. The result is a fairly smart establishment, with the low leather sofas in the room behind the L-shaped bar providing a snug nook in winter and the bright main bar only let down by a few too many spotlights. Stairs lead up to the Apollo concert room, a former Victorian music hall where pool is on offer. A convivial atmosphere is usually generated by the area's young creative types, fuelled by Adnams Bitter and Kölsch lager on tap, plus an excellent selection of gin – Gordon's Sloe, Hendrick's and Plymouth. *Function room. Games (pool table). Tables outdoors (10, pavement).* **Map 3 N4**.

Dollar Grills & Martinis
2 Exmouth Market, EC1R 4PX (7278 0077). Angel tube/Farringdon tube/rail/19, 38 bus. **Open** 6pm-1am Mon-Sat; 6pm-midnight Sun. **Food served** 6pm-midnight Mon-Sat; 6-11pm Sun. **Credit** MC, V.
A hip subterranean dive that's more Lost Vagueness than Las Vegas, certainly so after a few of the house cocktails. The styling is slick – red lights barely illuminate the bare brickwork and not one but four glitter balls hang over the bar. The mood is intimate, the lighting low and the jeans often slung even lower by the young things of Clerkenwell. It's best to grab a spot on one of the low leather sofas and let the waiter provide the liquid entertainment. Take your pick from a list of crisp Martinis or plump for one of the more entertaining options, such as a Porn Star (Stolichnaya vodka, vanilla vodka, vanilla and passion-fruit liqueur, with a shot of Champagne on the side) or a Show Girl (watermelon, passion fruit, cranberry and vodka). *Babies and children welcome. Bar available for hire. Music (DJs 8pm Fri, Sat; free). Restaurant. Tables outdoors (10, pavement).* **Map 3 N4**.

Dovetail
9 Jerusalem Passage, EC1V 4JP (7490 7321/ www.belgianbars.com). Farringdon tube/rail. **Open** noon-11pm Mon-Sat. **Food served** noon-3pm, 6-10pm Mon-Sat. **Credit** MC, V.
Unlike its Hackney-based sister the Dove, Dovetail serves only Belgian beer – 101 varieties of the stuff. Taps supply Leffe Blonde and Brune, Jupiler and Maes Pils, and the menu makes a good guidebook for the beer explorer. The

City

selection includes witbiers, gueuze (made from Lambic ale), pilsners, golden ales, amber beers, a sour red beer and 18 fruit beers that encompass cranberry, banana and mango flavours. Westmalle and Achel are among several Trappist beers, which fit in spirit with the stone-flagged floors and pew-style seating. A touch of light relief is provided by a set of framed Tintin prints. You'll need something to wash down with all that beer – perhaps something from the range of sausages (£7.50-£8.50) or steak and, of course, ale pie (£6.50)?

Babies and children welcome. Disabled: toilet. **Map 3 O4**.

Eagle
159 Farringdon Road, EC1R 3AL (7837 1353).
Farringdon tube/rail. **Open** noon-11pm Mon-Sat; noon-5pm Sun. **Food served** 12.30-3pm, 6.30-10.30pm Mon-Fri; 12.30-3.30pm, 6.30-10.30pm Sat; 12.30-3.30pm Sun. **Credit** MC, V.

Widely regarded as the first gastropub, this crowded, cosy venue attracts students, young professionals and hacks from the nearby *Guardian* offices. This could be attributed to the down-to-earth pubby environs and a fabulous music policy. On the other hand, it could be the drinks, which include continental white beers, Charles Wells beer on draught, and a surprisingly good wine list. The food is great too: small plates of tapas are available alongside a full menu of Modern European and Mediterranean fare. Chefs can be seen cooking in open view behind the polished wooden bar that runs along the back wall, which only adds to the relaxed vibe. Still a casual and laid-back masterpiece.

Babies and children admitted. Tables outdoors (4, pavement). **Map 3 N4**.

Easton
22 Easton Street, WC1X 0DS (7278 7608/www.the easton.co.uk). Farringdon tube/rail/19, 38 bus. **Open** noon-11pm Mon-Thur; noon-1am Fri; 5.30pm-1am Sat; noon-10.30pm Sun. **Food served** 12.30-3pm, 6.30-10pm Mon-Thur; 12.30-3pm Fri; 6.30-10pm Sat; 1-4pm, 6.30-9.30pm Sun. **Credit** MC, V.

The Easton has the gastropub thing down to a T: it's a one-room place, not over-renovated, with lovely retro wallpaper, regularly changing wall art, big windows and pub-style tables. The food majors in big flavours (robust lamb, chorizo and sausage cassoulet, organic Saltmarsh lamb with champ, red cabbage and mustard seed gravy) and is served in generous portions without fuss or frippery. No real ales – John Smith's? – but if Guinness and several lagers (Staropramen and Hoegaarden the best) don't hit the spot, bottles of Magners, Budvar, Tiger and Corona (£3) might. The small but well-chosen wine list (eight white, 11 red) proffers a bottle of full-bodied Tamaya viognier for £15.95 and several by the glass, including a fruity Andes Sur shiraz (£3.20/£4.25). The well-stocked bar (with a 'No Dancing' sign – for customers or bar staff?) serves house spirits for £3 to £3.70, including Knob Creek bourbon and Wood's Old Rum. Music? Al Green's all right by us.

Babies and children admitted (daytime). Music (DJs 9pm Fri; free). Tables outdoors (4, pavement). **Map 3 N4**.

Fluid
40 Charterhouse Street, EC1M 6JN (7253 3444/ www.fluidbar.com). Barbican tube/Farringdon tube/rail. **Open** noon-midnight Mon-Wed; noon-2am Thur; noon-4am Fri; 7pm-4am Sat. **Food served** noon-10pm Mon-Fri. **Happy hour** 5-7pm Mon-Fri. **Admission** £3 after 9pm, £5 after 10pm Fri, Sat. **Credit** AmEx, MC, V.

This Japanese-themed cocktail lounge could have been a kitsch disaster, yet Fluid is louche and sassy enough to pull it off. The mixmeisters at the helm have come up with intriguing cocktails such as a wasabi Martini, priced at £6 (or half that during weekday happy hours). Bottles naturally include Sapporo, Kirin and the ubiquitous Asahi, and there are a handful of wines for customers not wanting to go the whole Japanese hog. The menu consists of a tasty spread of sashimi, tempura and gyoza, with instructions on how to eat it – surely superfluous given sushi's welcome colonisation of menus across town. Entertainment comes in the form of Space Invaders games, a decent-sized downstairs area that lends itself to dancing, and house, electro or jazzy tunes depending on the night.

Babies and children admitted (until 9pm). Function room. Games (retro video games). Music (DJs 7pm Tue-Sat). Tables outdoors (3, pavement). **Map 3 O5**.

Fox & Anchor
115 Charterhouse Street, EC1M 6AA (7253 5075).
Barbican tube/Farringdon tube/rail. **Open** 7am-11pm Mon-Fri. **Food served** 7am-9pm Mon-Fri. **Credit** AmEx, MC, V.

Tarted up by Mitchells & Butlers, the Fox & Anchor is imposingly good-looking: the 1898 façade has pale green and blue tiles, with sinuous plant life ascending to a couple of gargoyles. There's even a floor mosaic. Inside, the no-smoking back section is the place to be, with a cluster of snugs accompanied by intricate 'gas' lamps, black-and-white photos of market traders and an antique tin of Fox's Glacier Mints; the main bar is an attractive 1970s refit in dark wood with traditional tiling. The pub's proximity to Smithfield market accounts for its early opening, and the all-day breakfasts are a half-notch above the norm, from Full English (£5.95) to an awesome Full Monty (Full English plus chips, black pudding, liver and a Guinness, £9.95). The fat conscious go veggie (£5.50) or have smoked salmon with scrambled eggs (£4.95). Draught options were Deuchars IPA, Greene King IPA, Landlord and Pride; a bottle of Rosemount Jigsaw costs a heavyish £7.95. Trade was quiet but steady for our midweek morning visit.

Babies and children admitted (until 9pm). Function room. No-smoking area. Tables outdoors (3, pavement). **Map 3 O5**.

Green
29 Clerkenwell Green, EC1R 0DU (7490 8010).
Farringdon tube/rail. **Open** noon-11pm Mon-Wed; noon-midnight Thur, Fri; 4pm-1am Sat; noon-10.30pm Sun. **Food served** noon-3pm, 6-11pm Mon-Fri; 6pm-midnight Sat; noon-4pm, 6-10.30pm Sun. **Credit** AmEx, MC, V.

There's a nice easy vibe to this pub-like bar, which attracts a mixed crowd of suited and more casually dressed customers. The solid wooden tables are accessorised with an enormous antique clock and handmade fairy lights that make use of paper cake cases. There's a decent group of beers on tap, including London Pride, Bitburger, Red Stripe and Amstel; the wine list is more than adequate; an interesting selection of spirits temptingly lines a shelf behind the bar; and the tapas menu is a big attraction (a more extensive lunch menu is available upstairs). Staff were very accommodating on our visit, and there's a free jukebox, though we couldn't figure out how to use it. A refreshing change from the many highly styled bars in the area.

Babies and children welcome. Disabled: toilet. Function room. Games (cards, dominoes). Music (DJ 7pm Sat, Sun; free). Tables outdoors (6, pavement). **Map 3 N4**.

Gunmakers

13 Eyre Street Hill, EC1R 5ET (7278 1022/www.the gunmakers.co.uk). Farringdon tube/rail. **Open** noon-11pm Mon-Fri, noon-5pm Sun. **Food served** noon-3pm, 6-10pm Mon-Fri, noon-5pm Sun. **Credit** AmEx, MC, V.

Duck into this side street off Clerkenwell Road, the Gunmakers is there with its bustling atmosphere and a decent line in filling pub grub. Local professionals tuck into lamb cutlets with puy lentils or goat's cheese and sunblush tomato risotto (mains are priced £7-£14), washed down by Greene King IPA, Pilsner Urquell or Bombardier. Wine drinkers have eight bottles each of red and white to choose from, plus port and a Spanish moscatel. Compact without feeling cramped, the building comprises a bar in the entry section and a space with dining tables up a few steps in the back. The pub has recently begun opening on Sundays, with a full lunch on offer, and puts on a quiz night. *Babies and children welcome (until 6pm). Quiz (7pm Mon; £2). Tables outdoors (10, conservatory).* **Map 3 N4**.

Hand & Shears

1 Middle Street, EC1A 7JA (7600 0257). Barbican tube. **Open** 11am-11pm Mon-Fri. **Food served** noon-3pm Mon-Fri. **Credit** AmEx, MC, V.

One of a glut of traditional pubs in the back streets around Cloth Fair, the Hand & Shears at least has a distinctive history. The pub in its present guise was constructed on the site of an alehouse built in 1123, which used to serve condemned prisoners their last drink before they were led to the scaffold at nearby Newgate. Perhaps because it has remained largely untouched by the refurbishing hand that's been so hard at work everywhere else in Clerkenwell, the pub has a slightly unconventional layout. It's divided into three small nooks, so there are plenty of corners to squeeze into if it's privacy you're after rather than people-watching. The mostly suited customers drink Courage Best and Directors, and Theakston Best, and sate their appetites with hearty steak or calamares and chips for around £5. *Function room. Games (darts). No piped music or jukebox. Quiz (weekly; call for details). Restaurant.* **Map 3 O5**.

Jerusalem Tavern

55 Britton Street, EC1M 5UQ (7490 4281/ www.stpetersbrewery.co.uk). Farringdon tube/rail. **Open** 11am-11pm Mon-Fri. **Food served** noon-3pm, 5-10pm Mon-Fri. **Credit** MC, V.

As the only London pub associated with the St Peter's Brewery, the Jerusalem serves exemplary booze: Mild, Old-Style Porter, Bitter and Golden Ale, as well as Bitburger and Suffolk Cyder, on draught, plus a full range of other St Peter's beers in bottles and a reasonable wine list. But the beer isn't left in the hands of middle-elderly beards. The place was so packed on a (clement, admittedly) February night that people were sitting on the window sills and minuscule tables outside, the clientele a fine mix of nationalities, genders, ages and professions. The pub divides into three areas: a benched front section is partitioned from the bar (whose happily wonky feel is exemplified by a single table isolated on a kind of balcony), then a bit of table space at the back. It's all pretty tight and cosy, the green-painted wood, chipped walls and candles working well with original tiles and a shopfront that dates back to 1810. *Babies and children admitted. Bar available for hire (weekends only). No piped music or jukebox. Tables outdoors (2, pavement).* **Map 3 O4**.

Leonards EC1

42 Northampton Road, EC1R 0HU (7278 9983/ www.leonards-ec1.co.uk). Farringdon tube/rail. **Open** 11am-midnight Mon-Thur; 11am-2am Fri, Sat. **Food served** noon-3pm, 6-10pm daily. **Credit** MC, V.

A feeling of space is one of the main features of Leonards: the main bar alone is quite wide-reaching, and there are two further rooms to explore, with a separate restaurant area. A tropical fish tank, pool table, table football and Jenga await those who wander. The slightly battered leather couches are comfortable, and bands (often of an indie guitar persuasion) play on Friday and Saturday evenings. The drinks aren't very inviting – Foster's, Stella and Carling – but the food menu is currently being revamped and the new chef is planning minted lamb and poached salmon to go with the current sharing platters of spring rolls and mini sausages (£12). *Babies and children welcome. Disabled: toilet. Function room. Games (pool, quiz machine, table football). Music (bands 8pm Fri, Sat; £3). TV (big screen).* **Map 3 N4**.

Match EC1

45-47 Clerkenwell Road, EC1M 5RS (7250 4002/ www.matchbar.com). Farringdon tube/rail. **Open** 11am-midnight Mon-Fri; 5pm-midnight Sat. **Food served** noon-11pm Mon-Fri; 6-11pm Sat. **Credit** AmEx, DC, MC, V.

Match forms the old guard of Clerkenwell bars, and much of its continued success is down to Dale DeGroff's definitive and frequently changing cocktail list. The menu begins by noting that 'There is no such thing as a chocolate Martini', but any disappointment arising from this is swiftly forgotten. The Miss Martini is a lip-smackingly indulgent mix of vodka, raspberries, Chambord and fresh cream, while the Stone Pole tops up delectable Zubrowka with apple and ginger juices, and sparkling ginger beer. Prices start at £6.25 and can reach £12, but here you get what you pay for. The space itself consists of a table-lined balcony overlooking a sunken standing and dancing space, which faces the excellently stocked and styled bar. Food-wise, sharing bowls for up to four people are a nice idea – they include mushroom risotto and shepherd's pie. *Babies and children admitted (before 5pm). Disabled: toilet. Tables outdoors (4, pavement).* **Map 3 O4**.

Medcalf

40 Exmouth Market, EC1R 4QE (7833 3533/ www.medcalfbar.co.uk). Angel tube/Farringdon tube/ rail/19, 38 bus. **Open** noon-11pm Mon-Thur, Sat; noon-12.30am Fri; noon-5pm Sun. **Food served** noon-3pm, 6-10pm Mon-Thur; noon-3pm Fri; noon-4pm, 6-10.30pm Sat; noon-4pm Sun. **Credit** MC, V.

This informal, dressed-down venue in the heart of Exmouth Market was a butcher's shop from 1912 until the turn of this century. Split into a restaurant with chunky wooden furniture on one side, and an even chunkier wooden bar on the other, it's as much about dining as it is about drinking – except on Friday nights, when dinner gives way to live music, and DJs and bands take over to play soul, ragga, disco and funky flavas. Trendy market locals come here for interesting wheat beers like Erdinger on draught, and there's a small but well-chosen selection of reasonably priced, mainly Old World wines. We enjoyed a light, crisp Navajas Bianco Rioja 2002 (£13.75) and a characterful Les Aureliens 1999 Triennes (£15). Food includes a changing, seasonal and mainly organic menu of suitably meaty British classics, such as pork belly with smoked black pudding and Granny Smith sauce.

City

Babies and children admitted (until 7pm). Disabled: toilet. Music (DJs 7pm Fri; free). Tables outdoors (5, garden; 6, pavement). **Map 3 N4.**

Meet

85 Charterhouse Street, EC1M 6HJ (7490 5790/ www.meetbar.co.uk). Farringdon tube/rail. **Open** 5pm-1am Mon, Tue; 5pm-3am Wed; noon-3am Thur; noon Fri-11am Sat; 6pm Sat-noon Sun; 8pm Sun-4am Mon. **Food served** 5-10pm Mon-Wed; noon-10pm Thur, Fri. **Credit** AmEx, MC, V.

Meet's big selling point is its location next door to Fabric, and it knows this – on Fridays and Saturdays it opens from 3am to 11am, to catch the outflow when its legendary neighbour shuts up shop. Being an udder's shake from Smithfield market has inspired punningly meaty decor: the bar is wrapped in cowhide, they have a bovine logo, and a bemusing print on one wall proclaims 'Meet food/Meet market/Meet behind the bikesheds'. Clerkenwell's standard-issue industrial feel rules. Spirits are the order of the day, with no draught beer available, but there's a variety of Martinis and other cocktails. The food served on the ground floor borrows from European and Asian menus – how about fillet of beef with wasabi mash (£16.50)? The two remaining floors are for drinking and dancing. *Disabled: toilet. Function room. Music (DJs 9pm daily; £5-£10 Fri-Sun). Tables outdoors (6, pavement).* **Map 3 O5.**

Old China Hand

8 Tysoe Street, EC1R 4RQ (7278 7678). Angel tube/ 19, 38, 341 bus. **Open** noon-midnight Mon-Thur, Sun; noon-1am Fri, Sat. **Food served** noon-3pm, 6-10pm Mon-Fri; 6-10pm Sat. **Credit** MC, V.

Formerly an Irish pub by the name of Mulligans, this venue has gone east and upgraded itself into a replica of a genteel living room with ethnic aspirations. Heavy carved wood furniture and pot plants give an African feel, although bamboo light shades have an affinity with the dim sum menu (£3.20-£6.80). An assortment of beers and ales impressively takes in a good chunk of the world: take your pick from Keo from Cyprus, Sri Lankan Lion Dark stout, Canadian Moosehead or Peruvian Cusqueña. Sweden stakes its place with Koppaberg pear cider, and England contributes three gluten-free beers. A skylight and electric piano are welcome touches of character, appreciated by the families who seemed very at home here. *Babies and children welcome. Function room. Games (board games). No-smoking area. Tables outdoors (2, pavement). TVs (big screen, satellite).* **Map 3 N3.**

Pakenham Arms

1 Pakenham Street, WC1X 0LA (7837 6933). Russell Square tube/King's Cross tube/rail. **Open** 9am-1am Mon-Sat; 9am-10.30pm Sun. **Food served** 9.30am-9pm Mon-Fri. **Credit** MC, V.

Opposite Mount Pleasant sorting office lies this freehouse. If real ales are your thing, you're sorted. As well as Greene King IPA, there are a couple of guest ales from Sharp's Cornish Brewery, such as the fruity Cornish Coaster and marvellously named Doom Bar. Most of the posties seemed to plump for a post-shift pint of lager on our last visit, with eyes down for a perusal of the day's papers or glued to the TV above the door beaming in Sky Sports. Banquettes line the edge of the main bar area, leaving a mildly disconcerting amount of empty space in the centre of the pub. Food is of the burgers and baguettes variety. *Tables outdoors (6, pavement).* **Map 3 M4.**

Peasant

240 St John Street, EC1V 4PH (7336 7726/ www.thepeasant.co.uk). Angel tube/Farringdon tube/rail/19, 38 bus. **Open** noon-11pm daily. **Food served** noon-10.45pm Mon-Sat; noon-10pm Sun. **Credit** AmEx, MC, V.

Owners Greg and Patrick Wright have made this a place where you'll want to linger, whether it's in the restaurant upstairs – where we've previously enjoyed excellent Mediterranean and innovative dishes and chummy service – or in the main bar, where the shabby-chic decor is even more comforting and apt. Vintage fairground posters and art adorn the walls, and original picture tiles remain from the pub's days as a Victorian gin palace. A hearthfire is lit on gloomy winter days and, if you don't bag a spot on the battered old sofa, tables by the large windows provide prime spots to spend a lazy Sunday – a chalkboard brunch menu runs from bagels to full roasts. A fine wine menu lists more than 16 varieties by the glass and there are almost as many bottled Belgian beers in stock. In the summer months there's a cute little garden. *Babies and children welcome. Games (board games). Restaurant (available for hire; no smoking). Tables outdoors (4, garden terrace; 5, pavement).* **Map 3 O4.**

Potemkin

144 Clerkenwell Road, EC1R 5DP (7278 6661/ www.potemkin.co.uk). Farringdon tube/rail. **Open** noon-11pm Mon-Fri; 6-11pm Sat. **Food served** noon-10.30pm Mon-Fri; 6-10.30pm Sat. **Credit** AmEx, DC, MC, V.

Free of decor clichés such as commie memorabilia or stills from Eisenstein's 1925 film, this is a vodka bar that proves its Russian credentials simply by its food and drink. Boasting 130 different types of vodka, the best thing to do is experiment – the smiley expat Russian bar staff will happily recommend something if you're feeling overwhelmed by the choice. The line-up of sipping herbal vodka should make you feel virtuous, as well as drunk, while there are more fruit and spiced varieties than zeros in Roman Abramovich's bank account. Downstairs the red and purple plush basement restaurant serves authentic Russian cuisine that's more than borscht and dumplings. It's just a shame the sense of home comfort doesn't run to the slightly bland feel of the bar itself. *Bar available for hire. Restaurant (no smoking). TV (big screen, satellite).* **Map 3 N4.**

St John

26 St John Street, EC1M 4AY (7251 0848/4998/ www.stjohnrestaurant.com). Farringdon tube/rail. **Open/food served** 11am-11pm Mon-Fri; 6-11pm Sat. **Credit** AmEx, MC, V.

The roomy ground-floor bar attached to the world-renowned British restaurant is one of the best options in the area for anyone interested in civilised drinking. The place isn't at all grand – punters sit on rickety wooden chairs, gaze at whitewashed walls and place their orders at the bar. The atmosphere is low-key but welcoming, and the wine list is a selection of very enticing French bottles at all price levels. There's also Amstel and Black Sheep, among others, on tap, and Budvar by the bottle, plus sherries, single malts and even an absinthe. Snack food is no-nonsense but ambrosial; the likes of roast beef sandwich, welsh rarebit and lentils with curd cheese come in large portions. If you order nothing else, try the wonderful own-made bread. One for the discerning drinker. *Babies and children welcome. Disabled: toilet. Restaurant.* **Map 3 O5.**

City

Sekforde Arms
34 Sekforde Street, EC1R 0HA (7253 3251).
Farringdon tube/rail. **Open** 11am-11pm Mon-Fri;
11am-6pm Sat; noon-6pm Sun. **Food served** noon-
9.30pm Mon-Fri; noon-3pm Sat, Sun. **Credit** MC, V.
Down a back street from relentlessly hip Clerkenwell Green
lies this unprepossessing Young's pub, in which the only
chalkboard you'll find is used to keep score for the darts.
Pictures of the Queen Mum and Prince Charles pulling
Wandsworth's finest adorn the walls, and the traditionalist
theme continues all the way from the swagged curtains
down to the swirly red carpet and Burnley FC pendant
hanging over the mantelpiece. The Yorkshire connection
comes from landlord Bill and his wife Wendy, who cheerfully man the pumps. Midweek they quench the thirst of
those seeking the simple pleasures of ale, no-nonsense pub
grub and an unpretentious vibe. Saturdays it's distinctly
local, but on Friday nights there's a more mixed clientele.
*Babies and children admitted (restaurant). Function
room. Games (darts). Quiz (sports, 2-3 per week; free).
Restaurant. Tables outdoors (5, pavement). TV.*
Map 3 O4.

Slaughtered Lamb
34-35 Great Sutton Street, EC1V 0DX (7253 1516).
Barbican tube/Farringdon tube/rail. **Open** noon-
midnight daily. **Food served** noon-10.45pm daily.
Credit AmEx, DC, MC, V.
Only two years old, the Slaughtered Lamb has comfortably established itself on the local bar scene. It occupies a
corner site in a newbuild, and the large windows let in
enough light to illuminate the spacious single-room bar,
populated by mismatched furniture and leather sofas, faux
Edwardian wallpaper and a few self-conscious quirks –
enormous painted paper lanterns hang from the ceiling like
a Mardi Gras planetarium. The drinks on offer are also out
of the norm, if not out of this world – Paulaner wheat beer,
Canadian Sleeman Honey Brown lager, Bombardier and
Madonna's favourite tipple, Timothy Taylor Landlord.
Downstairs, the black-painted cellar is the scene for a
variety of events, including film showings.
*Babies and children welcome. Disabled: toilet. Film
screening (9pm Sun; free). Function room. Tables
outdoors (3, pavement). TV (satellite).* **Map 3 O4**.

Smiths of Smithfield
*67-77 Charterhouse Street, EC1M 6HJ (7251 7950/
www.smithsofsmithfield.co.uk). Farringdon tube/rail.*
Open *Ground floor bar/café* 7am-11pm Mon-Wed;
7am-12.30am Thur, Fri; 10am-12.30am Sat; 9.30am-
10.30pm Sun. *Cocktail bar* 5.30-10.30pm Mon-Wed;
5.30pm-1am Thur-Sat. **Meals served** *Ground floor
bar/café* 7am-5pm Mon-Fri; 10am-5pm Sat; 9.30am-
5pm Sun. **Credit** *Both* AmEx, DC, MC, V.
Located in a listed building opposite Smithfield Market and
alongside Fabric, John Torode's vibrant, roomy venue is
sprawled over four floors. The impressive interior is done
up in New York-style industrial warehouse chic, with brick,
concrete, wood, steel, cast iron, glass and leather. The
ground floor, with its simple wood and leather furniture
and large picture windows, is where the main drinking and
casual dining area is. It serves contemporary British and
continental fare such as breakfasts, sandwiches, toasties,
salads, weekend brunches, juices, milkshakes and smoothies. A young after-work crowd creates plenty of buzz, and
the house Czech lager is popular. There's also a small red
cocktail bar on the first floor, which serves Champagne,
plus good, reasonably priced cocktails like flavoured

Martinis around the £6-£7 mark. Our Great Pear cocktail
(fresh pears, Poire William, St Evremond Champagne, £7)
was intensely fruity without being too sweet.
*Babies and children welcome (restaurant). Bar available
for hire. Disabled: toilet. Music (DJ 8pm Wed-Sat).
Tables outdoors (6, pavement; 8, terrace).* **Map 3 O5**.

Three Kings of Clerkenwell
7 Clerkenwell Close, EC1R 0DY (7253 0483).
Farringdon tube/rail. **Open** noon-11pm Mon-Fri;
7-11pm Sat. **Food served** noon-3pm Mon-Fri.
No credit cards.
Welcome to slacker HQ. A glorious pub, also known as the
Clerkenwell Green Social Club, where the idle, creative and
shambling souls of Clerkenwell congregate for happy pints
(London Pride, Young's Bitter, Old Speckled Hen, Scrumpy
Jack, the usual lagers) under the watchful eye of a (fake)
rhino head thrusting out over the open fire. These decorative oddities are complemented by ancient flyer-covered
walls of saffron and russet, apparently handpicked fresh
flowers and all manner of crazy crap – glitter balls, fairy
lights, candles, 'art'. When the place is heaving on a Friday
night, take a tip from the pampered pub cat and find a spot
in one of the two slightly grungy rooms upstairs. In one
you'll find an impressive shell chandelier and a glass
cabinet of snowdomes; the other boasts a Prestige jukebox
with one of the best playlists in town.
*Babies and children welcome (daytime only). Function
rooms. Games (board games). No-smoking area
(upstairs at lunchtime). TV.* **Map 3 N4**.

Trading House Bar
*12-13 Greville Street, EC1N 8SB (7831 0697/www.
thetradinghouse.net). Chancery Lane tube/Farringdon
tube/rail.* **Open** noon-midnight Mon-Fri. **Food served**
noon-10pm Mon-Fri. **Credit** AmEx, MC, V.
Situated in the heart of the diamond district, this will seem
the right place to come when a nine-pound cocktail (they
range from £7 to £11) seems as nothing compared to the
fortune you've just spent on baubles. The cocktails are daz-
zling, such as the Fire Rose (Stolichnaya vodka, Crème de
Framboise, fresh raspberry purée, fresh mint and lemon).
There are, thankfully, more reasonably priced wines, and
beers by the bottle, that can be supped within this sleek,
white and luxe bar with its Philippe Starck armchairs,
Conran lamps and paintings by YBAs. The decor – glazed
newsprint mixing soft porn and financial pages – is a good
indicator of the target customer; expect City slickers
unwinding and flirting, and the occasional mature bene-
factor wooing an immature companion.
*Babies and children welcome (until 6pm). Music
(musicians/open mic 7.30pm Fri; free). Restaurant
(no smoking). Tables outdoors (3, pavement).* **Map 3 N5**.

Vinoteca
*7 St John Street, EC1M 4AA (7253 8786/
www.vinoteca.co.uk). Farringdon tube/rail.* **Open**
11am-11pm Mon-Sat. **Food served** noon-2.45pm,
6.30-10pm Mon-Fri; 6.30-10pm Sat. **Credit** MC, V.
Vinoteca is a real find, lovely staff, a nice atmosphere
and one of the best wine lists we've seen in a London bar.
And it's no smoking. Instead of the usual wine bar mark-
up of 300 per cent or so, there's a fairly flat amount added
on – which means that even the most expensive bottle on
the list, cult Aussie wine Bass Phillips (1996), costs £96 to
takeaway but can be drunk in house for £110. The list of
220 wines, from ten suppliers, contains plenty of interesting bottles, and starts from just £4.50. There's plenty

City

of choice under £15, plus fancier bottles if you don't mind forking out. The wines by the glass are great too: more than a dozen, across a big range of styles, costing £2.49 to £8.99 for a 175ml glass. And the food? Chef Carol Craddock's menu isn't fine dining, it's bar food – of the bare-boned, seasonally adjusted sort served at St John (*see p120*) across the road, such as a simple but well-prepared Welsh rarebit with soft-boiled egg, grilled smoked bacon and watercress.

Babies and children welcome. Function room. No smoking. Tables outdoors (4, pavement). **Map 3 O5.**

Vivat Bacchus
47 Farringdon Street, EC4A 4LL (7353 2648/ www.vivatbacchus.co.uk). Chancery Lane tube/ Farringdon tube/rail. **Open**/food served noon-11.30pm Mon-Fri. **Credit** AmEx, DC, MC, V.
As the name suggests, Vivat Bacchus is a supremely posh wine bar. It's also an upmarket restaurant, with a wine cellar diners can venture into to choose a bottle from the 250 stocked. In the bar, wines by the glass kick off at £3.95, though you could pay £15.50 for a glass of 1997 Cordoba Crescendo (no, us neither). Sophisticated dark wood dominates the decor, with perfectly set tables and deli items displayed on shelves behind the bar (it's also possible to choose your own cheese to end the meal with – there's a cheese room here as well). The food menu features the likes of foie gras, grilled springbok and jus of this and that, and will set you back £13.50-£19.50 for a main.
Babies and children admitted. Bar available for hire (no smoking). Disabled: toilet. Function room. Wine Club (7pm Mon; £12.50-£15). **Map 4 N5.**

Well
180 St John Street, EC1V 4JY (7251 9363/www. downthewell.com). Farringdon tube/rail. **Open** 11am-midnight Mon-Thur; 11am-1am Fri; 10.30am-1am Sat; 10.30am-11pm Sun. **Food** served noon-3pm, 6-10.30pm Mon-Fri; 10.30am-4pm, 6-10.30pm Sat; 10.30am-4pm, 6-10pm Sun. **Credit** AmEx, MC, V.
The more mature, upmarket residents of the area all seem to be found in the Well, a neat bar-brasserie on St John Street. The cuisine proffered is along the lines of whole roast bream at £13.95 and seared calf's liver at £14.50. Beers on tap include Paulaner and the Czech Zatec, and chiller cabinets hold a couple of interesting specimens such as Old Speckled Hen and the Portuguese Sagres. Wines are more of a strong point, with eight reds and whites available by the glass, and plenty of alluring choices by the bottle. The ground floor is mostly taken up by deliberately worn-out wooden dining tables, with some stools available at the matt metal bar, while down in the basement matters take a sultrier turn with chocolate leather banquettes, moody lighting and two aquariums built into the walls.
Babies and children welcome. Bar available for hire. Games (chess). Music (DJ 7.30pm Fri; free). Tables outdoors (6, pavement). **Map 3 O4.**

Zetter
86-88 Clerkenwell Road, EC1M 5RJ (7324 4455/ www.thezetter.com). Farringdon tube/rail. **Open**/food served 11am-11pm Mon-Sat; noon-10.30pm Sun. **Credit** AmEx, DC, MC, V.
By the entrance of a minimalist Italian restaurant inside the fashionable Zetter, this chic, tiny bar is little more than a curved black marble bar with bar stools overlooking St John's Square. That doesn't stop it being an ideal place to gossip with a friend over cocktails, with a drinks list that focuses on Italian spirits like Grappa and Vin Santo, plus a lot of fresh fruit. Most are priced £7 to £8.50. We loved Poppy (Cointreau, limoncello and pink grapefruit juice, £8) and Zetter Martini (Italian strawberry grapes, vodka and Prosecco, £8.50). There are a few beers in the Beck's vein, and a fabulous international wine list that is, not surprisingly, very strong on Italian regional wines. Nibbles typically include veal-stuffed olives and farinata (thin chickpea flour pancakes), and water from the hotel's own well beneath the building provides a talking point.
Babies and children welcome. Disabled: toilet. Function rooms. Restaurant. Tables outdoors (14, pavement). **Map 3 N4.**

Also in the area...
Heads & Tails 64-66 West Smithfield, EC1A 9HE (7600 0700).
Hog's Head Cowcross Place, Cowcross Street, EC1M 6DH (7251 3813).
The Printworks (JD Wetherspoon) 113-117 Farringdon Road, EC1R 3AP (7713 2000).
Puncheon (Davy's) Unit 5, Cowcross Place, Cowcross Street, EC1M 6DQ (7250 3336).
Sir John Oldcastle (JD Wetherspoon) 29-35 Farringdon Road, EC1M 3JF (7242 1013).

Fleet Street, Blackfriars & St Paul's

The newspaper offices are long gone – and with them the long boozy lunches of the hacks. These days it's all worsted wool and testosterone thanks to the presence of financial instutions and law firms. You can still find some charm, however, at the stunning art deco **Black Friar**, the labyrinthine **Ye Olde Cheshire Cheese** or stylish Champagne bar **La Grande Marque**.

Balls Brothers
6-8 Cheapside, EC2V 6AN (7248 2708/www.balls brothers.co.uk). St Paul's tube. **Open** 11am-10pm Mon-Fri. **Food served** 11.30am-9pm Mon-Fri. **Credit** AmEx, DC, MC, V.
Part of a chain, yes, but a justly popular haunt still. Given its location in the lee of St Paul's, the decor is suitably restrained, a palette of browns from floor to simply decorated ceiling, complemented by some lovely Victorian tiling. The vibe is friendly and relaxed, with plenty of space over two floors for a suited clientele to enjoy a strong Eurocentric wine list (well priced too, from £14 a bottle) and a highly appealing evening tapas menu ranging from single plates for £3 to excellent sharing platters for just under a tenner. At lunchtimes, it's a classy oasis from the roaring traffic, with office groups enjoying simple mains that range from sandwiches to grilled salmon.
Children admitted (garden only). Separate area for hire, seats 70. Tables outdoors (16, courtyard). **Map 4 O6.**

Black Friar
174 Queen Victoria Street, EC4V 4EG (7236 5474). Blackfriars tube/rail. **Open** 11am-11pm Mon-Wed, Sat; 11am-11.30pm Thur, Fri; noon-10.30pm Sun. **Food served** noon-9pm daily. **Credit** AmEx, MC, V.
Against stiff competition, the Black Friar could be the most extraordinary in Nicholson's portfolio of historic pubs. Built in 1875, the pub had its interior remodelled in 1905

by Arts & Crafts Movement devotee H Fuller Clark; Henry Poole the pale green mosaic exterior. An odd triangular shape, the pub has a billowing white marble-topped bar, sleekly rounded chairs and an impressive fireplace with carved and bronze friars everywhere. The odd anteroom has a glorious gold and jade mosaic ceiling, lush carpet, and Victorian saws of the 'Haste is slow' variety. Drinkers get a good mix of real ales (Enigma and Hard Willie joined Pride, Landlord, Speckled Hen and Young's Bitter for our last visit), plus mulled wine (£2.50) in winter, and the usual Nicholson's food (fish 'n' chips, £6.95) is rounded out with 50p pickled eggs and pistachios. Already no smoking years ahead of the ban, it's a little shiny for comfort, but an art nouveau vision nonetheless.
No smoking. Tables outdoors (10, pavement). TV.
Map 4 O6.

Cockpit
7 St Andrew's Hill, EC4V 5BY (7248 7315).
Blackfriars tube/rail. **Open** 11am-11pm Mon-Sat; noon-2.30pm, 7-10.30pm Sun. **Food served** 11am-2.30pm, 5-9pm Mon-Fri. **Credit** MC, V.
When Will Shakespeare was still a struggling young playwright, a cockfighting pit stood on the corner now occupied by this old boozer. The interior remains red, although now it's faded paint and carpet rather than poultry gore; a tiny mock balcony looks like another nod to the old days but is actually modern fakery. Despite all the cockfighting memorabilia, this is a relaxed place where old geezers sit telling jokes at the bar while knocking back Courage or Adnams from the taps. A board in one corner shares 'Cockpit News' with the clientele – on our visit, a strange mix of musings about 'Princess Camilla' and rabbit-fur fashion. Will would have approved.
Games (fruit machine, shove-halfpenny). TV (satellite).
Map 4 O6.

Dion
Paternoster House, 65 St Paul's Churchyard, EC4M 8AB (0871 223 6186/www.dionlondon.co.uk). St Paul's tube. **Open** noon-11pm Mon, Tue; noon-2am Wed-Fri. **Food served** noon-11pm Mon-Fri. **Credit** AmEx, MC, V.
Blending in seamlessly with the retail outlets all around it, Dion is a goldfish bowl on a corner beside St Paul's, with views through its wraparound windows of the cathedral and the passing throng. Inside, it's all shiny steel, dark stonework and pale walls – a clean-lined space for clean-living City folk keen to slide into booths alongside the wall and get amiably sloshed on the decent, though expensive, selection of wines. Food choices go down well enough, with choices ranging from lamb cutlets and cottage pie to fig and ham salads or sushi, but, despite the happy hubbub on our visit, Dion's essential characterlessness may find people moving on to the next new spot when it appears.
Bar available to hire (weekends). Disabled: toilet. Function room. Music (jazz 8pm Wed; free). Tables outdoors (8, pavement). TVs (big screen, satellite). **Map 4 O6**.

El Vino
47 Fleet Street, EC4Y 1BJ (7353 6786/www.elvino. co.uk). Chancery Lane or Temple tube/Blackfriars tube/ rail. **Open/food served** 8.30am-9pm Mon; 8.30am-10pm Tue-Fri. **Credit** AmEx, MC, V.
Once a legendary journalists' hangout, now one of a mini-chain of four venues, El Vino plays host to venerable legal sorts from the nearby chambers, happy to gossip in a beautiful old bar where cigar smoke filters the yellowing light

Booze talking
Three Kings of Clerkenwell

You are?
Deke Eichler, landlord of the Three Kings of Clerkenwell (*see p121*).
How long have you had the pub?
I've been working here for 18 years. It was my dad's pub and I started working here after I finished school and I'm still here.
What's with the papier mâché decorations?
A couple of friends of one of our barmen used to have a company called Total Pap and the whole pub at one time was kitted out in papier mâché, but no longer. The pub sign still is theirs – Elvis, Kong and Henry VIII, who is part of Clerkenwell history – and there are other little bits and pieces left over.
And the snow domes upstairs – is that your collection?
They belong to Paul. He's probably our oldest regular. He's been here such a long time he now works here.
How would you characterise the crowd that drinks in here?
A bunch of wankers. No, sorry, couldn't resist that. Extremely varied, but mostly they're people that just like pubs. A lot of people come in here and say, 'Oh, it's like a real pub'. I don't want to use the word quirky, but anybody who drinks in a Wetherspoon's or Slug & Lettuce would see it as quirky. The personality here comes from whoever's behind the bar first of all, and who's in the bar, and then what's around them. Like, we don't have any machines in here because we don't like clicking things in the corner – but we do have a jukebox upstairs.

City

Planning a function?

Fuller's have more venues than you can shake a cocktail stick at!

We have an unrivalled selection of pubs and bars across the Square Mile and throughout London. Let us know what you are planning and we will provide the venue solution and all the help you need to make your function a success.

Contact us at: functions@fullers.co.uk
or ask for our function organiser on 020 8996 2000

(if the smoke gets too much, a rear space offers sanctuary). The glowing sign outside proclaims the rule of wine here, 'Spain Portugal France Germany – bottle, dozen or in cask', and the selection is both superb and well priced. Snug surrounds offer intimate corners, while a delightfully traditional kitchen might knock out the likes of pork chops with cranberry sauce or a ribald-sounding 'warm French tart'. The bar also serves as a shop counter for the wine, with prices as low as £5 a bottle.
No piped music or jukebox. No-smoking area. Restaurant (available for hire; no smoking). Tables outdoors (2, pavement). TV. **Map 4 N6.**

Evangelist

33 Blackfriars Lane, EC4V 6EP (7213 0740). Blackfriars tube/rail. **Open** noon-11pm Mon-Fri. **Food served** noon-9pm Mon-Fri. **Credit** AmEx, MC, V.
'Bar and Eating House' declares the sign for this modern corner hangout down an alley off Ludgate Hill – a utilitarian statement for a utilitarian place. Wood and metal dominate the long, thin, split-level interior, with a bustling kitchen at one end to provide viewing entertainment as well as simple, good-quality cooking such as grilled sea bass or lamb shank on pea and onion mash. About a dozen each of reds and whites jostle for drinking attention alongside a reasonable cocktail list but a poor beer selection. But then this is more a place to eat than just drink, and – like the nearby Ochre (*see below*) – is a hit with its target audience of City twenty- and thirtysomethings.
Babies and children welcome (lunchtime only). Disabled: toilet. Function room. Restaurant. TV (big screen). **Map 4 O6.**

La Grande Marque

47 Ludgate Hill, EC4M 7JU (7329 6709/www.lagrande marque.com). St Paul's tube/Blackfriars tube/rail. **Open/food served** 11.30am-11pm Mon-Fri. **Credit** AmEx, DC, MC, V.
On a corner of Ludgate Hill in one of the finest bank conversions in London, an ornate carved ceiling looks down on the racket. The special here is Champagne, with bottles filling the window as a come-on to the well-heeled local workers. While it's mainly bankers and legal types cramming into the wood-panelled surrounds to decide which of the array of sparklers to give a slice of their bonus to, there's a good choice of red and whites for the less affluent. Any overflow can drift downstairs past the framed wine posters to a less grand basement bar. Sandwiches are on offer, but for most the bubbles alone seem to do the trick.
Function room. **Map 4 O6.**

Livery

130 Wood Street, EC2V 6DL (7600 9624/www.the livery.co.uk). St Paul's tube/Bank tube/DLR. **Open/food served** 11.30am-midnight Mon-Wed; 11.30am-1am Thur, Fri. **Credit** AmEx, MC, V.
What used to be 'One of 2' – a pair of mediocre City bars – has changed into two contemporary bars, the Livery and the Wall (*see p137*). The Livery is split into three areas: there's a spacious ground floor with exposed brick walls, maroon banquettes, bright modern artwork, church candles, plants and dimmed lighting; a smaller, but similar-looking, Den in the basement; and Loft, a mezzanine. Wines include white Rioja, bottled beers like Leffe Blonde and Früli, and very reasonably priced cocktails (£3.95-£6). Food includes cheese boards, pâté platters, sandwiches, burgers, salads and Mediterranean-style sharing platters (£9.95-£12.95). Service is friendly and efficient, and on our

visit the place was crowded with young City slickers. The Loft and Den can be hired at no extra charge, making this an ideal place for reasonably priced birthday celebrations.
Babies and children welcome (until 5pm). Bar available for hire (weekends). Disabled: toilet. Music (DJs 7pm Thur, Fri; free). No-smoking area. Tables outdoors (4, pavement). TV (big screen). **Map 6 P6.**

Ochre

2-3 Creed Lane, EC4V 5BR (0871 223 5106). St Paul's tube/11, 15, 26, 76 bus. **Open** 11am-11pm Mon-Wed; 11am-midnight Thur; 11am-2am Fri. **Food served** noon-3pm, 6-10pm Mon-Fri. **Credit** AmEx, MC, V.
Particularly popular with City workers for both lunch and a post-work quickie, this low-ceilinged space is warmed by a brick-red colour scheme and huge windows. Seating includes a couple of sofas for early arrivals, and the music policy goes for chilled and funky – or rather what City types in their late twenties class as chilled and funky. You can't deny the place caters admirably for its core demographic with a number of quality touches. For food, fish cakes are smoked haddock and brie, and the steak boasts how well hung it is. Staff are friendly, and there's a fine cocktail list and decent wines. Shame beer options don't stretch beyond lager, but this remains a decent hideaway within a stone's throw of St Paul's.
Bar available for hire (weekends). Disabled: toilet. Function room. Music (DJ/musicians 9pm Fri; free). TV (big screen). **Map 4 O6.**

Old Bank of England

194 Fleet Street, EC4A 2LT (7430 2255). Chancery Lane or Temple tube. **Open** 11am-11pm Mon-Fri. **Food served** noon-9pm Mon-Thur; noon-8pm Fri. **Credit** AmEx, MC, V.
Once a flamboyantly grand old Victorian banking hall, this is now home to a Fuller's Ale and Pie House. The gorgeous soaring ceiling sports huge brass chandeliers, casting their light on to frescoed walls and an oval central bar that dispenses good beer and a so-so wine selection. The ornate surroundings perhaps merit more august food than the basic meat and fish dishes on the menu, but own-made pies include more ambitious options such as sweet potato and goat's cheese – appropriate, really, as the pub stands on the site of the Haunch of Venison, where Sweeney Todd reputedly enjoyed the odd pie himself. Despite its size, there are some cosy nooks, including a small balcony and a side room in which debtors once doubtless trembled.
Function rooms. No-smoking area. Tables outdoors (11, courtyard). **Map 4 N6.**

Old Bell Tavern

95 Fleet Street, EC4Y 1DH (7583 0216). Blackfriars tube/rail. **Open** 11.30am-11pm Mon-Fri. **Food served** noon-9pm Mon-Fri. **Credit** (over £10) AmEx, MC, V.
As a chalkboard sign in the etched glass entryway points out, the Old Bell was built by Sir Christopher Wren for his workmen while they were labouring on St Bride's Church; the pub backs on to the churchyard. A central bar divides the place in two, with a fire at the open end, while the most recent of many restorations has left it with fine woodwork and some stained glass. It's busy at lunchtimes, but the smell of extinguished candles and cleaning fluid greeted us at 10.30pm on a Wednesday. A decent range of Scotch and umbrellas to borrow suggest a core clientele of City gents, though there was only a table of wrecked students for our visit. They'd probably been on the Staropramen, but should have tried the draught ale: Landlord, Adnams

City

Bitter, Pride and guest ale Hard Willie. There's standard pub grub for lunch, and a £12.50 offer on sparkling rosé if Kirsty MacColl and the Scissor Sisters get you in the mood. *Babies and children welcome. Games (golf machine). No-smoking area. TV.* **Map 4 N6.**

Ye Olde Cheshire Cheese
145 Fleet Street, EC4A 2BU (7353 6170/www.yeolde cheshirecheese.com). Blackfriars tube/rail. **Open** 11am-11pm Mon-Sat; noon-2.30pm Sun. **Food served** noon-9.30pm Mon-Fri; noon-8.30pm Sat; noon-2.30pm Sun. **Credit** AmEx, DC, MC, V.
Another huge, historic Sam Smith pub, this 17th-century chophouse has real literary pedigree (Dickens, Mark Twain and Yeats all got squiffy here) but we've never warmed to the place, which seems gloomy and awkward rather than dimly intimate and intriguing. You enter from a side alley to find a cosy little bar on your right and the white table-cloths of the Chop Room (£9.95 steak and kidney pudding, £8.50 bangers and mash) on your left; straight through you'll get to the bigger Cheshire Bar; below are cellared antechambers on several levels before you hit the Cellar Bar proper for a standard pub lunch. Upstairs lie further bars and function rooms, even the Johnson Restaurant – Dr J lived in neighbouring Gough Square. Old brewery ads, prints of Johnson and a copy of the place's 1947 booze licence adorn dark-wood panelling on the upper levels; flag-stones and painted walls take over beneath. Drinks are the usual Samuel Smith lagers, bitter and Extra Stout. *Babies and children admitted (restaurant). Function rooms. No piped music or jukebox. Restaurant (no smoking).* **Map 4 N6.**

Punch Tavern
99 Fleet Street, EC4Y 1DE (7353 6658). St Paul's tube/Blackfriars tube/rail. **Open** 7am-11pm Mon-Wed; 7am-midnight Thur, Fri. **Food served** 7-10.30pm Mon-Fri. **Credit** AmEx, MC, V.
This venerable old boozer has been updated since *Punch* magazine was conceived here in the 1840s, while maintaining some of its Victorian atmosphere. The gorgeous tiled and mirrored entrance remains, but in place of the gaudy old red and green decor there's pastel yellow in the front bar, complemented by cooler tones in a rear dining space. Food rather than history has become a prime selling point, with a popular prix fixe menu mixing salads, casseroles and traditional favourites, washed down perhaps with a nice drop of well-kept Timothy Taylor. 'Team drinks' are organised for the City overspill keen to sup £75 Veuve Clicquot while playing board games thoughtfully placed on the mantelpiece above the roaring fire. *Babies and children welcome. Function room. Games (board games). Quiz (6.30pm 1st Mon of mth; £10 per team). No-smoking area (lunch). Wine tasting (monthly; call for details).* **Map 4 N6.**

Rising Sun
61 Carter Lane, EC4V 5DY (7248 4544). St Paul's tube/Blackfriars tube/rail. **Open** 11am-11pm Mon-Fri. **Food served** noon-3pm, 5.30-10.30pm Mon-Fri. **Credit** AmEx, DC, MC, V.
Set in a quiet alley between Blackfriars and St Paul's, this is a welcome haven from the bustle of the City. Antique pub memorabilia and old black-and-whites of Victorian London adorn bright yellow walls, with a fire crackling in one corner. Brass chandeliers above the dark-wood floor are further nods to tradition. So it's a disappointment that the bar offers nothing beyond lager and Guinness from the

taps. But there's a short, well-chosen wine list to go with a friendly atmosphere, and you can watch the world go by through the glass frontage if big-screen Sky doesn't appeal. *Babies and children admitted. Games (fruit machine). Restaurant. TV (big screen, satellite).* **Map 4 O6.**

Shaw's Booksellers
31-34 St Andrew's Hill, EC4V 5DE (7489 7999). St Paul's tube/Blackfriars tube/rail. **Open** noon-11pm Mon-Fri. **Food served** noon-9pm Mon-Fri. **Credit** AmEx, DC, MC, V.
You won't find any worthy tomes at this back-street hide-away near Blackfriars, just weathered clapboard walls and swirling old ceiling fans framing a spacious, high-ceilinged room scattered with old wooden tables. A relaxed mix of office workers enjoy dishes like duck, orange and anise risotto and beef stir-fry with lime and ginger from a short but punchy menu. An excellent wine list features the likes of a nice viognier for £12 a bottle, and there's also a great choice by the glass. Many choose to linger in the relaxed ambience that is aided by a chilled background soundtrack. The name, by the way, is testament to the space posing as a bookshop in the 1990s Brit-flick *The Wings of the Dove*. *Disabled: toilet. TV.* **Map 4 O6.**

Tipperary
66 Fleet Street, EC4Y 1HT (7583 6470/www.tipperary pub.co.uk). Blackfriars tube/rail. **Open** 11am-11pm Mon-Fri; noon-6pm Sat, Sun. **Food served** 11am-10pm Mon-Fri; noon-5.30pm Sat, Sun. **Credit** AmEx, MC, V.
When the Boar's Head (as it was then) was taken over by Dublin brewer SG Mooney in 1700, it became London's first Irish pub – it was evidently blessed with the luck of the Irish, as the old building had survived the Fire of London. Renamed after World War I, it's only right and proper to taste the Guinness once you've squeezed into the tiny, thin space – even if IPA is on offer, too, with Greene King having bought the place in the 1960s. Although the shamrock-decorated mosaic floor is pretty enough, there's better Guinness to be had in London. The clientele (a mix of youngsters and chinless legal eagles) and food in the equally tiny upstairs room share that lack of distinction. *Babies and children admitted. Function room. Games (fruit machine). TV.* **Map 4 N6.**

Viaduct Tavern
126 Newgate Street, EC1A 7AA (7600 1863). St Paul's tube. **Open** 11am-11pm Mon-Fri. **Food served** noon-6pm Mon-Fri. **Credit** AmEx, MC, V.
This ravishing little pub lights up one of the City's blandest locations. Opened in 1869, it takes its name from William Heywood's nearby Holborn Viaduct, then a beacon of Victorian engineering prowess. The traffic may roar just outside, but inside there's an air of restrained bonhomie. Not that the decor shows much restraint: a glorious red ceiling covered by swirling patterns, walls decorated with nouveau-esque maidens and antique mirrors. A U-shaped bar offers Fuller's beers such as ESB, Discovery and Chiswick, along with well-selected wines. It's little wonder, then, that this is a popular retreat for those in recent attendance at the neighbouring Old Bailey, whether celebrating justice done or drowning sorrows at a case lost. *Games (quiz machine). TV (big screen).* **Map 4 O6.**

Also in the area...
All Bar One 44-46 Ludgate Hill, EC4M 7DE (7653 9901).

Balls Brothers 5-6 Carey Lane, EC2V 8AE (7600 2720).
City Pipe (Davy's) 33 Foster Lane, off Cheapside, EC2V 6HD (7606 2110).
Corney & Barrow 3 Fleet Place, EC4M 7RD (7329 3141); 10 Paternoster Square, EC4M 7DX (7618 9520).
Davy's 10 Creed Lane, EC4M 8SH (7236 5317).
El Vino 30 New Bridge Street, EC4V 6BJ (7236 4534).
Jamies 34 Ludgate Hill, EC4M 7DE (7489 1938).
Knights Templar (JD Wetherspoon) 95 Chancery Lane, off Carey Street, WC2A 1DT (7831 2660).
Metropolis Bar & Grill (Pitcher & Piano) 2 Old Change Court, Peter's Hill, EC4M 8EN (7236 5318).
O'Neill's 2-3 New Bridge Street, EC4V 6AA (7583 0227).
Zuccato 4 Bow Lane, EC4M 9DT (7329 6364).

Hoxton & Shoreditch

These days the fins, mullets and Nathan Barleys are but a distant, laughable memory around the Shoreditch Triangle (formed by Old Street, Great Eastern Street and Shoreditch High Street). Some of the previously cutting-edge bars are looking pretty dated too, but it's still possible to find great design, fine drinks and interesting record bags around here – just don't come at the weekend. It's packed.

Anda de Bridge

42-44 Kingsland Road, E2 8DA (7739 3863/ www.andadebridge.com). Old Street tube/rail/26, 48, 55, 67, 149, 242, 243 bus. **Open** 11am-midnight Mon-Sat; noon-11pm Sun. **Credit** AmEx, DC, MC, V.
Nestled, unsurprisingly, under a railway bridge, this bar brings a little taste of Kingston, Jamaica, to Kingsland Road. Wooden blinds prevent passers-by from peering at the interior, which can be chilly and rather depressing unless it's late, when groups after one last drink bump up the temperature and brighten the mood. The painted concrete floor, tables modelled from industrial cable spools and dusty dried flowers aren't very alluring, and the hand-covered couches have certainly seen better days, but, if you're after friendly and unpretentious, there are worse places to down a pint of Amstel, Heineken, Guinness or Red Stripe. Or you might choose a bottle of Carib lager or even a Sorrel Daiquiri to accompany your soul food. Decent snacks such as fried plantain, and mains like ackee and salt fish with dumplings, are served against a reggae/dub/dancehall backdrop.
Babies and children admitted. Disabled: toilet. Music (DJs 8pm Fri, Sat). **Map 5 R3.**

Artillery Arms

102 Bunhill Row, EC1Y 8ND (7253 4683). Old Street tube/rail. **Open** 11am-11pm Mon-Fri; noon-11pm Sat; noon-10.30pm Sun. **Food served** noon-3pm Mon-Fri. **Credit** AmEx, MC, V.
Perfectly positioned for a stop after a walk around Bunhill Fields cemetery opposite – where both William Blake and John Bunyan are buried – this cosy pub attracts mostly office types from the Barbican area at weekday lunchtimes, and a relaxed mix of locals and wandering tourists at weekends. The tiny, central, dark-wood and stained-glass bar

(more of a kiosk, really) serves Fuller's ales (London Pride, ESB, Chiswick and Jack Frost) and pub grub such as 'Aussie burgers'. On one side a long, green banquette is set against a rough brick wall, on which are hung framed collections of military-themed cigarette cards, while the high stools ranged around the window-ledges offer views of two TVs, perennially tuned to sports. An escape is offered by the very pleasant upstairs room, with an old marble fireplace where logs blaze in midwinter.
Babies and children welcome. Disabled: toilet. Function room. Games (darts, fruit machine). No-smoking area. TV (satellite). **Map 5 P4.**

Bar Kick

127 Shoreditch High Street, E1 6JE (7739 8700/ www.cafekick.co.uk). Old Street tube/rail via 55 or 243 bus. **Open** noon-11pm Mon-Wed, Sun; noon-midnight Thur-Sat. **Food served** noon-3.30pm, 5-10pm Mon-Wed; noon-3.30pm, 5-11pm Thur, Fri; noon-11pm Sat; noon-10pm Sun. **Credit** AmEx, MC, V.
Sister establishment to Café Kick in Exmouth Market, this cosy, well-appointed bar has retro (think 1950s Italian) decor that marks it out as truly special. The focus – and source of much rowdy activity – is the fussball tables and two Sky Sports-tuned, flat-panel TVs, but you can linger on a battered leather sofa or at one of the Formica-topped tables just admiring the numerous national flags draped overhead. A zinc-topped bar dispenses a wide range of bottled European lagers – Superbock, Cruzcampo and Sagres among them – alongside cocktails, fresh fruit juices, smoothies, coffee and tea from their 'Brewhaha' menu. A good kitchen serves snacks like Serrano ham and manchego sandwiches, and hearty mains such as Toulouse sausages with mash and own-made onion confit, to an animated crowd of Shoreditch locals and off-duty suits alike.
Babies and children admitted (lunchtime only). Disabled: toilet. Entertainment: table football tournaments 7pm last Thur of mth; from £3. Function room. No-smoking area. Tables outdoors (4, terrace). TVs (big screen, satellite). **Map 5 R4.**

Barley Mow

127 Curtain Road, EC2A 3BX (7729 3910). Old Street tube/rail/55 bus. **Open** noon-11pm Mon-Fri; 4-11pm Sat. **Credit** MC, V.
Having resisted renovation for years, standing its ground against an encroaching tide of cutting-edge boutiques and designer furniture stores, the Barley Mow has finally had a makeover. It's nothing radical, mind – just a lick of paint and the removal of the heavy wooden gantry over the bar – so this corner institution retains its decidedly traditional feel. The stripped wooden floor, small tables and church-like pews up the cosiness ante, but the bar defies all expectations, offering ten wines (plus three Champagnes), draught Litovel, Leffe Blonde and organic Honey Dew, various bottled Belgian specialities (including the exotic Floris Chocolate) and, for drivers, Holsten non-alcoholic lager or Fentimans soft drinks. Upstairs, a small, fairy-lit snug gives laptop users free wireless internet access.
Babies and children admitted (until 6pm). Function room. Quiz (9pm Mon; £1). **Map 5 R4.**

Bar Music Hall

134 Curtain Road, EC2A 3AR (7729 7216). Old Street tube/rail. **Open** 9am-midnight Mon-Thur, Sun; 9am-1am Fri; 10am-1am Sat. **Food served** 9am-5pm, 6-10pm Mon-Fri; 10am-5pm, 6-10pm Sat; 11am-5pm, 6-10pm Sun. **Credit** (over £10) MC, V.

City

Princess. See p133.

City

Champagne of wheat beers because of its light flavours and fruity acidity; dark wheat beer Paulaner Dunkel, which has wheaty tartness and luscious malt tones; and, from Cologne, light and refreshing Küppers Kölsch. There are eight appealing German beers in total. Sadly, the cooking is far less impressive; although patriotically Bavarian and Austrian, it doesn't scale Alpine heights.
Babies and children welcome. Function rooms. Music (accordion player 7.30pm Thur; DJ 7.30pm Fri, Sat; both free). No-smoking area. Restaurant. TV (big screen, satellite). **Map 5 P3**.

Bedroom Bar

62 Rivington Street, EC2A 3AY (7613 5637). Old Street tube/rail. **Open** 7pm-midnight Thur; 7pm-2am Fri, Sat. **Food served** 7-10pm Thur-Sat. **Admission** £3 after 10.30pm Fri, Sat. **Credit** MC, V.
Enter the uninviting doorway next to the Comedy Café, climb the stairs and you'll find a surprisingly good-looking, well-appointed space, featuring the double iron bed (complete with animal-print pillows) that gives this bar its name tucked in next to the DJ booth. There's plenty of seating – long, brown leatherette banquettes around low coffee tables, a single chesterfield, leather-topped stools made from garbage tins – with the bare floor, cream-painted brickwork and wide windows reinforcing a sense of light and spaciousness. The upside-down tin pails that double as ceiling lights are a funky touch, as are the wall oil-slide projections, which accompany the mainly Euro-house music favoured by the DJs. A long, pinewood bar offers draught Kronenbourg, Leffe and Budvar, plus the bottled regulars, alongside boudoir-themed cocktails (Wet Spot, Sex On The Bed, ahem). A worthwhile stop.
Bar available for hire. Music (DJs 7pm Thur-Sat). **Map 5 R4**.

Bricklayer's Arms

63 Charlotte Road, EC2A 3PE (7739 5245/ www.333mother.com). Old Street tube/rail/55 bus. **Open** noon-11pm Mon-Thur; noon-midnight Fri, Sat; noon-10.30pm Sun. **Food served** noon-3pm, 6-11pm Mon-Fri; 2.30-11pm Sat; 1.30-9pm Sun. **Credit** MC, V.
The doughty character of this boozer (it predates the gentrification of Shoreditch by an ice age, though it's now in cahoots with Mother, *see p132*, and the Red Lion, *see p133*) and its shabby charm make up for the lack of imagination at the bar, where you'll find nothing more adventurous than Old Speckled Hen on tap or bottled Baltika and Corona. That 'the Brickies' is all about vibe is evident from the ancient wooden floor, the khaki parachute draped from the ceiling, the seating (old church pews, knackered pouffes, the odd empty beer keg), the local art (of varying quality) and the fact that no one ever gets around to taking down the Christmas lights. Its chaos is cheerful and well meaning, with plenty of fanzines and art exhibition/club pamphlets strewn along the window ledges and a good, well-patronised jukebox. In the dining room upstairs, a Thai kitchen serves decent food in a less anarchic atmosphere.
Jukebox. Restaurant (available for hire). **Map 5 R4**.

Cantaloupe

35 Charlotte Road, EC2A 3PB (7613 4411/ www.cantaloupe.co.uk). Old Street tube/rail/55 bus. **Open/food served** 11am-midnight Mon-Fri; noon-midnight Sat; noon-11.30pm Sun. **Credit** AmEx, DC, MC, V.

Formerly the site of the famous Brick Lane Music Hall, where the likes of Danny La Rue played, and most recently (and briefly) the Hell Bar, this establishment is now equal parts New York-styled grill and upmarket bar. It's a huge space dominated by a vast, stainless-steel-topped serving area, but smart design and decor – blonde wooden chairs and lacquered tables, black vinyl banquettes, muted lighting and trompe l'oeil graphics on one wall – create the illusion of warmth and intimacy. It may be out of step with the Shoreditch concept of cool, leaving it to be patronised chiefly by yuppies, but they seem happy with what's on offer: breakfasts, all-day snacks, hearty meat and fish dishes, and a Sunday roast with all the trimmings, plus an impressive drinks menu that includes Belgian draught and bottled beers, wines, Champagnes and cocktails. Jazz/funk bands occasionally play.
Babies and children welcome. Disabled: toilet. Music (jazz 8pm Mon; bands/DJs 8pm Tue-Sun). Tables outdoors (12, pavement). **Map 5 R4**.

Bavarian Beerhouse

190 City Road, EC1V 2QH (7608 0925/www.bavarian-beerhouse.co.uk). Old Street tube/rail. **Open** 11am-11pm Mon-Thur; 11am-1am Fri, Sat; 11am-10.30pm Sun. **Food served** 11am-10pm daily. **Credit** AmEx, MC, V.
It's like a Grayson Perry 'Claire' convention. The dirndls sported by the female staff may be traditional costume, but the effect of full skirt, bodice, lacy blouse and apron in an insalubrious, low-budget basement makes this dingy room look like a dive bar for cross-dressers. The intention is to evoke Bavaria – home of lederhosen, hearty German food, the Oktoberfest and great beer. The latter includes Munich's Erdinger Hefe-Weissbier, considered the

Now in its 11th year, this bar-restaurant, housed in a former light industrial building, was initially one of just three watering holes in Shoreditch, and the only one open at weekends. Now it has plenty of competition, but Cantaloupe seems to have no trouble holding its own. Noisily enthusiastic crowds still pack both the front bar area – with its hefty wooden tables and seating – and the back room (plump leather couches set around low, candlelit coffee tables) to the gunwales Thursday through Sunday nights. The range of bottled and draught brews includes König Ludwig wheat beer and organic cider, and there's an impressive list of wines and cocktails (including three non-alcoholic options). The restaurant in the back room is sensibly raised, separate from the hubbub of the lounge area, and focuses on hearty Mediterranean and Latin American fare.
Babies and children admitted (restaurant). Bar available for hire. Disabled: toilet. Music (DJ 8pm Fri-Sun; free). Restaurant (available for hire). **Map 5 R4.**

Catch

22 Kingsland Road, E2 8DA (7729 6097/ www.thecatchbar.com). Old Street tube/rail/55 bus. **Open** 6pm-midnight Tue, Wed; 6pm-2am Thur-Sat; 6pm-1am Sun. **No credit cards.**
Its location – a stone's throw from the 'Shoreditch triangle' – and the fact that it doesn't charge admission, explain why Catch (the street number is the clue to its name) often has a queue outside its door after kicking-out time. Amiable bouncers usher in a mixed crowd, who jockey for the seating spots (in raised, dark wooden booths and on leather couches under the window) or simply mob the bar for its draught lagers (Grolsch, Staropramen, Carling) and usual bottled brews. It's a pleasant if unprepossessing space, with one wall of old, white clapboard, fixed mirrors opposite and a pool table at the rear. As the evening advances, this is shifted aside to make space for enthusiastic booty shakers, who dance to DJs playing everything from disco to punk and R&B. Upstairs, a larger, L-shaped space often hosts live local and leftfield bands.
Function room (club upstairs). Games (pool table). Music (bands/DJs Tue-Sun; free-£5). **Map 5 R3.**

Charlie Wright's International Bar

45 Pitfield Street, N1 6DA (7490 8345). Old Street tube/rail/55 bus. **Open** noon-1am Mon-Wed, Sun; noon-2am Thur; noon-3am Fri, Sat. **Food served** noon-3pm, 5-10pm daily. **Admission** £3 after 10pm Fri, Sat. **Credit** MC, V.
Once the only place in Shoreditch where you could have one for the road after the pubs shut, Charlie Wright's is still happily holding its own. Fans are doubtless drawn more by its cheerful-to-chaotic atmosphere than its history, although it's hard not to like a bar run by a friendly, former Ghanaian weightlifter, whose framed photos are propped up by the bar. The long, slightly gloomy, yet oddly inviting space is divided by a wood-panelled wall and set with pub-issue tables and chairs, with one fussball table at the very back. The bar offers an excellent range of draught and bottled beers, with the emphasis on Belgian specialities (Leffe, Duvel, Chimay, Erdinger, Früli, Belle-Vue and more), but the kitchen has turned to Thailand for its inspiration and often attracts office workers for lunch during the week, long before the late revelry begins.
Babies and children admitted (until 7pm). Games (fruit machine, pool). Music (DJs 8pm Thur-Sun). Restaurant. TV (big screen, satellite). **Map 5 Q3.**

Cocomo

323 Old Street, EC1V 9LE (7613 0315). Old Street tube/rail/55 bus. **Open/food served** 5pm-midnight Mon-Sat. **Credit** MC, V.
The slightly scruffy, DIY attempt at Moroccan-themed decor is what makes Cocomo so cosy and welcoming. It's a tiny space – uncomfortably so at weekends, when you have to pick your way over bodies on floor cushions to reach the downstairs toilets – but, once you've settled here, it's easy to let the time slip by. At street level, the ambience is established via Moroccan lanterns, elaborately gold-framed mirrors and a generally agreeable music selection (thanks, in part, to the bar's association with DJ and label boss Rob Da Bank), while piles of flyers and a proliferation of posters advertising local events makes it feel like a community drop-in centre. The bar mixes mean Mojitos, Daiquiris and Martinis, but there are also draught Red Stripe, a range of bottled lagers (Hoegaarden, San Miguel, Beck's) and a choice of fruit smoothies for health freaks.
Music (DJs 8pm Thur-Sat; free). **Map 5 R4.**

Cube & Star

39A Hoxton Square, N1 6NN (7739 8824/www.the cubeandstar.co.uk). Old Street tube/rail. **Open** 5pm-midnight Mon-Thur; 5pm-1am Fri, Sat. **Food served** 5-11pm daily. **Credit** AmEx, MC, V.
Occupying the premises of the fêted former Shoreditch Electricity Showrooms, this new kid on the block introduces a decidedly swanky and sophisticated note to the neighbourhood. The street-level space is now a restaurant specialising in Nuevo Latino fare, with the lounge bar in the basement – where there's also a cigar humidor – complementing the decadent, pre-Castro Cuba theme. Almost every visible surface of this small, low-ceilinged space is padded – red walls, black leather armchairs, gold-framed couches, even the red velveteen, upholstered DJ booth – creating a cosy, cocoon-like vibe that suggests you've just wandered into the lounge of an upmarket Cuban hotel. Friendly, black-clad bar staff serve Mojitos, Daiquiris and the like alongside a range of bottled beers, including Corona, Pacifico, Kasteel Cru and Negra Modelo, to a soundtrack that is unsurprisingly heavy on Tropicália and bossa beats.
Bar available for hire. Music (jazz/funk 9.30pm Thur, Fri; £5-£10; DJs 9pm Thur-Sat; free). No-smoking area. **Map 5 R3.**

Dragon

5 Leonard Street, EC2A 4AQ (7490 7110). Old Street or Liverpool Street tube/rail. **Open** noon-11pm Mon, Sun; noon-midnight Tue, Wed; noon-1am Thur; noon-2am Fri, Sat. **Credit** (over £10) MC, V.
If it weren't for the fact that the door is usually left open, nothing would alert you to this unadvertised hideaway on an alley corner, slightly off Shoreditch's beaten track. Inside, you'll find a worn wooden floor, exposed brickwork, 1970s leather couches, mismatched armchairs and coffee tables, all under mellow lighting. A Lower East-Side vibe seems to be the aim and, to that effect, a long bar is the focus, with gleaming ranks of spirit and liqueur bottles watched over by a huge antlered deer's head. On quiet nights, one of the bar staff might well double as DJ, playing hip hop or electronica while serving standard draught lagers and bottled brews including Coors, Pacifico and Negra Modelo. Downstairs, grouped retro couches and strings of fairy lights beckon, offering space to lounge in comfort and providing a sharp contrast to the basic, graffiti-smothered toilet facilities.

City

Babies and children admitted (daytime). Music (DJs 8pm nightly; open mic 7pm 1st Sun of mth; both free). Tables outdoors (1, pavement). Map 5 Q4.

dreambagsjaguarshoes

34-36 Kingsland Road, E2 8DA (7729 5830/ www.dreambagsjaguarshoes.com). Old Street tube/rail. **Open** 5pm-midnight Mon; 5pm-1am Tue-Sat; 5pm-12.30am Sun. **Credit** MC, V.

The bar's surreal name is taken from its previous incarnation as two retail outlets, but there's little left of them except for the old shop signs outside. Concrete dominates, but the walls are softened with changing paint jobs (graffiti, manga figures and giant tattoos have all featured) and mellow lighting, while battered leather sofas under the windows provide relief from Formica tables with plastic chairs. The bar dispenses bottled Belgian specialities such as Leffe and Belle-Vue alongside cider and draught lagers, and there's a decent wine list, but the young crowds are more likely to swig back bottled standards while they listen to DJs playing everything from 1980s soft metal to rockabilly. Head downstairs and you'll find more beaten-up couches and exposed brickwork, but don't expect peace and quiet at the weekends – the place is usually packed. *Bar available for hire. Music (DJs 8pm Wed-Sun; free).* **Map 5 R3**.

Drunken Monkey

222 Shoreditch High Street, E1 6PJ (7392 9606/ www.thedrunkenmonkey.co.uk). Liverpool Street tube/ rail/35, 47, 242, 344 bus. **Open** noon-midnight Mon-Fri; 6pm-midnight Sat; noon-11pm Sun. **Food served** noon-11pm Mon-Fri; 6-11pm Sat; noon-10.30pm Sun. **Credit** AmEx, MC, V.

A combined dim sum eaterie and bar, this establishment provides a cosy and convivial environment for both. Heavy wooden tables and black leatherette banquettes flank the walls, which are covered with huge mirrors edged with gilt latticework. Dozens of large, red Chinese lanterns dominate the long space, while gold-framed calligraphy prints offset the dark wooden bar and crimson, crackle-painted wall opposite. The intimate Concubine Room provides space for just two tables but, up a few stairs, there's the larger Wu Dan dining area, where patrons can enjoy reasonably priced dim sum, barbecue, rice and noodle dishes. An extensive drinks menu offers French Kasteel Cru lager, Breton cider and Worthington's White Shield ale, alongside countless long and short cocktails, wines and Champagnes, while DJs play what the venue describes as 'music with soul for healthy digestion'. *Babies and children admitted. Function room. Music (DJs 8pm Wed-Sun; free). Restaurant.* **Map 5 R4**.

Fleapit

49 Columbia Road, E2 7RG (7033 9986/www.theflea pit.com). Old Street tube/rail. **Open/food served** 3.30-11pm Tue, Wed; 11.30am-11pm Thur-Sat; 9.30am-2pm Sun. **Credit** AmEx, MC, V.

'Organic food, drink and a little art' is what this airy, corner café-bar promises. The Pit out back is a space for art exhibitions and film screenings, but in front the setting is cream-painted brickwork, 1970s dining tables and chairs, retro leather couches and the odd recliner. Light meals such as goat's cheese and butternut squash frittata are served on funky 1970s crockery, alongside ethically traded coffee, fresh fruit/vegetable juices and a good selection of organic wines and micro brews, including NI wheat beer, Shoreditch Stout and Eco Warrior – all from Hoxton's

Pitfield Brewery. During the day, patrons are mostly local, groovy, young parents who treat the place like an extension of their own homes and talk is of toddlers and film treatments. Those in search of a quiet drink should take note: half the customers may be under the age of three. *Babies and children welcome. Disabled: toilet. Film screenings (check website for details). Function room. Internet access (free). Music (musicians monthly, check website for details). Tables outdoors (3, pavement).*

Foundry

84-86 Great Eastern Street, EC2A 3JL (7739 6900/ www.foundry.tv). Old Street tube/rail/55 bus. **Open** 4.30-11pm Tue-Fri; 2.30-11pm Sat; 2.30-10.30pm Sun. **No credit cards.**

Suggesting a sixth-form den as decorated by Glastonbury veterans, this converted bank is easily the most eccentric of the neighbourhood's bars. To say it's run-down is to seriously understate things, but that's as much a deliberate statement of Foundry's artistic intent as the result of a shoestring budget. A concrete floor, wobbly tables and mismatched chairs, battered sofas, old TVs perched on top of speaker stacks, banks of ancient computers, dolls and painted underpants suspended from the ceiling, amateur art, candles in empty wine bottles, yards of exposed cable and wiring strung overhead – all create an anarchic, community-spirited environment. The bar choices are equally out of the ordinary, with Pitfield Brewery's Eco Warrier, Shoreditch Stout and Hoxton Farmhouse Cider offered alongside draught Stella, Guinness, Boddingtons and Carling. Downstairs in the old vaults a wide variety of art is on display in ever-changing exhibitions. *Art exhibitions (free). Games (chess). Music (pianist 6pm Tue; free). Poetry readings (9pm Sun; free). Tables outdoors (5, pavement).* **Map 5 Q4**.

Fox

28 Paul Street, EC2A 4LB (7729 5708). Old Street tube/rail. **Open** noon-11pm Mon-Fri. **Food served** 12.30-3pm, 6.30-10pm Mon-Fri. **Credit** MC, V.

Its proximity to Moorgate, rather than the hub of Shoreditch, explains why this boozer is closed at weekends – there's simply no passing trade. The rest of the week, however, it's a popular workers' watering hole whose amiably scuffed warmth also draws in the odd local hipster. Glossy red and cream paintwork is offset by the weathered wood floor, wall panelling and jumble of wooden chairs and tables. The bar (the contemporary flowers are a nice touch) dispenses Hoegaarden and Bombardier alongside draught and bottled standards and features a substantial wine list. The hungry can order the likes of Welsh rarebit and beef and Bombardier pie at the bar, but upstairs in the dining room, the team behind the fêted Eagle (*see p118*) offers fancier fare such as razor clams or partridge and potato cake in slightly more formal surroundings. *Babies and children admitted (restaurant). Restaurant (available for hire). Tables outdoors (6, terrace).* **Map 5 Q4**.

George & Dragon

2 Hackney Road, E2 7NS (7012 1100). Old Street tube/ rail/55 bus. **Open** 5-11pm daily. **Credit** MC, V.

This charmingly scruffy, old-school boozer with a camp inflection may no longer attract the likes of Kathy Lette and Samantha Morton, who have both crossed its once notorious Sunday-night club off their gay hipster checklist, but it's still often packed to the rafters with party-minded punters. There's the requisite bare floor and

wooden tables and chairs, with heavy drapes and part-frosted windows to discourage passers-by from staring in, but it's the kitschy clutter that charms. Chinese paper parasols, fairy lights, glitter-covered guitars, gilt-framed paintings, a baby rocking horse and a cardboard cut-out of Cher all compete for space. Next to the pair of stuffed birds on the bar, the usual range of draught and bottled beverages (including Kronenbourg Blanc) is served. Small wonder that in 2005 the idiosyncratic George was part of the London in Six Easy Steps art installation at the ICA – complete with a working bar and DJs.
Disabled: toilet. Music (DJs 8pm nightly; free). **Map 5 R3**.

Great Eastern
54-56 Great Eastern Street, EC2A 3QR (7613 4545/ www.greateasterndining.co.uk). Old Street tube/rail/ 55 bus. **Open/food served** *Ground-floor bar* noon-midnight Mon-Fri; 6pm-midnight Sat. *Below 54 bar* 7.30pm-1am Fri, Sat. **Credit** Both AmEx, DC, MC, V.
Recently revamped, this venue has retained its decidedly upmarket vibe. Unlike many of its neighbours, it resisted the temptation to cram in more seating than the space can comfortably accommodate and the ground-floor bar feels elegant and airy. Dark wood (floor, tables, wall benches), leather and polished chrome predominate, offset by crimson chairs, a China-red feature wall and modern candelabra. The Eastern theme is carried through into the menu of the adjacent Dining Room. During the week, the street-level bar is a pleasant place to sup a pint of draught lager (Leffe and Hoegaarden included), peruse the cocktail menu or nibble on bar food such as baby pork ribs with black bean sauce. Downstairs, Below 54 plays host to a younger – though equally affluent – weekend clubbing crowd.
Babies and children admitted (weekend clubbing only). Bar available for hire. Music (DJs 9pm Fri, Sat; free). Restaurant (no smoking). **Map 5 R4**.

Griffin
93 Leonard Street, EC2A 4RD (7739 6719). Old Street tube/rail. **Open/food served** 11am-11pm Mon-Sat; noon-10.30pm Sun. **Credit** MC, V.
Among Shoreditch's countless self-consciously styled bars, the Griffin stands alone as an original, unreconstructed boozer. Cheerfully shabby and emitting a friendly, well-loved glow, its sole concession to decoration in decades has been the removal of the ancient carpet to reveal the bare boards beneath. Standard-issue wooden tables with stools, basic toilet facilities (just one cubicle for women), a tiny fireplace and a busy pool table confirm the venue's traditionalism. Its patrons, however, are mainly local media, music and fashion types, who settle in with a pint of draught (regulation ale and lager selections, plus Baltika and Kronenbourg Blanc) or choose from a list of ten wines. Above, the cosy lounge/cocktail bar with its sofas and odd armchairs provides escape from the downstairs crush, which can be unbearable on Friday and Saturday nights.
Babies and children admitted (until 7pm). Function room. Games (fruit machines, pool). Music (acoustic band 8pm 2nd Wed of mth; free; DJs 8pm Thur-Sat; free). Quiz (8pm 3rd Wed of mth; £1). TV (big screen, satellite). **Map 5 R4**.

Home
100-106 Leonard Street, EC2A 4RH (7684 8618/ www.homebar.co.uk). Liverpool Street or Old Street tube/rail. **Open** 5pm-midnight Mon-Wed; 5pm-2am Thur-Sat. **Food served** 6-10pm Mon-Sat. **Credit** AmEx, DC, MC, V.

Several ice ages ago, Home was the leader of the Shoreditch designer-bar pack, but tastes – and trends – change and it now feels decidedly dated. It still attracts hordes of off-duty office workers who'd likely feel alienated by the neighbourhood's newer, edgier options. The street-level area is now occupied by the restaurant, so drinking activity is downstairs. It's a pleasant enough space – divided up by settings of retro leather couches around low wooden tables, with swivel chairs at the bar, framed geometric mirrors and modernist art prints on the walls – but it's also utterly characterless. Not that Home's style-by-numbers approach bothers the young punters swigging bottles of Budvar, Sol and the rest on a Friday night while they shuffle around in the rowdy crush and eye up the talent on offer.
Disabled: toilet. Function room. Music (DJs 9pm-2am Thur-Sat; free). Restaurant (no smoking). TVs (big screen, digital, projector). **Map 5 R4**.

Hoxton Square Bar & Kitchen
2-4 Hoxton Square, N1 6NU (7613 0709). Old Street tube/rail. **Open** 11am-1am Mon-Thur, Sun; 11am-2am Fri, Sat. **Food served** noon-10pm daily. **Credit** AmEx, MC, V.
This is a fine space – huge front windows looking out on to patio seating, a distressed concrete bar, acres of squashy leather sofas and 1970s swivel chairs – but timing is key. At weekends, it attracts noisy throngs of identikit drinkers convinced Hoxton is still the coolest half mile on the planet, so weekday early evenings and Sunday afternoons are best. Bar food of grilled vegetable kebabs or mini-crabcakes is a plus, washed down with draught lagers such as Kirin and Sleeman Honey Brown, one of the many European bottled varieties or something from the wine list. Those with fatter wallets might be tempted by the adjoining restaurant, while anyone up for more than conversation will head for the vast back room on one of the club nights.
Babies and children welcome (until 6pm). Disabled: toilet. Film screenings (phone for details). Music (bands/DJs 9pm Thur-Sun; free-£5). Restaurant. Tables outdoors (4, patio). **Map 5 R3**.

Legion
348 Old Street, EC1V 9NQ (7729 4441/4442). Old Street tube/rail. **Open** 5pm-midnight Mon-Thur; 5pm-2am Fri; 7pm-2am Sat. **Credit** AmEx, DC, MC, V.
Part of the well-known Social mini-empire, the Legion places as much emphasis on music as booze, although you'd never guess from the often heroically inebriated, young (no one over 30, heaven forbid) crowds who pack the place out on Friday and Saturday nights. There's a good jukebox, niche DJs playing most nights, and occasional bands, although this long, cavernous space with its bare brick walls mitigates against decent sound. Seating – a mix of rough wooden tables with benches and soft leather couches – is usually set against one wall, but at busy times extra benches fill the room's centre, making negotiation to and from the packed bar a real test. Leffe, Belle-Vue and Hoegaarden have been added to the standard bar selection, and there's a reasonable wine list to accompany the bangers-and-mash style menu.
Disabled: toilet. Games (board games). Music (karaoke 9pm Tue; free; bands 8pm Wed; £3-£5; DJs 8pm Fri, Sat; free). **Map 5 R4**.

Light Bar & Restaurant
233 Shoreditch High Street, E1 6PJ (7247 8989/ www.thelight1.com). Liverpool Street tube/rail. **Open** noon-midnight Mon-Wed; noon-2am Thur, Fri;

City

6.30pm-2am Sat; noon-10.30pm Sun. **Food served** noon-10.30pm Mon-Fri, Sun; 6.30-11pm Sat. **Admission** *Upstairs bar* £2 Thur-Sat. **Credit** AmEx, DC, MC, V.
The rumble of tubes beneath is a reminder of this space's previous life as a railway warehouse. Not that you'd notice the sound on weekend nights; then, the bare brickwork and old tiles, concrete floor and high ceiling with ancient pulleys still attached resounds with the noise of the City hordes enjoying themselves. There's a good range of bottled lagers – Paulaner, Kasteel Cru, Duvel, Sleeman, Union and Früli – plus the usual draught choices, and an extensive wine list. Seating is at refectory-style tables with benches, on high stools or one of the few leather sofas. Those here for the long haul can refuel from the bar menu (burgers, oysters and so forth) or in the restaurant through the central double doors. Upstairs, the cocktail/lounge bar (open Fridays and Saturdays) features DJs, but don't go expecting anything on the cutting edge.
Babies and children welcome (restaurant). Disabled: toilet. Dress: no suits in upstairs bar. Function room (Mon-Thur, Sun only). Music (DJs Thur-Sat; free). Restaurant. Tables outdoors (9, courtyard). **Map 5 R5**.

Loungelover

1 Whitby Street, E2 7DP (7012 1234/www.lounge lover.co.uk). Liverpool Street tube/rail. **Open** 6pm-midnight Tue-Thur; 6pm-1am Fri; 7pm-1am Sat; 4-10.30pm Sun. **Food served** 6-11.30pm Tue-Fri; 7-11.30pm Sat; 4-10pm Sun. **Credit** AmEx, MC, V.
This bar is owned by the same concern as the celebrated Les Trois Garçons restaurant around the corner and shares its taste in divinely decadent decor. A wealth of extravagantly theatrical fixtures, fittings and accessories – fabulous chandeliers, a stuffed hippo's head, hot-house plants, a replica religious fresco adorning one wall, glass-topped tables, coloured Perspex lighting, red velveteen stools and faux Regency chairs, giant green coach lamps and candles – create a uniquely swish ambience. Mock croc-bound menus list cocktails by genre (Flower Power, Herbal Lover, Hot Lover, Virgin) and range between £7 and £11, but make no mention of the 12.5% 'service charge' added to your bill. If you fancy some sophistication or want to impress a date, Loungelover is perfect, but its attitude (unnecessarily snooty and superior, you sit where you're told to sit) and inflated prices rather spoil the effect.
Disabled: toilet. Music (DJs 7pm Fri, Sat; free). **Map 5 R4**.

Mother Bar

333 Old Street, EC1V 9LE (7739 5949/www.333 mother.com). Old Street tube/rail/55 bus. **Open** 8pm-3am Mon-Wed; 8pm-4am Thur, Sun; 8pm-5am Fri, Sat. **Credit** MC, V.
The 333 Club is owned – like the nearby Red Lion (*see p133*) and Bricklayer's Arms (*see p128*) – by uncrowned queen of Shoreditch, Vicki Pengilley, and its Mother Bar is a veritable institution. It's situated at the top of a dimly lit flight of stairs – where a sex-toy dispensing machine has been installed – and has gone for the seedy-glamour look. Hence the red patterned wallpaper, black padded bar, chess-board flooring, kinky mirrors and low lighting, all of which produce a friendly, anything-goes vibe at weekends, when the place is packed with late-night drinkers. Adjacent to the lounge area is the larger dance room, where DJs work the decks beneath a mirror ball. Beers are your basic draught Red Stripe and Guinness and bottled Staropramen. Queuing outside late at night, especially at weekends, is common. *Music (DJs 10pm daily; free).* **Map 5 R4**.

Owl & the Pussycat

34 Redchurch Street, E2 7DP (7613 3628). Bethnal Green or Liverpool Street tube/rail. **Open** noon-12.30pm Mon, Tue, Sun; noon-2am Wed-Fri. **Food served** noon-3pm Mon-Fri; 2-6pm Sun. **Credit** MC, V.
It may be only close to Shoreditch High Street, but this traditional pub is light years away from the area's hedonistic frontline, attracting a mixed crowd of local old timers, young arrivistes and off-duty workmen from nearby renovation sites. Floral carpet, faux leather chairs set around wooden tables and a collection of frosted mirrors, coach lamps and tatty wall posters are the decorative order of the day, with a bar billiards table completing the traditional picture. Sadly, the huge open fireplace doesn't look as if it's seen action for years. The bar selection sticks to the standards and there was no Drambuie to be had the night we visited, but the food is all hearty, own-cooked fare. The Carvery upstairs serves mainly traditional, carnivorous meals (including a Sunday roast with all the trimmings) and, during the summer months, you can sit at tables in the back garden.
Babies and children welcome (restaurant). Bar available for hire. Games (bar billiards, fruit machine). Tables outdoors (8, garden). **Map 5 R4**.

Pool

104-108 Curtain Road, EC2A 3AH (7739 9608/ www.thepool.co.uk). Old Street tube/rail/55 bus. **Open** noon-1am Mon-Thur; noon-2am Fri; 5.30pm-2am Sat; noon-midnight Sun. **Food served** noon-3pm, 5.30-10.30pm Mon-Fri; 5.30-10.30pm Sat; noon-10pm Sun. **Credit** AmEx, MC, V.
It may seem soulless, but Pool does exactly what its name suggests – with rather more flair and considerably better food than the competition, Elbow Room, over the road. At street level, there are just two tables for players and thus plenty of room to move. The rest of the space is taken up with small dining tables, a kitchen hatch serving Thai food and a well-stocked bar. Under its neon strip, busy staff dispense Hoegaarden from the draught options, bottled choices such as Savanna, Budweiser and Michelob, and a fair range of wines, cocktails and shooters. Plenty of booze, then, to lubricate the predominantly bridge-and-tunnel crowd that packs the vast, downstairs area at weekends to shoot pool or lounge around on the red, faux leather seating and bean bags while they check out the DJ action. Pool tables are free on Sundays.
Babies and children admitted (until 5pm). Games (3 pool tables; £6/hr before 6pm, £8 after 6pm; free Sun). Music (DJs 8pm Tue-Sun; free). Pool competition (7pm Mon; call for details). **Map 5 R4**.

Prague

6 Kingsland Road, E2 8DA (7739 9110/ www.barprague.com). Old Street tube/rail/55 bus. **Open/food served** 8am-midnight daily. **Credit** MC, V.
Billing itself as a 'bar/café/lounge', Prague is small and unprepossessing from the outside, but has much to recommend it, not least the warm, East European ambience its name implies. Wooden tables and chairs, exposed brickwork, red velveteen banquettes, a leather sofa and candlelight help establish the vibe, which is emphasised by the advertised list of 'Bohemian Suspects' – bottled Pilsner Urquell, Staropramen, Zatec, Krusovice and more – that appear alongside various vodkas and both dark and light draught Budvars. Two blackboards list over 30 cocktails, with exotic names like Applesinth and Love Junk

appearing beside the more familiar Mojito, while those on a mission might opt for one of many shooters. During the day, a gleaming Gaggia at the end of the brick bar dispenses coffees to laptop-toting patrons seeking quiet refuge from the roar of Kingsland Road traffic.

Babies and children welcome (until 6pm). Bar available for hire. Disabled: toilet. **Map 5 R4.**

Princess

76-78 Paul Street, EC2A 4NE (7729 9270). Old Street tube/rail. **Open** noon-11pm Mon-Fri; 5.30-11pm Sat; 12.30-5.30pm Sun. **Food served** 12.30-3pm, 6.30-10.30pm Mon-Fri; 6.30-10.30pm Sat; 1-4pm Sun. **Credit** AmEx, MC, V.

Previously a gloomy and unprepossessing old boozer, the Princess has been transformed into an elegant but welcoming gastropub, offering the likes of baked monkfish with warm saffron and pine nut tabouleh, and organic roast chicken. The old stained floorboards, candlelit wooden tables and chairs at street level are offset by dark cream paintwork, high latticed windows and a wrought-iron spiral staircase leading to the dining room. Potted plants and flowers on the bar are softening touches, but there's nothing twee about this place. Friendly bar staff dispense draught lagers including Hoegaarden, bottled brews such as Tiger and Peroni, organic cider and Deuchars IPA alongside the more familiar London Pride, while an extensive wine list (including three Champagnes) satisfies adventurous suits who've strayed from Moorgate. A contented glow is the overall ambience and small wonder – the Princess is royalty.

Babies and children welcome. Restaurant.
Map 5 Q4.

Red Lion

41 Hoxton Street, N1 6NH (7729 6930). Old Street tube/rail/55 bus. **Open** 6-11pm Mon-Sat; 6-10.30pm Sun. **Credit** MC, V.

Situated on the 'wrong' side of Hoxton Square, this once traditional East End boozer has had several makeovers in the past few years, but seems finally to have settled on an identity that fits. It's a tiny space, boasting just one leather couch with low coffee table, a few wooden, copper-topped tables with mismatched chairs, and two faux snakeskin numbers. In winter the welcome centrepiece is a roaring open fire, with Regency striped wallpaper, curtains, mirrors and a standard lamp completing the feeling of having stumbled into someone's lounge. The turntable deck crow-barred into one corner reminds you that you are in Hoxton; this is, in fact, sister establishment to Mother Bar (*see p132*) and the Bricklayer's Arms (*see p128*). The familiar range of draught and bottled beers (Guinness, Kronenbourg, Beck's) is dispensed from a tiny bar, while, upstairs, the Rare restaurant serves Thai food.

Bar available for hire. Music (DJs 8pm Fri-Sun; free). Tables outdoors (2, yard). **Map 5 R3.**

Reliance

336 Old Street, EC1V 9DR (7729 6888). Old Street tube/rail/55 bus. **Open** noon-11pm Mon-Thur, Sun; noon-2am Fri, Sat. **Food served** noon-9pm daily. **Credit** AmEx, DC, MC, V.

Part gastropub, part post-work watering hole, part late-night bar, the Reliance does an admirable job of being all things to all patrons. The worn floorboards, wooden seating and exposed brickwork lend the place something of a French bistro air, a feeling reinforced by a decidedly

City

T-Bar. *See p134.*

European bar that offers bottled Belgian specialities (Belle-Vue Kriek, Duvel) and draught Litovel, Hoegaarden or Leffe Blonde alongside London Pride, the blonde Fuller's Discovery and Adnams Bitter. There's an extensive wine list and, for driving drinkers, the Fentimans range. A blackboard menu offers both snacks and mains such as sirloin steak and a Sunday roast, all often served upstairs, away from the bustle at street level.
Disabled: toilet. Jukebox. **Map 5 R4**.

Smersh
5 Ravey Street, EC2A 4QW (7739 0092/www.smersh bar.co.uk). Liverpool Street or Old Street tube/rail. **Open** 5pm-midnight Mon-Sat. **Credit** (over £10) AmEx, DC, MC, V.
'From behind the Iron Curtain to behind Curtain Road' quips the promo for this tiny basement bar, whose name is that of the counter-espionage wing of the KGB, as described in early Bond novels. The Soviet-inspired theme and low ceiling make descending the staircase feel a little like entering a submarine – albeit a very warm and welcoming one. Red-painted walls, red seating in the cosy lounge area, Cold War newspaper cuttings in the (basic) toilets and Eastern European lubrication – absinthe, good German beers and an excellent range of Polish vodkas – complete the setting. Bar staff are laid-back and friendly, and regular DJs spin quality music, be it 1970s soul or Norwegian electronica. A curious – but cool and very cute – feature on the Shoreditch bar landscape.
Bar available for hire (Sat). Entertainment: DJs 7pm Mon-Sat. **Map 5 Q4**.

Sosho
2 Tabernacle Street, EC2A 4LU (7920 0701/ www.sosho3am.com). Moorgate or Old Street tube/rail. **Open** noon-10pm Mon; noon-midnight Tue; noon-1am Wed, Thur; noon-3am Fri; 7pm-4am Sat; 9pm-4am Sun. **Food served** noon-9.30pm Mon; noon-10.30pm Tue-Fri; 7-11pm Sat. **Credit** AmEx, DC, MC, V.
As part of the Match chain, Sosho shares its mission statement: 'to fix great drinks for a mixed crowd of grown-ups'. The emphasis is thus very much on cocktails (as selected by celebrated mixologist Dale DeGroff) and there are just three (bottled) beers on offer, although the wine list is quite respectable. Once hip, Sosho's look – dark floor, red walls with exposed brickwork, squashy leather sofas and low lighting in the street-level bar – is now tuppence plain, but it's an agreeable enough space, with a raised dais providing seating at black lacquered tables. Downstairs, there's a smaller lounge area, where brown leatherette banquettes and violently patterned wallpaper suggest 1970s après ski. Not that this bothers the City types who pour in from Moorgate to sup fancy cocktails on a Thursday and Friday, or maybe cut some rug under the glitter ball.
Babies and children welcome (daytime). Disabled: toilet. Function room. Music (DJs 9pm Wed-Sun; £3-£5 after 9pm Thur-Sun). **Map 5 Q4**.

Tabernacle
55-61 Tabernacle Street, EC2A 4AA (7253 5555). Old Street tube/rail. **Open** noon-midnight Mon-Wed; noon-1am Thur; noon-2am Fri; 6.30pm-2am Sat. **Food served** noon-10.45pm Mon-Fri; 6.30-10.45pm Sat. **Credit** AmEx, DC, MC, V.
This rather swish bar in a converted warehouse attracts a well-heeled crowd, rather than a cool one. The ground-floor space has been broken up with a metallic mesh curtain, creating two 'lounge' areas set with black lacquered tables

and a mix of cream and black seating. This is offset by the dark wood floor and exposed brickwork, with candles and back-lighting at the bar adding to the ambience. Guinness, Leffe, San Miguel, Foster's and Kronenbourg are all on tap, but the emphasis is very much on wine and cocktails. Bar snacks are served all day – a smart move, considering that some City workers are here for the long haul on Friday nights. Thereafter, many of these quasi-sophisticates head downstairs to the Lounge bar, where DJs play against a backdrop of bare brick and red leatherette.
Babies and children welcome (restaurant). Bar available for hire. Disabled: toilet. Music (DJs 7pm Thur, Fri; 8pm Sat; £3-£5). Restaurant (no smoking until 10.30pm). **Map 5 Q4**.

T Bar
56 Shoreditch High Street, E1 6JJ (7729 2973/ www.tbarlondon.com). Liverpool Street or Old Street tube/rail/8, 35, 48 bus. **Open** 9am-midnight Mon-Wed; 9am-1am Thur; 9am-2am Fri; 8pm-2am Sat; 11am-midnight Sun. **Food served** 9am-3pm, 5-9pm Mon-Fri; 11am-10pm Sun. **Credit** MC, V.
Housed inside the huge Tea Building (home also to a gallery and design agency), T may be unsettlingly quiet early on a Tuesday night, but, come midnight at the weekend, it will be rammed to the rafters with young revellers. They're here because there's plenty of room to dance and no admission charged to hear the name DJs who often play. Round, 1960s-styled black tables overhung with drop lights and a mix of black and white swivel chairs fill one half of the vast space; on the other, multicoloured box seating affords a good view of the dancefloor action. Draught and bottled beers and wine are available, but the focus is on cocktails, with the menu grouped not only into short, long and Champagne varieties, but also 'granddads' – although none of them will ever be seen shaking a leg here.
Babies and children welcome (Sun only). Disabled: toilet. Games (table tennis). Music (DJs 9pm Thur-Sat; free). **Map 5 R4**.

Wenlock Arms
26 Wenlock Road, N1 7TA (7608 3406/www. wenlock-arms.co.uk). Old Street tube/rail/55 bus. **Open** noon-1am Mon-Thur, Sun; noon-2am Fri, Sat. **Food served** noon-9pm daily. **No credit cards.**
Built in 1835 and opened as a pub a year later, the Wenlock Arms narrowly escaped being bombed into oblivion a century on by the Luftwaffe, who took out the local brewery but missed the nearby munitions factory. Perhaps that explains its perpetually cheerful ambience and unfaltering popularity, despite being situated in a bit of a no-man's land. The big draw here is the bewildering (to the layman) variety of speciality ales on offer, many of them with picturesque names like Top Totty, Hebridean Berserker, Pictish Claymore and Dark Star Nut Brown Ale. Darts, an open fire and a list of football fixtures testify to the traditional, community-based nature of the place, as does the fact that locals aged from seven to 70 pack in on Sunday afternoons for a sing-song round the old joanna.
Babies and children admitted. Function room. Music (blues/jazz 9pm Fri, Sat; 3pm Sun; free). Quiz (9pm Thur; free). TV (satellite).

Also in the area...
Elbow Room 97-113 Curtain Road, EC2A 3BS (7613 1316).
Masque Haunt (JD Wetherspoon) 168-172 Old Street, EC1V 9PB (7251 4195).

City

Medicine Bar 89 Great Eastern Street, EC2A 3HX
(7739 5173).
Pulpit (Davy's) 63 Worship Street, EC2A 2DU
(7377 1574).

Liverpool Street & Moorgate

For years there's been a dearth of decent drinking holes around here. Innumerable bar-u-like chains are rammed during the week only to shut over the weekend when the City's suits have vanished to the 'burbs. Happily, **Gramaphone** and the flamboyant **Commercial Tavern** have recently joined the **Golden Heart** on Commercial Street.

Commercial Tavern

142 Commercial Street, E1 6NU (7247 1888).
Aldgate East tube/Liverpool Street tube/rail. **Open**
5-11pm Mon-Sat; noon-10.30pm Sun. **Food served**
5-10pm daily. **Credit** MC, V.
From the outside, the Commercial looks like an old man's pub that's had an exterior touch-up. Step inside, though, and you'll need an inhaler to get your breath back. Someone let the maximalists loose, with baby-blue paintwork, a lobster-red BMX in a glass case and a little dog in a slouch chair being the immediate consequences. There are clusters of roof mirrors, lampshades and primary-coloured cuckoo clocks, not to mention Tour de France cycling wallpaper evidently purloined from a 1950s nursery. A smaller adjoining room, furnished only with a navy-blue baize pool table and matching lounger, doffs its flat cap to location with portraits of Mike Read and Den and Angie outside the Old Vic. Astonishingly, the bar is also enthusiastically run and well stocked – Black Sheep, Brains SA, Pride and Old Rosie Cloudy Cider on draught, and a prodigious array of spirits. Loud, a little self-conscious, but not a bit snooty.
Disabled: toilet. Function room. Games (pool). Tables outdoors (3, pavement). **Map 5 R5**.

George

*Great Eastern Hotel, 40 Liverpool Street, EC2M
7QN (7618 7400). Liverpool Street tube/rail.* **Open**
7am-11pm Mon-Fri; 7.30am-10.30pm Sat, Sun. **Food
served** 7am-4pm, 5-11pm Mon-Fri; 7.30am-4pm,
5-10.30pm Sat, Sun. **Credit** AmEx, DC, MC, V.
Part of the Great Eastern Hotel, Conran had a bit of fun when styling this understated pastiche of an Elizabethan drinking hall. Oak-panelled walls and ceilings conspire to make this one of the area's smarter pubs, with the heavy leaded windows keeping busy Bishopsgate at bay. The area's office workers are the main clientele, who huddle around the slightly incongruous high tables and stools. A small back room acts as an overflow, but here the Tudor touches are gone and have been replaced with a giant picture of a Robbie Williams album cover. Mead was off and the selection of ales wasn't particularly interesting, with Archers IPA and Morland Original the pick of the bunch.
Babies and children admitted. Function room. **Map 6 R6**.

Golden Heart

110 Commercial Street, E1 6LZ (7247 2158).
Liverpool Street tube/rail. **Open** 11am-11pm Mon-Sat;
11am-10.30pm Sun. **Credit** AmEx, MC, V.
Often the site of Tracey Emin's recurring work 'half-drunk pint', this has long been a popular haunt of the BritArt crowd, with the other local art controversialists Gilbert &

George sometimes popping in to mix it with the market traders and Brick Lane trendies. Dark wood panelling and floors, plus a roaring open fire in the saloon bar, provide the setting, with bits of art and photos of famous locals on the wall. The enduring character and popularity of the place is, however, thanks to landlady Sandra Esquilant. A local legend in her own right – confidante and surrogate mother of many BritArt *enfants terribles*, she was voted the 80th most important person in contemporary art a few years ago. The drinks – Adnams Bitter and Broadside remain on tap, to complement an uninspiring line-up of lagers – ensure creative juices are topped up.
Babies and children welcome. Function room. Jukebox.
Tables outdoors (4, pavement). TVs (big screen,
satellite).

Gramaphone

60-62 Commercial Street, E1 6LT (7377 5332/www.
thegramaphone.co.uk). Aldgate East tube/Liverpool
Street tube/rail. **Open** 11am-11pm Mon-Thur; 11am-
1am Fri; 7pm-1am Sat; 4-11pm Sun. **Food served**
noon-4pm, 6-8pm Mon-Fri. **Credit** AmEx, MC, V.
There had been little to excite drinkers at the south end of Commercial Street until Gramaphone reared its shiny head at the end of 2005. The corner bar-restaurant-club bucked the music trend followed by so many bars and, instead of electronic beats, two sets of DJ decks can usually be heard airing reggae, dancehall or the latest underground grime hip hop. If this all sounds too street, fear not – the decor is welcoming. Music legends stare from the black and white wall hangings that line the brickwork and low, curvy leather couches grace wooden block tables, perfectly positioned for a window-seat view of passing East End fashions. The broad wine list boasts a good range by the glass from £2.90, and there are pints of Bitburger, Guinness or Aspall Cider and bottles of Duvel, Leffe Blonde and Corona. With live comedy on Tuesdays, a Mediterranean tapas menu, cocktails and a basement club, there's every reason Gramaphone will play on.
Babies and children welcome (until 7pm). Comedy
(8pm Tue; £4). Music (DJ 7pm Thur-Sun; bar free;
club £4-£5). No-smoking area.

Jamies at the Pavilion

Finsbury Circus Gardens, EC2M 7AB (7628 8224/
www.jamiesbars.co.uk). Liverpool Street or Moorgate
tube/rail. **Open** 11am-11pm Mon-Fri. **Food served**
11am-3pm Mon-Fri. **Credit** AmEx, MC, V.
Finding a pleasant Jamies is as refreshing as finding a verdant oasis in the centre of the Square Mile, so this branch in the former clubhouse of the City of London Bowling Club on the edge of a well-manicured bowling green scores twice. The cute little premises is slightly raised, with windows that overlook the green providing the best spot to sit in an otherwise uninspired interior. So summer, when the patio in front of the bowling green is open, is the best time to sample a few glasses from the extensive wine list. The list itself is divided by grape variety, with a categories such as Eurostars, Anything But Chardonnay and Comfort Zone there to help when you don't feel like experimenting.
Bar available for hire. Dress: smart casual. Music (cover
band monthly, phone for details; free). Restaurant
(available for hire). TV (big screen). **Map 6 Q5**.

Poet

9-11 Folgate Street, E2 6EH (7426 0495). Liverpool
Street tube/rail. **Open** noon-11pm Mon-Fri. **Food**
served noon-3pm Mon-Fri. **Credit** AmEx, MC, V.

Just days after we go to press, the refurbished Poet will reopen, but we're glad to hear the details will remain much the same. Here a youngish crowd mixes rumpled suits with artfully distressed civvies, combining post-work mental fun with a dash of East End cool. Behind discreet front doors lies a surprisingly big pub, with decor that isn't afraid to have fun – candles in Affligem glasses, a dolls' house – and a couple of pool tables. The main bar is back-lit with bottles for cocktailing (the menu lists perhaps 20 options at about £7, six by the £18 jug); wines come a dozen of each, maybe half by the glass (from £2.95/£3.95/£11.45); and draught options include Bass, Old Speckled Hen, Kronenbourg Blanc and Staropramen. The likes of steak ciabatta with salad (£5) keep people on their feet, and the jukebox taps their toes with mainstream alternative music played the right kind of loud.

Babies and children welcome (until 9pm). Bar available for hire (Sat, Sun). Games (fruit machines, pool tables, table football). Poetry (8pm Mon; free). Restaurant (no smoking). Tables outdoors (15, garden). TV (big screen, satellite). **Map 5 R5.**

Public Life

82A Commercial Street, E1 6LY (7375 1631). Aldgate East tube/Liverpool Street tube/rail. **Open/food served** 11am-2.30am Mon-Thur, Sun; 11am-3am Fri, Sat. **Credit** AmEx, MC, V.
How could you best counter criticism that your bar is an absolute bog-hole? Easy, if it used to be a toilet in the first place. As a former public convenience, Public Life gets its defence in early and, to be fair, it's not such a shabby sub-terranean DJ bar. The entrance is easy to miss: sat in the shadow of Christ Church Spitalfields, all that can be seen at street level is a glass cube ringed by a wrought-iron gate. Inside the chequered tiled floor from its previous incarnation has been retained, with the bar now occupying the spot where the cubicles used to be. Budweiser and Stella are on tap, but drinks don't seem to be the main concern here. It's a small place (about 150 capacity), still a bit rough and ready, and while it may be situated underground the music policy can't be really be called the same. Depending on the night, expect to hear electro, techno or soul and funk.
Bar available for hire. Music (DJs 9pm Thur-Sat; £3-£8 Fri, Sat). Tables outdoors (6, pavement).

St Paul's Tavern

56 Chiswell Street, EC1Y 4SA (7606 3828). Barbican tube/Moorgate tube/rail. **Open** 11am-11pm Mon-Wed; 11am-midnight Thur, Fri. **Food served** noon-8pm Mon-Thur; noon-6pm Fri. **Credit** AmEx, MC, V.
This unpretentious boozer used to be the brewery tap for the Whitbread Brewery that stood next door from 1750 until a few years ago. The brewery is now offices and the pub has been taken over by Greene King. While the inoffensive bare-brick pillars, dark wooden floor and green and red colour scheme remain, we were disappointed by the absence of cask-conditioned ales for our most recent visit – on the night chippy staff seemed unable to tell us when they'd be back. A pity, since there's usually Greene King IPA, Old Speckled Hen and Morland Original (from the GK stable), plus two or three weekly changing guest ales at the back bar. Staropramen and Grolsch are the pick of the lagers. The pub has a more varied mix of punters than many others in the area, with suits in the minority on Friday night, and there was a bubbly atmosphere reminiscent of a student union bar.
Bar available for hire. Games (golf machines). No-smoking tables (lunchtime only). TVs. **Map 5 Q5.**

Ten Bells

84 Commercial Street, E1 6LY (7366 1721). Liverpool Street tube/rail. **Open** 11am-midnight Mon-Wed, Sun; 11am-1am Thur-Sat. **Credit** MC, V.
This regularly rammed boozer has a long and, at times, grisly history. Established in 1753, the pub is thought to have been the last place one of Jack the Ripper's victims was seen before she was murdered. Today it's a salubrious destination for the young and hip from nearby Brick Lane and Shoreditch, enticed by its scruffy charm. Old leather sofas take up a good part of the tiny single-room bar. Nicholas Hawksmoor's splendid Christ Church Spitalfields looms next door and, as you peer out through the large windows on to Commercial Street, gaggles of tourists on Jack the Ripper tours often gawp back in. There are limited options on draught, so go for the bottles, which include Russian Baltika beer and Brooklyn lager.
Quiz (7pm 1st Mon of mth; £1). Tables outdoors (4, pavement).

Vertigo 42

Tower 42, 25 Old Broad Street, EC2N 1HQ (7877 7842/www.vertigo42.co.uk). Bank tube/DLR/Liverpool Street tube/rail. **Open** noon-3pm, 5-11pm Mon-Fri. **Food served** noon-2.15pm, 5-9.30pm Mon-Fri. **Credit** AmEx, DC, MC, V.
Check in at reception, pass through X-ray machines and metal detectors, and then take a neon-illuminated express lift to this top-floor Champagne bar. The whole operation feels like the security checks before a flight, but once you've made it to your destination you'll be rewarded with staggering 360° views of London. The decor is also reminiscent of an airport executive lounge, and you shouldn't be surprised to find the bar populated by cooing couples and the

Tabernacle. See p134.

occasional office do. But it's the sight of London unfurled beneath you through floor-to-ceiling windows that is the main reason for visiting. The cheapest bottle of bubbly is £42, although there are choices by the glass. We suggest sticking to the fizz, as the Champagne cocktails at £10 each were the most indifferent we've tasted for some time. *Bar available for hire. Dress: smart casual. No cigars or pipes.* **Map 6 Q6.**

Wall Bar
45 Old Broad Street, EC2N 1HU (7588 4845).
Liverpool Street tube/rail. **Open** 11.30am-midnight Mon-Wed; 11.30am-1am Thur, Fri. **Food served** noon-10pm Mon-Fri. **Credit** AmEx, DC, MC, V.
This first-floor bar is owned by the same people as nearby Livery (*see p125*). It has a similar look to its sibling, with maroon banquettes, plants and church candles – plus a large centrepiece bar, huge mirrors, a pale-wood and granite floor, and fashionable talking loos. There's also generous terrace seating at the front, and an alfresco eating area at street level. Food and drink are exactly the same as the Livery, but the service was a bit lax and our barman didn't know how to make the Honey I'm Home (Galliano, vanilla vodka, passion-fruit syrup, passion-fruit juice and cream, £4.95): with supervision from a colleague, he made it up as he went along, and the result was distinctly odd. *Bar available for hire (weekends). Music (DJs 8pm Thur, Fri; free). No-smoking area. Tables outdoors (15, terrace). TV (big screen, satellite).* **Map 6 Q6.**

Also in the area...
All Bar One 18-20 Appold Street, EC2A 2AS (7377 9671); 127 Finsbury Pavement, EC2A 1NS (7448 9921).

Balls Brothers 158 Bishopsgate, EC2M 4LN (7426 0567); 11 Blomfield Street, EC2M 1PS (7588 4643); Gow's Restaurant, 81 Old Broad Street, EC2M 1PR (7920 9645); Mark Lane, EC3R 7BB (7623 2923).
Bangers (Davy's) Eldon House, 2-12 Wilson Street, EC2H 2TE (7377 6326).
Bishop of Norwich/Bishop's Parlour (Davy's) 91-93 Moorgate, EC2M 6SJ (7920 0857).
Boisdale Bishopsgate Swedeland Court, 202 Bishopsgate, EC2M 4NR (7283 1763).
City Boot 7 Moorfields High Walk, EC2Y 9DP (7588 4766).
Corney & Barrow 19 Broadgate Circle, EC2M 2QS (7628 1251); 5 Exchange Square, EC2A 2EH (7628 4367); 11 Old Broad Street, EC2N 1AP (7638 9308); 1 Ropemaker Street, EC2Y 9HT (7382 0606).
Cuban City Point, 1 Ropemaker Street, EC2Y 9AW (7256 2202).
Davy's 2 Exchange Square, EC2A 2EH (7256 5962).
El Vino 3 Bastion High Walk, 125 London Wall, EC2Y 5AP (7600 6377).
Hamilton Hall (JD Wetherspoon) Unit 32, The Concourse, Liverpool Street Station, EC2M 7PY
Hog's Head 25 St Mary Axe, EC3A 8LL (7929 0245).
Jamies 155 Bishopsgate, EC2A 2AA (7256 7279).
O'Neill's 31-36 Houndsditch, EC3A 7DB (7397 9841); 64 London Wall, EC2M 5TP (7786 9231).
Orangery Cutlers Gardens, 10 Devonshire Square, EC2M 4TE (7623 1377).
Pitcher & Piano 200 Bishopsgate, EC2M 4NR (7929 5914).
Slug & Lettuce 100 Fenchurch Street, EC3M 5JD (7488 1890); 25 St Mary Axe, EC3A 8LL (7929 0245); The Courtyard, Stoney Lane, E1 7BH (7626 4994).

Mansion House, Monument & Bank

There are still some decent bars and taverns to be found in among the chains in the historic financial quarter. Enjoy views of Sir Horace Jones's handiwork from **Leadenhall Wine Bar** or sample the subterranean delights of classy **Prism**.

Bar Bourse
67 Queen Street, EC4R 1EE (7248 2200/2211).
Mansion House tube. **Open** 11.30am-11pm Mon-Fri. **Food served** 11.30am-3pm, 5-10pm Mon-Fri. **Credit** AmEx, MC, V.
Bar Bourse is a bar going places. By summer 2006 it is aiming to integrate World Cup football punters into its cool subterranean surroundings of bar stools and Regency stripe banquettes in a bid to maximise the venue's evening appeal. In the meantime, the exceptionally welcoming team are rushed off their feet at lunchtimes (booking to eat is advisable) and busy for drinks in the early evening. Its main strength is the 60-strong wine list, which exists principally to accommodate the restaurant but is also available at the bar. All the classics are mixed here too, and very reasonable indeed at £6.50 (Martinis and short cocktails), £7 for long drinks and £8.50 for Bellinis and perfect French 75s from among a range of a dozen Champagne cocktails.

City

Babies and children admitted. Bar available for hire. Dress: smart casual. TVs (big screen, satellite). **Map 6 P7.**

Bell
29 Bush Lane, EC4R 0AN (7929 7772). Cannon Street tube/rail. **Open** 11am-10pm Mon-Fri. **Food served** noon-2.30pm Mon-Fri. **Credit** AmEx, MC, V.
In a square mile of superlatives, the Bell's claim to fame is impressive. This may or may not be the oldest pub in the City, but it at least feels as though it might be. The small, half-timbered saloon, decorated with ancient prints, yellowing walls and a slightly incongruous parquet floor, hasn't been messed with too badly down the years, at least when compared to some of the atrocities in the neighbourhood; that said, the addition of two TV screens at opposite ends of the room doesn't do the place any favours, though they've at least refrained from bringing in piped music. The beers are decent: five in total, on our visit, among them Spitfire and Wye Valley Hereford Pale Ale. *TV (satellite).* **Map 6 P7.**

Bonds Bar & Restaurant
Threadneedle Hotel, 5 Threadneedle Street, EC4R 8AY (7657 8088). Monument tube/Bank tube/DLR. **Open** 11am-11pm Mon-Fri; 10am-8pm Sat, Sun. **Food served** *Bar* noon-2.30pm, 6-10pm Mon-Fri. **Credit** AmEx, DC, MC, V.
Upmarket yet easy and comfortable, with very attentive and knowledgeable staff, this establishment – attached to the boutique hotel Threadneedle – handles its extensive cocktail list with élan and wit. A brief history of the cocktail is presented on the front of the menu, and the staff's attention to detail creates the feeling of being given VIP treatment on every visit. All the classics are here, with marvellous twists (anyone for a Breakfast Martini?). Comfy swivel chairs allow you that fun 'We've been expecting you, Meester Bond' arch-villain feeling, the mirror-top tables are deliciously decadent, and the bar, with foot rail and sundry perches, gives the room a fully integrated feel. Clean lines combine with high ceilings to create a sense of calm even when the place is buzzing. Thanks to the hotel, the restaurant is open for weekend breakfasts too, with sausages made to a special recipe. A class act.
Babies and children welcome (restaurant). Disabled: toilet. Function rooms (no smoking). Restaurant (no smoking). **Map 6 Q6.**

Bow Wine Vaults
10 Bow Churchyard, EC4M 9DQ (7248 1121). Mansion House tube/Bank tube/DLR. **Open** 11am-11pm Mon-Fri. **Food served** noon-3pm Mon-Fri. **Credit** AmEx, DC, MC, V.
A City institution for 25 years, BWV has decor that remains a proper fright, with light-wood panelling dressed in garish modern art. Luckily, substance triumphs over style. The bar is dutifully stocked and cocktail-ready, even if the largely blokey banking crowd seemed to prefer quaffing white wine while glancing at Sky Sports News. They cluster around a small, U-shaped serving area at which one can perch or stand while tucking into an excellent, no-nonsense bar menu featuring Cumberland sausage or sirloin steak sandwiches. But as the name suggests, wine is the real draw. French-dominated, but travelling the globe, and served, in the main, by the bottle, the house wines stand at a perfectly decent £13.50. The list pretty much covers the waterfront, but should your favourite be absent they are happy to order it for your next visit.

Babies and children admitted (restaurant). Restaurant (available for hire). Tables outdoors (14, pavement). TV (satellite). **Map 6 P6.**

Counting House
50 Cornhill, EC3V 3PD (7283 7123). Monument tube/Bank tube/DLR. **Open** 11am-11pm Mon-Fri. **Food served** noon-9pm Mon-Fri. **Credit** AmEx, DC, MC, V.
This grand Victorian building spent a century as a bank before Fuller's got hold of it in 1997. The job they did converting the main banking hall into a boozer won awards, but the exaggerated gestures (a mammoth central bar, huge tables) and tacky touches (staff uniforms, beer ads on the walls, an awful Heart FM-lite soundtrack) lend it the feel of a Las Vegas interpretation of a British pub. Still, there are good points, the beer chief among them – Chiswick and London Pride are among the five Fuller's ales on tap. The lunchtime and evening menus line the stomach effectively enough.
Disabled: toilet. Function room. Games (fruit machine). No-smoking area (lunchtime only). TV (big screen). **Map 6 Q6.**

Crosse Keys
9 Gracechurch Street, EC3V 0DR (7623 4824/ www.jdwetherspoon.co.uk). Monument tube/Bank tube/DLR. **Open** 9am-midnight Mon-Thur; 9am-1am Fri; 9am-7pm Sat. **Food served** 9am-11pm Mon-Fri; 9am-6pm Sat. **Credit** AmEx, MC, V.
The usual Wetherspoon deal – club nights for curry and steak, pack-'em-in tables and chairs, and the carrot of knockdown prices – applies here, only in much more conducive surroundings than are sometimes offered in the 'burbs (such as their hurried cinema conversion, Capitol, in Forest Hill). This former bank provides ample and luxurious space in every direction, even given the number of tables that have been crammed in. An oval island bar proudly displays its Cask Marque (there's Abbot on tap) and an Olympian array of international beers in bottles, even going so far as to keep a range of organic ciders. The enormous screen was playing the business news when we arrived. A cute touch, we thought, given the location, but it turned out later to have been mere coincidence: the screen is here to show sporting events, to which end the pub is open on a Saturday in this weekend boozer desert.
Babies and children welcome. Disabled: toilet. Function rooms. Games (fruit machines, golf machine, quiz machine). No-smoking area. TVs (big screen, satellite). **Map 6 Q7.**

Hatchet
28 Garlick Hill, EC4V 2BA (7236 0720). Mansion House tube. **Open** 11am-11pm Mon-Fri. **Food served** noon-2.30pm Mon-Fri. **Credit** MC, V.
The Hatchet is that now-endangered species, a pub that sells great beer to blameless chaps. Two small rooms, one in back with a fireplace and tables, the bar in front with a telly on a shelf and bar perches, are the stage for Greene King IPA and Abbot Ale. There's Angostura and fresh fruit behind the bar too, and a decent range of spirits, but though the bar is cocktail-willing, the punters are weak. And why shouldn't they be, with such well-kept beer? It's a friendly place, and the air is thick with enough blokey, beery nonsense to keep *Time Out's* 'Man Who Fell Asleep' contributor in copy for weeks ('Goalkeepers aren't really footballers', 'When she says that, I swear that beer will

come down my nose'). If you're happy to stand and have a pint and an inconsequential natter to relax and unwind, you are now entering old-school pub heaven.
Games (fruit machine). No piped music or jukebox. TV. **Map 6 P7.**

Lamb Tavern
10-12 Leadenhall Market, EC3V 1LR (7626 2454). Monument tube/Bank tube/DLR. **Open** 11am-11pm Mon-Fri. **Food served** noon-2.30pm Mon-Fri. **Credit** AmEx, DC, MC, V.
The arrival at the Lamb of transplanted Chicago cop John Wayne triggers a massive brawl in the long-forgotten 1975 movie *Brannigan*. Three decades on, this historic Leadenhall Market boozer maintains a rather more genteel existence under the Young's umbrella. In the pub's 18th- and 19th-century glory days, porter was poured for the market's meat, fish and fruit stallholders. A few remain today, but most of the local traders who drink here deal only in stocks and shares. The matey main space is little more than a room with a bar in it; there are tables on the gallery above, and a restaurant all the way at the top.
Function room. Games (darts, fruit machine). No-smoking area. No piped music or jukebox. Tables outdoors (5, pavement). **Map 6 Q6.**

Leadenhall Wine Bar
27 Leadenhall Market, EC3V 1LR (7623 1818). Monument tube/Bank tube/DLR. **Open** 11.30am-11pm Mon-Fri. **Food served** 11.30am-10pm Mon-Fri. **Credit** AmEx, MC, V.
The listed shopfronts at Leadenhall market are uniform throughout, but ascend the stairs of the original City tapas bar and you'll find an experience well above the high-street version. Even the stairway is all terracotta tiles and warm orangey-brown walls – so far, so tapas. The single room bar, however, with its drawing-room-red walls and elegant sash windows, fused with Spanish paintings and *objets d'art*, comes as something of a surprise – and a very pleasant one. The view of the high-up detail of the florid Victorian market outside is unique too. The marvellous buzz of the female-friendly bar (as opposed to the could-be-cheery, could-be-lairy drone of the bloke bar) is fuelled by a wide and affordable wine list. Top of the shop are a Rioja and a Sancerre at the £25 mark, with a drinkable chardonnay for a fiver a glass. You can also go native on the bubbles with Cava Cristal at £17.95. Wednesdays and Fridays are for paella (with jugs of sangria) and there's live flamenco on the first Thursday of each month.
Babies and children welcome. Function room. Flamenco (7.30pm 1st Thur of mth; free). No-smoking area. Restaurant. **Map 6 Q7.**

1 Lombard Street
1 Lombard Street, EC3V 9AA (7929 6611/ www.1lombardstreet.com). Bank tube/DLR. **Open** 11am-11pm Mon-Fri. **Food served** 5-10.30pm Mon-Fri. **Credit** AmEx, DC, MC, V.
Located in a converted bank, this spacious bar and brasserie (with a one-Michelin-star restaurant at the back) is classily done up in shades of cream. There's a circular bar in the centre of the brasserie, surrounded by high chairs for seating and a domed skylight. Early evening buzzes with City types enjoying cocktails, Champagne cocktails and Martinis with names like Wall Street, Bank Hall, FTSE 100 and Black Monday – all priced between £6.75 and £9. Blackberry cooler (mint-infused gin with fresh lime juice, mint leaves and blackberries, £7.50) was deliciously

refreshing. There's an extensive list of Old and New World wines, as well as fine wines from the restaurant's vault. Bar food includes mini-sausage platters (£9.95), tapas (£11.50 for a selection) and oriental snacks (£14.50). The surrounding brasserie offers an all-day menu, ranging from breakfasts to superior Modern European fare.
Babies and children admitted. Disabled: toilet. Function room. Restaurant (no smoking). **Map 6 Q6.**

Pacific Oriental
1 Bishopsgate, EC2N 3AB (7621 9988/www.pacific oriental.co.uk). Monument tube/Bank tube/DLR/ Liverpool Street tube/rail. **Open** 11.30am-11pm Mon-Wed; 11am-1am Thur, Fri. **Food served** 11.45am-3pm, 6-9pm Mon-Fri. **Credit** AmEx, DC, MC, V.
Beer comes in bottles here, with Tiger, Beck's and Heineken leading the way among the buzzy, lingering, knocking-off-work crowd. Even if the telly was blinking dumbly and unobserved, drowned by the sound system, this is still an easy venue in which to unwind from the day. The cocktails are mainly of the stupid variety – Slippery Nipple natch – but traditionalists can go for the well-mixed Mojito, a fine Bellini (Champagne cocktails come in at around £7) and the ubiquitous Cosmopolitan. On a Thursday night, however, the Chambord bottle remained unbothered, the punters preferring bottles of the yellow stuff and the affordable wines by the glass – from a range of around nine or ten each of red and white, although there is access on request to the more extensive cellar of the adjoining restaurant. There's even wireless internet access for those who just can't switch off from the nine-to-five.
Babies and children admitted (restaurant). Disabled: toilet. Function rooms. Music (DJ 8.30pm Thur, Fri; free). Restaurant (available for hire; no smoking). TV (big screen, satellite). **Map 6 Q6.**

Phoenix
26 Throgmorton Street, EC2N 2AN (7588 7289). Monument tube/Bank tube/DLR. **Open** 11am-11pm Mon-Wed; 11am-midnight Thur, Fri. **Food served** noon-4pm Mon-Fri. **Credit** AmEx, MC, V.
This Phoenix rises from the ashes of a smokeless fire: puffing on a gasper is strictly verboten throughout. Greene King IPA and Abbot stand with Adnams and Phoenix Ale on the bar, with the beer being the prime draw (Staropramen and Stella provide refreshment for the lager devotee). A lot of bar space is given over to alcopops, and there's a decent coverage of spirits, even if they don't stray into premium brand territory. The colour scheme of the L-shaped bar echoes the pub's surroundings (calling to mind nearby Leadenhall Market, and even the exposed air-conditioning pipes of the Lloyd's Building), and the high-arched windows allow you to see just how late it is. Indeed, the Phoenix may not be the best place to dig in for the night – rather it's an airy and comfortable stop-off before braving the 6pm exodus at Bank.
Disabled: toilet. Games (fruit machine). No smoking. TVs (big screen). **Map 6 Q6.**

Prism
147 Leadenhall Street, EC3V 4QT (7256 3888). Monument tube/Bank tube/DLR. **Open** 11am-11pm Mon-Fri. **Meals served** 11.30am-3pm, 6-10pm Mon-Fri. **Credit** AmEx, DC, MC, V.
This long, thin and surprisingly welcoming subterranean bar lies at the foot of a spiral staircase. Part of the Harvey Nichols chain, it's intimate, with light tones and wood surfaces, effortlessly blending ease and elegance. Their

City

scotches are intelligently listed by region and a fine selection of American whiskies (culminating in Blanton's Gold Edition at £16 a shot) is a veritable amber mine. Among the Champagne cocktails, reformed punks will smile at the Cham 69 (Champagne with Chambord and Amaretto). There's lager in bottles – Peruvian Cusqueña, plus Tiger and Peroni – with bottled Black Sheep Ale a nice touch. The tip of the wine list iceberg (which includes six each of reds and whites by the glass) features something for every pocket and occasion, with a more extensive list available on request. Cocktails, at just under £10, include an excellent Elder Statesman – Hendrick's gin, apricot brandy, crushed cucumber, elderflower and cloudy apple juice. *Babies and children welcome. Disabled: toilet. Function rooms. Tables outdoors (24, conservatory). TV (big screen).* **Map 6 Q6.**

TSP (The Samuel Pepys)

Stew Lane, High Timber Street, EC4V 3PT (7489 1871). Mansion House or St Paul's tube. **Open** 10.30am-11pm Mon-Fri; noon-3pm Sat. **Food served** noon-10pm Mon-Fri; noon-3pm Sat. **Credit** AmEx, MC, V.
The modernity of this place belies its venerable name – shortened now to TSP. Tucked away down the wonderfully named Stew Lane, where a seat puts you not so much by the river as over it. The interior is a seamless blend of old and new: slouchable sofas, dark-wood tables, exposed brickwork and judicious hints of steel here and there. The main selling point, though, are the fabulous views – downriver on one side, across to Tate Modern on the other. The drinks are good too: Deuchars IPA, Früli and Timothy Taylor Landlord stand in line with Leffe nearby. Even the gassy beer is dressed in its Sunday best, with Amstel and Heineken flowing from ornate earthenware taps, and there are decent selections of wine, rum and whisky (Scotch and bourbon). The staff are very friendly and all clad in black – they look like the Stranglers' grandchildren. Solid gastropub fare (including a monumental steak sandwich) rounds off an impressive operation.
Babies and children welcome. Disabled: toilet. Function room. Music (DJ 6.30pm Fri; free). Restaurant (no smoking). **Map 6 P7.**

Swan Tavern

Ship Tavern Passage, 77-80 Gracechurch Street, EC3V 1LY (7283 7712). Monument tube/Bank tube/DLR. **Open** 11am-11pm Mon-Fri. **Food served** noon-2pm Mon-Fri. **Credit** AmEx, MC, V.
Both the Swan and the Counting House (*see p138*) around the corner are Fuller's pubs serving Fuller's ale to a clientele dominated by City boys, but there the similarity ends. The Counting House could scarcely be grander, a massive, high-ceilinged room thick with braying conversation and cigar smoke. The Swan, conversely, claims to be the smallest pub in the Square Mile, its delightful downstairs marble-topped Ale Bar boasting a comfortable capacity in single figures. There's a bit more room – and, for that matter, a greater variety of drinks – upstairs in the Swan Bar, but a lot less charm. Be warned, though: staff have been known to shut up shop several hours before the advertised closing time.
No piped music or jukebox. TV. **Map 6 Q7.**

Throgmorton's

27A Throgmorton Street, EC2N 2AN (7588 5165). Bank tube/DLR/Liverpool Street tube/rail. **Open** noon-11pm Mon-Fri. **Food served** noon-8pm Mon-Fri. **Credit** AmEx, MC, V.

A London classic. It's also very nearly a complex, featuring dining room and deli as well as the brace of bars. Descend a faded Norma Desmond staircase, circling a wrought-iron lift shaft (the feel is of some Paris mansion block) and enter the Mosaic Bar (intricate tilework adorns the front of the counter). The atmosphere is gentleman's-clubby with modern overtones – Young's, Adnams, Spitfire and Leffe line up on the bar, with Früli white Belgian fruit beer a surprisingly exotic presence. Cross the chessboard floor to the welcoming carpeted area (with no-smoking area) and the mishmash of sofas and tables and chairs. The casualness of the clipboard menus belies a knowledgeable kitchen producing hearty fare and excellent grazing platters to share. Go one level down and the sports bar offers two pool tables, sport on TV, wood panels and (not very PC, this, and not for all that much longer) a deliciously appropriate aroma of tobacco. It's a miracle those City bods ever get any work done with this gem on their doorstep.
Babies and children welcome (restaurant). Bar available for hire (weekends). Games (2 pool tables). Restaurant (no smoking). TVs (big screen, satellite). **Map 6 Q6.**

Walrus & Carpenter

45 Monument Street, EC3R 8BU (7626 3362/ www.walrusandcarpenter.co.uk). Monument tube. **Open** 11am-11pm Mon-Fri. **Food served** noon-3.30pm Mon-Fri. **Credit** AmEx, DC, MC, V.
The Boozer (definition: full of blokes, good beer, bad carpet) isn't currently in rude health around here, so the front bar of the Walrus & Carpenter is a welcome institution, meeting all three criteria (Young's Bitter, Special and IPA in the good beer department). Rather like something out of Lewis Carroll (in whose *Alice Through the Looking Glass* the Walrus and Carpenter appeared), however, this rare institution morphs into three additional incarnations the deeper you look into it. Upstairs is the Gryphon (more Carroll) restaurant (traditional from its bubble and squeak to its bread and butter pudding); at the back is a wood-floored bar with ornate etched glasswork; and downstairs is a wine bar with a mosaic floor. Curiouser and curiouser.
Babies and children welcome (until 3.30pm). Bar available for hire. Function room. Games (darts, fruit machine, karaoke machine). Quiz (7pm last Tue in mth; £1.50). Restaurant (available for hire). TVs. **Map 6 Q7.**

Williamson's Tavern

1 Groveland Court, off Bow Lane, EC4M 9EH (7248 5750). Mansion House tube. **Open** 11am-11pm Mon-Fri. **Food served** noon-9pm Mon-Fri. **Credit** AmEx, MC, V.
Unlike many a 'history pub', this Nicholson's house wears its heritage lightly. It was once the residence of the man who inspired Shakespeare's Sir John Falstaff, as well as home to several Lord Mayors of London. The Williamson family tree is on the wall, tracing their ownership down to the early 20th century, but in the early 21st century the pub is still in good hands. Hand-written tasting notes on the guest ale pumps (Deuchars IPA) are a very nice touch, and there are Young's Bitter and London Pride too, alongside a jolly range of cheap and cheerful New World wines. A few tables sit outside in Bow Lane, but the pub is at its best of a dark evening, bringing out its warmly lit nooks and crannies to perfect effect. And, at no extra charge, there's even a ghost.
Function room. Games (fruit machine, golf machine). No-smoking area. Tables outdoors (4, pavement). TV (big screen). **Map 6 P6.**

Also in the area...

All Bar One 103 Cannon Street, EC4N 5AD (7220 9031).

Balls Brothers Bucklersbury House, Cannon Street, EC4N 8EL (7248 7557); Minster Court, Mincing Lane, EC3R 7PP (7283 2838); 2 St Mary at Hill, EC3R 8EE (7626 0321).

Bangers Too (Davy's) 1 St Mary at Hill, EC3R 8EE (7283 4443).

Bar Under the Clock (Balls Brothers) 74 Queen Victoria Street (entrance on Bow Lane), EC4N 4SJ (7489 9895).

City Flogger (Davy's) Fen Court, 120 Fenchurch Street, EC3M 5BA (7623 3251).

City FOB (Davy's) Lower Thames Street, EC3R 6DJ (7621 0619).

City Tup 66 Gresham Street, EC2V 7BB (7606 8176).

Corney & Barrow 44 Cannon Street, EC4N 6JJ (7248 1700); 2B Eastcheap, EC3M 1AB (7929 3220); 1 Leadenhall Place, EC3M 7DX (7621 9201); 12-14 Mason's Avenue, EC2V 5BT (7726 6030); 16 Royal Exchange, EC3V 3LP (7929 3131).

Davy's Unit 8, Plantation Place, Mincing Lane, EC3R 5AT (7621 9878).

El Vino 6 Martin Lane, off Cannon Street, EC4R 0DP (7626 6876).

Fine Line 1 Bow Churchyard, EC4M 9PQ (7248 3262); Equitable House, 1 Monument Street, EC3R 8BG (7623 5446).

Green Man (JD Wetherspoon) Bank Station, 1 Poultry, EC2R 8EJ (7248 3529).

Heeltap & Bumper (Davy's) 2-6 Cannon Street, EC4M 6XX (7248 3371).

Jamies 5 Groveland Court, EC4M 9EH (7248 5551); 107-112 Leadenhall Street, EC3A 4AA (7626 7226); 13 Philpot Lane, EC3M 8AA (7621 9577).

Number 25 (Jamies) 25 Birchin Lane, EC3V 9DJ (7623 2505).

O'Neill's 65 Cannon Street, EC4N 5AA (7653 9951).

Pitcher & Piano 28-31 Cornhill, EC3V 3ND (7929 3989).

Slug & Lettuce 25 Bucklersbury, EC4N 8DA (7329 6222).

Tower Hill & Aldgate

Drinking is distinctly old-school in this no-man's land between the river and the edge of the City, but if it's characters, a pint of Greene King IPA or Spitfire and some decent pub grub you're after...

Crutched Friar

39-41 Crutched Friars, EC3N 2AE (7264 0041). Tower Hill tube/Tower Gateway DLR. **Open** noon-11pm Mon-Fri. **Food served** noon-9pm Mon-Fri. **Credit** (over £10) AmEx, MC, V.

At first sight, the bar seems too small for this biggish Nicholson's house and its attendant throng at both lunch and knocking-off times. The excellent and cheery-under-pressure bar staff, however, make light work of the crowds. Entering by a sloped hallway, the pub has three spaces – two 'wings' with banquettes, tables and chairs that are popular with diners, and an L-shaped bar with adjacent beer garden. The garden is small, but a delicious spot for a naughty long lunch in summer. Greene King IPA and Spitfire sit alongside Staropramen on tap, with Leffe in bottles. Low-ceilinged but well-ventilated, there's little sign of cocktail activity, but all the highball bases are covered and there is a cheap and cheerful selection of wines. *Disabled: toilet. Games (golf machine). No-smoking area. Tables outdoors (7, garden; 3, patio). TV (big screen).* **Map 6 R7.**

City

Golden Heart. *See p135.*

Dickens Inn

St Katharine's Way, E1W 1UH (7488 2208). Tower Hill tube/Tower Gateway DLR. **Open** 11am-11pm Mon-Sat; noon-10.30pm Sun. **Food served** noon-10pm daily. **Credit** AmEx, DC, MC, V.

Timber beams. Beer barrels. Budweiser taps with mini TV screens built in. Huh? This wild clash of ye olde and high-tech is a must-see, at least for novelty value. And for what is essentially a tourist trap with booze for bait, it could be a whole lot worse. (History-seeking visitors take note: the building dates from the 1790s, but was wheeled to its current location in the late 1960s.) It's pricey, but is a perfect summertime boozer. This old, three-storey warehouse also offers food in the shape of Grill on the Dock and Pizza on the Dock. There's bar food too, from the Copperfield Bar – Dickens, it seems, like Jack the Ripper, is still a big draw. The beers aren't so much of an attraction, pretty much standard-issue lagers, with Bombardier for ale fans. The idyllic setting, however, keeps it on the map.

Babies and children admitted. Disabled: toilet. Function room. Games (fruit machine, quiz machine). Restaurant (no-smoking area). Tables outdoors (20, garden). TV (big screen).

Poet

82 Middlesex Street, E1 7EZ (7422 0000). Liverpool Street tube/rail. **Open** 11am-11pm Mon-Fri. **Food served** noon-3pm Mon; noon-3pm, 5-9pm Tue-Fri. **Credit** AmEx, DC, MC, V.

Large, single room bars can often feel like soulless affairs. The Poet staves off this feeling with a minimal, well-lit bar to pull focus, interesting lighting (hanging shades and chandeliers) and an array of window seats from which to view Original London Walks and their nightly pageant of Jack the Ripper tours. A bust of Shakespeare greets you at the door (having strayed from his usual stamping ground, he's nonetheless here in a professional capacity) and there's a big screen for big games. The food sits somewhere between Brown's and ABO, and on tap there's Greene King IPA and Budvar. Alcopops have elbowed their way to the front of the bar shelves – doubtless to meet the needs of a mixed on-the-way-home clientele that evidently includes every species of the office jungle – but the Poet remains pretty well stocked with grown-up spirits. There's a small but decent wine list too.

Babies and children admitted (until 5pm). Bar available for hire. Disabled: toilet. TVs (big screen, satellite). **Map 6 R6.**

Princess of Prussia

15 Prescot Street, E1 8AZ (7480 5304). Aldgate East or Tower Hill tube. **Open** 11am-midnight Mon-Fri. **Food served** noon-3pm Mon-Fri. **Credit** MC, V.

The area where the lines of the East End and the City begin to blur is something of a Twilight Zone for boozers of stature. A little dark wood room with corner bar and an adjoining lounge/dining room, done out in classic green and cream livery, provide a trad, bloke-heavy but in no way female-repellent atmosphere for an easy lunch or work post-mortem. Pictures of the local manor and Prussian army references nod to the pub's name and location. A mix of suits and civvies tuck into carefully presented jacket potatoes, sausages and sandwiches at lunch, and stand in the front bar of an evening putting the world to rights over Spitfire and Oranjeboom. A tiny little garden must surely be one of the City's great afternoon hideaways.

Babies and children admitted. Games (quiz machine). Tables outdoors (8, patio). TV.

Still & Star

1 Little Somerset Street, E1 8AH (7702 2899). Aldgate tube. **Open** 11am-11pm Mon-Fri. **Food served** noon-4pm Mon-Fri. **Credit** MC, V.

The ladies' lav here must, like Miss Haversham's front room, have remained undisturbed for 50 years: the only woman we encountered here was an unfeasibly grandly proportioned caricature called Hot Stuff, which adorned the fruit machine. The atmosphere, though, is very friendly and local, and the beer is superb – including Greene King IPA and Young's. The decor is hackneyed – horse brasses and beams – and, with the scant seating providing only a modicum of comfort, the preferred modus operandi of the clientele is consumption on the hind legs, even of the hearty lunchtime sandwiches that are made on site. An upstairs room provides a dartboard and some chairs and tables. If you're in the area for a honest-to-goodness pub, you won't do much better than this old shop.

Bar available for hire. Function room (no smoking). Games (darts, fruit machines). Tables outdoors (4, patio). TV.

White Swan

21 Alie Street, E1 8DA (7702 0448). Aldgate tube/Tower Gateway DLR. **Open** 11am-11pm Mon-Fri. **Food served** noon-3pm Mon-Fri. **Credit** AmEx, MC, V.

This gem of a boozer is another in the interesting hinterland between City and East End. Beer aficionados will find a haven in the small but perfectly formed L-shaped bar, coloured in the traditional Victorian livery of deep red and dark wood. Shepherd Neame Porter and Spitfire are on tap, with Oranjeboom and Asahi standing opposite. There's a no-nonsense array of spirits, perhaps indicative of a regular with a sweet tooth: sugary liqueurs take centre stage. The food is hearty stuff, served up with the ubiquitous chunky chip. A newspaper portrait of (that man again) Jack the Ripper is on the wall but, for a modern, made-over boozer, the place is mercifully free of pub tat. The place fills up with discerning beeros of an evening and chancers who really should be back in the office of an afternoon, drawn both by the fine ale and the excellent service. Within half an hour the place feels like your local.

Babies and children admitted. Games (quiz machine). No-smoking area (lunchtime).

Also in the area...

All Bar One 16 Byward Street, EC3R 5BA (7553 0301).
Bar 38 St Clare House, 30-33 The Minories, EC3N 1PD (7702 0470).
Corney & Barrow 37A Jewry Street, EC3N 2EX (7680 8550).
Fine Line 124-127 The Minories, EC3N 1NT (7481 8195).
Habit & New Waterloo Room (Davy's) Friary Court, 65 Crutched Friars, EC3M 2RN (7481 1131).
Hog's Head 171-176 Aldersgate Street, EC1A 4JA (7600 5852); 1 America Square, EC3N 2LS (7702 2381)
Jamies 119-121 The Minories, EC3N 1DR (7709 9900).
Liberty Bounds (JD Wetherspoon) 15 Trinity Square, EC3N 4AA (7481 0513).
Pitcher & Piano The Arches, 9 Crutched Friars, EC3N 2AU (7480 6818).
Vineyard (Davy's) International House, 1 St Katherine's Way, E1 9UN (7480 6680).

East

Bethnal Green

W hat have the inhabitants of Bethnal Green done to deserve their good fortune? They're inundated with excellent new pubs and bars – the **Camel**, **Green & Red** – and established favourites like the **Approach**, **Bistrotheque Napoleon Bar** or the **Florist** refuse to lose their lustre.

Albion
94 Goldsmith's Row, E2 8QI (0871 984 3403). Liverpool Street tube/rail then 26, 48 bus. **Open** noon-11pm daily. **Credit** MC, V.
The single-room Albion is easy to recognise – a big West Bromwich Albion badge is prominent on the outside corner of the triangular building. Within, there are decent draught options (Greene King IPA, Old Speckled Hen, Budvar and Stowford Press Cider) and a wine list that offers Concha y Toro cabernet sauvignon or chardonnay and a Rose d'Anjou as the house plonk (£3.50/£12). The counter has 'Jeff Astle (1942-2002) Bar' carved into it in tribute to the iconic striker, while memorabilia runs to a WBA clone black-and-white strip from Tirana. Barely clad ladies on Fashion TV upped the lad quotient, but an efficient, friendly young barmaid and a gaffer who bids you cordial farewell from his station at the head of the bar give a better sense of the place.
Games (darts, fruit machine). Quiz (8.30pm Thur; £1). Tables outdoors (6, covered terrace). TVs (big screen, satellite).

Approach Tavern
47 Approach Road, E2 9LY (8980 2321). Bethnal Green tube/rail. **Open** noon-11pm Mon-Sat; noon-10.30pm Sun. **Food served** noon-2.30pm, 6-9.30pm Mon-Fri; noon-9.30pm Sat; noon-4.30pm Sun. **Credit** MC, V.
The redoubtable Approach serves no less than five Fuller's pints on draught (Honey Dew, Discovery, Chiswick, Pride and ESB), along with Adnams Bitter and Czech beers Zubr and Litovel Classic and Premium. The clientele aren't your usual beer blokes, though, with suede-head barmaids serving everyone from half-starved student artists to a large chap in a suit. Above the classic cubby-holed bar there's a

stuffed fish, a brace of pheasants, a pair of those Scotties that advertise whisky, and a bust of Shakespeare; the rest of the lived-in interior is black wood, gently arched fanlights, pews, stools and comfier seats. Green tenting and heaters out front make for all-weather supping in the beer garden. The menu is a cut above standard pub grub (vegetarian shepherd's pie with goat's cheese mash, for example) and the soundtrack might veer from soul to Kraftwerk or the Clash.
Art gallery (noon-6pm Wed-Sun). Babies and children welcome. Quiz (8.30pm Tue; £1). Tables outdoors (6, garden; 9, heated terrace). TV.

Bistrotheque Napoleon Bar
23-27 Wadeson Street, E2 9DR (8983 7900/ www.bistrotheque.com). Bethnal Green tube/rail/ Cambridge Heath rail/55 bus. **Open** 5.30pm-midnight Mon-Sat; 11am-midnight Sun. **Food served** 6.30-10.30pm Mon-Sat; 11am-4pm, 6.30-10.30pm Sun. **Credit** AmEx, MC, V.
Bistrotheque is infused with the sort of effortless cool that wouldn't look out of place in New York's Meatpacking District. The venue incorporates a bar (Napoleon) and a cabaret room on the ground floor, and a rustic French bistro on the first. The dimly lit bar is furnished with comfortable grey seats and banquettes, and has exposed brick walls, opulent chandeliers and a large etched-glass mirror on dark-wood panelling behind the counter. Champagnes, wines and draught beer are available, but the hip and beautiful from the fashion, media, music and design industries that flock to the place prefer to sip the exquisite cocktails, meticulously blended by the friendly barman. All the cocktails are reasonably priced between £5 and £8.50, with most costing around £6.50. Our favourite is the simply sensational Passion Fruit Caipirinha, which is made with Germana cachaça, fresh passion fruit, passion-fruit syrup and lime (£6.50).
Disabled: toilet. Music (cabaret 9pm Wed-Sun; £5-£12). Restaurant. Tables outdoors (5, courtyard).

Camel
277 Globe Road, E2 0JD (8983 9888). Bethnal Green tube. **Open** noon-11pm Mon-Sat; noon-10.30pm Sun. **Food served** noon-9pm daily. **Credit** MC, V.
Destined to become a housing development but saved, in part, by local opposition, this lovely Victorian boozer was used as a kids' club for non-evacuated East End kids during World War II. A sensitive renovation retained its original brown-tile exterior and dark-wood bar, while updating it with retro lighting and striking wallpaper (from Chair, the Notting Hill home store). You'll find Adnams Broadside and Southwold real ales, Bitburger and Amstel lagers, and Guinness, as well as six different rums, five whiskies, nine decent red wines and the same number of white (all served by the glass). Food is handmade gourmet pies served with a pile of rich, buttery mash and minty mushy peas (£7.95; £8.95 for daily specials such as Jerusalem artichoke, stilton-like blue vinny, chestnuts, root vegetables). Tea, coffee and cakes are also available and, to top it all, the pub is a smoke-free zone. In Bethnal Green, the way to heaven is surely through the doors of the Camel.
Babies and children admitted. Bar available for hire. Games (backgammon, chess). No smoking.

Florist
255 Globe Road, E2 0JD (8981 1100/www.theflorist E2.co.uk). Bethnal Green tube/rail/8 bus. **Open** 2.30-11pm Mon-Fri; noon-11pm Sat, Sun. **Credit** MC, V.

This small, single-room establishment delicately balances pub comfort and bar sophistication. From the floral stained glass motif above the entrance to the upright piano at the back it's an East End local, but the sofas, easy chairs, low tables and odd text-based artworks on the back wall, not to mention a fireplace lit by three candles, feel more like a bar, complete with a diffident DJ gradually stepping up the pace from reggae to funk. The draught options are Bitburger, Heineken, Cruzcampo and, happily, Westons Cider, filled out with bottles of Belgian fruit beers and excellent spirits – on top of the half-dozen single malts and Zubrowka and Wyborow vodkas, we were given Ketel One vodka in our elegantly made Martini (£6.50). Come summer, you can sit on a bench-shelf along the outside wall.
Games (board games). Music (DJs 8pm daily; open decks 5pm Sun; free). Tables outdoors (2, pavement).

Green & Red

51 Bethnal Green Road, E1 6LA (7749 9670/www.green red.co.uk). Shoreditch tube/Liverpool Street tube/rail. **Open** 5pm-midnight Mon-Fri; noon-midnight Sat; noon-11.30pm Sun. **Food served** 6-11pm Mon-Fri; noon-11pm Sat; noon-10.30pm Sun. **Credit** AmEx, MC, V.
Well-conceived and well-run, Green & Red combines an almost evangelical commitment to fine tequila with a kitchen that produces great Mexican drinking food (tacos de carnitas, £6.50; chorizo asado, £4.50); it works equally well whether you're drinking or eating or just killing time with the papers. They take themselves seriously enough to offer tasting flights (three tequila shots, £12-£59.40), but not too seriously to have fun – witness the El Burro ('Moscow Mule Mexican-style', £6.60) or Lager-ita ('Two of our favourite drinks in one glass', £6.80). We enjoyed an excellent Michelada (Sol with lime juice and chilli, and served with a salted rim, £3.50) and a couple of different Margaritas (from £6) over a leisurely brunch in the ground floor Cantina Bar, where decor is a slightly odd combination of spaghetti western and industrial chic. Staff are charming, knowledgeable and enthusiastic. Impressive.
Babies and children welcome (restaurant). Disabled: toilet. Function room. Music (DJs 8pm Fri, Sat; free). Restaurant. Tables outdoors (6, terrace). TV. **Map 5 R4.**

Pleasure Unit

359 Bethnal Green Road, E2 6LG (7729 0167/www. pleasureunitbar.com). Bethnal Green tube/rail/8 bus. **Open/food served** 6pm-midnight Mon-Thur, Sun; 6pm-2am Fri, Sat. **Credit** MC, V.
This venue halfway along Bethnal Green Road mostly plays host to live-music events, plus a club night or two. Shake! is the long-running main event, a club night that cuts up the dancefloor with northern soul and Motown every month or so, while bands are a motley bunch who share a hatred of pigeon holes and usually a degree of commitment to coming up with amusing monikers for themselves. A retro aesthetic sets the design rules, with disco balls and psychedelic lights providing a groovy-grungy atmosphere. DJs play on several nights (your best bet is to check the website for listings), drinks are cheap and basic, and the crowd are an enthusiastic lot – round here, you really couldn't ask for much more.
Music (bands 8pm nightly; club nights Fri, Sat; £3-£5).

Redchurch

107 Redchurch Street, E2 7DL (7729 8333). Liverpool Street tube/rail then 8 bus. **Open** 5pm-1am Mon-Thur; 5pm-3am Fri; 11am-3am Sat; 11am-1am Sun. **Food served** Sat, Sun. **Credit** AmEx, MC, V.

East

Approach Tavern

A perennially busy wee bar despite, or perhaps because of, its location a little removed from the main drag of Truman Brewery drinkeries. If it's exciting drinks you hanker for, the Redchurch has put a great amount of effort into sourcing them from all over. Beer swillers can choose from Brooklyn lager, Crystal Wheat on tap, the Japanese Orion or Dutch Lindeboom. Whiskies and tequilas are a bit of a speciality, with a sizeable selection of both. A dozen sakes also stand on the crowded bar, and if you get carried away you can come back the morning after for a prairie oyster. The uncontrived decor encompasses retro neon tube lighting and chrome swivel bar stools, and weeknights have an easy aural ambience of slouchy reggae. Weekends welcome funky grooves spanning 1970s soul, disco, jazz and hip hop, and this is also when you can order Spanish-influenced food.
Babies and children admitted. Disabled: toilet. Music (DJs 9pm Thur-Sat; free). **Map 5 R4**.

Royal Oak
73 Columbia Road, E2 7RG (7729 2220). Old Street tube/rail/Bethnal Green tube/26, 48, 55 bus. **Open** 6-11pm Mon-Thur; noon-11pm Fri, Sun; noon-midnight Sat. **Food served** 6-10pm Mon-Fri; noon-10pm Sat; noon-9pm Sun. **Credit** AmEx, MC, V.
This is one of those old-fashioned pubs that have been taken over by trendy local residents, yet the overall feel is casually welcoming rather than posey. The big draws are an extensive wine list chalked on the wooden beams, and the gastropub-style menu boasting mussels with parmesan, oysters in cider and pumpkin soup with sage butter (from £4). Head to the upstairs dining area for a less crowded space to feast in. As well as San Miguel, Guinness and Kronenbourg Blanc on tap, there's Timothy Taylor Landlord and Adnams Bitter, and you'll be served by smiley and on-the-ball bartenders. If beer's not your bag, you could go for an ultra-fashionable vodka and pomegranate juice, or a hot toddy in the winter months. Music is intermittent and barely audible – great if you like to socialise without getting hoarse. All locals should be like this.
Babies and children admitted. Restaurant (no smoking). Tables outdoors (3, yard).

Sebright Arms
34 Coate Street, E2 9AG (7729 0937). Bethnal Green tube/rail/Cambridge Heath rail/55 bus. **Open** noon-11pm Mon-Wed, Sun; noon-midnight Thur; noon-2am Fri, Sat. **Food served** noon-4pm Sun. **Credit** AmEx, MC, V.
Down a slightly menacing alley just past Hackney City Farm resides this genuinely local East End boozer. A giant Frank Sinatra poster hangs on the little stage of an old-school drinking den that is all shabby velvet banquettes and fruit machines, plus a pub-sized pool table. Punters were in single figures on the Saturday night we ventured in, but it was all go downstairs according to an exceedingly friendly barwoman who informed us it had been privately hired. On Fridays singing acts grace the stage, and if you don't fancy them you can head to the basement where a DJ plays requests. The drinks available are pretty standard – Carlsberg, Strongbow and Guinness on tap, Courage Pale Ale and Smirnoff Ice in the fridge – but it's the atmosphere that you're here for. Complete the experience with a traditional Sunday lunch.
Babies and children admitted (restaurant). Function room. Games (fruit machine, pool table). Music (singer 9.30pm Fri, Sat, 3.30pm Sun; free). Restaurant. Tables outdoors (5, courtyard).

Booze talking
Camel

You are?
Matt Kenneston, co-owner with my partner Joe Hill of the Camel, Bethnal Green (*see p144*).
The Camel was a classic pub rescue, yes?
The pub had been closed for six years and the freeholder was trying to turn it into flats. A petition went round against it with 800 signatures. But we knew nothing about this until we took it over.
How did you get involved?
My mate Joe and I had talked about running pubs for years. We've always been sociable people – we like restaurants, we like pubs – and, like everybody else, you always think you can do it better.
And the pub comes with a bit of history?
In the first week after we opened, this old lady poked her head round the door and said, 'Have you still got those pictures?' There were these black and whites on the walls of old coach parties, which we kept. This was basically the Camel day trip to Margate. Talking to local people, it's '48, '49, possibly early '50s. One thing I'm really keen to do this year is recreate it: get everybody in period gear and head down, not to Margate, but Whitstable, put a more modern spin on it.
Does the piano get used?
It's a fairly new addition, £5 on eBay. It's not actually tuned. Just before Christmas we had this over-55s ladies' choir come down. They were fantastic. A friend of mine on piano and they did popular hits from the '40s – totally out of tune. Nearly as out of tune as the piano.
Any idea where the name comes from?
There was a regiment based here that had done service somewhere in Africa. We think maybe one of the old soldiers opened a pub... but I'm making it up, I really don't know.

East

Bow, Mile End & Stepney

Several pubs hereabouts have great reputations: the **Morgan Arms** is a fine gastro, while the **Palm Tree** remains astutely old-fashioned.

Bow Bells

116 Bow Road, E3 3AA (8981 7317). Bow Road tube/Bow Church tube/DLR. **Open** 11am-11pm Mon-Sat; noon-10.30pm Sun. **Food served** 11.30am-2.45pm Mon-Fri. **No credit cards**.

A few years ago, almost every sturdy old East End taproom was hidden behind frosted glass, impenetrable to prying eyes. Changes in fashion, as well as landlords' desire to draw new drinkers into their fading businesses, mean the brightly coloured Bow Bells is now fronted by clear glass, visible to all who pass it on this bleak stretch of the Bow Road. The pub itself still belongs to the 20th century, from the unpretentious decor and bright lighting to a basic range of ales and a food menu that can barely have changed since the 1960s. Drinkers range from geezers to students, all of them local and most of them friendly. *Function room. Games (darts, fruit machines, pool table). Music (DJs/karaoke 8.30pm Fri; Elvis impersonator 8.30pm last Sat of mth; all free). Quiz (9pm Wed; free). Tables outdoors (3, pavement). TV (big screen, satellite).*

L'Oasis

237 Mile End Road, E1 4AA (7702 7051/www.loasis stepney.co.uk). Stepney Green tube. **Open** noon-11pm Mon-Sat; noon-10.30pm Sun. **Food served** 9.30pm Mon-Sat; noon-9pm Sun. **Credit** MC, V.

L'Oasis went for the stripped-floor and blackboard menu conversion in 2000 – and it's been a great success. So much so, the boss reorganised the bar to make more room, and opened a 30-seat dining room upstairs. This shift towards eating has left the place feeling a little less pub-like, but it remains busy with a mix of locals and university types. There are still draught Landlord and Adnams Bitter for ale drinkers, Leffe, Guinness and Stella for other pint-swillers, and a long wine list and decent range of spirits for the rest. The cooking's solid rather than adventurous, but a certainly a step above pub grub; the soundtrack tends to blues or 1970s pop-rock. *Disabled: toilet. Function room. No-smoking area.*

Morgan Arms

43 Morgan Street, E3 5AA (8980 6389/www. geronimo-inns.co.uk). Mile End tube. **Open** noon-11pm Mon-Sat; noon-10.30pm Sun. **Food served** noon-3pm, 7-10pm Mon-Sat; noon-4pm Sun. **Credit** MC. V.

The Geronimo Inns group have quietly accumulated a sizeable portfolio of gastropubs over the last few years: 16 at the last count, scattered all over the capital. A few are merely ordinary, but others, such as the Morgan, have been done out with sympathy and imagination. Roughly half the room is given over to diners (the lively food is two or three cuts above standard gastro-fare); the remainder, a low-lit jumble of sofas, stools and armchairs, is left to drinkers supping on toothsome pints of Timothy Taylor Landlord or selections from the decent wine list. It can get very busy in here, but the staff are charm personified and the thirtysomethings who eat and drink here never make too much of a din. A very impressive operation. *Babies and children admitted (dining). Disabled: toilet. Tables outdoors (11, garden; 4, pavement).*

Palm Tree

127 Grove Road, E3 5BH (8980 2918). Mile End tube/8, 25 bus. **Open** noon-midnight Mon-Thur; noon-2am Fri, Sat; noon-1am Sun (last admission 10.45pm). **No credit cards**.

Standing in glorious isolation towards the top of Mile End Park (ignore the postal address and head off Grove Road into the park on Haverfield Road), this is unarguably one of east London's greatest boozers. The whole place is a relic in the best possible way: antique wallpaper, locals who turn up on Sundays wearing their Sunday best, staff who offer to pop your bag behind the bar even on busy evenings. Even the darts are old school: the quieter of the two bars boasts a London Fives board, rarely seen these days. On weekends, wannabe Matt Munros croon along with a jazz group in the corner; singalongs invariably ensue. In keeping with the period feel, the wine is best avoided, but there's always a decent ale on tap. A few Hoxton types show up on Saturdays, but the welcome is always warm, and the location is a real boon in summer, when you can spread out into the park. Absolute magic. *Music (jazz 9.45pm Fri-Sun; free). Tables outdoors (4, park).*

Also in the area...

Half Moon (JD Wetherspoon) 213-233 Mile End Road, E1 4AA (7790 6810).
Match Maker (JD Wetherspoon) 580-586 Roman Road, E3 5ES (8709 9760).

Clapton

Clapton isn't a part of Hackney that's been done many favours over the years – even the nature reserve is flat and relatively bleak marshland – but the following are all hospitable establishments.

Anchor & Hope

15 High Hill Ferry, E5 9HG (8806 1730). Clapton rail/253 bus. **Open** noon-11pm Mon-Sat; noon-10.30pm Sun. **No credit cards**.

This well-established neighbourhood pub is a breath of fresh air – literally. Perched on the side of the River Lea, with expansive views of Walthamstow Marsh Nature Reserve (and plenty of outside seating to enjoy them from), it's an unpretentious and friendly little watering hole. Decorated in colours inspired by the proximity of the Marshes (brown-painted wood, green fleur-de-lis-style wallpaper), its careworn interior is tiny, with one corner entirely given over to darts, which is taken very seriously by the regulars, many of whom appear in a large photo-montage of grinning punters that hangs by the loos. If darts isn't your thing, there's a games machine and, for sports fans, a TV on which to watch the match over a pint (ESB, London Pride and Hooky Bitter were on draught when we visited). Or just sit back and admire the views. *Babies and children welcome. Games (darts, fruit machine). TV.*

Eclipse

57 Elderfield Road, E5 0LF (8986 1591/www.the-eclipse.com). Hackney Central or Hackney Downs rail. **Open** 4-11pm Mon-Wed; 4pm-midnight Thur, Fri; 10.30am-midnight Sat; 10.30am-11pm Sun. **Food served** 10.30am-2pm Sat; 10.30am-12.30pm Sun. **Credit** MC, V.

The Eclipse sits on the corner of a back street that typifies the creeping gentrification that is overtaking Hackney, where redeveloped housing nestles cheek by jowl with grim housing estates. Reflecting this, the Eclipse fuses old and new: a mirror-backed bar, mini-palm trees and dark bamboo-wood panelling dominate the back bar, and pinewood workman's benches fill the brightly lit, smaller space by the entrance. Drinks are to suit every pocket and taste: cask ales (including Timothy Taylor Landlord, Harveys Sussex Best), draught lagers (mainly Belgian) and some unusual wines (Weltevrede sauvignon blanc, New Dog) are available alongside a noteworthy selection of spirits (absinthe, Appleton Jamaican rum, Zubrowka bison grass vodka). In fact, whatever you fancy – be it cocktails, slammers such as the Slippery Nipple (sambuca, Baileys and grenadine), or even a cup of Arabic caffeine-free tea – you'll find it here.
Babies and children welcome (until 6pm Sun). Games (board games, cards, dominoes). Tables outdoors (10, pavement).

Princess of Wales

146 Lea Bridge Road, E5 9RB (8533 3463). Clapton rail/48, 55, 56 bus. **Open** 11am-11pm Mon-Sat; noon-10.30pm Sun. **Food served** noon-2.30pm, 6-8.30pm Mon-Sat; noon-3.15pm Sun. **Credit** AmEx, DC, MC, V.
Pitched alongside a busy thoroughfare, where the edges of Leyton Marshes merge with the upper reaches of Clapton, the Princess of Wales is a welcome sight for the road-weary visitor to this industrial area. A broad, Tudoresque building, with pretty lamps outside, it has plenty of seating within, including leather settees on which you can lounge beside the open fire. The emphasis is on eating (food is served daily, and there's a Sunday roast with a vegetarian option) and sports (all major events are shown, and there's a darts corner, complete with pristine oche). This is a Young's pub and so are all the beers, with the seasonal St George's Ale a welcome arrival for our visit, but it feels a bit like a country hotel – or perhaps an upmarket Little Chef. Worth the trek in the summer months for the riverside patio.
Babies and children welcome (before 9pm). Games (fruit machines). Tables outdoors (15, patio). TV (satellite).

Docklands

If anywhere needed some characterful drinking options, it's the steel-and-glass temples of Docklands. Alas, much of what's on offer in the windy canyons around Canary Wharf is service-industry boozing geared to suits lunching or seeking out a quick snifter en route home. Only in the back streets of the Isle of Dogs are there signs of life, often with a gritty edge.

Cat & Canary

1-24 Fisherman's Walk, Canary Wharf, E14 4DH (7512 9187/www.fullers.co.uk). Canary Wharf tube/DLR. **Open** 11am-11pm Mon-Thur, Sat; 11am-midnight Fri; 11am-8pm Sun. **Food served** noon-3pm, 6-9pm Mon-Fri; noon-8pm Sat; noon-6pm Sun. **Credit** AmEx, MC, V.
Perched on a corner of the North Docks, the worn wood, dodgy carpets and dartboard in this Fuller's outpost don't quite fit with all the surrounding modernity. The traditional look is a transplant, though, using salvaged panels from a Victorian East End church. But even as a 1990s fake, it's the nearest you'll get to a reasonable pub in the vicinity, with decent beer options (London Pride, Jack Frost), hearty fare such as hot roast pork with brie, and a couple of cosy nooks. The view isn't bad either, with a couple of old boats bobbing incongruously in the lee of a skyscraper beyond a large terrace that offers plenty of summertime seating.
Disabled: toilet. Games (darts, fruit machines, golf machine, quiz machine). No-smoking area. Tables outdoors (20, terrace). TVs (big screen, satellite).

Ferry House

26 Ferry Street, E14 3DT (7537 9587). Island Gardens DLR. **Open** 11am-midnight Mon-Fri; 11am-midnight Sat; noon-11pm Sun. **Credit** MC, V.
The ferry to Greenwich has gone but there's been a hostelry hereabouts since Henry VIII's time. The present building, though, dates from the 1820s. Apart from the addition of a TV, not much has changed in a cosy interior lit by old globe lights and an antique fireplace. A locals' place, the Ferry House has a rough-hewn air that makes a welcome contrast to the colourlessness of nearby Canary Wharf. Modernity here means a new album on the jukebox. An unexpected nod to tradition is an old London Fives dart board, though most of the punters – a mix of oldsters and skiving yoof – seem happy just exchanging local chit-chat and exuding an air of solidarity against suits.
Games (darts). Music (karaoke 9pm Fri; free). Tables outdoors (3, pavement).

Gun

27 Coldharbour, Isle of Dogs, E14 9NS (7515 5222/ www.thegundocklands.com). Canary Wharf tube/DLR/ South Quay DLR. **Open** 11am-midnight Mon-Sat; noon-11pm Sun. **Food served** noon-3pm, 6-10.30pm Mon-Fri; noon-4.30pm, 6-10.30pm Sat; noon-4.30pm, 6-9.30pm Sun. **Credit** AmEx, MC, V.
This 18th-century Grade II-listed pub was strikingly restored after a fire around five years ago, and now attracts office-workers from nearby Docklands during the week, and young families at weekends. It certainly looks dramatic: there's a central bar constructed from dark wood, and the front room combines bar with formal dining area, complete with laid tables. The more informal, pubby back room has fireplaces, a limited number of alcoves, and a large terrace with great views over the Thames. There's an excellent choice of beers, including Young's Ordinary, Adnams Broadside and Brakspear Honeycomb; draught lagers include San Miguel, Hoegaarden and Guinness Extra Cold. There's a small selection of cocktails, and a broad selection of premium spirits, port, sherry and wines (including uncommon varieties such as Funtanaliras from Sardinia, £22.50, and 'wines of the week'). A separate pub menu includes hearty British fare such as a bookmakers' sandwich with fresh horseradish (£8.95) and rare-breed pork sausages with Lyonnaise potatoes and Pommery mustard sauce (£12.50). A complimentary rickshaw is available to transport you to and from Canary Wharf.
Babies and children welcome. Disabled: toilet. Function rooms. Tables outdoors (11, terrace).

Pier Tavern

299 Manchester Road, E14 3HN (7515 9528). Island Gardens DLR. **Open** noon-11pm Mon-Sat; noon-10.30pm Sun. **Food served** noon-3pm, 5.30-8.30pm Mon-Thur; noon-3pm Fri; noon-6pm Sun. **Credit** MC, V.
You probably associate rugger-buggers with upmarket west London gaffs, but this corner boozer is an East End outpost of the oval-ball game as result of its role as HQ of

East

Bistrotheque Napoleon Bar. *See p144.*

the Millwall Rugby Club. While the posh boys take over after Monday and Wednesday night training and post-match on Saturday, in between it's a locals' gaff, serving basic booze to a mix of teens and old-timers. Quizzes and live music are further evidence of its role as social hub for a fairly grim bit of post-industrial Docklands. The space itself is nothing much, though – worn wood floorboards and over-bright lighting, tempered by some nice black-and-white pics of old Dockland life.
Babies and children admitted (if dining). Function room. Games (fruit machine, games machine). Music (DJs 9pm Fri; live music 9pm Sat; free). Quiz nights (Tue). Tables outdoors (4, garden). TV (big screen).

Via Fossa
West India Quay, Canary Wharf, E14 4QT (7515 8549/www.viafossa-canarywharf.co.uk). West India Quay DLR. **Open** 11am-11pm Mon-Wed; 11am-midnight Thur-Sat; noon-10.30pm Sun. **Food served** 11am-10.30pm Mon-Wed; 11am-11.30pm Thur-Sat; noon-10pm Sun. **Credit** AmEx, DC, MC, V.
Carved out of one of the few old buildings not razed for office blocks – an old stone warehouse built by prisoners from the Napoleonic Wars – this is a promising warren of low-ceilinged, timbered rooms, offering hideaways for Docklands dalliance. A bizarre mishmash of chairs echo the colours of the rough-painted walls – yellow, orange, blue. The food and drink are, like the decor, a mixed bag – extensive food menu (mains £8-10), keenly priced cocktails (under a fiver) and a poor selection of beers. Table service is meant to add some class, as is the upstairs restaurant offering pub grub tarted up as posh nosh. A large terrace looks across a patch of water to the Cat & Canary.
Disabled: toilet. Function rooms. Music (DJ 7pm Sat; free). No-smoking area. Restaurant. Tables outdoors (45, quayside).

Waterman's Arms
1 Glenaffrid Avenue, E14 3BW (7093 2883). Island Gardens DLR. **Open** 11am-11pm Mon-Sat; 11am-10.30pm Sun. **No credit cards.**
Tucked away down a side-street on the southernmost part of the Isle of Dogs, this pub seems a world away from the nearby Docklands towers. Perched by a little inlet on the river, the Waterman's exudes welcoming solidity. Orange nouveau-style lights accentuate the warmth of a red-carpeted interior where the bar dispenses the likes of Young's and Adnams to locals and blow-ins in equally friendly style. A games area offers pool and, like the near-by Ferry House, an old-style London Fives dartboard. The separate restaurant space offers further comfort with its simple menu, while bar sandwiches don't mess with much more than 'cheese, ham or tuna'. A soundtrack of 1960s classics on the jukebox adds more vintage polish.
Games (darts, pool).

Also in the area...
All Bar One 42 Mackenzie Walk, South Colonnade, E14 5EH (7513 0911).
Bar 38 Unit C, 16 Hertsmere Road, India Quay, E14 4AX (7515 8361).
Corney & Barrow 9 Cabot Square, E14 4EB (7512 0397).
Davy's 31-35 Fisherman's Walk, Cabot Square, E14 4DH (7363 6633).
Fine Line 20-30 Fisherman's Walk, 10 Cabot Square, E14 4DM (7513 0255).
Jamies 28 Westferry Circus, E14 8RR (7536 2861).
Ledger Building 4 Hertsmere Road, West India Quay, E14 4AL (7536 7770).
Slug & Lettuce 30 South Colonnade, Canary Wharf, E14 4QQ (7519 1612).

Hackney

If the gentrification of Hackney means more places like the **Cat & Mutton** or the **Dalston Jazz Bar**, we're all for it; if it meant the loss of somewhere like the **Prince George**, we'd petition the Mayor.

Cat & Mutton
76 Broadway Market, E8 4QJ (7254 5599/www.cat andmutton.co.uk). Bethnal Green tube/rail then 106, 253 bus/London Fields rail/26, 48, 55 bus. **Open** 6-11pm Mon; noon-11pm Tue-Sat; noon-10.30pm Sun. **Food served** 6-10pm Mon; noon-3pm, 6-10pm Tue-Sat; noon-5pm Sun. **Credit** AmEx, MC, V.
If you were wondering where the 118 118 guys drink, well one of them appears to be serving behind the bar at this great local boozer. It's been regenerated just enough to get rid of the sticky carpets, expose the bare-brick walls, and add a cosy Moroccan sofa and plenty of mismatched wooden tables and chairs. A huge picture of a cat and a leg of lamb hangs above the happy locals who sit and sup from a decent range of wines (from £3 a glass) or from the tap (San Miguel, Red Stripe, Grolsch). In fact the pub's name originally referred to the cattle (no cats) and sheep that stopped off at London Fields before being herded on to Smithfields for slaughter. The gastro grub, served from an open kitchen, is good although not especially cheap (Sunday lunches are £12.50 a pop), but old-timers can still get themselves a bag of pork scratchings (£1) or a pint of prawns with mayo (£3.50).

Babies and children welcome (until 8pm). Disabled: toilet. Music (DJs 5.30-10.30pm Sun; free). No-smoking area (1st floor; available for hire). Tables outdoors (6, pavement).

Dalston Jazz Bar
4 Bradbury Street, N16 8JN (7254 9728). Dalston Kingsland rail. **Open** 5pm-1am Mon-Thur, Sun; 5pm-3am Fri, Sat. **No credit cards.**
For our money, DJB is all right. The cosy interior is ambiently lit, has a mishmash of squishy sofas, zinc tables and stools, a well-stocked bookshelf that offered (at random) *Labour in the Caribbean*, *Moses and the Mountain* and a couple of old copies of the Thomson local directory, and plays great tunes (Doris Day, Sarah Vaughn, Dean Martin). Friendly but professional bar staff serve you with nibbles (crisps, cheese and biscuits) and drinks from the bar – a collection of retro zinc kitchen cabinets and worktops filled and covered with spirits. There's a selection of draught options: Red Stripe, Hoegaarden, Bitburger, Staropramen and Erdinger, and a few decent wines, but the cognoscenti are here for the cocktails. Choose from a menu of 16 favourites, including the Caipirinha, Mojito and a lovely sweet Manhattan (bourbon, sweet vermouth, angostura bitters). At £4 are they the cheapest in London? More exotic ones cost £5.50. Midweek the atmos is laid-back and relaxed, but from Thursday the music cranks up, queues form round the block and the place rocks until 3am. *Music (DJs 8pm Fri, Sat; jazz 10pm nightly). Tables outdoors (7, pavement).*

Dolphin
165 Mare Street, E8 3RH (8985 3727). Hackney Central rail/48, 55, 254 bus. **Open** 11am-2am Mon-Thur, Sun; 11am-4am Fri, Sat. **No credit cards.**
The Dolphin has become something of a destination pub for those who've tired of the oh-so-trendy watering holes of Hoxton. The handsome island bar doesn't offer a great selection of drinks – choose from pints of Kronenbourg 1664, bottles of Beck's, Bud or alcopops, standard spirits or an odd unnamed glass of wine. Food is peanuts. Karaoke night can be painful: 'Achy Breaky Heart', closely followed by 'A Boy Named Sue' sung by a group of tragi-comic boozed-up, tattooed old geezers. So what's the draw? There's a separate pool room, the atmosphere is friendly and the crowd is as good a cross-section of locals as you'll find in Hackney. And what about the wonderful tiled walls? There's Arion, a famous lyrist, returning by ship to Lesbos. Threatened by his fellow sailors, he strummed his lute and dolphins (hence the name) drew near to carry him away to safety as soon as he jumped overboard. Sweet. *Games (fruit machine, pool). Music (DJs/karaoke 8pm Sat, Sun; free). TV (big screen, satellite).*

Dove Kitchen & Freehouse
24-28 Broadway Market, E8 4QJ (7275 7617/www.belgianbars.com). Bethnal Green tube then 55 bus/London Fields rail. **Open** noon-11pm Mon-Thur; noon-midnight Fri, Sat; noon-10.30pm Sun. **Food served** noon-3pm, 6-10pm Mon-Thur; noon-3pm, 6-10.30pm Fri; noon-10.30pm Sat; noon-10pm Sun. **Credit** MC, V.
Even during the day you'll find candles on mismatched tables reflecting in the chandeliers and mismatched mirrors, adding to the cosy feel of this dark wood, burgundy-walled hostelry. As well as a huge selection of Belgian beers, you'll find the likes of Powerstation Porter, Timothy Taylor Landlord and a guest cranberry Früli. The popularity of this local boozer (now forming a duopoly with Dovetail) means that, even with a big extension out the back and a non-smoking dining room, it's never that easy to get a table – particularly for Sunday lunch (booking recommended) when scores of roasts (including vegetarian) are served, as well as pint glasses of chubby chips or even whole chickens to share. The crowd is mixed: a few post-Saturday night clubbers who'd apparently been 'all decked out in Chloé perving at a few blokes' the previous night, along with plenty of old regulars who have been visiting this gem long before it registered on the trendies' radar. *Babies and children welcome (until 6pm). Games (board games). Music (jazz 7.30pm Sun; free). No-smoking area. Restaurant. Tables outdoors (6, pavement).*

Fox
372 Kingsland Road, E8 4DA (3215 2093). Dalston Kingsland rail/67, 149 bus. **Open** noon-11pm Mon-Sat; noon-10.30pm Sun. **Food served** noon-10.30pm Mon-Sat; noon-10pm Sun. **Credit** (over £5) AmEx, MC, V.
Describing itself as 'organic' might be thought a little cheeky, as only the meats and veg (maybe two-thirds of the food) and around half of the wine list is organic here. That said, there's a dearth of decent eat-and-drinkeries on this strip, so we welcome the Fox unreservedly. It's a huge, warmly lit space with bare-brick walls, battered leather sofas, wooden chairs and tables. Candles are set into the brickwork, and there's a cosy red-walled nook complete with chandelier and Venetian glass mirror for a more intimate experience. Service was friendly and a real effort has been made with the food – the extensive, monthly changing menu includes brunches, mains such as chargrilled organic ribeye with fat chips and béarnaise sauce, and tasty sharing platters. The Fox is child-friendly too: there's a special children's menu, as well as toys, crayons and high chairs. *Babies and children welcome. Bar available for hire. No-smoking area.*

Marie Lloyd Bar
Hackney Empire, 289 Mare Street, E8 1EJ (8510 4500/www.hackneyempire.co.uk). Bethnal Green tube/rail then 106 bus/Hackney Central rail/30, 55, 56, 277 bus. **Open** 4pm-1am Mon-Fri; 7pm-1am Sat; 7pm-midnight Sun. **Credit** MC, V.
Hanging inside this split-level theatre bar (it was pinched from outside in 2005) is Tracey Emin's fuschia neon sign 'Just Love Me', and the Lloyd (named after the much-loved Victorian music-hall artiste who used to perform at next-door's refurbed Hackney Empire) seems to be asking just that. It is attempting to attract more than just theatre customers, though trying to get through the door as they queued round around the block was a challenge. Within the slightly retro (1980s) interior a long bar serves up a small range of spirits and lagers/ales (Kronenbourg 1664, Greene King IPA and Fireside), as well as sandwiches between noon and 2.30pm, while on a small stage a Saturday night DJ mixed a decent dubby soundtrack. *Disabled: toilet. Function room. Music (DJs/bands 9pm Wed-Sat, 1st Sun of mth; free). No-smoking area.*

Pembury
90 Amhurst Road, E8 1JH (8986 8597). Hackney Central or Hackney Downs rail. **Open** noon-11pm daily. **Credit** MC, V.
This immense Victorian pile lay derelict for years, after the menacing pub on the ground floor closed in the 1990s. Apartment conversion or demolition seemed its most

East

likely fates, but 2006 saw the opening of this airy pub. The renovation is light and pleasant, if unremarkable. But as with sister pub, the Oakdale Arms, the drinks are the draw: 16 handpumps hold an ever-changing range of ales and ciders, alongside Belgian beers in bottles. Punters have been slow to head here, perhaps because the no-smoking policy arrived at the same time as a chilly winter; the lack of music doesn't help the slightly flat ambience. Still, early days; we wish it well. There are plans to add a kitchen; free wireless internet access has already arrived.

Babies and children welcome. Disabled: toilet. Games (bar billiards, board games, pool). No piped music or jukebox. No smoking.

Prince George

40 Parkholme Road, E8 3AG (7254 6060). Dalston Kingsland rail/30, 38, 56, 242, 277 bus. **Open** 5pm-midnight Mon-Thur; 5pm-1am Fri; noon-1am Sat; noon-11.30pm Sun. **Credit** MC, V.

A prince of pubs indeed. How about stepping through the door to be greeted by the sound of the Temptations' 'Law of the Land' (closely followed by Louis Jordan and Nina Simone), a real fire, friendly bar staff, drinks including six decent white/red wines (from £3.25 a glass), tap treats including Litovel, Litovel Premium, Flowers, London Pride, Adnams Bitter, Abbot Ale and a great range of spirits. As if that weren't enough, the dark wood church pews are usually filled with erudite George aficionados who might as easily give you a recipe as try to rope you in to the top Monday night quiz. Still no food here – and that's just how we like it. Don't go changin'.

Babies and children welcome (until 8.30pm). Games (board games, pool table). No-smoking area. Quiz (9pm Mon; £2 per team). Tables outdoors (10, heated forecourt). TV.

Royal Inn on the Park

111 Lauriston Road, E9 7HJ (8985 3321). Mile End tube then 277 bus. **Open** noon-11pm Mon-Thur; noon-midnight Fri, Sat; noon-10.30pm Sun. **Food served** noon-3pm, 6-9.30pm Mon-Fri; noon-9.30pm Sat; noon-6pm Sun. **Credit** MC, V.

Lying at the entrance to Victoria Park, the Royal Inn has a prime position and, on a sunny Sunday afternoon, is full to its lofty rafters with Sunday lunchers, post-park walkers and kids enjoying the nearby playground. The handsome bar serves six real ales (including Fuller's ESB, Chiswick, Porter and London), a range of continental beers (Litovel, Zubr, Leffe) and Scrumpy on tap, as well as a decent range of spirits. There's a good wine list too (with five by the glass), and the food is definitely a cut above the average pub fare (crispy pork belly with pease pudding, £11; roast red snapper with sweet potatoes, £11), which can be served in a no-smoking dining area. Sadly, on our Saturday night visit many of the church pew seats were eerily vacant. Perhaps because the famous jukebox was out of action and the fire wasn't lit (in spite of the bitterly cold weather without).

Babies and children admitted (restaurant). Disabled: toilet. Function rooms. Quiz (8.30pm Tue; £1). Restaurant (no smoking). Tables outdoors (30, garden).

Spurstowe

68 Greenwood Road, E8 1AB (7249 2500). Hackney Central rail. **Open** 4.30-11pm Mon-Thur; 4.30pm-midnight Fri; noon-midnight Sat; noon-10.30pm Sun. **Food served** 5-10pm Mon-Fri; noon-4pm Sat, Sun. **Credit** MC, V.

The venerable Prince George has been having things all its own way around this part of Hackney for a number of years, but the conversion of this corner taproom – a scruffy local and then a deeply tacky fun pub in its two most recent incarnations – has provided it with a measure of competition. It's run by the people behind the Londesborough in Stoke Newington, and looks it: the walls are exposed brick, the tables are sturdy and the drinkers are mostly New Hackneyites reaping the benefits of creeping gentrification. While the George is a drinkers' pub through and through, the Spurstowe is a bit calmer and a lot foodier: roasts on a Sunday, bangers and the obligatory fat chips during the week. Wash 'em down with a pint of respectably kept Flowers IPA, Tetley's or Black Sheep.

Babies and children welcome (until 6pm). Tables outdoors (18, garden).

Also in the area...

Baxter's Court (JD Wetherspoon) 282 Mare Street, E8 1HE (8525 9010).

Leyton & Leytonstone

This fairly unremarkable, residential area of London boasts some welcoming local pubs.

Birkbeck Tavern

45 Langthorne Road, E11 4HL (8539 2584). Leyton tube. **Open** 11am-11pm Mon-Thur; 11am-midnight Fri, Sat; noon-11pm Sun. **Food served** noon-6pm Mon-Sat. **Credit** AmEx, MC, V.

Walking to the Birkbeck from Leyton station takes a little patience, but the former hotel looks surprisingly bright and grand when you arrive. Even the smaller saloon bar is ample, and the freshly upholstered lounge bar big enough for people to play on both dartboards without catching sight of each other. The decor is traditional, but pristine, with an arrangement of dried flowers on the fireplace under the TV the most notable feature. Until, that is, you catch sight of the blackboard of ales: Archers Blarney Stoned, Warcops Raiders and Golden Wheat on our visit. The house wine was good too, and food that evening ran to ad hoc ham and tomato or red leicester cheese and onion rolls from an extremely helpful barmaid. A fine local.

Function room. Games (darts, fruit machine). Quiz (8.15pm Sun; £1). Tables outdoors (18, garden). TV.

North Star

24 Browning Road, E11 3AR (8989 5777). Leytonstone tube. **Open** noon-11.30pm Mon-Sat; noon-10.30pm Sun. **Food served** noon-3pm, 6-9pm Mon-Fri. **No credit cards.**

Set back from a side road off the main drag, the North Star looks like a country house, complete with half nets in the window. Through a door with lovely etched glass is the saloon and main bar, narrower than the sparsely furnished lounge next door. The decor is red patterned carpet and dark-brown tongue and groove, while the music (Blondie, ska, Snap!) suggested a seniority of clientele not borne out by the single table of students present on a Wednesday night. Draught options are solid (Deuchars IPA, Pride, Bombardier, Adnams Broadside), wines come four of each and a rosé at £2.60/£3.40/£10, and although there was no hint of a flame in the tiled fireplace the regular heaters kept the cold at bay. A cheery boozer – no more, no less.

Games (fruit machine). Tables outdoors (4, garden; 2, pavement). TV (digital, satellite).

East

Prospect of Whitby. *See p156.*

East

William IV
816 Leyton High Road, E10 6AE (8556 2460). Leyton tube/Walthamstow Central tube/rail. **Open** 11am-11pm Mon-Sat; noon-10.30pm Sun. **Food served** noon-3pm, 5-10pm Mon-Fri; noon-10pm Sat, Sun. **Credit** MC, V.
A grand old red-brick pub, this, dating back to 1897. It still advertises its microbrewery outside, though the barmaids knew nothing of it. Still, the Casque Mark is well deserved: Fuller's ESB and Pride, plus Leffe and the fizzies, were joined by quality guests Over the Moon and Dark Island. Despite the flags of St George outside, there's a comfy cross-section of local folk here. The pub itself is well buffed but familiar in its brewery mirrors and reproduction etchings, enlivened by a fire in each of the two rooms and some arched ceilings that, along with rubber plants along one wall, give the place a hint of the Victorian conservatory. Oddly, Julie Andrews and Barbara Streisand peer down from one of the walls – could they have preceded Madonna in realising the joys of British real ale?
Babies and children admitted (until 7pm). Games (board games, fruit machines). Music (blues 8.30pm Sun; jazz 8.30pm last Thur of mth; free). Tables outdoors (7, garden). TV (big screen, satellite).

Also in the area...
Drum (JD Wetherspoon) 557-559 Lea Bridge Road, E10 7EQ (8539 9845).
George (JD Wetherspoon) 155-159 High Street, E11 2RL (8989 2921).
Walnut Tree (JD Wetherspoon) 857-861 High Road, E11 1HH (8539 2526).

Limehouse
In the lea of the mighty financial edifices of Docklands proper, Limehouse is a quietly prosperous locale, with three decent – and very different – places to drink strung out along the same Thameside street.

Booty's Riverside Bar
92A Narrow Street, E14 8BP (7987 8343). Limehouse or Westferry DLR. **Open** noon-11pm Mon-Thur; noon-midnight Fri, Sat; noon-10.30pm Sun. **Food served** noon-9.30pm Mon-Fri, Sun; noon-7.30pm Sat. **Credit** AmEx, DC, MC, V.
The mellifluous sounds of Stevie Wonder could have seduced us into thinking this was a suburban wine bar had the music not lurched closer to Hi-NRG as the evening progressed. Romantically lush and a little camp (there's a pink flamingo outside), Booty's combines civilised pub (Greene King IPA, Pride, Staropramen, Caffrey's on draught) with relaxed wine bar. The setting is brilliant, with two cherished tables one step down at the river end of the bar, each providing a view of the Thames through paned, bottle-bottom windows. Low lights, red tablecloths and single flowers on the tables cultivate a smoochy atmosphere, but there is plenty of badinage at the stools by the bar at the back. Skip the reheated food, but drop in for weekend jazz nights when the place opens later.
Babies and children admitted. Games (fruit machine, quiz machine). Music (jazz 9pm Sat; free). Tables outdoors (2, pavement). TVs (satellite).

Black Bull. See p157.

Grapes

76 Narrow Street, E14 8BP (7987 4396). Limehouse or Westferry DLR. **Open** noon-3pm, 5.30-11pm Mon-Fri; noon-11pm Sat; noon-10.30pm Sun. **Food served** noon-2.30pm, 7-9pm Mon-Sat; noon-3.30pm Sun. **Credit** AmEx, MC, V.

Were you to imagine an historic riverside pub, this would be it: handsome etched-glass and greenery frontage; a wood-beams interior on the small side of cosy; model ships, a barometer, sea charts and porcelain plates as decoration; enjoyably old-fashioned Sunday roasts and quality beer (Marston Pedigree, Timothy Taylor Landlord, Adnams Bitter). There's even a pretty reliable Dickens connection: this could very well have been the model for the Six Jolly Fellowship Porters in *Our Mutual Friend*. The current premises date to 1720, although signs of modern life include a notice requesting that mobile phones be switched off, and a non-smoking area. The latter is in the riverside half of bar, and has an open fire. A rickety balcony extends over the Thames, equally rickety stairs lead up to a middling seafood restaurant and board games await those who forgot the papers.

Games (board games). No-smoking area. Restaurant.

Narrow Street Pub & Dining Room

44 Narrow Street, E14 8DQ (7265 8931). Limehouse DLR. **Open** noon-11pm Mon-Sun. **Food served** noon-10pm Mon-Sun. **Credit** MC, V.

We've never entirely warmed to the Narrow Street. The location couldn't be better: the pub is right on the mouth of Limehouse Basin, with mighty views of any boating action, it really comes into its own when the barbecue area is cranked up and bench seating overrun in summer. Inside, things are in the uncertain zone between style bar and posh pub. The dining area is moodily welcoming with tea lights and big paintings on the wall, but the drinking area is uncomfortably furnished and glossy without really impressing anyone. The draught options are Paulaner, Affligem, Amstel, Guinness and a couple of ordinary lagers, the wine list ascends from a house sauvignon blanc at £4.95 a glass, and the menu covers all bases with the likes of chocolate and black-eye pea soup alongside good burgers with fat chips.

Babies and children welcome. Disabled: toilet. Restaurant. Tables outdoors (36, riverside terrace).

Plaistow

There isn't much reason to visit Plaistow – most of the pubs bear forbidding 'No travellers, no students' signs – but the **Black Lion** makes the place worth a detour.

Black Lion

59-61 High Street, E13 0AD (8472 2351). Plaistow tube. **Open** 11am-3pm, 5-11pm Mon, Tue; 11am-11pm Wed-Sat; noon-10.30pm Sun. **Food served** noon-2.30pm, 5-7.30pm Mon-Fri. **Credit** MC, V.

In the setting of a traditional English coaching inn, the Black Lion's display of Oirishry may not seem propitious, but a glimpse of the 10-year Bushmill's on optic should set your mind at rest. Boozing is taken seriously here, with a chalkboard advertising past, future and present ales (Oakham Ales Bishops Farewell, Archers Winter

Olympics, plus Courage Best on our visit), a nice array of bloke-ish spirits (single malts, brandies) and wine that isn't priced for sipping (£2.50/£3.30/£9.50). A mixed bunch of drinkers sit at stools beside the long curved bar, or at tables in front of a single bench seat against the wall; more conventionally sociable seating is a few steps down to one side. Food is competitively priced (bacon and liver casserole, £5.50; leek and potato soup, £2). Very decent all round.
Babies and children admitted (until 7pm). Function room. Games (fruit machine, quiz machine). Tables outdoors (10, garden). TVs (satellite).

Stratford

Likely to be a prime beneficiary of 2012 Olympic funding, Stratford has actually been polishing up its act for years – which only goes to show how grim it used to be. Happily, both the **King Edward VII** and **Theatre Royal Bar** are mighty fine establishments.

King Edward VII
47 Broadway, E15 4BQ (8534 2313/www.kingeddie. co.uk). Stratford tube/DLR/rail. **Open** noon-11pm Mon-Sat; noon-10.30pm Sun. **Food served** noon-10pm Mon-Sat; noon-9pm Sun. **Credit** MC, V.
Dwarfed by its neighbours, this stocky little boozer belongs to a bygone era. Step inside and its compact interior (dark-wood panelling, brass fittings, wooden floors) reveals a 19th-century origin. Period details also abound in the large seating area at the back, where patrons mingle on comfy, chesterfield armchairs. Top marks go to the staff – no ashtray is left to overfill, and they take obvious pride in their wines (£12-£17 per bottle; £2.80-£4 per glass), all served in proper, smear-free glasses. On the night we visited, reds were mainly French, Italian and Chilean (Ponte Pietra merlot/corvina 2004; Oveja Negra cabernet sauvignon/ syrah 2004); whites included Ca' Marengo pinot grigio, and Ranch Series chardonnay 2002. They also stock real ales, including Bombardier and Hop Back Summer Lightning. King Eddie's Restaurant (formerly the upstairs bar) will sort out your munchies; daily specials for those with smaller appetites are available downstairs.
Babies & children welcome (restaurant). Quiz (8pm Sun; free). Music (acoustic/open mic 8pm Thur; free). Restaurant (no smoking). Tables outdoors (7, yard).

Theatre Royal Bar
Theatre Royal, Stratford East, Gerry Raffles Square, E15 1BN (8534 7374/www.stratfordeast.com). Stratford tube/rail/DLR. **Open** 11am-11pm Mon-Sat; noon-10.30pm Sun. **Food served** 12.30-9.30pm Mon; 12.30-8.30pm Tue-Sun. **Credit** MC, V.
Another reason (should you need one) to visit Stratford's 'pioneering' Theatre Royal is its bar. Housed in the theatre's original 1884 building, the bar's striking interior (original floor tiles, side lamps and framed photos of past productions adorn its vermilion walls) provides an eye-catching backdrop to an evening's merriment. Pumping beats, courtesy of the guest DJ (1980s funk the night we visited) makes catching up on the goss a bit of a challenge, but you'll be so busy noshing on the hearty Caribbean food (jerk chicken, mutton curry, Jamaican patties) you won't care. Real ales (Adnams, London Pride), cider (Magners) and plenty of alcopops are also stocked. As befits its thespian roots, entertainment is the name of the game here. There are regular free poetry evenings; a free weekly

comedy night; and regular DJ sets and live music – from acoustic jazz funk and R&B to Indian classical and hip hop. No wonder booking is advisable.
Babies and children welcome. Comedy (6-9pm Mon, last Sun of mth; free). Disabled: toilet. Music (bands/ solo musicians 6-9pm Mon-Fri, 1-4pm Sat, Sun; free). Poetry (7pm Sun; free). Restaurant. Tables outdoors (4, heated terrace).

Also in the area...
Goldengrove (JD Wetherspoon) 146-148 The Grove, E15 1NS (8519 0750).

Walthamstow

Walthamstow can seem like two completely different districts: the justly named and carefully preserved Walthamstow Village, where you'll find both the **Nag's Head** and the **Village**, and the rest – downbeat, suburban and typical of East London.

Flower Pot
128 Wood Street, E17 3HX (8520 3600). Walthamstow Central tube/rail. **Open** noon-11pm Mon-Sat; noon-10.30pm Sun. **Credit** MC, V.
Despite its name, there's nothing fragrant about this traditional boozer. The Flower Pot is strictly one for the lads, and local lads at that, who come to cheer on their favourite footie team. This is mainly a sports pub – two large TV screens ensure you catch all the (Sky) action. But sports aside, those in the know come for the draught beers (Leffe Blonde, Staropramen, Kronenbourg Blanc and Brahma for lager drinkers, plus Bass), as well as special promotions such as Früli apple beer and Floris passion-fruit beer (£1.50) 'while stocks last'. Surprisingly, there are wine lists on the tables, with around 16 wines, mostly Stowells (from £12); the lists include a helpful tasting guide. There's a decent amount of live entertainment – mainly 1960s and '70s tribute bands, plus DJ Smashy 'by public demand'. And if you fancy a flutter, there are regular race and auction nights.
Babies and children welcome (until 7pm). Games (board games, cribbage, retro gaming machine). Music (1960s and '70s tribute bands 8.30pm Fri, Sat; free). Quiz (8.30pm Sun; £1). Tables outdoors (10, garden). TV (big screen, satellite).

Nag's Head
9 Orford Road, E17 9LP (8520 9709). Walthamstow Central tube/rail. **Open** 4-11pm Mon-Fri; 2-11pm Sat; 2-10.30pm Sun. **Credit** MC, V.
Situated in the heart of Walthamstow Village, the Nag's Head looks a bit like a country hotel. A good layout inside ensures a feeling of space even when it's busy; there's plenty of seating, including sofas around one side of the bar for chilling, plus a heated patio and garden at the back. Black and white movie stills hang on the walls and tea lights dotted on the velvet-draped tables give the place an intimate feel – evidence of the new management's aim to make this a cut above your ordinary pub experience. Belgian fruit beers, real ales (Adnams, London Pride), plus some interesting wines mean there's plenty to wet your whistle. In terms of entertainment, there's good jazz on a Sunday afternoon. A good mix of locals and young professionals, plus incredibly friendly barmaids, give it a great buzz. You won't want to leave.

East

Belly-dancing classes (8.30pm Tue; £7). Life-drawing classes (7.30pm Mon; phone for details). Music (jazz 4-8pm Sun; free). Pilates classes (8pm Wed, 10.30am Sat; phone for details). Tables outdoors (8, heated patio; 20, heated garden).

Village

31 Orford Road, E17 9NL (8521 9982). Walthamstow Central tube/rail. **Open** noon-11pm Mon-Sat; noon-10.30pm Sun. **Food served** noon-3pm Mon-Fri; noon-4pm Sat, Sun. **Credit** MC, V.

You can't miss the Village – or rather you can't miss the huge billboard that advertises its approach. Which is just as well, as it's not otherwise the easiest place to find. Inside, a small, book-lined snug at the back redeems its otherwise traditional look. A banquette runs the length of one wall and there's just enough room for a couple of tables and chairs from which to admire the flagstones and garden furniture 'courtyard'. Real ales (Adnams, Greene King IPA, Directors, Old Hooky), plus all the usual suspects are present and correct. Campari is as exotic as it gets, and requesting it is guaranteed to flummox the staff. Sunday lunch is popular; standard pub grub (chicken casserole, 'giant' Yorkshire puds) is available weekdays. This popular boozer is good for a midweek catch-up with your mates, but, come the weekend, expect to shout to make yourself heard as *le tout* Walthamstow takes up residence.

Babies and children admitted (in snug and garden). Games (fruit machine, quiz machine). Quiz (8.30pm Tue; £1.50). Tables outdoors (14, garden). TV.

Wapping

H aunt of bristling pirates in the 16th-century, when the **Prospect of Whitby** was established, and home to Murdoch's News International from the 1980s – ah, the irony – Wapping is that now familiar mix of warehouse conversions and tough social housing.

Prospect of Whitby

57 Wapping Wall, E1W 3SH (7481 1095). Wapping tube. **Open** 11.30am-11pm Mon-Sat; noon-10.30pm Sun. **Food served** 11.30am-9.30pm Mon-Sat; noon-8.30pm Sun. **Credit** AmEx, DC, MC, V.

It's rare for a pub to be on the London tourist trail, but then the Prospect did start out around 1520, as the Devil's Tavern, and has changed little since the late 1700s. It's a good spot to combine rich history with a drink. And this place sure has history – where else can claim to be both the spot where England's first fuschia was exchanged for a noggin of rum in 1780 and the site of a 1950s armed robbery that resulted in the hanging of a public school villain called Scarface? The interior is wonderful too, with black stone floor and heavily carved old beams fighting for attention with memorabilia that mixes legal and nautical themes; we could have done, however, without the mild period stench that permeated the place on our visit. As you might expect of a former haunt of Dickens and Pepys, the beer's good – excellent Greene King IPA. The food veers between traditional daily specials under simple headings of 'Soup, Pie, Sausages' and modern offerings like asparagus tart or chicken tikka. A rather spruce alcove provides a brighter spot to admire the passing river traffic if you don't fancy sitting on the terrace.

Babies and children admitted. Function room. No-smoking area. Tables outdoors (7, garden).

Indo. See p158.

Town of Ramsgate
62 Wapping High Street, E1W 2PN (7481 8000).
Wapping tube/100 bus. **Open** noon-midnight daily.
Food served noon-9pm daily. **Credit** AmEx, MC, V.
This long, thin, twilit place is a welcoming beacon of
bonhomie amid nondescript Dockland buildings. Along
the dark wood walls, antique manuscripts and illustrations
nod to its rich nautical history – the name refers to the
tradition of Ramsgate fishermen landing their catch at the
adjacent Wapping Old Stairs, also the place where Captain
Kidd met his end and the infamous Judge Jeffreys nearly
met his end at the hands of a 17th-century lynch mob. Now
it's a welcoming spot in which to sup from a decent beer
selection (Adnams, Young's, Pride, as well as Leffe and
Hoegaarden) or, if the sun's out, grab a place on the tiny
terrace looking over the river to Rotherhithe. Veuve
Clicquot is available for anyone for whom the view and
history aren't rich enough.
Babies and children admitted (until 7pm). Quiz (8.30pm
Mon; £1). Tables outdoors (12, riverside garden). TV.

Whitechapel

Perfectly positioned to mop up some City
cash without losing the East End grittiness
everybody expects (and now wants to capitalise
on), Whitechapel manages to do boho (**Indo**),
sleek (**Lane**) and trad (**Pride of Spitalfields**),
all in a conveniently compact area.

Big Chill Bar
Old Truman Brewery, off Brick Lane, E1 6QL (7392
9180/www.bigchill.net). Aldgate East tube/Liverpool
Street tube/rail. **Open** noon-midnight Mon-Thur; noon-
1am Fri, Sat; 11am-11.30pm Sun. **Food served** noon-
11pm Mon-Sat; noon-10.30pm Sun. **Credit** DC, MC, V.
It's hard to imagine a more convivial crowd in the whole
of London's thriving bar scene – one of the reasons it was
on *Time Out*'s Best Bar shortlist in 2005. Located on the
hip, pedestrianised shopping and market area sandwiched
between Brick Lane and Commercial Street, this place
teems with passing trade and destination drinkers every
night. The prestige of the Big Chill's annual festival, plus
fine artistic touches such as low-slung leather seating,
patterned drapes, a chandelier and an incongruous bison
head all add to its allure. The snacks (burgers, pies and
late-night pizza) and cocktails (from £5.50) are popular, as
is the cider menu, featuring Westons on draught (£3.60)
and Savanna in bottles (£3). DJs play nightly, raising the
beat for dancing feet when the occasion demands it. With
the Big Chill House due to open in King's Cross as we went
to press, fingers are crossed that these amicable vibes
spread across the city.
Babies and children admitted (until 6pm). Disabled:
toilet. Music (DJs 7pm Tue-Sun; free). Tables outdoors
(4, patio).

Black Bull
199 Whitechapel Road, E1 1DE (7247 6707).
Whitechapel tube. **Open** 11am-11pm Mon-Sat;
noon-10.30pm Sun. **Food served** noon-3pm
Mon-Fri. **No credit cards**.
It looks like the Black Bull has been tarted up. Not that
first-time visitors would notice: there's the same cod Tudor
exterior, the same big booze hall within, wood furniture in
the main part and hideous pale green upholstery to one

East

side. The main attraction on our visit was Champions League football on a huge screen in the main bar (little relay screens keep those braving the green-ness informed), but it's the siren song of the pumps that's the real draw. This is, as far as we know, the only pub in London associated with the Suffolk-based Nethergate brewery. Which is a very good thing: savour, for example, Old Growler, Suffolk County, coriander-flavoured porter Umbel Magna or the wonderfully named Brewer's Drop. Always a pleasure.
Games (fruit machine, quiz machine). TV (big screen, satellite).

Exit
174 Brick Lane, E1 6RU (7377 2088). Shoreditch tube. **Open** 11am-11pm Tue-Sat; 11am-10.30pm Sun. **Food served** 11am-2pm, 6-9pm Tue-Sun. **No credit cards.**
There's nothing other-worldly about Exit, a cosily unpretentious bar that feels more like a café than an iniquitous drinking den. A sparse scattering of seats, a short menu (one pasta, one burger, one salad…) and a bar counter that comfortably sustains only a two-deep crowd don't detract from the atmosphere of easy-going serenity that prevails. Sweet-smelling joss sticks and a friendly, unrushed staff helps to make this narrow corridor a welcome respite from the bustle of shoppers and traders outside. At night the curtains are drawn and revellers can party until 3am, quaffing house wine at £3 a glass or a Maker's Mark and Coke for £4. At weekends the music leans to the funkier, more soulful end of the dance music spectrum, with live music on Tuesdays and Sundays.
Music (DJs nightly; live music Tue, Sun; free).

Indo
133 Whitechapel Road, E1 1DT (7247 4926). Aldgate East or Whitechapel tube. **Open** noon-1am Mon-Thur, Sun; noon-3am Fri, Sat. **Food served** noon-3pm, 6-9pm daily. **Credit** MC, V.
Changing art – often of a faintly salacious tenor – adorns the walls at Indo, where the light seems a little dimmed even at the middle of the day. Black and white floor tiles and a line of stools at the counter add a touch of bar elegance, while comfort comes as a quality £6.50 Sunday roast (£4.50 veggie), eaten from sofas drawn up to a low table at the window or at wooden tables with unmatched chairs. A loosely bohemian, mainly young, largely good-looking crowd deal with newspapers and roll-ups in a leisurely fashion, drinking draught (Pride, Hoegaarden, Budvar, San Miguel, Kronenbourg 1664, Red Stripe, Guinness, Carlsberg) or bottled beer (Sagres, Cooper's, Früli, Liefmann), wine (house £2.60/£3.40) and coffee (espresso, £1.30). A squad of spirit bottles lines up behind the bar, pourers at the ready, and the stereo delivers a nicely curated gallery of music, from free jazz and doo wop to the Kinks. Sheer quality.
Games (chess, dominoes). Music (DJs 8pm Sat, Sun; free). Tables outdoors (2, pavement). TV (big screen).

Lane
2-20 Osborn Street, E1 6TE (7377 1797/www.thelane bar.com). Aldgate East tube. **Open** noon-midnight Mon-Wed; noon-1am Thur, Fri; 6pm-1am Sat. **Food served** noon-3pm, 6-10pm Mon-Fri; 6-10pm Sat. **Credit** AmEx, DC, MC, V.
The Lane is simply too accommodating to feel as chic as it hopes to be. There seems to be half a dozen of everything: good draught beers (Amstel, Landlord, Sleeman Honey Brown), bottled beers, wines white and red, single malts, premium spirits, cocktails classic, cocktails house – it's all

laudably democratic, but leaves the Lane lacking that magic touch of individuality. Our Polish Spring Martini (Zubrowka, honey vodka, mint and a touch of apple, £6) was carefully and effectively mixed, the decor is functionally pitched between sleek bar and disco, and there's even a new menu to keep you going. But at midnight on the Saturday of our visit, the place was mainly boys in pressed shirts and jeans and girls in mini-dresses with thick gold belts. Decent, but strangely disjointed.
Disabled: toilet. Music (DJs 8pm Wed-Sat; free). TVs.

Pride of Spitalfields
3 Heneage Street, E1 5LJ (7247 8933). Aldgate East tube. **Open** 11am-11pm Mon-Sat; noon-10.30pm Sun. **Food served** noon-2.30pm Mon-Fri; 1-5pm Sun. **Credit** MC, V.
It's sometimes a relief to know there's a dyed-in-the-wool boozer just a skip from Brick Lane. As a Fuller's pub, the Pride can be expected to provide Pride and ESB, as well as two or three guest ales (Archers Village and Brewers Gold on our most recent visit). Apart from that, it's just a smoky little pub, with a pull-down screen for the football in the main room, and a tiny side room with a normal TV. The premises look a little like a suburban semi from the outside, and indoors a shiny cream-coloured plastic awning adds a slightly surreal edge to the food counter, but the clientele is a successful mix, with old East Enders alongside middle-class bohemians. When things get crowded in summer, there's a shelf outside to lean your pint on.
Babies and children admitted. Tables outdoors (4, pavement). TV (big screen, digital).

Vibe Bar
Old Truman Brewery, 91-95 Brick Lane, E1 6QL (7377 2899/www.vibe-bar.co.uk). Aldgate East tube/Liverpool Street tube/rail. **Open** 11am-11.30pm Mon-Thur, Sun; 11am-1am Fri, Sat. **Food served** 11am-3pm Mon-Thur; 11am-1am Fri, Sat; 11am-7pm Sun. **Admission** £3.50 after 8pm Fri, Sat. **Credit** AmEx, DC, MC, V.
Heaving on a wintry Tuesday, the original Brick Lane DJ bar is still doing a roaring trade. Original fans may occasionally fall by the wayside, lamenting over-exposure (read: overcrowding at weekends) and slight grubbiness, but fresh generations of bright young things are quick to fill the leather sofas that have been plonked at random in the saloon bar. Anyway, the lived-in look is glossed over by excellent cartoon murals. A range of pies has replaced the erstwhile Thai menu, but live music continues to feature regularly, the same DJs have been spinning here for years and, thanks to the row of offices above, the outdoor back benches still make you feel like you're sitting in a council estate. In spring the venue comes into its own, thanks to the large outdoor courtyard, which is the main focus of the Brick Lane summer festival. Draught and bottled options include Scrumpy and Guinness (£3), cocktails come in at £5.50.
Disabled: toilet. Function room. Music (bands 7.30pm Mon-Wed, Sun; DJs 7pm daily). Tables outdoors (70, courtyard and marquee).

Also in the area…
Goodman's Field (JD Wetherspoon) Mansell Street, E1 8AN (7680 2850).
Grapeshots (Davy's) 2-3 Artillery Passage, E1 7LJ (7247 8215).
Old Dispensary 19A Leman Street, E1 8EN (7702 1406).

East

North

Belsize Park & Swiss Cottage

We advise nearby Swiss Cottagers to think of themselves as 'Belsize Park borders' and head for the continental-style **Belsize**, modern gastro **Hill** or the superb **Washington**.

Belsize

29 Belsize Lane, NW3 5AS (7794 4910). Belsize Park tube. **Open** noon-11pm Mon-Sat; noon-10.30pm Sun. **Food served** noon-3pm, 6.30-10.30pm Mon-Thur; noon-10.30pm Fri, Sat; noon-9.30pm Sun. **Credit** MC, V.
Today's Belsize is a successful attempt at creating a modern, continental-style pub-cum-wine bar: the bar itself – very much the focus – is decorated to stylish effect with a hanging arrangement of wine glasses, while clean dark wood against fresh cream walls eschews the patterned decor of a traditional boozer. Tables are neatly arranged around the slick L-shaped interior (with posh pub nosh available at the back), and the smart punters are as likely to come here for a quick espresso seated at the bar as they are to sink a pint (of Leffe, Staropramen, Guinness or XXXX) on the comfortable seats that run along the window-backed walls. And the crowd isn't completely monotone, with the odd eccentric rocker still to be found here on occasion.
Babies and children welcome. Bar available for hire. Restaurant (available for hire; no smoking).

Hill

94 Haverstock Hill, NW3 2BD (7267 0033/www.geronimo-inns.co.uk). Belsize Park tube. **Open** 4-11pm Mon-Wed; 11am-midnight Thur-Sat; 12.30-11pm Sun. **Food served** 7-10.30pm Mon-Wed; noon-3pm, 7-10.30pm Thur-Sat; 12.30-9pm Sun. **Credit** MC, V.
The Hill has gone through various revamps, but the owners have finally settled on modern gastropub meets posh Parisian beauty. Beautiful antique chandeliers and jade green, gold leaf-decorated walls manage (just about) to give the place its contrived elegance (but any more mounted Renaissance-style busts and the word 'tacky' will enter the equation). The candlelit dining area with its flickering fireplace is – unusually – at the entrance; diners can expect an ambitious choice of pricey dishes, such as cold rare beef salad, and rock oysters. The drinks menu also seeks to impress, with an extensive range of wine, and quality choice of beers (Honey Dew, König Ludwig and Amstel on tap, and Peroni, Magners and Corona by the bottle). A posh brunch menu takes the place further from its Victorian pub roots. *Restaurant. Tables outdoors (20, garden).* **Map 8 G25**.

Sir Richard Steele

97 Haverstock Hill, NW3 4RL (7483 1261). Belsize Park or Chalk Farm tube. **Open** 11am-11pm Mon-Thur; 11am-midnight Fri, Sat; noon-11pm Sun. **Food served** noon-3pm, 6-10pm Mon; noon-3pm, 6-10.30pm Tue-Fri; noon-10.30pm Sat; noon-10pm Sun. **Credit** MC, V.
Worth seeking out on a wet and windy night as this one is as cosy as a pub gets: there are coal fires, little nooks with velvet and leather banquette seating, mismatched chairs and tables, and then there are the drinking options: Greene King Abbot Ale, Fuller's London Pride, Staropramen, Leffe, Scrumpy Cider and more on tap, plus a good range of bottles. There's plenty to hold the eye's gaze too, from the shelves of musty books to stained glass windows, animal heads, busts of historical figures, old advertising paraphernalia and, for sports fans, a couple of TV screens (which might explain the higher than usual male quotient on our visit). It's buzzy with a wide age range of punters and super-friendly bar staff. Oh! and the kitchen serves Thai food (or bowls of chips if you're in a hurry). A gem.
Music (R&B/rock 4pm, Irish music 9pm Sun; trad jazz 9pm Mon; acoustic blues/rock 9pm Wed, Thur; free). Games (fruit machine). Tables outdoors (16, patio). TVs (big screen, satellite).

Washington

50 England's Lane, NW3 4UE (7722 8842). Belsize Park or Chalk Farm tube. **Open** noon-11pm Mon-Thur; noon-midnight Fri, Sat; noon-10.30pm Sun. **Food served** noon-3pm, 5.30-10pm Mon-Fri; noon-10pm Sat; noon-9.30pm Sun. **Credit** AmEx, MC, V.
The Washington would definitely be in the running for prize of 'bar most likely to please all', despite being derided as 'yuppified' by some former regulars since its refurb in 2001. True, a younger, more contemporary vibe prevails, but the place still accommodates its old regulars. The original interior too has been treated with respect: Victorian mirrors with etchings of storks and reeds, and a carved mahogany bar still flamboyantly set the scene, while the high embossed ceiling has been preserved with a coat of glossy ruby-red. The well-priced food menu, featuring modern classics such as pork and leek sausages and mash (£7.50), pulls in a mixed band of happy punters, as do weekly comedy nights and helpful bartenders serving draught Beck's, Amstel and Staropramen, bottles of Früli and a large choice of wine. *Function room. Games (board games). Quiz (8pm Mon; £1.50). Tables outdoors (4, pavement). TV.*

Bounds Green

Once a Zone 3 desert for decent hostelries, Bounds Green now boasts two corkers.

Over the Hill

96 Alexandra Park Road, N10 2AE (8444 2524). Bounds Green tube. **Open/food served** 10am-3pm, 5pm-midnight Mon-Sat; 10am-6pm Sun. **Credit** MC, V.
This wine bar-cum-café on a mostly residential road has the cosy local feel of Amsterdam's brown bars, despite being a bit thrown together. Its rattan chairs, ceiling fans and jazz music probably seemed dead sophisticated

twenty years ago; now the feel is more 'charmingly ram-shackle'. Own-made cakes and great coffee in the day paves the way for a mixed local crowd of diners and drinkers in the evening. There are no draft ales or lagers; instead, wine, cocktails and alcopops are the order of the day. As diners continue to arrive, drinkers may feel themselves slightly squeezed, but the very friendly atmosphere and make-it-up-as-you-go-along feel make OTH the kind of place you'd be very glad to find if you'd just moved in around the corner.
Function room. Music (salsa classes 7.30pm Tue, Fri; £6). Tables outdoors (14, garden terrace).

Ranelagh

82 Bounds Green Road, N11 2EU (8361 4238). Bounds Green tube. **Open** noon-midnight daily. **Food served** noon-3pm, 5-10pm Mon-Fri; noon-10pm Sat, Sun. **Credit** AmEx, MC, V.
The residents of Bounds Green must be tickled-pink with the Ranelagh, whose recent refit has left it as smart and shiny as a new pin. For a suburban local, it's seriously funky, with fairy lights over the bar, a mishmash of retro office chairs, a heated terrace and a decent beer garden. The decor, which includes a huge wall of flock wallpaper surrounding a big fireplace, doesn't feel contrived; the young and enthusiastic punters look right at home. Proper burgers, fish finger sandwiches and Sunday roasts can all be washed down with speciality beers including Leffe, Hoegaarden, Erdinger and Sleeman Honey Brown, plus there's a good wine list. Throw in the popular quiz night on Thursdays and this is one of Zone 3's best.
Disabled: toilet. Quiz (8pm Wed; £1). No-smoking area. Tables outdoors (10, garden).

Camden Town & Chalk Farm

There are far too many dosser- and junkie-filled pubs in Camden. Here we list the alternatives – the cool, stylish, and 'destination' venues, plus a great, grimy gig venue (**Dublin Castle**), one for classical music (**Bartok**) and an honest-to-goodness old boozer (**Quinn's**). One of our faves, the **Hawley Arms** (2 Castlehaven Road, NW1, 7428 5979) is being refurbished at the time of writing, but should reopen in late spring 2006.

Bar Solo

20 Inverness Street, NW1 7HJ (7482 4611/www.solo bar.co.uk). Camden Town tube. **Open** 9am-midnight Mon-Thur, Sun; 9am-1am Fri, Sat. **Food served** 9am-11.30pm daily. **Happy hour** 5-7pm, 9-10pm daily. **Credit** MC, V.
Bar Solo has a reliable café-culture feel – less of a boozer, more a place to practise your Spanish and sip a glass of *vino*. Its continental feel has much to do with the airy restaurant area behind the bar, where clutches of couples (and their trendily dressed babies) lounge over excellent brunches or substantial Franglais mains. Bright orange walls, bizarre sculptures (look out for the golden buttocks) and large flower arrangements give it a decadent feel. The friendly, black-clad (Parisian) staff swan professionally between tables, and the owner stops to chat to regulars, rearranging the tulips on the little tables as he goes. Come nightfall, a week-long happy hour brings in a jovial post-work crowd for two-for-one cocktails, spirits and bottled beers. Get here early and squeeze into the sofa at the front.
Function room. Tables outdoors (2, terrace). **Map 8 H1.**

Bar Vinyl

6 Inverness Street, NW1 7HJ (7681 7898). Camden Town tube. **Open** 11am-11pm Mon-Thur; 11am-midnight Sat, Sat; 11am-10.30pm Sun. **Food served** noon-9pm Mon-Thur, Sun; noon-8pm Fri, Sat. **Credit** (over £10) AmEx, MC, V.
If ever there was a DJ bar-by-numbers, this would be it. There's always a cool kid spinning the decks at the back, you can buy your records downstairs and the crowd is exclusively young and urban. But Bar Vinyl does it so well, you can't help but love it. Squashed halfway along Inverness Street, the long, narrow room is covered in funky graffiti snaking from the walls on to the low ceiling. Small red tables and cube seats string out along the sides, where media and music types nod along to the pounding hip hop. At the curved, zinc-clad bar, friendly skater boys serve up draught Budvar and Hoegaarden, or muddle their way through a short cocktail menu. Food comes in the form of pizzas with adventurous toppings.
Babies and children welcome (until 5pm). Music (DJs 8pm Tue-Fri, day & evening Sat-Sun). Record shop (11.30am-7.30pm daily). Tables outdoors (2, pavement). **Map 8 H1.**

Bartok

78-79 Chalk Farm Road, NW1 8AR (7916 0595/ www.bartokbar.com). Chalk Farm tube. **Open** 5pm-3am Mon-Thur; 5pm-3.30am Fri; 1pm-3.30am Sat; 1pm-3am Sun. **Food served** 5-9pm Mon-Fri; 1-9pm Sat, Sun. **Admission** £3 after 11pm Fri; £4 after 11pm Sat. **Credit** MC, V.
This sultry, stylish bar has a quality which must be unique in London: it specialises in classical music. The setting is suitably classy, with low sofas, tartan armchairs, scarlet walls and crystal chandeliers. Tea lights flicker next to single lilies protruding from glass vases, and a posh, fashionable crowd sip on glasses from a well-chosen wine list. There are a couple of standard lagers and a small cocktail menu (proper meals at weekends), but this is a place for reclining elegantly in shadowy corners and pretending to understand the eccentric mix of music. Mondays is straight classics, but the rest of the week has DJs mixing up orchestral pieces, world music, opera, electronica and funk. Who knew that Chalk Farm could be so sophisticated?
Music (DJs 8.30pm Mon, Tue, Fri, Sat; bands 6pm Wed, Thur, Sun). **Map 8 G26.**

Bullet

147 Kentish Town Road, NW1 8PB (7485 6040/www. bulletbar.co.uk). Camden Town tube/Kentish Town tube/rail. **Open** 5.30pm-midnight Mon-Wed, Sun; 5.30pm-1am Thur; 5.30pm-2am Fri, Sat. **Admission** £3-£5 after 9pm. **Credit** MC, V.
This corner bar wouldn't turn too many heads in Soho, but tucked away on a junction between Kentish Town and Camden, it's a marvel. The wide, bare-brick and wine-red space, once a grim rockers' joint, has been transformed into a low-key cocktail bar, with stylish (if predictable) retro furniture and lamps. Pints seem to be the poison of choice for the mix of grown-up indie kids and office types hanging about on the sofas. Although the beer on tap is nothing remarkable, bottles include Cobra, Peroni and Mort Subite Framboise, and the good list of classic cocktails are handled competently by the swish bar staff. Musicians are a big draw, with popular indie nights run by indie45, plus acoustic sets and open mic nights.
Disabled: toilet. Music (salsa 7pm Mon, Tue; open mic 7pm Wed; bands 7pm Thur, Fri, Sun; DJ 7pm Sat). Tables outdoors (25, garden). **Map 8 J26.**

North

Camden Arms

1 Randolph Street, NW1 0SS (7267 9829). Camden Town tube. **Open** noon-11pm Mon, Tue, Sun; noon-11.30pm Wed, Thur; noon-midnight Fri, Sat. **Food served** noon-3pm Mon-Fri; noon-5pm Sun. **Credit** AmEx, DC, MC, V.

The Camden Arms lounges duskily between towering council estates and the railway line. This pub has a dark past: it was the site of Britain's last fatal duel, in 1843. But the interior, although suitably moody, is far too stylish for spectral concerns. The aubergine walls, original fireplaces and a wrought iron spiral staircase are lit up by 1970s lampshades and a glittering retro chandelier. A vague boudoir theme is offset by the resolutely young clientele, lazing on velvet chaise longues or squeezing around old-fashioned tables. There was no real food when we visited ('we're between chefs', the barman explained), but chips and dips go well enough with the standard draught beers or fruity cocktails. Appealingly languid during the week, things get hectic at weekends with ear-splitting house music, but you can escape to the paved beer garden.

Disabled: toilet. Function room. Restaurant. Tables outdoors (20, garden; 6, pavement). **Map 8 J26.**

Crown & Goose

100 Arlington Road, NW1 7HP (7485 8008). Camden Town tube. **Open** 11am-midnight daily. **Food served** noon-3pm, 6-10pm Mon-Sat; noon-9pm Sun. **Credit** AmEx, DC, MC, V.

This low-key gastropub is way off the usual Camden radar. It has its fair share of local fashion types, but look past the asymmetrical fringes and ironic ties and you'll see a cosy boozer serving some of the best pub grub in Camden. Location is its main plus, on quiet Arlington Road, well away from the main tourist drag. Inside, the fading green walls, dark wood and flickering candlelight seem ideal for clandestine trysts – and it's mostly couples that come here. Big bowls of handmade ravioli, tottering falafel burgers and excellent steaks are doled out from the busy open kitchen at the back. Although it gets very busy in the evenings, you rarely have to queue for a table. Standard beers are livened up by draught Leffe and San Miguel, and there's a good wine list – and wine-savvy serving staff.

Function room. Tables outdoors (4, pavement). **Map 8 J1.**

Cuban

Unit 23, Stables Market, Chalk Farm Road, NW1 8AH (7424 0692/www.thecuban.co.uk). Camden Town tube. **Open/food served** 10am-1am Mon-Thur; 10am-2am Fri, Sat; 10am-midnight Sun. **Credit** MC, V.

A Cuban bar, and not a Che Guevara poster in sight? Radical. Especially given its location, slap-bang in the middle of tourist-happy Camden Market. A couple of Cuban flags aside, what marks out the cavernous, bare-brick interior is the vast bar, stretching along an entire wall and backed by smooth cocktail-shaking bartenders. Hip-looking tourists and local trendies huddle over Mojitos on hidden sofas at one end, while couples – eyes glued to the wide screens where lithe bikini-clad Cubans writhe on beaches – munch their way through interesting tapas and Caribbean-style seafood at tables and in booths. The music is suitably Latin, with a few brave souls waggling their hips as the night wears on, oiled by the rum cocktails.

Bar available for hire. Babies and children welcome. Disabled: toilet. Music (bands 7pm Sun; DJ 8.30pm Fri, Sat; both free). Tables outdoors (11, pavement). TVs. **Map 8 H26.**

Dublin Castle

94 Parkway, NW1 7AN (7485 1773/www.bugbear bookings.com). Camden Town tube. **Open** noon-1am Mon-Thur; noon-2am Fri, Sat; noon-midnight Sun. **Happy hour** noon-6pm daily. **No credit cards.**

Grimy, sticky and beer-soaked, the Dublin Castle's red-painted and poster-plastered interior hasn't changed in years. And that's how the punters like it. But then no one comes here for the decor – the Castle is one of the best music venues in Camden. You can catch a handful of new acts here every night, and standards are high; this is, after all, where Madness, Travis and Blur first cut their teeth (signed posters adorn the walls). The handful of faded, vel-vet-covered banquettes at the front quickly fill up come nightfall, when the latest additions to North London's indie and rock scene down pints with their fans. In summer the smoky fug spills out on to Parkway, with indie-kids slopping their beers from plastic glasses.

Games (fruit machine). Music (indie/rock bands 8.30pm nightly; admission £4.50-£6). TV. **Map 8 H1.**

Enterprise

2 Haverstock Hill, NW3 2BL (7485 2659). Chalk Farm tube. **Open** 11am-11pm Mon-Sat; noon-10.30pm Sun. **Food served** noon-8pm daily. **Credit** MC, V.

Aside from the need for a few repairs and a good scrub, this pub is the perfect stop-off for a lazy afternoon pint. It attracts a bizarre mix: poetic types with their laptops, office workers downing post-work pints, and old rockers in battered leathers – although the reopening of the nearby Roundhouse should draw back an arty pre-theatre crowd. The drinks offering isn't at all bad, with a changing selection of guest beers and regular John Smith's and London Pride on tap, plus a suitably low-key menu (shepherd's pie, bangers and mash). Evenings can get frenzied, especially if there's a gig or comedy upstairs.

Comedy (8pm Mon, Wed, Sun, closed Aug; £4-£5). Function room. TV. **Map 8 G26.**

Lock Tavern

35 Chalk Farm Road, NW1 8AJ (7482 7163/www.lock-tavern.co.uk). Camden Town or Chalk Farm tube. **Open** noon-midnight Mon-Thur; noon-1am Fri, Sat; noon-11pm Sun. **Food served** noon-3pm, 5-10pm Mon-Fri; noon-5pm, 6-9pm Sat; noon-5pm Sun. **Credit** MC, V.

Don't be intimidated. OK, so the punters are fiercely fashionable, the staff icily gorgeous and the music almost too tasteful, but this is a brilliant boozer in a prime location. The gloomy interior – black floors, avocado walls – is surprisingly warm and comfy, with shiny black sofas and a long leather banquette facing the padded bar. At the back is an open kitchen where first-rate pies (£7.50 for a pint and pie at lunchtime) and big mains are served. Regular DJ sessions guarantee a full house most nights, but the media types (many from nearby MTV) are happy to spill out into the walled beer garden. Wear your finest jeans and trainers, and get here early to secure a pew. Upstairs is more intimate (and smokier), with a quiet roof terrace.

Babies and children welcome. Music (DJs 7pm Thur-Sat; 8pm Sun; free). Tables outdoors (8, roof terrace; 10, garden). TV (projector). **Map 8 H26.**

Lockside Lounge

75-89 West Yard, Camden Lock Place, NW1 8AF (7284 0007/www.locksidelounge.com). Camden Town tube. **Open** noon-midnight Mon-Thur, Sun; noon-1am Fri, Sat. **Food served** noon-10pm daily. **Credit** MC, V.

North

Lock Tavern. *See p162.*

Odd choice of name, this. Not the Lockside bit – you can't fault its waterside location. But it's distinctly un-loungey. It looks more like a trendily converted boathouse, with wooden tables strung along a narrow slice of a room, capped off with an airy, wooden ceiling. It's refreshingly free of leather sofas, too, although there is a pleasant sunken seating area at the far end. Blown-up photographs of tattooed and pierced Camden characters gaze from the walls, and the similarly adorned bar staff serve up great tapas and a wide range of bottled beers, plus some decent cocktails. Forget the inside, though – stretching around the outside is one of the best decks in Camden, overlooking the West Yard market. The backpack-toting hordes have caught on, so avoid in summer.
Games (video machine). Music (DJs 7pm Fri-Sun; free). Tables outdoors (10, terrace). **Map 8 H26**.

Lord Stanley

51 Camden Park Road, NW1 9BH (7428 9488). Bus 29, 253. **Open** 6-11pm Mon; noon-11pm Tue-Thur; noon-midnight Fri, Sat; noon-10.30pm Sun. **Food served** 7-10pm Mon; 12.30-3pm, 7-10pm Tue-Sat; 12.30-4pm, 7-9.30pm Sun. **Credit** AmEx, DC, MC, V.
A beacon in an otherwise dull residential corner, the Lord Stanley is a haven of good food and no-nonsense boozing. Its dreary green-tiled façade gives way to a comfortably dog-eared interior, with battered leather sofas, worn wooden floors, and chairs smoothed by years of use. A horseshoe-shaped bar dominates the centre, where old geezers in cloth caps slouch alongside bespectacled *Guardian* readers. Tucked behind the beer taps is a small open kitchen, where energetic chefs magic-up plates of crab linguine, roast lamb or posh sandwiches. There's an impressive wine list, but this feels more like a pints sort of place – Abbot Ale and Adnams bitter are pick of the bunch. In summer, the cooking moves al fresco with weekend barbecues in the garden.
Tables outdoors (10, garden; 5, pavement).

Lush

31 Jamestown Road, NW1 7DB (7424 9054). Camden Town tube. **Open** 1pm-midnight Mon-Sat; 1-11.30pm Sun. **Food served** 1-10pm daily. **Credit** MC, V.
It takes a few minutes to figure out why Lush is so pleasant. Yep, there are leather sofas and pleasingly chilled-out tunes. It's got nice high ceilings and attractive staff – all well and good, but it's hardly ground-breaking. Take a deep breath, though, and you'll notice the difference: it's the air. Lush recently turned smoke-free – although it's probably still the long cocktail list that draws in the regulars. This was previously the upmarket Blakes, and is now the sister bar to Islington's Lush. So no change in the well-heeled crowd and steep prices – best to come during the two-for-one happy hour. There's decent food, of the pasta-and-burger variety, plus good-value bar snacks. The Monkey Business comedy club is upstairs at weekends.
Comedy (8pm Sat; £10). Music (DJs 9pm Fri-Sun; free). Tables outdoors (10, pavement). **Map 8 H27**.

Monkey Chews

2 Queen's Crescent, NW5 4EP (7267 6406/www. monkeychews.com). Chalk Farm tube. **Open** 5-11pm Mon-Thur; 5pm-midnight Fri; noon-midnight Sat; noon-10.30pm Sun. **Food served** 5-11pm Mon-Sat; noon-10.30pm Sun. **Credit** MC, V.
Poking darkly from between estates, Monkey Chews is an odd discovery. It feels strangely secret – hard to find and dimly lit – and you get the feeling that they want to keep it that way. The blood-red walls, lit up by red lanterns and

flickering candles, are lined with creaky sofas and squishy armchairs which swallow up the young, slightly punky, regulars. Empty spirit bottles are lined up on ledges, and framed posters of Blues musicians and Samurais stare out from the gloom. Hushed conversations over pints of draught Grolsch, San Miguel and Tetley's set the tone, but things get noisier with Tuesday's open mic nights and DJs at weekends. At the back is a slightly musty restaurant serving French-style seafood beneath a gorgeous Victorian skylight.
Function room. Music (acoustic band 9pm Thur; DJs 9pm Fri, Sat; free). Games (quiz machine). Tables outdoors (5, pavement). TV (big screen, satellite). **Map 8 G25**.

Peachykeen

112 Kentish Town Road, NW1 9PX (7482 2300/ www.peachy-keen.com). Camden Town tube. **Open** 5-11.30pm Mon-Thur; 5pm-midnight Fri, Sat; 5-11pm Sun. **Food served** 5-9pm daily. **Credit** MC, V.
'Rizzo, how are you?' asks Sandi in *Grease*. 'Peachy keen, jelly bean,' says Rizzo. Quite some way from the cheer of Rydell High, there's thankfully no memorabilia pinned to the walls and no ageing T-Birds propped at the bar. In fact, PK is many-splendoured. White-walled and high-ceilinged, upstairs is mainly for standing and enjoying the cocktails; vodka and muddled passion fruit went together like ramalama in a refreshing 'Pink and Fluffy'. Downstairs is cosier: twinkly fairy lights illuminate low tables and comfortable beanbag stools. Drinks are delivered from the bar and, if you're feeling princely there's an enormous double bed in the corner. Cocktails are around £5, as are shareable snack platters. Most of the wines are available by the glass. Peachykeen deserves some custom, jelly bean, so get down there like greased lightni… You get the idea.
Bar available for hire. Function room. Music (DJs 8pm occasional Fri, Sat; free). **Map 8 J26**.

Positively 4th Street

119 Hampstead Road, NW1 3EE (7388 5380). Warren Street tube. **Open** noon-3pm, 5-11pm Mon-Wed; 5-11pm Thur-Sat. **Food served** noon-2.30pm Wed-Fri; 5-9pm Mon-Fri. **Credit** MC, V.
You don't expect to stumble into a sleek den of sophistication amid the high rises and four-lane traffic of Hampstead Road. Here it is though, a deep-red hybrid of a colonial Japanese gentlemen's club and a 1920s New York saloon bar. It's an oddly effective combination, with exotic fans swaying above a glossy art deco bar and rows of art nouveau mirrors. Besuited post-work groups loll in the red-leather cubby holes or perch on bar stools, with bowls of Japanese noodles to temper the offering of hot saké, alongside a wide range of draught beers (including Red Stripe, Leffe and Hoegaarden). The reasonably priced cocktails have an oriental twist, and music veers between blues and funk. Why is it named after a Dylan song though?
Music (DJs 9pm Fri, Sat; free). Specialities (cocktails).

Quinn's

65 Kentish Town Road, NW1 8NY (7267 8240). Camden Town tube. **Open/food served** 11am-midnight Mon-Wed, Sun; 11am-2am Thur-Sat. **Credit** AmEx, MC, V.
God bless Quinn's. In a sea of blonde wood and chrome, this is an island of old-fashioned pubbishness. There's no gastropub food, no stylish refit and absolutely no fashionistas. Instead, it does just what a proper pub should do: serves a great range of beers, has witty bar staff and lets you hide away in cosy crannies with your pint. Although there's an overall Irish theme (garish orange walls and hunting prints notwithstanding), Quinn's specialises in

Belgian and German bottled beers. There were a head-spinning 70 varieties at last count, plus 20 draught beers, and the barman was keen to chin-wag over their merits – like the difference between types of Kölsch, whether Früli tastes of strawberry ice-cream, and just how strong Duvel is (8.5% ABV, as you ask).

Music (DJs 8pm Fri, Sat; free). Tables outdoors (20, garden). TV (big screen, satellite). **Map 8 J26**.

Also in the area...

Camden Tup 2-3 Greenland Place, NW1 0AP (7482 0399).
Hog's Head 55 Parkway, NW1 7PN (7284 1675).
Ice Wharf (JD Wetherspoon) Camden Lock, NW1 7BY (7428 3770).

Crouch End & Hornsey

It's no surprise that there's a host of gastro enterprises in Crouch End, but what of poor relation Hornsey? The **Three Compasses** and the already popular **Viva Viva** may have nappy valleyers packing their three-wheel buggies and moving on.

Banners

21 Park Road, N8 8TE (8348 2930/www.banners restaurant.co.uk). Finsbury Park tube/rail then W7 bus. **Open** 11am-11.30pm Mon-Thur; 11am-midnight Fri, Sat; 11am-11pm Sun. **Food served** 9am-11.30pm Mon-Thur; 9am-midnight Fri; 10am-4pm, 5pm-midnight Sat; 10am-4pm, 5-11pm Sun. **Credit** MC, V.
This bustling hub is the epitome of a *Guardian*-reading middle-class bohemia. During the day the place is a café/restaurant/-cum-crèche where yummy mummies, tots in tow, natter over organic carrot cake and smoothies. But after nightfall it becomes an adults' playpen – it's worth calling ahead to reserve one of their roughed-up wooden tables or a stool at the bar. Bowls of freshly popped popcorn are to hand. But, thanks to the place's restaurant licence, you'll need to sample £3.50 worth of world-inspired cuisine from the good, veggie-friendly menu if you fancy trying one of Banners' eclectic array of global beers or an adulterated smoothie from their fun-filled range of cocktails. Service here is notoriously holier-than-though but the laid-back atmosphere keeps the locals coming back.
No-smoking tables (9am-7pm Mon-Fri).

Harringay Arms

153 Crouch Hill, N8 9QH (8340 4243). Finsbury Park tube/rail then W3, W7 bus. **Open** noon-11.30pm Mon-Thur, Sun; noon-12.30am Fri, Sat. **No credit cards.**
There's an old boot feel to this well worn-in little pub. It's not pretty to look at – with musty and dated wood-panelled walls – but for the clutch of regulars who kill hours there, downing pints of Guinness and real ale, that's part of the appeal. Since the brown sofa gentrification of all nearby pubs, the laddy Harringay Arms is the only real old boozer left and the feel here is almost affectedly old-school. Faded prints of Irish writers dot the walls, a telly rests haphazardly on beer crates and a sad ancient fruit machine sulks in the corner while the pock-marked dartboard gets all the attention. Unknown faces can be greeted with suspicion but once over the initial frostiness the intimate joint seems like a second front room.
Games (fruit machine). No piped music or jukebox. Quiz (9pm Tue; £1). Tables outdoors (4, garden). TV (satellite).

King's Head

2 Crouch End Hill, N8 8AA (8340 1028/www.down stairsatthekingshead.com). Finsbury Park tube/rail/ Crouch Hill rail. **Open** noon-midnight Mon-Wed, Sun; noon-1am Thur-Sat. **Food served** noon-3pm, 5-10pm Mon-Fri; noon-9pm Sat, Sun. **Credit** AmEx, MC, V.
Since its flock wallpaper and fancy lighting makeover a few years back, this central Crouch End pub has changed little. The place still looks like a confused cross between a slinky 1960s bar, old-school pub and your nan's front room. Seeing people trying to eat standard pub grub off ridiculously low tables at the back is always rather fun, but the best thing about this place is the legendary comedy club, Downstairs At The King's Head, erm, downstairs. As well as try-out nights (on Thursdays) and the weekends' Comedy Cabaret shows, this cellar also hosts Sunday afternoon jazz and weekly salsa nights. Back upstairs, TVs showing football, and perhaps more tellingly, rugby, fill the corners of the room, but the lively mixed crowd are friendly enough. Staropramen, Leffe, Hoegaarden and Adnams Broadside are all on tap at the well-stocked bar.
Comedy (8pm Thur, Sat, Sun; £6-£8). Disabled: toilet. Function room. Music (jazz 1pm-5pm Sun; £3). Salsa club (7pm-midnight Mon; £5).

Queen's

26 Broadway Parade, N8 9DE (8340 2031). Finsbury Park tube/rail then W3, W7 bus. **Open** noon-11pm Mon-Wed, Fri; noon-midnight Thur, Sat; noon-10.30pm Sun. **Food served** noon-8pm daily. **Credit** AmEx, MC, V.
Previously known as the Queen's Head, this once sturdy old boozer has now been given the gastropub overhaul. The results are impressive. The pool table, TV and old stage have been replaced by an open kitchen and eating area serving homely fare (shepherd's pie, sausage and mash) to a thirtysomething Crouch End crowd. Obligatory old leather sofas and casually scuffed tables abound but work well with the bar's lovely period features (etched glass, elaborate ceilings, polished woodwork) and huge windows to create an airy, laid-back and comfortable vibe. The new polished Queen's takes more pride in itself and offers an array of grown-up sprits at the huge island bar. As well as usual lagers, Leffe, Erdinger, Guinness and Strongbow are available on tap, as are four weekly-changing guest ales . A healthy selection of decently priced wines is also on offer.
Games (pool). Music (band 9pm Thur; free). Tables outdoors (7, garden). TVs (big screen, satellite).

Three Compasses

62 High Street, N8 7NX (8340 2729). Turnpike Lane tube then 144 bus. **Open** 11am-11pm Mon-Thur; 11am-midnight Fri, Sat; noon-11pm Sun. **Food served** 11am-10pm Mon-Sat; noon-9.30pm Sun. **Credit** MC, V.
High ceilings and plenty of glass, leather sofas, tea lights on tables, a no-smoking area… and pool tables round the back: clues to what attracts the youngish crowd. Beers on tap include Hoegaarden as well as Deuchars IPA, London Pride and regular real ale guests. Wine drinkers fear not, with 14 wines by the glass to suit any palate. Bar snacks of the chips with garlic mayo/mini falafel variety can be combined into sharing platters and although there is a full menu too, this does seem more of a drinkers' pub than anything. Newspapers, lattes and games from the bar all point towards the *Cold Feet* crowd, but the icing on the cake has to be the Saturday Hangover Cure brunch, served from 11am to 3pm: kedgeree or eggs benedict? The perfect local.
Games (board games, darts, pool, quiz machine). No-smoking area. Quiz (8pm Mon; £1). TV (big screen).

North

Viva Viva

18 Hornsey High Street, N8 7PB (8341 0999/www.
viva-viva.co.uk). Turnpike Lane tube then 144 bus.
Open 9am-2am daily. **Food served** 10am-11pm daily.
Credit MC, V.
Little has changed here and this community hub continues
to be charmingly eager to please. From its well-used notice-
board pinned with details of local yoga classes to the regular battle of the bands competitions, life coach workshops
and monthly singles nights (all published on its website),
the café-cum-bar-cum-tapas restaurant works hard to offer
something for everyone. And, run with the enthusiasm of
an American cheerleader, Viva Viva pulls it off. The decor
is big on primary colours and makes the most of a narrow
layout, with fairy lights, red lamps, leather banquettes and
bits of art. Viva Viva may be taking its community-centric
cue from the ever successful Banners (*see p166*) but what
it lacks in cool it makes up for with genuine friendliness
and a welcoming, unaffected atmosphere.
Disabled: toilet. Games (board games). Music (bands
8.30pm nightly; free). Tables outdoors (2, pavement).

Also in the area...

All Bar One 2-4 The Broadway, N8 9SN (8342 7871).
Tollgate (JD Wetherspoon) 26-30 Turnpike Lane,
N8 0PS (8889 9085).

Finsbury Park & Stroud Green

As well as the exquisite **Salisbury Hotel**,
cavernous **Old Dairy**, and the welcoming
Chapter One, the area is home to some of the
best beer in London, thanks to the **Oakdale Arms**.

Chapter One

143 Stroud Green Road, N4 3PZ (7281 9630/www.
chapteronebar.com). Finsbury Park tube/rail/210, W3,
W7 bus. **Open/food served** noon-midnight Mon-
Thur, Sun; noon-1am Fri, Sat. **Credit** AmEx, MC, V.
It's the law – all revamped London drinking establishments
must have red walls, exposed brickwork, leather sofas, club
chairs and an aspirant bistro menu. The boozer police won't
be nicking Chapter One anytime soon, but the slightly
hurried makeover (a mirrored door from a previous Latin
incarnation remains by the bar) hasn't prevented a welcoming atmosphere. All the usual suspects are on draught
(plus Kronenbourg Blanc) and there's also a big cocktail list,
favouring staff creations over the classics. A roaring fire
opposite the bar and sofas – plus long booths at the back
for diners – make everyone feel at home. With happy hour
every night and a good selection of roasts on Sundays, the
place is a welcome addition to the area.
Disabled: toilet. Music (DJs 9.30pm Fri, Sat; latino band
9.30pm occasional Thur; free). TV.

Oakdale Arms

283 Hermitage Road, N4 1NP (8800 2013). Manor
House tube/Seven Sisters tube/rail. **Open** noon-11pm
Mon-Sat; noon-10.30pm Sun. **Food served** noon-
2.15pm, 6-8pm Mon-Thur, Sat; noon-2.15pm, 6-9.30pm
Fri; noon-3.30pm Sun. **Credit** MC, V.
Nowhere with a London postcode can quite be said to be
in the middle of nowhere, but the Oakdale Arms, on an iso-
lated residential street in Harringey, comes pretty close.
When you eventually make it through the front door, you
may initially wonder why you bothered: the decor is faded

1970s pub style, and the atmosphere is (to say the least)
subdued. You're only here for the beer: good job it's among
the best in London. There are eight ales on the go at any
one time (including a number from Cambridge brewer
Milton), plus Cassels cider and all manner of Belgian brews.
The pub successfully fought off developers in 2005, but the
case looked set to return to court in 2006. The same owners
run the Pembury Tavern in Hackney.
Function room. Games (darts, pool). Jukebox. Quiz (8pm
Thur; free). Tables outdoors (4, garden). TV (satellite).

Old Dairy

1-3 Crouch Hill, N4 4AP (7263 3337). Finsbury Park
tube/rail/Crouch Hill rail. **Open** noon-11pm Mon-Sat;
noon-10.30pm Sun. **Food served** noon-9.30pm Mon-
Sat; noon-9pm Sun. **Credit** AmEx, MC, V.
This is one cavernous boozer. There are no less than seven
separate rooms, booths, parts – call them what you will –
to this converted dairy, and the milking frescoes outside,
cart filled with churns, and assorted agricultural ephemera
leave no doubts about the overall theme. The Dairy manages to make each different area feel like part of a whole,
mainly because you can see the huge central bar from
almost all of them. Locals, students and sports fans (there
are lots of TVs, and match fixtures are prominently displayed) quaff their beers happily – including König Ludwig
wheat beer in bottles and Young's, Bomber and Steinlager
on tap. Weekends see the space used for clubbing, with
Friday's indie night and Saturday's '70s/'80s disco a welcome local alternative to piling into the West End.
Babies and children welcome. Disabled: toilet. Function
rooms. Music (DJ 9pm Fri, Sat; free). Quiz (9pm Thur;
£1). Restaurant. TVs (big screen).

Salisbury Hotel

1 Grand Parade, Green Lanes, N4 1JX (8800 9617).
Manor House tube then 29 bus. **Open** 5pm-midnight
Mon-Wed; 5pm-1am Thur; noon-2am Fri, Sat; noon-
midnight Sun. **Food served** 6-10pm Mon-Thur; noon-
3pm, 6-10pm Fri, Sat; noon-5pm Sun. **Credit** MC, V.
If this former hotel turned pub and restaurant were located
in Notting Hill it would be nationally famous, but its remote
Green Lanes location keeps it at local-celebrity level. The
grand decor is reminiscent of a Victorian gentlemen's club,
with chequered marble flagstones, ornate woodwork over
the enormous bar and ceilings festooned with a craftsman's
touch. The dining room's bar has been converted into an
open-plan kitchen serving adventurous pub fare (vanilla
chicken and an excellent burger were two highlights) and
diners can admire the leaded skylight as they tuck in.
Elsewhere punters converse by the fire or take one of the
more secluded leather booths at the back for a more intimate
night. The excellent range of beers – two Litovels, Zubr and
several Fuller's ales on tap – is the icing on the cake.
Disabled: toilet. Music (jazz 8.30pm Sun; free). No-
smoking area. Restaurant (available for hire; no smoking).

Triangle

1 Ferme Park Road, N4 4DS (8292 0516/www.the
trianglerestaurant.co.uk). Finsbury Park tube/rail then
W3 bus/Crouch Hill rail. **Open/food served** 6pm-
midnight Tue-Fri; 11am-midnight Sat, Sun. **Credit** V.
This shabby triangular building houses one of the most
original venues in North London, the exterior giving little
clue to the delights inside. Coming in somewhere between
a Morrocan palace and a final-year art project, the most
distinctive feature of this bar and restaurant is its installation, featuring a raffia motorbike, a laid table, a bed and

North

a shopping bag… all stuck to the ceiling. On the real floor, the mirrored fireplace, metal furniture, hanging plants and numerous candles make for a surprisingly intimate feel. Towards the back patrons, cross-legged on the raised floor, tuck into meals from a catholic menu. Serious drinkers might complain about the absence of draught beers and the small wine list, but there's a good selection of bottled beers, including Kirin and Casablanca. And for sheer sensory overload, it's definitely worth a visit.

Babies and children welcome. Disabled: toilet. Games (board games). Tables outdoors (5, garden; 7, pavement).

Also in the area…
White Lion of Mortimer (JD Wetherspoon) 125-127 Stroud Green Road, N4 3PX (7561 8880).

Hampstead

Residents of one of the prettiest boroughs also have a clutch of superb bars and pubs where they can toast their good fortune. Notably the old-school **Ye Olde White Bear** and the wonderful **Holly Bush**, the only gay in the village **King William IV** and **Bar Room Bar** that keeps the kids happy.

Bar Room Bar
48 Rosslyn Hill, NW3 1NH (7435 0808/www.barroom bar.com). Hampstead tube. **Open** noon-11pm Mon-Sat; noon-10.30pm Sun. **Food served** noon-10.30pm Mon-Sat; noon-10pm Sun. **Credit** MC, V.
This used to be Hampstead's only decent bar for the under-forties; local competition has now arisen yet, ten years on, the place is still going strong. It is in fact part of a chain but, unlike its near namesake All Bar One, Bar Room Bar has decent music, a good mix of after-work drinkers and even a degree of charm. There's a small patio out the back which tends to be packed, come rain or shine, with groups of fresh-faced 'yoofs', but on the whole the punters are a casual gaggle of locals knocking back fairly priced glasses of merlot or pints of Hoegaarden and John Smith's. Tuesdays tend to be busy as everyone descends on the joint to take advantage of amazingly good value two-for-one pizzas.
Music (jazz, blues, soul, reggae 7pm Sun; free). Tables outdoors (10, garden; 3, pavement). TV.

Holly Bush
22 Holly Mount, NW3 6SG (7435 2892/www.hollybush pub.com). Hampstead tube. **Open** noon-11pm Mon-Sat; noon-10.30pm Sun. **Food served** 12.30-4pm, 6.30-10pm Mon-Fri; 12.30-10pm Sat; 12.30-9pm Sun. **Credit** MC, V.
Tucked away on one of the most beautiful corners of North London, a mere stone's throw from Hampstead tube but, atmospherically-speaking, a million miles away from the glare of the high street, the Holly Bush is a local institution. Aside from the addition of the rather uninspiring back room, little seems to have changed here since the place opened in the early 1800s. It's how a pub should be: intimate, friendly and with a diverse set of punters who huddle by the log fire, enjoying a relaxing pint and maybe a bite to eat. As well as the standard lagers there's also Fuller's, Harvey's Sussex and Adnams on tap, and the food – standard pub nosh (pies, sausage and mash) – is well executed and fairly priced. For those after more refinement, there's a plush, non-smoking dining room upstairs.
Babies and children welcome. Function room. Games (board games). Restaurant (no-smoking).

King William IV
77 Hampstead High Street, NW3 1RE (7435 5747). Hampstead tube. **Open** 11am-11pm Mon-Sat; noon-10.30pm Sun. **Food served** noon-10pm daily. **Credit** MC, V.
It's nice to a see that some shabby gems from Hampstead's past have survived the high street's transformation into a strip of garish mobile phone shops and estate agents (but for how long? We hear rumours that a refurbishment is on the horizon). The King William has for decades been the only gay pub in a famously queer part of town, yet the place is perhaps the straightest-feeling gay pub ever. In winter, occasional wanderers stumble in, none the wiser, plonk themselves by the fire and sip their pints alongside the low-key locals (sometimes signalling offence at the never-ending stream of pop classics). Summer is a busier affair, with the beer garden accommodating shoppers comparing designer purchases. The selection of beers and wine is fairly standard; food is more original, with a tasty line in crêpes.
Bar available for hire. Function room. Games (quiz machine). Quiz (9pm Thur; £2). No-smoking area. Tables outdoors (15, garden).

Magdala
2A South Hill Park, NW3 2SB (7435 2503). Hampstead Heath rail/24, 46, 168, C11 bus. **Open** 11am-11pm Mon-Thur; 11am-midnight Fri, Sat; noon-10.30pm Sun. **Food served** noon-2.30pm, 6-10pm Mon-Fri; noon-10pm Sat; noon-9.30pm Sun. **Credit** MC, V.
With the heath at the end of the road, the Magdala is ideally situated for a recuperative pint after a stroll, but is perhaps best known as the site of a shooting several decades back; the assailant, Ruth Ellis, subsequently became the last woman in Britain to be hanged. A framed *Evening Standard* documents the murder, and the bullet-holes are still visible on the outside wall. Yet, for a former crime scene, the place is very serene. There are two rooms: one is airy (and a bit uninspiring), the other cosy (with a fire) and both remain popular with that particular (dying?) breed: the old Hampstead liberal. There's a decent range of draught beers, from San Miguel to Leffe, as well as ales – London Pride and IPA – and a helpful wine list. The food ranges from reasonably priced sandwiches to roasts.
Function room. Games (board games, cards). Restaurant. Tables outdoors (4, patio).

Roebuck
15 Pond Street, NW3 2PN (7433 6871). Belsize Park tube. **Open** noon-11pm Mon-Thur; noon-midnight Fri, Sat; noon-10.30pm Sun. **Food served** noon-3pm, 5-10pm Mon-Fri; noon-4pm, 5-10pm Sat; noon-9pm Sun. **Credit** MC, V.
Upping the ante in a part of town starved of decent places for anyone still in their prime, the Roebuck is ideally placed to offer some much-needed style and cheer on a road dominated by the monstrous-looking Royal Free. Indeed, the hospital's medics are often to be found recharging on the sofas, coffee-in-hands, relaxing to a soundtrack of 6 Music-esque tunes. Downstairs there's a slick bar (available for hire), out the back a decent-sized beer garden, and while the decor is supremely trendy, service is with a smile rather than a sneer. There's a varied food menu (from grilled halloumi with couscous to burgers) and no less than 17 beers on tap, from Amstel to Staropramen, as well as a guest bitter which changes monthly according to customers' votes. Hey, they even do cocktails.
Function room. Games (board games). No smoking area. Tables outdoors (16, garden).

North

Spaniards Inn

Spaniards Road, NW3 7JJ (8731 6571). Hampstead tube/210 bus. **Open** 11am-11pm Mon-Thur; 11am-midnight Fri; 10am-midnight Sat; 10am-11pm Sun. **Food served** 11am-10pm Mon-Fri; 10am-10pm Sat, Sun. **Credit** AmEx, MC, V.

Probably one of London's most famous pubs (apparently highwayman Dick Turpin was a regular), the Spaniards dates back to the 16th century and looks and feels like a tavern from *Treasure Island*. Aided by the isolated location and the dim lantern lighting and galleon-style windows, you half expect a peg-legged chap with a parrot to stumble in. Instead, a mix of locals and homeward bound after-workers come by to enjoy decent food (from mussels in a Hoegaarden-flavoured cream to posh mushrooms on toast), and an admirable range of wines and beers (including Bombardier, Fuller's London Pride and Marston's Old Empire). It seems that every man and his dog finish their weekend stroll on the heath with a pint beside the fire here (or in the garden in summer), and the on-site dog wash tells them that they're welcome.
Babies and children admitted. Games (board games). Literary readings (poetry 8pm Tue; free). No piped music or jukebox. Tables outdoors (90, garden).

Wells

30 Well Walk, NW3 1BX (7794 3785/www.thewells hampstead.co.uk). Hampstead tube. **Open** noon-11pm Mon-Sat; noon-10.30pm Sun. **Food served** noon-3pm, 5-10pm Mon-Fri; noon-4pm, 7-10pm Sat; noon-4pm, 7-9.30pm Sun. **Credit** MC, V.

A few years back this was NW3's spot for under-age drinkers to get trollied. These days, however, the Well is a much classier affair. The decor is at the slick end of the standard gastropub kit, with deep-green walls, black leather sofas, dark wood and sleek lines. It's upmarket yet comfy, with a good range of wines and beers (including Abbot Ale, Wadworth 6X and Fuller's London Pride on tap). The daily-changing food menu is well-renowned, despite some tales of style over substance, and might include pan-fried salmon with mange tout or roast cod with grouper ravioli. But the best thing is its location, just a block from the heath; there are few better outdoor summer spots from which to sit and watch the world (and loads of golden retrievers) trundle by.
Babies and children admitted. Disabled: toilet. Function room. Music (jazz 8.30pm Mon; free). Restaurant (no smoking). Tables outdoors (15, patio).

Ye Olde White Bear

Well Road, NW3 1LJ (7435 3758). Hampstead tube. **Open** 11am-11pm Mon-Sat; noon-10.30pm Sun. **Food served** noon-9pm daily. **Credit** MC, V.

As the name may suggest, this is your standard, but still rather charming, old boozer: nondescript local photos hang on the dark-wood walls, there's a log fire and the bar staff are chatty and down-to-earth (ditto the clientele). All reasons that explain why the place is so popular, accommodating everyone from old men and their dogs to builders and young couples glad to have found a retreat away from the high street's shopping and schmoozing frenzy. As far as the drinks go, as well as all the usual lager suspects on tap, there's Suffolk's finest – Adnams Ale – and Young's. The food too is good, decently priced solid pub grub making this an ideal spot for filling up in before venturing out on to the heath.
Babies and children welcome. Games (board games). Quiz (9pm Thur; free). Tables outdoors (6, courtyard). TV (satellite).

Highgate

High on this particular hill a lonely goatherd would have no trouble finding a decent hostelry in which to enjoy a good pint and chat with betweeded locals. Those with more developed social skills will probably head for the **Boogaloo**.

Angel Inn

37 Highgate High Street, N6 5JT (8347 2921). Archway or Highgate tube. **Open** noon-midnight Mon-Fri; 11am-midnight Sat; noon-11pm Sun. **Food served** noon-4pm, 5-10pm Mon-Fri; 11am-10pm Sat; noon-9pm Sun. **Credit** MC, V.

A good example of how a reinvented drinking hole can still be atmospheric. This remains a proper pub, yet elements like the cylindrical lights above the bar, and the fish tank behind it, create a contemporary ambience enjoyed by smart, monied punters (the place is, after all, bang-smack in the centre of genteel Highgate Village). Posh pub credentials are enhanced further by tasteful theme-nights (Burns night on our visit) and by wine- and lager-of-the-week choices. Draught beer is mainly Belgian (including Früli, Leffe and Hoegaarden) or of the speciality ale variety (Timothy Taylor and Greene King), while bottles of Peroni, Beck's and Tiger are on hand for lager drinkers. Wines and whiskies are similarly well-chosen. Pistachios and olives replace the positively common peanut as drink accompaniments and, for proper food, there's a popular dining area for modern classics like steak and ale pie.
Disabled: toilet. Quiz (9pm Wed; £1). Tables outdoors (3, pavement). TV (big screen).

Boogaloo

312 Archway Road, N6 5AT (8340 2928/www.the boogaloo.org). Highgate tube. **Open** 6pm-midnight Mon-Wed; 6pm-1am Thur; 6pm-2am Fri; 2pm-2am Sat; 2pm-midnight Sun. **Food served** 6-9pm Mon-Fri; 2-7pm Sat, Sun. **Admission** £5 after 10pm Fri, Sat. **Credit** MC, V.

The sort of place that's surely accommodated many an unplanned 'late one', the Boogaloo is frequented by groups of sociable twenty- and thirtysomethings. Although you're bound to find ego (if you're looking for it) among the *NME*-reading, trendy crowd (with plenty of skinny jean-action, à la Pete Doherty, on our visit), the overriding feel is more laid-back than judgemental and the music more democratic than you might imagine with uplifting classics from the likes of Bowie and Dusty Springfield frequently blaring out from the famed jukebox, plus regular band appearances and DJ nights. Understated decor ('70s glass wall-lamps and music-related black-and-white photos) suits the mood; the beer selection is more pedestrian, favouring big-name brews. It's a fiver to get in on Fridays and Saturdays between 10pm and midnight, after which time a lock-in policy comes into play.
Babies and children welcome. Disabled: toilet. Music (country band 5.30-8.30pm Sun; free). Quiz (8.30pm Tue; £1). Tables outdoors (15, garden).

Bull

13 North Hill, N6 4AB (0845 456 5033/www.inthe bull.biz). Highgate tube. **Open** 5-11pm Mon; 11am-11pm Tue-Sat; 11am-10.30pm Sun. **Food served** 6-10.30pm Mon; noon-2.30pm, 6-10.30pm Tue-Fri; noon-3.30pm, 6-10.30pm Sat; noon-3.30pm, 6.30-9.30pm Sun. **Credit** MC, V.

Bull. *See p173.*

North

Located in a gorgeous Grade II-listed building, the Bull is clearly weighted in favour of food, with most of the ground floor set aside for upmarket dining (save for a small pre-meal bar). Seasonal ingredients are favoured for the wide range of ambitious British and French dishes. Upstairs is the 'pub' area (a popular space for private functions) serving real ales such as Timothy Taylor and Highgate IPA, plus Heineken, Leffe, Stella and Staropramen, all on tap. The wine list is, as you might imagine, extensive and features several vintage varieties, plus there's a quality choice of liqueurs. Nice touches like the real fire, the outside terrace at the front (complete with large wooden elephant) and amiable staff round the place off well.
Babies and children welcome. Function room. Games (chess, pool). Restaurant (no smoking). Tables outdoors (15, terrace). TV (big screen).

Flask

77 Highgate West Hill, N6 6BU (8348 7346). Archway or Highgate tube. **Open** noon-11pm Mon-Sat; noon-10.30pm Sun. **Food served** noon-3pm, 5-10pm Mon-Fri; noon-10pm Sat; noon-9.30pm Sun. **Credit** MC, V.
The type of pub sought after by filmmakers looking to create an English idyll on celluloid (Richard Curtis take note), the Flask is unarguably atmospheric in a rural and historic kind of way, and as perfect for cosy winter evenings (huddled inside the warren-like, candle-decorated interior) as it is for carefree late-summer afternoons after a day's activity on the heath (the garden is packed on Sundays). The beer line-up is as Belgium-heavy as at the nearby Angel Inn (*see p170*, owned by the same proprietor), with Leffe, Hoegaarden and Früli on tap alongside German beers Paulaner and Franziskaner. Speciality bottled beers include Chimay White Abby, Duvel and Mexican Dos Equus. Wine-drinkers will find a good range (of mainly New World varieties) to choose from. To soak up the booze, there's a popular food menu, and barbecues are sometimes held in the garden.
No-smoking areas. Tables outdoors (15, garden).

Wrestlers

98 North Road, N6 4AA (8340 4297). Highgate tube. **Open** 4.30pm-midnight Mon-Fri; noon-midnight Sat; noon-11pm Sun. **Food served** noon-4pm Sun. **Credit** MC, V.
Punters at the Wrestlers might experience something akin to a Mr Benn sensation when entering for the first time; the smell of burning wood, the squared dark-wood panelled walls, the hanging cast-iron spherical lights and the antlers above the fireplace immediately transport you to a 19th-century manor house reminiscent of Toad Hall – a surprise, as the exterior of the pub is classic 1920s London terrace. Tweed-jacketed locals propping up the bar and framed historic photos add to the rural, time-warped experience; round the other side, the plasma TV, plus banter from more contemporary locals, bring back a measure of normality. To drink, there's a large range of beer on tap – choose from the likes of Greene King IPA, Abbot Ale, Guinness, Staropramen and Young's Bitter, plus a good selection of wine and Champagne.
Bar available for hire. Games (board games). Tables outdoors (15, garden; 6, pavement).

Also in the area...

Gatehouse (JD Wetherspoon) 1 North Road, N6 6BD (8340 8054).

Holloway & Archway

Renowned for being more seedy than sought out, it's great to find some true gems around the Holloway Road in among the fast food eateries and junk shops. We particularly recommend **St John's** and the **Swimmer at the Grafton Arms**.

Coronet
338-346 Holloway Road, N7 6NJ (7609 5014/ www.jdwetherspoon.co.uk). Holloway Road tube. **Open** 9am-11.30pm daily. **Food served** 9am-11pm daily. **Credit** AmEx, DC, MC, V.
Impossible to miss with its art deco and neon exterior, the Coronet's façade looks very like a cinema – as indeed it was until 1983. The feeling persists inside, where original features have been retained, and with black-and-white blow-ups of golden-age movie icons and a brolly-shaped 1930s chandelier hovering over an old cinema projector. But it doesn't quite gel and you can't shake the feeling that it's a Wetherspoon pub. Of course, that's the draw for some: more than half a dozen real ales – Marston's Burton, Brains SA, Old Slug Porter, Abbot Ale – for less than two quid, G&Ts even cheaper, and choice international lagers like Budvar and bottles of Zywice. The food's likewise cheap and decent, if uninspiring. Which all probably explains the tables full of addled old men, students and a fair mix of locals.
Disabled: toilet. Games (fruit machines). No piped music or jukebox. No-smoking area. Tables outdoors (3, patio).

Landseer
37 Landseer Road, N19 4JU (7263 4658/www.the landseer.com). Archway tube/17, 43, 217 bus. **Open** noon-11pm Mon, Tue; noon-midnight Wed-Fri; 11am-midnight Sat; 11am-11pm Sun. **Food served** noon-4pm, 5-10pm Mon-Fri; 11am-4pm, 5-10.30pm Sat; 11am-9.30pm Sun. **Credit** AmEx, MC, V.
Like a beacon, light shines out of the wide bright windows of this classy gastropub that wraps around a residential corner. And inside, those same windows, along with the vaulted skylight and hanging plants, create a pleasantly airy space in which to while away an afternoon, seated on wooden pew chairs or benches at the chunky, stripped-pine tables, or on leather sofas in the small library nook with books and board games. Well-scrubbed thirtysomethings tuck into the unoriginal but tasty food (pan-roasted salmon, £10.25), washed down with one of a dozen wines by the glass (categorised by tastenotes rather than region). Decent ales are available too, including Greene King IPA and Pedigree.
Babies and children welcome. Games (board games). Restaurant (no smoking). Tables outdoors (15, pavement).

St John's
91 Junction Road, N19 5QU (7272 1587). Archway tube. **Open** 5-11pm Mon-Thur; noon-11pm Fri, Sat; noon-10.30pm Sun. **Food served** 6.30-11pm Mon-Thur; noon-2.30pm, 6.30-11pm Fri; noon-4pm, 6.30-11pm Sat; noon-4pm, 6.30-9.30pm Sun. **Credit** MC, V.
St John's stands out on drab Junction Road in more ways than one: its tile-clad exterior is prominently sited between two parallel streets, with windows on three sides making it a great place for afternoon drinking and people-watching. The food is terrific too, if a bit pricey, with starters such as seared scallops or a chunky game terrine with chutney, and venison steak leading the mains on our visit. It's the same menu in the back restaurant, where walls are covered in portraits – giving it the look of a 19th-century Parisian salon

– while tables are skewed about at all angles. The laid-back main room retains its original mouldings despite the standard paring-back exercise (with the usual mismatched wooden chairs and tables, plus a pair of leather sofas) and wraps around a prow-like bar, where Brakspear Special, Greene King Abbot Ale and Hoegaarden are all on tap.
Babies and children welcome. Tables outdoors (7, patio).

Settle Inn
17-19 Archway Road, N19 3TX (7272 7872). Archway tube. **Open** 11am-midnight daily. **Food served** noon-3pm, 6-10pm Mon-Fri; noon-9.30pm Sat, Sun. **Credit** MC, V.
Beyond Archway, the A1 starts feeling like a proper, desolate highway. So for local residents, this friendly pub is a godsend, with its low-key lighting, creamy textured walls and warm honey-coloured wood tones beckoning a mixed, youngish crowd. It ticks pretty much all the boxes for a decent local: good Thai food (plus a few pub standards) ordered from the open kitchen at the back; reasonably priced Flowers IPA, Bass and Hoegaarden on tap, with Staropramen the highlight of the lager brigade; simple decor, with framed prints overlooking the usual mismatched tables and chairs (plus a couple of wacky tall-backed chairs whose planks might have been rescued from a water mill); and a weekly quiz with a fair bit of interaction between the punters and the quizmaster.
Games (board games, quiz machine). Quiz (8.30pm Tue; free). TV (satellite).

Swimmer at the Grafton Arms
13 Eburne Road, N7 6AR (7281 4632). Holloway Road tube. **Open** noon-2.30pm, 5-11pm Mon-Thur; noon-11pm Fri, Sat; noon-10.30pm Sun. **Food served** 6-9.20pm Mon-Thur; noon-2pm, 6-9.20pm Fri; noon-5pm, 6-9.20pm Sat; noon-4pm Sun. **Credit** MC, V.
On a residential street opposite the Odeon cinema, this bijou pub is a real find. It's a long and narrow space done up in creamy yellow and black, modernised yet still retaining original features, like the ornate surround behind the bar and the high-backed wooden booths. The choice of lagers is a revelation, with unusual Czech brews Litovel and Zubr in the line-up, and there's Belle-Vue Kriek as well as home-grown ESB, Adnams and London Pride. A dozen wines by the glass go with a decent but not excessively 'gastro' menu, cooked up in the open kitchen. Games are popular too – ask for Scrabble and chess from the bar – but the real passion is reserved for the pub quiz; the winners can make off with over a hundred quid if there's a rollover.
Games (board games). No-smoking area. Quiz (9pm Mon; £2 per team). Tables outdoors (15, garden).

Islington

There is an enormous selection of bars to choose from in Islington, with new ones opening all the time – we're particularly excited about the games room at the **Baring** – so here we list Upper Street's finest as well as a canalside boozer, a tiny wine bar, organic gastropub, theatre pubs, pool bar...

Albion
10 Thornhill Road, N1 1HW (7607 7450). Angel tube. **Open** noon-11pm Mon-Sat; noon-10.30pm Sun. **Food served** noon-3pm, 5-9pm Mon-Fri; noon-9.30pm Sat; noon-8pm Sun. **Credit** MC, V.

You'd be forgiven for thinking you've been transported into a small rural village in the Yorkshire Dales, such is the serene, almost bucolic atmosphere exuded from nearby Barnsbury Square and the near total dearth of traffic. With a frontage concealed in ivy, and far enough off the beaten track for one to be able to enjoy a quiet ale without being surrounded by Upper Streeters, you'd probably be able to attain the same air of tranquility at the Albion as you would the nearby Yogabase on Liverpool Road. The interior is just the right side of quaint with pale green-wood panelled interiors and there's plenty of comfy seating. There's a decent selection of well kept beers (Greene King IPA, Bombadier, Erdinger and Staropramen) and a pleasingly rudimentary food menu of burgers and fish and chips, but it's probably more notable for its above average selection of vegetarian meals.
Games (quiz machine, fruit machine). No-smoking area. Tables outdoors (5, patio; 20, garden). TV. **Map 9 N1**.

Anam

3 Chapel Market, N1 9EZ (7278 1001/www.anambar. com). Angel tube. **Open** 6pm-midnight Tue, Wed; 6pm-2am Thur-Sat. **Snacks served** 6-11pm Mon-Sat. **Credit** AmEx, MC, V.
You've got to move slowly in this smart, Chapel Market retreat. And not just to appreciate its impeccably stylish, retro-inspired decor – nice though it is. This jazzy DJ/cocktail bar is so small and gets so crammed, that really you have no choice. Unsurprisingly, there's a vibrant intimate party vibe to the place – but this is not just down to the lack of space. There's finger food (veggie spring rolls, mixed charcuterie) on the menu and free popcorn at the bar, but it's the tantalising liquid concoctions courtesy of mixologists Simon Sheena and Filippo Lari that fuel the funky atmosphere. At around £8 each, they don't come cheap, but made with premium brand spirits and unusual ingredients (fresh chillies, fig liqueur) they're a decadent treat. Watch out for the cheeky glass window in the floor providing upskirt thrills for those in the basement lounge below.
Disabled: toilet. Function room. Music (DJs 8pm Thur-Sat; free). **Map 9 N2**.

Angelic

57 Liverpool Road, N1 0RJ (7278 8433). Angel tube. **Open** noon-midnight Mon-Thur, Sun; noon-1pm Fri, Sat. **Food served** noon-10pm Mon-Sat; noon-9.30pm Sun. **Credit** MC, V.
If you're looking for an old-school blokey bolthole, then you should probably head elsewhere. But if you want somewhere pleasant, airy and friendly to while away time, both day and night, the Angelic is hard to beat. There's something wonderfully welcoming about its huge windows, high ceilings and sofa tucked away by the fireplace. Plus, as well as a good selection of draught ales and wines, there's a juice bar. That, and its veggie-friendly gastropub menu, may make it the healthiest pub in London – which could explain why well over half the punters on our latest visit were female. The Angelic is so downright cheery that they even pipe stand-up comedy into the toilets. Pubs don't get much more civilised than this.
Bar available for hire. Disabled: toilet. Games (board games). TV (big screen). **Map 9 N2**.

Baring

55 Baring Street, N1 3DS (7359 5785). Angel tube/Old Street tube/rail. **Open/food served** 3pm-midnight Mon-Thur; 11am-midnight Fri; 10am-midnight Sat, Sun. **Credit** AmEx, MC, V.

Attempting to lure customers from the popular Rosemary Branch nearby, the Baring hosts weekly theme nights. The most popular is Thursday's excellent value 'quiz and curry for a fiver'. And since a renovation of the property last year, the Baring looks fantastic: simple beige and claret walls, well-chosen artwork, and a warming gas fire. A handful of staple main meals on the menu (bangers and mash £6.50, steak pie £7.90) is supplemented by a large number of daily-changing specials; at weekends, the £6.50 brunch is best. With Adnam's and London Pride at the bar, ale fans will be satisfied if not excited. As we were going to press, the Baring was also turning its entire upper floor into a games room, complete with Sky-equipped big screen and table football. Just in time to watch us crash and burn against Trinidad and Tobago in the World Cup.
Bar available for hire. Function room. Games (darts, pool). Quiz (7.30pm Thur; free). Restaurant (no smoking). TVs (big screen, satellite).

Barnsbury

209-211 Liverpool Road, N1 1LX (7607 5519/ www.thebarnsbury.co.uk). Angel tube/Highbury & Islington tube/rail. **Open** noon-11pm Mon-Sat; noon-10.30pm Sun. **Food served** noon-3pm, 6-10.30pm Mon-Fri; noon-4pm, 6-10.30pm Sat; noon-4pm, 6.30-9.30pm Sun. **Credit** AmEx, MC, V.
Nestled unassumingly next to a large Thai restaurant, the Barnsbury is an endearing pub that fits perfectly with the laid-back affluence of the neighbourhood. The decor is fresh and inviting, with pale walls displaying works by local artists, church pew seating, chandeliers made from wine glasses and vases of fresh flowers on the bar. Almost uniquely nowadays, there is no blaring music and no TV, meaning it's the perfect place for reading the Sunday papers or chatting with friends. Beers are represented by London Pride and Timothy Taylor, with a guest ale appearing monthly. Fellow drinkers tend to be a mixed bag of locals, providing a friendly atmosphere and constant burble of chatter. Food is generally upscale (lamb shank, sea bream fillet), and there's also a lovely walled garden for summer supping.
Disabled: toilet. No-smoking area. Tables outdoors (4, pavement; 6, garden). **Map 9 N1**.

Bull

100 Upper Street, N1 0NP (7354 9174). Angel tube. **Open** noon-midnight Mon-Wed, Sun; noon-1am Thur, Fri; 11am-1am Sat. **Food served** noon-3pm, 6-10pm Mon-Fri; 11am-10pm Sat; noon-9.30pm Sun. **Credit** AmEx, MC, V.
Like every other bar on Upper Street, there's an element of studied debauchery about this big airy pub. But here it's much easier to forgive. Ancient chaise longues, vintage leather car seats and random-sized tables team up with other dishevelled antiques market cast-offs and contemporary experiments (like a nice fairy-light lattice) to make the breezy pub feel like a communal living room. Cosy nooks and crannies give the impression of intimacy and encourage a buzzy, convivial atmosphere from the laid-back mixed crowd. There are Continental beers (like Franziskaner Weissbier, Küppers Kölsch and Caledonian Deuchars IPA available alongside other pub regulars and there's decent quality wine to help wash down gastro-pubby dishes. This mainstay is a real Sunday roast and papers sort of place. And happily enough, come the weekend, the Bull provides both.
Disabled: toilet. Games (board games, chess). Music (DJ 11am-3pm Sat; free). Quiz (7pm Wed; free). **Map 9 O2**.

North

Camden Head

2 Camden Walk, N1 8DY (7359 0851). Angel tube.
Open 11am-11pm Mon, Tue; 11am-midnight Wed,
Thur; 11am-1am Fri, Sat; noon-11pm Sun. **Food
served** noon-9.30pm daily. **Credit** MC, V.
Amid the antique shops and bistros of Camden Passage,
away from the frantic activity of Upper Street, the Head
looks and feels like a proper Victorian pub: frosted glass,
dark wood, (working) fireplace, (faux) gaslight fittings, banquettes – all contribute to the ambience. Outside is a paved
area with picnic table-style seating, perfect for watching the
ebb and flow of Islington on warm summer evenings, while
the performance space upstairs hosts regular comedy
nights. Beers include Bishops Tipple, London Pride and
Bombardier, but the drinks menu is often supplemented by
seasonal bevvies (hot toddies in winter, for instance). The
clientele are a friendly mixture of locals, trendies, students
and business folk, peppered by the occasional visit from an
Islington-based sleb. The Indie-heavy jukebox plays at a
sensible volume, so conversation is still possible. No surprise, then, that this is one of our favourite locals.
*Comedy (8.30pm Wed-Sun & alternate Mon; £3-£5).
Function room. Games (fruit machines, quiz machines).
Tables outdoors (12, heated garden). TVs.* **Map 9 O2.**

Canonbury Tavern

21 Canonbury Place, N1 2NS (7288 9881). Highbury
& Islington tube/rail. **Open** noon-midnight Mon-Fri;
11am-midnight Sat; noon-11pm Sun. Closed noon-5pm
in the winter. **Food served** noon-3pm, 5-10pm Mon-
Thur; noon-10pm Fri-Sun. **Credit** AmEx, MC, V.
Tucked away from manic Upper Street in the upmarket residential environs of Canonbury, this high-ceilinged local is
a hidden gem. Decked out with butcher's block tables, cosy
country-house sofas and leafy plants, the Tavern manages
to feel both snug and spacious. The red walls double up as
gallery space featuring interesting local artists and there's
a large games room with pool table (£1.50 a play) in which
to indulge in less highbrow pleasures. There's even a beer-
garden in the event of good weather. But it's the effortless
laid-back vibe here that really marks it out. From the comfort food (bangers and mash, vegan bean casserole, a Sunday
roast) on offer to the thirst-quenching range of drinks
(including Küppers Kölsch, Erdinger Weissbeir and Veuve
Clicquot Champagne) and the refreshingly friendly bar staff,
the Tavern makes an ace place for a chilled-out pint.
*Games (fruit machine, pool table). Quiz (8pm Tue; £1).
Tables outdoors (34, garden). TV.* **Map 9 I26.**

Colebrookes

69 Colebrooke Row, N1 8AA (7226 7517/www.cole
brookes.co.uk). Angel tube. **Open/food served** 11am-
midnight Mon-Wed, Sun; 11am-1am Thur; 11am-2am
Fri, Sat. **Credit** AmEx, MC, V.
This teeny weeny wine bar tucked away off Essex Road is
a very grown-up affair. Opened at the latter end of 2005, the
living room-sized bar sits on the site formerly occupied by
a pizzeria. There are some bottled beers, spirits and classic
cocktails on offer, but the bulk of the drinks menu is made
up of thirty or so wines – ranging in price from £15 to £45
a bottle – that complement the antipasti-inspired sharing
platters also served. The staff seem to know their stuff and
fall over themselves to be helpful. On our last visit, a
Spanish guitarist added to the toasty, intimate vibe, but at
other times, jazz, blues and Parisian swing waft through
the room (see website for details). Colebrookes is a very
sweet and honest proposition and a welcome change from
the usual brash peacocks that inhabit this part of town.

*Bar available for hire. Games (board games). Music
(classical solos 7pm Sun; DJs 8pm Sat; jazz band 8pm
Wed; all free).* **Map 9 O1.**

Compton Arms

4 Compton Avenue, N1 2XD (7359 6883). Highbury
& Islington tube/rail. **Open** noon-11pm Mon-Sat; noon-
10.30pm Sun. **Food served** noon-2.30pm, 6-8.30pm
Mon-Fri; noon-4pm Sat, Sun. **Credit** MC, V.
This stubborn backstreet local refuses to change. Which for
once is a very good thing. Free of Islingtonian pretension
and the area's usual concessions to trendiness, there's an
earthy lowliness about this neighbourhood hub that's whol-
ly inviting. From the hanging baskets outside to the chatty
barmaids and exposed beams within, entering is like being
transported to a friendly country local. Everyone seems to
know each other and with no background music to shout
over, the place buzzes with warm conversation. With Greene
King ales (IPA, Abbot) and a good choice of lagers (including Kronenbourg, Stella, Foster's) to keep thirsts quenched,
its amiable vibe and homely dishes (like game casserole), the
Compton Arms remains the perfect evening getaway.
*Babies and children welcome (until 8.30pm, separate
area). No piped music or jukebox. Quiz (8.30pm Sun;
free). Tables outdoors (10, garden). TV (big screen,
satellite).* **Map 9 O26.**

Crown

116 Cloudesley Road, N1 0EB (7837 7107). Angel tube.
Open noon-11pm Mon-Sat; noon-10.30pm Sun. **Food
served** noon-3pm, 6-10pm Mon-Fri; noon-10pm Sat;
noon-9pm Sun. **Credit** AmEx, MC, V.
'Please depart in a discreet and elegant manner' requests the
sign on the porch. But unruly patrons are unlikely here.
Tucked off a square in the heart of genteel Barnsbury, the
Crown is home to a well-heeled, yet mixed crowd. With glossy
woods and etched glass, period plasterwork and a roaring
fire, the front room of this elegant yet cosy saloon is usually
buzzing. Service is friendly and an open kitchen serves hearty
(gastro)pub fare. You have to open a tab before you order
food in case you leave without paying, and judging by our
steak and ale pie (too much potato; tough, fatty meat) you
understand why. Still, the own-made fish cakes fared better,
and there's a good range of wines and beers, including
Fuller's ales, Jack Frost, Honey Dew and Discovery on tap.
Games (board games). Tables outdoors (6, patio).
Map 9 N1.

Drapers Arms

44 Barnsbury Street, N1 1ER (7619 0348/www.the
drapersarms.co.uk). Angel tube/Highbury & Islington
tube/rail. **Open** noon-11pm Mon-Sat; noon-10.30pm
Sun. **Food served** noon-3pm, 7-10pm Mon-Sat; noon-
3pm, 6.30-9.30pm Sun. **Credit** AmEx, MC, V.
Set a few streets back from Upper Street, in the heart of
Barnsbury, the crisp and airy Drapers Arms is a pleasant
place to enjoy a quiet few drinks. But this isn't exactly a pub.
With its clean decor offset with mirrors and tasteful flower
display it's more a classy restaurant take on a gastro-pub
and as such can seem a little lifeless. But it's this calm atmosphere and the excellent food from the fish-centric menu that
draws the well-to-do crowd. A few lit candles, a real fire and
a sofa under the skylight in the back lend the place warmth
and there's a great wine list and a good selection of beers
and ales on tap (Beck's, Carlsberg, Foster's, Paulaner,
Speckled Hen, Courage Best as well as a guest ale).
Restaurant (no smoking). Tables outdoors (20, garden).
Map 9 N1.

Duchess of Kent

441 Liverpool Road, N7 8PR (7609 7104/www.
geronimo-inns.co.uk). Highbury & Islington tube/
rail. **Open** noon-11pm Mon-Wed, Sun; noon-midnight
Thur-Sat. **Food served** noon-3pm, 7-10pm Mon-Fri;
noon-4pm, 7-10.30pm Sat; noon-10pm Sun. **Credit**
MC, V.

Embraced into the Geronimo mini-chain bosom a few years
back, this old local really doesn't feel like a chain pub.
Matching its gentrified neighbourhood with its 'scruffy
chic' style, this is a pub of two very welcoming halves. A
huge leather sofa under airy windows greets you by the
front door, while two real fires and a clutch of old books
and board games help give the place that front room feel.
The cosy L-shaped back room is dotted with chunky tables
where jovial thirtysomething punters tuck into gastropub
fare (the likes of cream of celeriac soup and pan-fried trout).
There's an extensive wine list and a well-stocked bar boasting IPA, Timothy Taylor Landlord, Bitburger, Amstel,
Budvar Original and König Ludwig on tap. The service is
as warm as the atmosphere.
Disabled: toilet. No-smoking area. Tables outdoors
(10, pavement). **Map 9 N1**.

Duke of Cambridge

30 St Peter's Street, N1 8JT (7359 3066/www.duke
organic.co.uk). Angel tube. **Open** noon-11pm Mon-Sat;
noon-10.30pm Sun. **Food served** 12.30-3pm, 6.30-
10.30pm Mon-Fri; 12.30-3.30pm, 6.30-10.30pm Sat;
12.30-3.30pm, 6.30-10pm Sun. **Credit** MC, V.
On first inspection, the Duke is a standard late '90s pub
conversion. Bare floors, huge windows, mismatched chairs,
an open kitchen – all conspiring to create an impression of
intensely studied casualness. If that were as far as it went,
this would be just another painfully hip gastropub, but the
Duke's selling point is its organic credentials. The beers,
wines, soft drinks and food are all organically produced
(with any exceptions carefully pointed out). Be prepared
for organic prices, though: a pint bottle of Sam Smith's
organic lager costs £5, and food isn't exactly cheap. But
you can't argue with the credentials – products are carefully sourced from small suppliers. High ceilings in the
large main room can make it draughty on quiet nights, but
this doesn't seem to deter the cool crowd who pack the
place out at weekends. A word of warning: the bar staff
seem to cope rather better with crowds than the kitchen
and waiting staff do.
Babies and children welcome. No-smoking area.
Restaurant (available for hire; no smoking). Tables
outdoors (5, pavement). **Map 9 O2**.

Elbow Room

89-91 Chapel Market, N1 9EX (7278 3244/www.the
elbowroom.co.uk). Angel tube. **Open** 5pm-2am Mon;
noon-2am Tue-Thur; noon-3am Fri, Sat; noon-midnight
Sun. **Food served** 5-11pm Mon; noon-11pm Tue-Sun.
Admission £5-£6 after 8pm Thur; £2 9-10pm, £5 after
10pm Fri, Sat. **Credit** MC, V.
Pool halls don't come glossier than this. Part of a chain of
temples to American-style pool, this retro-chic bar (think
'70s wood panelling, curved leather booths, and chrome)
features rows of baize-covered pool tables – including a
black table in the VIP room – on which to rack up some
frames. As the evening and week progress, things get livelier and waiting for your turn on a table can take ages. But
ping-pong and an open dancefloor serving eclectic beats
provide welcome distractions for a trendy, clubby crowd
that is still too young to enjoy their beer sitting down.

Drinks here are similarly unsophisticated mainly featuring lagers (Coors, Carling) and fluorescent cocktails, which
are sold two-for-one between 5pm and 8pm. There's a
regular student night (Wednesday) and club nights are
posted on the website.
Disabled: toilet. Music (DJs 9pm Wed-Sat; bands 9pm
Thur). Function room. **Map 9 N2**.

Filthy McNasty's

68 Amwell Street, EC1R 1UU (7837 6067/www.filthy
macnastys.com). Angel tube. **Open** noon-11pm Mon-
Sat; noon-10.30pm Sun. **Food served** noon-3pm Mon-
Fri. **Credit** MC, V.
That Pete Doherty tended bar here says a lot about this
effortlessly scuffed-up boozer. Its crimson walls have had
a recent lick of paint but the Irish pub, tucked away in the
residential back streets of Angel, is still the epitome of elegant slumming. Trendy mags and French books are there
for perusal in the cosy front bar while the signed rock
posters – including a glossy signed photo of the Libertines
in the back lounge – hint at the bar's rock pedigree. As well
as the usual lagers, there's Guinness and Adnams on tap
and a fine selection of single malts. A mix of young hipsters and weathered locals add to the pub's rough-hewn
charm while staff are amiably down to earth. Thai food is
served during the day but at night the hungry must content themselves with tasty Irish Tayto crisps.
Disabled: toilet. Function room. Literary readings
(phone for times; free). Music (bands, phone for dates;
free). Tables outdoors (7, pavement). TV (big screen).
Map 9 N3.

Green

74 Upper Street, N1 0NY (7226 8895/www.the-
green.co.uk). Angel tube. **Open** 4pm-midnight Mon-
Wed; 4pm-1am Thur; noon-2am Fri; 11am-2am Sat;
11am-midnight Sun. **Food served** 5-11pm Mon-
Wed; 5pm-midnight Thur; noon-midnight Fri; 11am-
midnight Sat; 11am-11pm Sun. **Credit** MC, V.
This straight-friendly gay bar is a relative newcomer on
the Islington landscape. A self-professed everyman of a
bar, it aspires to be a place to eat, drink and be merry away
from the scrutinising eyes outside on Upper Street, and
prides itself on its welcoming vibe. And in a trendy Conran-
esque way, it succeeds. Catering to a hip, young-ish crowd,
it's a friendly, intimate spot. Leather banquettes and small
café-style tables and chairs run up the sides of the bar,
while a vast mirror opposite the bar lends an impression
of space to the long, narrow room. The stylish continental
atmosphere is echoed both in its menu (with moules
marinière, and chargrilled squid) and beers, with
Cruzcampo and Paulaner lagers, among others, on tap.
There's a good selection of bottled beers too, and a selection of colourful cocktails.
Disabled: toilet. Music (DJs 9pm Thur-Sat; free; pianist
7.30pm Mon; free). Quiz (8.30pm Tue; £1). **Map 9 O2**.

Hemingford Arms

158 Hemingford Road, N1 1DF (7607 3303).
Caledonian Road tube/rail. **Open** 11am-11pm Mon-
Sat; noon-10.30pm Sun. **Food served** 12.30-2.30pm,
6-10.30pm Mon-Fri; 6-10.30pm Sat; 12.30-4pm, 6-10pm
Sun. **Credit** MC, V.
This tardis-like boozer is a world away from the quiet,
affluent Barnsbury community that it serves. Behind the
ivy-covered exterior is a enchanting little curiosity shop of
a pub where time seems to have stood still. Victorian ads
clutter the walls and gilded vintage birdcages hang from

North

Prince. *See p188.*

the ceiling above the huge island bar. Tables tucked away in nooks and crannies throughout the pub – one behind a scruffy old bookcase, another by a big fireplace – give the place a cosy amber warmth which complements its gregarious atmosphere. As well as the usual pub spirits and lagers (Stella, Foster's) draught ales are well represented (IPA, Directors, London Pride, Timothy Taylor Landlord and Adnams Broadside) and there's a handful of wines to choose from. Decent Thai food keeps the thirtysomething trendy locals happily sated.
Games (fruit machine). Music (bands 9pm Mon, Fri-Sun; free). Quiz (9pm Thur; £1). Tables outdoors (6, pavement). TVs (satellite). **Map 9 M26.**

Hen & Chickens Theatre Bar
109 St Paul's Road, N1 2NA (7704 7621/www. henandchickens.com). Highbury & Islington tube/rail. **Open** 4pm-midnight Mon-Wed; noon-1am Thur-Sat; noon-midnight Sun. **Credit** MC, V.
Holding court on Highbury Corner, the Hen & Chickens is a working fringe theatre and comedy club but you wouldn't guess by looking at it. There are no faded photos of forgotten productions adorning the walls. Instead, all glossy old woods and cream paint, this has a fresh, young feel about it. Fairy-lights give the place a warm, welcoming glow and flatter original fittings like the period tiling. Straddling the gorge between the area's ramshackled old boozers and swanky uber-fashionable bars, both in decor and available drinks, this relaxed establishment offers a decent range of spirits alongside the usual premium lagers (Grolsch, Staropramen), a few ales (Bombardier and Caledonian Deuchars IPA) and Addlestones Cider on tap. The wine list too is healthy and there are also a few bottles of 'champers' for those devil-may-care moments. Smoky beats serenade the relaxed hipsterish crowd.

Comedy (8pm Mon, Sun; £6-7). Music (DJs/bands 10.30pm Fri, Sat; free). Theatre (eves Tue-Sat, box office 7704 2001; £6-£10). Games (fruit machine, pinball machine, quiz machine). Tables outdoors (3, pavement). **Map 9 O25.**

Hope & Anchor
207 Upper Street, N1 1RL (7354 1312). Highbury & Islington tube/rail. Ground floor **Open** noon-11pm Mon-Sat; noon-10.30pm Sun. **Food served** noon-4pm daily. *Basement* **Open** 8.30pm-1am Mon-Sat; 8pm-midnight Sun. *Both* **Credit** MC, V.
Like a Camden pub plonked into the heart of Islington, this institution is a grizzled spit-and-sawdust rock pub. The down-at-heel Victorian boozer is an open rebellion against the poserism of Upper Street. The cavernous basement venue was the setting for Frankie Goes To Hollywood's *Two Tribes* and *Relax* videos, and still plays host to up-and-coming rock acts – as well as the odd gob-and-all punk revival night. The jukebox, however, is normally pitched somewhere between the Pixies and Joy Division (with the volume on full-whack). Stella, Foster's, IPA, and Guinness are on tap, there's a spacious games room upstairs (with pool and table football) while the ground floor houses what could be Upper Street's only fruit machine.
Disabled: toilet. Games (fruit machines, pool, table football, video games). Music (bands 8.30pm nightly; £4.50-£6; DJs 11pm Thur-Sat; free). **Map 9 O26.**

House
63-69 Canonbury Road, N1 2DG (7704 7410/www. inthehouse.biz). Highbury & Islington tube/rail. **Open** 5-11pm Mon; noon-11pm Tue-Sat; noon-10.30pm Sun. **Food served** 6.30-10.30pm Mon; 12.30-2.30pm, 6.30-10.30pm Tue-Fri; 12.30-3.30pm, 6.30-10.30pm Sat; 12.30-3.30pm, 6.30-9.30pm Sun. **Credit** MC, V.

The House manages to do cosy and classy at once, which explains why it's never empty, even on a wintry Tuesday night. Understated decor provides the backdrop: white walls, dark wood and beautiful floral displays. On our mid-week visit the soundtrack was mellow, the squishy leather sofa near the fire was free, and a fine glass of De Loach pinot noir (£5.25) went down a treat. A chalkboard lists half a dozen white and red wines as well as six Champagnes while the full list also includes a short but interesting list of cocktails variously muddled, shaken, topped and stirred, from a Sherbet Raspberry (raspberries, lemon vodka and chambord topped with ginger beer) to a classic Mojito. There's a smart dining area round the other side of the bar where interesting, well-executed food can be enjoyed.
Babies and children admitted. Disabled: toilet. Tables outdoors (6, garden). **Map 9 O26.**

Island Queen

87 Noel Road, N1 8HD (7704 7631). Angel tube. **Open** noon-11pm Mon-Fri; noon-11pm Sat; noon-10.30pm Sun. **Food served** noon-4pm, 6-10.30pm Mon-Thur; noon-10.30pm Fri, Sat; noon-10pm Sun. **Credit** MC, V.
A gem set in the gentrified backstreets of Islington. There's plenty to recommend the Island Queen, from the decor (high ceilings, Victorian flourishes, velvet drapes) and the laid-back atmosphere to the decent wine list and interesting eating options. If the ground floor is too busy, there's an upstairs lounge that's usually a bit quieter. In terms of food, think locally sourced pub grub, with Sunday roasts (£8.90), fish and chips (£7.50) and even afternoon tea. Beers include London Pride and Hoegaarden alongside Früli and Küppers Kölsch. The jukebox is a nice mix of indie and mainstream, there's a quiz night on Tuesdays and the clientele is a jolly combo of dressed-up and dressed-down locals. Our only gripe is that the staff seemed stand-offish, but that could have been a blip. We'll just have to go back to find out.
Function room (no smoking). Quiz (8pm Tue; £1). Tables outdoors (8, pavement). TV. **Map 9 O2.**

Keston Lodge

131 Upper Street, N1 1QP (7354 9535/www.keston lodge.com). Angel tube. **Open** noon-midnight Mon-Wed, Sun; noon-1am Thur; noon-2am Fri, Sat. **Food served** noon-3pm, 5-10pm Mon-Fri; noon-5pm, 6pm-10pm Sat, Sun. **Admission** £3 after 10.30pm Fri, Sat. **Credit** MC, V.
Exposed pipework, raw concrete, pegboard and exposed screwfixtures announce that the Lodge is definitely not a pub. You could easily be in a trendy bar in New York, Hong Kong or Sydney. The internationalist flavour carries over to the drinks list, which eschews real ale and best bitter in favour of Martinis, Bellinis and a good selection of wine. The post-industrial decor is softened by the presence of booths, armchairs and couches normally occupied by businessfolk or trendies, but the atmosphere is convivial and conducive to hanging out. Fresh produce from Borough Market features prominently on the daily-changing food menu; starters in the £4-£6 range and mains mainly between £6 and £8 are positive bargains by gastropub standards. Managing to pull off the difficult trick of being trendy without being pretentious, the Keston gets our vote of approval.
Music (DJs 9pm Thur-Sat; 8.30pm Sun). **Map 9 O1.**

King's Head

115 Upper Street, N1 1QN (7226 0364/www.kingshead theatre.org). Angel tube/Highbury & Islington tube/rail. **Open** 11am-1am Mon-Thur; 11am-2am Fri, Sat; noon-1am Sun. **Food served** *(pre-booked theatre dinner only, £16 3 courses)* 7-8pm Tue-Sat. **No credit cards.**

Legendary for its in-house theatre, where some of today's stars of British stage and screen cut their teeth (as evidenced by the 'headshots' covering the red walls), the King's Head is also a good place for those in search of a proper pint. Adnams, Tetley and Wadworths provide the bitters and ales (there's not a lager tap in sight). Wine is also given short shrift (it comes in two colours, but that's about the limit of choice), but the usual selection of spirits and mixers is available. Spotlights staring down at drinkers (composed of equal parts locals, business-types and trendies), and flip-down seating are further nods to the King's theatrical roots. The atmosphere is friendly and relaxed, helped in no small part by the refreshing absence of sport TV and booming music. We like.
Bar available for hire. Disabled: toilet. Function room. Music (bands 10pm nightly; £3 after 10pm Fri, Sat). Tables outdoors (2, pavement). Theatre (box office 7226 1916). **Map 9 O1.**

Marquess Tavern

32 Canonbury Street, N1 2TB (7354 2975). Highbury & Islington tube/rail. **Open** noon-11pm Mon-Sat; noon-10.30pm Sun. **Food served** noon-3pm, 6-10pm Mon-Sat; noon-9pm Sun. **Set meal** £10 for 2 courses Mon-Thur. **Credit** MC, V.
Despite its stone's-throw proximity to the fashionable bar haven of Essex Road, the Marquess Tavern boasts an unpretentious vibe. Blissfully forsaken by the trendy hordes, it's a community pub where down-to-earth locals prop up the huge bar, chatting to the landlord. Recent renovations have highlighted the Victorian boozer's original features: there are well-preserved fireplaces and the invitingly mellow vibe of the back room draws attention to the room's airy, high ceiling. Lined with old-fashioned pub benches and dotted with comfortable sofas, the red-painted-wood panelled front room is cosy at night and, thanks to its large windows, bright by day. Sky Sports plays unobtrusively in the background and there are board games to help while away the night. Young's bitters and beers are available on tap to boost an unexceptional selection of bottled beers, spirits and wines.
Babies and children welcome (before 6pm). Games (board games, fruit machine). Quiz (1st Mon of month, 8pm, £2). Restaurant (available for hire). Tables outdoors (4, patio). TV (big screen, satellite). **Map 9 P26.**

Medicine Bar

181 Upper Street, N1 1RQ (7704 9536/www.medicine bar.net). Angel tube/Highbury & Islington tube/rail. **Open** 5pm-midnight Mon-Thur; 5pm-2am Fri; 2pm-2am Sat; 2pm-midnight Sun. **Admission** £4 after 9.30pm Fri, Sat. **Credit** MC, V.
The longstanding good-time Medicine Bar remains the preserve of the young. With its black lacquered floor and oppressively dark walls this hugely popular spot is a heady sort of place. And the pumping soundtrack (spicy soul through to cutting edge electro house, courtesy of big name DJs) only adds to the intensity. Large fronds of greenery, particularly in the bar's gothic conservatory-like front, are a soothing antidote to the sensory overload, but it's the claustrophobic air of decadence that draws the fashion-conscious twentysomething crowd. There are a handful of round tables and obligatory scuffed sofas but this is essentially a standing, drink-in-hand sort of place. Come the weekend club nights, the place is bursting at the seams. Beck's, San Miguel and Guinness are on tap, and there's a basic wine list.
Function room. Music (DJs 8.30pm Thur-Sun). Tables outdoors (10, pavement). **Map 9 O1.**

North

Mucky Pup

39 Queen's Head Street, N1 8NQ (7226 2572/www.
muckypup-london.com). Angel tube. **Open/food**
served 4-11pm Mon-Thur; noon-1am Fri, Sat;
noon-11pm Sun. **Credit** AmEx, MC, V.
Voted the most dog-friendly bar in Britain by the Dog
Trust, dog walker services are the only thing advertised
on the pub's notice board, painted paw prints decorate the
walls and Iggy, the bar's very own tiger-striped mutt,
seems to run the place. There's an unpretentious earthi-
ness that defines both the dressed-down boozer itself and
its laid-back locals. A well-stocked, rock-heavy jukebox
keeps the atmosphere alive, while low sofas and roughed-
up old benches (and free Wi-Fi) give the place its homely
feel. There's a separate area for pool and darts and the
small courtyard is pleasant in summer. As well as the usual
pub lagers there's Castle Eden and IPA on tap. And of
course your four-legged friend is more than welcome.
Babies and children admitted (until 9pm). Bar available
for hire. Games (board games, darts, pool). Jukebox.
Quiz (8.30pm Wed; £1.50). Tables outdoors (3, garden).
TV. **Map 9 O2**.

Narrow Boat

119 St Peter Street, N1 8PZ (7288 0572). Angel tube.
Open 11am-midnight Mon-Sat; noon-midnight Sun.
Food served noon-3pm, 5-9.30pm Mon-Fri; noon-
9.30pm Sat, Sun. **Credit** MC, V.
We gave this place a lukewarm review last year, but things
have improved markedly since then. An extensive refit has
resulted in a comfortable and elegant pub with wonderful
views over the Regent's Canal from the full-length windows.
These slide away in warmer months, but even on winter
evenings it's a lovely place to come, the reflection of light
from canal boats creating a twinkly atmosphere (chesterfield sofas, candlelight and flowers complete the effect). The
plasma screens we lamented last time are still there but were
mercifully switched off. The range of drinks is good, with
guest ales and an affordable, though laminated, wine list.
The food menu – more burger and steaks – appears less pre-
cious than before too. A welcome return to form.
Babies and children welcome (until 8pm). Function
room. Games (board games, chess, fruit machines).
Music (DJs 7pm Fri; Irish band 8.30pm Thur; free).
Quiz (8.30pm Sun, £1). No-smoking area. Restaurant.
TVs (big screen, satellite). **Map 9 P2**.

Northgate

113 Southgate Road, N1 3JS (7359 7392). Bus 76, 141.
Open 5-11pm Mon-Thur; 5pm-midnight Fri; noon-
midnight Sat; noon-10.30pm Sun. **Food served** 6.30-
10.30pm Mon; noon-4pm, 6.30-10.30pm Sat;
noon-4pm, 6.30-9.30pm Sun. **Credit** MC, V.
Formerly the Junction Tavern – known for hosting amateur boxing matches – this joint now aspires to something
rather more sophisticated. From the heated picnic tables
that fill its cute courtyard to the small paintings trapped
in Perspex that dot its cream walls, plus the mismatched
scuffed tables and chairs, everything about the Northgate
screams 'gastropub'. The menu (pan-roasted lamb chops,
beef tomatoes stuffed with wild mushrooms) backs this up.
Time has clearly been taken over the selection of wine on
offer, while Guinness and regular-changing guest ales complement the usual selection of lagers. Trendy background
beats give the place a lively vibe while soft spotlights and
chunky candles warm up the canteen-like space. The
mixed crowd seem to approve.
Restaurant. Tables outdoors (10, patio).

Old Queen's Head

44 Essex Road, N1 8LN (7354 9993/www.theold
queenshead.com). Angel tube. **Open** noon-midnight
Mon-Thur, Sun; noon-2am Fri, Sat. **Food served**
6-11pm Mon-Fri; noon-9pm Sat, Sun. **Credit** MC, V.
This old Bessie of a corner pub has just had a fabulous
revamp courtesy of Fabric's Steve Blonde and the Medicine
Bar's Rob Wheeler. The hugely impressive sixteenth-cen-
tury carved fireplace, a quirky antler chandelier, and vintage wooden artefacts (including a meticulously made
gothic wooden cabinet behind the bar) lend an opulent
hunting lodge feel to the place. Dark, racing green walls
and the seemingly ubiquitous flock wallpaper make the
spacious room feel cosy, but huge front windows allow for
lots of light and world gazing. A trendy young crowd chill
at the many low-slung sofas and stubby coffee tables, guzzling beers and cocktails (no ales), to eclectic sultry beats.
Meanwhile upstairs, in the decadent boudoir-esque party
room, DJs play a warm-up set before they head off to head-
line Fabric (weekends).
Art exhibitions. Function room. Games (table football).
Music (acoustic band twice monthly; £2; DJs 9pm Fri,
Sat; £3 after 10pm Fri, after 9pm Sat). Tables outdoors
(3, garden; 3, pavement). TV (satellite). **Map 9 O1**.

Old Red Lion

418 St John Street, EC1V 4NJ (7837 7816/www.oldred
liontheatre.co.uk). Angel tube. **Open** noon-midnight Mon-
Thur; noon-1am Fri, Sat; noon-11pm Sun. **Food served**
noon-3pm Mon-Fri; noon-6pm Sun. **Credit** MC, V.
An unpretentious pub serving good drinks in a friendly
and efficient manner: what more could you ask for? There
are no leanings towards gastropub here; the food is defiantly sarnies, bangers and Sunday roasts (although the
presence of herbal tea was noted). Red walls, slightly tired
blue sofas, tables and chairs make up the decor, while the
clientele is a mixture of regulars, theatre-goers (there's a
small theatre upstairs), students and Upper Street trendies,
all of whom seem to appreciate the relaxed feel. An etched
glass partition separates the saloon from the public bar
(our tip: the saloon – a bit cosier). Beers include 6X and
Abbot Ale, with lagers of the Leffe and Staropramen ilk.
A welcome antidote to over-designed pubs.
Games (board games, fruit machine). Tables outdoors
(3, patio). Theatre (occasional comedy/new writing Mon;
plays Tue-Sun; £8-£12). TV (satellite). **Map 9 N3**.

Rosemary Branch

2 Shepperton Road, N1 3DT (7704 2730/www.
rosemarybranch.co.uk). Bus 21, 76, 141. **Open** noon-
11.30pm Mon-Thur; noon-midnight Fri, Sat; noon-
10.30pm Sun. **Food served** noon-3pm, 6-9.30pm
Mon-Sat; noon-6pm Sun. **Credit** MC, V.
This hidden gem has been an ale house since 1594, yet the
contemporary look is far from Elizabethan. An eccentric
old grandma of a place, it's a community hub (and a theatre). Art adorns the walls, courtesy of the local artists that
frequent the old watering hole, and large models of World
War II planes hang (somewhat inexplicably) from the ceiling. Paul Whitehouse's BBC series *Happiness* was shot
here and the feel remains down-to-earth. Rosemary Branch
is a haven for both beer and music lovers, with Leffe,
Litovel and a sturdy selection of Fuller's ales on tap and
eclectic tunes emanating from the jukebox. There's also
hearty food (own-made shepherd's pie) and a warming fire.
Function room. Games (board games). Quiz (8.30pm
Tue, Thur; £1). Theatre (7.30pm Tue-Sat; £8-£10).
Tables outdoors (12, patio). TV (big screen). **Map 9 P1**.

North

Salmon & Compass

*58 Penton Street, N1 9PZ (7837 3891/www.salmon
andcompass.com). Angel tube.* **Open** 4pm-2am Mon-
Thur, Sun; 4pm-4am Fri, Sat. **Food served** 4-10pm
daily. **Happy hour** 5-8pm Mon-Fri. **Admission**
£3 after 9pm, £5 after 11pm Fri, Sat. **Credit** AmEx,
MC, V.

This Chapel Market establishment may have a quaint olde
pub name, but you'll not find exposed beams nor hearty
cask ales here. With its shiny metallic surfaces and the
flash illuminated bar juxtaposed against rough open brickwork this is, as its clean-lined decor suggests, a trendy-beer
and cocktail spot. A few doors down from the Elbow Room
(see p175), the Salmon attracts a similarly young, clubby
crowd for whom sitting down is not a priority. Which is
just as well as, save for a bench, some stools and the odd
armchair, there are few places to park. Instead, most of the
bar is earmarked for shaking your thang: music is a priority here. With live beat-box and acid jazz performers, and
weekly funk, hip hop and breakbeat nights, there's never
a quiet moment.

*Games (board games). Function room. Music (bands
9pm Thur; DJs 8pm daily). Tables outdoors (5,
pavement). TV (big screen, satellite).* **Map 9 N2.**

25 Canonbury Lane

*25 Canonbury Lane, N1 2AS (7226 0955). Angel
tube/Highbury & Islington tube/rail.* **Open** 5-11pm
Mon-Fri; noon-11pm Sat, Sun. **Food served** 6-10pm
Mon-Thur; noon-3.30pm Sat; 1-4.30pm Sun. **Credit**
MC, V.

With its soothing soul soundtrack, strings of fairy lights
and abundance of white marble, this is a sensuous seduc-
tress of a bar. Attention to detail is important here: fresh
cut flowers stand in mismatched vases, candles dot the low,
tiny tables and crystal chandeliers dangle from the high
ceiling, lending the place an elegant boudoir feel. And at
the end of this small, narrow watering hole is an intimate
fairy-grotto of a room, decadently decked out in red fabrics. Even the barman looks like a Hollywood romantic
lead. Tapas is served to an effortlessly good-looking crowd
and washed down with a choice of 25 red and white wines,
or pints of Stella, Grolsch, Kronenbourg and Staropramen.
But it's the cocktail menu offering – 25 mouth-watering
concoctions – that really impresses. Ask nicely, and the
Johnny Depp-alike might mix you up something special.
Tables outdoors (5, conservatory). **Map 9 O26.**

Warwick

*45 Essex Road, N1 2SF (7688 2882/www.the
warwickbar.com). Angel tube.* **Open** 5pm-midnight
Mon-Thur; 5pm-1am Fri; 2pm-1am Sat; 2pm-midnight
Sun. **Credit** MC, V.

From the super cool tunes in its jukebox (DFA, Talking
Heads and, erm, Chas 'n' Dave) to the mishmash of Formica
tables, glitterballs and sofas, this funky Essex Road bar has
a thrift-store chic vibe that's very New York. Formerly a gay
bar, it's now run by Dan Beaumont and Sarah Warwicker,
who previously managed the nearby Social and it seems
they've brought the said bar's trendy, laid-back customers
with them. It's hard to move about in the long narrow boozer (especially when rammed at the weekend) but there's usually breathing room at the back. Drinks-wise, there's crisp
Baltica beer on tap and the usual lagers, plus a small selection of wines. But cocktails are the forte here, and range from
Bloody Marias to seasonal concoctions such as hot toddies.
*Disabled: toilet. Function room. Jukebox. Music (DJs
7pm Thur-Sun; free).* **Map 9 O2.**

Winchester

*2 Essex Road, N1 8LN (7704 8789/www.thewinchester
bar.co.uk). Angel tube.* **Open** noon-midnight Mon-Wed;
noon-2am Thur, Fri; 10am-3am Sat; 10am-10.30pm Sun.
Food served noon-10pm Mon-Fri; 10am-10pm Sat,
Sun. **Credit** AmEx, DC, MC, V.

Self-consciously – but endearingly – eccentric, the
Winchester is a riot of antlers, landscape paintings, worn
wood, brick and mirrors. What appears from the entrance
to be a narrow space, widens at the back to accommodate
tables, leather banquettes and armchairs. Tea lights in red
glass holders give the place a dark, ruddy glow. The overall feeling is relaxed, a mood helped by the friendly staff
and local punters who are trendy without being pretentious. The place is part-owned by Fabric founder Steve
Blonde, and DJs provide tunes on Fridays (£3 after 10pm)
and Saturdays (£4 after 10pm). Drinks include prosecco, a
good range of cocktails (from £6.50), a run-of-the-mill selection of beers on tap (Beck's, Foster's, Guinness) and a reasonable wine list. Brunch, lunch and dinner are served and
there's also a range of snacks such as nachos and olives.
*Babies and children welcome (until 6pm). Function
room. Music (DJs 9pm Thur-Sat; free-£3).* **Map 9 O2.**

Also in the area...

Angel (JD Wetherspoon) 3-5 Islington Street,
N1 9LQ (7837 2218).
Bierodrome 173-174 Upper Street, N1 1XS
(7226 5835).
Elk in the Woods (Bar Chocolate) 37 Camden
Passage, N1 8EA (7226 3535).
Glass Works (JD Wetherspoon) N1 Centre,
21 Parkfield Street, N1 0PS (7354 6100).
Lush 235 Upper Street, N1 1RU (7704 6977).
O'Neill's 59 Upper Street, N1 0NY (7704 7691).
Pitcher & Piano 68 Upper Street, N1 0NY (7704
9974).
Slug & Lettuce 1A Islington Green, N1 2XH
(7226 3864).
Social 33 Linton Street, N1 7DU (7354 5809).
Walkabout 56 Upper Street, N1 0NY (7359 2097).
White Swan (JD Wetherspoon) 255-256 Upper
Street, N1 1RY (7288 9050).

Kentish Town & Tufnell Park

This part of town has seen an explosion of decent
bars. Take the **Abbey**, the **Assembley House** and
the **Bull & Last** or the excellent **Junction Tavern**,
which have joined the quirky Pineapple and leafy-
gardened **Vine**.

Abbey

*124 Kentish Town Road, NW1 9QB (7267 9449).
Kentish Town tube/rail.* **Open** 11am-midnight Mon-
Thur; 11am-1am Fri; 9am-1am Sat; 9am-midnight Sun.
Food served noon-3.30pm, 6-10pm Mon-Thur; noon-
3.30pm, 6-10.30pm Fri; 9am-10.30pm Sat; 9am-10pm
Sun. **Credit** MC, V.

Nuzzling up against the grubby end of Kentish Town, the
Abbey doffs its cap to passing locals in need of gastro fare
and low-key jazz. They respond in droves, piling into the
long, high-ceilinged room and walled beer garden throughout the week. The pace remains gentle, though, with families and couples sharing chunky tables and leather

North

benches. The decor is vaguely industrial-chic – bare brick walls, exposed ventilation shafts – mellowed by globe lights. The small menu of burgers and fish and chips is unadventurous, and there are no draught ales, but there's a good Italian-heavy wine list, and fans of Belgian beers fare well with 20 different bottles available. Sundays draw in couples who are attracted by the brunch or roasts and can pore over papers and nod along to jazz musicians. *Function room. Music (bands 8pm Tue, 7.30pm Sun; DJs 9pm Fri; free). Restaurant (available for hire). Tables outdoors (10, garden). Map 8 J25.*

Assembly House
292-294 Kentish Town Road, NW5 2TG (7485 2031). Kentish Town tube/rail. **Open** noon-11.30pm Mon-Thur; noon-midnight Fri, Sat; noon-10.30pm Sat. **Food served** noon-3pm, 6-10pm Mon-Fri; noon-10pm Sat, Sun. **Credit** MC, V.
Thanks to a recent refurb, this sprawling pub feels something like a grand country-house hotel crossed with an All Bar One. Gilt Corinthian columns hold up the double-height patterned ceiling and antique-looking tables are widely spaced. But on our visit, the wall of ornately etched Victorian mirrors was incongruously obscured by a football match on the giant pull-down screen; we escaped to the lovely side room, where a massive skylight hovers over leather sofas snuggled up to a fireplace. The friendly staff serve Greene King IPA, Abbot Ale, Scrumpy Jack and at least one notable lager (Budvar) but the menu, with an American/Tex-Mex bent, seemed keenly priced. The place may still be finding its feet, and might be a bit raucous if a metal band is playing at the nearby Forum, even if only on the way to the Pineapple or the Vine.
Babies and children admitted. TVs (big screen, satellite).

Bull & Last
168 Highgate Road, NW5 1QS (7267 3641). Kentish Town tube then 214, C1, C2, C11 bus/Gospel Oak rail. **Open** 11am-11pm Mon-Sat; 11am-10.30pm Sun. **Food served** noon-3pm, 6.30-10pm Mon-Fri; noon-10pm Sat; noon-9.30pm Sun. **Credit** MC, V.
Many's the happy punter who has stumbled on this welcoming pub after a stroll on nearby Hampstead Heath. And what's not to be happy about? The burgundy walls, dark wood from floor to ceiling and candles guttering away give the place a warm and cosy vibe, and there's a comfy leather sofa next to the fire. The food – also served upstairs in a dining room of widely spaced tables for two – is a similarly warming line of British gastro fare, such as roast belly of pork with caramelised onion mash (£10.25). There's a good variety of tipples too, with Pilsner Urquell the lager of choice plus Westons Organic Cider by the bottle and Greene King IPA and London Pride on tap, and the increasingly standard North London trio of Leffe, Hoegaarden and Guinness. Good luck getting one of the pavement tables on a sunny day.
Babies and children welcome. Function room. Tables outdoors (5, pavement).

Dartmouth Arms
35 York Rise, NW5 1SP (7485 3267/www.dartmouth arms.co.uk). Tufnell Park tube. **Open** 11am-11pm Mon-Fri; 10am-11pm Sat; 10am-10.30pm Sun. **Food served** 11am-10pm daily. **Credit** MC, V.
There's a homely feel to the Dartmouth, done up in muted olive tones, weathered wainscoting and with a stag's skull over the fireplace. The locals seemingly know the bar staff on a first-name basis. It can be a bit blokey when the football's on, but that's balanced by the landlord shucking oys-

ters at the bar, works by local artists on the walls and the smoke-free saloon at the back, which is home to occasional wine-tastings, a fiendish fortnightly quiz and families sitting down to brunch or Sunday roasts. Cider is a feature, with Aspall Suffolk Cyder on tap and an intriguing selection by the bottle, as are real ales – usually a representative or two of the Adnams family and a succession of guest beers. The food's just shy of gastro, and reasonably priced, featuring the likes of rabbit pie, mussels and bangers and mash. *Restaurant (available for hire). Quiz (8pm alternate Tue; £1). TV (big screen, satellite).*

Junction Tavern
101 Fortess Road, NW5 1AG (7485 9400/www.junction tavern.co.uk). Tufnell Park tube. **Open** noon-11pm Mon-Sat; noon-10.30pm Sun. **Food served** noon-3pm, 6.30-10.30pm Mon-Fri; noon-4pm, 6.30-10.30pm Sat; noon-4pm, 6.30-9.30pm Sun. **Credit** MC, V.
You might mistake this for a restaurant, with its regimented tables and chairs visible through the front windows, and it would be fair enough, as the pricey gastro fare alone, such as seared yellow-fin tuna (£13.50), done to a turn, makes a visit worthwhile. Head to the back half however, with its dark-wood panelling and carved pilasters, and the place feels more like a proper pub, the punters looking more casual as the space spills down into a large conservatory and on to the lamp-warmed, umbrella-shaded garden. It's a place for sitting rather than congregating at the bar, where they had Deuchars IPA and three Tring Brewery bitters. There were also 20-or-so barrels stacked up ready for their seasonal beer festivals, with Addlestones Cloudy Cider as a bonus.
Tables outdoors (15, garden).

Lord Palmerston
33 Dartmouth Park Hill, NW5 1HU (7485 1578/www. geronimo-inns.co.uk). Tufnell Park tube. **Open** 11pm Mon-Sat; noon-10.30pm Sun. **Food served** 12.30-3pm, 7-10pm Mon-Sat; 1-4pm, 7-9pm Sun. **Credit** MC, V.
Stripped-back old boozers converted to gastropubs are hardly a rarity in North London, but they went to town on the idea here. There's nary a decoration on the pale grey-green walls and the ambient noise is from well-offish drinkers and diners. The former have reason to rejoice as management seems to have recently ditched the Young's for a regularly changing sampler of real ales (Tim Taylor Landlord, Deuchars IPA, Sharp's Doom Bar), added Bitburger Pils and Budvar Dark to the lager list, and maintained a comprehensive choice of more than a dozen wines by the glass (including a pair of rosés). The food's up to scratch, too, with substantial portions of gastro fare chalked up on a big blackboard. In summer, the swathe of picnic tables out front makes for interesting people-watching, though you can also sit in the secret garden at the back.
Tables outdoors (5, garden; 13, pavement).

Oxford
256 Kentish Town Road, NW5 2AA (7485 3521/www. realpubs.co.uk/theoxford). Kentish Town tube/rail. **Open** noon-11.30pm Mon-Thur; noon-midnight Fri, Sat; noon-10.30pm Sun. **Food served** noon-3.30pm, 6-10pm Mon-Fri; noon-5pm, 6-10pm Sat; noon-9pm Sun. **Credit** MC, V.
The matt black exterior may not be particularly inviting but, once inside, Oxford's large south-facing windows provide plenty of natural light and fat yellow candles and new paired lampshades cast a warm glow at night. The requisite leather sofas and mismatched wooden furniture are scattered around the front room, where a melee of spiffy after-work drinkers settle along the lengthy bar. But the

gleaming open kitchen is the allure for many. Sit in the quieter back room, surrounded by black-and-white photos, to consume good-sized portions of updated British and continental gastro fare. There's around a dozen bottles of both red and white wine (nearly half of them by the glass), and Tim Taylor Landlord and Old Speckled Hen on tap. *Music (jazz Mon 8.30pm; free). Tables outdoors (6, pavement).*

Pineapple
51 Leverton Street, NW5 2NX (7284 4631/www.the pineapplelondon.com). Kentish Town tube/rail. **Open** noon-11pm Mon-Sat; noon-10.30pm Sun. **Food served** 1-3pm, 7-10pm Mon-Sat; 1-4pm Sun. **Credit** MC, V. Devilishly hidden away on a residential street, this gem of a pub is mostly frequented by casually dressed locals who have the wherewithal to find it. Mirrors with (pineapple) etchings, and the dark-wooden surround behind the bar immediately announce the place's Victorian heritage, as do the mouldings, velvety red banquettes and worn wooden tables. The pineapple theme continues throughout, with shaped lamp bases, sculptures and, in the hall leading back to the glass-covered atrium, framed labels from tins, all saluting the spiky fruit. Further back, the walled-in, paved garden is a pleasant spot to sample the gastro menu, which might include a chunky game terrine, crayfish risotto, or well-executed standards of the sausage and mash ilk. Wash this down with Pedigree, Young's, Hoegaarden or Leffe. The menu is also available in an elegant dining room upstairs. *Function rooms. Games (backgammon, cards, chess, darts). Quiz (8.30pm Mon; £1). Restaurant. Tables outdoors (9, garden; 16, pavement).* **Map 8 J24.**

Progress Bar
162 Tufnell Park Road, N7 0EE (7272 2078/www. progress-bar.co.uk). Tufnell Park tube. **Open** 4pm-midnight Mon-Wed, Sun; 1pm-3am Thur-Sat. **Food served** 6-9pm Mon-Fri; 1-9pm Sat, Sun. **Happy hour** 7pm-midnight Thur. **Credit** MC, V. There's often a gaggle of lads and ladettes outside the unprepossessing exterior towards the end of the week, indicative of the young and sometimes-raucous atmosphere that fills this stripped-back pub. A large central bar serving the usual lager suspects (though there's Kirin and Asahi in bottles), standard cocktails (£5.50) and just the one bitter (Adnams Broadside – off when we visited) divides the two main rooms, which are decked out with low tables and leather cubes and old-style waiting-room sofas. It scores well on the billiards front, with four tables in a side room wrapped by a night skyline mural, and the good-sized garden is also a hit in summer. The Progress also hosts frequent gigs, including a mid-week open-mic night and comedy once a month. *Function room. Games (American pool; free Tue, Thur; £6/hr Mon, Wed, Fri-Sun). Music (DJs 9pm Thur-Sun; free; bands 8pm Tue, Wed, Fri, Sat; £3-£5). Tables outdoors (15, garden). TVs (big screen, satellite).*

Torriano
71-73 Torriano Avenue, NW5 2SG (7267 4305). Kentish Town tube/rail. **Open** noon-11pm Mon-Sat; noon-10.30pm Sun. **Food served** noon-10.30pm Mon-Sat; noon-10pm Sun. **Credit** MC, V. Tucked away in a residential backwater, the fresh looking façade suggests yet another North London gastropub. Not so. Inside, the one main space is pleasantly unpretentious and local in feel, with a square central bar, a charcoal-painted concrete floor and sea-blue and green distempered walls that (oddly) hint at an Eastern European connection.

Booze Talking
Pineapple

You are?
Chloë Powell, landlady of the Pineapple, Kentish Town (*see left*).
There aren't many young women running pubs.
I absolutely adore it but it's a 24-hour job. My home life, my social life and my work life is all just one big life now. I'm always the Pineapple landlady whatever I'm doing. I'm quite young to be doing this but I don't see why you can't, as long as you've got a certain amount of authority.
So you're a strict disciplinarian then?
I say to the staff they can spill drinks or knock things over and I don't care, as long as they're nice to the customers. There's nothing slick about the Pineapple, it's all a bit 'Aargh', but I think people like the eclectic nature of it all.
So who drinks in the Pineapple?
Did you hear about that film *Scenes of a Sexual Nature* with Jude Law and Sophie Okonedo? That guy over there wrote it. We get lots of that in here. Bohemian, arty. Ken Stott drank in here. He's moved to Clerkenwell now, but a guy wrote a film with him in mind and approached him in here and he ended up doing the film. Over pints in the Pineapple the whole project got put together. I love that.
Do you know why it's called the Pineapple?
The pineapple was a symbol of opulence and welcome. People coming back from the New World would stick one on their front gate so people could welcome them home. Someone's just written a history of the fruit and launched her book here. It's amazing the amount of stuff the pineapple is used on. We don't allow any form of branding. 'We'll give you 150 free kegs of beer if you'll put this mirror up on the wall.' No, just the Pineapple, that's our branding. I can't go anywhere without pineapple-spotting. 'Yes, Chloë, it's a pineapple. Very good.'

North

Other than toasted sandwiches and Sunday fry-ups, there's not much in the way of food. This place is more about drinking, with friendly regulars imbibing a range of beers that include Pedigree, London Pride, Hoegaarden and Guinness on tap, plus a decent-enough range of wines. If you really must satisfy those hunger pangs, there are weekend barbecues in the back garden, weather permitting. *Babies and children admitted. Quiz (8.30pm Mon; £2). Tables outdoors (4, garden). TV.*

Vine

86 Highgate Road, NW5 1PB (7209 0038/www.the vinelondon.co.uk). Tufnell Park tube/Kentish Town tube/rail. **Open** noon-11pm Mon-Thur; noon-midnight Fri, Sat; noon-10.30pm Sun. **Food served** noon-3pm, 6-10pm Mon-Sat; noon-10pm Sun. **Credit** AmEx, MC, V. Picnic tables in front of the Vine's Edwardian façade hint at one of its key selling-points – a leafy, covered garden out the back. In cooler months, however, the interior is just as appealing, being stripped back enough to highlight features like the chandelier and bow windows at the front, and the roaring fireplace in a side room that's decorated with ethnic pillows strewn on leather sofas. The eye-catching zinc-topped bar draws in a collection of thirtysomething professional and media types, supping Old Speckled Hen or Greene King IPA, or one of the nine wines by the glass. The menu suits them well: there's whitebait as a bar snack. Upstairs is a Moroccan-themed dining room with lanterns and potted palms.
Babies and children welcome. Function rooms. Tables outdoors (22, garden).

Kilburn

Once the stout and shamrock centre of London, Kilburn's gentrification continues apace with the **Kilburn Pub & Kitchen** joining the superb old-school boozers like the **Black Lion**.

Black Lion

274 Kilburn High Road, NW6 2BY (7624 1424/www. blacklionguesthouse.com). Kilburn tube. **Open** 2pm-midnight Mon-Thur; 11am-12.30am Fri, Sat; 11am-11.30pm Sun. **Food served** noon-3pm, 6-10pm Mon-Fri; 11am-10pm Sat; noon-9.30pm Sun. **Credit** MC, V. Pints of Guinness trembled in the hands of traditionalists a few years back when the Black Lion closed for a refurb. They needn't have worried. This Victorian drinking palace – ornate, handsome, almost baroque – still sets bar standards in the area. The Grade II-listed interior has been mercifully restored rather than scrubbed, preserving the quintessentially pubby feel. Adnams Broadside is on tap, with Hoegaarden alongside, and the wine list is extensive and reasonable (the bar benefits from the adjacent dining room). Cocktails on a blackboard namecheck the popular classics, but you can be sure that the upbeat staff will not be fazed by any drinks request. As the clock creeps up to midnight, the vast, packed bar somehow manages to achieve the intimacy of a cosy front room. The perfect pub? As near as it gets.
Babies and children welcome (until 6pm). Restaurant (no smoking). Tables outdoors (6, garden).

Kilburn Pub & Kitchen

305-311 Kilburn High Road, NW6 7JR (7372 8668/ www.thekilburn.com). Kilburn tube/Brondesbury rail. **Open** noon-11pm Mon-Wed; Sun; noon-midnight

Thur-Sat. **Food served** noon-3pm, 5.30-10pm Mon-Thur; noon-9.30pm Fri, Sat; noon-6pm Sun. **Happy hour** 5-8pm daily. **Credit** AmEx, MC, V.
Something of a saloon feel has been created here, despite modernisation. Low level red-hued lighting fights – and wins – a battle with big windows, creating an atmospheric space, even at lunchtime. Solid offerings take the form of affordable Thai, while liquids on tap cover most bases (but are a little light in the real ale department): John Smith's, Guinness, Leffe and Amstel are all available. The sofas positively eat you up, and it's an easy place in which to spend an entire night in the company of Irish legends – a nod to the area's traditional immigrant community – such as Van Morrison and Samuel Beckett, whose portraits hang on the walls.
Music (DJs 7.30pm Sat; free). TV (big screen, satellite).

North London Tavern

375 Kilburn High Road, NW6 7QB (7625 6634). Kilburn tube. **Open** noon-11pm Mon-Wed; noon-midnight Thur-Sat; noon-11pm Sun. **Food served** noon-3.30pm, 6.30-10.30pm Mon-Fri; 12.30-4.30pm, 6.30-10.30pm Sat; 12.30-9.30pm Sun. **Credit** MC, V.
The NLT is a whole lorra pub. This despite the signature scrubbed floors of gastro-dom, the spouted spirits behind the bar and the vase of outlandish lilies on the counter. The overall impression is that modernising touches have been added gradually, with the place evolving quite naturally into the perfect hybrid pub-bar it is today. The exterior is painted in a shade of Guinness black, and 'dark wood' is the interior theme, with big windows removing any suggestion of claustrophobia that the colour scheme might engender. Brakspear Special and Black Sheep Bitter are both on tap, alongside Leffe (now almost de rigueur for any self-respecting establishment), and the tidily stocked bar hasn't been downgraded by any spontaneous cocktail whims.
Babies and children welcome. Disabled: toilet. Function room. Restaurant. Tables outdoors (5, pavement). TV.

Power's Bar

332 Kilburn High Road, NW6 2QN (7624 6026). Kilburn tube/Brondesbury rail. **Open** noon-11pm Mon-Sat; noon-10.30pm Sun. **No credit cards.**
Despite being converted just a decade ago, Power's has a bohemian and clandestine feel that suggests a much more well-established haunt. The cacophony of mismatched tables, chairs and church pews seems to have been there forever, while the tortured (and, frankly, not very good) fresco in the back could have been daubed in exchange for beer in a real life version of the Stella Artois advert. There's live music, often traditional Irish, often of a pretty high standard, the Guinness is good and there's an impressive array of whiskies. Crowded and sometime raucous, the place is surprisingly welcoming. If you're looking for shillelaghs on the wall, head for O'Starbucks or the like. Good music and decent beer devotees, however, need look no further.
Jukebox. Music (acoustic 9pm Tue, Wed; DJs 8.30pm Thur-Sat; Irish band 4-7pm Sun; all free). TV.

Salusbury

50-52 Salusbury Road, NW6 6NN (7328 3286). Queens Park tube/rail. **Open** 5-11pm Mon; noon-11pm Tue-Sat; noon-10.30pm Sun. **Food served** 7-10.15pm Mon; 12.30-3.30pm, 7-10.15pm Tue-Sat; 12.30-3.30pm, 7-10pm Sun. **Credit** MC, V.
A mixed clientele occupies this modern local. Although the outside resembles something of a Dickensian shop, inside

the feel is much more contemporary. Mix 'n' match tables and chairs and bare wood surfaces may be standard issue for boozer-to-bar conversions, but this place has managed to retain an authentic atmosphere, while at the same time becoming a versatile local of the new-school variety. The comfortable space is easy to relax in, whether waiting for friends, cosying up intimately by the open fire, or for an evening of quaffing with your mates at the pavement tables in summer. Adnams bitter and Broadside are on tap, while the wine list features a good range of reasonably priced varieties. Lunch deals are often available , with food served either in the bar or the snug, dark dining room.
Babies and children welcome (until 7pm). Restaurant (no smoking). Tables outdoors (4, pavement).

Maida Vale & St John's Wood

With more than its fair share of pub gems, like the bucolic **Clifton**, Maida Vale just got a few more including the superb gastro **Salt House** and the perfectly formed **E Bar**.

Bridge House
13 Westbourne Terrace Road, W2 6NG (7432 1361). Warwick Avenue tube. **Open** noon-11pm Mon-Sat; noon-10.30pm Sun. **Food served** noon-10pm Mon-Sat; noon-9.30pm Sun. **Credit** (over £5) AmEx, MC, V.
Home to the Canal Café Theatre (launch pad for Rory Bremner and others), this former old-school boozer has enjoyed a fabulous (but borderline tarty?) makeover in recent times, turning the bar into a space every bit as adventurous as the famed News Revue show it hosts upstairs. Red lights dangle over the bar like your wild aunt's earrings, and the place is strewn with a rag-tag band of sofas, perches, stools and tables. Yet despite all the fun and frivolity, the place is serious about drink, with Früli, Abbot Ale, Leffe and Adnams Broadside on tap, wines by the glass, and a bar stocked well enough to handle even the most theatrical booze-up. Genuinely welcoming, both day and night, the place is as lovely on a winter's afternoon as it is entertaining on a buzzing summer's evening.
Disabled: toilet. Fringe theatre (7.30pm & 9.30pm Mon-Sat; 7pm & 9pm Sun; phone to confirm times; £7-£9). Games (board games). Tables outdoors (8, terrace).

Clifton
96 Clifton Hill, NW8 0JT (7372 3427). St John's Wood tube. **Open** noon-11pm Mon-Sat; noon-10.30pm Sun. **Food served** noon-3pm, 6-9pm Mon-Sat; noon-4pm Sun. **Credit** AmEx, MC, V.
This 170-year old pub in a comfy Georgian villa is a bucolic retreat in a stern, grand street. The great beers (draught Küpper Kölsch, Leffe, Young's, London Pride, Früli and Staropramen), good wines (eight of each colour by the glass and bottle, including Viognier Les Jumelles £4.50/£13.25 and Siglo Rioja £4.50/£13.25) and fine food (including handmade pies) would lure in any pub – here, the trappings are equally attractive. Edward VII (depicted over the fire, with a letter notifying his lying in state) and mistress Lillie Langtry, also illustrated, conducted their love affair here. They would still melt in today's relaxed wooden interior, with its sunken dining room, conservatory and lounge. There's also a terrace, patrolled by the lovely pub cat, whom you should not feed despite protestation. The cat has now been joined by a pub dog.
Babies and children welcome (until 7pm). Games (board games). Tables outdoors (12, garden).

Duke of York
2A St Anne's Terrace, NW8 6PJ (7722 1933). St John's Wood tube. **Open** 11am-11pm Mon-Sat; noon-10.30pm Sun. **Food served** noon-10.30pm Mon-Sat; noon-10pm Sun. **Credit** MC, V.
Sitting on the corner of two adjoining terraces this European-style brasserie has just a few hints of its old pub façade. Inside there's a strange mismatch of wooden tables and chairs, long leather bench seating and washed brown walls interspersed with artexing splattered on and covered with twigs. Most of the finishing touches are eastern, with wooden Indian Shutters and Persian wrought-iron trellising on the windows and sinuous Habitat-esque lamps competing with North African hanging coloured glass lanterns. The cuisine is a fusion of modern British and European; there is an 18-strong wine list that includes a delicate clean and fruity pinot grigio, £14.95, with Old Speckled Hen and Hoegaarden on tap. The music is strictly MOR, which seems to suit the well-to-do middle-aged crowd that comes here.
Babies and children welcome (until 8pm). Restaurant (no-smoking tables). Tables outdoors (8, pavement).

E Bar
2 Warrington Crescent, W9 1ER (7432 8455). Warwick Avenue tube. **Open** 5-11pm Tue-Fri; noon-11pm Sat; noon-10.30pm Sun. **Food served** 5-10.30pm Tue-Fri; noon-10.30pm Sat; noon-10pm Sun. **Credit** MC, V.
Both tapas and cocktail lounge, the subterranean E Bar is a welcome addition to Little Venice's bar portfolio. The dinky little place may be small, but it is perfectly formed, and the cocktail menu is comprehensive and confident. The Long Island Iced Tea is billed as being made 'the proper way', and does not disappoint. Tapas – excellent and imaginative – go for £3.50 for one or £9.50 for three. If you're in a grazing mood, the bountiful sharing platters of cheese and meat or seafood are great value at £20. Alfresco tables are available at ground level in summer, but the best spots in the house are the deliciously clandestine hideaways – with banquettes and soft cushions – away from the atrium (where DJs spin an eclectic range of music) at the bottom of the stairs.
Function rooms. Games (backgammon, chess). Tables outdoors (20, terrace).

Elgin
255 Elgin Avenue, W9 1NJ (7624 2602). Maida Vale tube. **Open** 9.30am-11pm Mon-Thur; 10.30am-midnight Fri, Sat; 10.30am-11pm Sun. **Food served** Bar 10.30am-10pm Mon-Sat; 10.30am-9pm Sun. Restaurant noon-3pm, 6-10pm Mon-Sat; noon-9pm Sun. **Credit** MC, V.
This long, slender, one room bar makes the best of the available space, with low stools and tables near the door, perches against the windows and a comfortable hideaway area at the back. Bare wood floors and exposed brick walls are the order of the day and the place is nicely lit during the evenings, when it feels cosy despite the large windows (the resultant natural light is a great boost for a daytime flick through the paper). Summery pitchers of Sea Breeze and Sangria are available (for around £14) and the wine list is egalitarian both in terms of selection and price. Beer heads are catered to with London Pride and Hoegaarden on tap. The Elgin's upstairs dining room was enjoying a refurb at the time this guide went to press, but light bites (like ciabatta-bread sandwiches) were available in the bar.
Games (board games). Restaurant (no smoking). TV.

North

Graze

215 Sutherland Avenue, W9 1RU (7266 3131/
www.graze.co.uk). Maida Vale tube. **Open** 6pm-1am
Tue-Sun. **Food served** 6pm-12.30am Tue-Sun.
Credit AmEx, DC, MC, V.
Does exactly what it says on the tin on the food front, with
tapas-style fare the order of the day. If hops are your thing,
Budvar and Kronenbourg are available in bottled form,
but it's the cocktails that set the tone, with classics,
Champagne versions and fads all taken on with aplomb,
to be imbibed at the long, elegant bar. The place also does
a great Sunday brunch with traditional English at a decent
£8. This isn't the easiest of joints to 'swing by' though:
after 11pm food must be ordered with drinks as a condi-
tion of their licence, and on live music nights (like the
Thursday's TFI club night – an ironic misnomer) there's
a £10 cover charge.
Bar available for hire. Music (DJ 8pm Thur-Sun; free;
reggae band 8pm Tue; free).

Ordnance

29 Ordnance Hill, NW8 6PS (7722 0278). St John's
Wood tube. **Open** noon-11pm Mon-Sat; noon-10.30pm
Sun. **Food served** noon-2pm, 6-9pm Mon-Thur; noon-
2pm, 6-9.30pm Fri, Sat; noon-5pm Sun. **Credit** MC, V.
One of the loveliest pubs around, with a garden that surrounds it on three sides, making it perfect for lazy summer afternoons, and a roaring winter fire with sink-in
sofas for colder nights. Aside from the front main bar area
there is a cosy no-smoking back room and an adjoining
conservatory, all coloured in peachy pastel shades and
adorned with Greco-Roman portraits. Above the mismatch of furniture hang large branches dripping with
fairy lights, and at the bar there's a good range of reasonably priced Sam Smith's beer and ales. There's decent
pub grub too, such as a seafood platter, £9.95, or Sunday
roasts from £7.25 to £9.95.
Babies and children welcome. No piped music or
jukebox. No-smoking area. Tables outdoors (9, garden).

Prince Alfred & Formosa Dining Rooms

5A Formosa Street, W9 1EE (7286 3287). Warwick
Avenue tube. **Open** 11am-11pm Mon-Sat; noon-10.30pm
Sun. **Food served** noon-3pm, 6-10.30pm Mon-Sat;
noon-4pm, 6-10pm Sun. **Credit** AmEx, MC, V.
A fascinating testimony to the British class system, this:
the half-moon bar is divided into five delicious little snugs,
each with its own minature door, which were originally
intended to keep the classes and sexes apart. History les-
son over, this beautiful Victorian treasure is now characterised by super-modern, efficient and friendly service, an
excellent range of premium spirits and over 20 different
wines by the glass. On draught there's Affligem and
Paulaner wheat beer, with Cruzcampo in bottles. The food
is fast and fresh in the bar, but if eating is your principal
aim, head for the dining room (where booking is almost
essential, thanks to the chef's excellent reputation) for modern British/European fare. The pub area has a great local
feel when full – which it often is. Lucky locals.

Salt House

63 Abbey Road, NW8 0AE (7328 6626). St John's
Wood or Kilburn Park tube. **Open** noon-11.30pm
daily. **Food served** noon-10.30pm daily. **Credit**
AmEx, MC, V.
This venerable old pub restaurant has seen several guises
in the past few years but has reverted back to its original

name with new ownership. The spruced-up front main pub
area has large windows surrounded by burnt wood and
peach pastel walls adorned with arty posters and large mirrors, packing in a crowd of well heeled thirtysomethings
enjoying Greene King IPA, Abbot Ale, Hoegaarden and
Budvar on tap. There are two dining areas (at the back and
upstairs) serving a good range of uncomplicated hearty
gastropub fare such as casserole of corn fed chicken,
cannellini beans and winter greens. There's an excellent
wide-ranging wine list with over 60 examples to sample
such as a lovely dry Brouilly Domaine Cret des Garanches,
£22.50. The stylish terrace outside gains a cover, so that
it can be used in all weathers.
Restaurant. Tables outdoors (12, terrace).

Star

38 St John's Wood Terrace, NW8 6LS (7722 1051).
St John's Wood tube. **Open** 11am-11pm Mon-Sat;
noon-10.30pm Sun. **Credit** MC, V.
With row upon row of opulent mansions served by myriad
locals gastropubs you might wonder where the ordinary folk
who inhabit the odd tower blocks nearby go to for a swifty.
The answer is this place – a quintessentially British pub
with some eccentric touches – such as the wonderfully kitsch
portrait of a Scottie dog in military commander's uniform.
The decor of green rag-rolled ceilings and red marble wallpaper is covered in pictures of sporting heroes or stars of the
silver screen, while a mahogany and marble fireplace is
presided over by an elaborate gold candelabra and clock. At
the square central bar you can try Worthington draught and
cream plus Bass and Carlsberg Export.
Games (fruit machine). Jukebox. Tables outdoors
(5, patio). TV (big screen).

Warrington Hotel

93 Warrington Crescent, W9 1EH (7286 2929).
Maida Vale tube. **Open** 11am-11pm Mon-Thur;
11am-midnight Fri, Sat; noon-10.30pm Sun. **Food**
served noon-2.30pm, 6-10pm daily. **Credit** MC, V.
The Warrington is surely one of London's most beautiful
hostelries. A great night (or Sunday afternoon) can always
be had here, but this is one of those venues (like Edinburgh's
Café Royal) that seems to be more atmospheric earlier in
the day, when it's practically deserted. The outlandishly
ornate main bar area is both grand and cosy, the ornate
horseshoe-shaped bar dispensing guest ales alongside regulars such as Fuller's ESB, John Smith's, London Pride and
Deuchars IPA, while a smaller bar area with TVs and a
dartboard ghettoises the sports crowd, leaving the main bar
as a haven for proper drinking and thinking. Thai food is
available upstairs. Rumoured to have once been a brothel,
this handsome pub seems to be enjoying a more respectable
time period, but remains a London original.
Games (darts, fruit machine, quiz machine). No piped
music or jukebox (main bar). Restaurant (no smoking).
Tables outdoors (12, courtyard). TV (big screen, satellite).

Waterway

54 Formosa Street, W9 2JU (7266 3557/www.the
waterway.co.uk). Warwick Avenue tube. **Open** noon-
11pm Mon-Sat; noon-10.30pm Sun. **Food served** 12.30-
3.30pm, 6.30-10.30pm daily. **Credit** AmEx, MC, V.
Although unprepossessing from the outside, this place is
a true delight for a warming beverage after a winter walk
alongside the canal. Scandinavian in feel, in summer the
sizeable outside deck area overlooks the barges bobbing
on the canal; it's as close to idyllic as an urban space surrounded by tower blocks can be. The elegant, modern

North

restaurant is the raison d'être, but the bar is also an easy space to occupy, whether for coffee, or a carefully made cocktail mixed with premium ingredients (the Norsk – muddled blackberries, gomme, fresh lemon juice and Smirnoff Norsk – in particular, stands out). Beer drinkers are offered Budvar, Flowers and Hoegaarden, and the wine list is pretty classy. Bar food includes steamed mussels for less than a tenner, while in summer frequent barbecues attract a host of revellers.
Bar available for hire. Restaurant (available for hire). Tables outdoors (20, garden).

Muswell Hill & Alexandra Palace

There may not be much to shout about but when one of the destinations offers the best views in London, bar none, you have to take notice.

Phoenix
Alexandra Palace Way, N22 7AY (8365 4356). Wood Green tube/Alexandra Palace rail/W3 bus. **Open** *Winter* 10.30am-8pm Mon-Thur; 10.30am-11pm Fri, Sat; 10.30am-10.30pm Sun. *Summer* 10am-11pm daily. **Food served** 11.30am-5pm daily. **Credit** MC, V.
With its faux-marble columns, giant spherical lightbulbs and huge industrial mural, the Phoenix tries to hark back to Alexandra Palace's Victorian heyday – not altogether successfully. Depending on what's on at Ally Pally, you could be supping your standard lager, Everards Sun Chaser or London Pride alongside with blinged-up boxing fans, antiques buyers or a selection of the nation's more dedicated knitters. But the reason the place is listed here is very simple: the view. Neither Primrose Hill nor Hampstead Heath can boast a pub which gives you a clear view all the way to Canary Wharf and beyond, from inside the bar. On a sunny summer's day, seated at one of the outside tables, it's a sheer joy.
Disabled: toilet. Function rooms. Tables outdoors (50, garden terrace). TV.

Victoria Stakes
1 Muswell Hill, N10 3TH (8815 1793/www.victoria stakes.co.uk). Finsbury Park tube/rail then W3, W7 bus. **Open** 5-11pm Mon-Thur; noon-midnight Fri, Sat; noon-10.30pm Sun. **Food served** 6-10.30pm Mon-Thur; noon-4pm, 6-10.30pm Fri, Sat; noon-9pm Sun. **Credit** AmEx, DC, MC, V.
Pubs located at major road junctions don't tend to have distinguished reputations. The Victoria Stakes, however, is no shoebox in a car park, being an elegant bar with a huge covered outdoor eating area and a restaurant upstairs. The heavy drapes, rugs and dark woods are leavened by some discreet modern lighting, so that the small, split-level bar never feels oppressive. Food's the order of the day here: there's a bar menu, but it's also possible to order from the restaurant menu (complete with table service), so that diners generally outnumber drinkers here. Those without an appetite can still enjoy Leffe and bottled Duvel or choose from an extensive wine list. It's a great place for a hearty lunch after a weekend trip to Alexandra Park.
Babies and children welcome. Games (board games). Music (acoustic band 8pm 1st Mon of mth; free). No-smoking area. Restaurant (no-smoking tables). Tables outdoors (20, garden).

Prince Alfred & Formosa Dining Rooms

North

Also in the area...

O'Neill's 87 Muswell Hill Broadway, N10 3HA (8883 7382).
Wetherspoons Unit 5, Spouter's Corner, High Road, N22 6EJ (8881 3891).

Primrose Hill

In spite of its class-A celeb count, there are more traditional than ground-breaking destination bars in the 'Hill, but when the **Engineer** or the **Lansdowne** is your local, who's complaining?

Albert

11 Princess Road, NW1 8JR (7722 1886). Chalk Farm tube. **Open** 11am-11pm Mon-Sat; noon-10.30pm Sun. **Food served** noon-2.30pm, 6.30-10pm Mon-Fri; noon-10pm Sat; noon-9.30pm Sun. **Credit** AmEx, MC, V.
Still as traditional as ever from the outside (the exterior resembles *Eastenders'* Queen Vic), the Albert's interior is now all wooden floors and friendly young Aussies behind the bar yet the place eschews the more self-conscious trend-setting of its neighbours. Simple decor creates a space where nothing is superfluous, and the same could be said of the standard drinks selection, which nevertheless covers most bases and seems to please the mixed, laid-back crowd of locals (it's not just literary types here, and the place is extremely family-friendly). The lovely beer garden plus pavement tables at the front are a definite plus come summer, and theme nights, including a quiz night on Tuesdays, plus pie and fish 'n' chip nights, are a further draw.
Babies and children welcome. Games (board games). Tables outdoors (16, garden). **Map 8 G1.**

Engineer

65 Gloucester Avenue , NW1 8JH (7722 0950/www.the-engineer.com). Chalk Farm tube/31, 168 bus. **Open** 9am-11pm Mon-Sat; 9am-10.30pm Sun. **Food served** 9-11.30am, noon-3pm, 7-11pm Mon-Fri; 9am-noon, 12.30-4pm, 7-11pm Sat; **Credit** MC, V.
The Engineer has enjoyed its current incarnation, as one of London's most stylish gastropubs, since 1995 and the food is certainly a large part of the draw here, with breakfast (eggs Benedict or buttermilk pancakes anyone?), lunch (organic cheeseburger?) and dinner (organic rib eye steak?) menus wooing locals and food critics alike. The carved wooden bar is beautifully kept (decorated with vases of flowers) and hosts a choice selection of drinks, including an excellent range of trendy spirits and a classy wine list. The wallpapered, homely, scrubbed interior has many fine touches, and the good-looking, new-bohemian clientele often catch sight of themselves in the antique wall mirrors; for the more laid-back experience, there's a gorgeous, heated patio out the back, while for those seeking more formality, there's an art-themed dining room.
Babies and children welcome. Disabled: toilet. Function rooms. No-smoking area (lunch Sun). **Map 8 G1.**

Lansdowne

90 Gloucester Avenue, NW1 8HX (7483 0409). Chalk Farm tube. **Open** 5-11pm Mon; noon-11pm Tue-Sat; noon-10.30pm Sun. **Food served** 7-10pm Mon; 12.30-3pm, 7-10pm Tue-Sat; 12.30-4pm, 7-9.30pm Sun. **Credit** MC, V.
The Lansdowne's vibe is provided largely by its clientele: either charming and characterful or rather egocentric and

irritating, depending on who is describing them, it's unarguably the loud guffawing that frequently sets the tone here (often driving the more low-key – read 'less posh' – customers to the safe haven near the fireplace). Staff take it in their stride, attempting to remain jovial. Drinks-wise, there's a good wine selection (scribbled up on the blackboard) and a standard selection of beers (including Tiger, Everards and Staropramen) and spirits. Olives provide the culinary accompaniment but for more substantial fare, own-made pizzas and pasta dishes can be had in the upstairs dining room.
Babies and children welcome. Disabled: toilet. Restaurant. Tables outdoors (8, pavement). **Map 8 G26.**

Pembroke Castle

150 Gloucester Avenue, NW1 8JA (7483 2927). Chalk Farm tube. **Open** 11am-11pm Mon-Sat; noon-11pm Sun. **Food served** noon-3pm, 6.30-9.45pm Mon-Fri; noon-6pm Sat, Sun. **Credit** AmEx, MC, V.
Although the Pembroke doesn't break new ground in terms of atmosphere or decor (think pine floors, gilt mirrors, and bunches of lilies), its friendly staff, decent-enough grub and high ceilings create a laid-back, sociable space in which a large variety of people unwind (from suits to fashionistas to odd-balls). Timothy Taylor Landlord is available alongside a more familiar line-up of lagers (such as London Pride, Grolsch and Carling) and spirits. A grandiose staircase leads up to a function room housing a large-screen TV, but perhaps the most mentionable feature of this pub is its spacious beer garden at the back, popular all year round due to its patio heaters but, not surprisingly, especially busy in summer with post-park punters.
Games (fruit machine; quiz machine). Tables outdoors (25, terrace). TVs (big screen, satellite). **Map 8 G26.**

Princess of Wales

22 Chalcot Road, NW1 8LL (7722 0354). Chalk Farm tube. **Open** 11am-11pm Mon-Sat; noon-10.30pm Sun. **Food served** noon-3pm, 7-9.30pm Mon-Sat; noon-5.30pm Sun. **Credit** AmEx, MC, V.
As the only pub in the area to still be resisting the modern refurb, the Princess houses an assortment of Primrose Hill originals shaken out of the nearby boozer-turned-gastropub joints with which it makes no attempt to compete. This pub is happy enough with its busy walls crammed with pictures, its well-worn seating, and its male-dominated clientele. The drinks selection doesn't need to be fancy, and it isn't (London Pride and Adnams), although the wine list does offer some surprises. But for those looking for traditional values over style, this friendly spot comes up trumps. Further draws are live jazz, and a basement bar.
Babies and children welcome. Function room. Music (jazz, 8.30pm Thur; noon Sun; free). Quiz (9pm Tue; £1). Tables outdoors (10, patio garden; 5, pavement). TV. **Map 8 G1.**

Queens

49 Regent's Park Road, NW1 8XD (7586 0408/www.geronimo-inns.co.uk). Chalk Farm tube. **Open** 11am-11pm Mon-Thur; 11am-midnight Fri, Sat; noon-10.30pm Sun. **Food served** noon-3pm, 7-10pm Mon-Thur; noon-3pm, 7-10.30pm Fri, Sat; 12.30-4pm, 7-9pm Sun. **Credit** MC, V.
The displays of bottled fruits and the wicker baskets filled with dried shrubs (plus various assorted knick-knacks) give this gastropub a rustic feel. Run by Young's since 1991, it's nonetheless a pub with its own flavour. Tight and intimate, it houses a band of well-established regulars, and

manages to avoid the pretentiousness of nearby spots. The beers on offer include a good-enough range, with Young's on draught, plus Red Stripe and Hoegaarden (although we've had the odd duff pint of bitter on occasion), and the wine selection is pretty broad too. Enjoy a glass of red with your pheasant casserole (sitting by the fireplace); alternatively, the richly textured dining room upstairs boasts its own little balcony.
Tables outdoors (3, balcony; 3, pavement). **Map 8 G1.**

Stoke Newington

It's all around Church Street, and the **Shakespeare, Fox Reformed**, and beer-lovers' **Rose & Crown** are still going strong, but happily we now find gastro action at the **Alma** by Newington Green.

Alma

59 Newington Green Road, N1 4QU (7359 4536/ www.the-alma.co.uk). Highbury & Islington tube/rail/ Canonbury rail . **Open** 5-11pm Mon-Wed; noon-11pm Thur-Sat; noon-10.30pm Sun. **Food served** 7-10.30pm Mon-Wed; 12.30-3pm, 7-10.30pm Thur, Fri; 1-4pm, 7-10.30pm Sat; 1-4pm, 7-10pm Sun. **Credit** MC, V.
Sitting in the Alma on a sunny afternoon sinking a pint or two can be a visually arresting experience. The vast bay windows that sweep across the bar's front look out onto a solid wall of lush greenery, despite the pub being slap-bang on the main bendy bus artery to Stamford Hill. Light pours through like a hazy, golden, big-budget beer commercial, perfect for freelance afternoons flicking through the dailies or working on the novel. Which pretty much sums up the clientele. Availability of tables can be squeezed when the food side of things is at its most popular. The kitchen is increasingly hit and miss (matching the service on occasion), but the odd miracle does emerge from it. Courage and Director's are available on draught, but the lager selection, headed by Kronenbourg, is largely unremarkable.
Babies and children welcome. Bar available for hire. Games (board games). Music (pianist 4pm alternate Sun; free). No-smoking area. Quiz (8pm 3rd Mon of mth; £1). Tables outdoors (4, pavement; 8, courtyard).

Auld Shillelagh

105 Stoke Newington Church Street, N16 0UD (7249 5951). Stoke Newington rail/73, 476 bus. **Open** 11am-11pm Mon-Sat; noon-10.30pm Sun. **Credit** MC, V.
The exterior of this pub, resplendent with its claret façade and mirrored signage, is the prettiest in the area. It looks pocket-sized but in fact, like many of the bars along Church Street, it's thin but very long and benefits from a massive dog-friendly backyard. OK, so the crowd isn't particularly cutting edge, but the twenty and thirtysomethings mix well with the ageing 'oirish' barflys, with little in the way of clique to intimidate a Shillelagh newbie. Come for the Guinness, widely considered to be the best in North London by stout connoisseurs. Perfectly pulled black stuff, or a John Smith's or Foster's if you are that way inclined, complement Friday night music sessions and a good craic throughout the week.
TV (big screen, satellite).

Daniel Defoe

102 Stoke Newington Church Street, N16 0LA (7254 2906). Stoke Newington rail/73, 393, 476 bus. **Open** 1-11.30pm Mon; 1pm-12.30am Tue-Fri; noon-12.30am Sat; noon-11.30pm Sun. **Food served** 1-9.30pm Mon-Thur; 1-7pm Fri; noon-7pm Sat, Sun. **Credit** MC, V.

The Defoe is blatantly anti-fashion in a knick-knacky kind of way, yet still manages to draw in a crowd more at home in the aspirational bars of Shoreditch than supping Bombardier, Directors or Eagle ale (although the appearance of Japanese Kirin lager lends an interesting twist). But what the place lacks in cool it makes up for in warmth. OK, so the landlord may not smile much but you never feel anything less than welcome. And with game pie and some great sausage options on the food menu, and a sleeping dog by the roaring fire, all seems well with the world. The small backyard is nothing more than an afterthought, but the pub's front and back rooms are big enough to make getting an inside table a good possibility. File under 'cosy'.
Games (fruit machine). Tables outdoors (10, garden). TV.

Fox Reformed

176 Stoke Newington Church Street, N16 0JL (7254 5975/www.fox-reformed.co.uk). Stoke Newington rail/ 73, 393, 476 bus. **Open** 5-11pm Mon-Fri; noon-11pm Sat, Sun. **Food served** 6.30-10.30pm Mon-Fri; noon-3pm, 6.30-10.30pm Sat, Sun. **Credit** AmEx, DC, MC, V.
It's hard to find fault with the Fox, a lovely wine bar. OK, maybe the lighting could be a little gentler, and sometimes the (thankfully unobtrusive) music is a bit off-key, but the only real problem is the difficulty in securing a table. As evident by the mountains of corks in the windows the emphasis here is on wine, with some adventurous varieties peppering a menu that also does some of the best food on Church Street. A simple steak or 'variation on sausage and mash' is all that's needed. The Fox's hosts, Robbie and Carol, have run the bar for over 20 years and have a loyal crowd of regulars.
Entertainment (backgammon club 7.30pm Mon; book club, phone for details; wine-tasting club 7pm alt Thur; £30 a year). Games (board games). No-smoking tables. Tables outdoors (5, heated garden).

Lion

132 Stoke Newington Church Street, N16 0JX (7249 1318/www.massivepub.com). Stoke Newington rail/ 73, 476 bus. **Open** 3-11pm Mon, Tue; 3pm-midnight Wed-Sat; noon-10.30pm Sun. **Credit** AmEx, MC, V.
Ground Zero for Stoke Newington social life. The main room has, with the removal of its stained glass partition, opened up a lot and there's now regular cabaret and comedy upstairs. The back yard offers an escape from the big-screen footie on match days, and even though they don't do food they'll supply you with cutlery and plates and a very drinkable Hazy View chenin blanc if you want to order in from a comprehensive menu of local delivery firms. Bombardier joins Foster's, Kronenbourg, San Miguel and Guinness on tap. The core clientele is made up of trainerspotter boys with ironic beards, and their girlfriends.
Comedy (8pm Thur; £5). Function room. Music (open mic 8.30pm Wed; free). Quiz (8.30pm Mon; £1). Tables outdoors (8, garden). TV (big screen, satellite).

Londesborough

36 Barbauld Road, N16 0SS (7254 5865). Stoke Newington rail/73 bus. **Open** 4.30-11pm Mon-Thur; 4.30pm-midnight Fri; noon-midnight Sat; noon-10.30pm Sun. **Food served** 5-10pm Mon-Fri; noon-4.30pm, 5-10pm Sat, Sun. **Credit** MC, V.
Not the most intimate of places despite an open fire and a decent amount of soft furnishings, the Londesborough is still a gleaming example of what's possible when it comes to gentrifying an old boozer. A chalkboard wine list covers all of the grape bases and the draught is diverse enough

North

(Sidestreet, Pedigree, Adnams and Harveys on one side, Staropramen, San Miguel and Hoegaarden on the other) to satisfy most tastes. The backyard has had a Soho House-style makeover with a swish barbecue area and some very posh garden furniture, and when the sun shines it can often feel like a chic private party. The down side (for the child-free) is the proliferation of toddlers who seem to invade every Sunday afternoon, and a blaring sound system at night. *Babies and children welcome (until 6pm). Music (DJs 8pm Fri, Sat; free). Tables outdoors (12, garden).*

Prince

59 Kynaston Road, N16 0EB (7923 4766/www.prince pub.com). Stoke Newington rail/73, 106 bus. **Open** noon-11pm Mon-Thur; noon-midnight Fri, Sat; noon-10.30pm Sun. **Food served** noon-2.30pm, 5-10pm Mon-Fri; noon-4pm, 5.30-10pm Sat; noon-4pm, 5.30-9pm Sun. **Credit** MC, V.

The Prince is a temple to the colour palettes of Farrow and Ball, drenched in dark gothic shades with a once-radical industrial-looking zinc bar. The effect is rather elegant. The narrow L-shaped room gives up over half of its floor space to well heeled couples and families dining, so when there's a run on spicy gourmet burgers from the kitchen you might find yourself standing near the fireplace or edged into the small garden. The food can be excellent but comes at a premium. Service is always nothing less than friendly and there's a decent range on draught: Stella, Carlsberg, Guinness, Staropramen, Leffe, Hoegaarden, San Miguel, London Pride, Bass and IPA, in addition to a solid wine list. Somewhat incongruous with its upmarket image, the Prince's weekly pub quiz is a delight.
Babies and children welcome (until 5pm). Quiz (8.30pm Tue; £1). Tables outdoors (8, garden). TV.

Rose & Crown

199 Stoke Newington Church Street, N16 9ES (7254 7497). Stoke Newington rail/73, 393, 476 bus. **Open** 11.30am-midnight Mon-Sat; noon-midnight Sun. **Food served** noon-2.30pm Mon-Fri; noon-3.30pm Sat, Sun. **Credit** MC, V.

The R&C feels like an historic country pub while its rich wood-panelled interior, with seats fashioned from beer barrels, resembles the captain's quarters of a tall ship. It certainly wouldn't benefit from any licks of modernity; it revels in handsome '30s fustiness. There's a coal fire, unobtrusive TV for match days and a dining area that does overwhelmingly generous and tasty portions of pie, though late on a Sunday the roasts tend to be a little overdone. Very much a beer lovers' pub, there is a fantastic and well tended selection of draught including Budweiser, Holsten Export, Martin's Pedigree, Fuller's London Pride, Theakston XP and IPA as well as one guest ale.
Games (fruit machine, quiz machine). Quiz (8.30pm Tue; £1). TV (satellite).

Shakespeare

57 Allen Road, N16 8RY (7254 4190). Bus 73, 141, 476. **Open** 5-11pm Mon-Fri; noon-11pm Sat; noon-10.30pm Sun. **Credit** MC, V.

The most archetypal Stokey pub of them all is tucked away in a residential enclave like a well-kept wonderful secret. There's uncomfortable church pew seating, Morrissey on the (free!) jukebox, pickled eggs and a clientele that runs the gamut from musicians to cycle couriers. Most newcomers become instant regulars. It's all quite, quite fabulous in a slightly spit-and-sawdust kind of way, though the unpolished interior isn't without a few knowing theatrical

flourishes and there's a rather tatty backyard and picnic tables behind the railings on the street for those summer moments. It can get a little rowdy late in the evening, but never scary. The booze is taken as seriously as the ambience, with an exemplary draught selection of Guinness, Hoegaarden, Leffe, Scrumpy Jack, Litovel, London Pride, Adnams, and Discovery as well as a guest ale.
Babies and children welcome (until 7pm). Games (board games, cards, cribbage, dominoes). Quiz (8.45pm Mon; £1). Tables outdoors (12, covered garden). TV (satellite).

Also in the area...

Rochester Castle (JD Wetherspoon) 145 High Street, N16 0NY (7249 6016).

West Hampstead

It's not exactly teeming with bars here: thank goodness for **No.77**.

Gallery

190 Broadhurst Gardens, NW6 3AY (7625 9184). West Hampstead tube/rail. **Open** 4-11pm Mon; 4-11.30pm Tue-Thur; noon-midnight Fri, Sat; noon-11pm Sun. **Food served** 5-9pm Mon-Fri; 12.30-4.30pm, 6-9pm Sat, Sun. **Happy hour** 5-7pm daily. **Credit** DC, MC, V.

This stylish compact bar is set out on three levels, with the shrewd addition of an ornate wrought iron balcony area to maximise space. The large windows, topped with art deco stained glass, open out onto the street in summer months. The Gallery has a distinctly colonial air from the whirring overhead fans to the dark-wood floors and rich maroon walls – though they are adorned with Hitchcock posters and fairly naff impressionist art. The atmosphere is relaxed with a mixture of low music and chat from the young well-heeled crowd enjoying Erdinger, Leffe and Kirin at the bar, while a more intimate candle-lit restaurant downstairs serves a fusion of British and modern European cuisine.
Games (board games). Restaurant (no-smoking area).

No.77 Wine Bar

77 Mill Lane, NW6 1NB (7435 7787). West Hampstead tube/rail. **Open** 6-11pm Mon; noon-11pm Tue; noon-midnight Wed-Sat; noon-10.30pm Sun. **Food served** 6-10.30pm Mon; noon-10.30pm Tue; noon-11.30pm Wed-Sat; noon-10pm Sun. **Credit** MC, V.

Unlike many bars of this type, No.77 is stylish but unpretentious which makes it exceptionally charming. The walls are hung with African art, carvings and lovingly signed sports shirts. The four separate areas, although on ground level, have a cavernous subterranean feel but the friendly staff help to give the place a warm atmosphere. Decent food includes fish pie (£10.45), and some sumptuous desserts. There's only Budvar on tap but an excellent wine list more than makes up for this with nearly 40 wines, most by the glass, including very popular La Serre sauvingon blanc (£15.40). A popular venue for rugger matches.
Function room. Tables outdoors (8, pavement).

Also in the area...

Eclipse West Hampstead 283-285 West End Lane, NW6 1RD (7794 7817).
Walkabout O₂ Centre, 255 Finchley Road, NW3 6LU (7433 6570).
Wetherspoons O₂ Centre, 255 Finchley Road, NW3 6LU (7433 0920).

North

South

Balham

Balhamites enjoy the best of all worlds as the area's gentrification continues: gastro delights at the **Balham Kitchen & Bar**, perhaps, or comedy at the **Bedford**.

Balham Kitchen & Bar
15-19 Bedford Hill, SW12 9EX (8675 6900/www. balhamkitchen.com). Balham tube/rail. **Open** 8am-midnight Mon-Thur; 8am-1am Fri, Sat; 8am-10.30pm Sun. **Food served** 8am-11pm Mon-Fri; 8am-4.30pm, 5.30-11pm Sat; 8am-4.30pm, 5.30-10pm Sun. **Credit** AmEx, MC, V.
Upstairs, this Soho House outpost is more kitchen than bar, with most of the seating area given over to a restaurant that is lined with leather-studded bench seating and typically a dressed-up clientele. Here, the flatscreens play old black-and-white movies to a funky, disconnected soundtrack and light emerges from wire-and-driftwood lampshades. Confit duck dips a leg into bubble and squeak for £12, coq meets vin at £11 and lamb racks in at £14 (restaurant prices, then). The largely Old World wine list offers five of both red and white, plus a couple of rosés, all available by the glass from £5. If there are no seats at the stainless steel bar with its inset ice buckets, check out the downstairs 'playroom'; playfully decorated with faux animal skins, the obligatory leather sofas, white cubes of light and a Perspex bar.
Babies and children welcome. Disabled: toilet. Function room. Music (DJ 10pm Fri, Sat; free). No-smoking area. Tables outdoors (6, pavement). TV (big screen, satellite).

Bedford
77 Bedford Hill, SW12 9HD (8682 8940/www.the bedford.co.uk). Balham tube/rail. **Open** 10am-midnight Mon-Thur, Sun; 10am-2am Fri, Sat. **Food served** noon-3pm, 7-10pm Mon-Sat; noon-5pm, 7-10pm Sun. **Credit** MC, V.
Not so much a pub as an entertainment centre, the multi-roomed Bedford is a perfect example of how large pubs can diversify. The main room has an open fire, live music most evenings (sometimes involving the house piano) and discreet flatscreens above the bar, plus an open food-counter serving dishes like own-made burgers (£7.95) or corn-fed poussin, herb couscous and rocket pesto (£11.95). The balconied back room is in the round and a perfect venue for watching sport or the comedy. Friday nights see the Banana Cabaret take over this and the ornate Victorian upstairs room, with four comics circulating between the two. Other nights in the upstairs section include even salsa classes. There's 6X, Young's, Courage and London Pride on tap, plus the usual lagers. If these bits of the pub sound a bit posh, there's a separate spit-and-sawdust wing.
Babies and children admitted (until 6pm). Comedy (9pm Tue; £3; 7.30pm Fri; £8-£12; 6.30pm Sat; £12-£15). Dance (line dancing 7.30pm Mon; £5; swing classes 8pm Tue; £8-£10; salsa classes 7.45pm Wed; £5). Disabled: toilet. Function rooms. Games (board games, fruit machines). Music (bands 9pm Mon, Tue, Thur; free; acoustic 9pm Wed; free; jazz 8pm Sun; £5). Nightclub (11.15pm-2am Fri, Sat; £5). Quiz (8.30pm Wed; £1). TV (big screen, satellite).

Exhibit
12 Balham Station Road, SW12 9SG (8772 6556/ www.theexhibit.co.uk). Balham tube/rail. **Open** 11.30am-11pm Mon-Thur; 11.30am-midnight Fri, Sat; 11.30am-10.30pm Sun. **Food served** noon-3pm, 7-10.30pm Mon-Sat; noon-4pm Sun. **Credit** AmEx, MC, V.
This squat, modernist cube comprising bar, first-floor restaurant and second-floor sometime cinema makes no apologies for abutting the Sainsbury's car park – nor should it. 'Music to Watch Girls By' creates a chilled mood and, in the unlikely event of there being no people-watching opportunities, the splendid fish tank set into the back wall is always diverting. Low light and equally low seating sneak under the stairs and lounge by the gas fire, while backlit walls of images of grass and autumn leaves similarly mellow the metrosexual crowd. The cocktail menu offers mango Mai Tais, Daiquiris and Cosmopolitans from £6. The user-friendly wine list is laid out by the grape, with six of each colour by the glass. Draught beers include Kirin, Budvar and Amstel, and bottles include Bombardier, banana-flavoured bitter, Erdinger weissbier and Duvel.
Babies and children admitted (until 7pm). Disabled: toilet. Film screenings (8.45pm Tue; £5). Function room. Restaurant (no smoking). Tables outdoors (8, garden; 12, pavement).

Grove
39 Oldridge Road, SW12 8PN (8673 6531). Clapham South tube/Balham tube/rail. **Open** 11am-midnight Mon-Sat; noon-11pm Sun. **Food served** noon-10.30pm Mon-Sat; noon-9.30pm Sun. **Credit** MC, V.
The Grove keeps itself to itself in the no-man's land between Balham and Clapham South. It is not easy to stumble across, a fact most of the genteel regulars quietly applaud, slightly smug in their seclusion. The Grove is a Young's pub whose potted plants, wisteria pergola and subtle colour scheme scream outdoor sophistication and give a fitting introduction to the ornate ceilings and door frames, two-tone battleship grey and muted turquoise walls, and open fire inside. The front bar is a deep blood-red and furnished with leather sofas. Cherry Belle-Vue, Kronenbourg Blanc and Leffe Blonde prop up the usual draught suspects and there is a whole range of bottled Young's ales. Eleven of each colour wine range from £12 to £42 per bottle, with around half available by the glass.
Babies and children admitted (restaurant). Games (board games). Quiz (8pm alternate Sun; £2). Restaurant (no smoking). Tables outdoors (9, terrace).

Also in the area...

Balham Tup 21 Chestnut Grove, SW12 8JB (8772 0546).

Moon Under Water (JD Wetherspoon) 194 Balham High Street, SW12 9BP (8673 0535).

Battersea

There's no shortage of bars around Battersea, but we're especially fond of the **Artesian Well**, **Le Bouchon Bordelais**, the **Dovedale** and, above all, the exemplary **Dusk**. And although the Tea Rooms des Artistes is no more, hurrah for its replacement, **Lost Society**.

Artesian Well

693 Wandsworth Road, SW8 3JF (7627 3353/ www.artesianwell.co.uk). Clapham Common tube/ Wandsworth Town rail. **Open** 5pm-3am Fri, Sat. **Credit** AmEx, MC, V.
The Artesian Well is a phantasmagorical production; a cross between *Lord of the Rings* and Dante's *Inferno*, spread over five bars on three levels – gargoyles, unicorns, devils and angels leap out from a backdrop of red velvet drapes and decadent scenes from ancient history. Four of the five rooms are mainly for private hire, the louche Sofa Bar and Speed Room at ground level visible from a hexagonal glass panel in the floor of the Moody Room upstairs, adjacent to the Red Room. When open to all at weekends, the main Front Bar has an atmosphere not unlike the hedonism depicted on the walls, as DJs pump funky house and other happy dance music to queues of paying punters. Funny to think that this was the Nag's Head until fairly recently.
Disabled: toilet. Function rooms. Music (DJs 9.30pm Fri, Sat; £3-£5). **Map 11 K16**.

Corum

30-32 Queenstown Road, SW8 3RX (7720 5445/ www.corumrestaurants.com). Battersea Park, Queenstown Road or Clapham Junction rail/77, 137, 156, 345 bus. **Open** 5pm-3am Mon-Fri; noon-3am Sat, Sun. **Food served** 5pm-midnight Mon-Fri; noon-midnight Sat, Sun. **Credit** AmEx, MC, V.
There have been some changes at the Corum. The recently foodie operation has moved away from the culinary side of things, kicked off its slingbacks and relaxed into its role as a chic lounge bar. Food is still available, but the menu headings say it all: Simple and Tasty, Bigger and Better, Sweet and Sexy. It adds up to a steak sandwich with salad and mustard dressing in ciabatta for £8.95. The capacity has been increased to 250, but it is open to debate how much room is needed midweek when the thirtysomething clientele prefers to frequent the place at weekends. In Corum's favour, a late licence runs even at the start of the week, and you can count on a good wine list and reasonably priced cocktails every day. Funky house music is spun on the decks on Fridays.
Disabled: toilet. Music (DJs 10pm Fri, Sat; free). No-smoking area. Tables outdoors (6, pavement).

Dovedale House

441 Battersea Park Road, SW11 4LR (7223 7721). Battersea Park rail/44, 49, 344, 345 bus. **Open** noon-11pm Mon-Thur, Sun; noon-midnight Fri, Sat. **Food served** noon-3pm, 6-10pm Mon-Fri; noon-4pm, 6-10pm Sat, Sun. **Credit** MC, V.

Now well established, the Dovedale is a handy hangout in what was a forgotten corner of Battersea. Local photographers are happy with it too – their work adorns the pale walls, beneath ornate chandeliers. Commanding your immediate attention, though, is the golden Buddha sitting proudly behind a curvaceous bar. Another bar, newly installed, stands in a beer garden embellished with ironwork sculpture, accessed through an intimate patio. Inside or out, the range of beers is excellent: Paulaner wheat beer, Sleeman, Adnams and various bottled options. The wine list is equally extensive and nicely priced – Stump Jump grenache shiraz at £17.70, for example. The mosaic-styled open kitchen serves simple, tasty fare: a Dovedale bacon-and-cheese burger with red onion, tomato, gherkins and lettuce costs £6.50. The smart, young professional crowd pack in for free jazz nights on Sundays.
Babies and children welcome. Disabled: toilet. Games (football table). Music (jazz 8pm Sun; free). Tables outdoors (15, garden).

Dusk

339 Battersea Park Road, SW11 4LF (7622 2112/ www.duskbar.co.uk). Battersea Park rail. **Open** 6pm-12.30am Mon-Wed; 6pm-1.30am Thur-Sat. **Food served** 6-10.30pm Mon-Sat. **Credit** AmEx, MC, V.
The most notable thing about Dusk is not the awards showered on it – from ourselves included – but its prices. For less than a bland burger from inferior kitchens round the corner, you can tuck into yakitori chicken with red pepper dipping sauce, or tiger prawn skewers with mirin dip. For the price of a nameless vodka with carton orange juice nearby, you can sip award-winning and inventive concoctions created from high-end brands and fresh fruit. 'Affordable luxuries' the PR blurb calls it – and it's right. A candlelit dark-wood interior is set into three spaces: a lounge with leather cube chairs; a VIP/members' section, roped off and always crowded; and a large back area. Recommended are cocktails – Ketel One Citron, lemongrass-infused Wyborowa and Woodford Reserve – and the reserve wine list which includes a crisp Oyster Bay pinot noir (£29) and a deliciously dry Chablis Domaine Moloussin Moreau (£26). Ali Akkache's Med- and Oriental-influenced dishes (about £5), exotically dipped and drizzled, comprise the sharing platters (£14-£18). Add oysters to the seafood variety for the £21 full monty. Exceptional.
Dress: smart casual. Music (DJs 9pm Wed-Sat; free). Tables outdoors (10, terrace).

Fox & Hounds

66-68 Latchmere Road, SW11 2JU (7924 5483). Clapham Junction rail. **Open** 5-11pm Mon; noon-2.30pm, 5-11pm Tue-Thur; noon-11pm Fri, Sat; noon-10.30pm Sun. **Food served** 7-10.30pm Mon-Thur; 12.30-3pm, 7-10.30pm Fri, Sat; 12.30-4pm, 7-10pm Sun. **Credit** MC, V.
A top-notch gastropub this, doing justice to the ground floor of an impressive Victorian building. The backdrop is impeccable too: dark red ceilings are supported by ornate black columns set on a rough wooden floor, vintage mirrors adorn the walls. Good taste is extended to the rustic modern European cuisine, with delicate touches added to dishes such as risotto with mixed peppers, balsamic molasses and parmesan (£7.50) and daily specials chalked up on the blackboard. The young, professional crowd have little problem finding a wine to accompany their meal – the list is long and varied – and ales include Harveys Best and Deuchars IPA. A good continental lager would be welcome, but it's a minor criticism. The summer garden and gentle

South

clatter from the open kitchen provide welcome diversions from the trains rattling over the nearby railway bridge on this otherwise bleak stretch of Battersea pavement. *Babies and children admitted (until 7pm). Disabled: toilet. Tables outdoors (10, garden). TV.*

Halo

317 Battersea Park Road, SW11 4LT (7801 8683). Battersea Park or Queenstown Road rail. **Open** 6pm-midnight Mon-Thur; 6pm-2am Fri, Sat. **Credit** MC, V.
Soon to celebrate its first anniversary, this decorative style bar is a poorly kept secret. It doesn't help that it plays host to all manner of performances on any given night of the week. Spoken word, stand-up, short plays or live music make up the constantly changing programme – there's even a grand piano set on the small stage in the corner, a cue for local musicians to come up and tinkle on Tuesday evenings. DJs blast out tribal house at weekends. The tasteful decor, around an island bar, of candelabra and sculptures, displays local artwork. On offer are standard beers plus Pilsner Urquell and Hoegaarden, and a few wines, but no kitchen as yet. A regular boho crowd add to the relaxed, underground ambience. A boon in often bland Battersea. *Bar available for hire. Music (DJs 8.30pm Fri, Sat; free; jazz quartet 8.30pm Mon; £3-£5).*

Holy Drinker

59 Northcote Road, SW11 1NP (7801 0544/www.holy drinker.co.uk). Clapham Junction rail/35, 37 bus. **Open** 4.30-11pm Mon-Thur; 4.30pm-midnight Fri; noon-midnight Sat; 1-11pm Sun. **Credit** MC, V.
Little change at this landmark trendy drinkerie, one of Battersea's first style bars. Comfortable and fashionable, the Holy Drinker is a neat combination of wine bar and style bar, its loyal crowd of regulars more demanding and discerning than your average Battersea hooray. Just look at the beer fridge, from which colourful continental labels beckon; the draught options are equally attractive: Old Speckled Hen and Summer Lightning for ale lovers, Schneider Weisse and Hahn the less-common light options. There is a good selection of wine and bubbly by the glass. Not much is offered by way of food, but that matters little to the somewhat boho mob who slouch on the couches towards the back, enjoying a reliably interesting soundtrack of mainly ambient dance music. *Babies and children admitted (until 7pm). Tables outdoors (4, pavement). TV.*

Iniquity

8-10 Northcote Road, SW11 1NT (7924 6699/www. iniquitybar.com). Clapham Junction rail. **Open** 5-11pm Mon-Wed; 5pm-midnight Thur, Fri; 3pm-midnight Sat; 3-10.30pm Sun. **Food served** 5-10.30pm Mon-Fri; 3-9.30pm Sat, Sun. **Credit** AmEx, MC, V.
Iniquity is a cut above other Northcote Road contenders by dint of the attention paid to quality and detail on its comprehensive and imaginative cocktail list. In-house mixologist and manager Tim Oakley (Sand, Babington House, People's Republic) conjures up creative and classy combinations such as Sour Susie (pisco and prunes) and Bees Knees (with Manuka honey vodka) for a well-heeled crowd. The bar promises 'salacious sinning', but the nearest you'll get is by sampling the Porn Star Martinis. Sassy waitresses will serve you at your table if you can't be bothered with the bar throng. The lacquer, leather and thick red drapes give the place a cosy feel in winter and there's a small outside area for when the sun is shining. There's a standard tapas, sharing dish and bar food menu and pro-

motional offers such as beer and a burger for £8.50 when the big screen is rolled out for this area's beloved rugby. The sound system pumps out run-of-the-mill funky house. *Disabled: toilet. Tables outdoors (10, terrace). TV (big screen).*

Latchmere

503 Battersea Park Road, SW11 3BW (7223 3549). Battersea Park or Clapham Junction rail/44, 49, 344, 345 bus. **Open** noon-11pm Mon-Sat; noon-10.30pm Sun. **Food served** noon-3pm, 5-10pm Mon-Fri; noon-9pm Sat, Sun. **Credit** MC, V.
This large and popular drinking hole sits on the busy junction of Battersea Bridge Road and Battersea Park Road, and is a welcome escape from the traffic. It's a vintage space, with dark polished-wood panels softly lit by candles and side lamps, and battered and studded sofas clustering around the fireplace to one side. Upstairs, the Latchmere theatre is one of London's best fringe venues; there's nothing better after a spot of theatre than a debate over a pint, and the draught here includes Young's and Adnams Bitter, John Smith's and Kronenbourg; in bottles, there's Stella, Budvar, Michelob and others, alongside alcopops. The beer garden is pleasant in summer – barbecues are available on request. *Babies and children admitted (until 7pm). Games (fruit machines, quiz machine). Quiz (9pm Thur; £1). Tables outdoors (10, garden). Theatre (nightly; box office 7978 7040). TVs (big screen, satellite).*

Le Bouchon Bordelais

5-9 Battersea Rise, SW11 1HG (7738 0307). Clapham Junction rail/35, 37 bus. **Open** 10am-11pm Mon-Thur; 10am-1am Fri, Sat; 10am-10.30pm Sun. **Food served** 10am-10pm daily. **Credit** AmEx, MC, V.

South

A high-standard, authentically French brasserie, Le Bouchon runs equally as well as a bar, its snacks and light meals superbly executed, its commitment to televised sport ensuring a mix of clientele from either side of the Channel. The all-French wine list begins with a house Petit Mas (£3.50/£5/£13.95), with eight other varieties by the glass and a long selection by the bottle, Pouilly-Fuissé Michel Delorme (£39) and Château Rahoul Graves (£35) the priciest. Standard cocktails (£5.50) include a Bouchon of Cointreau, cassis, cranberry juice and Champagne; Kronenbourg is the draught beer of choice. Lunch and evening menus are similar and Gallic in tone: a dozen snails in garlic and parsley butter (£6.95), moules marinière (£7.95), steak-frites (£9.50). Mention must be made of the superior breakfasts, oeuf Florentine (poached egg, spinach, cheese and mornay sauce, £4.80) a fine example. Desserts are creations of equal finery, rum baba and chantilly (£5.50) and a tasty range of fruit and cream tarts. A weekend lunchtime crèche is a boon for the arriviste families on this side of Clapham Common.
Babies and children welcome. Disabled: toilet. Function room. No-smoking area. Restaurant. Tables outdoors (15, terrace). TV (big screen, satellite).

Lost Society
697 Wandsworth Road, SW8 3JF (7652 6526/www. lostsociety.co.uk). Clapham Common tube/77, 77A bus. **Open** 5pm-1am Tue-Thur; 4pm-2am Fri; 11am-2am Sat; 11am-1am Sun. **Food served** 5-11pm Tue-Thur; 4-11pm Fri; 11am-11pm Sat, Sun. **Credit** AmEx, MC, V.
What was the Tea Room des Artistes has been made even more alluring with modish chandeliers, but still feels louche, hidden and intimate. The drinks list includes some interesting bottled beers (German wheat beers, English ales and fruity Belgians), but the cocktails are best of all. There's a choice of eight bourbons and whiskies, top-brand gins and vodkas for Martinis; and classics line up with modern creations, such as Berrylicious (berries crushed with cachaça, vanilla syrup and limes, £6) – a very long, well-made drink. The food too might bring a smile to Gordon Ramsay's lips. Lamb shank was tender and beautifully cooked; retro-sounding chicken supreme was made contemporary with Taleggio cheese stuffing and thyme-scented new potatoes. DJ sets start at 8pm from Thursday to Saturday, in the loft where Rob da Bank once played. Let's hope it doesn't get too popular – taxis of idiots from Chelsea would ruin this south-side gem.
Music (DJs 8pm Thur-Sun; free). Tables outdoors (20, garden; 10, terrace). **Map 11 K16**.

Masons Arms
169 Battersea Park Road, SW8 4BT (7622 2007). Battersea Park rail/137, 417 bus. **Open** noon-11pm Mon-Sat; noon-10.30pm Sun. **Food served** noon-3pm, 6-10pm Mon-Fri; noon-5pm, 6-10pm Sat; noon-5pm, 6.30-9pm Sun. **Credit** AmEx, MC, V.
Under a railway bridge opposite Battersea Park station is not where you'd expect to find a gastropub of this quality. Warm in winter, airy in summer, the Masons is a pub for all seasons. Unmatching candlelit wooden tables are set on a rough floor, against a backdrop of oak panels, pale yellow walls and columns decorated with ironworks. A young smart set float in on the delightful aromas from the large open kitchen, which produces such delights as poached smoked haddock with Indian-spiced cauliflower and leeks (£12.50) or baked portobello mushrooms with couscous (£9). You've plenty of choice for accompanying wine or beer. Select a fine, peachy Yalumba viognier (£17)

South

Garrison. *See p196.*

or pint of Pride or Leffe, and settle back. Style bars are in abundance deeper into Battersea, so it's nice to find a high-quality, old-fashioned alternative.
Babies and children welcome (until 6pm). Disabled: toilet. Restaurant (no smoking). Tables outdoors (6, pavement).

Matilda

74-76 Battersea Bridge Road, SW11 3AG (7228 6482/www.matilda.tv). Clapham Junction rail then 319 bus/South Kensington tube then 45 or 345 bus. **Open** noon-1am daily. **Food served** noon-3pm, 6-10.30pm daily. **Credit** AmEx, MC, V.

A delightful bar-cum-restaurant a few hundred yards from Battersea Bridge, Matilda has a refined but relaxed air, and gives guests a warm reception. The interior is a subtle mix of mint green and vanilla, with interesting tapestries hung around the compact but extensively stocked bar. The food served in the back-room restaurant (booking essential) is good, but there's also a more casual bar menu that offers picks from the chef's specials board, along with a fine choice of Italian hams and bread. The wine list is well thought out too, and there's a small number of beers on tap: Pilsner Urquell, Amstel and Adnams Bitter. Well worth a visit.
Babies and children admitted. Disabled: toilet. Function room. No-smoking area. Tables outdoors (5, garden; 5, pavement). TV.

Microbar

14 Lavender Hill, SW11 5RW (7228 5300/www. microbar.org). Clapham Common tube/Clapham Junction or Wandsworth Road rail/77, 77A, 137, 159 bus. **Open** 6pm-midnight Mon-Fri; 4pm-midnight Sat, Sun. **Food served** 6-10pm Mon-Fri; 4-10pm Sat, Sun. **Credit** MC, V.

Beer is the reason to come to this splendid little bar – beer, genial staff and a funky little atmosphere. With more than a hundred beers on offer from every part of the world (Alaska!), it's handy that the huge list is as informative as the chatty, knowledgeable bar crew, who are happy to make recommendations. Unsurprisingly, Belgian brews feature highly, Westvleteren 8 and 12 ('This is beer perfection. This is beer bliss.'), Boon Gueuze (you don't want to know about the preparation), Rochefort 8... There are plenty of American types too: Anchor Liberty on draught and Anchors by the bottle, and Goose Island Honkers (isn't that rude?) from Chicago. Funky music, low lighting and cosy leather sofas create a laid-back atmosphere and encourage you to sample widely. Just remember it's a long walk home.
Bar available for hire. Games (backgammon, chess, cards). Quiz (8pm alternate Wed; £2).

S Bar

37 Battersea Bridge Road, SW11 3BA (7223 3322). Sloane Square tube then 19, 49, 319 bus/Clapham Junction rail. **Open** noon-midnight Mon-Thur; noon-2am Fri, Sat; noon-11pm Sun. **Food served** noon-3pm, 6-10pm Mon-Fri; noon-10pm Sat; noon-6pm Sun. **Credit** AmEx, MC, V.

More laid-back than the contemporary exterior would suggest, this place is well laid out and welcoming. Big wooden tables offer plenty of seating options, and the fresh flowers and fish tank integrated into the wall are nice touches. There is a good selection of imported spirits along with a reasonable wine list and the regular draught beers. The food menu is typical pub fare: sandwiches, salads, platters.

A large plasma screen shows sport but, at one end of the bar, is easy to avoid if it isn't your thing. Popular with younger locals, but chilled enough for all to enjoy.
Babies and children admitted (until 6pm). Disabled: toilet. Function rooms. Music (DJs 8pm Fri, Sat; free). TVs (big screen, satellite).

Woodman

60 Battersea High Street, SW11 3HX (7228 2968). Clapham Junction rail then 319 bus. **Open** 11am-11pm Mon-Thur; 11am-midnight Fri; 10am-midnight Sat; 11am-10.30pm Sun. **Food served** noon-3pm, 6.30-10pm Mon-Fri; 10am-3pm, 6.30-10pm Sat; 1-5pm, 6.30-10pm Sun. **Credit** MC, V.

Situated at the residential end of Battersea High Street, a quiet area when considered in relation to Battersea Park Road, the Woodman is a lovely space, where traditional is placed alongside modern to create a real haven. The front bar greets the entrant with good draught beers (Tanglefoot, Badger, Hofbräu) and a small open fire. The back opens up to a long yet cosy room, delicately lit by fairy lights and clearly well loved. There is a great beer garden that is open in summer; during the winter, make the most of the sturdy cooking: fish pies, own-made burgers and decent steaks. Satellite TV is available, but doesn't dominate the place. Well worth an extra few yards' stroll.
Babies and children welcome. Quiz (8.30pm Mon; £1). Tables outdoors (10, garden). TVs (satellite).

Also in the area...

All Bar One 32-38 Northcote Road, SW11 1NZ (7801 9951).
Asparagus (JD Wetherspoon) 1-13 Falcon Road, SW11 2PL (7801 0046).
Fine Line 33-37 Northcote Road, SW11 1NJ (7924 7387).
Le Bouchon Lyonnais 38-40 Queenstown Road, SW8 3RY (7622 2618).
Pitcher & Piano 94 Northcote Road, SW11 6QW (7738 9781).
Slug & Lettuce 4 St John's Hill, SW11 1RU (7924 1322).

Bermondsey & Rotherhithe

This area goes from strength to strength, thanks to the lovely **Garrison** and the **Hartley**, but you can also mess about in a boat on the **Wibbley Wobbley**, sup a decent pint at old-school boozers or kick back and enjoy the view at the **Mayflower**.

Blacksmith's Arms

257 Rotherhithe Street, SE16 5EJ (7237 1349). Canada Water or Rotherhithe tube. **Open** noon-11pm Mon-Thur, Sun; noon-midnight Fri, Sat. **Food served** noon-2.30pm, 6-10pm Mon-Thur; noon-2.30pm, 6-10.30pm Fri; noon-10.30pm Sat; noon-10pm Sun. **Credit** AmEx, MC, V.

Located 50 yards west of the middle of nowhere, this Tudor-style boozer is never going to pull in much passing trade, but it fulfils its role as a local with aplomb. The horseshoe bar counter displays a small plaque commemorating the level reached by water during the great flood of 1928, and on top you'll find pumps of London Pride, Discovery, ESB and the usual selection of lagers. Reasonably priced Thai cuisine (shallow-fried king prawns with panang curry sauce,

£8.50) is available in the cosy rear dining area, resplendent with an open fire; there are also very popular Sunday roasts (£6.75). Large beer barrels are dotted around and the rough terracotta walls above wood panelling are covered by old pictures that give a great insight into a bygone time of busy riverside life.
Babies and children welcome. Games (fruit machines). Tables outdoors (3, garden). TV.

Garrison

99-101 Bermondsey Street, SE1 3XB (7089 9355/ www.thegarrison.co.uk). London Bridge tube/rail. **Open** 8am-11pm Mon-Fri; 9am-11pm Sat; 9am-10.30pm Sun. **Food served** 8.30am-3.30pm, 6.30-10pm Mon-Fri; 9-11.30am, 12.30-4pm, 6.30-10pm Sat; 9am-11.30am, 12.30-4pm, 6-9.30pm Sun. **Credit** AmEx, MC, V.
This country kitchen of scrubbed wood and pastel shades, filled with French and Swedish Victoriana, is very popular with local professionals from marketing, music and fashion. Grabbing a perch at one of the tall tables with wooden dividers is of paramount importance, since there's no room to stand, but a basement is available for the overspill (it doubles up as a cinema that can be used for parties). The menu changes every eight weeks (with an additional daily changing special menu), offering a healthy mix of gastropub fare including rabbit leg stew, creamed barley and tarragon, with savoy cabbage (£11.90). A varied wine list is on offer – the St Chinian Château le Dourine (£20) is very good and there are some expensive fine wines and Champagnes.
Disabled: toilet. Function room. Jukebox. No-smoking area.

Hartley

64 Tower Bridge Road, SE1 4TR (7394 7023/www. thehartley.com). Borough tube/London Bridge tube/rail. **Open** noon-midnight Mon-Thur; noon-2am Fri; 11am-2am Sat; noon-11pm Sun. **Food served** noon-3pm, 6-10pm Mon-Fri; 11am-4pm, 6-10pm Sat; noon-7pm Sun. **Credit** AmEx, MC, V.
Gaze through the wooden Venetian blinds hanging in these picture windows and you'll see an old jam factory, the source of this cool gastropub's name. Unfortunately, the long bar counter, backed by bare brick and terracotta walls, dispenses a rather bland selection of beer, with no real ales – at least Bass Premium, Leffe and Duckstein are available by the bottle. There's a solid wine list and an array of reasonably priced cocktails: the Tuscan Mule is claimed to be better for refreshment than Pimm's. The food is varied, adventurous and reasonably priced, with organic produce used whenever possible and vegetarians well catered for. The crispy grilled lemon thyme-stuffed mackerel with warm mustard sauce, chive potato and buttered spinach (£12.50) was delicious. For entertainment, live musicians regularly play on Tuesday nights and free internet access is available to the clientele of professional and well-heeled regulars. Why wait till tomorrow for jam?
Babies and children admitted. Entertainment (live music 8pm Tue; free). Function room. Games (board games). No-smoking area.

Mayflower

117 Rotherhithe Street, SE16 4NF (7237 4088). Rotherhithe tube. **Open** *Winter* 11am-3pm, 5.15-11pm Mon-Thur; 11am-11pm Fri, Sat; noon-10.30pm Sun. *Summer* 11am-11pm Mon-Sat; noon-10.30pm Sun. **Food served** *Winter* noon-2.30pm, 6.30-9.30pm Mon-Sat; noon-9pm Sun. *Summer* noon-9.30pm Mon-Sat; noon-9pm Sun. **Credit** MC, V.

The menu at this rather touristy riverside boozer is in the form of an old newspaper detailing the place's history – and the history is impressive: the pub sits next to the quay from which the Pilgrim Fathers set sail to the New World in 1620. In 1957 the pub was restored and manages to retain an authentic feel with black wood panelling, large oak beams, a brick open fireplace and the odd nautical item. At the bar, Abbot, Old Speckled Hen, Ruddles County and Greene King IPA are on offer with the usual array of nitro-keg lagers. The food is less than keenly priced: mature cheddar on a bed of house salad came in at an astonishing £9.95, so we recommend settling for a pint of ale, and either finding a cosy corner or heading on to the pleasant terrace.
Babies and children admitted (restaurant). Quiz (8.30pm Tue; £1). Restaurant (no smoking). Tables outdoors (25, riverside jetty).

Wibbley Wobbley

Greenland Dock, Rope Street, SE16 7SZ (7232 2320). Canada Water or Surrey Quays tube. **Open** noon-11pm Mon-Sat; noon-10.30pm Sun. **No credit cards.**
This welcoming, low-key, tranquil little floating pub, moored in Greenland Quay, was once co-owned by the late Malcolm Hardee, one of the founding fathers of alternative comedy. A slip and slide on the gangplank takes you inside to a low-ceilinged little bar, bedecked with old coins and banknotes, with red bench seating running down each side. Little crescent lights shine on high-tide clocks, naval pennants and the centrepiece ship's compass; warmth is supplied by an open stove fire. On tap Greene King IPA, Old Speckled Hen and Hoegaarden line up alongside the usuals, and, if sandwiches don't suffice, food is available upstairs in the café, which has river views.
Babies and children welcome (until 8pm). Games (quiz machine). Restaurant (no smoking). Tables outdoors (12, pontoon).

Also in the area...

All Bar One 34 Shad Thames, Spice Quay, Butlers Wharf, SE1 2YG (7940 9771).
Pommeler's Rest (JD Wetherspoon) 196-198 Tower Bridge Road, SE1 2UN (7378 1399).
Surrey Docks (JD Wetherspoon) 185 Lower Road, SE16 2LW (7394 2832).

Blackheath & Lee

Blackheath Village (the cluster of streets around the station) is where most of the drinking action is: the **Princess of Wales** is a terrific boozer, **Railway** caters to barflies and **Zero Degrees** draws both the pint-thirsty and the peckish. Further afield, the comfortable **Crown** is on Burnt Ash Hill in Lee.

Crown

117 Burnt Ash Hill, SE12 0AJ (8857 6607). Lee rail. **Open** 11am-11pm Mon-Thur; 11am-midnight Fri, Sat; noon-10.30pm Sun. **Food served** noon-9.30pm daily. **Credit** MC, V.
Alcove or alfresco, the Crown provides a convivial spot for Young's ale drinkers (Special and St George's on pumps, Waggledance and Double Chocolate Stout in bottles) and hearty diners. A menu of traditional food (5.30-9.30pm, sandwiches to 10.30pm) includes all-day brunch, Cumberland sausages and cod in a batter of Young's beer, plus Sunday roasts in winter and summer salads (£4.95)

in the warmer months, best enjoyed in the garden. Under new management since summer 2005, the Crown has a large car park for those arriving from the nearby South Circular turn-off, a 'strictly no children' policy in the bar and a room available upstairs for functions. Sunday quiz nights are almost as popular as the karaoke ('be a star for five minutes') on Fridays. Another sign suggests a take-away beer service, four bottles for a fiver – then again, not even your living room would be as homely.
Disabled: toilet. Function room. Games (darts, fruit machine). Music (karaoke 9pm Fri; band 9pm Sat; both free). Quiz (8.30pm Sun; £1). Tables outdoors (12, garden). TV (big screen).

Crown

47-49 Tranquil Vale, SE3 0BS (8852 0326). Blackheath rail. **Open** 11am-11pm Mon-Sat; noon-10.30pm Sun. **Food served** noon-9pm daily. **Credit** AmEx, DC, MC, V.
The loungey makeover of the historic Crown feels somewhat incongruous. On the corner of a gentle slope lined with estate agents and restaurants that leads into Blackheath Village, the Crown was a staging-post inn in the 18th century. Blackheath has some serious sporting heritage (the oldest open rugby union club in the world plays here), so it's unsurprising that the pub remains rugby-centric, attracting a thirtysomething, professional clientele, but the introduction of low sofas in one alcove and an open-plan bar area mean that it has lost its pub gravitas. The ales – Bombardier, Greene King IPA, Courage Best, Deuchars IPA – remain the same, and the wine selection by the glass (Chablis Ropiteau £3.95/£14, Châteauneuf-du-Pape Chais du Bâtard £4.30/£15.30) exemplary. Superior pies and pastas underscore the well-priced food menu, best enjoyed on the small triangle of bar tables on the front terrace in summer.
Babies and children welcome (until 8pm). Games (fruit machines, video games). Tables outdoors (8, pavement). TV (satellite).

Hare & Billet

1A Elliot Cottages, Hare & Billet Road, SE3 0QJ (8852 2352). Blackheath rail. **Open** 11am-11pm Mon-Thur; 11am-midnight Fri, Sat; noon-11pm Sun. **Food served** noon-3.30pm, 5.30-9pm daily. **Credit** MC, V.
Four centuries of history help, but this former coaching inn needed substantial upgrades to its dining options to attract punters away from the ever-growing number of quality pubs and bars located closer to Blackheath Village. It shouldn't worry. Set on the other side of the heath by the local rugby and football pitches, the H&B fills its cosy, rustic interior every day of the week. Greene King IPA and Flowers attract the ale suppers, six types of each colour (Chablis Ropiteau £16.95, red Fleurie £16.95) attract the wine sippers and foodies now have a deli board to peruse. The seafood sandwich (£6.45) boasts crab claws and crayfish tails, while mains include 28-day aged sirloin steak with a jenga tower of chips (£10.95) and beer-battered cod loin with the same ubiquitous jenga chips (£7.45). Whatever the place's gastronomic status, the dartboard remains sacrosanct.
Babies and children admitted (lunch only). Games (darts, quiz machine). No-smoking area. TV (big screen).

Princess of Wales

1A Montpelier Row, SE3 0RL (8297 5911). Blackheath rail. **Open** noon-11pm Mon-Sat; noon-10.30pm Sun. **Food served** noon-3pm, 5-9pm Mon-Fri; noon-9pm Sat; noon-8pm Sun. **Credit** MC, V.

Since its 21st-century makeover, this is easily the best pub in Blackheath. Without losing sight of its history (a sign in the side alcove still indicates where England players gathered before rugby's first international in 1871) or its heritage (named after Caroline of Brunswick), the Princess now revels in its role as a funky gastropub appealing to all social classes. It's a place where you can be served draught Paulaner, Kirin, Früli, Shepherd Neame Spitfire or Young's by a sympathetic, spiky-haired, nose-pierced bar girl, while nodding to well-chosen DJ rhythms or indie jangle, and peruse a menu of pan-fried sea bass and own-made pesto mash (£9.70) or breaded camembert and redcurrant jelly (£3.80). Given its size (comfortable, heath-facing front bar area, wide corridor with its own bar, plus a conservatory), it's the perfect place to spread out on a Sunday, when they honey-roast the legs of pork (£8.90), herb-crust the ribeye steak (£8.90) and provide tons of newspapers.
Babies and children welcome (until 5pm). Conservatory available for hire. Disabled: toilet. Games (fruit machine, golf machine). Quiz (8.30pm Tue; £1). Tables outdoors (30, garden).

Railway

16 Blackheath Village, SE3 9LE (8852 2390). Blackheath rail. **Open** noon-11pm Mon-Wed; noon-midnight Thur; noon-1am Fri, Sat; noon-10.30pm Sun. **Food served** noon-10pm Mon-Fri; noon-8pm Sat, Sun. **Credit** AmEx, MC, V.
Ever more popular, the lively Railway offers many attractive sins. Its continental lager selection appeals to reasonably discerning beer drinkers, taps of Paulaner, Küppers Kölsch, Budvar, Leffe and Staropramen lining the long bar counter that separates the communal front area from the intimate back one, now behind beaded curtains. Plenty of Belgian bottled varieties too. Pumps of Shepherd Neame Spitfire, Greene King IPA and Adnams Broadside attract ale drinkers. Bin-end and classy wines, chalked up over the bar, include a Spy Valley sauvignon blanc (£13) and Pouilly-Fumé Fouassier (£18). Light bites, burgers in focaccia and sandwiches are served during the day. DJ decks are set up at the front for weekend sessions. But most of all, the Railway is where people mingle, some in an inebriated, provocative fashion. It's not Club 18-30 – by Blackheath station, it's too sophisticated for that – but there's an undercurrent of lust, most certainly, a sense of trains passing and picking up passengers.
Disabled: toilet. Music (DJ 8pm Sat, Sun; free). Tables outdoors (5, garden).

Zero Degrees

29-31 Montpelier Vale, SE3 0TJ (8852 5619/www.zero degrees.co.uk). Blackheath rail. **Open** noon-midnight Mon-Sat; noon-11.30pm Sun. **Food served** noon-11pm Mon-Sat; noon-10.30pm Sun. **Credit** AmEx, MC, V.
This microbrewery, bar and restaurant goes from strength to strength. While the bar counter underneath the huge vats of hand-crafted beers gets busier, punters queue for a table in the sunken dining area where zinging wood-fired pizzas are served – new varieties include porcini mushroom (£7.95), peri peri chicken (£7.95) and smoky Mexican (with authentic spicy sausage, £8.95). Recently introduced salads include a Cajun king prawn type (£8.50) and the kilo pots of mussels (£12.25) come in Thai green curry and Thermidor (with brandy, wine, cheddar and mustard) sauces. As for the speciality beers, at a uniform and welcome £2.50 a pint (or £15.50 for a five-litre party keg, £85 a 50-litre one), they come in four types: black, wheat, pilsner and pale ale. The light, open-plan drinking area pro-

South

vides two floors of bar tables and space for private conversation, despite a huge screen for sports. A general party atmosphere hums around the mixed clientele. *Babies and children welcome. Restaurant (available for hire; no smoking). TV (big screen, satellite).*

Also in the area...

Edmund Halley (JD Wetherspoon) 25-27 Lee Gate Centre, Burnt Ash Road, SE12 8RG (8318 7475). **O'Neill's** 52 Tranquil Vale, SE3 0BH (8297 5901).

Borough & Southwark

Borough Market's continuing success keeps this area lively. The hordes of gastronomes will be delighted to find the **Brew Wharf** has joined the oenophiles' **Wine Wharf**, while a liquid breakfast at the **Market Porter** is guaranteed to give them a rose-tinted view of working life hereabouts. And a visit to the **Royal Oak** gives you a rose-tinted view of... well, everything.

Brew Wharf

Brew Wharf Yard, Stoney Street, SE1 9AD (7378 6601/www.brewwharf.com). London Bridge tube/rail. **Open** 11am-11pm Mon-Sat; 11am-4pm Sun. **Food served** noon-10.30pm Mon-Sat; noon-4pm Sun. **Credit** MC, V.
Just beyond Borough Market is Brew Wharf, the latest addition to the Vinopolis enterprise, and one of the few signs of life once the lively market has shut its stalls for the day. A treat for drinkers of real ale, Brew Wharf boasts its own microbrewery (a rarity in London), which is on display for restaurant-goers, and beer tastings can be arranged. Smart, sophisticated and inviting, it is all housed in huge dock arches. There is plenty of seating indoors, as well as a decked seating area with heaters outside. The microbrewery produces one ale made with Fuggles hops and another with Goldings, a nod to the nearby Hop Exchange which made Borough famous for its Kentish hops. There is a variety of imported bottled beers too, including Rochefort and de Koninck, and wines and Champagnes are available by bottle and glass. The kitchen, shared with the neighbouring Wine Wharf (*see p199*), produces bar snacks.
Babies and children admitted. Disabled: toilet. Function room. Restaurant (no smoking). Tables outdoors (10, pavement). TVs (big screen).

Bridge House

218 Tower Bridge Road, SE1 2UP (7407 5818). Tower Hill tube/London Bridge tube/rail. **Open** 11.30am-11pm Mon-Sat; noon-10.30pm Sun. **Food served** 11.30am-10pm Mon-Sat; noon-9.30pm Sun. **Credit** AmEx, MC, V.
This light and spacious regenerated former grainstore benefits from amiably helpful staff and its commercial links to Suffolk-based brewery Adnams, which not only supplies the exceptional real ales that were being enjoyed by lunchtime diners on our visit, but also furnishes a vast range of globally sourced fine wines. The decor is unobtrusive, with pale-wood tables and chairs joined by several purple-covered settees for loungers. Outside, massive glass constructions rise where future punters – with the taste and pocket for, say, Australian Canoe Tree shiraz/cabernet red combo or Argentinian Viña Paraíso viognier to accompany their whole smoked baby chicken

or beer-battered haddock with mustard sauce – will toil. At night, the view through the tall windows comes into its own when the new County Hall and the glimmering blocks banking the Thames provide a soothing light show. *Babies and children admitted (restaurant). Disabled: toilet. Function room. Restaurant (no smoking).*

George Inn

77 Borough High Street, SE1 1NH (7407 2056). London Bridge tube/rail. **Open** 11am-11pm Mon-Thur; 11am-midnight Fri, Sat; noon-10.30pm Sun. **Food served** noon-3pm, 5-10pm Mon-Fri; noon-4pm, 5-10pm Sat; noon-4pm Sun. **Credit** MC, V.
The George Inn should work. As London's sole surviving galleried coaching inn, it ticks many of the right boxes. Fabulous monochrome façade? Check. Warren of wonky, interlinked rooms with no right angles? Check. Oak beams and lattice windows galore? Affirmative. Perfectly acceptable traditional English grub and ales – Greene King and Everards among them – are available. And yet the crassness of the pack-'em-in mentality behind the decision to swamp the cobbled courtyard with a swathe of pallid wooden tables and sore-thumb patio heaters extends to the barbecue-style light-fittings and cretin-friendly ephemera within. Add to this smirk-worthy claims of erstwhile regulars like Dickens and Shakespeare – used to come in with Churchill, don't you know – and you begin to realise that the aim is to entice tourists, and that the George Inn's past has got more going for it than its present. *Babies and children admitted. Function rooms. Games (darts, fruit machine). No-smoking area (lunch). Tables outdoors (35, courtyard).*

Lord Clyde

27 Clennam Street, SE1 1ER (7407 3397). Borough tube. **Open** 11am-11pm Mon-Fri; noon-11pm Sat; noon-8pm Sun. **Food served** 11am-2.30pm, 5.30-11pm Mon-Fri. **Credit** AmEx, DC, MC, V.
Hidden in a street so small that even its abbreviated name is barely visible in the *A to Z*, the Lord Clyde is well worth seeking out. Literally warm and welcoming, the place was chock-full on our winter lunchtime visit. Above the bar, a flatscreen TV nestles among old barrels and cider flagons as easily as the locals mix with office bods, drawn by the hospitality of the Fitzpatricks, who have run the place for the last 50 years. The lamb is chopped and the potatoes are new on the traditional menu of lunchtime fare, which can be enjoyed in the main bar area or in the cosy, four-table backroom. Beers include the ever-reliable Spitfire. A thoroughly genuine and delightful place. *Babies and children admitted (until 9pm). Function room. Games (darts, fruit machines). TVs (big screen, satellite).*

Market Porter

9 Stoney Street, SE1 9AA (7407 2495). London Bridge tube/rail. **Open** 6-8.30am, 11am-11pm Mon-Fri; noon-11pm Sat; noon-10.30pm Sun. **Food served** noon-3pm Mon-Fri, Sun. **Credit** AmEx, MC, V.
Real ale lovers swear by the Market Porter. A constantly evolving menu of ludicrously monikered delights attracts beer-hunters throughout the day, with fans of the liquid breakfast welcomed from six in the morning thanks to the venue's proximity to Borough Market. The recent refurbishment was sensitive enough not to put off the legion of regulars, used to solid wooden tables, the odd barrel and a spectacular variety of mottled complexions. The service is invariably friendly – astoundingly so in the evenings when,

Market Porter

even during the winter months, customers spill out on to the pavements, yet the bartenders are more than willing to offer samples of the day's available beverages to the curious. All of which guarantees enduring success for a unique hostelry that entirely merits its popularity.
Babies and children welcome (restaurant). Disabled: toilet. Function room. Games (fruit machines). Restaurant.

Royal Oak

44 Tabard Street, SE1 4JU (7357 7173). Borough tube. **Open** 11am-11pm Mon-Fri; 6-11pm Sat; noon-6pm Sun. **Food served** noon-3pm, 5-9.30pm Mon-Fri; 6-9.30pm Sat; noon-5pm Sun. **Credit** MC, V.
No wonder this place is a popular location for real-ale get-togethers! Tight and exclusive links to the Sussex brewery Harveys guarantee imbiber-friendly quality as much as the welcoming service and surroundings prompt devotion. Multiple awards jostle for position with framed theatre posters, old photos of moustachioed bartenders and traditional prints on the maroon mock-flock walls in two bijou bars, furnished with chunky tables, green leather settees and several rocking chairs. Space is so tight the latest accolade from the Society for the Preservation of Beers as the Wood's Greater London Pub of the Year 2006 has yet to find a permanent location. Perhaps the unpretentious and cheery atmosphere was encapsulated in the following exchange: [Bar lady] 'D'you want ice wiv thet, gel?' [Regular] 'Oh yer, I larve all the trimmins!' Special.
Disabled: toilet. Function room. No piped music or jukebox.

Shipwrights Arms

88 Tooley Street, SE1 2TF (7378 1486). London Bridge tube/rail. **Open** 11am-midnight Mon-Thur; 11am-1am Fri, Sat; noon-10.30pm Sun. **Food served** noon-3pm Mon-Fri; noon-4pm Sat, Sun. **Credit** AmEx, MC, V.
The heavy drapes and the high ceiling – not to mention the punters – have seen plenty of nicotine action in this popular watering hole, a mere stone's throw from London Bridge. Nautical ephemera abounds – model ships atop the bar look like they could date from the pub's 19th-century debut, framed knots and river-life bric-a-brac adorn the maroon walls, and a 6ft-square tiled depiction of a shipwright backed by a particularly choppy Thames catches the eye. Customers, eager to get stuck into the Adnams, Spitfire and usual lagers, throng the high, dark-wood, square bar that dominates the centre of the room. Food is available at lunchtimes, and the thought occurs that strict enforcement of the anti-tobacco laws would inevitably result in the absence of edibles rather than of smokes.
Babies and children admitted (until 7pm). Function room. Games (darts, fruit machines, quiz machines). Tables outdoors (3, pavement). TVs (big screen, satellite).

Wine Wharf

Stoney Street, Market, SE1 9AD (7940 8335/www. winewharf.com). London Bridge tube/rail. **Open** 11.30am-11pm Mon-Sat. **Food served** noon-10pm Mon-Sat. **Credit** AmEx, DC, MC, V.
This paradise for wine lovers with a taste for experiment nestles alongside Vinopolis. Enthusiastic and informative staff help you to negotiate a vast list of some of the finest

vinicultural products the world has to offer. In the red corner, Mexico provides an eminently quaffable La Cetto Nebbiolo. Lovers of dry white could plump for, rather than suffer from, a Nobilis Ritinitis from Greece. The menu is standard global contemporary, with a charcuterie platter, Thai fish cakes and enchiladas available for consumption on soft sofas in industrial-chic surroundings: bare-brick walls, chunky beams and heavy metal. An upstairs section is accessible via a staircase that looks as if it was lifted from a trawler – fitting, perhaps, given that it is possible to go overboard by ordering a 1953 Château d'Yquem Sauternes for £916.50 as a precursor to a 1927 Taylor's Vintage Port, a relative snip at £655.
Babies and children admitted (until 8pm). Disabled: toilet. Music (jazz 7.30pm Mon; free). Venue available for hire.

Zakudia
River Level, 2A Southwark Bridge Road, SE1 9HA (7021 0085/www.zakudia.com). London Bridge tube/rail. **Open/food served** noon-11pm Mon-Wed, Sun; noon-1am Thur-Sat. **Credit** AmEx, MC, V.
This accommodating and increasingly popular riverside bar allows customers to take in constantly changing riverside views while sampling an impressive range of cocktails from the standard Cosmopolitan to the particular Miss Thames – 'fresh raspberries muddled with Stoli Razberi, topped with cranberry and apple juice'. Zakudia's raison d'être is contained within its name, a word that strongly implies the concept of sharing and could perhaps be translated as 'conviviality'. So tables are round, as are the muted green or red suede-covered stools, and diners are encouraged to order dishes – a new chef has engendered a move towards tapas-style offerings – that can be sampled in groups. African-themed paintings, with wildlife to the fore, adorn the walls. Giraffe-like humans should not be put off by the rather low ceilings, but rather enjoy the warmth of the service and the splendid vistas.
Babies and children welcome (until 6pm). Disabled: toilet. Music (jazz 7pm Tue; DJs 7pm Thur-Sat; free).

Also in the area...
All Bar One 28-30 London Bridge Street, SE1 9SG (7940 9981).
Balls Brothers Hay's Galleria, Tooley Street, SE1 2HD (7407 4301); Hop Cellars, 24 Southwark Street, SE1 1TY (7403 6851).
Borough Bar (Jamies) 10-18 London Bridge Street, SE1 9SG (7407 6962).
Cooperage (Davy's) 48-50 Tooley Street, SE1 2SZ (7403 5775).
Heeltap & Bumper (Davy's) Chaucer House, White Hart Yard, Borough High Street, SE1 1NX (7407 2829).
Mughouse (Davy's) 1-3 Tooley Street, SE1 2PF (7403 8343).
Skinkers (Davy's) 42 Tooley Street, SE1 2SZ (7407 9189).
Slug & Lettuce 32-34 Borough High Street, SE1 1XU (7378 9999).

Brixton & Streatham

Despite the continuing presence of fine traditional pubs like the **Effra** or the **Trinity Arms**, a new breed of watering holes has followed the fading **Dogstar** to prominence: **Brixton Bar & Grill**, **Hive** and **Mango Landin'** among them. Brixton also boasts a clutch of hot clubs, for which see our Clubs section, starting on p246.

Brixton Bar & Grill
15 Atlantic Road, SW9 8HX (7737 6777/www.bbag. me.uk). Brixton tube/rail. **Open** 4.30pm-midnight Tue, Wed; 4.30pm-1am Thur; 4.30pm-2am Fri, Sat; 3.30-11pm Sun. **Food served** 6pm-midnight Tue-Sat; 4-10.30pm Sun. **Credit** MC, V.
This bar is a class act – friendly but slickly run, with an excellent drinks list. Bitburger and Stella are on draught, but bottled beers include the malty Anchor Steam Beer from San Francisco (£3.50) and organic St Peter's Best Bitter from Suffolk (£4.50). Cocktails start at a reasonable £5.75, and a house Bbag Royale (strawberry purée, Frangelico and lemon juice topped with Mumm, £7) was perfectly mixed. The wine list is well balanced between the Old and New World, with about a third by the glass. Billecart-Salmon Champagne (£35 a bottle) is a rare treat in a neighbourhood bar like this. Most people eat here, choosing dishes such as spiced sweet potato chips with soured cream (£4) or lamb cutlets with yoghurt mint sauce (£5) from the tapas-style menu. The decor is Spanish-influenced, with a mix of low seats and high wooden tables. Candlelight softens the atmosphere in the evenings, and a DJ plays soul and funk on weekends. There's a Backgammon Club on Tuesday nights, when you can also play chess, snakes and ladders or draughts.
Disabled: toilet. Music (DJs 9pm Fri, Sat; free). Tables outdoors (4, pavement).

Dogstar
389 Coldharbour Lane, SW9 8LQ (7733 7515). Brixton tube/rail. **Open** 4pm-2am Mon-Thur; noon-4am Fri, Sat; 11am-2am Sun. **Food served** 6-11pm Mon-Sat; noon-8pm Sun. **Admission** £5 after 10pm Fri, Sat. **Credit** MC, V.
Once the most popular bar in Brixton and a Saturday-night destination for non-locals, this bar's star has definitely faded of late. Brixtonians have more choice in watering holes these days and aren't always looking for the pump-'em-up, pack-'em-in experience the Dogstar was once famous for. Nonetheless, this local institution still draws a youngish clientele for its regular DJ nights, which range from roots reggae to Latin. The bar offers the usual beers and spirits, with £3 shooters a popular option. The first-floor Caribbean restaurant has now closed, but in its place there's a function room for parties. By day, when there's plenty of room on the comfy sofas and at the big wooden tables, the Dogstar has an easygoing vibe, and a big-screen TV has been added for those who want to watch the footie. The traditional Sunday lunch (£7.50) remains popular, and if you feel like a change from Yorkshire pudding you'll find salt cod fritters or roti with goat curry (£5.50) on the menu.
Babies and children admitted (until 6pm). Disabled: toilet. Function room. Music (DJs 9pm Mon-Sat, 3pm Sun). Tables outdoors (5, garden). TVs (big screen, satellite).

Effra
38A Kellet Road, SW2 1EB (7274 4180). Brixton tube/rail. **Open** 3-11pm daily. **Food served** 3-10pm daily. **No credit cards.**
A traditional-style corner pub, decked out Victorian style, the Effra is a popular haunt for many of Brixton's older Afro-Caribbean residents, except when there's live music

(jazz, reggae, ska) and then a younger, more diverse crowd of locals and visitors turns up. Whatever the mix, the vibe remains laid-back and low-key, with everyone just doing their thing in true Brixton tradition. Pool and dominoes are popular pastimes, fuelled by regular deals on pints and pitchers of beer. On tap, you'll find Stella, Grolsch, Carling and particularly good Guinness. If you're feeling peckish, there are a few, mostly Jamaican dishes on offer, such as jerk chicken. The place was given a lick of paint in 2005, but nothing much really changes at the Effra, which makes it refreshingly different from many of the capital's other drinking venues and deserving of its loyal clientele.

Games (dominoes). Music (8.30pm Tue-Thur, Sat, Sun; free). Tables outdoors (3, garden). TV.

Far Side

144 Stockwell Road, SW9 9TQ (7095 1401). Stockwell tube/Brixton tube/rail. Open noon-11pm Mon-Thur; noon-3am Fri, Sat; noon-10.30pm Sun. Food served noon-2.30pm, 6-9pm Mon-Sat; noon-8pm Sun. Credit MC, V.

Located just beyond Brixton Academy, the Far Side is a modern pub that attracts diverse punters. Two open fires and big wooden tables make it a cosy venue in winter, while a beer garden at the back opens up the space in summer. There's a fair range of beers on tap (Staropramen, Leffe Blonde, Hoegaarden, Stella and Guinness), and a wide selection of bottled beers, including Brahma and Belle-Vue Framboise. The shortish wine list covers Old and New World, with most sold by the glass. The food is standard stuff but fairly priced, especially the generous plate of wedgy cayenne-dusted chips (£3.50) and organic Sunday roast in winter (barbecues are offered in summer). A big plasma screen makes the Far Side popular for sports fans, although there are sofas and comfy chairs tucked away in nooks and crannies if you want to escape the action.

Babies and children welcome (until 7pm). Music (DJs/bands 9.30pm Fri, Sat; free). Tables outdoors (16, garden). TV (big screen, satellite).

Hive

11-13 Brixton Station Road, SW9 8PA (7274 8383/ www.hivebar.net). Brixton tube/rail. Open noon-midnight Tue-Thur, Sun; noon-3am Fri; 11am-3am Sat. Food served noon-10pm Tue-Sat; noon-7pm Sun. Credit MC, V.

Hive's tiny but airy downstairs café/restaurant has already created quite a buzz among fashionable Brixtonistas, though it only opened in late 2005, and the bar that sits above it has received the same high praise. Small and perfectly formed, this is an intimate space with subtle decor. Beers on tap include Stella, Heineken and Guinness, while Corona, Peroni and the French Kasteel Cru come in bottles. The cocktails start at a reasonable £6 and are mixed with real skill and a smile. The bartender who served us was also more than happy to come up with a bespoke concoction. Vodka fans can enjoy Wyborowa Single Estate, and, if bubbles are your tipple, Prosecco is offered by the glass and bottle in addition to Champagne (Moët et Chandon and Veuve Clicquot). Leather sofas and pouffes make this a comfortable space, while DJs playing imaginative sets add to the laid-back but cool vibe. Hive deserves to do well and should become a destination bar for in-the-know Londoners as well as locals.

Babies and children admitted (restaurant). Music (DJs 8pm Tue-Thur, 10pm Fri, Sat; free). Restaurant. Tables outdoors (3, pavement).

Hope & Anchor

123 Acre Lane, SW2 5UA (7274 1787). Clapham North tube/Brixton tube/rail. Open noon-11pm Mon-Thur, Sun; noon-1.30am Fri, Sat. Food served noon-3pm, 6.30-10pm Mon-Sat; noon-5pm Sun. Credit MC, V.

This Young's pub, located halfway between Brixton and Clapham, is refreshingly down-to-earth and eclectic in its clientele. On a weeknight, you might find a mix of football fans watching a game on the big-screen TV, old-timers enjoying a quiet pint, lone souls absorbed in a newspaper or friends having a giggle. All seem to mingle quite happily, thanks in part to the spacious layout of the Hope and Anchor and the friendly, easygoing staff. Aside from Young's seasonal ales, you won't find anything out of the ordinary at the bar, though the gin and tonic was generously strong for a pub like this. On the food front, dishes such as grilled halloumi and chorizo sausages and mash are chalked up on a blackboard menu. The pretty beer garden at the back, with a Japanese maple tree and children's play area, is extremely popular in summer. Comedy and cabaret will resume once the room where they're held has been refurbished, hopefully by summer.

Babies and children welcome. Disabled: toilet. Function room. Tables outdoors (40, garden). TV (big screen, satellite).

Living

443 Coldharbour Lane, SW9 8LN (7326 4040/www. livingbar.co.uk). Brixton tube/rail. Open noon-2am Mon-Thur, Sun; noon-4am Fri, Sat. Happy hour 5-9pm daily. Admission £5 after 10pm Fri, Sat. Credit AmEx, MC, V.

If you're looking for a lively, up-for-it bar in the centre of Brixton, full of like-minded types ready to party, this two-floor venue located on Coldharbour Lane will deliver. The atmosphere is pretty raucous on Friday and Saturday nights, when most of the clientele have come for DJ sets that could be bhangra, Cuban or house. To kick off the evening, a happy hour and several two-for-one deals get everyone nicely lubricated. Red Stripe, Bitburger and Hoegaarden are on tap, and there's a lengthy cocktail list, including jugs (£12). Hunger pangs can be put to rest with snacks such as bruschetta (£4) and veggie pâtés served with organic bread. Living is a popular venue for private parties and, if you really want to let your hair down, pole-dancing classes are on offer.

Babies and children welcome (until 9pm). Disabled: toilet. Entertainment (film screenings; pole-dancing classes; phone for details). Music (DJs 9pm nightly). Tables outdoors (3, pavement).

Mango Landin'

40 St Matthew's Road, SW2 1NL (7737 3044/www. mangolandin.com). Brixton tube/rail then 2, 3, 133, 159 bus. Open 5.30-11.30pm Mon-Wed; 11am-midnight Thur; 10am-3am Fri, Sat; 11am-11.30pm Sun. Credit AmEx, MC, V.

This bar, which was formerly a pub called the Hope, then a branch of Babushka, is a good example of what Brixton does best: provide hip but laid-back venues for all sorts of customers. With its yellow exterior and tropically themed interior, Mango Landin' adds a bright splash of colour to the local bar scene. The cocktails are suitably fruity and the standard beers on offer well priced. Music is a big draw, with DJ sets ranging from Miss Feelgood's feline funk to ska Cubano, as well as regular live reggae. Much more than just a bar, Mango Landin' hosts an organic food market on Saturdays (10am-2pm), tango lessons and quiz nights. Don't

South

be put off by the location (on the corner of a housing estate), as this is a characterful bar that's well worth a visit. Children are made particularly welcome during the day. *Babies and children welcome. Games (board games, chess, table football). Market (10am-2pm Sat). Music (band/DJ 9pm Thur-Sat, 5pm summer Sun; free). Quiz (8pm 1st & 3rd Tue of mth; £2). Tables outdoors (20, garden). Tango classes (8pm Wed; £6).*

Prince
467-469 Brixton Road, SW9 8HH (7326 4455/ www.dexclub.co.uk). Brixton tube/rail. **Open** noon-2am Mon, Wed; noon-midnight Tue, Thur; noon-4am Fri; 11am-4am Sat; 11am-midnight Sun. **Food served** noon-10.30pm Mon-Fri; 11am-10.30pm Sat, Sun. **Credit** AmEx, MC, V.
The brief reincarnation as Harlem proved that if Brixtonites and visitors really wanted West London, then they'd go there. Now reincarnated as simply the Prince, this large gastropub (soon to be larger when the upstairs conversion/DJ hotel/members' club is complete) is sitting much more naturally in its south London location. Great food, reasonable prices and a new relaxed drinking/dining situation have made it far more welcoming than it was under the constraints of its predecessor. In addition wi-fi access and top quality tunes make it a popular meeting spot, day or night, with Brixton's media/music community. Sunday roasts, happy hours and lunch deals plus an impressive Champagne list, stylish cocktails and good DJ roster turn it from café society to night-time hot spot as the sun goes down over Brixton.
Babies and children admitted (until 9pm). Disabled: toilet. Function room. Music (DJs 8pm daily; free). No-smoking area. Tables outdoors (12, garden). TV (big screen).

SW9
11 Dorrell Place, SW9 8EG (7738 3116). Brixton tube/rail. **Open** 10.30am-11pm Mon-Wed; 10.30am-midnight Thur; 10.30am-1am Fri, Sat; 11am-5.30pm Sun. **Food served** 11am-10pm Mon-Sat; 11am-5.30pm Sun. **Happy hour** 4.30-7pm Mon-Fri. **Credit** AmEx, MC, V.
Tucked down a side street opposite Brixton tube, this small venue is a little jewel. An intimate bar by night and easy-going café by day, its relaxed atmosphere has made it a long-standing hit with locals. A happy hour that kicks off at 4.30pm every weekday afternoon attracts a steady after-work crowd, while live music (jazz, samba, soul) and DJs step up the beat at the weekend. The bar is predictably but well stocked (Stella, Staropramen, Leffe and Guinness are on tap), and a good number of wines are offered by the glass. Snacks ordered from the bar are generously proportioned for the price (a plate of chilli-beef nachos, £6.50, was big enough for four). SW9's outside area is heated in the winter and provides some much-needed space in the summer, as this venue can get very crowded. Clubbers recovering from the night before regularly pitch up on Sunday mornings, when SW9 serves hearty breakfasts, good coffee and hair-of-the-dog refreshers.
Babies and children admitted (until 5pm). Music (9pm Fri, Sat). Tables outdoors (16, heated patio).

Trinity Arms
45 Trinity Gardens, SW9 8DR (7274 4544). Brixton tube/rail. **Open** 11am-11pm Mon-Thur, Sun; 11am-midnight Fri, Sat. **Food served** noon-3pm Mon-Fri. **Credit** MC, V.

Set on the corner of a quiet square off Acre Lane, this well regarded watering hole is a local institution and one many regulars would like to keep a secret. Built in 1840, the Trinity is a traditional pub unaffected by the passing trends of central Brixton – which isn't to say it has no personality of its own. Quiet and low-key, the pub has an old-school barman (attired in shirt and tie) who serves a loyal clientele of older-generation Brixtonians and newcomers looking for a no-frills, no-attitude drinking experience. There's a selection of Young's ales on offer (Waggledance, the seasonal Winter Warmer), as well as good single malt whiskies, including Glenlivet. A small terrace at the front, with wooden tables, makes this the perfect spot for a mellow summer evening pint.
Babies and children welcome (garden only). Games (fruit machine). No piped music or jukebox. Tables outdoors (8, garden; 6, pavement). TV.

Urban Retreat
56 Atlantic Road, SW9 8PX (0871 332 2905). Brixton tube/rail. **Open** 11am-11pm Mon-Wed; 11am-midnight Thur-Sat; 11am-6pm Sun. **Food served** 11am-10pm Mon-Sat; 11am-5pm Sun. **Credit** AmEx, MC, V.
Tiny but full of character, Urban Retreat is a well-frequented café called Lounge by day (weekend breakfasts are especially popular) and a laid-back bar by night. Mostly filled with locals looking for a chilled-out atmosphere, Urban Retreat rarely fails to deliver. There aren't many beers on draught (Carling, Grolsch and Guinness), but bottled varieties are more plentiful. The wine list is short but fairly priced, starting at £9.95 for a bottle of drinkable French vin de pays. The decor is chrome, neon and leather, but somehow it all blends together harmoniously. There's local art for sale on the walls; if you arrive in the day check out the Bettie Morton gallery a few doors down. Plans are afoot to extend the bar area and obtain a later licence, which should start pulling in even more hip Brixtonians.
Babies and children welcome. Bar available for hire. Disabled: toilet. Music (jazz 8pm Wed; free). No-smoking area.

White Horse
94 Brixton Hill, SW2 1QN (8678 6666/www.whitehorse brixton.com). Brixton tube/rail then 59, 118, 133, 159, 250 bus. **Open** 5pm-1am Mon-Thur; 2pm-3am Fri; noon-3am Sat; noon-1am Sun. **Food served** 5-10pm Mon-Fri; noon-9pm Sat; noon-10pm Sun. **Credit** AmEx, MC, V.
Part scruffy boozer, part style bar and part rave, the White Horse is a likeably mixed-up beast. Outside peak hours, you can grab a sofa, scan the pleasant, open interior, which mixes crumbling bricks and groovy artwork, and munch on the reasonable food (including tempura onion rings and Jamaican jerk chicken). In the evening, things get louder, with DJs till late on Fridays and Saturdays. When these early hours get busy, the atmosphere is cheerfully riotous, with the battered boards full of dancing feet, the toilets resembling a damp bombsite and the DJs doing populist tricks like playing Michael Jackson after half an hour of pounding house. The drinks selection is fairly standard: San Miguel and Scrumpy Jack the most exciting options on tap; standard cocktails starting at £5; a shortish wine list on which most are sold by the glass. The atmosphere is cool but not snobby, and balls on the pool table (£1.20) clunk with a reassuring regularity.
Disabled: toilet. Games (board games, pool table). Music (DJs 9pm Fri, Sat; jazz/funk 5pm Sun; free). Tables outdoors (6, courtyard). TV.

South

Windmill

*22 Blenheim Gardens, SW2 5BZ (8671 0700/www.
windmillbrixton.co.uk). Brixton tube then 49, 59, 118,
133, 159, 250 bus.* **Open** 11am-midnight Mon-Thur;
11am-1am Fri, Sat; noon-11pm Sun. **No credit cards.**
If you're looking to hear the next big indie band just before
they break, you should probably venture to the back streets
of Brixton. Over the past few years, the Windmill has built
up a well-deserved reputation as one of London's coolest
music venues, giving groups such as British Beef and Dr
Dog the chance to impress a discerning muso crowd. Entry
is dirt cheap (around £3) and so is the beer (all standard
stuff), which is what everyone drinks. This is a totally no-
frills space, and pretty much standing room only, although
there a few tables and chairs. The Windmill can get seriously crowded, with long queues at the bar, so it's not the
place to come if you're a thirsty, impatient sort. But serious
indie fans will be in their element. If you look young, you
may be asked to show some ID at the door.
*Babies and children welcome (until 7pm). Disabled:
toilet. Games (fruit machine). Music (8pm nightly;
£3-£4). Tables outdoors (4, garden; 4, pavement).
TV (big screen).*

Also in the area...

Beehive (JD Wetherspoon) 407-409 Brixton Road,
SW9 7DG (7738 3643).
Crown & Sceptre (JD Wetherspoon) 2A Streatham
Hill, SW2 4AH (8671 0843).
Holland Tringham (JD Wetherspoon) 107-109
Streatham High Road, SW16 1HJ (8769 3062).

Camberwell

The impressive variety of drinking options in
Camberwell caters to a rich mix of residents.
Sun & Doves appeals to arty environmentalists, the
Hermit's Cave to lovers of the honest-to-goodness
pub, the **Old Dispensary** to the upwardly comfortable
and **Funky Munky** to just about everybody.

Castle

*65 Camberwell Church Street, SE5 8TR (7277 2601).
Oval tube/Denmark Hill rail/12, 35, 68, 176, 185, 345
bus.* **Open** noon-midnight Mon-Thur, Wed; noon-2am
Fri, Sat. **Food served** noon-10pm Mon-Sat; noon-
9.30pm Sun. **Credit** AmEx, DC, MC, V.
As with all boozer-to-bar conversions from here to Forest
Hill, the Castle has been scrubbed bare, clean and white,
but staves off the new homogeneity with the wit and elan
of some quirky and light-hearted decor touches: look out
for the paranoid-looking stuffed fox guarding the door. The
sense of fun spreads naturally to the breezy staff who serve
up a good range of libations from a price list headed 'The
Damage'. Adnams Broadside is on tap, and although this
isn't a cocktail bar per se, the spirit spread is deep and wide,
strong on flavoured vodkas and whiskies. They lay on a
superb Sunday brunch and roast, and for those who want
to add a *Friends* feel to their dipsomania, there's a big old
chesterfield opposite the open fire. If you don't like any of
it, you can fill out a comment card – all clean comments
are subsequently displayed on the wall.
*Babies and children welcome (until 7pm). Comedy (8pm
alternate Mon; £4). Function room. Games (board
games). Music (DJs 9pm Thur-Sun; free). TVs (big
screen, satellite).*

Funky Munky

*25 Camberwell Church Street, SE5 8TR (7277 1806).
Denmark Hill rail/12, 36, 171, 176, 185, 436 bus.*
Open noon-midnight Mon-Wed, Sun; noon-2am Thur;
noon-3.30am Fri, Sat. **Food served** noon-6pm Tue,
Sat, Sun; noon-10pm Wed-Fri. **Happy hour** 5-7pm
daily. **Credit** MC, V.
The Funky Munky is all things to all barflies. For a Sunday
brunch and Bloody Mary with some discreet 1940s swing
playing to help with the comedown, it is perfect. For lunch
any day of the week, its tapas-bar-ish decor and imaginative, broadly modern European menu is an easy and comfortable combination. For a cocktail in the 5-7pm happy
hour, the FM is hard to beat. (Traditionalists take note: the
cocktails err on the modern side. Tiramisu Martini, anyone?) After 9pm from Wednesday through the weekend,
the place is suddenly a banging DJ bar. There's London
Pride for the beeros and San Miguel on tap for lager heads.
Check. Dance lessons? Can do. The atmosphere reflects the
general buzz of Camberwell and the pally staff are never
less than welcoming. In short, the best, most fun chameleon
in the whole of south-east London.
*Babies and children welcome. Dance classes (tango
7.45pm Mon; £6-£8). Function room. Music (DJs 9pm
Wed-Sun; free). Tables outdoors (6, pavement).*

Hermit's Cave

*28 Camberwell Church Street, SE5 8QU (7703 3188).
Denmark Hill rail/12, 36, 171 bus.* **Open** 10am-
midnight Mon-Wed; 10am-2am Thur-Sat; noon-
midnight Sun. **Food served** noon-4pm daily. **No
credit cards.**
The Cave typifies the rude health of Camberwell bar culture, being a perfect example of how an old-school shop
needn't go all pseudo-gastro to attract custom. Crumblies
and trendies rub happy shoulders in this beautifully preserved corner boozer that feels at once local and metropolitan, traditional and modern. It's a beer aficionado's
heaven, with Gravesend Shrimpers Bitter and Spitfire
pumped alongside Leffe and Hoegaarden. The food on offer
is really hearty, stick-to-your-ribs fare. And while this is
the pubbiest of pubs, with its ornate etched windows and
open fire, exotica is hinted at in the shape of a Galliano bottle that looks to be in full use – the Hermit's Cave isn't a
bar that is easily caught out. Empty Maker's Mark bottles
adorn the top of the bar, like trophies of grand nights of
yore – and a testimony to the great range of whiskies.
*Babies and children welcome (lunch only). Tables
outdoors (3, pavement). TV (big screen, satellite).*

Old Dispensary

*325 Camberwell New Road, SE5 0TF (7708 8831).
Elephant & Castle tube/rail then 12 or 176 bus/Oval
tube then 36 or 436 bus.* **Open** noon-midnight Mon-
Thur; noon-1am Fri, Sat; noon-11pm Sun. **Food
served** noon-3pm, 6-10pm Mon-Fri; noon-10pm Sat,
Sun. **Happy hour** 5-7pm Mon-Fri. **Credit** AmEx,
DC, MC, V.
The interior of this slick operation resembles a 1920s cocktail bar given a makeover in 1975 and then perfectly preserved. Mirror- and marble-topped tables give the place an
air of decadence, while a huge – and deliciously ostentatious – chandelier, slung from an octagonal skylight, lights
up the proceedings. Gilt-framed blackboards advertise promotions – happy hour and DJs – and mirrors seem to double the size of the place. There's Leffe and Guinness on the
taps, but the cocktails provide too much of a distraction
for such everyday fare. Knowledgeable staff mix your

every whim in ideal surroundings: indeed, say the words 'cocktail' and 'bar' to the uninitiated, and this is the kind of joint that will appear in their mind's eye. It's not the most comfortable of eating spaces – the stools, perches and banquettes are more designer bag than nosebag – but as a cocktail bar, it completes Camberwell's set of almost everything the drinker could desire.

Babies and children welcome. Disabled: toilet. Music (DJs 9pm Thur-Sat; free). TV (big screen).

Sun & Doves

61-63 Coldharbour Lane, SE5 9NS (7733 1525/ www.sunanddoves.co.uk). Brixton tube/rail then 35, 45, 345 bus/Loughborough Junction rail. **Open** noon-11pm Mon-Thur, Sun; noon-midnight Fri, Sat. **Food served** noon-10.30pm Mon-Sat; noon-5.30pm Sun. **Credit** MC, V.

This madeover corner pub sets out to be a gallery and even a community resource as well as a bar-diner. And it succeeds on all fronts. In a single large, airy and bright room, one can dine on everything from beans on toast to tuna steak on red chard with lemon vinaigrette. The wines travel the world from New to Old, and the massive beer garden is a huge draw in the sunshine months. The menu claims to offer 'the best cocktails this side of the river'; if their truly outré Bloody Mary with Guinness is anything to go by, this may be no idle boast. The bar doubles as a gallery space showing contemporary artists, hosts acoustic music nights and even runs a wine-appreciation course. You want more? Then hit the website for tips on how to reduce your environmental impact – an issue the guv'nor is deeply committed to. Indeed, only the Sun's lack of beds will stop you from never going home again. An absolute one-off.

Art exhibitions. Babies and children welcome. Music (musicians 8.30pm Sun; free). No-smoking area. Restaurant. Tables outdoors (20, garden; 6, pavement).

Also in the area...

Fox on the Hill (JD Wetherspoon) 149 Denmark Hill, SE5 8EH (7738 4756).

Catford

Catford has a bad image, bad transport links and a load of blokey pubs. Thank providence, then, for giving locals the wonderful **Rutland Arms**.

Blythe Hill Tavern

319 Stanstead Road, SE23 1JB (8690 5176). Catford or Catford Bridge rail. **Open** 11am-11pm Mon-Sat; noon-10.30pm Sun. **No credit cards.**

They keep a good pint of Guinness at the Blythe. This unusually shaped bar falls into three unique spaces, with two open fires. It thrums to the sound of the horses on TV in the afternoon, and buzzes with disparate and engaging locals of an evening. There's Irish folk music of a Thursday night and a free quiz on a Monday, with a crate of beer as top prize. The pub's genuine Irishness is worn lightly – free from all traces of Green Beer tat – and is reflected in a wider-than-average range of Irish whiskeys, in the true warmth of the welcome and in a deep-set professionalism that springs from the old days of the pub trade. The bar is subtly stocked with a non-showy array of drinks and mixers that wait patiently for even the most exotic request, but it is at being a great traditional corner pub that the place excels.

Babies and children welcome (until 7pm). Games (darts, fruit machine). Music (Irish traditional 9pm Thur; free). Quiz (9pm Mon; free). Tables outdoors (20, garden). TV (big screen, satellite).

Rutland Arms

55 Perry Hill, SE6 4LF (8291 9426). Catford or Catford Bridge rail then 181 or 202 bus. **Open** noon-11pm Mon-Sat; noon-10.30pm Sun. **Food served** noon-10pm Mon-Sat; noon-2.30pm Sun. **No credit cards.**

With traditional pubs it's all too easy to confuse old school with dog-eared and raggedy. Don't make that mistake with the Rutland, which is one of the capital's finest jazz pubs. Looking like just another London shebeen from the outside, this comfortable and welcoming L-shaped pub is a hidden treasure. That old-time combo of trad jazz and real ale (Saturday nights; modern jazz is on Tuesday night and Sunday lunch) ensures that fans of both make this something of a Mecca. The bar fairly swings with Young's Bitter and Special sitting in alongside Bass, Adnams and Fuller's – and although the jazz bill doesn't feature so many famous names, it still hits the spot every time. Near the door, in what could almost be a separate bar in this spacious, high-ceilinged hostelry, there's a dartboard and telly to satisfy the blokes. This is a character-packed house that typifies all that's great in London pub culture.

Function room. Games (darts, fruit machines). Music (trad jazz 8.30pm Sat; modern jazz 8.30pm Tue, 1pm Sun; R&B 8.30pm Thur; free). Quiz (1st Sun of mth; £1). Tables outdoors (2, pavement). TV (satellite).

Also in the area...

London & Rye (JD Wetherspoon) 109 Rushey Green, SE6 4AF (8697 5028).

Tiger's Head (JD Wetherspoon) 350 Bromley Road, SE6 2RZ (8698 8645).

Clapham

Clapham may well have the best range of boozers in the whole of south London, with **Clapham North** and **Grafton House** our favourites among the newcomers.

Arch 635

15-16 Lendal Terrace, SW4 7UX (7720 7343/ www.arch635.co.uk). Clapham North tube/Clapham High Street rail. **Open** 5pm-midnight Mon-Thur; 5pm-2am Fri; 4pm-2am Sat; 4pm-midnight Sun. **Credit** (over £10) AmEx, MC, V.

Inside a railway arch, Arch 635 has gone to great efforts to provide an industrial-themed drinking space to suit a wide range of drinkers, but remains essentially the preserve of those who like their pubs loud – painfully so at weekends. Chopped in two, with a small bar in the middle serving both areas, the decor borrows from a number of styles, and features original brickwork punctuated with bright sheets of stainless steel, and a large Roy Lichtenstein-inspired mural with manga overtones brightening up the wall behind the convivial, cocktail-shaking bar staff. A superior selection of draught lagers, among them San Miguel, joins impressive cocktails and wines, and a fridge is well stocked with bottles including the superb Baltika from Russia and the wonderful Californian Anchor Steam beer.

Disabled: toilet. Games (pool, table football). Music (DJs 10pm Fri, Sat; free). TV (satellite). **Map 11 L16.**

South

Brixton Bar & Grill. *See p201.*

Bar Local

4 Clapham Common Southside, SW4 7AA (7622 9406/www.barlocal.co.uk). Clapham Common tube. **Open** 5pm-midnight Mon-Fri; noon-midnight Sat; noon-11.30pm Sun. **Food served** 5-10pm Mon-Fri; noon-10pm Sat, Sun. **Credit** MC, V.

As long and thin as many of the people who like to be seen in it, Bar Local remains the choice of good-looking Londoners who drop by every night for hip booze, knock-out burgers and ear-bursting DJs. Imagine an art gallery full of alcohol on a submarine in Brighton and you've sort of got this place in one. Heading up the beers are a catwalk of fashionable drinks including the delicious bottled brothers Asahi and Asahi Black, Leffe and Staropramen on tap, and a better-than-average list of cocktails. With the exception of the aforementioned burgers, forget the food and treat this one as a storming boozer where talking takes second place to looking the part. Non-smokers should know that, until the laws are finally sorted out, the air gets incredibly smoky on busy nights.

Music (DJs 8pm Thur-Sun). **Map 11 L17**.

Bread & Roses

68 Clapham Manor Street, SW4 6DZ (7498 1779/ www.breadandrosespub.com). Clapham Common or Clapham North tube. **Open** noon-11pm Mon-Thur; noon-midnight Fri; 11am-midnight Sat; 11am-10.30pm Sun. **Food served** noon-3pm, 7-9.30pm Mon-Fri; noon-4pm, 6-9.30pm Sat; 1-7pm Sun. **Credit** MC, V.

The fabulous Bread and Roses attracts a mixed and charming clientele thanks entirely to it being one of the best pubs in London – it's as simple as that. Run by the inspired Workers' Beer Company, the decor is simple throughout, offering a choice of smoking and no-smoking rooms with lots of sharp angles and big mirrors, plus a number of thoughtful additions including a comical jelly bean machine in the main bar. Beer runs the gamut from bottled Hoegaarden to draught Leffe to Adnams, and there's a number of classy cocktails to keep the City types fuelled and happy. In true gastropub style the food is bold and experimental, featuring several blackboard favourites and a popular Saturday Sausage Sizzler BBQ. Entertainment includes live music and occasional stand-up comedy, and they've also thoughtfully put in wireless internet throughout the building. A truly wonderful place to spend your money, any time of day or night.

Babies and children welcome (until 9pm). Disabled: toilet. Function room. Games (board games). Music (band monthly; check website for details). No-smoking area (conservatory). Quiz (8.30pm Mon; £2). Tables outdoors (8, conservatory; 15, heated garden; 8, patio). **Map 11 L16**.

Clapham North

409 Clapham Road, SW9 9BT (7274 2472). Clapham North tube. **Open** 11am-midnight Mon-Wed; 11am-2am Thur-Sat; noon-midnight Sun. **Food served** 11am-10pm Mon-Sat; noon-10pm Sun. **Credit** AmEx, MC, V.

Pandering primarily to a nouveau riche estate agent Saturday night crowd, Clapham North offers the authentic Kronenbourg and cocktail experience in a predominantly vertical drinking environment. During the day the place is popular for its admirable food, including changing daily specials, American breakfast and a limited range of vegetarian dishes, and is a genuinely nice place to spend quality time with friends. Sunday mornings are given over to smoked salmon and pricey salads, while Thursday, Friday and Saturday nights witness possibly the strangest

Babies and children welcome (until 8.30pm). Disabled: toilet. Function room. Games (board games). Quiz (8pm 1st Mon of mth; £1; 7pm Sun; free). Tables outdoors (8, enclosed terrace). TVs (big screen, satellite). **Map 11 L17.**

Grafton House

13-19 Old Town, SW4 0JT (7498 5559/www. graftonhouseuk.com). Clapham Common tube. **Open** 11am-1am daily. **Food served** noon-10.30pm daily. **Credit** AmEx, MC, V.

A delightfully spacious bar and restaurant, Grafton House is popular with the Clapham A-list and a whole host of local media professionals, and is currently making waves all over south London. The designers must have had a ball putting this place together. It's littered with big red sofas and features by far the best people-watching windows on Old Town. Marble floors, tropical hardwoods, thoughtful lighting and quirky toilets all fit together to create a thoroughly relaxed atmosphere in which to sink a battalion of fancy drinks. As well as the now obligatory list of neon-tinted cocktails, the biggest pull here is the bottled Kasteel Cru, a delicious French lager made from Champagne yeast. DJs hit the decks at the weekends, and on Friday and Saturday nights the place is buzzing with crowds of sophisticated drinkers, making either getting here early or booking a table wise precautions.

Babies and children welcome. Disabled: toilet. Music (jazz 6pm Thur, Sun; DJs 7pm Fri, Sat; both free). Restaurant (no smoking). TVs (big screen, satellite). **Map 11 K16.**

Landor

70 Landor Road, SW9 9PH (7274 4386/www.landor theatre.com). Clapham North tube/Clapham High Street rail. **Open** noon-11.30pm Mon-Thur; noon-midnight Fri, Sat; noon-10.30pm Sun. **Food served** noon-2.30pm, 6-9.30pm Mon-Fri; 1-8.30pm Sat; 1.15-5pm Sun. **Credit** MC, V.

Situated on what was once dubbed Murder Mile, Landor epitomises the area's recent rise to prosperity. This superb theatre bar is now safely out of the doldrums of the last couple of years, thanks to the efforts of enlightened new management. The indifferent barmaids are gone and this detritus-filled epic boozer is a fabulous place to eat, drink, watch football on the large screen or shoot a few games of pool on one of three tables. Tradition is upheld by draught Abbot and Greene King IPA, while the fridges stock a staggering array of bottles from pale ale to Peroni. Food choices include monster burgers, organic beef, Indian platters and a recommended Sunday roast lunch, best eaten in the pleasant beer garden, during the summer months. A genuinely nice mix of people drink here, including die-hard locals, students, and the occasional celebrity, though the altogether wonderful vibe can make finding a seat problematic some evenings. Highly recommended.

Comedy (8pm 3rd Sun of mth; £6-£10). Games (fruit machines, 3 pool tables, quiz machine). Music (cabaret 8pm 2nd Sun of mth; £6-10). Quiz (8pm 1st Sun of mth; £2). Tables outdoors (12, garden). Theatre (7.30pm Tue-Sat; £7-£10). TVs (big screen, satellite). **Map 11 M16.**

Prince of Wales

38 Old Town, SW4 0LB (7622 3530). Clapham Common tube. **Open** 5-11pm Mon-Wed; 5pm-midnight Thur; 5pm-1am Fri; 1pm-1am Sat; 1-11pm Sun. **Credit** AmEx, MC, V.

door policy in London – a frenzied, bouncer-controlled gridlock by the corner entrance takes place a few metres to the left of a second set of entirely unmonitored doors. However you choose to get in, quality DJs are on hand to spin an upbeat blend of 1970s oddities, jazz funk and chill-out amid something reminiscent of an Essex school reunion. All awfully good fun, and highly recommended.

Babies and children welcome. Disabled: toilet. Music (DJs 8pm Thur, 9pm Fri, Sat, 5pm Sun; free). Nosmoking area. Tables outdoors (5, terrace). TVs (big screen, satellite). **Map 11 M16.**

Coach & Horses

173-175 Clapham Park Road, SW4 7EX (7622 3815/ www.barbeerian-inns.com). Clapham Common tube. **Open** noon-11am Mon-Wed; noon-midnight Thur-Sat; noon-10.30pm Sun. **Food served** noon-2.30pm, 6-9.30pm Mon-Fri; noon-3pm, 6.30-9pm Sat; 12.30-5pm, 7-9pm Sun. **Happy hour** 6-7pm Thur-Sat. **Credit** MC, V.

The Coach and Horses is a tastefully updated trad pub, frequented by rugby fans and a lively after-work crowd kept happy on draught real ales including London Pride, Spitfire and Old Speckled Hen. The draught lagers include San Miguel and Red Stripe, the weekend cocktails are a popular hit, and there's a well-chosen (albeit small) selection of obscure Scotch whisky. If you fancy more than a pickled egg, the specials board offers a diverse selection of posh mains, your granny's favourite stodgy puddings and celebrated Sunday lunches. The proprietors have maintained a minimalist attitude to decor, by sprinkling the bookshelves with hardback copies of *Reader's Digest* and chucking a vase of fresh flowers on the bar. During the summer hardcore drinkers can brave the elements and tip back drinks next to one of the busiest roads in the area.

In an area dominated by big identikit pubs and the merry young professionals that frequent them, this tiny, mellow place sticks out like a sore thumb. The occasionally morose indie soundtrack (the Cure are prominent) helps, but the POW's defining feature is its tat: a multitude of pots hangs from the ceiling, a surfboard juts towards one of the small windows, a sofa is backed with a pair of skis and two halberds, and the toilets are neighboured by a statuette and a deer's head. It's an amiable mess – the pub is just far too relaxed to feel wacky, with the (mostly local) clientele ignoring the clutter to concentrate on chatting and booze. The wine is limited, but regular ales include Landlord and Bombardier, and there's a nice mix of lagers, including Hoegaarden. Thursday is quiz night, and you can watch the buses roll past and top up your tan at outside seating.
Babies and children admitted (until 9pm). Benches outdoors (4, pavement). Quiz (8pm Thur; free). TV. **Map 11 M16.**

Royal Oak

8-10 Clapham High Street, SW4 7UT (7720 5678). Clapham North tube. **Open** noon-11pm Mon-Thur; noon-midnight Fri; noon-1am Sat; noon-10.30pm Sun. **Food served** noon-10.30pm daily. **Credit** MC, V.
Straight out of the final episode of *Twin Peaks*, this former spit-and-sawdust watering hole has been radically transformed into something altogether more contemporary, thanks to the addition of a coat of white paint, thumping tunes and an assortment of postmodern Londoners. Shoe-staring students and colourful cabbies vie for limited space over draught Kronenbourg, Stella, Bud and Adnams, while web designers and their wives drop in for large plates of venison sausage and mash, halloumi snacks and a surprisingly good selection of wines. A garage has been transformed into an intimate drinking area (accessed somewhat alarmingly via the gent's toilet at the back) and waitresses ferry drinks hither and thither – the whole effect is really enjoyable. It's just a shame they have to play the music so ear-breakingly loud after the sun goes down.
Babies and children welcome (until 6pm). Tables outdoors (4, pavement). TV (big screen, satellite). **Map 11 M16.**

Sand

156 Clapham Park Road, SW4 7DE (7622 3022/ www.sandbarrestaurant.co.uk). Clapham Common tube/35, 37 bus. **Open** 6.30pm-2am Mon-Thur; 6.30pm-3am Fri, Sat; 6.30pm-1am Sun. **Food served** 6.30-11pm daily. **Admission** £5 after 9pm, £8 after 11pm Fri, Sat. **Credit** MC, V.
A magnificent oasis of quirky sophistication, this desert-themed establishment for high-flyers is an absolute pleasure to drink in. Khaki minimalism throughout, including a sparse collection of pots, some oriental ironwork, the clever use of housing-estate breeze blocks and an enormous egg timer behind the bar ensure the atmosphere is always relaxing – precisely what you want when you're paying these kind of prices. With the exception of draught Leffe, everything worth drinking comes in a bottle, including perfectly chilled Staropramen, Beck's, Corona and £100 Krug Grande Cuvée NV-Reims. Divided into three main areas, Sand has a friendly ground-floor bar bristling with impeccable bar staff, dancing downstairs and a members-only upstairs room. Not surprisingly, queues reach communist country proportions at the weekends, and booking a table is highly recommended.
Disabled: toilet. Function room. Games (board games). Music (DJs 10.30pm Wed-Sat). Tables outdoors (7, roof terrace). TV (big screen). **Map 11 L17.**

Tim Bobbin

1-3 Lilleshall Road, SW4 0LN (7738 8953). Clapham Common or Clapham South tube. **Open** noon-11pm Mon-Wed; noon-midnight Thur-Sat; noon-10.30pm Sun. **Food served** noon-3pm, 7-10pm Mon-Sat; 12.30-4pm, 7-9.30pm Sun. **Credit** MC, V.
This charming little local, named after a lewd 18th-century caricaturist, mixes boozer and bar quite nicely. Fawn walls are covered in Bobbin's creations: hands wandering under girls' skirts and inebriated craftsmen retching on tables. A mixed clientele enjoy the candlelight, chatting by the open fire, some tucking into large portions of rustic food in the brick conservatory with open kitchen at the back – rosemary-braised haggis with traditional neeps and tatties (£10.50) is a prime example of the winter fare. The wine list is reasonably priced, and Bombardier, London Pride and the usual lagers feature on tap. Funky modern jazz plays in the background, interrupted by the popular and informal quiz on Sundays.
Games (darts). Quiz (8pm Sun; free). Restaurant (no-smoking area). Tables outdoors (2, pavement). TVs.

Windmill on the Common

Windmill Drive, Clapham Common Southside, SW4 9DE (8673 4578/www.windmillclapham.co.uk). Clapham Common or Clapham South tube. **Open** 11am-midnight Mon-Sat; noon-11pm Sun. **Food served** noon-3pm, 6-10pm Mon-Fri; noon-11pm Sat; noon-10pm Sun. **Credit** AmEx, DC, MC, V.
This vast Young's pub and hotel is an institution for the hordes that gravitate to Clapham Common throughout the year. A somewhat depressing collection of draught beer and nothing better than bottled Waggledance confirm the place is little more than a large provincial hotel, complete with airport bar carpets, country house furnishings and bursts of modern art on the walls. But, surprisingly, this just doesn't matter. Location alone means it attracts one of the strangest mixes of people in any pub in the area, giving the place a surprisingly healthy buzz. Equally surprising is the fact that the Windmill is a great place to eat, featuring an English-leaning menu offering everything from mussels in white wine to fish and chips to – count them – three different types of ploughman's. If you bring your dog, they'll even provide it with its own bowl of water.
Babies and children welcome (conservatory or restaurant). Disabled: toilet. Function room. Games (fruit machine). Quiz (8pm Sun, winter; £1). Restaurant (no smoking). Tables outdoors (12, garden). TV (big screen, satellite). **Map 11 K18.**

Also in the area...

Bierodrome 44-48 Clapham High Street, SW4 7UR (7720 1118).
Fine Line 182-184 Clapham High Street, SW4 7UG (7622 4436).
Revolution 95-97 Clapham High Street, SW4 7TB (7720 6642)

Crystal Palace & Sydenham

For an area most famous for a glasshouse that burned down in the 1930s, you're looking at some surprisingly chic new drinking options. **Mansion** foremost among them. There's even a hidden Algerian treasure: **Numidie.**

Bluebottle

79 Westow Hill, SE19 1TX (8670 0654). Crystal Palace rail. **Open** 5pm-midnight Mon; noon-midnight Tue, Wed; noon-1am Thur, Sun; noon-2am Fri; noon-3am Sat. **Credit** MC, V.

This large-fronted establishment on the corner of Westow Hill has all the markings of a modern pub makeover, without losing some of the old habits. For a start, it has the giveaway lower-case all-in-one title over the front door; once inside, the spacious, relaxing brown and beige interior with big leather armchairs and open fire give the game away. A back area doubles as dancefloor and TV lounge for the big-screen matches at weekends, when the place turns into a pulling paradise, ferocious bouncers on the door. See what we mean about old habits dying hard? Daytime, though, and weekday evenings, it's a pleasant enough local, ideal for an afternoon's spin at table football. *Babies and children admitted (until 4pm). Function room. Games (table football). Music (8pm Thur-Sun; free). Tables outdoors (12, garden). TV (big screen).*

Dulwich Wood House

39 Sydenham Hill, SE26 6RS (8693 5666). Sydenham Hill rail/63, 202 bus. **Open** 11am-11pm Mon-Wed; 11am-midnight Thur-Sat; noon-10.30pm Sun. **Food served** noon-10pm Mon-Sat; noon-4pm Sun. **Credit** MC, V.

This solid landmark boasts historical touches. Its name derived from the ancient Dulwich Woode, loved by Byron when attending school in the area, the Dulwich was designed and built a century ago by Joseph Paxton, who was responsible for the Crystal Palace which stood down the road until the fire of 1936. In any case, this is a sturdy, much-loved boozer with a clutch of wood-panelled rooms inside and an expanse of lawn with a fine beer garden and children's play area in summer. It's a Young's pub, so expect the brewery's usual range of beers and ales at the bar, along with a decent menu of reasonably priced standard pub dishes and daily changing specials. *Games (fruit machines, quiz machine). Quiz (7.30pm Mon; £1). Restaurant (no smoking). Tables outdoors (50, garden). TV.*

Mansion

255 Gipsy Road, SE27 9QY (8761 9016). Gipsy Hill rail. **Open** noon-11pm Mon-Thur, Sun; noon-1am Fri, Sat. **Food served** noon-4pm, 6-10pm Mon-Thur; noon-4pm, 6-10pm Fri; noon-5pm, 6-10.30pm Sat; noon-5pm, 6-9.30pm Sun. **Credit** MC, V.

Long overdue an update, this monolithic old boozer opened at the end of 2005 and welcomes a new generation of 'Gypsies'. A grand piano (more mellow jazz than 'Roll out the barrel') sets the tone in a tasteful, dimly lit interior of cream walls, brown-leaf wallpaper, dark wood and gilded candelabra. Professionals and young couples are delighted with the eclectic, reasonably priced Thai/trad British menu (stir-fried roast duck with bamboo shoots and ginger,£9.50, monster burgers , £9). The bar dispenses house Mansion ale, along with Flowers IPA, Hoegaarden and Leffe and a range of cocktails (£6) and shooters (£3.50). A decent wine list (10 white and red, 2 rosé, from £12 to £27) plugs the gaps. Packed to the rafters for Tuesday's quiz night; there's live jazz on alternate Mondays. The Mansion (sister pub to the Rye in Peckham, *see p220*) is worth travelling for. *Babies and children welcome (until 6pm). Disabled: toilet. Function room. Music (pianist 5pm Sun; free). No-smoking area. Over 21s only after 6pm. Quiz (8pm Tue; £2). Tables outdoors (15, garden).*

Numidie

48 Westow Hill, SE19 1RX (8766 6166/www. numidie.co.uk). Gipsy Hill rail. **Open** 6pm-midnight Tue-Sun. **Credit** MC, V.

This little-known cellar bar beneath the Algerian restaurant of the same name is a gem. Candlelit tables, peeling pictures and bust sofas filling the many nooks and crannies comprise the decor, as well as a pocket-sized Zinedine Zidane hanging from the ceiling. Hamed, your friendly barman for the evening, dispenses pints of Staropramen or little bottles of Casablanca beer. The bar snack menu features well-made curiosities such as squid stuffed with crabmeat and pan-fried spinach (£5.50) and merguez sausage with harissa (£4.50). Wines are mainly French, although the two house glasses (£3.50) are of South American origin, a Chilean sauvignon blanc and an Argentinian shiraz. Mention must be made of the original cocktails (£5.50-£6), examples of which include a Berbère Cup of Wild Turkey 8 and fresh lemon, a Creole Daisy of Creole Shrub orange rum and coconut, and a Maurèsque of Zubrowka Bison Grass vodka muddled with coriander and almond syrup. *Babies and children welcome (restaurant). Bar available for hire (Tue-Thur). Restaurant (no smoking).*

Also in the area...

Postal Order (JD Wetherspoon) 32-33 Westow Street, SE19 3RW (8771 3003).

Deptford

The taverns along the historic High Street where Marlowe caroused and finally met his doom are no more. Welcome with open arms, then, new addition the **Last Lick**.

Dog & Bell

116 Prince Street, SE8 3JD (8692 5664/www.thedog andbell.com). New Cross tube/rail/Deptford rail. **Open** noon-11pm Mon-Sat; noon-10.30pm Sun. **Food served** noon-3pm, 6-9pm Mon-Fri; 2-4pm Sun. **Credit** MC, V.

Now decorated with some unusual art in stone tablets in the busy side room, the landmark Dog and Bell – sat in a dark passage between Deptford and Greenwich – is still best known for its eclectic beers and cheap prices. Incumbents include British Bulldog, Harry Jack's Three Rivers and Over The Moon, all in the £2.10-£2.30 price range (you can't buy a packet of Rizlas in W11 for £2.10), and there are Beck's and, Fuller's ESB and London Pride too. Running round the walls an unusual collection of plates with caricatures of famous chefs on them keeps watch over proceedings, but don't worry: no nouvelle cuisine here. Honest, well-turned-out pub grub keeps honest, well-turned-out regulars happy. There are authentic retro touches (the political map of India, the bar billiards table) but, this being Deptford, nobody pays much attention. There's drinking to be done. *Bar available for hire. Disabled: toilet. Games (bar billiards). Quiz (8pm Sun; £1). Tables outdoors (6, garden). TV.*

Last Lick

189 Deptford High Street, SE8 3NT (8320 2340/ www.thelastlick.com). Deptford rail. **Open** 11am-11pm Mon-Thur, Sun; 11am-2am Fri, Sat. **Food served** 11am-3pm, 6-9pm Mon-Fri; 11am-9pm Sat, Sun. **Credit** MC, V.

South

A new bar has arrived in the pub wilderness of Deptford High Street. In its day, when Marlowe was murdered here or a sozzled Peter the Great was ridden home in a wheelbarrow, this was nothing but pubs. Now, *cada nada*. Not that the Last Lick, name included, will be to everyone's taste. Neither Marlowe, Peter the Great nor a certain type of Deptfordite would like a wine bar and bistro anywhere near them, this one a small, gleaming room of light wood with a slice of paved back garden. It has an extensive menu of foreign bottled beers, some 30 varieties changed every six weeks (Isle of Skye Black Cuillin? Dorothy Goodbody's Our Glass?). Surprisingly, there are only a dozen wines, most by the glass, including a Waipara West chardonnay (£3.90/£15.60) from New Zealand and a Domaine Ruet Brouilly (£14.50). Cocktails are stupid cheap at £4, and superior weekday lunches include steamed haddock stuffed in jacket potatoes (£5.50) and Chinese-style bream on noodles (£6).
Babies and children admitted. Bar available for hire. Disabled: toilet. Music (jazz 9pm 1st and 3rd Sat of mth; free). Tables outdoors (12, garden).

Live Bar

41-42 Deptford Broadway, SE8 0PL (8469 2121/ www.livebar.co.uk). Deptford Bridge DLR/53, 177 bus. **Open** noon-11pm Mon, Tue; noon-2am Wed-Sun. **Food served** noon-10pm daily. **Credit** AmEx, MC, V.
A reasonably priced pasta selection and line of dining tables is the latest addition to this successful, late-opening party bar set in an old bank on the main road out of Deptford to Dover. Apart from that, little change – why should there be? A clubby crowd packs out the main room with its large, main bar counter, DJ decks and pictures of Charlie Parker and stills from *Betty Blue* on the walls. Most dive into pints of San Miguel, Kronenbourg or Foster's, despite the modest cocktail menu of standards (£5.50). There's a back room for pool and a side room occasionally open for overspill. A substantial new housing development just the other side of the nearby DLR station might change Deptford's demographics but not this bar, attracting up-for-it punters from Woolwich and beyond.
Comedy/variety shows (8pm Wed; free). Function room. Games (pool). Music (DJs, local bands 9pm Wed-Sun; free). TV.

Dulwich

Dulwich is another area with a spate of new establishments: among them, the renewed **Palmerston** is much improved and **Inside 72** an absolutely terrific find.

Clock House

196A Peckham Rye, SE22 9QA (8693 2901). East Dulwich or Peckham Rye rail/12, 197 bus. **Open** 11am-midnight Mon-Sat; noon-11pm Sun. **Food served** noon-2.30pm, 6-8.30pm Mon-Fri; noon-8.30pm Sat, Sun. **Credit** MC, V.
Opposite Peckham Rye, its front terrace a boon in summer, this local landmark is a popular choice with the more discerning of recent arrivals to SE22. Inside, the Clock House, filled with timepieces, is neither gentrified nor gastro. A safe and solid offering of salads and jackets is served from a buffet bar, supplemented by a daily changing board of specials, and best partaken in the upper dining area, the no-smoking zone for the time being. A main bar and back area fitted with a skylight are done out in green, embell-

ished with stuffed birds and fish. As for beers, there's Young's Special and Pilsner, guest ales such as St George's and Waggledance, standard lagers and Hoegaarden. All of a decent range of wines are available by the glass.
Babies and children welcome (patio). Disabled: toilet. No-smoking area. Tables outdoors (20, patio).

Crown & Greyhound

73 Dulwich Village, SE21 7BJ (8299 4976). North Dulwich rail/P4 bus. **Open** 11am-11pm Mon-Wed, Sun; 11am-midnight Thur-Sat. **Food served** noon-10pm Mon-Sat; noon-9pm Sun. **Credit** AmEx, MC, V.
Once two separate pubs, the Crown for the gentry and the Greyhound for the peasants, today this is the only pub for everyone in Dulwich Village – and there is no need for any other. A grand frontage is set back from the main road, behind which hide four saloon areas around a polished wood and stained-glass bar, each creaking with armchairs and daintily carved bench seats. Beers include Tom Wood's Old Timber, Marston's Pedigree, de Koninck and Früli, but many people come here for the food alone, enjoyed in a newly refurbished dining area with an open kitchen. An expansive two-tiered beer garden and terraced area comes into its own for barbecues and Sunday lunches in summer. The carvery is legendary, serving up hulking great roasts of lamb, beef or pork (£9).
Babies and children welcome. Disabled: toilet. Function room. Restaurant (no smoking). Tables outdoors (50, garden).

East Dulwich Tavern

1 Lordship Lane, SE22 8EW (8693 1316). East Dulwich rail/12, 40, 176, 185 bus. **Open** 11am-midnight Mon-Thur; noon-1am Fri, Sat; noon-11.30pm Sun. **Food served** noon-9pm daily. **Credit** MC, V.
Another refurb, this pub has scrubbed out the Victorian heritage of the original building with chocolate-brown decor and harlequin floor tiles. Unkind, perhaps, because the building has lent it a neat L-shape, with a back bar and split down the middle. To the left, picture windows give natural light to modern art; to the right, an open fire and intimate side area partitioned by silk oriental drapes are in stark contrast to TV sport and banging rock music. A prime location on the corner of up-and-coming Lordship Lane ensures a packed house of young revellers, narrowly the right side of raucous, who enjoy draught Grolsch, Guinness and Young's and a few wines by the glass. More fuss is made of the food, such as roasted sea bass with coriander, crème fraiche baby potatoes and artichokes (£12.95). There's table football to even an old score should things have not gone well on the big screen.
Babies and children welcome (until 6pm). Disabled: toilet. Games (quiz machine, table football). Restaurant. Tables outdoors (5, pavement). TVs (big screen, satellite).

Franklins

157 Lordship Lane, SE22 8HX (8299 9598/www. franklinsrestaurant.com). East Dulwich rail/40, 176, 185 bus. **Open** noon-11pm Mon-Wed; noon-midnight Thur-Sat; noon-10.30pm Sun. **Food served** noon-10.30pm Mon-Sat; 1pm-10pm Sun. **Credit** AmEx, MC, V.
This popular local gastrobar didn't need a recent external makeover to reveal its previous existence as corner boozer the Victory – communal pub elements reside in the busy front area. The back section has long been given over to an open kitchen and dining area. What is on offer is perhaps slightly expensive and overly ambitious takes on

modern British cuisine. One example from our most recent visit was pig's cheek, chicory and snails at £12.50, with the side dishes extra. It's a nice place to dine, all the same – its dimly lit bare-brick walls adorned with works by local artists. If you're just after a simple snack and a standard beer or one of eight wines by the glass, sink into a leather sofa and take in the neighbourhood vibe.

Babies and children welcome. Disabled: toilet. Function room. Restaurant (no-smoking area). Tables outdoors (3, pavement).

Inside 72

72 Lordship Lane, SE22 8HF (8693 7131). East Dulwich rail. **Open** noon-midnight Mon-Sat; noon-10.30pm Sun. **Food served** noon-3pm, 7-10pm Mon-Sat; noon-4pm Sun. **Credit** MC, V.

In an area inundated in overpriced, snobby mediocrity, this friendly, unpretentious little retro bar would be a credit to any part of London. Here, it's an oasis for those who care about where they drink and who they drink with. Amid tatty stone walls plastered with art, film posters and automatons – the boss has a thing for robots, just look behind the bar – well-chosen rock 'n' roll noise inspires conversation without drowning it out. Occasional theme nights (Hendrix, for example) bring a few bods out of the woodwork. The draught beer selection could be more imaginative, but there's no faulting the bottles: Erdinger, Chimay, Duvel, Anchor Steam and Hoegaarden, among others. The food available is mainly of the burger and chilli variety, with roasts on Sundays.

Games (board games, cards).

Liquorish

123 Lordship Lane, SE22 8HU (8693 7744/www.liquorish.com). East Dulwich rail/40, 176, P13 bus. **Open** 5pm-midnight Mon-Thur; 5pm-1am Fri; 11am-1am Sat; 11am-11.30pm Sun. **Food served** 6-11pm Mon-Fri; noon-5pm, 6-11pm Sat, Sun. **Credit** AmEx, MC, V.

This popular sliver of space somehow manages to be split into two, one part a sleek cocktail bar, the other a simple diner. DJ decks are discreetly positioned towards the back for after-dark vibe control, when bare bulbs of different sizes hanging at various lengths illuminate primary-coloured walls and bar stools apparently fashioned by Henry Moore. Here a young set fuel up on two dozen superbly mixed classic and original cocktails (all £6). Liquorish's signature (£6), for example, comprises cucumber vodka, pear purée and coriander shaken with apple and lychee juice, topped with Champagne; a Honey Pie features honey vodka, Drambuie and apricot liqueur. A global choice of beer is available by the bottle; the wine choice does little wrong. Food is simple and locally sourced where possible, with bar snacks available for DJ sessions on Friday and Saturday. Couples and families play backgammon and Connect 4 over the course of the afternoon.

Babies and children welcome (lunch). Bar available for hire. Games (board games). Music (DJ 9pm Fri, Sat; musicians 6pm alternate Sun; both free). Tables outdoors (8, terrace).

Palmerston

91 Lordship Lane, SE22 8EP (8693 1629/www.the palmerston.co.uk). East Dulwich rail/185, 176, P13 bus. **Open** noon-11pm Mon-Thur; noon-midnight Fri, Sat; noon-10.30pm Sun. **Food served** noon-2.30pm, 7-10pm Mon-Thur; noon-2.30pm, 7.30-11pm Fri; noon-3pm, 7-11pm Sat; noon-4pm Sun. **Credit** MC, V.

Booze talking
Royal Oak

You are?
Frank Taylor, co-landlord of the Royal Oak, Borough (*see p199*), where the bar had a sign reading, 'Lager drinkers served only when accompanied by a responsible adult'.

What persuaded the CAMRA judges to make the Royal Oak their pub of the year in 2005?
I suppose it's all sorts of things. The decor. The ambience. The ashtrays being clean. The size of the barmaid's boobs [the Royal Oak has an all-male staff]. And the beer – Harveys for a start sells itself, it's a very popular beer, and we're the only Harveys pub in London.

So everyone's here because of the Harvey's.
Well, if you look at the till at the end of the evening, we're an incredibly beer-oriented pub. A smidgen of lager and Guinness and cider. But it's just basically beer.

Don't publicans make more profit on lager?
True, it costs much less to make and look after lager. If the pub trade wants to make cask ale a going concern we've got to put up prices. That's probably why we can't afford holidays.

So are Royal Oak drinkers all CAMRA men?
A lot of people think real ale drinkers just sniff and twirl and scribble and write. By and large I find CAMRA people OK. As long as you pull them a full pint and they don't think you're ripping them off, they're very easy to look after.

The Royal Oak has a different atmosphere to most of the other pubs around Borough.
It's the cobwebs, the dust, the shiny carpets. People like squalor. No, we look after the pub. It's the atmosphere and the crowd. Go into some pubs and no one's talking to anybody. Some Sundays I go down Brick Lane and call in the Pride of Spitalfields and that's a wonderful place. Everybody talks to each other. That's what I think it's like here. At least, I hope it is.

South

All the recent changes to the former geezer boozer the Lord Palmerston have been for the better. A friendly atmosphere pervades a mixed clientele of regulars, professionals and young families – that and the aroma of award-winning food. Large cascading lights are set to dim, oak panels and leather bench seats provide a little gravitas, and relaxed soul music soundtracks the main bar. The back no-smoking area with its lovely skylight is where the food is served. It's not cheap, mind you – Moroccan spiced lamb with couscous, baba ganoush, harissa and minted yoghurt is £13.75, and little is under £10. A decent accompanying Argentinian malbec is £17. No cocktails yet at the bar – they're promised soon – but for now there is a selection of good ales: Timothy Taylor Landlord, London Pride and Greene King IPA.

Babies and children welcome. Music (jazz/soul 7pm Sun; free). No-smoking area. Tables outdoors (5, pavement).

Forest Hill

Nothing much to see here. Bar action centres on traffic-hexed streets focused on the station, and nothing outshines the **Dartmouth Arms**.

Dartmouth Arms

7 Dartmouth Road, SE23 3HN (8488 3117/www.dartmoutharms.com). Forest Hill rail/122, 176, 197 bus. **Open** noon-midnight Mon-Sat; noon-11.30pm Sun. **Food served** noon-3.30pm, 6.30-10pm Mon-Sat; noon-9pm Sun. **Credit** AmEx, MC, V.
After its revival as a rather decent gastropub under Michael Richards of Fire Station (*see p106*) fame, the Dartmouth seems out of place in this shabby stretch of south London. A beer garden with a pear tree in the middle adds to the incongruity. Inside, red 1960s-style Perspex lights are surrounded by pristine white walls (did Forest Hill ever do pristine?) dotted with pictures of coffee cups. Under Paul Newbury, who earned his spurs in the kitchens of Tate Modern, the weekly changing menu has come on in leaps and bounds. The open-plan kitchen turns out fine and well-priced takes on robust modern European cuisine (squid and black pudding risotto, £5; potted hot smoked trout with toasted sourdough, £4.50). For drinks, there's Brakspear Bitter, London Pride and Old Speckled Hen on draught, Baltika and Budvar by the bottle, standard cocktails under a fiver and 30 types of wine, eight by the glass (from £2.90/£10.95).
Babies and children welcome. Disabled: toilet. Restaurant (no smoking). Tables outdoors (10, garden).

Railway Telegraph

112 Stanstead Road, SE23 1BS (8699 6644). Forest Hill rail/122, 185 bus. **Open** 11am-11pm Mon-Thur; 11am-midnight Fri, Sat; noon-10.30pm Sun. **Food served** noon-2.30pm, 6-9.30pm Mon-Sat; 1-3pm Sun. **Credit** AmEx, MC, V.
Jutting out on to the South Circular, this large Shepherd Neame pub was once favoured by bikers (whatever happened to them?) and now fills with local bods, their girlfriends, wives and offspring. Communal would be a fair term. They seem happy to gather between its peach walls and stripy curtains, and look forward to the various types of entertainment put on by the management. There's karaoke, of course, competitions at the man-sized pool table that fills a side area, quiz nights, darts, any number of board games and a free jukebox (try finding a good tune, though). Why, you needn't bother with Pontins this year.

And although either would provide bog-standard pub grub of the large battered cod variety, you can bet your bottom dollar that only the Railway would have Swiss Hürlimann, Dutch Oranjeboom, and Shepherd Neame Spitfire and Master Brew on draught. Sky Sports also pulls in the crowds, the garden attracts young mums eager for an RTD-fuelled break at weekends.
Babies and children admitted (until 7pm). Games (board games, darts, fruit machines, pool, quiz machine). Music (bands/DJs/karaoke alternate Sat; free). No-smoking area. Quiz (8.30pm Thur; £2). Tables outdoors (3, pavement; 11, garden). TV (big screen, satellite).

Also in the area...
Capitol (JD Wetherspoon) 11-21 London Road, SE23 3TW (8291 8920).

Greenwich

These days Greenwich has a real buzz about it, especially at the weekends when visitors throng to the market and historical attractions. Family pub lunches at the **Ashburnham Arms** and **Trafalgar Tavern** still have their place, but the ostentatious **Inc Bar** and excellent **Greenwich Union** and **Polar Bar** are also now established.

Ashburnham Arms

25 Ashburnham Grove, SE10 8UH (8692 2007). Greenwich rail/DLR. **Open** noon-11pm Mon, Wed, Sun; noon-midnight Tue, Thur-Sat. **Food served** noon-2.30pm, 6-9pm Tue-Sat; noon-8pm Sun. **Credit** MC, V.
There have been few changes here, but if it ain't broke, don't fix it. A lovely neighbourhood pub, this, well run, well staffed, well stocked. Shepherd Neame beers and Oranjeboom lager are quietly consumed in the cosy space around the main bar, while a narrow corridor and conservatory lend themselves to convivial dining. Mains in the £7 range include honey-roast red pepper chicken salad, blackened salmon fillet, and pizzas such as a Leyumi (roast vegetables) and Piccante (spicy meatball pepperoni). The Sunday roasts (£6.50) are unsurprisingly popular, as are the children's meals (£4.75) and desserts (£3.75). Eight wines are served, two by the glass; they include a decent chenin blanc and rioja Crianza at £15 each.
Babies and children welcome (conservatory). Games (board games). Quiz (9pm Tue; free). No-smoking area. Tables outdoors (6, garden; 12, patio).

Bar du Musée

17 Nelson Road, SE10 9JB (8858 4710/www.bardumusee.com). Cutty Sark DLR. **Open** noon-midnight Mon-Thur; noon-2am Fri; 11am-2am Sat; 11am-midnight Sun. **Food served** noon-3pm, 6-10pm Mon-Fri; 11am-4pm, 6-10pm Sat, Sun. **Credit** MC, V.
Brunches, lunches, free half bottles of wine – the Greenwich Inc management, now running almost every landmark bar in the vicinity, does everything to bring people in to the spacious dining conservatories at the back of the Bar du Musée. And come they most certainly do, even though the mixed reviews also keep on coming. But still locals use it as a late-opening, louche hangout, foxy to a fault, intimate, candlelit and conspiratorial around a well-kept bar counter. It's where couples can fire a flagging relationship over a pricey bottle of Châteauneuf-du-Pape or singletons – quite often ladies of a certain age on a mission à deux, chatting

ferociously while eyeing up the talent – can order up a modest glass of house white and feel at ease. There's even a second-base option in basement form. Parisian decorative touches add to the mystique.

Babies and children welcome. Function room.
Restaurant. Tables outdoors (20, garden).

Coach & Horses

13 Greenwich Market, SE10 9HZ (8293 0880).
Greenwich rail/DLR/Cutty Sark DLR. **Open** 11am-11pm Mon-Thur; 11am-midnight Fri, Sat; noon-10.30pm Sun.
Food served noon-10pm daily. **Credit** MC, V.
Market pub and gastrobar, the Coach is a successful modernisation of a familiar local. Beer garden tables cover a corner space of Greenwich's covered crafts market, while a slightly upmarket, young professional crowd is attracted inside the pub by the daily changing menu. Quality starters included, on the day of review, mussels in white wine (£5) and goat's cheese and onion tartlet (£6), but bottles of Heinz ketchup are defiantly plonked on each of the small wooden trestle tables, for use in the traditional fish and chips (£9). With restaurant prices in force, the current weekday lunchtime two-course offer of £10 is worth considering. Taps of Paulaner, Leffe, Shepherd Neame and Bombardier line the quarter-moon bar counter, although many prefer to choose from the two dozen wines, six of each colour by the glass – perhaps an Oveja Negra chardonnay (£15.70) from Chile or a Australian Stump Jump grenache shiraz (£17.70).
Babies and children admitted (until 9pm). No-smoking area. Tables outdoors (12, patio).

Cutty Sark Tavern

4-6 Ballast Quay, SE10 9PD (8858 3146). Greenwich rail/DLR/Cutty Sark DLR. **Open** 11am-11pm Mon-Sat; noon-10.30pm Sun. **Food served** noon-9pm Mon-Fri, Sun; noon-10pm Sat. **Credit** MC, V.
The contrast between the modern waterfront housing development and this historic hostelry couldn't be more striking. 'A Georgian Free House c1695' says the sign, although the Cutty Sark Tavern may have been built a century later. In any case, it feels traditional: real ales (Black Sheep, Adnams Broadside, Shepherd Neame Spitfire, Timothy Taylor Landlord) on offer, beer-barrel tables, maritime knickknacks, low ceiling. The menu is brazenly trad too – 10oz gammon steak (£7.45), beef and Broadside pie (£7.95) and minted lamb steak (11.95) – and best devoured in the spacious first-floor area accessed by a wooden staircase. Some tables are set by river-view windows, while summer sees ten Thameside terrace tables come into their own. A half-decent choice of wines (around £13 a bottle) sees a few ladies join the mainly manly ale-drinking clientele.
Babies and children welcome. Games (fruit machine). Jukebox. Tables outdoors (10, riverside terrace). TV (satellite).

Greenwich Park Bar & Grill

1 King William Walk, SE10 9JY (8853 7860). Greenwich rail/Cutty Sark DLR/108, 177, 180, 472 bus. **Open** 11am-11pm Mon-Fri; 10am-11pm Sat, Sun. **Food served** 6.30-9.45pm Mon-Thur; noon-4pm, 6.30-9.45pm Fri-Sun. **Credit** MC, V.
The omnipotent Greenwich Inc group opened its latest venture by the grand main gates of Greenwich Park in 2005. It comprises a ground-floor bar, upstairs restaurant and a top-floor lounge for hire, with a lovely view of the park. Floral motifs are etched on to the windows and menu covers, upon which is written 'our food is blooming marvellous' and 'our wines have wonderful bouquets'. Of course,

given its location, the GPB&G will be popular. An easy walk from the park's playground, it has a well-priced children's menu (£2.95/mains); for adults, a high-standard bar menu includes warm pastrami on rye (£4.95) and, at weekends, five kinds of bagel (£2.80). The problem is the large bar itself, which is devoid of character. It needs living in, and a dozen wines by the glass, ten by the bottle (£16-£40), will help. The raised area of wicker chairs facing the park is the decorative exception to an otherwise bland interior. Beers are no surprise, either. And what's the scoop with the turquoise chandeliers?
Babies and children welcome (until 7pm). Disabled: toilet. Function room. Restaurant (no smoking). Separate room for parties, holds 50. Tables outdoors (6, courtyard; 4, pavement).

Greenwich Union

56 Royal Hill, SE10 8RT (8692 6258/www.greenwich union.co.uk). Greenwich rail/DLR. **Open** noon-11pm Mon-Fri; 11am-11pm Sat; noon-10.30pm Sun. **Food served** noon-10pm Mon-Fri; noon-9pm Sat, Sun. **Credit** MC, V.
Ray Richardson's bright artwork of the footballer looking heavenward is as iconic a Greenwich landmark as the beers at this Meantime Brewery flagship. Alistair Hook, who learned his age-old trade in Munich, has made a wonderful success of this bar since it opened in 2001. Seven house draught beers are proudly named in block capitals over the small rectangle of bar counter: Pilsener, Blonde, Kölsch, Wheat, Union, Raspberry and Indian Pale Ale (£2.50-£3.60), each with its own fresh, tangy flavour. But it's not just that – there's a relaxed, enjoyable, unsnobby atmosphere throughout. A similar venture in Clapham might have been unbearable; here, next to a Young's pub, it works. Richardson aside, decor is kept to a few framed copies of the *Picture Post* in the comfortable back area. There are foreign bottled beers too (Aventinus, Westmalle Trippel and American microbrews such as Sierra Nevada), wines (Laroche Chablis, £21.95; Spy Valley pinot noir, £21.95) and well-conceived dishes, either mains (sea bass and tuna seafood velouté, £8.90) or tapas (golden chicken breast skewer, £3.95). Even the coffee is well sourced.
Babies and children admitted (until 9pm). Music (live music 8pm Mon; free). No-smoking area. Tables outdoors (12, garden). TV.

Inc Bar & Restaurant

7 College Approach, SE10 9HY (8858 6721/www.inc bar.com). Cutty Sark DLR/177, 180, 286 bus. **Open** 6pm-1.30am Wed-Sat; 6pm-12.30am Sun. **Food served** 6-10pm Wed-Sun. **Credit** MC, V.
Another of the mighty Greenwich Inc's outposts, this ostentatious bar on the first floor of a spacious building was designed by Laurence Llewelyn-Bowen in a style meant to recall the slums and splendour of Victorian-era Greenwich. At the front there's a large area with jewels, antique clocks, plasma screens and a bar counter – as well as dining areas in a sunken pit and on the balcony. There are a number of smaller bars at the back – one has swirly patterned carpet and granny furniture, another is a dimly lit room with tastefully pornographic Victorian wallpaper. Reasonably priced cocktails (£6) are popular with the fashionable young locals who make up the clientele, as are the large selection of single malts and wines by the glass. And the heaven-and-hell-themed toilets are just beautiful.
Function rooms. Music (funk band 8pm Wed; DJs 9.30pm Thur-Sat; 6pm Sun; free). Over-21s only. TVs (satellite).

South

North Pole

131 Greenwich High Road, SE10 8JA (8853 3020/ www.northpolegreenwich.com). Greenwich rail/DLR. **Open** noon-midnight Mon-Wed; noon-1am Thur; noon-2am Fri, Sat; noon-11pm Sun. **Food served** noon-10pm daily. **Happy hour** 4.30pm-midnight Mon-Thur; 4-8pm Fri, Sat; 4-11pm Sun. **Credit** AmEx, DC, MC, V.

As popular as ever, this three-level bar, nightclub and restaurant halfway between Greenwich and Deptford attracts a party crowd. OK, it means bouncers on the door, but the atmosphere in the ground-floor bar room is chatty. Fashion TV plays over the bar while a disco ball casts light over a three-area space that comprises an intimate side alcove, bar stools opposite the bar counter and low sofas by the main door. The cocktail list is 30-strong: Gin Martinis made with Hendrick's, Grey Goose vodka with Mozart dark chocolate liqueur and double cream in a Raised In The Gateaux, with prices kept at £6 despite the quality on offer. Most people opt for beers – Staropramen, Hoegaarden, Caffrey's – although the wine list of two dozen varieties (Billaud-Simon Chablis, £28; Château Liversan Haut-Médoc, £34.50) isn't shabby. Superior Lite Bites (Thai fish cakes, risotto) in the £5 range and mains (£6-£7) such as Lincolnshire sausage and chips are informed by the high-standard continental restaurant upstairs. Basement club the South Pole runs Thursday through Saturday.
Babies and children welcome. Function room. Music (DJs 8.30pm Thur-Sat; jazz 8pm Sun; free). Restaurant (no-smoking area). Tables outdoors (8, pavement). TV (big screen).

Polar Bar

13 Blackheath Road, SE10 8PE (8691 1555/www.polar bar.co.uk). Greenwich rail/DLR/Deptford Bridge DLR. **Open** noon-1am Mon-Wed, Sun; noon-2am Thur; noon-3am Fri, Sat. **Food served** noon-10pm daily. **Admission** £3 after 9pm Thur; £5 after 9pm Fri, Sat. **Credit** MC, V.

A busy little late-opening DJ bar this, right next to the Magistrates' Court on the hill up to Blackheath, at the Greenwich–Deptford border. There's nothing fancy about it, but nothing scruffy either. You'll find a bright bar counter in one corner, dispensing draught Grolsch and Korenwolf, and glasses (£5.50) or jugs (£12) of 'long & cool' cocktails (including a Polar Bar Cooler with dark rum and a Polar Bar Cola with Cointreau), plus half-a-dozen types of wine (sauvignon blanc, tempranillo) at £14 a bottle. At the other end are a pool table, sports TV screens and DJ decks ready for action. Reasonably priced mains and tapas keep a young, clubby clientele replete.
Babies and children welcome (until 8pm). Music (karaoke 9pm Tue; DJs 9pm Mon, Wed-Sun). Tables outdoors (15, garden). TVs (big screen, satellite).

Richard I

52-54 Royal Hill, SE10 8RT (8692 2996). Greenwich rail/DLR. **Open** 11am-11pm Mon-Sat; noon-10.30pm Sun. **Food served** noon-9pm daily. **Credit** MC, V.

This Young's pub hasn't had to change a bit since the success of the adjoining Greenwich Union (*see p213*). It's as traditional as ever: framed pictures of high-picking outings from 1955; roast topsides of beef with all the trimmings (£8.95); treacle sponge (£3.95) for pudding. If anything, business here is on the up. It has an older clientele, Sky Sports is turned down and the usual range of Young's ales is supped reflectively. Prime seats are at the table in the bay window overlooking Royal Hill, the couple of tables in front

of it or, in summer, in the extensive back garden where children can be let loose. There are wines too, decent merlots and chardonnays in the £14 bracket.
Babies and children admitted (garden). Chess club (6pm Tue; free). No piped music. Quiz (8pm Sun; £1). Tables outdoors (15, garden; 2, pavement). TV.

Trafalgar Tavern

Park Row, SE10 9NW (8858 2909/www.trafalgar tavern.co.uk). Cutty Sark DLR/Maze Hill rail. **Open** noon-1am Mon-Thur; noon-2am Fri, Sat; noon-midnight Sun. **Food served** noon-10pm Mon-Sat; noon-5pm Sun. **Credit** MC, V.

With the proud addition of a statue of Horatio on the riverside cobblestones by the entrance, the Trafalgar's 2005 battle anniversary celebrations coincided with an upmarket approach to its catering. Still 'home to the famous whitebait dinners', the Tavern has trendified its food offerings in the bar and two restaurants. As for the bar itself, little has changed. The TT is a landmark, thanks to the Thames lapping against its wall and busy tourist trade. It isn't authentic (it was only built in 1837) but, restored in regal style in 1968, it does feel historic. Framed black-and-white photos of maritime scenes and portraits of braided admirals around a sturdy wooden interior help. In the three-space candlelit bar, Flowers IPA, London Pride, Marston's Pedigree and Boddingtons are the ales on offer. A new menu offers the house speciality of whitebait with paprika mayo (£8.95); you'd pay almost as much for the £8 club sandwich with chips (sorry, frites) and salad.
Babies and children welcome (until 7pm). Function rooms. Restaurant (no smoking). Tables outdoors (20, riverside). TV (big screen, satellite).

Also in the area...

Davy's Wine Vaults 161 Greenwich High Road, SE10 8JA (8853 0585).
Gate Clock (JD Wetherspoon) Cutty Sark Station, Creek Road, SE10 9RB (8269 2000).

Herne Hill

Snuggled around the south and eastern side of lovely Brockwell Park, betwixt Brixton and Dulwich, Herne Hill has recently started to gain a sense of itself. Gentrification has forced up property prices and greatly increased the drinking (and eating) options. Within two minutes' stumble of the train station, you'll find at least half a dozen varied boozing possibilities.

Commercial

210-212 Railton Road, SE24 0JT (7501 9051). Brixton tube/rail then 3, 196 bus/Herne Hill rail. **Open** noon-midnight daily. **Food served** noon-3pm, 5-10pm Mon-Fri; noon-10pm Sat; noon-9pm Sun. **Credit** AmEx, MC, V.

Here's proof that not all pub chains are the same. Mitchells & Butlers totally transformed the once-grotty Commercial at the end of 2004, and it's now Herne Hill's best and most popular boozer. There's lots of polished wood, brass details, big windows, comfortable couches and real fires blazing away on chilly nights. The drink prices are pretty steep, but the range on offer is exemplary: 12 or so wines of each colour (starting at £11); excellent beers (Bombardier, Spitfire, Paulaner, Früli, Küppers Kölsch,

Staropramen, Hoegaarden, de Koninck, Leffe) and even a choice of six or so gins (the wonderful Tanqueray Ten among them). Food, too, is well pitched and not too ambitious – the likes of chicken and bacon burgers, served with thick wedges, mussels or kebabs.
Babies and children welcome. Disabled: toilet. Games (board games). No-smoking area. Tables outdoors (5, garden).

Escape Bar & Art
214-216 Railton Road, SE24 0JT (7737 0333/www. escapebarandart.com). Herne Hill rail/3, 196 bus. **Open** 10am-midnight Mon-Wed, Sun; 10am-1am Thur; 10am-2am Fri, Sat. **Food served** 10am-3pm, 5-9pm Mon-Fri; 10am-9pm Sat, Sun. **Credit** (minimum £5) MC, V.
Janus-faced Escape is Herne Hill's most versatile venue. By day it's colonised by the the buggy brigade; by night it transmogrifies into the coolest bar in the area. Turntables at the back welcome some serious DJs from Wednesday to Sunday, including the former Specials' supremo Jerry Dammers and various members of Alabama 3. Gulpener is the pick of the few draught beers on offer; cocktails are more popular choices. Food-wise, there are some excellent pizzas and ciabattas on offer, and the carrot cake is a dream. The bar itself is big and airy, with plenty of space but an oddly temporary feel to it – it always feels like the staff can't quite work out where to

put the furniture. Other elements in the mix: an internet terminal that can be used for free by customers, board games, and regularly changing art exhibitions from local and international artists. Service could do with being more reliably friendly, though.
Art (exhibitions monthly). Babies and children welcome (until 6pm). Games (board games). Music (DJs 8pm Wed-Sun; free). Tables outdoors (3, pavement). Wine tasting (phone for details).

Half Moon
10 Half Moon Lane, SE24 9HU (7274 2733). Herne Hill rail/68 bus. **Open** noon-11pm Mon-Thur; noon-1.30am Fri, Sat; noon-10.30pm Sun. **Credit** AmEx, DC, MC, V.
Last refuge for unreconstructed drinkers in majorly reconstructed Herne Hill, the stubbornly blokey Half Moon spits in the face of gastro-dom and thumbs its nose at stripped boards and Belgian beers. The fact that former British and European boxing champion Clinton McKenzie's Boxercise gym (www.mckenzieboxercise.com) is on the Half Moon's first floor sets the tone; and there's a music venue at the back that pulled in some big names in the late 1970s and early '80s. The pub itself is a Victorian gem: high of ceiling, dark of wood panelling, softened by etched glass, and with some seriously beautiful painted glass in the back snug. The bottled and tap beers are fairly predictable –

Hermit's Cave. *See p204.*

South

Courage Directors and Best, Beck's, Kronenbourg, John Smith's, Guinness, Foster's – but then you don't really come to the Half Moon for innovation.
Function room. Games (darts, pool). Music (bands 8pm Fri, Sat; £3-£5). Quiz (8pm Tue; £1). Tables outdoors (12, pavement). TV (big screen, satellite).

Number 22
22 Half Moon Lane, SE24 9HU (7095 9922/www. number-22.com). Herne Hill rail/3, 37, 68 bus. **Open** noon-11pm Mon-Sat; noon-10.30pm Sun. **Food served** noon-4pm, 6-10.30pm Mon-Sat; noon-4pm, 6-10pm Sun. **Credit** MC, V.
The area's drinking scene has moved on apace in recent years, and slick Number 22 has slipped neatly into the niche marked 'trendy yet friendly upmarket tapas bar'. It's more Spanish-influenced than truly Spanish: Iberian bottles dominate the reds (starting at £14), but there are more Italian than Spanish offerings among the whites. There is, though, draught Cruzcampo and a choice of six superb sherries (bone-dry La Guita Manzanilla is the perfect aperitif; £3.50 a glass). Unsurprisingly, given that there's ex-Match Group expertise at work here, the selection of spirits behind the bar is flawless; the cocktails are impressive too. Small of space but big of personality (the browns and blues and 1970s retro chic decor somehow don't seem dated here), and with lovely, friendly staff as well. Look on the website for details of wine-tasting and cocktail workshops.
Babies and children admitted. No smoking. Tables outdoors (4, patio; 2, pavement).

Prince Regent
69 Dulwich Road, SE24 0NJ (7274 1567). Herne Hill rail. **Open** noon-11pm Mon-Wed; noon-midnight Thur-Sat; noon-10.30pm Sun. **Food served** 7-10pm Mon; noon-3pm, 7-10pm Tue-Sat; noon-7pm Sun. **Credit** MC, V.
SE24's quota of earthy boozers is shrinking by the day. Once a jovial if nondescript joint across from Brockwell Lido, the Prince Regent is the latest place to succumb to gentrification – but it's been done with admirable subtlety. The floors are, naturally, stripped boards, and there are classy touches like an abundance of fresh flowers and oil-burning lamps on the tables. The partially sectioned-off restaurant area serves high-quality grub along the lines of goat's cheese salad, mussels and steaks. There's a good range of wines from £11 a bottle, but the beer selection is pretty pedestrian (Staropramen, Stella, Greene King IPA, Grolsch, Hoegaarden).
Babies and children admitted (until 7pm). Bar available for hire. Disabled: toilet. Function room. Restaurant (no smoking). Quiz (8pm Tue; £2). Tables outdoors (12, garden). TV (big screen).

Pullens
293-295 Railton Road, SE24 0JP (7274 9163). Herne Hill rail/3, 196 bus. **Open/food served** 8.30am-11pm Mon-Fri; 9am-11pm Sat; 9am-10.30pm Sun. **Happy hour** 5-7pm Mon-Fri. **Credit** MC, V.
It's not all change in Herne Hill. Pullens has been here from way before the area got its first loft conversion and, with aplomb, it continues to fulfil its multifaceted role: restaurant, bar, breakfast spot, gathering place, coffee shop. Inside, it's stereotype bistro, with plenty of wood and brick, a restaurant space to one side and a diminutive bar to the other. Pullens really comes into its own in fine weather, when its tables spill out on to the pavement area outside the rail station. The wine list features a dozen or so bottles of red and white, and while there's no beer

on draught, bottles include St Peter's Ale, Everards Tiger and Bishops Finger. Of the food, it's best to go for the snackier items and excellent breakfasts.
Babies and children welcome. Restaurant (no smoking). Tables outdoors (10, pavement).

Kennington, Lambeth & Oval
While this section covers a vast tract of south-east London, much of the area is just estate pub after estate pub – neighbouring Camberwell feels far, far away. The gastro **White Hart** is a welcome new arrival.

Beehive
60 Carter Street, SE17 3EW (7703 4992). Kennington tube/12, 68, 68A, 171, 176, P5 bus. **Open** 11am-11pm Mon-Sat; noon-10.30pm Sun. **Credit** MC, V.
It's a bit of a trek from Kennington tube, past rows and rows of housing estates, but it's worth it to reach this little treasure of a local. Food is no longer served here, but that doesn't detract from the substantial merits of the place. It's effectively in two sections, with pastel-shaded wood panels below peach walls that are adorned with modern art. Mellow music allows mixed groups to chatter by candlelight. The oval central bar is well stocked with Old Speckled Hen, London Pride, Directors and Kronenbourg Blanc; a small but varied wine list, mostly under £10; and a fine selection of over 40 whiskies, including Lagavulin 16-year-old single malt. At the back of the main bar are pictures of former prime ministers and presidents and an illustration of the House of Commons, hinting at a radical political past.
Babies and children welcome (until 7pm). Tables outdoors (30, patio). TV.

Dog House
293 Kennington Road, SE11 6BY (7820 9310). Kennington or Oval tube. **Open** 11.30am-midnight Mon-Thur, Sun; 11.30am-2am Fri, Sat. **Food served** noon-3pm, 6-10pm Mon-Fri; noon-10pm Sat, Sun. **Credit** MC, V.
At the junction of two of Kennington's main arteries, this friendly picture-windowed bar is an attractive mix of gastro and bohemian. Festooned with seemingly uncontrollable houseplants and embellished with some arty photographs on the rough mustard walls, the two-room interior has a relaxing, communal feel – there's a single mums' knitting club on Saturdays. Both bar and kitchen are run as a serious business. Draught Abbot, Black Sheep, Leffe and Hoegaarden and a varied, reasonably priced wine selection are provided by one; mains such as braised lamb shank with butternut squash and rosemary gravy (£8.50) by the other. Upstairs is a cosy space with leather sofas which accommodates a modest offering of local live bands.
Babies and children welcome (upstairs). Function room. Games (board games). Knitting group (2pm Sat; free). Music (jazz/latin 8.30pm alternate Tue; musicians 6pm alternate Sun; both free). Tables outdoors (20, pavement). TV.

Greyhound
336 Kennington Park Road, SE11 4PP (7735 2594). Oval tube. **Open** 11am-2am daily. **Food served** noon-3pm Mon-Fri; noon-4pm Sun. **Credit** AmEx, MC, V.

Hibernian in character, the corner Greyhound accommodates – nay, encourages – an eclectic clientele from the Oval neighbourhood. There are cricket fans, of course – the famous ground only a ten-minute walk away – and the Test summer of 2005 was marked by live Radio 5 broadcasts from here. Thesps from a couple of nearby drama schools drift in from time to time, while Chilean poets gather and gabble passionately. More prosaically, plasma screens dot the long narrow walls: the Greyhound is known as a place to watch TV sport, as reflected by the memorabilia of signed bats and sweaters. A busy bar counter beneath a low wood-beamed ceiling offers London Pride, Directors and Courage Best, behind it a rare and extensive range of Irish whiskey, including Connemara, Locke's and Tyrconnell. Traditional pub food runs to hearty roasts (£6) on a Sunday, when equally traditional Irish music pipes up in the evening.
Games (fruit machine, golf machine). Music (Irish music 9pm Sun; free). TV (big screen, satellite).

Prince of Wales
48 Cleaver Square, SE11 4EA (7735 9916/www.
shepherdneame.co.uk). Kennington tube. **Open** noon-11pm Mon-Sat; noon-10.30pm Sun. **Food served** noon-2.30pm, 6-9pm Mon-Thur; noon-2.30pm Fri, Sat; noon-3pm Sun. **Credit** AmEx, MC, V.
Tucked away in a little square, a brisk walk from Kennington Park Road, lies this homely little local, built in 1901. Its hush-hush location made it a notorious hangout for gangsters and sneaky politicians hiding out from rumble and rumour. Since its takeover by Kent's Shepherd Neame Brewery, it's become a cosy safe haven for the double-income family to discuss interior design and swap school-run tales. At the bar, as you would expect, there's a good range of ales on tap such as Spitfire, Kent's Best and Original Porter, with the now rare sight of Oranjeboom for lager lovers. Food is also available, with a main menu backed up by daily changing specials of traditional British food including the excellent pie of the day at £6.95.
Tables outdoors (3, pavement).

Three Stags
67-69 Kennington Road, SE1 7PZ (7928 5974).
Lambeth North tube/159 bus. **Open** 11am-midnight daily. **Food served** noon-7.30pm Mon, Sun; noon-10pm Tue-Sat. **Credit** MC, V.
This spacious corner boozer has been here for centuries. Charlie Chaplin's father drank himself to death at the bar, sending his son to the poorhouse. A recent revamp has seen the no-smoking booth at the back named Chaplin Corner, although little else is made of the historical connection. Tourists form the bulk of the daytime clientele, the World War II memorabilia a thematic continuation of the attraction diagonally opposite, the Imperial War Museum. Here, though, they can be introduced to traditional draught ales, such as Greene King IPA, Abbot and Old Speckled Hen, and superior pub grub in the £7-£8 range. Locals arrive after work, either office workers or residents here for regular jazz nights (note the small stage with an upright piano).
Babies and children welcome (until 8pm). Disabled: toilet. Games (fruit machine). Music (jazz 8pm Mon; free). No-smoking area. Tables outdoors (5, pavement). TV.

White Hart
185 Kennington Lane, SE11 4EZ (7735 1061).
Kennington tube/196 bus. **Open** noon-11pm Mon-Wed; noon-1am Thur-Sat; noon-10.30pm Sun. **Food served** noon-3pm, 6-10.30pm Mon-Fri; noon-4pm, 6-10.30pm Sat; noon-9pm Sun. **Credit** MC, V.

Set on the corner of a busy intersection, the once tediously themed La Finca is now a cool green gastropub that attracts a wide range of people from actors to MPs (or are they the same?). The spacious rectangular bar has raised seating areas around the edges for diners and an open kitchen at the far end that dispenses a lunch, dinner and weekend menu of modern British and European cuisine, such as smoked haddock with bubble and squeak, poached egg and mustard cream (£10) with some impressive steaks imported from a ranch in Texas. There's also an impressive 40-strong wine list and a couple of real ales on pump (Timothy Taylor Landlord and Deuchars IPA, with Kronenbourg Blanc the best of the rest). Free internet access is also available. Judging from the packed crowd on our visit, this one could be around for some time. We especially liked the three-foot fezzes doubling up as lampshades above the dining area.
Babies and children welcome. Function room. No-smoking area. TVs (big screen, satellite).

Lewisham

The **Dacre** is a treasure and, together with the **Jolly Farmers**, bucks the trend of god-awful drinking dens that litter (literally) the area.

Dacre Arms
11 Kingswood Place, SE13 5BU (8852 6779). Lewisham DLR/rail then 321 bus/Blackheath rail. **Open** noon-11pm Mon-Sat; noon-10.30pm Sun. **No credit cards.**
Walk up Dacre Park from the 321 bus stop on Lee High Road, past a boarded-up pub and grim housing blocks, to Kingswood Place third on the left – what you'll find is the epitome of pub bonhomie. A home-from-home for a cross-section of regulars, the Dacre Arms is done out with dark-wood panelling, rust-coloured banquettes, matching stools and armchairs, and browsable bric-a-brac. Pictures of trams in Deptford High Street, cigarette card collections and a variety of Arsenal paraphernalia blend in with the living-room feel. Old couples and blokes who know their beer enjoy a glass of the usual. Ales are the main attraction (Greene King IPA, Bombardier and Deuchars IPA), the best lagers bottled and European and found in the fridge. A tidy, enclosed beer garden is a boon in summer.
Games (fruit machine). Tables outdoors (16, garden). TV.

Jolly Farmers
354 Lewisham High Street, SE13 6LE (8690 8402).
Ladywell rail/54, 75, 185 bus. **Open** 10am-11pm Mon-Fri; 11am-11pm Sat; noon-10.30pm Sun. **Food served** noon-3.30pm Mon-Fri; 12.30-5pm Sat; 12.30-2.45pm Sun. **Credit** MC, V.
A new name, new management – but this lovely old pub remains pretty much the same. Who would change its wooden-beamed interior, dotted with beer barrels, and shelves crammed with oddities? And who would dare tamper with the choice of ales? Served from a long, narrow bar counter between the square-shaped front and back areas, K&B Sussex and Ringwood Forty Niner, Stonehenge Green and Orkney Raven satisfy ale drinkers spoilt for choice, while the best lager varieties are bottled, Belgian and behind the bar. A friendly, local crowd, including many an off-duty worker from Lewisham University Hospital next door, can tuck into well-priced pub grub in the back area. The three-course Sunday lunch is unsurprisingly popular at £8 a throw.

Prince of Wales. *See p207.*

Babies and children welcome (until 7pm). Games (cribbage, fruit machine, quiz machine). No-smoking area. Tables outdoors (6, garden). TV.

Also in the area...
Watch House (JD Wetherspoon) 198-204 High Street, SE13 6JP (8318 3136).

New Cross

The success of this area can be experienced first-hand in the marvellous **Montague**, tiny **Walpole**, or unofficial students' union bar **Hobgoblin**.

Hobgoblin
272 New Cross Road, SE14 6AA (8692 3193). New Cross Gate tube/rail/36, 89, 136, 171, 177 bus. **Open** 11am-11pm Mon-Sat; noon-10.30pm Sun. **Food served** noon-8.30pm Mon-Thur; noon-4pm Fri-Sun. **Happy hour** (students with ID only) 2-8pm Mon-Fri. **Credit** MC, V.

More Goldsmiths' student hangout than real ale haunt, even though it's a Wychwood Brewery house, the Hobgob directly opposite New Cross Gate station is a large and busy local rendezvous. Essentially it's a post-work or pre-party venue, with enough scuffed wooden tables to accommodate blokes gawping at Sky Sports on the corner televisions, and broad enough to serve Thai food and nitro-keg lagers alongside Wychwood, Greene King IPA and Bombardier from the island bar counter. In keeping with the spirit of things, a jukebox spills out indie and glam rock classics, but couples staggering in with heavy bags of shopping from the vast nearby Sainsbury's wouldn't feel out of place. For summer there's a beer garden out back. *Babies and children welcome (until 7pm). Disabled: toilet. Games (fruit machines). Music (DJs 8pm Mon, Fri, Sat; free). Tables outdoors (8, conservatory; 12, garden). TV.*

Montague Arms
289 Queens Road, SE15 2PA (7639 4923). New Cross or New Cross Gate tube/rail. **Open** 7.30-11.30pm Mon, Tue; 7.30-midnight Thur-Sat; noon-11pm Sun. **Food served** noon-5pm Sun. **No credit cards.**

An idiosyncratic gem. Stuck out on a bend of the main road between Peckham and Europe, the Montague has by tradition attracted coachloads of tourists bound for Dover. Somewhere in the attics of neat homes across Holland must be snaps of this weird English pub, with its zebra heads and maritime knick-knacks – perhaps even a group shot with laconic Stan, the landlord. It's not only Eurostar and easyJet that have changed the dynamic of this low-ceilinged anomaly – locals, who 20 years ago would have scoffed at the Casio entertainment provided by Peter 'Two Moogs' London from the main stage, now cherish and patronise it. On Sundays, when medieval hulks of meat are slavered in gravy and served to the compact row of dining tables, you can't move. There are pheasant and trout too. Occasional gigs bring a fresh crowd from Goldsmiths College, happier with the standard lagers than the Black Sheep and Deuchars IPA preferred by older regulars. *Games (fruit machine). Music (live music 9pm Sat, 1.30pm Sun; free).*

Walpole Arms

407 New Cross Road, SE14 6LA (8692 2080). New Cross tube/rail. **Open** 11am-midnight Mon-Thur; 11am-2am Fri, Sat; noon-midnight Sun. **Food served** 12.30-10pm daily. **Credit** MC, V.
The New Cross success story of the last five years, the Walpole was an old geezers' boozer by New Cross station until it was transported 50 years into the early 21st century by a change of decor (shiny wood, dinky table lights, sofas, low bar counter) and clientele (students from nearby Goldsmiths, party people in their early 20s); the lovely tiling remains, thank heavens. Thai food is another innovation, accompanied by draught San Miguel, John Smith's, Kronenbourg Blanc, a couple of wines and a few cocktails. The front terrace comes into its own after April, although the view is of lorries and coaches to Bratislava pulling up at the traffic lights before hurtling down the A2. Always busy, the Walpole doesn't need to lay on any entertainment, but you'll find music nights nevertheless. *Games (board games, fruit machine). Music (jazz 8.30pm Wed; karaoke 9pm Thur; 1970s night 9pm Sat; open mic 6-9pm Sun; all free). Tables outdoors (3, covered terrace). TVs (big screen, satellite).*

Peckham

S lowly, slowly. Since last year we've doubled the number of decent bars in Peckers that we'd recommend you spend an evening in. **Bar Story** and **Page 2** are upping the profile of the area substantially. Ale-drinkers are already well aware of the superior **Gowlett Arms** and for foodies and families (until 6pm at least) there's the **Rye Hotel**.

Bar Story

213 Blenheim Grove, SE15 4QL (7635 6643/www. thesassoongallery.co.uk). Peckham Rye rail. **Open** 4pm-midnight Mon-Thur; 11am-midnight Fri-Sun. **Food served** 4-10pm Mon-Thur; noon-10pm Fri-Sun. **Credit** MC, V.
Set under the arches right near Peckham Rye station, Bar Story's sparse interior of concrete floor, unplastered walls and wooden benches is reminiscent of a 1950s classroom, but it's also a warm and lively space in which to meet. There are only two beers on tap, Amstel and Guinness, and these have to be served outside under an umbrella;

the bottled variety (Duvel, Chimay White, Budvar and London Pride, pricey at over £3) and the enormous range of cocktails chalked up over the bar (from £5) pick up the slack. The kitchen is also behind the bar – the modern Med food (pasta, salmon, twofers on Tuesday) is simple and freshly prepared. There's a large outdoor area with palm trees and railway sleepers for seating. The rotating DJs, live music and independent film nights attract a trendy young crowd. After popular films at the Multiplex opposite and on summer nights, the place is heaving. *Art (exhibitions). Babies and children admitted. Function room. Music (DJs 7pm Thur-Sun; free). Tables outdoors (8, patio).*

Gowlett Arms

62 Gowlett Road, SE15 4HY (7635 7048/www.the gowlett.com). East Dulwich or Peckham Rye rail/12, 37, 40, 63, 176, 185, 484 bus. **Open** noon-midnight Mon-Thur; noon-1am Fri, Sat; noon-11.30pm Sun.
Food served 6.30-10.30pm Mon; 12.30-2.30pm, 6.30-10.30pm Tue-Fri; noon-10.30pm Sat; noon-9pm Sun.
Credit MC, V.
Tucked away on the corner of a residential street, the Gowlett Arms was awarded CAMRA's South East London pub of the year award for 2005. With Adnams Bitter and three guest ales from Batemans, Skinner's and Shepherd Neame (plus Hoegaarden and Leffe Blonde on tap), this is a pub that takes its beer seriously. The wine list is 100% organic and priced from £10 to £16 a bottle. Stone-baked pizzas are a speciality, served whole at evenings and on weekends, and by the slice for lunch and takeaways. There's a heated, covered terrace, a pool table (Tuesday night is competition night), plus high chairs and toys for children. It's a relaxing kind of place, with smoochy jazz during the day, broadsheets and mellow tunes from the DJ at weekends. Local art on the walls lends a sympathetic touch. *Babies and children welcome (until 9pm). Disabled: toilet. Games (board games, pool, retro games machines). Music (DJs 4pm Sun; free). Quiz (8.30pm Mon; £1). Tables outdoors (4 benches, heated terrace). TV.*

Page 2

57 Nunhead Lane, SE15 3TR (7732 5366). **Open** 3pm-midnight Mon-Thur; 3pm-2am Fri; noon-2pm Sat; noon-midnight Sun. **Food served** 5-10pm Mon-Fri; noon-10pm Sat, Sun. **Credit** MC, V.
Five minutes' walk from the Rye, Page 2 is waiting to be discovered by the Peckham and East Dulwich crowd. Softly lit and snugly furnished, it has a relaxed atmosphere and offers a genuine welcome. The landlord even seems to enjoy his job, and nothing apparently is too much trouble. The food, though, is the main attraction. A new catering manager draws on a rotating team of chefs and the menu changes daily, offering Jamaican jerk tuna and traditional Ulster fry breakfasts along with traditional own-made pies and bangers and mash. Everything, including the soda bread, is freshly prepared on the premises and, at under £7 for a main meal, is fantastic value. Drink options are not nearly as extensive. The wine list is short, three each of red and white, tap beers include Hoegaarden, Guinness and Tetley's Extra Cold, but the dark-wood bar, open fire and warmed nuts more than make up for it. *Babies and children admitted (until 8pm). Function room. Music (blues/jazz band 9pm Fri; DJ 9pm Sat; free). Quiz (9.30pm Thur; £1). Tables outdoors (4, pavement). TV (big screen).*

Rye Hotel

31 Peckham Rye, SE15 3NX (7639 5397). Peckham Rye rail/12, 37, 63 bus. **Open** noon-11pm Mon-Thur, Sun; noon-1am Fri, Sat. **Food served** noon-4pm, 6-10pm Mon-Fri; noon-5pm, 6-10pm Sat, Sun. **Credit** MC, V.
Glittering with fairy lights, candles and an open fire, the Rye Hotel is an inviting place on a winter's evening; for summer, a marquee extension at the back accommodates the overspill. An excellent modern European/Thai menu features specials such as seared swordfish or tuna steak in the £10 range, though you can still order steak and chips from the permanent menu; the white chocolate cheesecake (£4) is a winning choice among the desserts. Adnams, Guinness, Hoegaarden and Leffe are the better of the tap beers, while wines range from £11.50 (house white or red) to £29 (Craigow pinot noir). Decorated with fresh flowers and local art, the Rye attracts two-salaried young parents at weekends – their children tend to take over the place during the day. After 6pm, however, nobody under 21 is allowed in. This is Peckham after all.
Babies and children welcome (until 6pm). Quiz (8pm Wed; £1). Tables outdoors (40, garden).

Also in the area...

Kentish Drovers (JD Wetherspoon) 71-79 Peckham High Street, SE15 5RS (7277 4283).

Putney

Better known for fine boozers with lovely Thameside views, such as the **Duke's Head**, than for decent gastro fare, it's good to see **Coat & Badge** and **Putney Station** trying to redress the balance.

Coat & Badge

8 Lacy Road, SW15 1NL (8788 4900/www.geronimo-inns.co.uk). Putney Bridge tube/Putney rail/14, 39, 74, 85 bus. **Open** 11am-midnight Mon-Sat; 11am-10.30pm Sun. **Food served** noon-3pm, 6-10.30pm Mon-Fri; noon-4pm, 6-10.30pm Sat; noon-4pm, 6-9.30pm Sun. **Credit** MC, V.
This fetching pub (part of the Geronimo group) set off Putney High Street provides a welcome respite from the Saturday shopping hordes. Tranquil decor and spacious, comfortable seating attract the local young smart set, who while away spare afternoons over a glass from the varied wine list. Named after the Doggett's Coat and Badge rowing race, inaugurated in the 17th century and still run today, the pub is covered in the names of previous winners, alongside suitable pictures of boats and coves. On this visit the excellent, frequently changing menu featured baked sea-bass fillet with olives, fennel, capers and slow-roast lemons for £12.50, to be enjoyed in a dining area at the back. In summer, a large, pretty patio, complete with palm tree, is the ideal spot for a G&T.
Babies and children welcome (until 7pm). Disabled: toilet. Function room. Games (board games). Quiz (8pm Mon; £1). Tables outdoors (25, terrace). TV.

Duke's Head

8 Lower Richmond Road, SW15 1JN (8788 2552). Putney Bridge tube/22, 265 bus. **Open** 11am-midnight Mon-Thur; 11am-1am Fri, Sat; noon-midnight Sun. **Food served** noon-10pm Mon-Fri; 11am-10pm Sat; noon-4.30pm, 5-10pm Sun. **Credit** AmEx, MC, V.

This is a grand old Victorian pub, set on the bank of the Thames and divided into main three areas. Each has its own function. The public bar is the ideal place to watch rugger with a pint of Young's in hand. The larger saloon bar is a more genteel affair, with its open fire and framed sketches of scenic Thames views on the walls – you could almost be in the drawing room of a country manor. The vast dining room, equipped with almost equally large windows, offers wonderful views across the river, where rowers pass for the Oxford–Cambridge Boat Race. A scattering of tables on the riverside patio give a better vantage point, should the weather hold.
Games (table football). No piped music or jukebox. Over-21s only. Tables outdoors (9, riverside patio). TVs (big screen, satellite).

Half Moon

93 Lower Richmond Road, SW15 1EU (8780 9383/ www.halfmoon.co.uk). Putney Bridge tube/Putney rail. **Open** noon-11pm Mon-Sat; noon-11pm Sun. **Credit** MC, V.
An endearing mix of students, post-punk dissidents and charming old codgers frequent this barn-like Young's boozer. The pictures covering the main bar are a *Who's Who* of pub rock circa 1965-1975, highlighting the good and the bloody awful that have graced the 200-capacity back room. These days it's tribute bands, re-runs and and unsigned acts that are belting out the racket, and when there's no live performance an excellent jukebox offers a soundtrack of rock and pop classics. The Half Moon has an unashamedly scruffy individuality, a welcome change from the homogeneous theme pubs and style bars springing up all over this part of the world.
Games (board games, fruit machines, pool, quiz machine). Music (bands 8.30pm nightly; from £2.50; jazz 2-5pm Sun; free). Tables outdoors (8, garden).

Putney Station

94-98 Upper Richmond Road, SW15 2SP (8780 0242/www.brinkleys.com). East Putney tube. **Open** 11am-11pm Mon-Sat; 11am-10.30pm Sun. **Food served** noon-11pm Mon-Sat; noon-10.30pm Sun. **Happy Hour** 5-7pm daily. **Credit** MC, V.
Most commuters walk on by this establishment, next door to East Putney station, just like the song says – the decor could date back as many decades. It's a shame, since the wine list is adventurous and well priced. They could have picked up a decent Chablis JM Brocard for £14.50, or a good cocktail at £5-£6, £3 if they happened to be passing between 5pm and 7pm. Meals are outlined on separate lunch and dinner menus – mains (£11-£13) include roast duck breast with sautéed shiitake mushrooms, pak choi, new potatoes and red wine jus. These can be taken in the silver-and-grey upper dining level, but if you're looking for company you'll have to join the smart young crowd at the front bar. Here a change of blinds and some Roxy Music have brought the Putney Station forward a decade.
Babies and children welcome. Disabled: toilet. Function room. No-smoking area. Restaurant. Tables outdoors (3, pavement).

Whistle & Flute

46-48 Putney High Street, SW15 1SQ (8780 5437/ www.fullers.co.uk). Putney Bridge tube/Putney rail. **Open** 11am-11pm Mon-Sat; noon-10.30pm Sun. **Food served** noon-4pm, 5-10pm Mon-Fri; noon-5pm, 6-10pm Sat; noon-5pm, 6-9pm Sun. **Credit** AmEx, MC, V.

This old NatWest bank, now part of the Fuller's brewery chain, is the least anonymous of the bland watering holes on Putney High Street. Weary shoppers collapse into large, welcoming leather sofas beside big wooden tables, in an interior made cosier by crimson walls, heavy drapes and candlelight. As you would expect from a Fuller's pub, the Whistle has a decent selection of ales on tap, including some brewed on particular anniversaries – a talking point for you while you sup. The wine is well priced and uncomplicated food culminates in a superior Sunday lunch. Work by local artists is displayed, and there are two televisions that are largely ignored in favour of conversation. *Babies and children welcome (until 6pm). Disabled: toilet. Games (fruit machine, quiz machine). No-smoking area. TVs (big screen, satellite).*

Also in the area...
O'Neill's 90-90A High Street, SW6 3LF (7384 3573).
Railway (JD Wetherspoon) 202 Upper Richmond Road, SW15 6TD (8788 8190).
Slug & Lettuce 146-148 Putney High Street, SW15 1SL (8785 3131).
Walkabout 14-16 Putney High Street, SW15 1SL (8785 3081).

South Norwood

If it weren't for the wonderful **Oceans Apart**, life in South Norwood would scarcely be worth living.

Oceans Apart
152 Portland Road, SE25 4PT (8663 8881/www. oceanapart-bars.com). Norwood Junction rail/30, 197, 312 bus. **Open** 11am-midnight Mon-Sat; noon-10.30pm Sun. **Food served** noon-10pm daily. **Credit** AmEx, DC, MC, V.
The Portland Road is a succession of closed-down boozers and dubious watering holes deserving the same fate, so it's a godsend to find this cool, relaxing, music-driven bar – oceans apart, indeed, from the local competition. Enough quirky touches stand out from the blond wood to make a good first impression and confirm Oceans' definition of itself as a style bar: cute little illuminated pod tables, comfy toffee-coloured sofas and a picture-framed fire. As well as DJs at weekends, there have been live music spots on Thursdays that move to the beer garden for summer weekends. At the bar draught Leffe stands out from the usuals and there's a reasonably priced cocktail list to work through. South Norwood could do with more bars like this. *Babies and children welcome (until 7.30pm). Disabled: toilet. Games (board games, fruit machines). Music (DJs 7pm Fri, Sat, 1pm Sun; free). Tables outdoors (20, garden). TVs (big screen).*

Also in the area...
William Stanley (JD Wetherspoon) 7-8 High Street, SE25 6EP (8653 0678).

Stockwell

Along with **Bar Estrela**, another bright star has joined Stockwell's firmament in the shape of the refurbished **Royal Albert**. Real ale fans will find they're not disappointed in the **Priory Arms**.

Bar Estrela
111-115 South Lambeth Road, SW8 1UZ (7793 1051). Stockwell tube/Vauxhall tube/rail. **Open** 11am-11pm daily. **Food served** noon-10.45pm daily. **Credit** AmEx, MC, V.
The Estrela (star) shines as the most prominent and popular of the Portuguese bars along this stretch of the South Lambeth Road. The interior is simple and functional, with an L-shaped bar in the corner draped in assorted bright Portuguese football scarves. Below-counter are authentically prosaic pastries and those little dishes full of breaded and battered bite-size shapes of fish, cheese and potato. If you need something more substantial, there's a comprehensive selection of local delicacies such as carne de porco em molho de cogumelos (pork with clams, £9.50), followed by a tasty dessert like molotof com molho de ovos (eggwhite soufflé). Dining takes place in a back room dominated by onerously gloomy Portuguese commentary, whether it's describing Benfica or slight drizzle on Tuesday. In summer, continental bar tables spread over a small triangle of outside pavement. The beer on draught is, naturally, Sagres and Ceres. *Babies and children welcome. Tables outdoors (10, pavement).*

Canton Arms
177 South Lambeth Road, SW8 1XP (7582 0965/ www.barbeerian-inns.com). Stockwell tube. **Open** 11am-11pm Mon-Sat; noon-10.30pm Sun. **Food served** noon-2.30pm, 6-9.30pm Mon-Fri; 12.30-3pm, 6.30-9pm Sat; 12.30-4pm, 7-9pm Sun. **Happy hour** 6-7pm Fri, Sat. **Credit** MC, V.
This comfortable neighbourhood local, standing on the edge of Little Portugal, is a pub of contrasts. The octagonal bar counter stretches around the two halves of lounge area. On one side, big-screen football viewers can watch the game in comfort while tucking into saffron, asparagus and baby pumpkin risotto at £7.50; on the other, a more bookish crowd settle in half-moon leather chairs by the bookcase, puffing on a Charatan own-made Corona from the cigar machine. Above, a skylight is emblazoned with a knight in armour who, surrounded by pictures of Swiss heraldry, is at least taking a stab at authenticity amid all the incongruity, given the pub's name and all. Pub quizzers and a younger, livelier crowd in the evening can down happy-hour cocktails and munch on twofer burgers, though most are happy to settle for a pint of Greene King or Pride. Oh yes, and there's table football as well. *Babies and children welcome (until 8pm). Games (quiz machine, table football). Tables outdoors (8, patio). TV (big screen, satellite).*

Circle
348 Clapham Road, SW9 9AR (7622 3683). Clapham North or Stockwell tube. **Open** noon-11pm Mon-Fri; noon-1am Sat; noon-10.30pm Sun. **Food served** noon-2.30pm, 6.30-9.30pm Mon-Thur; noon-2.30pm, 6-9pm Fri; 1-4pm Sat; noon-5pm Sun. **Credit** MC, V.
Due for a revamp in early 2006, this mauve mongrel of lounge bar and pub sits on a corner of the main drag between Clapham and Stockwell. As its interior and furniture are totally dominated by yesterday's brown, a revamp seems wise. Sturdy wooden tables and low cube pouffes are warmed by two open fires, with boxy alcove seats along one side leading out to a beer garden. The menu from the open kitchen has already had a makeover: witness the nori-wrapped roasted salmon tranche served on wasabi mash at £7.50. The clientele is pretty mixed:

South

couples in their mid-30s for Sunday lunch, twentysomethings taking over on Friday and Saturday nights when DJs man the decks. Leffe, Hoegaarden and Pilsner Urquell on tap compete with a well-priced wine list and the usual shooters and cocktails with daft names.
Function room. Games (board games). Music (DJs 8pm Fri, Sat; free). Tables outdoors (16, garden). TVs (big screen, satellite). **Map 11 M16**.

Priory Arms
83 Lansdowne Way, SW8 2PB (7622 1884). Stockwell tube. **Open** 11am-11pm Mon-Sat; noon-10.30pm Sun. **Food served** noon-9pm Mon-Sat; 12.30-5pm Sun. **Credit** MC, V.
Beer mats of past guest brews cover the bar and adjoining wall, a testament to what the Priory Arms is all about. Whether it's ale, lager, wheat beer or cider, you're catered for in spades at this lovely little neighbourhood free house. Six real ales were available for this visit, including Harveys Sussex Best, Godfather's and Timothy Taylor Landlord, as well as countless other bottled reasons for this being mentioned so often in CAMRA dispatches. The place is cosy to the point of crowded, but at a drop of sunshine you can sit outside on the quiet residential street. Food, such as Thai red curry with roast duck (£7.25), can be washed down with one of the 15 fruit wines on offer. Upstairs there is occasional live music – jazz, blues, country – at weekends, and on Sunday afternoons intense backgammon sessions are followed by the equally serious quiz.
Function room. Games (fruit machine; backgammon club, Sun afternoon; chess club, Wed afternoon). Quiz (9pm Sun; free). Tables outdoors (8, patio). TVs (satellite).

Royal Albert
43 St Stephen's Terrace, SW8 1DL (7840 0777). Stockwell tube. **Open** noon-11pm Mon-Sat; noon-10.30pm Sun. **Food served** noon-2.30pm, 5-9.30pm Mon-Fri; noon-9.30pm Sat, Sun. **Credit** MC, V.
This bar on the corner on one of Stockwell's quieter side streets has been completely refurbished, with the expected change from pub to funky bar now complete. All remnants of the past boozer are now eradicated, although God knows what they've done with those old codgers who used to prop up the corner – perhaps they've been hidden behind the large mirrors, leather sofas, low tables and plasma screens that have been set into beige and crimson walls. Young couples sit by the bookshelves and open fires chatting quietly, while funky music plays in the background. Leffe and Hoegaarden have been added to the usual lager pumps, and Pride and a guest ale are on offer for discerning drinkers. The new kitchen should also be up and running by now, meaning the transformation is complete.
Babies and children welcome. Function room. Games (darts, pool table, quiz machine, volleyball). Music (DJ 7pm 1st Fri of mth; free). Tables outdoors (16, garden; 3, pavement). TV (big screen, satellite).

Surprise
16 Southville, SW8 2PP (7622 4623). Stockwell tube/Vauxhall tube/rail. **Open** 11am-11pm Mon-Sat; noon-10.30pm Sun. **Food served** noon-3pm Mon-Fri, Sun. **Credit** MC, V.
Perched on the edge of Larkhill Park, this Young's pub is a completely different proposition on a summer's afternoon to a winter's evening. During warmer months the front terrace area comes into its own, hosting barbecues and boules evenings. Cyclists and dog-walkers use the place all year

round, but it has an eerie feel on a bleak night in January – maybe it's the thought of walking home through ill-lit greenery. Inside, two communal rooms lead from the tiny dog-leg main bar, which is lined with the usual Young's pints. The back room with its open fire is home to caricatures of the more interesting regulars. Pub grub is basic, consisting mainly of jackets and sandwiches.
Games (board games, boules pitch, fruit machine). Tables outdoors (12, patio). TV (satellite).

Tooting

A little more downmarket than neighbouring Balham, Tooting nonetheless boasts the historic charms of the **King's Head** and the more contemporary pleasures of **smoke**.

King's Head
84 Upper Tooting Road, SW17 7PB (8767 6708). Tooting Bec tube. **Open** 11am-11pm Mon-Wed, Sun; 11am-midnight Thur-Sat. **Food served** noon-10pm daily. **Credit** AmEx, MC, V.
A Grade II-listed building built by WM Bruton in 1896, the King's Head has an ornate Victorian frontispiece that defines it as a classic London watering hole. Peering through the etched glass, the first impression is of a down-at-heel old man's pub, but walk through the green and

Commercial. *See p214.*

South

cream tiled hallway and you see a vast space, its soul cleverly preserved by three distinct areas divided by Victorian wood panelling. The front is predominantly for dining (check out the steak and Speckled Hen ale pie, £7.95) and the main bar for drinking. Both areas have a slightly jaded feel, mixed crowd, old-style carpet and traditional pub tables. The more contemporary rear is for playing pool on purple baize and lounging on colourful leather cubes and sofas in front of the football. Draught Stella, Leffe, Hoeegarden and Budvar are joined by real ales London Pride and the more interesting Deuchars.
Comedy (8pm Thur; £6). Function room. Games (pool, quiz machine). Music (covers band 8pm Sat; free). Quiz (8pm Sun; £1). Tables outdoors (11, patio). TV (big screen, satellite).

smoke bar diner
14 Trinity Road, SW17 7RE (8767 3902/www. smokebardiner.com). Tooting Bec tube. **Open** 5pm-midnight Mon-Thur; noon-1am Fri, Sat; noon-10.30pm Sun. **Food served** 5-10pm Mon-Fri; noon-10pm Sat, Sun. **Credit** MC, V.
The highlight of the Tooting bar scene is the minimalist and funky smoke, a stone's throw from Tooting Bec station. It is no surprise that it is also the nearest of Tooting's bars to the more upmarket Balham. Giant sepia prints of sporting icons line the wall, an upbeat electro soundtrack sets the tone and a young, unselfconsciously fashionable crowd drapes itself over the low leather sofas. Long, thin, more clandestine seating and 1960s lampshades define the brick dog-leg nook before the converted courtyard. There's also a glass brick-lined dining area with bench seating, stylish walnut-veneer tables and obligatory football flatscreens. The wine list favours the New World and offers four of each by the glass. Unusually, they also serve well-priced bottles of prosecco and Cava (£15/£17.50). Food comes international tapas-style: check out the pan-fried figs with halloumi (£3.75).
Disabled: toilet. Function room. Music (DJs 8pm Fri, Sat; free). TV (big screen, satellite).

Trafalgar Arms
148 Tooting High Street, SW17 0RT (8767 6059). Tooting Broadway tube. **Open** noon-midnight Mon-Wed, Sun; noon-1am Thur-Sat. **Food served** noon-9.30pm daily. **Credit** MC, V.
Set back from the High Street in squat, double-fronted Georgian grandeur is the detached and somewhat jaded Trafalgar Arms. The front courtyard offers summer seating on standard outdoor tables, but sadly no attempts have been made to desterilise the area with flower beds and shrubbery. Inside is similarly in need of a little TLC, but it is still popular – particularly with a half gay/half straight male crowd including staff from St George's hospital. The best of the mismatched seating is next to the gas fireplace, but there are also large tables for groups and cute, converted Singer sewing tables for couples. The dark-wood bar serves a standard selection of drinks and the board games are rather tired, but the food is good, honest pub grub. Plaques and framed manuscripts relive the Battle of Trafalgar.
Babies and children admitted (until 9pm). Games (board games, fruit machines). No-smoking area. Quiz (7pm Sun; £2). Tables outdoors (20; pavement).

Also in the area...
JJ Moon's (JD Wetherspoon) 56A High Street, SW17 0RN (8672 4726).

Vauxhall

A well-established centre of the capital's gay scene, yet Vauxhall has little to offer drinkers – apart from the very decent **Fentiman Arms**.

Fentiman Arms
64 Fentiman Road, SW8 1LA (7793 9796/www. geronimo-inns.co.uk). Vauxhall or Oval rail/tube. **Open** noon-11pm Mon-Thur; noon-midnight Fri, Sat; noon-10.30pm Sun. **Food served** noon-3.30pm, 7-9.30pm Mon-Fri; noon-4pm, 7-10.30pm Sat; noon-4pm, 7-9.30pm Sun. **Credit** MC, V.
The Fentiman Arms, part of the Geronimo Group, is a welcoming spot, occupying a cosy corner site between elegant townhouses in the moneyed niche of the Oval. Here chattering classes abound, a younger crowd filling the comfy corners by the bookshelves in the evening. Others gather around the square bar counter. The quality food is concocted with herbs and vegetables from the contemporary kitchen garden at the back, creating dishes such as salmon, fennel and thyme pie (£8.50). All in all, it's satisfying in a two-income coupley sort of way – Bombardier, Deuchars or Hoegaarden for him, a half-score of reasonably priced wines for her... even the toilets are marked fentimen and fentiwomen. A revamp's due for spring 2006.
Babies and children admitted. Function room. No-smoking area. Quiz (8pm Tue; £1). Tables outdoors (15, garden). TV (satellite).

Wandsworth

Wandsworth has a clutch of decent hostelries popular with its well-heeled young families. River views are only part of the **Hope**'s continuing charm, while the **Ship** is one of south London's finest pubs. The chic little **Freemasons** keeps the foodies happy. Ditto **ditto**.

Alma
499 Old York Road, SW18 1TF (8870 2537/ www.thealma.co.uk). Wandsworth Town rail. **Open** 11am-11pm Mon-Wed; 11am-midnight Thur-Sat; noon-11pm Sun. **Food served** noon-4pm, 6-10.30pm Mon-Sat; noon-4pm, 6-10pm Sun. **Credit** AmEx, MC, V.
Directly opposite the railway station, this green-tiled pub with numerous balconies and a flagpole on top takes its name from the battle for Crimea. The large central circular bar serves Young's ales from the nearby brewery, along with Staropramen and Hoegaarden, and a lively twentysomething after-work crowd sprawl out on the battered sofas that line the walls or rest their elbows on the big, wooden, antique cold cupboard. Behind it, ceramic tiled tablets commemorate the 1854 battle and there are big mirrors above an open fire. A quiet restaurant at the back serves good gastropub fare, made with produce from owners Charles and Linda Gotto's farm. A decent variety of Champagnes too.
Babies and children welcome. Disabled: toilet. Function room.

ditto
55-57 East Hill, SW18 2QE (8877 0110/www.doditto.co. uk). Wandsworth Town/Clapham Junction rail. **Open** noon-11pm Mon-Sat; noon-10.30pm Sun. **Food served** noon-2.30pm, 6.30-11pm Mon-Fri; noon-11pm Sat; noon-9pm Sun. **Credit** MC, V.

This long rectangular bar-restaurant has established itself as a local favourite. Its owners have done well, given the lack of natural light, to overcome any feeling of dinginess with pale walls, candles and lovely saggy sofas. The tiny bar serves up classic cocktails made from spirits distilled locally, such as Monkey Shoulder triple-malt whisky. Draught beers include Staropramen and there are some interesting small plates on offer, such as crayfish tempura with a sweet chilli dipping sauce for £3.75. The private dining room, which doubles as a children's play area during the day, and a more formal dining section running alongside the bar pull in moneyed locals with a classic European menu prepared by new executive chef Lee Glenn. *Babies and children admitted (until 5pm in play area). Function room. Music (acoustic singer 8pm Wed; free). Restaurant (no-smoking tables). TV (big screen, satellite).*

East Hill

21 Alma Road, SW18 1AA (8874 1833/www.geronimo-inns.co.uk). Wandsworth Town rail. **Open** 11am-11pm Mon-Sat; noon-10.30pm Sun. **Food served** noon-3pm, 6-10pm Mon-Fri; noon-9pm Sat, Sun. **Credit** MC, V.
Another venue in the Geronimo Group chain, this corner pub – tucked away down a back street – has had a recent makeover and now resembles a country kitchen. The bar counter of mock drawers and cupboard festooned with strings of garlic are in stark contrast to the place's previously gaudy appearance. Open bookcases help break up the space, where you can flop into a comfy leather sofa next to an open fire with *Dombey and Son* or a Snoopy annual. A spot at one of the rustic kitchen tables allows you to try a daily special, like smoked salmon and spinach spaghetti with garlic cream sauce (£8.50); there are three types of deliboard selection too. Four real ales include Broadside and Sharp's Doom Bar, and there's New Zealand Steinlager, Russian Baltika and an extensive wine list.
Babies and children admitted. Games (board games). Quiz (8pm Sun; £1). Tables outdoors (4, paved area). TVs (satellite).

Freemasons

2 Wandsworth Common Northside, SW18 2SS (7326 8580). Clapham Junction rail. **Open** noon-11pm Mon-Sat; noon-10.30pm Sun. **Food served** noon-3pm, 6.30-10pm Mon-Fri; 12.30-3.30pm, 6.30-10pm Sat; 12.30-4pm, 6.30-9.30pm Sun. **Credit** AmEx, MC, V.
This chic little bar on the north side of Wandsworth Common brings in good-looking, well-bred twentysomethings by the bucketload. They must follow the smell from the open kitchen – or have a sixth sense for stylish decor. And whether those well-bred noses are sniffing out vegetarian or meaty delights, the menu is terrific: spicy sweet potato and coconut soup with own-made bread (£4.50)... outstanding! Draught ales such as Everards Tiger and (in winter) Sleigh Bell – plus Früli, Leffe and Hoegaarden on tap – are complemented by interesting bottled options such as JW Dundee's Honey Brown Lager, Früli Apple and Subal, a Thai blend of sparkling wine. The place is always crammed, so arrive early for a spot on a comfy leather sofa. *Babies and children welcome (restaurant). Quiz (7.30pm Mon; £1). Restaurant (no smoking). Tables outdoors (11, patio).*

Hope

1 Bellevue Road, SW17 7EG (8672 8717). Wandsworth Common rail. **Open** noon-midnight Mon-Sat; noon-10.30pm Sun. **Food served** noon-10pm Mon-Sat; noon-9pm Sun. **Credit** AmEx, MC, V.

First-time visitors to the Hope tend to perch on a high stool at the bar for a lovely view through picture windows across Wandsworth Common – but the young, upmarket regulars snuggle into leather chairs and sofas in the main, triangular lower level. For intimacy there's also a small sunken section hidden away beside the bar. You'll find a decent choice of beers (Küppers Kölsch, Fuller's Jack Frost in winter, Deuchars) augmented by regularly changing guest ales. You can take tea with some organic carrot cake or a scone at the afternoon table near the bar, and there are healthy drinks such as pomegranate juice for those on detox. A menu of comfort food standards features the sturdy likes of Sicilian beef casserole with roasted root vegetables, and there are any number of wines to wash it down with. Book a table for the popular quiz on Monday nights.
Disabled: toilet. Games (space invaders). Quiz (8.30pm Mon; £5/team). Tables outdoors (15, patio). TVs.

Nightingale

97 Nightingale Lane, SW12 8NX (8673 1637). Clapham South tube/Wandsworth Common rail. **Open** 11am-midnight Mon-Sat; noon-11pm Sun. **Food served** noon-10pm daily. **Credit** MC, V.
Built by Thomas Wallis in 1853, the Nightingale has collected more money for good causes than almost any other pub in the UK – it has a whole wall dedicated to photos of sponsored guide dogs. This is sacrosanct, surviving a recent makeover that saw tartan seats and mustard walls covered in framed Edwardian comic sketches join a modern open fireplace. Local, middle-aged regulars get a smile and their Young's served swiftly – the house beer is also used in such food options as the Young's Champion steak and mushroom pie from an otherwise unsurprising menu. Even a couple of the old boys who have been drinking here since Wallis's day may not have noticed the narrow passage that leads into a delightful roofed garden at the back, where twinkling blue lights are draped over the greenery. *Babies and children admitted (no-smoking area). Games (board games, darts, fruit machine). No-smoking area. Quiz (7.30pm 1st Tue of mth; £1). Tables outdoors (12, garden). TV.*

Ship

41 Jew's Row, SW18 1TB (8870 9667/www.theship.co.uk). Wandsworth Town rail. **Open** 11am-midnight Mon-Sat; noon-midnight Sun. **Food served** noon-10.30pm Mon-Sat; noon-10pm Sun. **Credit** AmEx, DC, MC, V.
The approach (past wasteland punctuated with a bus garage and McDonald's) is an incongruous build-up to one of the best pubs in south London: the Ship. It's one of a number currently owned by farming couple Charles and Linda Gotto (of Alma fame, *see p223*) – although Young's are soon to take it back. The Gottos have been running a tidy ship, while keeping the pub's original unpolished character. There's a large, trendy, yellow-and-scarlet conservatory and a ship's boiler funnel supporting the ceiling in the sunken area – this was a real dockers' pub in the past. Today the upmarket element can dine on loin of pork (from the Gottos' own farm) with bubble and squeak and glazed apples (£11.95), while sipping on a Terra Mater cabernet sauvignon Reserva (£17), in an adjoining restaurant with open kitchen. Another long-tabled dining area sits in the quieter front bar, full of books and odd antiquities. You can also sup from the usual range of Young's ales while contemplating the trek back across no-man's land.

South

Babies and children admitted (before 7pm). Function room. Games (board games). No piped music or jukebox. Restaurant (no smoking). Tables outdoors (30, riverside garden). TV (big screen, digital, plasma).

Wimbledon

Wombles will find the best pubs are off-Broadway and away from the High Street, such as the fine **Crooked Billet** or the **Fox & Grapes** by the Common, Southfields' wonderful gastro **Earl Spencer**, or one of our faves, the **Sultan**.

Alexandra
33 Wimbledon Hill Road, SW19 7NE (8947 7691). Wimbledon tube/rail. **Open** *Pub* 10am-11pm Mon-Wed; 10am-midnight Thur-Sat; noon-11pm Sun. *Wine bar* noon-11pm Mon-Wed; noon-midnight Thur; noon-1am Fri, Sat; noon-11pm Sun. **Food served** *Wine bar* noon-9.30pm Mon-Sat; noon-9pm Sun. **Credit** AmEx, DC, MC, V.
The Alexandra is Wimbledon's principal commuters pub, and in the early evening it fills up with an assortment of worn but jovial workers, freshly disgorged from Waterloo and Vauxhall. The need to please a wide variety of drinkers is evident in the large interior, which stretches from the dim, traditional pub that occupies the southern half of the place to a wine bar, replete with French impressionist prints and a pretty decent wine selection, that fills the northern annexe. This dichotomy means the Alexandra never really feels like a unified venue, but everyone seems happy enough, and the older locals at the bar give the place a slight but significant feeling of community. There's a pleasant roof garden and a well-kept selection of Young's beers, and the wine bar has a restaurant section for those who end up staying long enough to miss dinner.
Disabled: toilet (wine bar). Games (fruit machine, quiz machine, golf machine). Music (rock covers band 9.30pm Fri, Sat £5 after 9.30pm). No-smoking areas. Quiz (7.30pm alternate Tue; £1). Tables outdoors (15, roof garden; 6, pavement). TVs (big screen, satellite).

Common Room
18 High Street, SW19 5DX (8944 1909/ www.jamiesbars.co.uk). Wimbledon tube/rail. **Open/food served** 11am-11pm Mon-Thur; 11am-midnight Fri, Sat; 11am-10.30pm Sun. **Credit** AmEx, MC, V.
For our Sunday visit, the Common Room buzzed with boisterous young punters quaffing white wine or lager in accordance with gender. A special offer Chilean Carmen cabernet sauvignon rosé (£4.75/£6.75/£18) caught the eye, and a dozen of each colour are listed, from £3.25/£4.50/£13 for a Two Oceans Cape Red or Broken Rock chenin blanc. Non-wine choices are meagre – bottled Warsteiner beating any of the draughts – and the decor is standard Jamies (the chain to which the bar belongs): dark leather, wood tables, tea lights, giant plasmas for sport. Food menus (platters at £9.50 or £16.50, fat chips £4.50, whitebait £5) were whisked away at about 10pm, by which time almost all the chalkboard options had been scratched out. The locals were animated, veering raddled; the Common Room itself comfy, veering common.
Babies and children admitted (until 8pm). Games (board games). No-smoking area (until 4pm). Tables outdoors (12, patio). TV (big screen, satellite).

Crooked Billet
14-15 Crooked Billet, SW19 4RQ (8946 4942). Wimbledon tube/rail. **Open** 11am-11pm Mon-Sat; noon-10.30pm Sun. **Food served** noon-10pm Fri, Sat; noon-9pm Sun. **Credit** MC, V.
Wimbledon Village's quieter western edge is often a better bet for boozing than its self-conscious centre. The Crooked Billet is the best of the bunch, with a wood and stone interior that looks as old as the hills, a blazing winter fire, a pleasant green for summer drinking (shared with the neighbouring Hand in Hand) and an assortment of fruity, if rather uncertain, legends (a ghostly Irishwoman has been spotted in the cellar, while Oliver Cromwell's father is said to have died here). The back room offers hearty food, although most of the well-off locals congregate in the atmospheric bar, dogs mooching idly around their feet. Wimbledon Common is just round the corner, making the Billet a fine pit-stop, but in truth it's a wonderfully convivial pub for anyone in search of good old-fashioned drinking. Alongside the familiar Young's range, there's Hoegaarden and Kronenbourg Blanc, and a predictably substantial wine list is chalked up over the bar.
Babies and children welcome (until 9pm). Restaurant (available for hire; no smoking). Tables outdoors (5, patio). TV.

Earl Spencer
260-262 Merton Road, SW18 5JL (8870 9244/www. theearlspencer.co.uk). Southfields tube. **Open** 11am-11pm Mon-Sat; noon-10.30pm Sun. **Food served** 12.30-2.30pm, 7-10pm Mon-Sat; 12.30-3pm, 7-9.30pm Sun. **Credit** AmEx, MC, V.
A short walk from Southfields tube, the Earl Spencer is everything a gastropub should be. Refurbished in 2003, it has filled its large space tastefully, with two open fires under gold-leafed ceilings beckoning a discerning crowd in winter and tables outside in summer. It's the kitchen that attracts return custom – the menu changed twice daily and the bread baked fresh on the premises. Much is Brit-based, any given day featuring six superbly composed starters (£6) and six mains (£10). On our visit, there was beer-battered ox tongue and lamb's brains with gribiche sauce or marinated octopus and Chinese broccoli with soy, ginger and chilli dressing, followed by slow-roast belly of pork, cabbage-braised cannelloni beans with white wine and rosemary or Italian sausage and sage risotto, rocket and parmesan. The wines are varied and come a dozen by the glass from a list of 40 reds and whites, from a Cuvée du Baron (£2.60/£10) to a bottle of Cuvée Antique Chablis (£25) and Châteauneuf-du-Pape (£30). Good cask-conditioned ales too (Hook Norton, Bombardier, Spitfire), plus Beck's for lager drinkers.
Babies and children welcome. Function room for parties. Tables outdoors (10, patio).

Fire Stables
27-29 Church Road, SW19 5DQ (8946 3197). Wimbledon tube/rail then 93, 200, 493 bus. **Open** 11am-11pm Mon-Sat; 11.30am-10.30pm Sun. **Food served** noon-4pm, 6-10.30pm Mon-Sat; noon-4pm, 6-10pm Sun. **Credit** MC, V.
This gastropub still proudly displays its 2001 *Time Out* award, and the place hasn't aged too badly. There's an open, brushed metal kitchen by the entrance and spacious, distressed tables among leather slob sofas through the drinking area, with the room given pleasant focus by a pair of lovely fires set into shiny metal surrounds; a back dining area is less well used. The clientele range from smoochy couples to boisterous birthday party groups. Helpful gel-

South

spiked staff cope well with food detritus, and booze options (Pride, Paulaner and Affligem the pick of the draughts; wine running to more than a dozen each, half by the glass) and food are pretty good (chicken liver parfait with red onion and blood orange marmalade; lambburger with big chips). *Babies and children welcome. Disabled: toilet. No-smoking area. Restaurant. TV.*

Fox & Grapes

9 Camp Road, SW19 4UN (8946 5599). Wimbledon tube/rail. **Open** 11am-11pm Mon-Thur; 11am-midnight Fri, Sat; noon-10.30pm Sun. **Food served** noon-9.45pm Mon-Sat; noon-9.30pm Sun. **Credit** MC, V.

It may have a London postcode, but the Fox and Grapes feels like a country pub. The Common stretches out in three directions, and even the relative hubbub of Wimbledon Village is a healthy tramp away. As such, it's hardly a party joint (on our last visit Jack Johnson hummed quietly through the speakers), but it attracts a mixed crowd. They congregate in the main room, with huge ceiling and large tables, and the dimmer food-orientated side room, where bashing your head on the beams is a real possibility. Unlike the decor – which is so old school that even the 1990s tennis posters look out of place – the food takes its cues from the Mediterranean (buffalo mozzarella and sun-dried tomatoes) as well as pub staples (deep-fried whitebait). Most patrons eschew lager for the impressive wine list and ales including Directors, Courage and Hogs Back TEA. *Babies and children admitted (until 8pm). Function room. No-smoking area. TV (big screen, satellite).*

Leather Bottle

538 Garratt Lane, SW17 0NY (8946 2309/www. leatherbottlepub.co.uk). Earlsfield rail. **Open** 11am-midnight Mon-Sat; noon-11pm Sun. **Food served** noon-3pm, 6-10pm Mon-Fri; noon-10pm Sat; noon-8pm Sun. **Credit** MC, V.

There's been a popular change of direction at this sturdy 18th-century country pub. The pretty front patio is still festooned with flowers, but the back area has been converted to a smoke-free dining room, and a mezzanine is now in place – candlelit and adorned with surrealist art – while a bar outside serves the 450-capacity beer garden in summer. New band nights, two pool tables, table football, board games… all have helped bring a younger crowd into this Young's pub, set on seemingly endless Garratt Lane. The menu has been revamped too. You can still get a Sunday roast, but also dishes such as nori- and tempura-battered fillet of whiting served with sugar snaps, chips and sweet chilli sauce (£9.50). As an alternative to the usual Young's range and standard lagers, a small but varied wine list includes a tasty Côte de Imaz Reserva rioja at £18.75. *Babies and children admitted (garden play area only). Disabled: toilet. Games (board games, pool, table football). Music (guitarist 9pm fri; free). Tables outdoors (garden). TV (satellite).*

Prince of Wales

2 Hartfield Road, SW19 3TA (8946 5369). Wimbledon tube/rail. **Open** noon-midnight daily. **Food served** noon-10pm daily. **Credit** MC, V.

Like many a railway pub, this place can feel like everyone's in transit – an impression the games machines do little to dispel. Happily, some through traffic hangs around in the evening, joined by an assortment of locals, giving the place a pleasant buzz. There's nothing out-of-the-ordinary here: a big area in front of the bar where punters mill and mix, a non-smoking mezzanine that gets a little smoky, a reasonable range of food (including burgers, pasta and wedges), some decent ales (including Skullsplitter) and a wine list that allows room for manoeuvre. But the POW does the basics better than any of the chain pubs around, and its unpretentious hubbub makes it comfortable whether you're nursing a midweek pint or indulging in a Saturday quaff-fest. *Disabled: toilet. Function room. Games (fruit machine, quiz machine). Music (karaoke 8pm Thur; free). No-smoking area. Tables outdoors (3, courtyard). TVs.*

Suburban Bar & Lounge

27 Hartfield Road, SW19 3SG (8543 9788/www. suburbanbar.com). Wimbledon tube/rail. **Open** 5-11pm Mon-Thur; 5pm-midnight Fri; 2pm-midnight Sat; 5-10.30pm Sun. **Credit** AmEx, MC, V.

The former Hartfield's Wine Bar has gone for the IKEA approach to cocktails – pile 'em up, knock 'em out cheap (£3.90-£4.90). Mojitos and Margaritas come in raspberry and strawberry flavours, cranberry juice (and Red Bull) feature highly in the vodka types, and there are categories such as 'Retro '70s' and 'Ice Cream'. The Champagne (£6) varieties include a Kir Royale without crème de cassis. It's popular, of course, because before too long everyone is off their face, partying and copping off, not copping off and drinking more. Music is provided (loudly) by an Xfm playlist or the mercifully quieter Adelphi Road Acoustic Duo every other Sunday. Oh, and the wines are pretty good: 15 well-chosen ones including a Chablis le Colombe at £25. *Disabled: toilet. Music (funk/soul/indie rock 8pm Sun; free). Tables outdoors (8, garden). TV (big screen).*

Sultan

78 Norman Road, SW19 1BT (8542 4532). Colliers Wood or South Wimbledon tube. **Open** noon-11pm Mon-Thur; noon-midnight Fri, Sat; noon-11pm Sun. **Credit** MC, V.

Proud and deserved winner of the *Time Out* Best Pub award in 2005, the Sultan (which is named after the great racehorse of the 1830s) is a magnet for lovers of real ale. It's a place that has no truck with modern fripperies, focusing instead on great beer and the provision of a warm and comfortable environment in which to sup it. The only Hop Back Brewery pub in London, you'll find Entire Stout, GFB and Summer Lightning on draught (or takeaway as singles or polypins). To tempt non-beeroes there are four reds, four whites and a rosé (£2.50 a small glass), or house-spirit doubles at £2.30. Two fires kept the busy saloon bar cosy, but the larger public bar (named after an extra from *The Archers*) was also full on a Friday night. A cabinet of trophies and picture of famous darts' dieter Andy 'The Viking' Fordham suggest darts are taken seriously here, but otherwise the entertainment is all down to you. Perfect. *Disabled: toilet. Games (board games, darts). Quiz (8.30pm Tue; £1). Tables outdoors (8, garden).*

Also in the area…

All Bar One 37-39 Wimbledon Hill Road, SW19 7NA (8971 9871).

Colliers Tup 198 High Street, SW19 2BH (8540 1918).

Eclipse 57 High Street, SW19 5EE (8944 7722).

O'Neill's 66 The Broadway, SW19 1RQ (8545 9931).

Walkabout 74-78 The Broadway, W19 1RQ (8543 8624).

Wibbas Down Inn (JD Wetherspoon) 6-12 Gladstone Road, SW19 1QT (8540 6788).

South

West

Acton

The **Grand Junction Arms** is an unexpected find in an altogether unpromising neighbourhood for thirst-quenching excitement.

Grand Junction Arms

Acton Lane, NW10 7AD (8965 5670). Harlesden tube. **Open** *Front bar* 11am-11pm Mon-Sat; noon-10.30pm Sun. *Back bar* noon-11pm Mon-Thur; noon-1am Fri, Sat; noon-10.30pm Sun. **Food served** noon-9pm Mon-Sat; noon-4pm Sun. **Credit** AmEx, MC, V.
Set in a semi-suburban industrial hinterland in the shadow of McVities, it's hard to imagine a more prosaic location for a pub – which makes the Grand Junction Arms even more of an oasis. In addition to the relatively small main bar, quickly filled on weekday lunchtimes by nearby workers from the call centres and courier depots, there are a couple of more spacious, high-beamed candlelit rooms – each with an open fire – from where you can gaze out on to a large beer garden and the Grand Union Canal beyond (the pub was originally set up to serve the moored harbour boats). Standard offerings are on tap, including Young's Export and a couple of seasonal ales, plus there's solid pub grub available, and major sports events are shown in the main bar.
Disabled: toilet. Games (fruit machines, 3 pool tables). Music (karaoke 8pm Fri; free). Tables outdoors (20, garden). TVs (widescreen).

Barnes & Mortlake

With ample opportunity for pint-in-hand riverside relaxing, the **Sun Inn** is idyllically positioned; **Ye White Hart** and the **Ship** are prime Boat Race viewing spots, and the **Coach & Horses** offers relief from the quaintness of it all.

Bull's Head

373 Lonsdale Road, SW13 9PY (8876 5241/www. thebullshead.com). Hammersmith tube then 209 or 283 bus/Barnes Bridge rail. **Open** 11am-midnight Mon-Sat; noon-11pm Sun. **Food served** noon-2.30pm, 6-10.30pm daily. **Credit** AmEx, MC, V.

This recently refurbished – but still quaint – riverside pub has hit upon the successful mix of jazz and Thai food, consumed in equal quantities on a nightly basis. The jazz element came first, with bearded toe-tappers flocking here since 1959 to catch the likes of Humphrey Lyttelton and Nelson Rangell. The splendid green and red curries were a later addition, and are now complemented by a selection of more than 200 wines, 32 different types of Champagne and over 80 malt whiskies. Few watering holes in the vicinity can compete with such choice. There are real ales too, supped by dog walkers and flat-capped locals in the daytime. You'll find more of a buzz on Sunday afternoons, when jazzsters pack the newly sponsored 100-capacity Yamaha Jazz Room.
Babies and children admitted (family area). Function room. Games (board games). Music (jazz 8.30pm Mon-Sat; 1pm, 8.30pm Sun; £5-£15). No-smoking tables. Tables outdoors (3, terrace). TVs (big screen).

Coach & Horses

27 Barnes High Street, SW13 9LW (8876 2695). Hammersmith tube, then 209 or 283 bus/Barnes Bridge rail. **Open** 11am-midnight Mon-Sat; noon-midnight Sun. **Food served** noon-11pm daily. **Credit** MC, V.
A throwback to local boozers of times past, the unpretentious Coach & Horses has avoided the battered leather sofas, scuffed wooden flooring and mismatched chairs refit – making it something of a rarity in these parts. Part of the Young's chain, this is still a place for working folk. Hardy old regulars play darts and talk over their respective football teams' failings over a pint of Special. The bubbly staff serve from behind a semicircular bar supported by beer barrels, and the open fire and old bench seats make for a cosy atmosphere (although there's an trek across the courtyard to the toilets outside). What's more, there's a paddock to the rear for nippers and big-screen entertainment, plus an attractive beer garden for summer barbecues and floodlit *boules*.
Babies and children admitted (play area, garden). Games (boules). Tables outdoors (40, garden). TV.

Ship

10 Thames Bank, SW14 7QR (8876 1439). Mortlake rail. **Open** 11am-11pm Mon-Sat; noon-10.30pm Sun. **Food served** noon-3pm, 6.30-9.30pm daily. **Credit** AmEx, DC, MC, V.
This pleasant riverside pub is serendipitously located right by the finish line for the Oxford and Cambridge Boat Race, held in April. For the rest of the year, it's overpowered not by students, but by the smell of beer from the adjoining Budweiser brewery. Few seem to mind. Junkshop knick-knacks decorate a cheery interior built around a welcoming log fire, with pop hits of yesteryear pouring out of a jukebox or, worse, a dodgy covers-band. Rugger fans, accountants and workmen trade witty retorts at the bar supping in unison from the modest range of draught ales, including London Pride, Bombardier and at least one guest ale per month. There's an equally modest but adequate wine list plus pub grub such as chicken tikka or rump steak at £7.95. A small dining area overlooks the beer garden and river.
Games (board games, fruit machines, quiz machine). Music (covers band 9pm Sat; free). Quiz (9pm Tue; free). Tables outdoors (25, garden). TV (satellite).

Spencer Arms

237 Lower Richmond Road, SW15 1HJ (8788 0640). Putney Bridge tube. **Open** 10am-midnight daily. **Food served** noon-2.30pm, 6.30-10pm Mon-Fri; noon-3pm, 6.30-10pm Sat; noon-2.30pm, 6.30-9.45pm Sun. **Credit** MC, V.

The interior of this Victorian pub is awash with green pastel shades and dark wood, creating a pleasant combination of traditional boozer and modern gastropub. Here, comfortable West London meets the Putney river brigade. The food is the main attraction, from robust, unfussy lunchtime bacon butties (£5.20) to hearty dinners of roast pheasant, creamed celeriac and beetroot leaf (£11). Real ales include Broadside and Jack Frost, with Bitburger and Amstel for the lager drinkers. A number of the wines and Champagnes are available by the glass. In the main dining area, remnants of Victoriana come into view as you sink into an old sofa, with a stuffed buffalo's head mounted above the open fire. A younger bunch take over the place on Friday nights, entertained by a lounge DJ, but all is back to normal for traditional roasts on Sunday lunchtimes.
Babies and children admitted (until 9pm). Bar available for hire. Disabled: toilet. Games (board games). Music (jazz duo 9pm occasional Tue-Thur; free). Restaurant (no smoking). Tables outdoors (8, pavement). TVs.

Sun Inn

7 Church Road, SW13 9HE (8876 5256).
Hammersmith tube then 209 or 283 bus/Barnes Bridge rail. **Open** noon-11pm Mon-Thur; noon-11.30pm Fri, Sat; noon-10.30pm Sun. **Food served** noon-3pm, 6-10pm Mon-Thur; noon-10pm Fri, Sat; noon-8.30pm Sun. **Credit** AmEx, MC, V.
This is the most popular pub in the area, thanks to its picturesque setting by the village pond and piss-easy Tuesday quiz nights. A cosy ambience is played out to a soundtrack of laid-back modern jazz and low-key disco, attracting a smart, young crowd. Open fires, cream and brown furnishings with snug corners and dim lighting from kitsch lampshades do the rest. Sharp young bar staff serve a good range of beers including Spitfire and Deuchars IPA, plus a guest ale and Belgian and fruit beers aplenty. The wine list is more than adequate and the menu features curiosities such as stuffed pesto chicken with Parma ham, vegetable ragoût and couscous (£8.80) or a light sharing menu featuring the likes of calamari with sweet chilli sauce (£4.50), to nibble by the piano.
Babies and children admitted (until 7pm). Games (video game). No-smoking tables. Quiz (9pm Tue; £1). Tables outdoors (15, terrace).

Ye White Hart

The Terrace, Riverside, SW13 0NR (8876 5177).
Barnes Bridge rail/209, 419 bus. **Open** 11am-midnight daily. **Food served** noon-3pm, 6.30-10pm Mon-Sat; noon-9pm Sun. **Credit** MC, V.
Standing for over 300 years, this majestic old pub appears to be coming apart at the seams – but in a charming way, with high-beamed ceilings rising over expansive windows. Once a Masonic lodge, it was extensively rebuilt at the turn of the last century when a wooden balcony was added to provide a ringside seat for the Boat Race. It's a prime spot on warm summer days too, when natural light floods through, or near the warming glow of an open fire on winter nights. Gnarled regulars sup Young's ales – although there's also a superb, comprehensive wine list (note the mounted awards) to choose from – and all is well with the world. A riverside terrace and towpath complete the idyllic picture here.
Function room. Games (fruit machine). Music (jazz 8pm Sun, winter only; free). Tables outdoors (6, balcony; riverside terrace; 8, garden; 8, tow path). TV (big screen, satellite).

West

Sam's Brasserie & Bar. *See p232.*

Paradise by Way of Kensal Green.
See p238.

Chiswick & Kew

Real-ale drinkers are spoiled for choice with the primary source of Fuller's ales close by. The **Mawson Arms** has the best range. The river is also a draw, as is top nosh for post-Gardens refuels.

Bell & Crown

11-13 Thames Road, Strand-on-the-Green, W4 3PL (8994 4164). Gunnersbury tube/rail. **Open** 11am-11pm Mon-Sat; noon-10.30pm Sun. **Food served** noon-3pm, 6-9pm Mon-Sat; noon-7pm Sun. **Credit** AmEx, DC, MC, V.
This traditional riverside boozer draws a mixed crowd of old-timers and wide-eyed youngsters into its garishly decorated interior, drawn not by the lurid decor but by the large windows and riverside terrace behind. You need to be here with the worm-catching bird to get a seat outside on a hot summer's day. Unsurprisingly, Fuller's (whose brewery is nearby) supply the ales – also used in the steak and London Pride ale pie (£8.75). The calf's liver, black pudding and smoked bacon with mashed potato (£11.95) is another excellent choice. Other beers include Anniversary Ale, Chiswick Bitter and Discovery as well as Stella, Grolsch, Caffrey's and Guinness. The wine list favours Australia and South Africa with most of the 20-odd bottles available by the glass.
Babies and children admitted (until 7pm). No-smoking area. Tables outdoors (10, riverside patio).

Bollo

13-15 Bollo Lane, W4 5LR (8994 6037). Chiswick Park tube. **Open** noon-11pm Mon-Sat; noon-10.30pm Sun. **Food served** noon-3pm, 6-10pm Mon-Fri; noon-3.30pm, 6-10pm Sat; noon-10pm Sun. **Credit** MC, V.

This characterful backstreet L-shaped pub is best enjoyed on bustling weekends; catch it at the wrong time in the week and the empty dining area can drain the pub of atmosphere. When busy, however, it's a great spot, particularly for Sunday lunch during the summer on the south-west facing front terrace. Blackboards above the bar show six of each wines by the glass; Greene King, Budvar and Abbot Ale are the draught stars (and draughts is one of the many board games available). Tables are typically large and good for reading the daily papers (supplied), while tucked behind the dining area is a more comfortable spot where folk play board games while lounging on the large leather banquette. Food is posh pub grub: pot-roast pheasant with bread sauce and savoy cabbage (£8.95) and sautéed mushrooms on garlic bread with a poached egg (£4.95).
Babies and children admitted. Tables outdoors (12, pavement).

City Barge

27 Strand-on-the-Green, W4 3PH (8994 2148). Gunnersbury tube/rail/Kew Bridge rail. **Open** 11am-11pm Mon-Sat; noon-10.30pm Sun. **Food served** noon-3pm, 6-9.30pm Mon-Sat; noon-8.30pm Sun. **Credit** AmEx, DC, MC, V.
Not a barge at all – but it is on the river – this place is entered either by the riverside walkway or the main car park behind and has been an operating pub since medieval times. The split level creates several different bars, characterised by tiled floors, open fires and baskets of condiments on the tables. The pub grub may be basic but the spread of ales is strong, with Adnams, Bombardier and a good selection from the Fuller's range. The low-ceilinged downstairs bar is more atmospheric (and popular) and the wines are reasonably

priced – particularly the Sancerre at £15. A handful of tables overlook the river on the waterside terrace and make a sublime spot for sun-kissed drinking.
Babies and children admitted (until 9pm). Games (quiz machine). No-smoking area. Tables outdoors (6, riverside terrace).

Coach & Horses
8 Kew Green, TW9 3BH (8940 1208/www.coachhotel kew.co.uk). Kew Gardens tube/rail. **Open** 11am-midnight Mon-Sat; 11am-11pm Sun. **Food served** noon-2.30pm, 7-10pm Mon-Sat; noon-9pm Sun. **Credit** AmEx, MC, V.
This old Tavern Hotel has refreshed many a weary traveller with its position near the bridge on Kew Green, and continues to be a popular watering hole after a tour of nearby Kew Gardens. Young's supply the ales with a good variety of seasonal specials on tap including the eponymous Kew Brew which simply has to be sampled in-situ. The pub grub is on the posher side of things, with burgers, fresh fish and steaks at prices ranging from £10 to £15. Food can be eaten anywhere inside the pub, but there is a separate dining wing – complete with open fire – for those after a more formal experience. The full English breakfast, Bloody Mary and weekend sports-watching facilities come highly recommended.
Disabled: toilet. Games (board games, fruit machines, quiz machine). Restaurant (no smoking). Tables outdoors (6, patio; 8, garden). TV (big screen, satellite).

Devonshire House
126 Devonshire Road, W4 2JJ (8987 2626/www.the devonshirehouse.co.uk). Turnham Green tube. **Open** noon-11pm Tue-Sat; noon-10pm Sun. **Food served** noon-3pm, 7-10.30pm Tue-Sat; noon-3pm, 7-9.30pm Sun. **Credit** AmEx, MC, V.
This squat period corner house, marooned in a sea of anonymous architecture just north of the A4, is well worth a visit. Its modern interior is characterised by dark wood panelling, leather furniture, giant candles in bell jars and minimalist Thai-style candelabras. The coffee tables are old tea chests and the elegant touches extend to several open gas fires. Hoegaarden, London Pride, Stella and Strongbow are pulled from the pumps along with Foster's and Guinness Extra Cold. The separate and highly renowned dining area offers such treats as spinach soup with poached egg and truffle oil (£4.95), duck egg sunny side up with foie gras (£7.95) and rabbit stew (£11). A third of the 40 wines are available by the glass, with the selection featuring a good blend of Old and New World, with several mid-price options.
Babies and children welcome. Bar available for hire. Tables outdoors (10, garden; 4, pavement).

Inn at Kew Gardens
292 Sandycombe Road, Kew, TW9 3NG (8940 2220/ www.theinnatkewgardens.com). Kew Gardens tube. **Open** 11am-11pm Mon-Thur, Sun; 11am-midnight Fri, Sat. **Food served** noon-3pm, 6-10pm Mon-Fri; noon-10pm Sat; noon-9pm Sun. **Credit** AmEx, MC, V.
This large pub at the foot of the Kew Gardens Hotel has benefited from a thoughtful and tasteful renovation; subtly dividing spaces up by different decor and furniture has clearly paid off here. The hardened locals have their unpretentious space, there's a more relaxed area with leather sofas to the left of the bar and an informal dining room of high stools and tables behind it. It doesn't end there, however, with formal dining to the rear and a spiral staircase leading to a sexy leather seating section, populated by the

young and beautiful. An imaginative food menu is comprised of dishes like basil and shellfish risotto and home-baked pork scratchings. San Miguel bolsters the lagers and Magners cider makes a rare appearance at the pumps. Young's supply a good cast of ales and the wine list numbers over 40.
Babies and children welcome. Disabled: toilet. Function room. Restaurant (available for hire; no smoking). Tables outdoors (8, garden; 4, terrace). TVs (big screen, satellite).

Mawson Arms
110 Chiswick Lane South, W4 2QA (8994 2936). Turnham Green tube. **Open** 11am-8pm Mon-Fri. **Food served** noon-3pm Mon-Fri. **Credit** MC, V.
Mention that this pub closes at 8pm and is not open at weekends and it's hard to show excitement about the prospect of visiting; add the fact that it's almost on top of one of the busiest roundabouts in London, and enthusiasm is sure to wane even further. However, when you find out that said pub is the starting point of the adjoining Fuller's brewery tour, with the freshest and widest selection of Fuller's ales in town, the reasons for Mawson Arms's popularity become clear. Portraits of esteemed Fullers share wall space with old photos of the brewery in an otherwise unremarkable space. The roll-call of draught ales reads London Pride, Chiswick Bitter, ESB, Discovery and Champion Ale, plus a vast bottled selection. A good starting point for an evening's tour of riverside watering holes.
Function room. No-smoking area. TV.

Old Pack Horse
434 Chiswick High Road, W4 5TF (8994 2872). Chiswick Park tube. **Open** 11am-11pm Mon-Sat; 11am-10.30pm Sun. **Food served** noon-10pm Mon-Sat; noon-9pm Sun. **Credit** AmEx, MC, V.
Dominating the Chiswick High Road with its classic red-brick four-storey frontispiece, the Pack Horse is one of the better pubs on the main drag. Discovery, ESB, Jack Frost and London Pride share tap space with Leffe, Scrumpy Jack and Strongbow and the cider selection is further bolstered by bottled Magners. The Fuller's bottled range is strong, with a few guest beers like Hock and Tiger. Adventurous souls may want to try a bottle of Thai wine (£10.50). It's a big space sub-divided into saloon bar, dining area that's been extended into the old courtyard to form a Thai restaurant, and more comfier leather seating areas by the two open fires. Old theatre programmes from the now-extinct Chiswick Empire add interest to the walls. It draws a mixed crowd of regulars throughout the week and is a busy spot at the weekend.
Games (fruit machines). Restaurant (no smoking). Tables outdoors (6, pavement; 5, garden).

Pilot
56 Wellesley Road, W4 4BZ (8994 0828). Gunnersbury tube/rail. **Open** noon-11pm Mon-Sat; noon-10.30pm Sun. **Food served** noon-3pm, 6.30-10pm Mon-Fri; noon-10pm Sat; noon-9.30pm Sun. **Credit** AmEx, MC, V.
Pop art depictions of iconic music and movie stars line the walls of this buzzing neighbourhood pub, with its high-ceilinged, modernised Victorian interior and high-octane vibe. The mix of Hoegaarden, Leffe Blonde, Staropramen, London Pride and organic Fuller's Honey Dew keeps drinkers lubricated. There's an adequate wine selection of ten of each colour ranging from £11.50 to £21 which includes sauvignon blanc from Chile's Bio-Bio valley, quietly tipped as the next big thing. Hand-cut chips (£2.50),

West

Spanish chorizo, poached egg, shallot vinegar and rocket salad (£6.50) and beetroot risotto with fresh greens and butternut squash (£9.50) show an imaginative and well-executed menu. In the summer, the courtyard garden is the perfect sheltered spot to drink late into the night. *Babies and children admitted (until 7pm). Disabled: toilet. Function room. Tables outdoors (12, garden). TV.*

Sam's Brasserie & Bar

11 Barley Mow Passage, W4 4PH (8987 0555/www. samsbrasserie.co.uk). Chiswick Park tube. **Open** 9am-11pm Mon-Sat; 9am-10.30pm Sun. **Food served** noon-3pm, 6.30-10pm Mon-Fri; 9am-4pm, 6.30-10.30pm Sat; 9am-4pm, 6.30-10pm Sun. **Credit** AmEx, MC, V.
Atypical for Chiswick is this warehouse-style space with large windows, exposed brick walls and steel ventilation shafts offset by softer touches like the giant lampshades, colourful flowers and comfy leather sofas. The smart brasserie is to the rear, with views into the bustling kitchen, while the steel bar and surrounds gives an industrial feel to the drinking space at the front. Staropramen, Leffe and Guinness are the only draught selections, but there's a good range of bottled beers including Asahi, Lapin Kulta, Aspall Suffolk Cyder, Zatec and London Pride. The focused cocktail list includes a strawberry, honey and lavender Martini (£6.50) but the wines are the stars with 60 bottles, priced from £12.50 to £85. There are nine varieties available by the glass including, unusually, a 2003 Châteauneuf-du-Pape (£6.75) and a 2003 Pouilly-Fumé (£6.50). *Babies and children welcome. Disabled: toilet. Music (jazz band 7pm occasional Sun; free). Restaurant (no smoking).*

Swan

Evershed Walk, 119 Acton Lane, W4 5HH (8994 8262). Chiswick Park tube/94 bus. **Open** 5-11pm Mon-Fri; noon-11pm Sat; noon-10.30pm Sun. **Food served** 7-10.30pm Mon-Fri; 12.30-3pm, 7-10.30pm Sat; 12.30-3pm, 7-10pm Sun. **Credit** MC, V.
This Victorian swan can hold its neck high, serving as it does some of the best pub food in Chiswick. The menu changes daily but can include treats like antipasti of poached salmon aïoli or smoked duck breast with olive tapenade (£6-£7), followed by pork tenderloin with Parma ham (£12.50). The background music can only just be heard over the hum of expectant voices, and rickety furniture in the dining area adds to the character. Drinkers congregate on cosy leather sofas around the gas fire in winter, while the good-sized patio garden makes this a top spot for lazy summer days. London Pride, Adnams and Broadside mix it up with Hoegaarden and San Miguel on tap and a respectable wine list has bottles from £10.50 to £32, with six each available by the glass. *Babies and children welcome (until 7pm). Tables outdoors (30, garden).*

Also in the area...

All Bar One 197-199 Chiswick High Road, W4 2DR (8987 8211).
Pitcher & Piano 11 Bridge Street, TW9 1TQ (8332 2524).

Ealing

The cosy **Red Lion** has been refuelling actors from nearby Ealing Film Studios for years. A new wave is characterised by **Baroque**'s Maori-inspired menu.

Baroque

94 Uxbridge Road, W13 8RA (8567 7346/www. baroque-ealing.co.uk). West Ealing rail. **Open** noon-11pm Mon-Thur; noon-2am Fri, Sat; noon-10.30pm Sun. **Food served** noon-3pm, 6-10pm Mon-Sat; noon-5pm Sun. **Credit** MC, V.
The main change to this tasty little bar on an uncongenial bit of the Uxbridge Road is the introduction of authentic Maori food. Traditional cooking methods are used, namely the *hangi*, where food is placed on the ground in baskets surrounded by hot rocks, and slow-cooked. This makes meat deliciously smoked and tender, such as in the *hangi*-smoked lamb rump with *kumara* (a New Zealand sweet potato) mash, buttered cabbage, carrots and baby spinach (£12.95). Antipodean specialities have stretched to the cocktails (£6) too, such as the unappealingly named Sheep Dip, just to show that Baroque hasn't lost its party edge. Pictures of the Manhattan skyline stand out beneath a purple ceiling, while a trendy, young crowd jiggles about to DJs and manages to make conversation during the Sunday brunch jazz sessions. *Music (DJ 10pm Fri, Sat; jazz 2-5pm Sun; free). Tables outdoors (5, garden).*

Castlebar

84 Uxbridge Road, W13 8RA (8567 3819/www. castlebar.co.uk). Ealing Broadway or West Ealing tube. **Open** 8am-midnight Mon-Wed; 8am-1am Thur-Fri; 10am-1am Sat; 11am-midnight Sun. **Food served** noon-2.30pm, 6-9.30pm Mon-Fri; noon-4pm, 6-9.30pm Sat; noon-5pm Sun. **Credit** MC, V.
Below a 1960s tenement block, this former rough old boozer is now a funky gastrobar. In summer or winter, people gather in the new heated outside area – despite the view of the Uxbridge Road traffic – a no-smoking rule having cleared the main bar. DJs work the place at weekends, and Monday's quiz nights are popular with the articulate young clientele. But most come here for the food. Impeccably served and presented, it includes superior versions of pub standards in the £10 range: Guinness and oysters, or grilled tuna with vegetable ratatouille, rocket and red pepper sauce are often options, and the house burgers come highly recommended. Often a gastro-makeover is viewed suspiciously by locals, but this one seems to be most welcome. Leffe, Staropramen and Hoegaarden are on tap. *Babies and children admitted (until 6pm). Disabled: toilet. Music (DJs 9.30pm Sat; free). Quiz (8pm Mon; £2). Tables outdoors (17, garden). TV.*

Drayton Court

2 The Avenue, W13 8PH (8997 1019/www.fullers. co.uk). West Ealing rail. **Open** 11am-11pm Mon-Thur; 11am-midnight Fri, Sat; noon-11pm Sun. **Food served** noon-3pm, 5-9pm Mon-Fri; noon-9pm Sat, Sun. **Credit** AmEx, MC, V.
The popularity of this huge space hasn't diminished of late; if anything, the major refit two years back has helped people to find a seat and more privacy. As you enter, an open fire beckons to the left, in a room comfortably decked out with leather furniture and embellished with an ironwork chandelier. To the right, a main bar on two levels features a balcony overlooking a large beer garden and children's play area. Grown-ups play at the back of the bar, with a pool table and screens for live sporting action. As you would expect from a Fuller's pub, there are well-kept ales – house ESB, London Pride, Chiswick and Jack Frost – and the usual lagers. Wines come in 15 varieties and pub grub includes regularly changing specials. Add in the jazz and quiz nights, and everyone goes home happy.

Babies and children admitted (until 9pm). Disabled: toilet. Function room. Games (1 pool table). Music (jazz 8pm 3nd or last Wed of mth; free). No-smoking area. Tables outdoors (40, garden). TVs (big screen, satellite).

Ealing Park Tavern

222 South Ealing Road, W5 4RL (8758 1879). South Ealing tube. **Open** 5-11pm Mon; 11am-11pm Tue-Sat; noon-10.30pm Sun. **Food served** 6-10pm Mon; noon-3pm, 6-10pm Tue-Sat; noon-3.45pm, 6-9pm Sun. **Credit** AmEx, MC, V.

This former South Ealing student haunt (as the Penny Flyer) is now well established as a gastropub. The beautiful old place is probably breathing a sigh of relief. Opera now plays in the background as afternoon sunlight streams onto the oak-panelled walls and well-heeled customers compare the quality of the Moorish fish casserole (£12.50) to the goat's cheese tart (£8) (one of several vegetarian choices). Dining can be enjoyed at the tapas bar near an open fire, in intimate booths or, after April, in the spacious, 25-table garden. The selection of ales matches the food, with Doom Bar, Deuchars IPA and Grand Union Honey Porter, dark and light; Leffe and Hoegaarden feature among the lighter options. In the evening Puccini makes way for jazz and Latin music and a slightly younger crowd.
Babies and children welcome. Restaurant (no smoking). Tables outdoors (25, garden).

Red Lion

13 St Mary's Road, W5 5RA (8567 2541). South Ealing tube. **Open** 11am-11pm Mon-Sat; noon-10.30pm Sun. **Food served** noon-3pm, 7-9.30pm Mon-Sat; 12.30-5pm Sun. **Credit** AmEx, MC, V.

As confirmed by the brass plaque by the front door, this place is known by many as Stage Six, being Ealing Film Studio's equivalent of a golf club's '19th hole' (the studios were numbered one to five). Actors and technicians have been frequenting this comfortable and friendly place for decades, and the decor reflects this, with stills and posters of Ealing stars. Daytime regulars are commendably eccentric (with many a tale to tell); after dark, the place fills with punters from the *Star Wars* generation. Own-made food is top quality – expect the likes of fillet of beef and Guinness pie, green beans and home fries (£11.95). Being a Fuller's pub, the draught ale options are Chiswick, London Pride and ESB, plus its recent introduction, Discovery Blonde, possibly named after a leading lady in a Dirk Bogarde film.
Disabled: toilet. Tables outdoors (15, garden).

Also in the area...

Hog's Head 46-47 The Mall, Ealing Broadway W5 3TJ (8579 3006).
O'Neill's 23-25 High Street, W5 5DB (8579 4107).

Fulham & Parsons Green

With the riverside to the busy King's and Fulham Roads within its boundary, options abound in Fulham. Parsons Green is home to the **White Horse** – one of London's finest boozers, despite its often sloaney flavour.

Aragon House

247 New King's Road, SW6 4XG (7731 7313/ www.aragonhouse.net). Parsons Green or Putney Bridge tube/22 bus. **Open** 11am-11pm Mon-Sat;

noon-10.30pm Sun. **Food served** noon-3pm, 6-10pm Mon-Fri; noon-9pm Sat, Sun. **Credit** AmEx, DC, MC, V.

Named after Catherine of Aragon, who lived in a manor house on this site during the 16th century, Aragon House occupies a handsome, late 18th-century terrace on the South side of Parsons Green. Inside, 'Tudor' touches abound and, while the overall effect is a bit kitsch, the bar is extremely comfortable. Squashy sofas, long wooden tables, friendly staff and a laid-back vibe all encourage weekend newspaper reading. Customers mostly fall into the twenty- to thirty something, well-dressed, prosperous looking bracket. A variety of beers is on offer, an interesting wine list (prices starting at £12.50) and a number of Champagnes (£6.50 for a glass). Lunch and dinner are served (with a good selection of hearty dishes, like minted lamb chop with parsley mash, £9) as well as brunch and full English breakfast. There are sometimes barbecues in the garden.
Function rooms. Tables outdoors (5, garden; 12, patio).

Elk Bar

587 Fulham Road, SW6 5UA (7385 6940/www.elk bar.com). Fulham Broadway tube. **Open** noon-11pm Mon-Wed, Sun; noon-midnight Thur-Sat. **Food served** noon-9pm daily. **Credit** MC, V.

Elk-themed, this smart, dark bar has antlers on the walls and elk-burger on the menu. On a Saturday lunchtime visit, the bar was pretty empty, with a few couples wandering in for brunch or a beer. However, the place gets busier come nightfall, buffering Fulham Broadway's rowdy rugger buggers. Cocktails (around £5, pitchers £12.90) include Elk's own (elderflower cordial, squeezed lime & Absolut Kurrant) and a variety of spirits are offered by the bottle. Food-wise, a selection of simple platters are available (barbecue-themed, antipasti, meze) for around the £11 to £12 mark, plus pub grub-type dishes including cod and chips, and Caesar salad. Smiley, helpful young bar staff make very decent cappuccinos. There's also a garden area, plus regular screening of live sports events.
Disabled: toilet. Music (DJs 7pm Thur-Sat; free). Tables outdoors (12, garden). TV (big screen).

Finch's

190 Fulham Road, SW10 9PN (7351 5043). Earl's Court, Fulham Broadway or South Kensington tube/14 bus. **Open** 11am-midnight Mon-Sat; noon-midnight Sun. **Food served** noon-10pm Mon-Sat; noon-5pm Sun. **Credit** MC, V.

Finch's is very much a sports viewer's pub, with a number of screens throughout the pub showing a variety of matches (Scotland versus Wales was in progress on our visit). On match days, blue-shirted Chelsea supporters (the football ground is a stone's throw away) regularly fill the space, spilling out on to the pavement. Run by Young's Brewery, the pub offers (not surprisingly) a variety of Young's beers (plus the usual favourites – Guinness, Stella) and a short wine list. Reasonably priced dishes are also available, including Sunday specials (roast beef, lamb shank) plus a special chip menu. A Victorian pub with beautiful original tiling and a stained-glass skylight providing evidence of former grandeur, Finch's is not for those who dislike sport.
Games (fruit machines). TV (big screen, satellite).

Fox & Pheasant

1 Billing Road, SW10 9UJ (7352 2943). Fulham Broadway tube. **Open** 11am-11pm Mon-Wed; 11am-midnight Thur-Sat; noon-10.30pm Sun. **Food served** noon-2.30pm Mon-Fri. **Credit** MC, V.

West

A small street off the Fulham Road (and almost next to the Chelsea football ground), is the location of the Fox & Pheasant. With its low ceilings, wooden beams, smoky walls, patterned carpets and open fires, this pub just needs a village green outside to be completely authentic. Abbot Ale and Greene King's IPA are on offer, as is a daily changing menu of 'good English food' although, sadly, food is not served in the evening. With no blaring music, this is a relaxing proper pub with a good atmosphere and a garden and terrace at the back – it's something of a surprise. One note of caution, when Chelsea are playing at home it can get very busy; avoid match days if you're after a quiet pint.
Games (darts). Tables outdoors (8, heated garden). TV.

La Perla
803 Fulham Road, SW6 5HE (7471 4895/www.cafe pacifico-laperla.com). Parsons Green tube. **Open** 5-11pm Mon-Fri; noon-11pm Sat; noon-10.30pm Sun. **Food served** 5-10.15pm Mon-Fri; noon-10.30pm Sat; noon-9.45pm Sun. **Happy hour** 5-7pm daily. **Credit** AmEx, MC, V.
A Mexican-themed bar and restaurant, La Perla is all terracotta walls, ceiling fans and Mexican beer posters. The bar serves a wide range of tequilas: blanco (young un-aged tequila), reposado (aged in oak for up to 12 months), anejo (aged for more than a year), plus top-of-the-range Premium tequilas. Mexican beer, and flavoured Martinis and Margaritas also feature. For something solid, a range of tortillas, quesadillas, fajitas and taquitos provide a good way of mopping up the booze, though some dishes could be described as lacking authenticity – sweet soy duck quesadillas (soy duck, Edam cheese, onion and smoked chilli marmalade), for instance. However, after an evening on the 'tequila flights', it's doubtful you'll care too much.
Restaurant.

Mitre
81 Dawes Road, SW6 7DU (7386 8877/www.fulham mitre.com). Fulham Broadway tube. **Open** noon-11pm Mon-Sat; noon-10.30pm Sun. **Food served** noon-3pm, 6-9.30pm Mon-Sat; 1-4pm, 6-9.30pm Sun. **Credit** AmEx, MC, V.
Independent and family run, the Mitre is a spacious, comfortable pub, with an attractive conservatory/terrace area to the rear. Busy on the Sunday of our visit, with customers of all ages, the pub offers a good range of beers and wines (ten reds, ten whites, all reasonably priced at under £21.50, plus rosé and sparkling wine). A good place for lunch – main courses might typically include poached brill or honey-roasted ham (with prices normally between £8 and £13), while a bar menu offers light snacks (the likes of devilled whitebait) as well as salads and sandwiches. There's no pounding music and the plasma screens are kept to a low volume. A good 'Sunday-with-the-family' type of place, the Mitre is winner of the Greater London Award for Excellence 2003-4.
Babies and children welcome (until 7pm). Disabled: toilet. No-smoking area. Tables outdoors (30, garden). TV (satellite).

Wandsworth Bridge Tavern
360 Wandsworth Bridge Road, SW6 2TY (7610 9816). Fulham Broadway tube/Wandsworth Town rail. **Open** noon-midnight Mon-Thur, Sun; noon-1am Fri, Sat. **Food served** noon-3pm, 6-9pm Mon-Thur; noon-3pm Fri; 1-4pm Sat, Sun. **Credit** MC, V.
Set on a busy and rather unprepossessing section of road, the Wandsworth Bridge Tavern doesn't have the most attractive of locations. Nevertheless, the place fights

Booze talking
White Horse

You are?
Mark Dorber, landlord of the White Horse, Parsons Green (*see p236*).
How long have you had this place?
I'm coming up for a 25-year involvement. A dear friend took over the pub on the 15 June 1981 and I was one of her helpers. I was between university degrees and this was a summer job – I just carried on helping.
Has the pub always been known for real ales?
It wasn't until the mid-'80s that we started to branch out with more interesting bottled beers. We started stocking guest beers and guest cask ales, and also held beer festivals. The first in 1982, which we've run every year since, was an old ale festival, featuring as many beers that tasted of old England as possible.
What is an 'old England' taste?
Something with high alcohol content, low bitterness, a fruitiness that comes with warm top fermentation and that's rich in aroma and malt flavour. These are beers that have had anything from a month to a year's maturation. Beers that have undergone subtle changes in the cask, as wine does.
How many beers do you have on?
We have around 75 bottled beers, and hope to move up to 150 very soon. And 20 beers on draught all the time. It means we have a huge palette of flavours to work with. The restaurant has made that the very heart of its appeal – a beer and a wine suggestion against each dish.
Is there a growing appreciation of real ale?
The more exciting new flavours and beers, yes, but overall it seems the market is declining. When I first came here we sold 20 barrels of cask ales a week. Now we're selling about 14 a week. Unless we get three Chelsea home games on the trot – those lads drink a lot of ale.

West

against this disadvantage by offering a host of activities (Salsa classes, jazz singers, a pub quiz, speed-dating). The pub itself is large and high ceilinged, with plenty of open brickwork, an open fire, comfy sofas, low tables, plus lots of newspapers. And there's a terrace at the back too. Beers include Greene King IPA, Abbot Ale and Speckled Hen. Serving an interesting selection of wines, the owners have also come up with a nice idea for Sunday lunch: whole roast chicken plus trimmings (£24 but suitable for four sharing). A couple of whinges – too much dismal grey paint and loads of match-showing plasma screens.

Bar available for hire. Games (board games, poker, table football). Music (DJ 8.30pm 3rd Sat of mth; free; jazz duo 2pm last Sun of mth; free). Quiz (8pm Thur; £2). Salsa class (7.30pm Mon; £5). Tables outdoors (6, garden). TV (big screen, satellite).

White Horse
1-3 Parsons Green, SW6 4UL (7736 2115/www. whitehorsesw6.com). Parsons Green tube. **Open** 11am-midnight Mon-Sat; 11am-11pm Sun. **Food served** noon-10.30pm Mon-Fri; 11am-10.30pm Sat, Sun. **Credit** AmEx, MC, V.

If you're in the Parsons Green area and looking for top-quality beer, the White Horse is an absolute godsend. It serves Harveys Sussex Best Bitter, Adnams Broadside and Fuller's ESB, plus a huge variety of other draught and bottled British and international beers (20 on draught and another 75 in bottles, according to the landlord – and we're in no position to gainsay him). Food is also a strong point, with emphasis on British fare like hot smoked pheasant and steak and ale pie. Prices are not especially low, but quality is good. A free house, the White Horse is large and generally very crowded, so you sometimes have to wait a time to get served at the bar. Also known as the 'Sloaney Pony', it can be something of a hang-out for hoorays. The space outside sometimes hosts barbecues in summer.
Babies and children admitted. Disabled: toilet. Function room. No piped music or jukebox. Restaurant (no smoking). Tables outdoors (50, garden).

Also in the area...
Fulham Tup 1 Harwood Terrace, SW6 2AF (7610 6131).
Oyster Rooms Fulham Broadway, SW6 1AA (7471 0310).
Pitcher & Piano 871-873 Fulham Road, SW6 5HP (7736 3910).
Slug & Lettuce 474-476 Fulham Road, SW6 1BY (7385 3209).

Hammersmith, Ravenscourt Park & Stamford Brook

Socially diverse Hammersmith is a mix of the raw and the genteel, a fact reflected in its watering holes. With plenty of choice on the High Street and by the river, the pick of the bunch is the **Old Ship** – a marriage of views, outdoor space and lively folk.

Blue Anchor
13 Lower Mall, W6 9DJ (8748 5774). Hammersmith tube. **Open** 11am-11pm Mon-Sat; noon-10.30pm Sun. **Food served** noon-3pm, 6-9pm Mon-Fri; noon-4pm, 6-9pm Sat, Sun. **Credit** MC, V.

Dating from 1722, the sleepy riverside boozer where Gustav Holst allegedly penned his *Hammersmith* is an unashamedly boaty establishment; being a mere paddle-length from the Thames, it has every right to be. More or less untouched since the '60s, the diminutive and thread-bare crimson and mahogany interior has been jollied-up with 19th-century black-and-white photographs and knick-knacks hanging from the ceiling (mind your head on the tricycle). A conservative selection of lagers and bitters are on tap (with little bottled backup) – the best of the bunch being a good San Miguel and the ever reliable Brakspear. The food menu too is rather disappointing: although good-value, dishes are unimaginative. But on cold days, the upstairs function room is a lovely spot, with views of the Hammersmith Bridge and jets arriving at Heathrow. Grab an outdoor pew by the water in warm weather.
Babies and children admitted (until 6pm). Function room. Tables outdoors (10, riverside). TV.

Brook Green Hotel
170 Shepherd's Bush Road, W6 7PB (7603 2516/ www.brookgreenhotel.co.uk). Hammersmith tube. **Open** Ground floor bar 8pm-midnight Wed-Fri; 6pm-1am Sat; 7pm-midnight Sun. *1st floor bar* 7am-11pm Mon-Thur; 8am-11pm Fri, Sat; 8am-10.30pm Sun. **Food served** *1st floor bar* 7am-9.30am, noon-3pm, 6-10pm Mon-Thur; 8am-10am, noon-3pm, 6-10pm Fri, Sat; noon-4pm, 6-10pm Sun. **Credit** AmEx, DC, MC, V.

An exquisitely preserved Victorian monster (size-wise), Brook Green is not your classic hotel bar – it's more a pleasantly old-fashioned, well-preserved pub, with plenty of room to unwind on an array of large leather sofas. A wide selection of Young's beer and other tipples to hand; recommended is the honey-flavoured Waggledance, available both on tap and bottled. Tiger beer is also stocked, as well as draught Guinness, Strongbow and a lacklustre selection of spirits. Food ranges from a bowl of olives for two quid to an inventive set menu, featuring the likes of Thai fish cakes and bangers and mash. Sky Sports, a dartboard, a coal fire and summer barbecues in the courtyard are welcome extras. Downstairs, a more modern and intimate club hosts jazz to comedy to blues.
Comedy (8pm Thur; £5). Disabled: toilet. Function room. Music (DJ & swing dancing 7pm Sun; blues 8pm Fri; jazz 8pm Wed; £5-£7). No-smoking area. Tables outdoors (12, garden). TVs (big screen, satellite).

Dove
19 Upper Mall, W6 9TA (8748 5405). Hammersmith or Ravenscourt Park tube. **Open** 11am-11pm Mon-Sat; noon-10.30pm Sun. **Food served** noon-2.30pm, 5-9pm Mon-Sat; 12.30-4.30pm Sun. **Credit** AmEx, MC, V.

Selling drinks since Hammersmith was a dozy hamlet, this 17th-century masterpiece started out as a coffee shop before moving on to bigger things. William Morris lived next door, Hemingway and Graham Greene both drank here, and the *Guinness Book of Records* bestowed an award on the microscopic front bar (127cm x 239cm) back in 1989. Today's Dove comes with three additional sections, all sumptuously scruffy, plus an outdoor Thames-side terrace. A Fuller's pub, the bar stocks the usual dark suspects; Budweiser in the fridge supplements an appalling range of draught lagers, but there's a refreshingly well-stocked selection of wines, and a good supply of pub grub. On top of its lovely river view, the Dove keeps the eyes and minds busy with a superb selection of old local photographs.
No piped music or jukebox. Tables outdoors (15, riverside terrace).

paraphernalia, the decor remains a little bland. On a more positive note, the place is light, spacious and comfortable, with a main bar area as well as a separate non-smoking restaurant. While a fairly standard selection of beers is on offer, wines (mainly New World) are competitively priced, starting at just over £10. Food is nice and simple – salmon fillet, tuna steak, Thai green curry – and also reasonable price-wise, with a special menu for children. Noisy TV screens throughout the main bar area can be irritating. *Babies and children admitted. Disabled: toilet. Function rooms. Games (games machine). Restaurant (no smoking). Tables outdoors (17, riverside terrace; 7, balcony). TV (big screen, satellite).*

Salutation

154 King Street, W6 0QU (8748 3668/www.fullers. co.uk). Hammersmith tube. **Open** 11am-11pm Mon-Thur, Sat; 11am-midnight Fri; noon-10.30pm Sun. **Food served** noon-2.30pm, 5.30-9.30pm daily. **Credit** MC, V.
Take a 17th-century coaching house, add draught Bacardi Breezer, potted palms, horrid Europop and a suburban conservatory and the result is the Salutation (or the 'Sally', as the locals call it). A unique tiled frontage and chain-independence (unusual around here) – plus the fact that the late Queen Mother once pulled a pint here – seem to be the main marketing tools. The Grade II-listed anomaly pours a fine draught Grolsch and stocks a good number of Fuller's beers including London Pride and ESB. Sky football courtesy of a large pull-down screen, big comfy sofas, and large open spaces set the scene, with young lads in red ties collecting the refreshingly disparate crowd's empties. The slightly masculine feel makes this a better bet as part of a pub-crawl rather than somewhere to spend an entire evening. *Babies and children welcome (until 6pm). Games (arcade machine, quiz machine). Tables outdoors (24, garden). TV (big screen).*

Also in the area...

Bar 38 1 Blacks Road, W6 9DT (8748 3951).
Plough & Harrow 120-124 King Street, W6 0QU (8735 6020).
William Morris 2-4 Swan Island, King Street, W6 0QA (8741 7175).

Kensal Green

Gastropubs are a clear reflection of this area's boho gentrification, with beautiful **William IV** and the **Paradise** favoured spots for trendy locals.

Astons

2 Regent Street, NW10 5LG (8969 2184). Kensal Green tube. **Open** noon-11pm Mon-Thur; noon-midnight Fri, Sat; noon-10.30pm Sun. **Food served** noon-10pm daily. **Credit** MC, V.
Now re-established after its overhaul, Aston's does especially big business over the Notting Hill Carnival weekend, (despite being off the main trail); on normal week nights, however, the place is still often quite empty and quiet. The traditional-feel large space includes a courtyard out back for dancing, drinking and sunning; the bar area, inside, is somehow more awkward in mood (despite the comfy sofas and fireplace), like a teenager trying to find his or her cool. Bar staff seemed a bit jittery and snappy on our visit; the drinks selection is pretty unexciting, with Beck's on tap and two dozen varieties of wine, many by

Wych Elm. *See p239.*

Hope & Anchor

20 Macbeth Street, W6 9JJ (8748 1873). Hammersmith tube/266 bus. **Open** 11am-11pm Mon-Sat; noon-10.30pm Sun. **No credit cards**.
The Hope and Anchor continues to avoid gastropub refurbishment – perhaps saved by its side street location – remaining an old-fashioned boozer. The 1930s Grade II-listed building (on CAMRA's list of London pubs with historic interest) houses a pool table, a dartboard and a good crew of venerable regulars inside its wood-panelled interior; most punters seem to know each other and share a laugh. And while the selection of beers on offer is fairly pedestrian (with Guinness, Foster's, Kronenbourg and John Smith's on tap, and Beck's and Budweiser in bottles), no one could accuse it of being pretentious; this is a simple, honest pub with helpful, pleasant service. It'll never win any awards, but you suspect that the locals want to keep it exactly as it is. *Babies and children welcome. Games (darts, fruit machines, pool). Jukebox. Music (musicians 8.30pm Sat; free). Tables outdoors (8, garden). TVs (big screen, satellite).*

Old Ship

25 Upper Mall, W6 9TD (8748 2593/www.old shipw6.co.uk). Hammersmith, Ravenscourt Park or Stamford Brook tube. **Open** 8am-11pm Mon-Sat; 8am-10.30pm Sun. **Food served** 8am-10.30pm Mon-Sat; 8am-10pm Sun. **Credit** AmEx, MC, V.
You can almost dip a toe in the Thames from the Old Ship. A top choice for a Sunday afternoon, this riverside spot does get very crowded on fine days. Inside, cream-wood panelling predominates and, despite the nautical

West

London Apprentice. *See p240.*

the glass. Separated from the main bar, the dining room, also with a fireplace, serves standard but very reasonably priced Thai food. DJs and their soulful house beats pull in a few more people at weekends.
Babies and children welcome. Tables outdoors (3, pavement; 15, patio).

Greyhound
64-66 Chamberlayne Road, NW10 3JJ (8969 8080). Kensal Green tube/Kensal Rise rail. **Open** 6.30-11pm Mon; noon-11pm Tue-Thur; noon-midnight Fri, Sat; noon-10.30pm Sun. **Food served** 6.30-10pm Mon; 12.30-3.30pm, 6.30-10.30pm Tue-Sat; 12.30-7pm Sun. **Credit** MC, V.
Created from two separate premises, the Greyhound has been artfully aged and mismatched to give the appearance that it was always thus. Cream walls covered with music and film posters sit above blackened wood panelling. One half is a bar, the other a dining area. Subdued red lighting and friendly staff create a pleasant and inviting ambience, bonhomie also generated by regular offers – like a Lidgate's meat or veg pie, green beans and gravy with a glass of ale, lager or wine (£5.50) – on the traditional, British-based menu. It's a music industry fave, with a mixed, moneyed clientele choosing from draughts (Bitburger, Adnams Explorer), Belgian bottled beers, or some two dozen wines, many by the glass. Theme nights are popular, as is the Irish music on Sundays. The beer garden is busy in summer.
Babies and children welcome. Disabled: toilet. Games night (7.30pm 4th Sun of mth; free). Music (DJ 7.30pm 1st, 3rd Sun of mth; free). Quiz (7.30pm 2nd Sun of mth; £5 per person). Restaurant (no smoking). Tables outdoors (7, pavement; 15, garden).

North Pole
13-15 North Pole Road, W10 6QH (8964 9384/www. massivepub.com). Latimer Road or White City tube. **Open** noon-midnight daily. **Food served** noon-3pm, 6-9.30pm Mon-Thur, Sat; noon-4pm, 6-9.30pm Fri, Sun. **Credit** AmEx, DC, MC, V.
Two different crowds frequent this unpretentious gastropub. During the week middle-aged regulars and BBC staff run the show (when it's a popular lunch spot), while at weekends a younger, lively clientele flocks around the main bar. The place seems to cater to all types, however. The candlelit dining area, with large gilded mirrors and an open kitchen, keeps the weekday visitors interested with an upmarket daily-changing specials menu – the best offering on our visit was garlic and rosemary-marinated pork steak with sweet apple mash and caramelised onion (£9.95). Seating is often at a premium here, with evening events including DJ competitions and end-of-month carnivals, where conversation has to be yelled over a pint of Kronenbourg Blanc, Bombardier or a guest ale.
Music (7pm last Sat of mth; free). Restaurant (available for hire; no smoking). Tables outdoors (6, pavement).

Paradise by Way of Kensal Green
19 Kilburn Lane, W10 4AE (8969 0098). Kensal Green tube/Kensal Rise rail/52, 302 bus. **Open** 12.30pm-midnight Mon-Thur; 12.30pm-2am Fri, Sat; noon-11.30pm Sun. **Food served** 12.30-4pm, 7.30-11pm Mon-Sat; noon-9pm Sun. **Credit** MC, V.
This extremely likeable corner pub gives off the impression of being a very upmarket squat. Named after a GK Chesterton eulogy to an English drunkard (the poem is

painted across the front of the bar), this endearingly eccentric Gothic paradise seems to have taken its decorative influences from the local graveyard, with grey walls and a large stone angel in the corner. There's a lovely side room, with worn-out armchairs, an open fire and theatrical green velvet drapes. A dining area at the back is covered with works by local artists, large gilded mirrors and assorted Buddhas. The crowd is equally mixed. Draught beers include Old Speckled Hen, Spitfire and Hoegaarden, and food is Mediterranean, Asian and resoundingly British on popular Sunday lunchtimes. A summer garden is also a draw. *Babies and children welcome. Function room. Tables outdoors (10, garden). TV (widescreen).*

William IV

786 Harrow Road, NW10 5LX (8969 5944/www. williamivlondon.com). Kensal Green tube. **Open** noon-11pm Mon-Wed; noon-midnight Thur; noon-1am Fri, Sat; noon-10.30pm Sun. **Food served** noon-3pm, 6-10.30pm Mon-Wed; noon-3pm, 6-11pm Thur, Fri; noon-4pm, 6.30-11pm Sat; noon-4.30pm, 7-9.30pm Sun. **Credit** MC, V.

A haunt for staff from the nearby music industry offices – look out for the odd celeb – the William IV had a successful makeover of late. A backdrop of wood panelling and deep blue or maroon walls (depending on which section you're in) offset the open fires surrounded by mosaics of broken glass, creating a smart but homely feel. The menu has been expanded to incorporate Brit-tinged tapas dishes, such as chorizo with potato wedges (£5) or grilled swordfish with green tomato chutney (£7). There's a wide choice of booze: wines feature well-priced Iberian offerings (a decent rioja at £15.75) and beers include Cruzcampo to complement the Leffe and Hoegaarden. Ale drinkers choose between Fuller's London Pride and at least one guest. There's comedy on the first Thursday of the month, and DJ sets every weekend. *Babies and children welcome (until 7pm). Comedy (8.30pm 1st Thur of mth; £5). Music (DJ 9.30pm Fri, Sat; free). Tables outdoors (30, garden).*

Kingston

With continued development along this Thames stretch, Kingston's boozers are in a constant state of renewal. As well as riverside options, **Wych Elm** is renowned for its well-kept ales.

Boaters Inn

Canbury Gardens, Lower Ham Road, Kingston-upon-Thames, KT2 5AU (8541 4672/www.jazzatthe boaters.co.uk). Kingston rail. **Open** 11am-11pm Mon-Sat; noon-10.30pm Sun. **Food served** noon-9.30pm Mon-Sat; noon-9pm Sun. **Credit** AmEx, MC, V.

Kingston's recent riverside building spree has given the Thames all manner of snazzy new flats, but not too many options for the discerning drinker. The Boaters, set on a tranquil, tree-lined swathe of grass a few minutes walk from the town centre, feels a world apart. Inevitably in summer everyone wants a piece of the action, with the riverfront busy with dog walkers, rowers and Frisbee throwers, while drinkers sit on pub benches or stretch out on the grass. The efficiently unexceptional interior has a large L-shaped bar, ensuring there's never too much of a scrum to get served, while bright chalk marks out the many entertainments on offer: if the middle-aged regulars get bored of their pinot grigio, IPA, Adnams and Brakspear, or the pleasant grub, there's a long-running jazz night every Sunday.

Babies and children admitted. Games (board games, fruit machines). Music (jazz 8.30pm Sun; free). Restaurant (no smoking). Tables outdoors (30, riverside patio). TV.

Canbury Arms

49 Canbury Park Road, Kingston-upon-Thames, KT2 6LQ (8255 9129/www.thecanburyarms.com). Kingston rail. **Open/food served** 9am-11pm Mon-Sat; 10am-10.30pm Sun. **Credit** MC, V.

Before a change of management, overhaul and relaunch in the middle of 2005, the Canbury was just a simple local boozer. Now you walk in, past a coat stand and a chest of drawers laden with tea and fruit, to whitewashed walls and a neat bar. The effect is a bit hotel lobby-ish but the venue, which now stretches to a heated annexe, wears its new skin well enough, plying coffee and sandwiches to families during the day and a decent range of wine and ales (including Landlord and Sussex Best) to a mostly middle-aged clientele in the evening. Food is an obvious focus – even the kids' menu includes crudités – and on our visit you could choose cheese and red onion marmalade on focaccia or a vegetable strudel. The cheery bar staff, meanwhile, ensure that the Canbury makes up in civilised comfort what it lacks in earthy charm. *Babies and children admitted (separate room). Games (board games). Tables outdoors (8, forecourt; 12, garden).*

Wych Elm

93 Elm Road, Kingston-upon-Thames, KT2 6HT (8546 3271). Kingston rail. **Open** 11am-3pm, 5pm-midnight Mon-Fri; 11am-midnight Sat; noon-11pm Sun. **Food served** noon-2.30pm Mon-Sat. **No credit cards.**

Wych Elm's CAMRA awards (including 2005 joint pub of the year for Kingston and Leatherhead) are certainly merited: this likeable Fuller's pub not far from Richmond Park offers some superbly kept Chiswick Bitter and dangerously drinkable ESB, among others. 'I've only sent one pint back in eight years,' confirmed one regular. 'They were very apologetic.' The beer, though, is just one of many appealing features of this idiosyncratic bar. Toby jugs are mounted on the deep red walls of the L-shaped interior, there are plants rearing out of their pots and into the corridors, while the amiable Spanish landlord greets the many regulars with a wave and plays cribbage on quiet nights. What's more, there's lunchtime pub grub, a big screen and a decent dartboard, tucked away to the side of the pub. *Games (darts, fruit machine). Tables outdoors (8, garden). TV.*

Also in the area...

Kingston Tup 88 London Road, KT2 6PX (8546 6471).
O'Neill's 3 Eden Street, KT1 1BQ (8481 0131).

Richmond, Isleworth & Twickenham

In this historically significant part of town there are plenty of atmospheric, centuries-old boozers to be enjoyed. The award-winning **Red Lion** is a magnet for real ale aficionados, while idyllic background sounds of leather on willow are par-for-the-course at the **Cricketers**, overlooking Richmond Green.

West

Austin's A Bar & Restaurant

93 Colne Road, Twickenham, Middx, TW2 6QL (8898 8000). Twickenham or Strawberry Hill rail. **Open/food served** 6pm-midnight Tue-Thur; noon-midnight Fri, Sat; noon-6pm Sun. **Credit** AmEx, DC, MC, V.
Twickenham's most stylish bar is tucked down an unexceptional suburban street, helping to insulate it from the rugby vibe that predominates elsewhere. Inside, the walls are decorated with pop art images of Ali, Jagger and the Queen, and the civilised dining space at the front backs on to a small, atmospheric drinking area with groovy red couches. It's obvious that a great deal of effort has been put into this place, from the tasteful decor to the sweets, aftershave and towels in the toilets (the wobbly tables must be an anomaly). On our Friday night visit the bar was surprisingly quiet, however. There's a fair selection of draught beers, and a more extensive, cheerily written wine list, plus Mediterranean-influenced food that's well-regarded and a back garden that looked promising even in midwinter.
Babies and children admitted. Restaurant (available for hire; no smoking). Tables outdoors (8, garden).

Coach & Horses

183 London Road, Isleworth, TW7 5BQ (8560 1447). Syon Lane rail. **Open** 11am-11pm Mon, Wed, Thur; 11am-midnight Tue; 11am-1am Fri, Sat; noon-10.30pm Sun. **Food served** noon-3pm, 6-10pm Mon-Fri; noon-10pm Sat; noon-6pm Sun. **Credit** AmEx, MC, V.
This inn was once a stopover on the main coaching route to the West Country. Now, sat close to Syon Park but closer to the clatter of the main road, the Coach & Horses presents a jumbled mix of signifiers, with elements like the bridle on the wall looking rather out of place next to the cutely stylised door to the neighbouring restaurant. Still, the circular bar is graceful and the front room hosts an impressive array of music groups – with everything from rock covers to jazz frequently blaring out. The drinks selection is standard Young's fare, and the Thai-influenced food (including sesame chicken fillet with pad thai, and haddock and chips) is simple but well executed. There's a pleasant beer garden out back and a quiz night on Thursdays.
Babies and children admitted (until 8pm). Games (cards, darts, fruit machines). Music (jazz/folk 9.30pm Mon, Tue, Fri, Sat; 2.30pm Sun; free). Quiz (Wed 9pm; £1). Tables outdoors (12, courtyard). TV (big screen, satellite).

Cricketers

The Green, Richmond, TW9 1LX (8940 4372). Richmond tube/rail. **Open** noon-11pm Mon-Sat; noon-10.30pm Sun. **Food served** noon-2.30pm Mon-Fri; noon-3pm Sat, Sun. **Credit** AmEx, MC, V.
Not many pubs boast a cricket team that plays outside their front door. In the summer months, when not hosting a sports event, the Green is often teeming with plastic-glass wielding Cricketers' punters. Inside, the place combines pub traditionalism (check out the black-and-white photos on the wall and the splendid chunky benches outside) and wine bar-style (the back section features comfy sofas, candles and Dali prints). To add to the hotchpotch, there's a big screen TV and rather underwhelming, wafting music, but it's this very neutrality that makes it a popular meeting spot, pulling in a diverse crew: we shared the bar with some middle-aged women, a clutch of lads and four girls in their twenties merrily discussing their underwear. There's a function room and some perfectly pleasant Greene King IPA and Abbot.
Comedy (8.30pm Wed; £5). Function room. Games (fruit machine, quiz machine). No-smoking area. Tables outdoors (3, pavement). TV (big screen).

Eel Pie

9-11 Church Street, Twickenham, TW1 3NJ (8891 1717). Twickenham rail. **Open** 11am-11pm Mon-Wed; 11am-midnight Thur-Sat; noon-10.30pm Sun. **Food served** noon-4pm daily. **Credit** MC, V.
This splendid old pub may not be located on nearby Eel Pie Island (where the Rolling Stones regularly gigged; the Mystery Jets are currently doing their best to bring a bit of rock 'n' roll back to the area) but it does sit on Church Street, a winding pedestrianised road that heads down to the river and brims with character. The walls in the lounge are lined with plates and mirrors, giving the place a bit of a tea room vibe; during the rugby, however, it feels a good deal less refined. The bar eschews commercial lagers for a well-kept selection of ales, including Badger, Tanglefoot and Sussex – which goes down well with the regulars. The billiards table has sadly now been scrapped but the pub quiz – the hardest in Twickenham? – takes place every Thursday.
Quiz (9pm Thur; £1). TVs (big screen, satellite).

London Apprentice

62 Church Street, Isleworth, TW7 6BG (8560 1915). Isleworth rail. **Open** *Winter* noon-11pm Mon-Sat; noon-10.30pm Sun. *Summer* 11am-11pm Mon-Sat; noon-10.30pm Sun. **Food served** *Winter* noon-3.30pm, 6-9.30pm Mon-Fri; noon-5pm, 6-9.30pm Sat; noon-9pm Sun. *Summer* noon-5pm, 6-9.30pm daily. **Credit** AmEx, DC, MC, V.
Nearby Richmond and Twickenham may have better reputations when it comes to riverside drinking, but this fine spot, lying between Isleworth and St Margarets, certainly provides some competition. With a large terrace that juts out onto the Thames, the beer garden has a very open feel. Inside, things are more secluded, with the main room stretching around a long bar, punctuated by barrel tables and snugs and with a fire in the far corner. Local legend suggest that it's been a convivial space for some time: both Henry VIII and Charles II are said to have held trysts here. Given the place's history, the decor is rather unoriginal, with an England rugby jersey on the ceiling and old signs on the walls, and beers include Adnams, Pride and Bombardier alongside Foster's and Kronenbourg.
Function room. Games (fruit machine, video games). Music (traditional Irish folk 8.30pm Mon, Wed; free). Tables outdoors (10, riverside terrace). TV (big screen).

Old Ship

3 King Street, Richmond, TW9 1ND (8940 3461). Richmond tube/rail. **Open** 11am-11.30pm Mon-Wed; 11am-midnight Thur-Sat; noon-11pm Sun. **Food served** noon-9pm daily. **Credit** AmEx, DC, MC, V.
One glance at the menu (which features sausage and mash, pasta with tomato sauce and the frightening-sounding 'chilli mountain') should be enough to tell you that, despite the 2004 refit, this warm and creaky Young's pub is not rushing to change its spots. The interior is divided into two separate rooms, one of which stretches back into a small (and usually covered) beer garden. The decor of beams and model ships, with an open fire in winter, treads the line between genuine history and cheerful tat. There's even a polished ship's lever with settings by the stairs. It's all very pleasant, and manages to feel engagingly intimate despite its weekend hubbub and central location – on a busy afternoon, you can nurse your drink, peek at bustling shoppers through the stained-glass doors and feel quietly smug.
Function room. Games (fruit machine, skittles). Quiz (7pm Sun; £1). Restaurant (no-smoking area). Tables outdoors (7, garden). TVs (big screen, satellite).

West

Prince's Head

28 The Green, Richmond, TW9 1LX (8940 1572).
Richmond tube/rail/St Margarets rail. **Open** 11am-
11pm Mon-Sat; noon-10.30pm Sun. **Food served**
noon-9pm Mon-Sat; noon-6pm Sun. **Credit** MC, V.
Attracting a slightly older and more local crowd than the
neighbouring Cricketers, this laid-back Fuller's pub is also
a better bet – that is, if you're a keen football fan. Any televised match provides the excuse for getting out the big
screen here, whether you're a follower of the Spanish league
or Soccer AM. For non footie-led punters, however, it's easy
enough to escape around the sides of this lovely old building, full of gilt-edged mirrors and dark, rich hues. The section to the right is more food-orientated, with everything
from char-grilled chicken and chorizo salad to Irish stew on
offer, although if you're looking for booze-fuel, the tasty
nachos will keep you going for a while. The Fuller's staples
of Chiswick, Pride and ESB are present and reliably served.
*Games (fruit machine). No-smoking area. Tables
outdoors (6, pavement). TVs (big screen, satellite).*

Red Lion

*92-94 Linkfield Road, Isleworth, TW7 6QJ (8560 1457/
www.red-lion.info). Isleworth rail.* **Open** 11am-11pm Mon-
Thur, Sun; 11am-midnight Fri, Sat. **Food served** 11am-
11pm Mon-Fri; 12.30-4.30pm Sun. **No credit cards.**
For all its CAMRA awards, this boozer – round the corner
from Isleworth station – doesn't look very impressive: the
carpet is raggedy, the signs are peeling and the back room
is too open to be intimate. The overall feel is of a pub that
hasn't had a refurb since the early '60s. But if you're looking for battered charm, the Red Lion has it in spades.
Likeable touches abound, from the vaguely nonsensical mes-
sage board ('if pigs could fly they would be poultry') through
to an admirable assortment of games and helpful bar staff.
On our visit, they cheerfully suggested we try the cider ('it's
6.8%') but we stuck with the ales – including a very fine
Rebellion. There's a separate Belgian beer menu and a regular music programme, and barbecues over the summer.
*Beer festivals (live music and family events, call for
dates). Games (backgammon, board games, cards, chess,
darts, pool). Music (rock, country bands 8.30pm Sat,
Sun; free). Quiz (9pm Thur; £1). Tables outdoors (20,
garden). TVs (satellite).*

White Cross

*Water Lane, Richmond, TW9 1TJ (8940 6844/www.
youngs.co.uk). Richmond tube/rail.* **Open** 11am-
midnight Mon-Sat; noon-10.30pm Sun. **Food served**
noon-3.30pm Mon-Sat; noon-4pm Sun. **Credit** MC, V.
Recalling a monastery that was this site's previous occu-
pant, the White Cross's huge illuminated sign towers over
both the river and the nearby Slug & Lettuce, which – in
summer at least – doesn't stand a chance against this local
institution that's been packing in the crowds like nobody's
business for generations. There are separate entrances for
low and high tide, but during the spring you'll occasionally
have to wade in anyway. Bay windows, a fire in winter, and
a secluded upstairs lounge, just perfect for a relaxing drink,
make up the lovely interior. And the quality of the Young's
beers and the spotless toilets provide good enough reasons
to stick about.
No piped music or jukebox. Tables outdoors (15, garden).

Also in the area...

All Bar One 11 Hill Street, TW9 1SY (8332 7141).
O'Neill's 28 The Quadrant, TW9 1DN (8334 0111).

Slug & Lettuce Riverside House, Water Lane, TW9
1TJ (8948 7733).
Twickenham Tup 13 Richmond Road, TW1 3AB
(8891 1863).

Shepherd's Bush

The **Havelock Tavern** was being refurbished as
we went to press. The pubs listed below are
good signs in an area notable only for a half-decent
music venue and proximity to the BBC.

Albertine

*1 Wood Lane, W12 7DP (8743 9593/www.gonumber.
com/albertine). Shepherd's Bush tube.* **Open** 10am-
11pm Mon-Thur; 10am-midnight Fri; 6.30-midnight Sat.
Food served noon-10.30pm Mon-Fri; 6.30-10.30pm
Sat. **Credit** MC, V.
Opposite the splendid Defectors Weld, the equally attractive
Albertine creates a hub of classy bonhomie, a world away
from the grotty flotsam and jetsam nearby. The interior is
candlelit and bistro-like, providing two floors for relaxed
chat between young professionals perusing the daily changing menu (spinach and ricotta tortellini, £6.10, and chicken,
mushroom and tarragon casserole, £8.30) were on the menu
on our visit. To say that the wine list is extensive is doing
Albertine a disservice: 50 reds and 40 whites by the bottle
(£11-£30), half of them by the glass (£2.90-£5.10), and a
handful by the half bottle (£9.25-£18.80). French and New
World varieties dominate but you will be guided knowl-
edgeably and without pretension. There are 30 fine wines
too, plus port, sherry and bottled beers (Budvar, Timothy
Taylor Landlord and Marston's Pedigree). A selection of 20
cheeses rounds off a perfect evening here.
Function room. Games (board games).

Anglesea Arms

*35 Wingate Road, W6 0UR (8749 1291). Goldhawk
Road or Ravenscourt Park tube.* **Open** 11am-11pm
Mon-Sat; noon-10.30pm Sun. **Food served** 12.30-
2.45pm, 7-10.30pm Mon-Sat; 12.30-3.30pm, 7-10pm Sun.
Credit MC, V.
A pleasant sanctuary from the exhaust fumes of the nearby
Goldhawk Road, the Anglesea is ideal for a Sunday afternoon, when the versatile kitchen comes into its own. Well-
behaved media types are joined by the odd stray for pints
of prawns in the non-smoking brick dining area, which is
brightened by a skylight and a large, colourful mural. The
menu easily expands to seared fillet of sea bass, braised fennel, leeks and cucumber sauce bourride (£13.95), accommodating upmarket desserts such as chocolate fondant with
ginger ice-cream. The wine list is suitably extensive and ales
include London Pride, Greene King IPA and Old Speckled
Hen. Hang your hat on the stag's antlers, sink into a
Chesterfield and relax.
*Babies and children welcome. No-smoking area. Tables
outdoors (5, pavement).*

Bush Bar & Grill

*45A Goldhawk Road, W12 8QP (8746 2111/www.bush
bar.co.uk). Goldhawk Road tube.* **Open** noon-11.30pm
Mon-Sat. **Food served** noon-3pm, 5.30-11.30pm Mon-
Sat. **Credit** AmEx, MC, V.
A whitewashed passageway off the Goldhawk Road, lined
with red strip lights, leads you to this chichi hideaway
of savvy cocktails and upmarket edible treats. Around

West

twenty inventive house cocktails (£6.50) – a Bam Bam of Wild Turkey, orange and sugar or a Black Manhattan of crushed blackberries, cherry juice, sweet Vermouth and rye whiskey – complement a similar number of superbly concocted classics. A raised dining area, filled with rows of benches, canopied by a soaring ceiling, is where you tuck into confit duck leg and cannelloni bean cassoulet (£14.25) or roast guinea fowl with broccoli purée (£12.75). Much fuss is made over the beef – naturally reared, three-week aged – and desserts are equally impeccable. Faultless.

Babies and children welcome. Disabled: toilet. Function room. Tables outdoors (9, courtyard).

Crown & Sceptre

57 Melina Road, W12 9HY (8746 0060/www.fullers. co.uk). Goldhawk Road or Shepherd's Bush tube. **Open** noon-11pm Mon-Sat; noon-10.30pm Sun. **Food served** noon-3pm, 6-9.45pm Mon-Fri; noon-9.45pm Sat; noon-8.45pm Sun. **Credit** AmEx, MC, V.

Locals pack this tastefully decorated Victorian Fuller's pub, filling every available table, with chairs tightly crammed in. Legroom is something of a luxury in the open-plan seating area, but the natural light flooding in from the tall windows helps to compensate. The corner bar is more ramshackle still, serving carefully poured pints of Pride and Honey Dew, plus Leffe or Kirin Ichiban for light beer drinkers. Further round, a more contemporary open kitchen turns out superior pub grub, the daily-changing menu featuring familiar mains (£9 to £12) like lamb stew with rocket mash and sweet potato crisps, plus curiosities such as ostrich steaks and wild boar. Leather pews alongside provide comfort for couples perusing the photocopied menus on clipboards.

Babies and children admitted. Disabled: toilet. Quiz (9pm Mon; £1). No-smoking area. Tables outdoors (10, garden; 3, pavement). TV.

Defectors Weld

170 Uxbridge Road, W12 8AA (8749 0008/www. defectors-weld.com). Shepherd's Bush tube. **Open** noon-midnight Mon-Thur; noon-1am Fri, Sat; noon-11.30pm Sun. **Food served** noon-3pm, 5-10pm Mon-Fri; noon-10pm Sat, Sun. **Credit** MC, V.

Tastefully decorated, this large, brown-fronted two-storey modern corner pub attracts a lively, unpretentious crowd. The stylish downstairs is effectively split into two parts: the front is brown with leather seats, fresh flowers, an open fire and an eccentric picture of the bar staff; the back is more intimate, with candlelit seating, exceptionally soft armchairs and small wooden booths illuminated by low-slung fabric lights. The bar serves draught London Pride, Greene King IPA, Leffe and Hoegaarden, frosted glasses provided where necessary. Upstairs is a rather smart cocktail lounge with table service. The food in either is exemplary if pricey, generally classy versions of pub classics. A commendable music policy is not confined to the DJs at weekends.

Disabled: toilet. Music (DJs 9pm Fri-Sun; free). No-smoking area.

Seven Stars Bar & Dining Room

243 Goldhawk Road., W12 8EU (8748 0229/ www.sevenstarsdining.co.uk). Goldhawk Road tube/94, 237 bus. **Open** 11am-11pm Mon-Wed, Sun; 11am-midnight Thur-Sat. **Food served** noon-3pm, 6-10pm Mon-Sat; noon-10pm Sun. **Credit** MC, V.

A rather swish, spacious gastrobar this. The express lunch menu (noon to 3pm) is a scaled-down version of its evening counterpart, giving the kitchen a chance to practise its rib-eye steak with flat mushrooms and slow roasted tomatoes

(£11.90) or pan-fried salmon with mashed potatoes (£11.50) before the post-work rush. There are sandwiches too – steak and mixed leaves (£6), for example, and some wicked desserts including a sticky toffee square with vanilla ice-cream (£5). Among the ten wines (eight by the glass) there's a basic Cuvée des Amandiers (£2.95/£4.25/£11.95) and Marqués rioja (white £16.95; red £24.95). A small clutch of draught beers include Tetley's, Hoegaarden and Pilsner Urquell. All is enjoyed on shiny wooden pews or comfy sofas, against an effective backdrop of framed Soviet propaganda handbills on stark white walls.

Babies and children admitted. Disabled: toilet. Restaurant (no smoking). Tables outdoors (3 long tables, garden).

Vesbar

15-19 Goldhawk Road, W12 8QQ (8762 0215). Goldhawk Road or Shepherd's Bush tube. **Open** 11am-11pm Mon-Thur; 11am-midnight Fri; 10am-midnight Sat; 10am-10.30pm Sun. **Food served** 11am-10.30pm daily. **Credit** AmEx, DC, MC, V.

Vesbar tries its best to funk up the shabby neighbourhood. Warhol art on the walls, with caramelised chicken, Parma ham and Cumberland sausage among the ten handmade, stone-baked pizzas, and a long zinc bar offering Fuller's Honey Dew beer, Leffe and Hoegaarden – all over the heads of much of the clientele. Still, the place is big enough to hide away in (in fact, you could hide an army in here), so call up a cocktail (apple Martinis with Bison Grass vodka or spiced Mojitos, £5.75 to £5.95), a large glass of Oyster Bay sauvignon blanc (£5.30) or zinfandel Cutler Crest (£4.25) and pretend the Goldhawk Road isn't there. If you're here to see a band at the nearby Empire, the bar does pre-concert specials of steak burgers to your table in 15 minutes (for £7.85).

Disabled: toilet. Function room. Games (board games).

Also in the area...

Central Bar (JD Wetherspoon) West 12 Shopping Centre, Shepherds Bush Green, W12 8PH (8746 4290).
Davy's White City Units 4 & 5, Media Centre, White City Media Village, Wood Lane, W12 7ST (8811 2862).
O'Neill's 2 Goldhawk Road, W12 8QD (8746 1288).
Walkabout 56 Shepherds Bush Green, W12 8QE (8740 4339).

Southall

Glassy Junction

97 South Road, Southall, UB1 1SQ (8574 1626). Southall rail. **Open** 11am-11.30pm Mon-Wed; 11am-1am Thur; 11am-2am Fri, Sat; noon-11pm Sun. **Food served** noon-10.30pm Mon-Wed; noon-midnight Thur-Sat; 12.30-10pm Sun. **No credit cards.**

An exotic anomaly, this. According to the somewhat reticent barman, this is still the only pub in the UK to accept Indian rupees. That aside, the Glassy is a tripped-out Bollywood experience, with a spectacularly tasteless gold and velvet colour scheme, pictures of India's biggest film stars and a faux-jewel encrusted display on the back of the main door. Indian beers on tap, including Lal Toofan, and decent offerings from the curry kitchen keep punters satisfied well into the evening. Worth a visit for the decor alone.

Babies and children admitted. Games (pool tables). TV.

Chain, chain, chain

In March 2006 the Campaign for Real Ale (CAMRA) celebrated their 35th anniversary by announcing a record 80,000 members: people who, in the words of chief executive Mike Benner, want 'to make sure consumers of real ale will always have a powerful voice'. Could the rumours be true? Is real ale about to trade in its Arran jumper for a crocheted shrug? A renewed endorsement of Timothy Taylor Landlord by Madonna may not amount to much (indeed killjoys would argue Gordon Brown's Progressive Beer Duty of 2002 has done more to stimulate the diversity of British beer by encouraging small producers), but even fickle broadsheet fashion pages seem to be joining in the fun.

What does this have to do with chain pubs? In trying to bring you the best of London's bar culture since 1998, we've become increasingly reluctant to waste space on identikit pubs dreamed up in boardrooms, lamenting each Dog & Duck that fell into the maw of the irrepressible All Bar One. ABO's success at drawing women into bars with the now tired formula of picture windows, sleek Scandinavian decor and a slim choice of wine must be applauded – but gender balance in drinking culture is damn close to being achieved and it's surely time to move on from places designed to be undemanding and dependable. Can we really be expected to get excited by Slug & Lettuce, when the bars are described thus on their own website: 'All look slightly different, open at different times and run different local events…'?

Though nominally differentiated, most JD Wetherspoon pubs are undistinguished booze halls, but the beer is cheap, varied and, almost without exception, of very good quality. So where a particular Wetherspoon catches our fancy, we review it in full.

Mitchells & Butlers, owners of O'Neill's and All Bar One, carry out more interesting work under their Nicholson's moniker. Their restoration of many of the City's historic pubs is a joy, even though the identikit menus rapidly become tedious and the choices of guest ale can get pretty repetitive.

Some loosely affiliated groups of pubs are proving a success. In such cases we review individual pubs – you'll notice, for example, a scattering of fine gastropubs of the Geronimo group through this book. Brewery pubs (Young's, say, or Fuller's) also get reviews when of sufficient quality or interest, though Fuller's Fine Line appears below.

Branches appear at the end of the relevant geographical section under the 'Also in the area' subheadings. They may not delight you, but they probably won't appal. So here is a brief overview of the major chains.

All Bar One
www.mbplc.com/allbarone
That All Bar One was a pioneer in its time makes it no less of a bore now: huge windows, pine-saturated interiors, lots of seating and enormous bar counters with a very average selection of beers and a slightly better array of wines.

Balls Brothers
www.ballsbrothers.co.uk
The original Balls Brothers wine bars were cellars, with wood panels and drawing room prints, catering for City slickers. Newer venues have a more contemporary feel and are aimed at a younger, more mixed crowd. House wine lists tend to be strong on Old World favourites.

Bierodrome
www.belgo-restaurants.com
Belgo began in 1992 with a quirky restopub in Camden. The three Bierodromes that followed (Clapham, Holborn and Islington) share the same wide spread of Belgian beers backed by huge platters of mussels and chips, or sausage in beer sauces, but venues tend to be too noisy, corporate and tanked up for fine-ale connoisseurs.

Corney & Barrow
www.corneyandbarrow.com
Corney & Barrow's City wine bars are sleek and sexy, just like their clientele. You'll find a substantial mix of designer beers, but the real draw is a wine list offering nearly 80 by the glass. Food is modern eclectic brasserie fare.

Davy's
www.davy.co.uk
Davy's started trading as a wine merchant's in 1870 and has run wine bars since the 1960s. Their compact wine selection is enhanced by plenty of own-label options. There's no particular house style and interiors can vary from spit and sawdust to gleaming and spotlit – indeed, Truckles of Pied Bull Yard (*see p31*) has a bit of both.

Fine Line
www.thefineline.co.uk
Fuller's take on the style bar follows the All Bar One blueprint: big windows, pale wood. Menus are sensibly unambitious, with mains at around £7-£14. The company's excellent draught beers are largely sidelined in favour of decent wines. Fine Line are notably female-friendly.

hog's head
www.laurelpubco.com
Conceived as a chain serving real ales and Belgian beer, the Hogsheads (note the rebranded title) faded once its begetters, Whitbread, sold it on. The accent is now on lager, alcopops and cheap food. The only cask-conditioned ale available at many branches is London Pride.

Jamies
www.jamiesbars.co.uk
Jamies branches vary dramatically in stature and setting, from one beside the Thames at Westferry Circus to the unique pavilion bar of a lawn bowling club (*see p135*). Decor is smart and modish, and the undaunting wine list represents countries of the Old and New World. Food is better than average, ranging from nibbles to mains.

JD Wetherspoon
www.jdwetherspoon.co.uk
Cheap booze, no smoking, no music and quick-serve canteen cuisine at bargain prices – no wonder Tim Martin's chain now has 600 pubs nationwide. We like them for their devotion to real ale and for the out-of-the-ordinary premises some of the pubs occupy, including a cinema, a ballroom and a chapel-turned-theatre. Low prices mean a core clientele of students and male pensioners. JDW's 'bright, brash and fun' offshoot Lloyds No.1 might be an acquired taste.

Corney & Barrow

O'Neill's
www.mbplc.com/oneills
'The largest Irish bar brand in the world', brags the Mitchells & Butlers website, which means identical multi-boothed emporiums of crass craic, littered with Emerald Isle trinkets. Guinness, Murphy's and Caffrey's are all on tap, although most punters seem to dig into the lager; food is of the Irish stew variety. Surprisingly, O'Neill's are not often frequented by the Irish.

Pitcher & Piano
www.pitcherandpiano.com
All Bar One's lairier cousin, P&Ps – again with the pine – tend to attract office bods on the lash: hectic, smoky and noisy, they're clearly a whole lot of fun for those in the mood. Paulaner, Staropramen have joined Pedigree, Hoegaarden and bottles of Kasteel Cru or Leffe Blonde.

Slug & Lettuce
www.slugandlettuce.co.uk
Back in the early 1980s Hugh Corbett's Slug & Lettuce chain introduced such revolutionary concepts as windows people could see through, non-sticky carpets and edible food. Now owned by Laurel pubco (the people behind hog's head), revolutionary they ain't. Expect suits, evenly split between sexes, and an age range older than All Bar One.

Tup
www.massivepub.com
Also founded by Hugh Corbett (but now owned by the Massive pubco), the Tups are smart, airy and very proud of their support of local and national rugby. Branches avoid identikit anodynity and, although beers tend to be standard, they're customer-friendly.

Walkabout Inn
www.walkabout.eu.com
Antipodean visitors pack these Australian-themed party joints, along with tourists, lost souls and the just plain unadventurous. If you're not attracted by the Sheilas and surfer boys, you might be by late weekend closing – 3am most nights at the branch on Charing Cross Road and Shaftesbury Avenue. Perhaps surprisingly, a Walkabout opened on Putney High Street at the end of 2005.

Chain, chain, chain

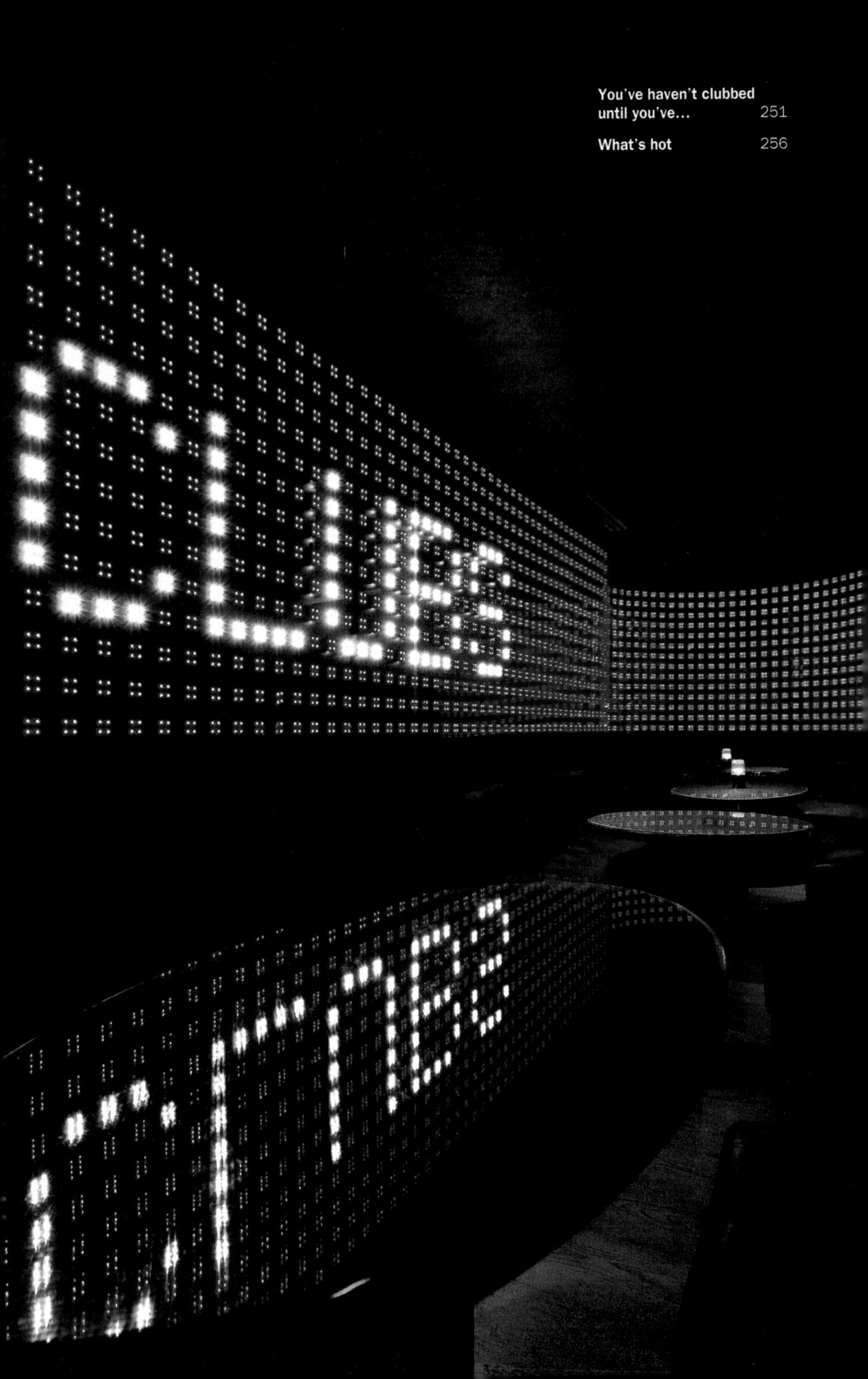
Clubs

Clubs

End. See p248.

If you're into clubbing, then London's your nirvana, Mecca and promised land all rolled into one. It's great to sample the delights in other cities (festivals in Barcelona, minimal house in Berlin) but nothing can touch our capital, which is why DJs are desperate to play here, and our nightclubs cram the lists of the best in the world. No question, our nightlife has been on a bit of a roll the past couple of years, and it looks set to get even wilder. At *Time Out*, we're amazed by the number of new parties and venues opening their doors every other week, and our jaws drop at the sight of the queues that continue to wrap about the block – whether it's NagNagNag at the **Ghetto** every Wednesday night, Bugged Out at the **End** on a Saturday, or Secretsundaze at (shhh!) a secret East End boozer on a summery Sunday afternoon. The summer of 2005 saw the Italians and Spanish take over many a club, determined to go for it in a Balearic fashion, which meant the rise and rise of the afterparty and Sunday clubbing, and also a never-ending stream of zanily clad ravers; this trend looks set to skyrocket in 2006. The last year has also seen 24-hour drinking introduced in London and, despite middle-England concerns about a return to Tudor-styled debauchery, very little changed except that places opening till dawn can now serve alcohol until they close.

Aquarium

256-260 Old Street, EC1V 9DD (7251 6136/www.club aquarium.co.uk). *Old Street tube/rail.* **Bar Open** noon-11pm Mon-Wed, Sun; 11am-midnight Thur, Fri; 1pm-midnight Sat. **Food served** noon-8pm daily. *Club* **Open** 10pm-3am Mon-Wed, Sun; 10pm-4am Thur-Sat. **Admission** £5-£20. *Both* **Credit** (bar only) MC, V.
You might not think to pop your bikini into your dinky handbag when getting ready to go out disco dancing, but this is one club that lives up to its name: it is apparently the only club in the country with its own swimming pool and bubblelicious jacuzzi. Lifeguards are on hand (as are fluffy towels) if you fancy a spot of synchronised swimming, but for more traditional frugging the 500-capacity

space has two dancefloors and a great lounge bar where you'll usually find a sofa to fall into. Achingly cool Old Street is just outside, but parties here are more tongue-in-cheek fare. Carwash keeps on keeping on – the unstoppable 1970s funkfest still sends clubbers to their dressing-up box (but no wigs!) every Saturday.
Map 5 Q4.

Barfly

49 Chalk Farm Road, NW1 8AN (7691 4244/www. barflyclub.com). *Camden Town or Chalk Farm tube.* **Open** 7.30pm-midnight Mon-Thur; 7.30pm-3am Fri, Sat; 7.30-11pm Sun. **Admission** £5-£8. **No credit cards.**
Sure, it's part of the Barfly chain, but cast away any thought of All Bar One: it's a small-gig venue that goes all out to support new talent. This is Camden, so expect balding once-were-rockers moshing against girls in designer vintage and skinny jeans in two rooms with the essential bare-brick walls and odd tattered posters. Club nights feature plenty of squealing guitar action, but are some of the best you'll find in town. The outrageously fun Filthy Dukes are here every other Saturday with their rock 'n' roll circus, Kill 'Em All Let God Sort It Out, plus the once-monthly Saturday argument between guitars and club culture that is Transmission and, the club to watch, Adventures Close to Home on the first Friday of the month.
Map 8 H26.

Bar Rumba

36 Shaftesbury Avenue, W1V 7DD (7287 6933/www. barrumba.co.uk). *Piccadilly Circus tube.* **Open** 9pm-3am Mon; 6pm-3am Tue; 8pm-3am Wed; 8pm-3.30am Thur; 7pm-4am Fri; 9pm-3.30am Sat; 8.30pm-2.30am Sun. **Admission** £3-£12; free before 9pm Tue, Fri; free before 8.30pm Thur. **Credit** (bar only) AmEx, MC, V.

Clubs

Check at which Blag Club you're meeting your mates: there's another in the Canalot Studios on Kensal Road, and the newest on Holland Park Road. All three microclubs are more bar than club, but plenty of people come to dance even when it gets squishy – and with a capacity of just 100, that happens pretty fast. Tucked away (up a floor in Notting Hill; behind some nondescript doors on Kensal Road), the first two have Indonesian-minimalist decor, while the newest goes for a Hindu theme, and since many people come as part of a big guest-list group, it often feels like you're walking into a friendly party.
Map 10 A7.

Canvas
King's Cross Goods Yard, off York Way, N1 0UZ (7833 8301/www.canvaslondon.net). King's Cross tube/rail. **Open** 8pm-2am Thur, Fri; 10pm-6am occasional Sat. **Admission** £12.50-£20. **Credit** (bar only) MC, V.
While the nearby Key and Cross are open all weekend, every weekend, Canvas is open as and when promoters fancy biting off a whole lot of space. It easily accommodates 3,000 if all three rooms and two bars are open, and, bit by bit, the owners have added swanky touches throughout (velvet sofas, enormous gilt mirrors, plenty of flowers) that make it feel less like a monolithic warehouse. There's a new Ibizan-styled terrace too, crammed full of palms, plaster fountains and barbecues in the summer. Thursdays and Fridays remain the stonkingly successful Roller Disco (where Madonna filmed the fabulously kitsch skate session in her video for 'Sorry').

Cargo
83 Rivington Street, EC2A 3AY (7749 7844/www.cargo-london.com). Old Street tube/rail/55 bus. **Open/food served** 6pm-1am Mon-Thur; 6pm-3am Fri, Sat; 6pm-midnight Sun. **Admission** £6-£10 (depending on DJ/band). **Credit** AmEx, MC, V.
While much of Shoreditch concerns itself with how you look while you're dancing, Cargo's only concern is what you're dancing to. This converted railway arch maximises its space. Come in off the street and hang a left for the excellent small restaurant that serves up bite-sized street food, or keep going for the large bar with its raised lounge in the corner. The main room jumps to locally grown hip hop at Friends & Family, or grooves to world moves at Ross Clarke's Destination Out. Whatever your taste – nu jazz and soul, wah wah guitars or scratchtastic DJs – Cargo satisfies in spades. Summertime sees the garden smoke with barbecues too.
Map 5 R4.

Cross
Arches, 27-31 King's Cross Goods Yard, N1 0UZ (7837 0828/www.the-cross.co.uk). King's Cross tube/rail. **Open** 11pm-5am Fri, Sun; 10pm-6am Sat. **Admission** £12-£20. **Credit** (bar) MC, V.
What occupied just two railway arches over a decade ago has since expanded to five and a garden: a cavernous venue for house lovers who quite like dressing up, thank you. Its nights aim for the middle of the road and create huge queues: Renaissance, XPress2's Muzik Xpress, and the Italo-house Vertigo are all regulars here. The crowd is good-looking, friendly and unafraid to wear sunglasses, and there's a big quotient of Italian and Spanish clubbers. The walls might be bare bricks, but the rest is pure style: enormous leather sofas, red drapes, elevated seating areas and lots and lots of plants. It really does make you think (as it proudly states): 'Who needs Ibiza when you can have the Cross?'

They say that they're a fave with Londoners, and we have to agree. Open since 1993, but still going strong, this basement venue is home to some of the most respected sessions in town. Their 'happy hour' goes on for hours, and don't fret if you don't nab one of the booths: this place was made for groovin' on the dancefloor with the lights down low. Barrio Latino fires out hot 'n' heavy reggaeton sounds each and every Tuesday, Movement continues to ride at the top of the junglist tree every Thursday, while you'll need your finest old school tracksuit for the weekly Wednesday Sportswear Jam, the hip hop equivalent of School Disco!
Map 8 H26.

Bethnal Green Working Men's Club
42 Pollards Row, E2 6NB (7739 2727). Bethnal Green tube/8, 55 bus. **Open** 8pm-2am Thur, Fri; 10am-2am Sat; 10.30am-2am Sun. **Admission** £5 after 8pm Fri, Sat. **Credit** MC, V.
As Shoreditch becomes ever more full of, well, bridge 'n' tunnellers, the really cool stuff has been moving further east, and the BGWMC is currently riding that particular wave. Admittedly, not much has changed in the 50 years that the place has been open: it's still a small school-hall-type room with a stage, a dancefloor and a bar (selling cheap drinks) that's seen better days, but it's certainly attracting the young turks of clubland with their mad cabaret nights. Viva Cake is monthly Saturdays and offers a jive class, free tea and cakes, and rock 'n' roll bands to bop to, while Whoopee! run their monthly Friday's Hip Hip, with its crazy burlesquey cabaret acts.

Blag
First Floor, 68 Notting Hill Gate, W11 3HT (7243 0123/www.blagclub.com). Notting Hill Gate tube. **Open** 7.30pm-1am Wed-Sat; 8pm-12.30am Sun. **Admission** £5 after 9pm. **Credit** MC, V.

Clubs

EGG

*200 York Way, N7 9AX (7609 8364/www.egglondon.
net). King's Cross tube/rail then free shuttle bus from
York Way.* **Open** 10pm-10am Fri; 10pm Sat-2pm Sun.
Admission free-£15. **Credit** (bar only) MC, V.
If only all clubs could be as good-looking as EGG. There
are three floors inside to play on: the loft bar, boasting gorgeous red leather banquettes to lounge on; a middle floor
that comes straight out of a warehouse dance studio, with
a flashy disco-lit bar if you (ahem) lose your way on the
dancefloor; and the basement, which is half art gallery and
half super-swanky apartment. A well-designed outdoor
terrace and courtyard – complete with bar, Astroturf and
loungers by the paddling pool – is simply perfect for
sunny weather. In recent months, the EGG afterparty
Jaded has put the venue back on the map (Sunday mornings were never so scary, or so much fun), while Playtime
continues to twist out the filthy electro sounds once a
month, and house legend Robert Owens holds a monthly
residency at Journeys.

Electrowerkz

*7 Torrens Street, EC1V 1NQ (7837 6419/www.
electrowerkz.com). Angel tube.* **Open** 10pm-6am
Fri; 10pm-7.30am Sat; times vary on weekdays.
Admission £5-£15. **No credit cards**.
At one end of the London nightlife spectrum, you
have West End glamour. At the other? Welcome to
Electrowerkz. It's more than a tad skanky: you certainly
don't want to fall on the floor, or come here shod in anything you can't wash (or even throw away). Not that you'd
be allowed in on Saturday nights if your feet were dressed
in anything but black: Electrowerkz is home to Slimelight,
the capital's biggest Goth night (both modern and traditional variants welcome). You have to be a member to get
in, and can only apply by turning up (they like to check
you out in person). Saturdays aside, Soul Jazz host their
popular reggae night, 100% Dynamite, here, and there
are also regular one-off events, particularly showcasing
electronica labels.
Map 9 N2.

End

*18 West Central Street, WC1A 1JJ (7419 9199/www.
endclub.com). Holborn or Tottenham Court Road tube.*
Open 10pm-3am Mon; 10.30pm-3am Wed; 10pm-4am
Thur; 10pm-5am Fri; 10pm-7am Sat; phone for details
Sun. **Admission** £5-£16. **Credit** (bar only) MC, V.
Winner of *Time Out's* 2006 Live Award for best venue,
the End may be in the West End, but it remains at the
forefront of all things leftfield in the world of electronica.
The main room boasts an island DJ booth that a few
jocks loathe but most love (they can be adored from
all angles, you see), while the Lounge is a fierce little
room that can outpace the main room when it fires up.
The upstairs industrial bricks 'n' steel AKA bar (*see p27*)
gets dragged into the party every Saturday when all three
rooms become 'As One' for the likes of the ever-kicking
electro techno Bugged Out, Laurent Garnier's all-night
residency, the breaks mayhem of Chew the Fat, or tech-
house fun at Underwater. However, it's Monday night's
Trash that everyone keeps talking about. Run by Erol
Alkan (also the resident DJ), it's a meeting of indie and
dance, with frequent ahead-of-the-curve live acts. The
Trash dress code – thrift shop meets haute couture – is
as cutting-edge as the music, and evidence of effort made
is a basic requirement for entry.
Map 1 L6.

Fabric

*77A Charterhouse Street, EC1M 3HN (7336
8898/www.fabriclondon.com). Farringdon tube/rail.*
Open 9.30pm-5am Fri; 10pm-7am Sat. **Admission**
£12-£15. **Credit** MC, V.
The easiest way to work out if you're past it or still down
with the kids is to head to Fabric. If you refuse to leave
the dancefloor till dawn, rock on, raver. But if you find the
sardine-like crowds and bassbin-destroying soundsystem
too much to bear, well… Fabric has been billing DJ and live
talent most haven't even heard of yet for six years now;
Fridays bring in leftfield breaks, D&B and hip hop while
Saturdays get all electro, minimal and tech-house. Although
the two enormous rooms are hard to leave, the small room
upstairs always rewards seeking (look out for the staircase,
which despite being long and wide, can be surprisingly hard
to find in a venue full of them). With a capacity of 1,500 it
can sometimes feel like you need a map – but getting lost
and making new friends on the stairs is half the fun. If you
turn up just as the pubs are closing, expect huge queues.
Map 3 O5.

Fridge

*1 Town Hall Parade, Brixton Hill, SW2 1RJ (7326
5100). Brixton tube/rail. Bar* **Open** 6pm-2am Mon-
Thur; 6pm-4am Fri; 8pm-4am Sat; 8pm-3am Sun.
Happy hour 6-10pm daily. **Admission** free before
10.30pm then £5-£10 Fri, Sat; £3 occasional Sun.
Club **Open** 10pm-6am Fri, Sat. **Admission** £12-£18.
Both **Credit** (over £10) MC, V.
Fridge remains London's hard-dance mecca with enough
lights and lasers to send the glo-stick wielding party kids
crazy. The atmosphere's anarchic: it's a veritable home
from home for nutters who, depending on the night, range
from dreadlocked trancers to water-bottle-carrying, furry-
booted ravers. One or two nights lean to out-and-proud gay
parties, but the rest are straight-up, hard-dance marathons.
Which is just the way they like it.
*Music (DJs 10pm nightly; open mic/musicians 8pm
Tue). Tables outdoors (4, pavement).*

Ghetto

*5-6 Falconberg Court, W1D 3AB (7287 3726/www.
ghetto-london.co.uk). Tottenham Court Road tube.*
Open 10.30pm-3am Mon-Wed, Sun; 10.30pm-4am
Thur, Fri; 10.30pm-5am Sat. **Admission** £1-£7.
No credit cards.
Done out in raving red, this fabulously sweaty basement
venue is home to two of London's hippest electro synth
fests. NagNagNag might not make headlines these days, but
there's no doubt it has one of the most forward-thinking
music policies around and remains one of the capital's best-
loved parties with the talented JoJo de Freq playing bang-
up-to-date (not banging) electro and techno, and Johnny
Slut mixing up old and new electro-disco. Friday's Cock
(mostly gay, though straight-friendly) is not as cutting-
edge but works hard to outdo Nag for sheer energy: it's the
night that prompted gay bible *Attitude* to dub Ghetto 'a
welcome break from your typical homo hangout'.
Map 7 K6.

Heaven

*Under the Arches, Villiers Street, WC2N 6NG
(7930 2020/www.heaven-london.com). Embankment
tube/Charing Cross tube/rail.* **Open** 10am-6am Mon,
Wed, Fri, Sat. **Admission** £2-£12. **Credit** (advance
booking only) AmEx, MC, V.

Clubs

The Home of Funk

Carwash

London   Paris   Lausanne

www.carwash.co.uk

0870 246 1966

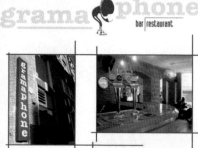

You haven't clubbed until you've...

- Found yourself mesmerised by four-lane traffic hell in Vauxhall at 10am with several topless blokes (your new bestest pals), waiting to get into a gay club.
- Complained that the Hoxton and Shoreditch scene ain't what it used to be.
- Lost your friends at Fabric only to find them at the end of the night sitting in a stairwell you didn't even know existed.
- Stumbled, ahem, bright eyed and bushy tailed out of a West End club at closing time and hung your head in shame as the streetcleaners stare.
- Suffered severe outfit envy at Trash at the End.

- Felt the bass make your jeans stand straight at jungle parties Metalheadz or Grace at Herbal.
- Decided against going home, and hit a boozer instead. And then found yourself sitting on the same leather sofa all afternoon.
- Felt physically sick on looking at the bill for your first round of drinks at, oh, most London clubs.
- Made a new best friend on the night bus home, only to completely forget about them until you scroll through your mobile phone several weeks later.
- Fallen over at Rollerdisco, reached for the laser at Turnmills or lounged on the terrace at EGG.

Ask anyone who raved in London's earliest days about Heaven, and they're likely to go misty eyed and talk about hearing the likes of Grooverider and Fabio cutting their DJ teeth. Fast forward a decade, and it's mostly 'the most famous gay club in the world'. The main room is super-club-sized, while towards the back, the Soundshaft is a much smaller affair that has a wrap-around balcony to throw shapes on; there's also a diner and a VIP room with fishtanks and red velvet seats. Nights are usually loudly and proudly gay, with Saturday nights heaving with sweating men. You're still likely to find supersized hard dance parties down this way, with the occasional four-room D&B extravaganza to boot.
Map 2 J7.

Herbal

10-14 Kingsland Road, E2 8DA (7613 4462/www. herbaluk.com). Old Street tube/rail/55 bus. **Open** 9pm-2am Tue-Thur, Sun; 9am-3am Fri, Sat. **Admission** £3 after 10pm Wed; £3-£5 Thur; £4-£8 Fri, Sat; £6-£8 Sun (women free before 11pm). **Credit** MC, V.
While the rest of Shoreditch might jump on the last cool bandwagon to motor on by, this two-floored venue keeps its eye firmly on keeping things quality. Both rooms are small (the main room fits 300 at a squeeze, the top floor barely 200) and perfectly worn with bare brick and reclaimed timber, but the money's in the system, and don't the crowd just love it? Soul II Soul bring the love and good times here one Saturday a month, while Goldie's Metalheadz (which started ten years ago over in Hoxton Square) does real bassbin damage once a month. Grooverider's Grace fires every Sunday, especially on public holidays, Spitkingdom keeps attracting the mic botherers every Tuesday, and there are plenty of house nights to keep things varied.
Map 5 R3.

Jamm

261 Brixton Road, SW9 6LH (7274 5537/www.brixton jamm.org). Brixton tube/rail. **Open** 5pm-2am Mon-Thur; noon-6am Fri, Sat; noon-2am Sun. **Admission** £3-£8. **Credit** AmEx, DC, MC, V.
It took a while, but Jamm has finally established itself as one of Brixton's best-loved nightclubs. It's a minor schlep from Brixton tube (perhaps not ideal to wander alone in a drunken fashion – you'd make easy pickings) before you come across a carpark with the venue at the back. There's a huge outdoor terrace that they haven't made much of (but no doubt will one day) and, despite the indoor palms, it's still the right side of rundown: there's a lounge area kitted out with sofas, a few plants, posters and a good-sized bar. The main room was made for small gigs and blistering club nights, with a small stage and a bar running the length of one side. Basement Jaxx lay on their monthly Inside Out parties here (they drape white acid house sheets over the bare walls), Twisted Melon do just that one Friday a month, and there are regular positive action parties too.
Disabled: toilet. Function rooms. Music (DJs/live music 7pm Thur-Sun). Tables outdoors (8, terrace yard). TV (big screen, satellite).

Kabaret's Prophecy

16-18 Beak Street, W1F 9RD (7439 2229/www. kabaretsprophecy.com). Oxford Circus tube. **Open** 11pm-3am Mon, Wed, Thur-Sat. **Admission** (men only) £15 Mon, Wed, Thur, Sat. **Credit** MC, V.
Does the West End need any more exclusive and swanky nightclubs? Apparently so. New kid on the Soho block, it's a late-night luxury space that accommodates just 130 party people, and the monochromatic moving-image walls made up of LED screens certainly add to the wow factor. Kabaret's Prophecy doesn't open until 11pm, and the DJs here reach for dancefloor-friendly R&B and commercial sounds. It's advisable to make sure that your name's down on the guestlist to guarantee entry (which is easily done via their website). You can book tables but, of course, there's usually a minimum spend at the bar. Shimshad Khalid is the owner and usually works the door: it pays to work a cracking smile.
Map 2 J6/7.

Key

King's Cross Freight Depot, off York Way, N1 9AA (7837 1027/www.thekeylondon.com). King's Cross tube/rail. **Open** 11pm-5am Fri; 10pm-6am Sat; 6am-1pm Sun. **Admission** £7-£15. **Credit** (bar only) MC, V.
When we heard they were opening up a second room at the Key, we nearly cried: the beauty of this tiny club was, well, that it was tiny. Deep sighs of relief all round when the new 'Chandelier' room only added to the excellent space. Part of the complex of clubs behind King's Cross railway station, and at the far end of a cobbled lane (slippery when wet, be warned), the crowning glory remains the discotastic flashing dancefloor. All of the monthly parties are a treat, whether it's the blistering electro of Deepdownanddirty or thumping tech-house of Mulletover. Just don't get there before midnight: this is a super late-night dance space.

Ministry of Sound
Every Friday
& Saturday

Switch every Friday.
featuring in 2006:
Jazzy Jeff
Rahzel
Pete Rock
Gilles Peterson
Tony Touch
DJ Zinc
Friction
Guru
Shy FX
Bryan Gee
Cash Money
Artificial Intelligence
Shortee Blitz
The Rogue Element
Soul of Man
Roots Manuva
Mampi Swift
Friendly
DJ Maseo
DJ Haul & Mason
plus many more...

Saturday Sessions.
featuring in 2006:
Deep Dish
Sander Kleinenberg
Steve Angello
Groove Armada
Dan Ghenacia
Pete Tong
DJ Sneak
Yousef
Jon Carter
Nic Fanciulli
Paul Woolford
Funk D'Void
Little Louie Vega
Josh Wink
Tim Sheridan
Smokin Jo
John Dalhback
Mr. C
Cassius
Desyn Masiello
plus many more...

www.ministryofsound.com/club

Key. *See p251.*

KOKO

*1A Camden High Street, NW1 9JE (7388 3222/
www.koko.uk.com). Mornington Crescent tube.*
Open 9.30pm-4am Fri; 10pm-4am Sat. Call to check
other times. **Admission** free-£15. **Credit** (bar) MC, V.
Famous for being the Camden Palace (we wish they'd go
back to the old name; KOKO is a bit daft), where many
music legends did legendary things, it was allowed to
run down in quite depressing fashion. Opulent in an old-
fashioned way – gloss claret and gold paint, plenty of
Greek gods holding up columns – KOKO is all about vertical levels. You'll no doubt get lost in the many stairwells
as you try to get from balcony over here to balcony over
there. The sound system works for both DJs and live
shows. Fridays are all about Club NME, which gets some
scream-worthy bands in, but Saturdays is a random mix
of Sunday Best, Guilty Pleasures and hard dance raves.
Map 8 J2.

Lucky Voice

*52 Poland Street, W1F 7NH (7439 3660/www.lucky
voice.co.uk). Oxford Circus tube.* **Open/food served**
6pm-1am Mon-Fri; 3pm-1am Sat. **Credit** AmEx, MC, V.
Karaoke has become inexplicably fashionable, and this
upscale karaoke bar is the result of an idea that its owner
Martha Lane Fox had when she was laid up in hospital
after a major accident. There's a small, stylish bar decorated in contemporary red and black Japanese design
motifs at the front. It offers reasonably priced oriental
cocktails like Sen Chai Bellini (green tea Bellini) from
£6 – most of which are good, but some a little weak and
watery. There's a good selection of saké and shochu
sold only by the bottle, making them much more expensive. The karaoke rooms have no stage and are very
cramped, but they offer a comprehensive playlist and
friendly waitress service (rates for hiring the rooms vary).
Oriental bar snacks like steamed vegetable gyoza are
not sensational, but work well.
Map 1 J6.

Madame Jo Jo's

*8-10 Brewer Street, W1S 0SP (7734 3040/www.
madamejojos.com). Piccadilly Circus tube.* **Open**
10pm-3am Wed, Fri; 9pm-3am Thur; 7pm-3am Sat.
Admission £5-£15. **Credit** (bar only) AmEx, MC, V.
Those who find Madame Jo Jo's love it: the opulent red decor
makes it stand out from the Soho crowd, spinning several
entertainment plates (cabaret, comedy and club). Highlights
here include Keb Darge's legendary, ten-year strong Deep
Funk – the last word in rare funk singles, and a legacy of
the capital's '80s rare groove scene – while Mark 'S-Express'
Moore holds an ace, bursting electronic Glitz party that
trips through the decades for a custom-kitted crowd.
Map 7 K6.

Mass

*St Matthew's Church, Brixton Hill, SW2 1JF (7738
7875). Brixton tube/rail.* **Open** 8.30pm-3am Thur;
10pm-6am Fri; noon-7pm, 10pm-6am Sat. Call to check
other times. **Admission** £4-£15. **No credit cards.**
Former Prime Minister John Major was married on the
steps just outside, but since then, this space has become a
bastion for genre-defying hedonism. Legendary reggae
broadcaster David Rodigan has made his Wednesday reggae session an essential one, hitting the spot for a local mul-
ticultured crowd with soundclash greats such as Saxon
Sound. Plenty of psy-trance and junp up D&B promoters
get the most out of the three rooms, including Tasty and
Chichime for the laser-reachers.

Medicine

*89 Great Eastern Street, EC2A 3HX (7739 5173/
www.medicinebar.net). Old Street tube/rail/55 bus.*
Open/food served 5-11pm Mon-Wed; 5pm-2am
Thur, Sat; 4pm-2am Fri. **Happy hour** 5-9pm Mon-Fri.
Admission £4-£6 after 9pm Fri, Sat. **Credit** MC, V.
A perfect example of when a bar is also a club. This ground
floor bar heaves with the post-work City crowd – try to
get the loft floor at the back which can also be hired for

Clubs

small parties – before making room later on for the cooler Shoreditch crowd who come for Little Issst, the electro pint-sized happening once a month, Norman Jay's regular all night long sessions, and Tim Deluxe's AT which sees the ginger-mega producer welcome his DJ mates. The basement is much bigger than you expect walking down the stairs, and is no stranger to rocking sweatfests. While nothing spectacular to look at, it works at keeping its music policy on the right side of cool.
Map 5 Q4.

Ministry of Sound

103 Gaunt Street, SE1 6DP (7740 8600/www.ministry ofsound.com). Elephant & Castle tube/rail. **Open** 10pm-3am Wed; 10.30pm-5am Fri; 11pm-7am Sat. **Admission** £5 Wed; £12 Fri; £15 Sat. **Credit** (bar) MC, V.
The most famous clubbing brand in the world, with perhaps Pacha coming a close second; it's difficult to get away from the feeling that it isn't a club, it's a corporation. Once inside, it's as far removed from the days of raves as it's possible to get although the sound is gobsmackingly great and DJs have said that they play there just to hear what their records really sound like. The main room (the 'box') could be confused with a warehouse, albeit a very clean one, while the bar with its overlooking balcony is often just as heaving as the main room. A recent rejig of the club nights have seen Fridays go all bass happy with hip hop, breaks and D&B at Switch, while Saturdays keep flipping between house clubs like Pete Tong's Pure Pete Tong, and Club Class.

Neighbourhood

12 Acklam Road, W10 5QZ (7524 7979/www. neighbourhoodclub.net). Ladbroke Grove or Westbourne Park tube. **Open** 8pm-2am Thur-Sat; 5pm-midnight Sun. **Admission** £5-£15. **Credit** (bar) MC, V.
No doubt missing Ben Watt (who also took his very special soundsystem when he left in 2005), they're nonetheless still working to keep this spot under the Westway, previously occupied by Subterrania, rocking. While not much has changed in looks – the beloved balcony upstairs is still a great feature – there are now lots of convivial seating areas if you aren't in a moving-and-grooving kinda mood. Saturdays are One Starry Nights, which nods towards soulful, quality house music, but Fridays work to differing beats depending on who is booked. Regulars include the glam-house Tokyo Disco, Groove Armada's Andy Cato, Mylo and Felix da Housecat.
Map 10Az5.

93 Feet East

150 Brick Lane, E1 6QN (7247 3293/www.93feet east.com). Aldgate East tube/Liverpool Street tube/rail. **Open** 5-11pm Mon-Thur; 5pm-1am Fri; noon-1am Sat; noon-10.30pm Sun. **Admission** £5-£10 after 9pm Fri, Sat. **Credit** (bar) MC, V.
We'd sell our granny to get this place a late licence, but till the devil says 'hell yeah', 93 Feet East continues to be slightly hampered by having to close at 1am. Still, they make the most of what they've got, and when that includes a great courtyard that wraps right around the back, a large balcony terrace, a bar crammed full of squishy sofas, a loft and a main space that works well as a cinema, gig venue or club, they're clearly on to a winner. During winter months, Rock&Roll Cinema sees people reclining in red vintage cinema seats before Lindyhopping across the dancefloor to the likes of Vincent Vincent & the Villians, while every Sunday all year round, Deano's Alphabetti Spaghetti has the music policy decided by a single letter of the alphabet. The first Saturday of the month is It's Bigger Than, which is one of our fave clubs in London, with resident Deven Miles set for big things thanks to his clever re-edits.

Notting Hill Arts Club

21 Notting Hill Gate, W11 3JQ (7460 4459/www. nottinghillartsclub.com). Notting Hill Gate tube. **Open** 6pm-2am Mon-Fri; 4pm-2am Sat; 4pm-1am Sun. **Admission** £5-£8. **Credit** (bar) MC, V.
It's the kind of space that really shouldn't work in posh Notting Hill but thankfully does (they need all the help they can get, right?). It's not fancy, in fact it's quite plain, and only fits in a few hundred people – if everyone gets up close and personal – but it's got some of the best far-flung sounds in town. You could tour the globe without ever leaving this basement club: Berlin electronica (Client's Being Boiled); Asian beats and desi rhythms (Nihal's Bombay Bronx); Latin flavours (Brazilian Love Affair) and even a Craft Night.
Map 10 B7.

Pacha

Terminus Place, SW1E 5NE (7833 3139/www.pacha london.com). Victoria tube/rail. **Open** 10pm-5am Fri; 10pm-6am Sat. **Admission** £15-£25. **Credit** (bar) MC, V.
Everyone knows that Pacha in Ibiza is one of the world's very best clubs. Those chasing the double cherry logo to Victoria, though, are in for a shock. Sure, once you get in, it's glitzy and sleek; but it's nowhere near as massive as its Balearic counterpart, and the Astroturf terrace overlooks a bus depot. The main room works well, on occasion, with a large raised platform for exhibitionists, and the baby room upstairs is perfectly formed. They've struck a successful chord with glammed-up house nights that see queues running for miles: Kinki Malinki, Defected, Gate 21. It often costs £20 just to get through the door, which says a lot about the clientele: more big spenders than cool clubbers.

Penthouse

1 Leicester Square, WC2H 7NA (7734 0900/www.the penthouseclub.co.uk). Leicester Square tube. **Open** *Club* 10pm-2am Wed-Sat. **Admission** £15 before 11pm, £20 after 11pm Wed-Fri; £20 Sat. **Credit** (bar) MC, V.
Just as Hoxton is always encumbered with 'London's trendy Hoxton' in the tabloids, the Penthouse collected the prefix of 'London's exclusive' soon after opening thanks to a steady stream of glossy celebs falling out of the door (it's a stumble away from the Odeon which regularly hosts UK film premières). On the same site as the doomed superclub, Home, there are three floors that make up the space. On the 6th, the 'boutique nightclub', with space for just a couple of hundred designer-clad young things (the old things can stay by the bar ordering endless bottles of champagne) and some snakeskin sofas, the 7th is the restaurant, while the 8th is the laughably over the top members bar. How Not To Decorate are surely on their way.
Map 7 K7.

Plan B

418 Brixton Road, SW9 7AY (7733 0926/www.plan-brixton.co.uk). Brixton tube/rail. **Open** 5pm-2am Tue-Thur, Sun; 5pm-4am Fri, Sat. **Admission** £5 after 10pm Thur; £5 after 9pm, £7 after 11pm Fri, Sat. **Credit** AmEx, MC, V.
Make no mistake: this small venue has been punching above its weight since opening in 2002. The Funktion One soundsystem stands up to the blistering hip hop and funk

talent that work hard to put it through its paces every Friday, while Saturday's B Side leans more to house and soulful talent that keep the party jumping, and this is where Mike Skinner (The Streets) holds his irregular Beats parties. The ceiling's low (more like a bunker, really), but the venue's done to a high spec. The high bar spans the entire back wall and serves the usual bottled beers, some inspired cocktails and generously poured measures of spirits.

Plastic People

147-149 Curtain Road, EC2A 3QE (7739 6471/www. plasticpeople.co.uk). Liverpool Street or Old Street tube/ rail/8, 55, 133, 344 bus. **Open** 10pm-2am Thur; 10pm-3.30am Fri, Sat; 7.30pm-midnight Sun. Times vary, check website. **Admission** £5-£10. **No credit cards.** Plastic People subscribes to the old-school line that says all you need for a kicking party is a dark basement and a sound system. But what it lacks in size and decor it makes up for in sound quality (the rig embarrasses those in many larger clubs) and some of London's most progressive club nights. On the last Thursday of the month Forward showcases the latest developments in dub-step, two-step and grime; Friday nights see Rory Phillips (Erol Alkan's right-hand man at

Trash) go it alone with And Did We Mention Our Disco; flagship Saturday night Balance treads a middle ground of Latin, jazz, hip hop, house and techno; and the second and last Sundays of the month see Co Op roll out future jazz and broken beats. Ben Watt holds Buzzin' Fly Sunday night parties every now and then, while Forward hammers the filthy grime sound one Thursday a month. **Map 5 R4.**

Scala

275 Pentonville Road, N1 9NL (7833 2022/www. scala-london.co.uk). King's Cross tube/rail. **Open** 10pm-5am Fri, Sat. **Admission** £6-£15. **Credit** (over £10) MC, V.
This dual-purpose venue manages to tick the right music boxes both as a club and a live venue. The variety of nights and gigs mean the Scala is bound to appeal to everyone at some point, but the layout and design are also well thought out. A balcony and mezzanine-type levels provide great views of the stage, which has been graced by acts including the Scissor Sisters and Franz Ferdinand. Weekends are given over to club nights: all-inclusive gay regular Popstarz is on Fridays, Pure Old Skool is on the last

What's hot

Nightlife is a fast-moving and fickle beast, and nowhere is more fast-moving (or fickle) than London. What to listen to, where to listen to it, and – clothes crisis alert! – what to wear while you're dancing to it? It's enough to make you hole up and never leave your sofa. Crucial mistake, though: there's a world of exciting, brand new happenings that you just shouldn't miss. Take a gander at what we think are the biggest trends in clubland right now, and get out there...

Minimal house

What they play at Ibiza's infamous Monday-morning knees up, Circo Loco at DC10, and championed at clubs like Secretsundaze at secret East End locations and All Over My Face at the Key. Deep electronic house from the likes of Berlin's Get Physical Records and London's Superfreq, and it continues to fly off the shelves at record shops. Which can only mean a maximal backlash is just around the corner.

Strange locations, strange times

Time was, you would head out on a Friday or Saturday evening for a night's disco dancing, and be home again by dawn (unless you were a dirty stop-out, of course). There just wasn't anywhere else to go, unless you were invited back to some illegal bash or other. The rise and rise of secret afterparties coupled with 24-hour licensing has resulted in promoters going wild with where they put on parties and at what time. One-off parties in decommissioned churches or in converted arches in the City that run until 9am, or weekly afterparties that have really put EGG on the map make normal clubbing hours seem, well, a bit of a yawn.

Dressing up, up, up

Converse trainers, baggy jeans and a record label T-shirt? That look is so over it's practically retro. Following the electroclash explosion in 2002 and the indie revival of late, it's now tea dresses and plenty of coloured eye-shadow for the girls, cravats and smart haircuts for the boys, even if you're going to a sweaty, dance-till-way-past-dawn warehouse rave.

Let's go to the hop

Fancy a bit of retro dancefloor action? Forget cheesy 1980s chart trash, it's all about partying like it's 1929. Afternoon tea dances at Viva Cake at Bethnal Green Working Men's Club; vintage jazz at the Rakehell's Revels in the West End; swing bands at Lady Luck and 2TooMuch. Learn a few Lindy hop moves and you'll be the belle of the ball. Failing that, just pose in pearls and lashings of red lipstick or a vintage tuxedo like everyone else.

Partying outdoors

OK, so shimmying in sunglasses outside is hardly a novel concept, but this year promoters have pushed the ingenious boat right out in a bid to get people jumping around to beats in the fresh air. Ravers no longer have to schlep to fields hundreds of miles away. Clapham Common, Hyde Park – even the old King's Cross Freight Depot and Brockwell Lido – host outdoor parties during the spring, summer and autumn months. Come winter, clubs like EGG and Canvas keep their terraces open (and heated!) too. Every boozer worth going to has a beer garden or sizeable terrace that's put to good use with a pair of decks and a sound system. Moral of the story? Never, ever leave home without those sunglasses.

Clubs

Plastic People

Saturday of the month, and garage and funky house nights also feature. It all adds up to a nomination for a *Time Out* Live Award in 2006.

seOne
41-43 St Thomas Street, SE1 3QX (7407 1617/www. seonelondon.com). London Bridge tube/rail. **Open** 10pm-6am Fri, Sat. **Admission** £10-£18. **Credit** (advance bookings) AmEx, MC, V.
It may be absolutely huge, often damp and leave a weird mark at the bottom of your jeans after a night out, but these arches boast some of the best loos in London, which goes a long way in our book. The promoters usually open up two arches and a chill out space, but just three rooms need a few thousand to fill them. When they're rammed, it's all 'back in the day' rave, with a cracking atmosphere and plenty of space for lasers. Clubs go from old school happy hardcore raves to the Hum Allnighters and psychedelic trance parties.

Telegraph
228 Brixton Hill, SW2 1HE (8678 0777/www.the brixtontelegraph.co.uk). Brixton tube, then 45, 59, 118, 133, 159, 250 bus. **Open** noon-2am Mon-Thur; noon-4am Fri; noon-6am Sat; noon-midnight Sun. **Food served** 5.30-11.30pm daily. **Credit** AmEx, MC, V.
One of south London's most relaxing hangouts, for which you'll be thankful after the hill-climb to get there. The layout is designed for multi-space enjoyment; fill up on Thai food at the chunky wooden tables before moving on to the bar. Then, in one corner, you can warm up to a DJ before retiring to the air-conned club. If it all sounds rather grand, it is – and don't local SW2 dwellers appreciate it. (Be warned that in the cold light of day, the shabby interior gives a slightly different impression; early drinkers may notice the tatty wallpaper.) Thursday is Hunk Pappa's Pure Reggae. *Babies and children admitted (until 6pm). Function room. Games (fruit machines, pool table). Music (DJs 9pm nightly; bands 8pm nightly; £5-£15). Quiz (8pm Thur; free). Tables outdoors (4, pavement). TV (big screen, satellite).*

333
333 Old Street, EC1V 9LE (7739 5949/www.333 mother.com). Old Street tube/rail. Bar **Open** 8pm-3am Mon-Wed; 8pm-4am Thur, Sun; 8pm-1am Fri, Sat. *Club* **Open** 8pm-3am Wed; 10pm-4am Thur, Sun; 10pm-5am Fri, Sat. **Admission** £5-£10. *Both* **Credit** (bar only) MC, V.
Not many people know that the 333 was a gay bar before Tubbs West thought that it would make a cracking straight venue back in 1996. Some ten years later, and the queues still form in rain, hail and shine, thanks to constantly evolving programming that, recently, has taken in grime in the form of Straight Outta Bethnal and given a home to the Queens of Noize noisy guitar bashes most Fridays. Three floors (dark basement, big main, Mother bar upstairs, all filled with oh-so-cool party people) lay on everything from Jamaican dancehall to jazz-tinged house, electro-disco to drum 'n' bass – usually all on the same evening. **Map 5 R4.**

Turnmills
63B Clerkenwell Road, EC1M 5PT (7250 3409/www. turnmills.co.uk). Farringdon tube/rail. **Open** 8pm-1am Wed; 9pm-3am Thur; 10.30pm-7.30am Fri; 10pm-6am Sat, 6am-2pm Sun. **Admission** £12-£15. **Credit** (bar only) MC, V.
Some great clubs have resided here: Trade, Heavenly Social, Headstart, the Gallery… Despite questionable Mediterranean decor (what's wrong with warehouse-rave?), the main room still has an acid house feel, helped by its rectangular shape, lasers and the fact that it's usually pitch black. The small room is tucked away under some stairs, and there can be some irritating bottlenecks (who thought to put a bar right by a major thoroughfare?); the top room is part neo-classic, part Ibizan nightspot. The other rooms out the back have been opened in recent months thanks to Together, which once a month basically throws a festival inside the venue. Tim Sheridan's Veryveryverywrongindeed is just that, starting as it does every Sunday morning at 6am. **Map 3 N4.**

Clubs

Where to go for...

Index

Index

Index

A-Z Index

Index

Index

Index

Index

Index

Advertisers' Index

**Please refer to relevant sections for
addresses & telephone numbers**

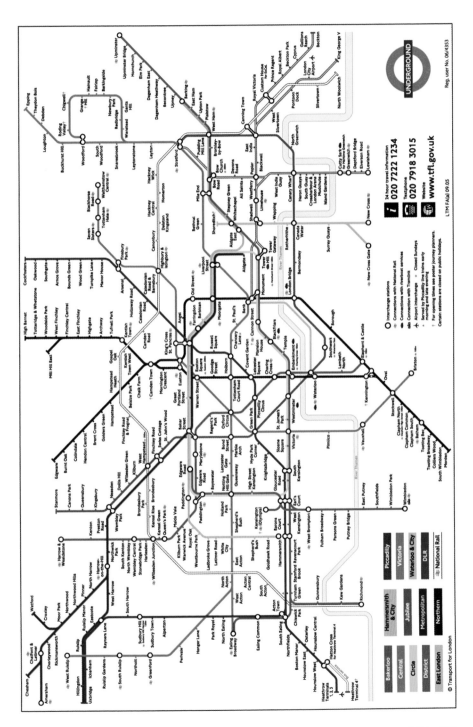

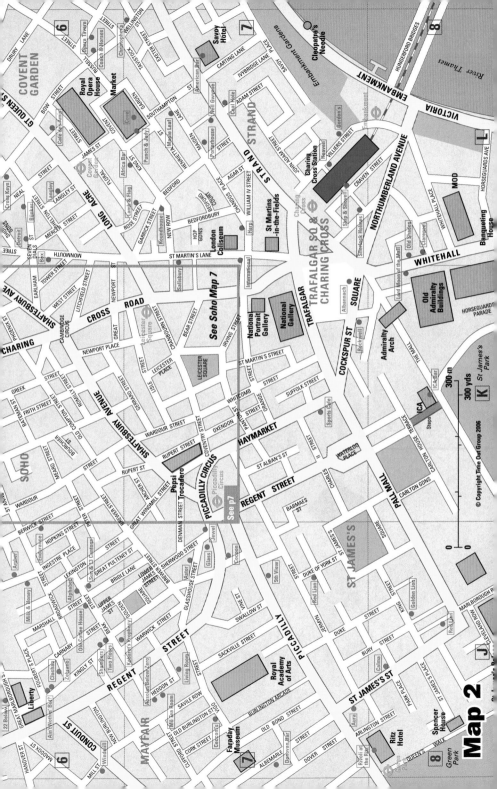

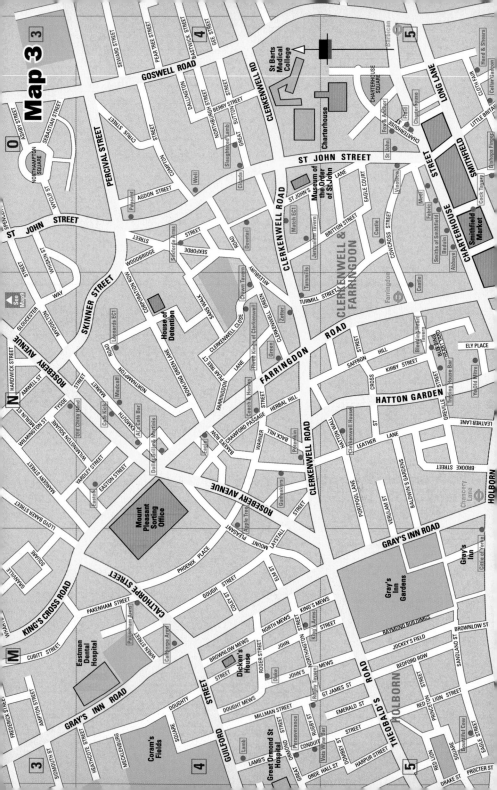

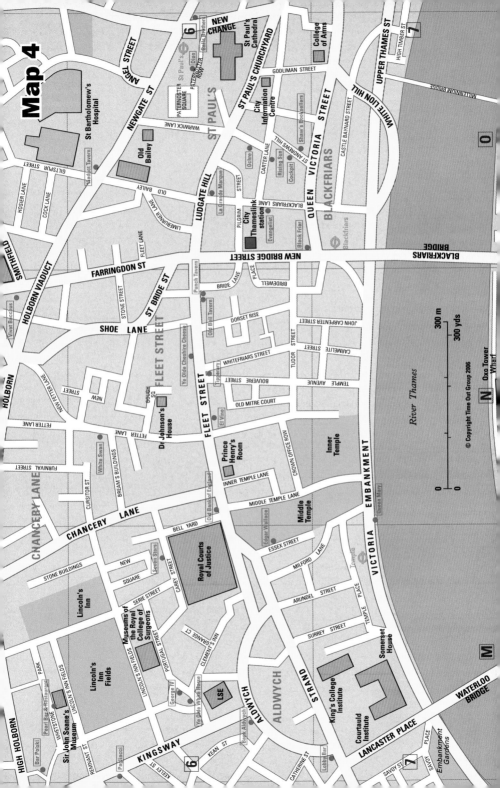

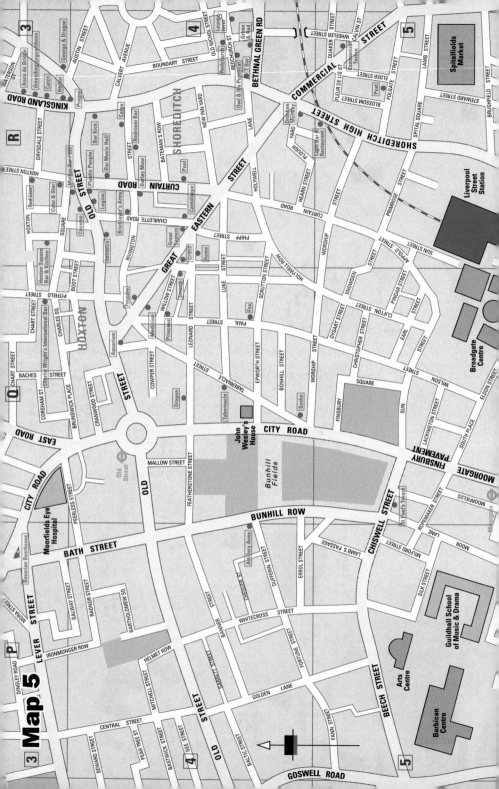

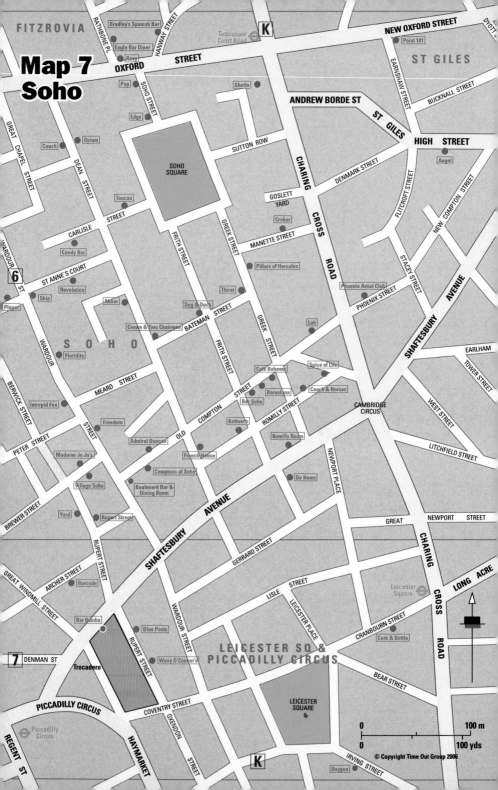

Map 10
Notting Hill

Map 11
Clapham

© Copyright Time Out Group 2006